# Why Do You Need This New Edition?

1. Thirty-eight new readings—many written within the last five years—address the controversial topics of today. Subjects range from the changing nature of gender in contemporary society to the economy and the financial crisis to how technology is changing not just how we communicate, but how we think.

2. A new Chapter 15, Passing the Buck—Our Economy in Crisis? explores the complex issues that contributed to the current financial crisis and the challenges many young adults now face upon graduation.

3. A new Chapter 16, Our Lives Online, delves into the ways technology is changing us—our brains, our speech, and our personal relationships.

4. A new Chapter 17, Human Rights and Wrongs takes a look at some of the arguments around human rights, including Gitmo, the Middle East, and immigration and deportation issues.

5. Written in an accessible style with clearly stated definitions that help you more readily understand key terms and concepts, the new edition of *Dialogues* includes enhanced discussions of the Rogerian approach to argument as well as the Toulmin method.

6. Student sample essays, including six new essays, provide you with helpful models that show you how fellow students completed their assignments.

7. The chapter, Using Visual Arguments, includes new sample photos, print ads, editorial cartoons, and graphs for discussion—all aimed at helping you strengthen your ability to influence and persuade.

8. The Documentation Guide for MLA and APA features the most recent updates with expanded coverage on using electronic sources. That section includes two annotated and fully documented student essays—one brand new, the other newly updated, and each incorporating visual images.

PEARSON
Longman

P9-DTP-997

# DIALOGUES

## An Argument Rhetoric and Reader

SEVENTH EDITION

**GARY GOSHGARIAN**
Northeastern University

**KATHLEEN KRUEGER**

**Longman**

Boston   Columbus   Indianapolis   New York   San Francisco   Upper Saddle River
Amsterdam   Cape Town   Dubai   London   Madrid   Milan   Munich   Paris   Montreal   Toronto
Delhi   Mexico City   Sao Paulo   Sydney   Hong Kong   Seoul   Singapore   Taipei   Tokyo

Executive Editor: Suzanne Phelps Chambers
Development Editor: Anne Leung
Senior Marketing Manager: Sandra McGuire
Production Manager: Stacey Kulig
Project Coordination, Text Design, and Electronic Page Makeup: PreMediaGlobal
Cover Design Manager: Wendy Ann Fredericks
Cover Designer: Nancy Sacks
Cover Image: © Exactostoc/SuperStock
Photo Researcher: Rebecca Karamehmedovic
Senior Manufacturing Buyer: Roy Pickering
Printer and Binder: Edwards Brothers
Cover Printer: Lehigh Phoenix Color

For permission to use copyrighted material, grateful acknowledgment is made to the copyright holders on pp. 641–643, which are hereby made part of this copyright page.

Library of Congress Cataloging-in-Publication Data

Dialogues: an argument rhetoric and reader / [edited by] Gary Goshgarian, Kathleen Krueger.—7th ed.
    p. cm.
    Includes index.
    ISBN 978-0-205-78845-3 (alk. paper)
    1. English language—Rhetoric.   2. Persuasion (Rhetoric)   3. College readers.   I. Goshgarian, Gary.
II. Krueger, Kathleen.   III. Title.
    PE1431.D53 2010
    808'.0427—dc22

                                                                                2010033232

Copyright © 2011, 2009, 2007 by Gary Goshgarian and Kathleen Krueger

All rights reserved. No part of this publication may be reproduced, stored in a retrieval system, or transmitted, in any form or by any means, electronic, mechanical, photocopying, recording, or otherwise, without the prior written permission of the publisher. Printed in the United States.

1 2 3 4 5 6 7 8 9 10—DOC—13  12  11  10

**Longman**
is an imprint of

www.pearsonhighered.com

ISBN-13: 978-0-205-78845-3
ISBN-10:    0-205-78845-9

# Contents

             an Investigator                                    241

       Sources of Information    241
           Primary Sources    242
           Secondary Sources    243
       A Search Strategy    243
           Choosing Your Topic    244
           Getting an Overview of Your Topic    244
           Compiling a Working Bibliography    245
       Sample Entries for an Annotated Bibliography    246
       Locating Sources    247
           Finding Periodicals    247
           Finding Books    248
           Finding Internet Sources    249
       Evaluating Sources    251
           Print Sources    251
           Electronic Sources    252
       Taking Notes    256
           Summary    257
           Paraphrase    258
           Quotation    258
       Drafting Your Paper    259
           Incorporating Your Research    260
           Attribution    260
       Revising and Editing Your Paper    262
       Preparing and Proofreading Your Final Manuscript    262
       Plagiarism    263
       DOCUMENTATION GUIDE: MLA and APA Styles    266
       Where Does the Documentation Go?    266
       Documentation Style    266
       A Brief Guide to MLA and APA Styles    267
           Books    268
           Periodicals    271
           Internet Sources    272
           Miscellaneous Sources    274
       SAMPLE RESEARCH PAPERS    275

           Shannon O'Neill, "Literature Hacked
               and Torn Apart: Censorship in
               Public Schools" (MLA) (student essay)    276
           Dan Hoskins, "Tapped Out: Bottled
               Water's Detrimental Side" (APA) (student essay)    283

# Preface

*Dialogues: An Argument Rhetoric and Reader* focuses on promoting meaningful discussion, that is, the effective exchange of opinions and ideas. In this book, we move away from traditional models of confrontation and dispute and, instead, promote ways to create dialogue by examining different points of view with an open mind. This exploration of multiple perspectives on an issue helps students reach informed positions and develop their own compelling cases. While dialogue and consensus are encouraged, we realize that not all arguments can be resolved to everyone's satisfaction. However, understanding the principles of persuasive writing and the techniques of argument provides students with the tools to engage productively in negotiation. And although students may not always reach a consensus of opinion, they will be able to discuss diverse issues in a thoughtful and productive way.

## New to This Edition

The seventh edition reflects the efforts of the previous edition to teach students how to create effective arguments. At the same time, we continue to encourage discussion and understanding rather than confrontation and dispute. For this edition we have incorporated the insights and suggestions of many instructors who used the last edition. Some changes to this edition include:

### The Rhetoric

Each of the rhetoric chapters has been revised and updated, and they include new study and discussion questions and expanded apparatus. Furthermore, we have added new sample readings (student and professional) with analyses and replaced others in these chapters. Likewise, we have refreshed some examples and discussion in the visuals chapter. Finally, the examples of documentation using electronic sources have been updated and expanded in the "Documentation Guide: MLA and APA Styles," which concludes with two annotated and fully documented sample student essays, each incorporating visual devices.

### The Reader

Part Two contains over sixty essays and visuals, many which are new to this edition, and written or created within the last five years. We extensively revised several chapters, including "Gender Matters," "Race and Ethnicity," and "University Life." We kept readings that reviewers said worked very well in class, and added new ones based on their suggestions and feedback.

In addition to magazines and journals, today's students increasingly find their information online. Online social networks such as Facebook and Twitter have created online communities through which students connect and share information. Blogs, which operate as online diaries, present viewpoints and invite others to discuss ideas and experiences.

This edition includes a few readings pulled from blogs, reflecting the new ways we create and share points of view.

Writing assignments that follow each section encourage students to address issues further, prompting them to formulate critical responses to the different points of view expressed in the section. Some questions include suggestions for using the Internet to explore a topic more fully and to aid research.

## Organization of the Book

As the title indicates, this book is divided into two parts. The rhetoric section consists of nine chapters explaining the strategies of reading and writing arguments. The reader section consists of eight thematic units containing over sixty essays that present a challenging collection of thought-provoking contemporary arguments.

### Part One: The Rhetoric

Part One of the book is designed to stimulate critical thinking, reading, and writing, and to introduce students to research skills. It explores how issues are argued while emphasizing the actual process of persuasive writing, from brainstorming exercises to shaping the final product. Each of the nine chapters in Part One focuses on a particular facet or principle of persuasive writing, including a new visuals chapter that addresses how visuals can act as arguments in and of themselves, or as auxiliary support for written arguments.

Chapter 1 offers an overview of argumentation, clarifies key terminology, and introduces the processes of debate, dialogue, and deliberation. Chapter 2 focuses on critical reading, presenting a series of activities designed to help students evaluate arguments and recognize their primary components. An extensive section on testing arguments for logical fallacies ends the chapter. Chapter 3 discusses how to begin writing arguments. It helps students find worthwhile and interesting topics to write about by demonstrating techniques for brainstorming, limiting topics, and formulating claims. Chapter 4 examines the presence of audience, encouraging students to think about the different kinds of readers they may have to address. This chapter suggests ways to evaluate readers' concerns and strategies to reach different audiences.

Chapter 5 focuses on the organization of the argument essay by analyzing two basic types of arguments—position and proposal. Outlining is reviewed as a tool to ensure effective organization. Chapter 6 considers the importance of evidence. We demonstrate that the effectiveness of a writer's argument largely depends on how well the writer uses evidence—facts, testimony, statistics, and observations—to support his or her ideas. Chapter 7 introduces the socially constructed Toulmin model of logic as a way of testing the premises of the writer's argument.

Chapter 8 explores the principles of visual argument in art, advertisements, editorial cartoons, photographs, and ancillary graphics such as charts and tables. Focusing on developing visual literacy skills, the chapter shows students how to apply the tools of critical analysis to the many visual arguments they encounter every day. Finally, Chapter 9 discusses research strategies, including locating and evaluating print and electronic sources, note-taking, and drafting and revising argument essays. The Documentation Guide provides documentation formats and annotated sample student papers for both MLA and APA styles.

## Part Two: The Readings

With over sixty contemporary essays and visuals, the readings offer a wide range of challenging and stimulating issues that we think will be of interest both to students and instructors. The topics are selected to encourage discussion, and attempt to represent the diversity of opinion connected to the controversial issues we face today.

The goal of Part Two is to examine broad themes that offer diverse points of view, including consumerism, gender, technology, race, religion, the economy, human rights and personal rights. Each of chapter presents a variety of readings that provide multiple viewpoints surrounding an issue. Charts, graphs, cartoons and photographs are interspersed through the chapter to demonstrate the importance of visual information in framing and supporting arguments.

## Study Apparatus

The study apparatus of the book is designed to help students thoughtfully consider the issues, their own opinions on these issues, and how they might engage in meaningful dialogue. Questions encourage critical thinking about each article's content and style. Each chapter in Part Two features an introduction to the chapter theme and its subsections. A brief headnote to each reading provides students with context and pertinent information regarding the reading. "Before You Read" and "As You Read" questions help frame the reading. Following each reading are "Questions for Analysis and Discussion" that stimulate thinking on the content, argument, and writing strategies of the author. Some questions ask students to consider how other authors in the section would respond to a particular essay's argument or evidence, encouraging critical thinking across the theme or chapter. "Writing Assignments" follow the end of each subsection of readings, helping students to synthesize the information they have read and their own opinions.

# Supplements

### PEARSON
mycomplab ▯

The only online application to integrate a writing environment with proven resources for grammar, writing, and research. MyCompLab gives students help at their fingertips as they draft and revise. Instructors have access to a variety of assessment tools including commenting capabilities, diagnostics and, study plans, and an e-portfolio. Created after years of extensive research and in partnership with faculty and students across the country. MyCompLab offers a seamless and flexible teaching and learning environment built specifically for writers.

## Instructor's Manual

The Instructor's Manual has been updated to assist and guide instructors as they teach each chapter. In addition to summarizing how instructors might teach each chapter, the manual provides answers to all the questions in the textbook. Questions from each reading that are particularly appropriate for class discussion are indicated in boldface, with suggestions on how instructors might use specific questions to stimulate class dialogue.

## Acknowledgments

Many people behind the scenes deserve much acknowledgment and gratitude. It would be impossible to thank all of them, but there are some for whose help we are particularly grateful. First, we would like to thank all the instructors and students who used the first five editions of *Dialogues*. Their continued support has made this latest edition possible. Also, we would like to thank those instructors who spent hours answering lengthy questionnaires on the effectiveness of the essays and who supplied many helpful comments and suggestions in the preparation of this new edition: Marcia Allen, University of Maryland University College; Desire Baloubi, Shaw University; Candace Boeck, San Diego State University; Cathy Brostrand, Mt. San Jacinto College; Gert Coleman, Middlesex County College; William Donati, University of Nevada, Las Vegas; Kurt Harris, Southern Utah University; Tom Hemmeter, Arcadia College; Debra Johanyak, University of Akron; James M. Lang, Assumption College; Glenda Mora, Gavilan University; Joan Naake, Montgomery College; Eric S. Norment, Bridgewater State University; Phyllis Pae, Lakeland Community College; Robert Stafford, Cuyamaca College; and Jule Wallis, Wayne State University.

A very special thanks goes to Kathryn Goodfellow, for her extraordinary contribution in locating articles and writing the study apparatus for Part Two, as well as for her considerable work creating the Instructor's Manual. We would also like to thank Kristine Perlmutter for her assistance in formulating some of the questions in Part Two, and Amy Trumbull for her tireless help in securing permissions.

Finally, our thanks to the people at Longman Publishers, especially our editor, Suzanne Phelps-Chambers, her ever-efficient editorial assistant, Erica Schweitzer, and Anne Leung, our development editor. We are very appreciative of their fine help.

*Gary Goshgarian*
*Kathleen Krueger*

# PART ONE

# Strategies for Reading and Writing Arguments

# Understanding Persuasion: Thinking Like a Negotiator

Think of all the times in the course of a week when someone tries to convince you of something. You listen to the radio on the way to school or work and are relentlessly bombarded by advertisements urging you to buy vitamins, watch a particular television show, or eat at the new Mexican restaurant in town. You open a newspaper and read about the latest proposals to lower the drinking age, raise the age for retirement, and provide tax relief for the poor. The phone rings and the caller tries to sell you a newspaper subscription or to convince you to vote for candidate X. There's a knock on your bedroom door and your sister wants to borrow a CD and the keys to your car. Whether the issue is as small as a CD or as important as taxes, everywhere you turn you find yourself called on to make a decision and to exercise a choice.

If you think about all these instances, you'll discover that each decision you finally do make is heavily influenced by the ability of others to persuade you. People who have mastered the art of argument are able to influence the thoughts and actions of others. Your ability to understand how argument works and how to use it effectively will help you become aware of the ways in which you are influenced by others, as well as become more persuasive yourself. Anyone can learn to argue effectively by learning the techniques needed to create successful arguments.

This book is designed to help you achieve two goals: (1) to think critically about the power of other people's arguments and (2) to become persuasive in your own arguments.

## Argument

Broadly speaking, *persuasion* means influencing someone to do something. It can take many forms: fast-paced glittering ads, high-flying promises from salespeople, emotional appeals from charity groups—even physical threats. What will concern us in this book is *argument*— the form of persuasion that relies on reasoning and logical thought to convince people. While glitter, promises, emotional appeals, and even veiled threats may work, the real power of argument comes from the arguer's ability to convince others through language.

Because this is a book about writing, we will concentrate on the aspects of persuasion that most apply in writing, as opposed to those that work best in other forms (advertisements or oral appeals, for instance). Although written arguments can be passionate, emotional, or even hurtful, a good one demonstrates a firm foundation of clear thinking, logical development, and solid supporting evidence to persuade a reader that the view expressed is worth hearing. The ultimate goal might be to convince readers to change their thinking on an issue, but that does not always happen. A more realistic goal might be to have your listeners seriously consider your point of view and to win their respect through the logic and skill of your argument.

Most of what you write in college and beyond will attempt to persuade someone that what you have to say is worthy of consideration, whether it's a paper stating your views on immigration laws, an analysis of "madness" in *King Lear,* a letter to the editor of your school newspaper regarding women's varsity basketball, or a lab report on the solubility of salt. The same demands of persuasion and argument will carry into your professional life. Such writing might take the form of business reports, memos to colleagues, progress reports on students, medical evaluations, results of a technical study, proposals, maybe even a sales speech. In searching for a job or career, you might have to sell yourself in letters of inquiry.

The success or failure of those attempts will strongly depend on how well you argue your case. Therefore, it's important that as a college student you learn the skills of writing persuasive arguments. Even if you never write another argument, you will read, hear, and make them the rest of your life.

# What Makes an Argument?

Arguments, in a sense, underlie nearly all forms of writing. Whenever you express ideas, you are attempting to persuade somebody to agree with you. However, not every matter can be formally argued. Nor are some things worth the effort. So, before we go on to discuss the different strategies, we should make clear which subjects do and do not lend themselves to argument.

## Facts Are Not Arguable

Because facts are readily verifiable, they can't be argued. Of course, people might dispute a fact. For instance, you might disagree with a friend's claim that Thomas Jefferson was the second president of the United States. But to settle your dispute, all you have to do is consult an encyclopedia. What makes a fact a fact and, thus, inarguable, is that it has only one answer. It occurs in time and space and cannot be disputed. A fact either *is* or *is not* something. Thomas Jefferson was the third president of the United States, not the second. John Adams was the second. Those are facts. So are the following statements:

- The distance between Boston and New York City is 214 miles.
- Martin Luther King, Jr.'s birthday is now celebrated in all 50 states.
- I got a 91 on my math test.
- The Washington Monument is 555 feet high.
- The Japanese smoke more cigarettes per capita than any other people on earth.
- My dog Fred died a year ago.
- Canada borders the United States to the north.

All that is required to prove or disprove any of these statements is to check with some authority for the right answer. Sometimes facts are not easily verifiable. Consider for instance, "Yesterday, 1,212,031 babies were born in the world" or "More people have black hair than any other color." These statements may be true, but it would be a daunting, if not impossible, challenge to prove them. And what would be the point?

## Opinions Based on Personal Taste or Preference Are Not Arguable

Differing opinions are the basis of all argument. However, you must be careful to distinguish between opinions based on personal taste and opinions based on judgments. Someone who asks your "opinion" about which color shoes to buy is simply seeking your color preference—black versus brown, say. If someone asks your "opinion" of a certain movie, the matter could be more complicated.

Beyond whether or not you liked it, what might be sought is your aesthetic evaluation of the film: a judgment about the quality of acting, directing, cinematography, set design—all measured by critical standards you've developed over years of movie-going. Should you be asked your "opinion" of voluntary euthanasia, your response would probably focus on moral and ethical questions: Is the quality of life more important than the duration of life? What, if any, circumstances justify the taking of a life? Who should make so weighty a decision—the patient, the patient's family, the attending physician, a health team?

The word *opinion* is commonly used to mean different things. As just illustrated, depending on the context, opinion can refer to personal preference, a reaction to or analysis of something, or an evaluation, belief, or judgment, all of which are different. In this text, we categorize all these different possibilities as either opinions of taste or opinions of judgment.

*Opinions of taste* come down to personal preferences, based on subjective and, ultimately, unverifiable judgments. Each of the following statements is an opinion of taste:

- George looks good in blue.
- Pizza is my favorite food.
- Brian May of the group Queen is the greatest living rock guitarist.
- Video games are a waste of time.

Each of these statements is inarguable. Let's consider the first: "George looks good in blue." Is it a fact? Not really, since there is no objective way to measure its validity. You might like George in blue, whereas someone else might prefer him in red. Is the statement then debatable? No. Even if someone retorts, "George does *not* look good in blue," what would be the basis of argument but personal preference? And where would the counterargument go? Nowhere.

Even if a particular preference were backed by strong feelings, it would not be worth debating, nor might you sway someone to your opinion. For instance, let's say you make the statement that you never eat hamburger. You offer the following as reasons:

1. You're turned off by the sight of ground-up red meat.
2. When the meat is cooked, its smell disgusts you.
3. Hamburgers remind you of the terrible argument that broke out at a family barbecue some years ago.
4. You once got very sick after eating meatloaf.
5. You think beef cattle are the dirtiest of farm animals.

Even with all these "reasons" to support your point of view, you have not constructed an argument that goes beyond your own personal preference. In fact, the "reasons" you cite are themselves grounded in personal preferences. They amount to explanations rather than an argument. The same is true of the statements about pizza, musicians, and video games.

## Opinions Based on Judgments Are Arguable

An *opinion of judgment* is one that weighs the pros and cons of an issue and determines their relative worth. That "something" might be a book, a song, or a public issue, such as capital punishment. Such an opinion represents a position on an issue that is measured against standards other than those of personal taste—standards that are rooted in values and beliefs of our culture: what's true and false, right and wrong, good and bad, better and worse. Consequently, such an opinion is arguable.

In other words, personal opinions or personal preferences can be transformed into bona fide arguments. Let's return to the example of hamburger. Suppose you want to turn your own dislike for ground meat into a paper persuading others to give up eating beef. You can take several approaches to make a convincing argument. For one, you can take a health slant, arguing that vegetarians have lower mortality rates than people whose diets are high in animal fat and cholesterol or that the ingestion of all the hormones in beef increases the risk of cancer. You might even take an environmental approach, pointing out that the more beef we eat, the more we encourage the conversion of woodlands and rain forests into grazing land, thus destroying countless animals and their habitats. You can even take an ethical stand, arguing from an animal-rights point of view that intensive farming practices create inhumane treatment of animals—that is, crowding, force-feeding, and force-breeding. You might also argue that the killing of animals is morally wrong.

The point is that personal opinions can be starting points for viable arguments. But those opinions must be developed according to recognized standards of values and beliefs.

# The Uses of Argument

Many arguments center on issues that are controversial. Controversial issues, by definition, create disagreement and debate because people hold opposing positions about them. And, most of the time, there are more than two sides. Depending on the issue, there may be multiple opinions and perspectives. Because these views are often strongly held, we tend to view argument only in the form of a *debate,* an encounter between two or more adversaries who battle with each other over who is right. The media does much to contribute to the way we picture argument, particularly in the area of politics.

Every four years or so, the image returns to our television screens. Two candidates, dark-suited and conservatively dressed, hands tightly gripping their respective podiums, face off for all of America to watch. Each argues passionately for his or her solution to war, the economy, environmental crises, poverty, educational failings, high taxes, and countless other problems. Each tries desperately to undermine the arguments of the opponent in an effort to capture the votes of those watching. It's a winner-take-all debate, and it's often the image we see in our minds when we think of argument.

Argument *is* a form of persuasion that seeks to convince others to do what the arguer wants. Argument allows us to present our views and the reasons behind those views clearly and strongly. Yet argument can serve more productive purposes than the above illustration. Although argument can be a debate between two or more opponents who will never see eye-to-eye, in the world outside presidential debates and television sound bites argument can also begin a *dialogue* between opposing sides. It can enable them to listen to each other's concerns and to respond in a thoughtful way. Rather than attempt to demolish their opponent's arguments, these negotiators can often arrive at positions that are more valuable because they try to reconcile conflicting viewpoints by understanding and dealing directly with their opponent's concerns. Through the practice of *debate, dialogue,* and *deliberation,* real change can happen. In this chapter, we explore these three essential elements of argument and explain how they will enable you to be more effective when you write to persuade others.

## Debate

Think for a moment of all the associations the word *debate* suggests to you: winning, losing, taking sides, opposition, and competition. Debate is how we traditionally think of argument. It is a situation in which individuals or groups present their views as forcefully and persuasively as possible, often referring to their opponents' arguments only to attack or deride them. Practiced with just this goal in mind, debate can serve the purpose of presenting your position clearly in contrast to your opposition's, but it does little to resolve controversial issues. Focusing too much on the adversarial qualities of debate can prevent you from listening and considering other viewpoints. You can become so preoccupied with defeating opposing arguments that you fail to recognize the legitimacy of other opinions. This may lead you to ignore them as you fashion your own argument.

Consider the last time you debated an issue with someone. Perhaps it was an informal occasion in which you attempted to convince that person of your point of view. It may have been about an instructor or the best place to spend spring break or what movie to see. Your aim was to persuade the other person to "see it your way," and, if it was a typical debate, you were successful only if the other individual acquiesced. Debates are traditionally won or lost, and losers often feel frustrated and disappointed. Even more important, reasonable concerns on the losing side are often overlooked or not addressed. Debate does not provide a mechanism for compromise. It is not intended to provide a path toward common ground or a resolution in which all parties achieve a degree of success and positive change is made. Although some issues are so highly contentious that true consensus can never be achieved, an effective argument must acknowledge and respond to opposition in a thoughtful and productive manner.

But debate is an important way to develop your arguments because it allows you to explore their strengths and weaknesses. It can be a starting point for argument rather than a conclusion. Debate contains some of the essential elements of argument: Someone with a strong opinion tries to demonstrate the effectiveness of that view, hoping to persuade others to change positions or to take a particular course of action. When we debate, we have two objectives: to state our views clearly and persuasively and to distinguish our views from those of our opponents. Debate can help us develop our arguments because it encourages us to *formulate a claim, create reasons to support it,* and *anticipate opposition.*

### Formulating Claims

The claim is the heart of your argument. Whether you hope to protest a decision, change your readers' minds, or motivate your audience to take action, somewhere in your argument must be the assertion you hope to prove. In an argument essay, this assertion or claim functions as the *thesis* of the paper, and it is vital to the argument. The claim states precisely what you believe. It is the *position* or opinion you want your readers to accept or the action you want them to take. Thus, it's very important to state your claim as clearly as possible. It will form the basis for the rest of your argument.

Claims often take the form of a single declarative statement. For example, a claim in an argument essay about homelessness might look like this:

> If we look further into the causes of homelessness, we will discover that in many cases it is not the homeless individual who is at fault but rather conditions that exist in our society that victimize certain individuals.

A claim for an essay about teen pregnancy might be stated even more simply:

> People who blame the rise in teenage pregnancies on the sexual references in popular music ignore several crucial realities.

Sometimes writers signal their claims by certain words: *therefore, consequently, the real question is, the point is, it follows that, my suggestion is.* Here's an example:

> Therefore, I believe that scientists can find other effective ways to test new medicines and surgical techniques other than relying on helpless laboratory animals.

Because some arguments make recommendations for solving problems, your claim might be framed as a conditional statement that indicates both the problem and a consequence. This can be accomplished with split phrases such as *either . . . or, neither . . . nor, if . . . then.* For example,

> If we continue to support a system of welfare that discourages its recipients from finding employment, the result will be a permanent class of unemployed citizens who lack the skills and incentives to participate in their own economic benefit.

Claims must have support to convince a reader, so they are often followed by "because" statements—that is, statements that justify a claim by explaining why something is true or recommended or beneficial:

> Outlawing assisted suicide is wrong because it deprives individuals of their basic human right to die with dignity.

Formulating your claim when you debate is a first step for three basic reasons:

1. It establishes the subject of your argument.
2. It solidifies your own stand or position about the issue.
3. It sets up a strategy on which your argument can be structured.

There are no hard-and-fast rules for the location of your claim. It can appear anywhere in your essay: as your opening sentence, in the middle, or as your conclusion. However, many writers state their claim early in the essay to let their readers know their position and to use it as a basis for all the supporting reasons that follow. In later chapters, we will look at strategies for arriving at a claim and ways to organize your reasons to support it effectively.

## Creating Reasons

We have all seen a building under construction. Before the roof can be laid or the walls painted or the flooring installed, the support beams must be carefully placed and stabilized. Reasons are the support beams of an argument essay. Whether your claim will be considered correct, insightful, or reasonable will depend on the strength and persuasiveness of your reasons.

Reasons answer some basic questions about your claim:

1. Why do you believe your claim to be true?
2. On what information or assumptions do you base your claim?
3. What evidence can you supply to support your claim?
4. Do any authorities or experts concur with your claim?

You can derive reasons from personal experience, readings, and research. Your choices will depend on your claim and the information and evidence you need to make your reasons convincing. Let's use one of the examples from our discussion about claims to demonstrate what we mean:

**Your Claim:** Outlawing assisted suicide is wrong because it deprives individuals of the basic human right to die with dignity.

**Question 1:** Why do you believe your claim to be true?

**Response:** When individuals are terminally ill, they suffer many indignities. They lose control of their bodily functions and must be dependent on others for care. A prolonged illness with no hope of recovery causes the individual and family members to suffer needlessly. When death is imminent, individuals should be given the right to decide when and how to end their lives.

**Question 2:** On what information or assumptions do you base your claim?

**Response:** I believe that no individual wants to suffer more than necessary. No one wants to lose his or her independence and have to rely on others. Everyone wants to be remembered as a whole human being, not as a dying invalid.

**Question 3:** What evidence can you supply to support your claim?

**Response:** This is based on personal examples and on readings about how terminal illness is dealt with in hospitals and clinics.

**Question 4:** Do any authorities or experts concur with your claim?

**Response:** Yes, many authorities in the field of medicine agree with my claim. I can use their statements and research to support it.

By examining the responses to the questions, you can see how reasons can be created to support your claim. The answer to the first question suggests several reasons why you might be opposed to outlawing assisted suicide: the indignities suffered by the terminally ill, unnecessary suffering, the right to control one's own fate. Question 2 explores your assumptions about what the terminally ill might experience and provides additional reasons to support your claim. The third and fourth questions suggest ways to support your claim through personal examples, references to ideas and examples found in readings related to your topic, and the support of experts in the field.

*Credibility* is an essential element in creating reasons. To be a successful debater, you must be believable; you must convince your audience that you are knowledgeable about your subject and that the facts, statistics, anecdotes, and whatever else you use to support your reasons are accurate and up-to-date. This means constructing your reasons through research and careful analysis of all the information available. For example, if you argue in an essay that there are better ways to run the U.S. Post Office, you will need to understand and explain how the current system operates. You can use the facts and statistics that you uncover in your research to analyze existing problems and to support your ideas for change. Being thoroughly informed helps you present and use your knowledge persuasively. Acquainting yourself with the necessary information will make you appear believable and competent. In later chapters, we will discuss how to formulate reasons to support your claim and how to evaluate evidence and use it effectively.

Another way to achieve credibility is to avoid logical fallacies, which will undermine the logic or persuasiveness of your argument. *Logical fallacies,* a term derived from the Latin *fallere,* meaning "to deceive," are unintentional errors in logic or deliberate attempts to mislead the reader by exaggerating evidence or using methods of argument that appeal to prejudice or bias. In Chapter 2, we will review the most common forms of logical fallacies so you can recognize them in the arguments of others and avoid them in your own writing.

## Anticipating Opposition

Because debate anticipates opposition, you need to be certain that your reasons can withstand the challenges that are sure to come. Your goal as a successful debater is not only to present your reasons clearly and persuasively but to be prepared for the responses of people holding other views. For instance, in an essay on discrimination in women's collegiate sports, you may state that the operating budget of the women's varsity basketball team at your school is a fraction of that for the men's team. As evidence, you might point to the comparative lack of advertising, lower attendance at games, and lesser coverage than for the men's team. Unless you anticipate other perspectives on your issue, your argument could fall apart should someone suggest that women's basketball teams have lower budgets simply because they have smaller paying audiences. Not anticipating such a rebuttal would weaken your position. Had you been prepared, you could have acknowledged that opposing point and then responded to it by reasoning that the low budget is the cause of the problem, not the result of it. Putting more money into advertising and coverage could boost attendance and, thus, revenue.

In short, it is not enough simply to present your own reasons, no matter how effectively you support them. Unless you are familiar with opposing reasons, you leave yourself open to being undermined. To make your case as effective as possible, you must acknowledge and respond to the strongest reasons that challenge your own. To present only the weakest points of those who disagree with you or to do so in a poor light would likely backfire on your own credibility.

The following are strategies we recommend to help you become more aware of views that are different from your own and ways you might respond to them.

### "Yes, but . . ." Exchanges

One way to be aware of the reasons on the other side is to research your topic carefully. After you've done some reading, a useful method to explore the way others might respond to your ideas is to engage in a "Yes, but . . . " exchange. Imagine you are face-to-face with someone holding a different position and, as you run down the list of your own reasons, his or her response is "Yes, but . . . [something]." What might that "something" be? Your task is first to acknowledge the validity of the other individual's viewpoint, and then to respond to that idea with reasons of your own. Consider, for instance, how a debate about affirmative action programs might proceed. You begin:

> Affirmative action programs discriminate against white males by denying them employment for which they are qualified.

From what you've heard and read, your opponent might respond this way:

> Yes, there are probably instances in which white males have lost employment opportunities because of affirmative action programs, but without these programs minority candidates would never be considered for some job openings regardless of their qualifications.

Another reason might be:

> Race and gender should not be considerations when hiring an applicant for a job.

From your readings, you may uncover this opposing reason:

> Yes, in an ideal society race and gender would never be factors for employers, but since we don't live in such a society, affirmative action programs ensure that race and gender don't become negative considerations when an individual applies for a job.

> Imagining your debate in a "Yes, but . . . " exchange will help you work through a number of possibilities to strengthen your reasons in the light of opposition and to become more aware of other viewpoints.

### Pro/Con Checklists

Another method to help you become more aware of opposing viewpoints is to create a pro/con checklist. Making such a checklist is useful for several reasons. First, it helps you solidify your own stand on the issue. It puts you in the position of having to formulate points on which to construct an argument. Second, by anticipating counterpoints you can better test the validity and strength of your points. By listing potential resistance you can determine the weak spots in your argument. Third, tabulating your own points will help you decide how to organize your reasons—which points to put at the beginning of your paper and which to put in the conclusion. Depending on the issue, you may decide for the sake of impact to begin with the strongest point and end with the weakest. This is the strategy of most advertisers—hitting the potential customer right off with the biggest sales pitch. Or you may decide to use a climactic effect by beginning with the weakest point and building to the strongest and most dramatic. Last, by ordering your key points you can create a potential framework for constructing your argument. Page 00 shows an example of a pro/con checklist.

## Sample Pro/Con Checklist

CLAIM: Human cloning should be outlawed because it is unnecessary and unethical.

| PRO | CON |
|---|---|
| Human cloning is unnecessary because we have better ways to treat infertility. | Current fertility treatments are very expensive and are often unsuccessful. |
| Because we have too many unwanted children in the world already, we should not create more. | People have a right to have their own children. |
| Cloning is an unnatural process. | It is no more unnatural than many of the ways we currently treat infertility. |
| Human cloning will devalue the uniqueness of each individual. | A clone will still be a unique and separate human being. |

# Moving from Debate to Dialogue

Debate is an important step in constructing an argument. It propels us to find a strong position and to argue that position as effectively as possible. But if we define argument as only debate, we limit the potential power of argument in our society. One common misconception is that all arguments are won or lost. This may be true in formalized debates, but in real life few arguments are decided so clearly; and when they are, the conflicting issues at the heart of the debate can persist and continue to create dissent among individuals and groups. The prolonged tensions and sometimes violent confrontations that surround the issue of abortion may be the outcome of a debate that supposedly was resolved by a Supreme Court decision, *Roe* v. *Wade,* but remains a continuing problem because the debate did not engender a dialogue in which conflicting sides listened to each other and reconsidered their views from a more informed perspective. Argument must do more than provide an opportunity to present one's views against those of an opponent. We need to use it as a vehicle to explore other views as well and to help us shape a process in which change can happen and endure.

# Dialogue

Take another moment to consider words that come to mind when you think of *dialogue:* discussion, listening, interaction, and understanding. By definition, a dialogue includes more than one voice, and those voices are responsive to each other. When we have a dialogue with someone, we don't simply present our own views. We may disagree, but we take turns so that no one voice monopolizes the conversation. The object of a dialogue is not to win or lose; the object is to communicate our ideas and to listen to what the other person has to say in response.

For example, you may find a policy in a particular class regarding make-up tests unfair. Since your instructor seems to be a reasonable person, you visit her office to discuss your objections. Your dialogue might proceed like this:

**You:** Professor, your syllabus states that if a student misses a test, there are no make-ups. I think that this is unfair because if a student is genuinely ill or has an important conflict, the student will be penalized.

**Professor:** I can understand your concern, but I have that policy because some students use make-ups to gain extra time to study. And, by asking other students about the questions on the test, they gain an advantage over students who take the test when it's scheduled. I don't think that's fair.

**You:** I hadn't thought of that. That's a good reason, but I'm still worried that even if I have a legitimate excuse for missing a test, my grade in the course will suffer. What can I do if that happens?

**Professor:** Let me think about your problem. Perhaps there's a way that I can be fair to you and still not jeopardize the integrity of my exams.

**You:** What if a student provides a physician's note in case of illness or a few days' advance notice in case of a conflict? Would you be able to provide an alternative testing day if that should happen?

**Professor:** That might be a good way to deal with the problem, as long as the make-up could be scheduled soon after. I'm going to give this more thought before I decide. I appreciate your suggestions. Stop by tomorrow and we can come to an agreement.

This hypothetical dialogue works because each participant listens and responds to the ideas of the other. Each has an important stake in the issue, but both focus on finding constructive ways to deal with it rather than trying to prove that the other is wrong. As a result, a compromise can be reached, and each person will have made a contribution to the solution.

When we move from debate to dialogue, we move from an arbitrary stance to one that allows for change and modification. Dialogue requires that both sides of the debate do more than simply present and react to each other's views in an adversarial fashion; it demands that each side respond to the other's points by attempting to understand them and the concerns they express. Often it is difficult for those participating in a debate to take this important step. In such cases, it will be your task, as a student of argument, to create the dialogue between opposing sides that will enable you to recognize common concerns and, if possible, to achieve a middle ground.

Creating a dialogue between two arguments involves identifying the writers' claims and key reasons. This is a skill we discuss in Chapter 2, when we look at strategies for reading and analyzing argument essays.

## Deliberation

*Deliberate* is a verb that we don't use very much and we probably don't practice enough. It means to consider our reasons for and against something carefully and fully before making up our minds. We often speak of a jury deliberating about its verdict. Jury members must methodically weigh all the evidence and testimony that have been presented and then reach a judgment. Deliberation is not a quick process. It takes time to become informed, to explore all the alternatives, and to feel comfortable with a decision.

*Deliberation* plays an important part in the process of developing arguments. *Debate* focuses our attention on opposition and the points on which we disagree. *Dialogue* creates an opportunity to listen to and explore the arguments that conflict with our own. Deliberation, the careful consideration of all that we have learned through debate and dialogue, enables us to reach our own informed position on the conflict. Because we have participated in both debate and dialogue, we have a more complete understanding of the opposing arguments, as well as the common ground they may share. We are able to take the concerns of all sides into account.

Deliberation does not always resolve an issue in a way that is pleasing to all sides. Some issues remain contentious and irreconcilable, so that the parties are unable to move beyond debate. And, just as a jury sometimes reaches a verdict that is not what either the defense or the prosecution desires, deliberation does not ensure that all concerns or arguments will be considered equally valid. However, deliberation does ensure that you have given the arguments of all sides careful attention. And, unlike a jury, you have much broader parameters to determine your position. You do not have to decide *for* or *against* one side or the other. Your deliberations may result in an entirely new way of viewing a particular issue or solving a problem.

Consider, for example, a debate about whether a new football stadium should be built in a city experiencing economic problems, such as high unemployment and a failing public school system. One side of the debate may argue that a new stadium would result in additional jobs and revenue for the city from the influx of people who would come to watch the games. Another side may argue that the millions of dollars intended to subsidize a new stadium would be better spent creating job-training programs and promoting remedial education for schoolchildren. Your deliberation would involve several steps:

1. Becoming informed about the issue by reading and researching the information available
2. Creating a dialogue by listening to the arguments of all sides in the debate and trying to understand the reasons behind their claims
3. Weighing all the arguments and information carefully
4. Determining your own position on the issue

Your position might agree with one side or the other, or it might propose an entirely different response to the situation—say, a smaller stadium with the extra funds available to the schools, or a delay in the construction of a stadium until the unemployment problem is solved, or an additional tax to fund both, and so on. It would then be your task to convince all sides of the value of your position.

Deliberation enables you to use argument productively. It allows you to consider all sides of a problem or issue and to use your own critical analysis to find a way to respond.

As you learn more about writing your own arguments, you'll find that debate, dialogue, and deliberation can help you identify different perspectives, search for shared concerns, and develop your own position on an issue.

## Review: Basic Terminology

**Argument Essay**

An essay that attempts to convince or persuade others through reason, logic, and evidence to do what the writer wants or believe as the writer wishes.

**Claim**

The statement in your essay that expresses your position or stand on a particular issue. The claim states precisely what you believe. It is the viewpoint you want your readers to accept or the action you want them to take.

**Reasons**

The explanation or justification behind your claim. To be effective, reasons must be supported by evidence and examples.

**Debate**

The act of presenting your claim and reasons, and challenging and being challenged by someone who holds a different viewpoint. Debate often focuses on differences between opponents rather than shared concerns and values.

**Dialogue**

The act of listening and responding to those who hold viewpoints that are different from your own on a particular issue. The object of a dialogue is to find common ground by trying to understand other viewpoints while sharing your own. It is intended to reduce conflict rather than promote it.

**Deliberation**

The careful and informed consideration of all sides of an issue before reaching a conclusion or position on it. Deliberation can result in the resolution of a contentious issue.

# Taking a "War of Words" Too Literally
*Deborah Tannen*

The following essay provides important insights into the ways in which we often approach argument in our society. This article by Deborah Tannen is adapted from her book, *The Argument Culture: Moving from Debate to Dialogue,* which explores how U.S. culture promotes a warlike, adversarial approach to problem-solving. Tannen is a professor of linguistics at Georgetown University. She is the author of the bestsellers *You Just Don't Understand: Women and Men in Conversation* and *Talking from 9 to 5: Women and Men in the Workplace.* As you read Tannen's article, think about whether you have had experiences similar to those Tannen describes, when disagreements could have been settled more successfully through dialogue and thoughtful deliberation than through conflict.

1   I was waiting to go on a television talk show a few years ago for a discussion about how men and women communicate, when a man walked in wearing a shirt and tie and a floor-length skirt, the top of which was brushed by his waist-length red hair. He politely introduced himself and told me that he'd read and liked my book *You Just Don't Understand*, which had just been published. Then he added, "When I get out there, I'm going to attack you. But don't take it personally. That's why they invite me on, so that's what I'm going to do."

2   We went on the set and the show began. I had hardly managed to finish a sentence or two before the man threw his arms out in gestures of anger, and began shrieking—briefly hurling accusations at me, and then railing at length against women. The strangest thing about his hysterical outburst was how the studio audience reacted: They turned vicious— not attacking me (I hadn't said anything substantive yet) or him (who wants to tangle with someone who screams at you?) but the other guests: women who had come to talk about problems they had communicating with their spouses.

3   My antagonist was nothing more than a dependable provocateur, brought on to ensure a lively show. The incident has stayed with me not because it was typical of the talk shows I have appeared on—it wasn't, I'm happy to say—but because it exemplifies the ritual nature of much of the opposition that pervades our public dialogue.

4   Everywhere we turn, there is evidence that, in public discourse, we prize contentiousness and aggression more than cooperation and conciliation. Headlines blare about the Starr Wars, the Mommy Wars, the Baby Wars, the Mammography Wars; everything is posed in terms of battles and duels, winners and losers, conflicts and disputes. Biographies have metamorphosed into demonographies whose authors don't just portray their subjects warts and all, but set out to dig up as much dirt as possible, as if the story of a person's life is contained in the warts, only the warts, and nothing but the warts.

5   It's all part of what I call the argument culture, which rests on the assumption that opposition is the best way to get anything done: The best way to discuss an idea is to set up a debate. The best way to cover news is to find people who express the most extreme views and present them as "both sides." The best way to begin an essay is to attack someone. The best way to show you're really thoughtful is to criticize. The best way to settle disputes is to litigate them.

6   It is the automatic nature of this response that I am calling into question. This is not to say that passionate opposition and strong verbal attacks are never appropriate. In the words of Yugoslavian-born poet Charles Simic, "There are moments in life when true invective is called for, when it becomes an absolute necessity, out of a deep sense of justice, to denounce, mock, vituperate, lash out, in the strongest possible language." What I'm questioning is the ubiquity, the knee-jerk nature of approaching almost any issue, problem or public person in an adversarial way.

7   Smashing heads does not open minds. In this as in so many things, results are also causes, looping back and entrapping us. The pervasiveness of warlike formats and language grows out of, but also gives rise to, an ethic of aggression: We come to value aggressive tactics for their

own sake—for the sake of argument. Compromise becomes a dirty word, and we often feel guilty if we are conciliatory rather than confrontational—even if we achieve the result we're seeking.

8    Here's one example. A woman called another talk show on which I was a guest. She told the following story: "I was in a place where a man was smoking, and there was a no-smoking sign. Instead of saying 'You aren't allowed to smoke in here. Put that out!' I said, 'I'm awfully sorry, but I have asthma, so your smoking makes it hard for me to breathe. Would you mind terribly not smoking?' When I said this, the man was extremely polite and solicitous, and he put his cigarette out, and I said, 'Oh, thank you, thank you!' as if he'd done a wonderful thing for me. Why did I do that?"

9    I think the woman expected me—the communications expert—to say she needs assertiveness training to confront smokers in a more aggressive manner. Instead, I told her that her approach was just fine. If she had tried to alter his behavior by reminding him of the rules, he might well have rebelled: "Who made you the enforcer? Mind your own business!" She had given the smoker a face-saving way of doing what she wanted, one that allowed him to feel chivalrous rather than chastised. This was kinder to him, but it was also kinder to herself, since it was more likely to lead to the result she desired.

10   Another caller disagreed with me, saying the first caller's style was "self-abasing." I persisted: There was nothing necessarily destructive about the way the woman handled the smoker. The mistake the second caller was making—a mistake many of us make—was to confuse ritual self-effacement with the literal kind. All human relations require us to find ways to get what we want from others without seeming to dominate them.

11   The opinions expressed by the two callers encapsulate the ethic of aggression that has us by our throats, particularly in public arenas such as politics and law. Issues are routinely approached by having two sides stake out opposing positions and do battle. This sometimes drives people to take positions that are more adversarial than they feel—and can get in the way of reaching a possible resolution. . . .

12   The same spirit drives the public discourse of politics and the press, which are increasingly being given over to ritual attacks . . . I once asked a reporter about the common journalistic practice of challenging interviewees by repeating criticism to them. She told me it was the hardest part of her job. "It makes me uncomfortable," she said. "I tell myself I'm someone else and force myself to do it." But, she said she had no trouble being combative if she felt someone was guilty of behavior she considered wrong. And that is the crucial difference between ritual fighting and literal fighting: opposition of the heart.

13   It is easy to find examples throughout history of journalistic attacks that make today's rhetoric seem tame. But in the past such vituperation was motivated by true political passion, in contrast with today's automatic, ritualized attacks—which seem to grow out of a belief that conflict is high-minded and good, a required and superior form of discourse.

14   The roots of our love for ritualized opposition lie in the educational system that we all pass through.

15   Here's a typical scene: The teacher sits at the head of the classroom, pleased with herself and her class. The students are engaged in a heated debate. The very noise level reassures the teacher that the students are participating. Learning is going on. The class is a success.

16   But look again, cautions Patricia Rosof, a high school history teacher who admits to having experienced just such a wave of satisfaction. On closer inspection, you notice that

only a few students are participating in the debate; the majority of the class is sitting silently. And the students who are arguing are not addressing subtleties, nuances or complexities of the points they are making or disputing. They don't have that luxury because they want to win the argument—so they must go for the most dramatic statements they can muster. They will not concede an opponent's point—even if they see its validity—because that would weaken their position.

17    This aggressive intellectual style is cultivated and rewarded in our colleges and universities. The standard way to write an academic paper is to position your work in opposition to someone else's. This creates a need to prove others wrong, which is quite different from reading something with an open mind and discovering that you disagree with it. Graduate students learn that they must disprove others' arguments in order to be original, make a contribution and demonstrate intellectual ability. The temptation is great to oversimplify at best, and at worst to distort or even misrepresent other positions, the better to refute them.

18    I caught a glimpse of this when I put the question to someone who I felt had misrepresented my own work: "Why do you need to make others wrong for you to be right?" Her response: "It's an argument!" Aha, I thought, that explains it. If you're having an argument, you use every tactic you can think of—including distorting what your opponent just said—in order to win.

19    Staging everything in terms of polarized opposition limits the information we get rather than broadening it.

20    For one thing, when a certain kind of interaction is the norm, those who feel comfortable with that type of interaction are drawn to participate, and those who do not feel comfortable with it recoil and go elsewhere. If public discourse included a broad range of types, we would be making room for individuals with different temperaments. But when opposition and fights overwhelmingly predominate, only those who enjoy verbal sparring are likely to take part. Those who cannot comfortably take part in oppositional discourse— or choose not to—are likely to opt out.

21    But perhaps the most dangerous harvest of the ethic of aggression and ritual fighting is—as with the audience response to the screaming man on the television talk show—an atmosphere of animosity that spreads like a fever. In extreme forms, it rears its head in road rage and workplace shooting sprees. In more common forms, it leads to what is being decried everywhere as a lack of civility. It erodes our sense of human connection to those in public life—and to the strangers who cross our paths and people our private lives.

## QUESTIONS FOR DISCUSSION AND WRITING

1. Do you agree with Tannen's assertion that public discussions about controversial issues have been turned into "battles and duels" by the media? Why or why not? Look through current newspapers or magazines for evidence of this trend. Do other forms of media, such as television and radio, also encourage the same?
2. How has the "argument culture" affected our ability to resolve issues? Think of current controversies that have been negatively affected by the

tendency of some to defend their own "turf" rather than listen and respond constructively to others with differing views?

3. Tannen cites a woman who called in to a talk show and questioned whether her conciliatory approach to a potential conflict was the best course of action (paragraphs 8 and 9). In your journal, discuss your own experiences confronting someone whose behavior you found unacceptable. What approaches proved successful for you? Do you agree with Tannen that the woman was wise to avoid conflict?

4. In your own experience, have you found that schools and teachers promote and reward students who engage in heated debate with other students, as Tannen contends in paragraphs 18 to 20? Do you think this strategy discourages students who are uncomfortable with this confrontational behavior? Have you found that a "winner-take-all" approach to argument is a productive way to solve disagreements? What problems can arise from this approach? Any benefits?

## SAMPLE ARGUMENTS FOR ANALYSIS

Read the following two essays to find the basic components in writing arguments and to practice debate, dialogue, and deliberation. After you have read each essay carefully, respond to these questions about them:

1. Identify each writer's claim and restate it in your own words. What do you think is the writer's purpose in writing the essay?

2. What reasons does each writer use to support his claim? Make a list of the reasons you find in each essay. Are the reasons convincing?

3. Find examples of the ways each writer supports those reasons. How convincing is the evidence he presents? Is it pertinent? reliable? sufficient? Is it slanted or biased?

4. Does the writer acknowledge views about the subject that are different from his own? Where does he do this? What is the writer's attitude toward those who hold different views? Does he try to understand those views or does he respond only negatively toward them?

5. Using debate, dialogue, and deliberation, complete the following activities individually or in small groups:

   a. To become acquainted with opposing reasons, write a "yes, but . . ." exchange or a pro/con checklist.

   b. Using your checklist or exchange, create a dialogue between two or more opposing sides on the issue that attempts to find points of disagreement as well as common ground or shared concerns among them. Look for opportunities for each side to listen and respond constructively to the other.

   c. Deliberate. Review the reasons and examples from a number of perspectives. What reasons on either side do you find the most compelling? What concerns have particular merit? How can you balance the interests of all sides of the issue? Formulate a claim that takes into account what you have learned from listening and considering several perspectives and provide reasons to support it.

# The Case Against Tipping

*Michael Lewis*

Many people have strong views about tipping. Some consider it an optional act of kindness to express appreciation for good service, an additional expense over what they have already paid. For others it is an essential part of their day's wages, and thus their income. The following essay by Michael Lewis explores this dichotomy. Lewis is a contributing editor at *Vanity Fair* and the author of several bestselling books including *Liar's Poker* (1990), *Moneyball: The Art of Winning an Unfair Game* (2004), and most recently, *Home Game: An Accidental Guide to Fatherhood* (2009).

As you read this article, which originally appeared in the *New York Times Magazine* in 1997 and was updated by the author for this edition, think about your own attitudes toward the practice of tipping. What motivates a tip? If you have ever been on the receiving end, did you find that relying on others' generosity for your income left you vulnerable to their whims?

1  No lawful behavior in the marketplace is as disturbing to me as the growing appeals for gratuities. Every gentle consumer of cappuccinos will know what I'm getting at: Just as you hand your money over to the man behind the counter, you notice a plastic beggar's cup beside the cash register. "We Appreciate Your Tips," it reads in blue ink scrawled across the side with calculated indifference. The young man or woman behind the counter has performed no especially noteworthy service. He or she has merely handed you a $2 muffin and perhaps a ruinous cup of coffee and then rung them up on the register. Yet the plastic cup waits impatiently for an expression of your gratitude. A dollar bill or two juts suggestively over the rim—no doubt placed there by the person behind the counter. Who would tip someone a dollar or more for pouring them a cup of coffee? But you can never be sure. The greenbacks might have been placed there by people who are more generous than yourself. People whose hearts are not made of flint.

2  If you are like most people (or at any rate like me), you are of two minds about this plastic cup. On the one hand, you do grasp the notion that people who serve you are more likely to do it well and promptly if they believe they will be rewarded for it. The prospect of a tip is, in theory at least, an important incentive for the person working behind the counter of the coffee bar. Surely, you don't want to be one of those people who benefit from the certain hop to the worker's step that the prospect of a tip has arguably induced without paying your fair share of the cost. You do not wish to be thought of as not doing your share, you cheapskate.

3  And these feelings of guilt are only compounded by the niggling suspicion that the men who run the corporation that runs the coffee shops might be figuring on a certain level of tipping per hour when they decide how generous a wage they should extend to the folks toiling at the counters. That is, if you fail to tip the person getting you that coffee, you may be directing and even substantially affecting that person's level of income, especially in today's down economy.

4  That said, we are talking here about someone who has spent all of 40 seconds retrieving for you a hot drink and a muffin. When you agreed to buy the drink and the muffin you

did not take into account the plastic-cup shakedown. In short, you can't help but feel you are being had.

5    There in a nutshell is the first problem with tipping: the more discretion you have in the matter the more unpleasant it is. Tipping is an aristocratic conceit—"There you go, my good man, buy your starving family a loaf"—best left to an aristocratic age. The practicing democrat would rather be told what he owes right up front. Offensively rich people may delight in peeling off hundred-dollar bills and tossing them out to groveling servants. But no sane, well-adjusted human being cares to sit around and evaluate the performance of some beleaguered coffee vendor.

6    This admirable reticence means that, in our democratic age at least, gratuities are inexorably transformed into something else. On most occasions where they might be conferred—at restaurants, hotels and the like—tips are as good as obligatory. "Tipping is customary," reads the sign in the back of a New York City taxi, and if anything, that is an understatement. Once, a long time ago, I tried to penalize a cabdriver for bad service and he rolled alongside me for two crowded city blocks, shouting obscenities through his car window. A friend of mine who undertipped had the message drummed home more perfectly: a few seconds after she stepped out of the cab, the cab knocked her over. She suffered a fracture in her right leg. But it could have been worse. She could have been killed for . . . undertipping! (The driver claimed it was an accident. Sure it was.)

7    There, in a nutshell, is the second problem with tipping: the less discretion you have in the matter, the more useless it is as an economic incentive. Our natural and admirable reluctance to enter into the spirit of the thing causes the thing to lose whatever value it had in the first place. It is no accident that the rudest and most inept service people in America—New York City cabdrivers—are also those most likely to receive their full 15 percent. A tip that isn't a sure thing is socially awkward. But a tip that is a sure thing is no longer a tip really. It's more like a tax.

8    Once you understand the impossibility of tipping in our culture, the plastic cup on the coffee-bar counter can be seen for what it is: a custom in the making. How long can it be before the side of the coffee cup reads "Tipping Is Customary"? I called Starbucks to talk this over, and a pleasant spokeswoman told me that this chain of coffee bars, at least, has no such designs on American mores. The official Starbucks line on their Plexiglas container is that it wasn't their idea but that of their customers. "People were leaving loose change on the counter to show their gratitude," she said. "And so in 1990 it was decided to put a tasteful and discreet cup on the counter. It's a way for our customers to say thanks to our partners." (Partners are what Starbucks calls its employees.)

9    Perhaps. But you can be sure that our society will not long tolerate the uncertainty of the cup. People will demand to know what is expected of them, one way or the other. Either the dollar in the cup will become a routine that all civilized coffee buyers will endure. Or the tasteful and discreet cup will disappear altogether, in deference to the straightforward price hike.

10    A small matter, you might say. But if the person at the coffee-bar counter feels entitled to a tip for grabbing you a coffee and muffin, who won't eventually? I feel we are creeping slowly toward a kind of baksheesh economy in which everyone expects to be showered with coins simply for doing what they've already been paid to do. Let's band together and ignore the cup. And who knows? Someday, we may live in a world where a New York City cabdriver simply thanks you for paying what it says on the meter.

————————————

1. Do you think Lewis has had much experience in a job that relies on tips? What evidence can you find to demonstrate this?

2. Do you agree with Lewis? In your journal, respond to Lewis's ideas by exploring your own views on tipping. What experiences have you had that support your own view?

# Women Soldiers Crucial to US Mission

*Paula Broadwell*

American fighting forces are engaged in brutal engagements in two countries, Iraq and Afghanistan. We have all seen film footage of our military men and women kiss their families goodbye as they prepare to deploy. We have also seen news footage of the wars. Yet what we don't see on the evening news are women in fatigues, women toting automatic weapons, women rushed from battle or from an IED attack to medical facilities. It's almost always male soldiers. But what is the full reality? Who are engaged in combat? Who are the targets of an IED? Yes, women are serving, but their roles are barely visible. In this piece, West Point graduate Paula Broadwell explains that while official policy prevents women from serving in combat, women are there. And she argues strongly that modern military policy should be revised to reflect this reality. Broadwell is a research associate at Harvard University's Center for Public Leadership and serves on the board of Women in International Security. This article originally appeared on the op-ed page of the *Boston Globe* on August 26, 2009.

1   Recent headlines about whether G.I. Jane should be serving in combat or combat units—a violation of official policy—touched a nerve with women warriors.

2   A group called the Center for Military Readiness has been lobbying Congress to restrict women's roles in war. But in fact, today's wars have already decided when and where women are to be deployed. Instead of restricting women's opportunities, it is time for Pentagon leadership to consider codifying the reality of the role of women in combat. Defense Secretary Robert Gates should keep time with the beat of reality on the ground.

3   On today's battlefield, there is little differentiation between "front" and "rear" area operations. Whether they are in "combat units" or not, women are on the front lines, and they are invaluable. Period. By not acknowledging that in official policy, we diminish the sacrifices and contributions these women make every day.

4   Women have played an increasing role in recent wars, and the trend is likely to continue. Over 7,000 women served in Vietnam. In the first Persian Gulf War, 33,000 women deployed to the Gulf. Since Sept. 11, more than 220,000 of our total deployed forces have been women.

5   Even as the military fights wars in Iraq and Afghanistan, the class that entered West Point in 2008 contained more women than any other class since women first came to the academy in 1976. Higher-ranking women are also pursuing combat command experience for promotion opportunities. If we prohibit women from acquiring that experience, they

will never earn the same status as their male counterparts—although they may be doing effectively the same jobs.

6    Putting those concerns aside, our thin-stretched military can ill afford to keep women out of combat zones. Excluding women from combat units—infantry, armor, special operations, and some artillery units—hurts those units, because there are simply not enough male soldiers to fill their forward support companies.

7    Stability operations, peacekeeping, and counterinsurgency are unequivocally the norm for today's military and tomorrow's. These operations require winning local populations' hearts and minds, and female soldiers are well equipped to engage with the half of the population that shares their gender. The generation of soldiers who grew up in this complex environment understands that having well-trained women helps accomplish the mission. Officially restricting such a key resource from the front lines is naive and counterproductive—as many of our closest allies have recognized.

8    Myriad examples of the unofficial policy illustrate women's increasingly important front-line role in the no-boundary combat zone. In some special operations units, women are essential for cover and approach missions—and can easily and should morph into the assault elements if appropriate. Marine Female Engagement Teams (FETs) in Afghanistan also reflect the changing nature of counterinsurgents. An all-female unit of 46 Marines, the FET is the military's latest innovation in its competition with the Taliban for the populace's loyalty. Afghan women are viewed as good intelligence sources, and more open to the basics of the military's hearts-and-minds effort—including hygiene, education, and an end to the violence.

9    Without a doubt, this is a complex question with a lot of attendant emotion. Assuming women can meet physical requirements, one of the remaining concerns centers on the potential for women to be disruptive to combat unit cohesion. Experience in Iraq and Afghanistan has proven otherwise. According to a member of the well-disciplined Special Forces, elite women have integrated smoothly into many operations without disruption.

10    Human sexuality will always present a challenge to organizational discipline. In an isolated combat unit, it could present challenges, and long-term infantry operations in isolated outposts could create a situation where issues of sex impede an organization's survival skills. But on forward-operating bases, managing sexual issues should be like managing routine personnel issues. Banning sex is futile and impossible; the best approach is to set rules regarding fraternization, maintain awareness of relationships within the command, and strictly and fairly discipline transgressors.

11    At this point, the question is not whether women should be serving in combat, but whether we have enough women at all for today's wars.

12    We are ready, and we are already there.

### QUESTIONS FOR DISCUSSION AND WRITING

1. Have you served in the military or does a family member or close friend serve in the military? Prior to reading this essay, what was your opinion about women in combat? Was this based on personal experience? the experience of a friend or relative? your ideas about gender roles? or on arguments

you've heard in the media? Did this essay change your thinking or challenge your ideas on the subject? How is your opinion the same or different than before reading this piece?

2. In your own words summarize the claim or the assertion that Broadwell makes in this piece. What prompted her to express her ideas about the role of women in the military?

3. List three arguments Broadwell makes supporting the role of women in combat. Then classify each piece of evidence whether it be statistics, personal experience, events in recent history or a personal judgment. Which argument did you find the most convincing? Which argument was the least convincing? Why?

4. Does what you know about Broadwell's background make her credible, neutral' or biased when it comes to arguing about women in combat? Explain.

5. Broadwell discusses the argument that women can be disruptive to combat unit cohesion. Does she acknowledge one or both sides of the issue? Does this strengthen or weaken her argument?

## EXERCISES

1. Try to determine from the following list which subjects are arguable and which are not.
   a. Letter grades in all college courses should be replaced by pass/fail grades.
   b. Sororities and fraternities are responsible for binge drinking among college students.
   c. Lobster is my favorite seafood.
   d. Professor Greene is one of the best professors on campus.
   e. Children are better off if they are raised in a traditional nuclear family.
   f. Advertisements now often appear in commercial films using a strategy called product placement.
   g. Minorities make up only 10 percent of upper management positions in corporate America.
   h. The earth's population will be 7 billion by the year 2011.
   i. Juveniles who commit serious crimes should be sent to adult prisons.
   j. Last night's sunset over the mountains was spectacular.
   k. Advertisers often mislead the public about the benefits of their products.
   l. AIDS testing for health care workers should be mandatory.
   m. Bilingual education programs fail to help non-English-speaking children become part of mainstream society.
   n. Scenes of the nativity often displayed at Christmastime should not be allowed on public property.
   o. The tsunami that struck Asia in December of 2004 is the worst natural disaster in recorded history.
   p. Couples should have to get a license before having children.

q. Given all the billions of galaxies and billions of stars in each galaxy, there must be life elsewhere.

r. Secondhand smoke causes cancer.

2. In your argument notebook, create a pro/con checklist for the following topics. Make two columns: pro on one side, con on the other. If possible, team up with other students to brainstorm opposing points on each issue. Try to come up with five or six solid points and counterpoints.

a. I think women are better listeners than men.

b. If a juvenile is charged with a serious crime and his/her parents are found to be negligent, the parents should be charged with the crime as well.

c. "Hard" sciences such as math are more difficult than "soft" sciences such as sociology.

d. There should be a mandatory nationwide ban of cigarette smoking in all places of work including office buildings, restaurants, bars, and clubs.

e. The university should reduce tuition for those students who maintained an A average during the previous year.

f. ROTC should be made available to all students in U.S. colleges and universities.

g. The majority of American people support prayer in school.

h. Mandatory national ID cards would reduce the threat of terrorism in this country.

3. Use one of these topics to construct a dialogue in which the object is not to oppose the other side but to respond constructively to its concerns. As a first step, analyze the reasons provided by both sides and make a list of their concerns, noting whether any are shared. Then create a dialogue that might take place between the two.

4. Write about a recent experience in which you tried to convince someone of something. What reasons did you use to make your claim convincing? Which were most successful? What were the opposing reasons? How did you respond?

# 2

# Reading Arguments: Thinking Like a Critic

We read for a variety of purposes. Sometimes it's to find information about when a particular event will take place, or to check on the progress of a political candidate, or to learn how to assemble a piece of furniture. Other times we read to be entertained by a favorite newspaper columnist, or to discover the secrets behind making a pot of really good chili. But if you've ever picked up a book, a magazine article, a newspaper editorial, or a piece of advertising and found yourself questioning the ideas and claims of the authors, then you've engaged in a special kind of reading called *critical reading*. When you look beyond the surface of words and thoughts to think about the ideas and their meaning and significance, you are reading critically.

Critical reading is active reading. It involves asking questions and not necessarily accepting the writer's statements at face value. Critical readers ask questions of authors such as these:

- What do you mean by that phrase?
- Can you support that statement?
- How do you define that term?
- Why is this observation important?
- How did you arrive at that conclusion?
- Do other experts agree with you?
- Is this evidence up-to-date?

By asking such questions, you are weighing the writer's claims, asking for definitions, evaluating information, looking for proof, questioning assumptions, and making judgments. In short, you are actively engaged in thinking like a critic.

## Why Read Critically?

When you read critically, you think critically. Instead of passively accepting what's written on a page, you separate yourself from the text and decide what is convincing to you and what is not. Critical reading is a process of discovery. You discover where an author stands on an issue, and you discover the strengths and weaknesses of an author's argument. The result is that you have a better understanding of the issue. By asking questions of the author, by analyzing where the author stands with respect to others' views on the issue, you become more knowledgeable about the issue and more able to develop your own informed viewpoint on the subject.

Critical reading not only sharpens your focus on an issue, it also heightens your ability to construct and evaluate your own arguments. That will lead you to become a better writer because critical reading is the first step to critical writing. Good writers look at the written word the way a carpenter looks at a house—they study the fine details and how those details connect to create the whole. It's the same with critical reading. The better you become at analyzing and reacting to another's written work, the better you are at analyzing and reacting to your own, by asking: Is it logical? Are my points clearly stated? Do my examples really support my ideas? Have I explained this term clearly? Is my conclusion persuasive? In other words, critical reading will help you use that same critical eye with your own writing, making you both a better reader and a better writer.

Additionally, as you sharpen your skills as a reader and a writer, you will also develop your critical skills as an interpreter of arguments embodied not in words but in visual images. As you will see in Chapter 8, argumentation is not limited to verbal presentation. Photographs, political cartoons, and advertisements, among others, express potent and persuasive arguments in visual imagery.

Even though you may already employ many of the strategies of critical reading, we'd like to offer some suggestions and techniques to make you an even better critical reader.

## Preview the Reading

Even before you begin reading, you can look for clues that may reveal valuable information about the subject of the article, the writer's attitude about the subject, the audience the writer is addressing, and the purpose of the article. As a prereading strategy, try to answer the following questions:

1. *Who is the writer?* Information about the writer is sometimes provided in a short biographical note on the first or last page of the reading. The writer's age, education, current profession, and professional background can tell you about his or her experience and perspective on the subject. For instance, a physician who is writing about assisted suicide may have a very different attitude toward that subject than an individual who has a degree in divinity. A writer who has held a high-ranking position in a government agency or a political appointment will bring that experience to bear in a discussion of a political issue. A writer's background and professional training can provide knowledge and credibility; you may be more inclined to believe an expert in a field than someone with little or no experience. However, direct experience can also limit the writer's perspective. A review of this information before you read can help you better evaluate the writer as an authority.

2. *Where was the article originally published?* Often the publication in which the article originally appeared will indicate the writer's audience and purpose. Some publications, such as scholarly journals, are intended to be read by other professionals in a particular field. Writers for such a journal assume that readers are familiar with the terminology of that profession and possess a certain level of education and

experience. For example, an author writing about cancer research in a scholarly medical journal such as the *Journal of the American Medical Association (JAMA)* would assume a high degree of medical expertise on the part of the readers. An author writing about the same cancer research in *Newsweek* would provide a greatly simplified version with little medical terminology. Popular magazines you see at newsstands are designed to communicate to a larger, more general audience. Writers make an effort to explain difficult concepts in terms an inexperienced reader can understand. Knowing where the article was originally published will prepare you for the demands of the reading. It may also prepare you for the writer's point of view. Publications are usually designed for a specific audience. The *Wall Street Journal,* for example, has a readership largely comprising people interested in the economy, business, or investments. The articles in it reflect the concerns and interests of the business community. In contrast, an article appearing in *High Times,* a publication that endorses the use and legalization of marijuana, has a very different set of readers. By familiarizing yourself with the publication in which the article originally appeared, you can learn much about the writer's likely political and professional opinions, knowledge you can use to judge the credibility of his or her argument.

3. *When was the article originally published?* The date of publication can also provide background about what was happening when the article was published. It will indicate factors that might have influenced the writer and whether the evidence used in the reading is current or historical. For instance, an article written about the economy during a recession would be strongly influenced by factors of high unemployment and business failures. The writer's argument might not be as convincing during a period of growth and stability. Some readings are timeless in their consideration of basic truths about people and life; others can be challenged about whether their arguments still apply to current circumstances.

4. *What does the title reveal about the subject and the author's attitude toward it?* The title of an article often indicates both the subject of the article and the writer's attitude toward it. After you have identified the subject, look carefully at the words the writer has used to describe it. Are their connotations negative or positive? What other words do you associate with them? Does the title make reference to another written work or to a well-known slogan or familiar saying? Sometimes writers use their titles to suggest a parallel between their subject and a similar situation in recent times or a particular event in history. An article about the possibility of an annihilating nuclear attack in 2020 might be titled "Hiroshima in the Twenty-First Century." These choices are deliberate ways to inform readers about a writer's views and ideas on a subject. By considering the language in the title, you will be more aware of the writer's intent.

Let's try a preview of the first reading in this chapter. By carefully reading the introductory paragraph, you can learn the following information:

*Preview Question 1: Who is the writer?* As the introduction tells us, Henry Wechsler is the director of the College Alcohol Studies Program at the Harvard

School of Public Health. His professional title suggests that he is knowledgeable about alcohol use, particularly at the college level, because he directs a program that studies this area. You are about to read an essay, then, written by an expert in the field of alcohol research.

*Preview Question 2: Where was the article originally published?* By reading further in the paragraph, you find that the article was originally published in the *Boston Globe*. This is a widely circulated newspaper located in a major American city. The writer would expect the article to be read by a large cross-section of people with diverse economic and educational backgrounds. Because Boston is the city where Harvard and many other colleges are located, readers might have a special interest in issues that affect the college community.

*Preview Question 3: When was the article originally published?* The introduction tells you that the article first appeared on October 2, 1997. Although this was written some 13 years ago, the topic is still relevant to current concerns.

*Preview Question 4: What does the title reveal about the subject and the author's attitude toward it?* The title of the article, "Binge Drinking Must Be Stopped," suggests an emphatic and nonnegotiable attitude on the part of the author.

As you can see, your preview of the article has provided much valuable information that will help prepare you to begin the critical reading process.

## Skim the Reading

Just as an athlete would never participate in a competitive event without first stretching his or her muscles and thoroughly warming up, you will find that successful critical reading is a process that benefits from a series of activities aimed at increasing your understanding of the writer's ideas. The first time through, you may wish to skim the reading to get a general idea of its subject and intent. Further readings should be slower and more thoughtful so that each reason presented can be analyzed and evaluated and each idea judged and considered. Now that you have previewed the material about the author, the original publication and date, and the title, you are ready to skim the reading to find its basic features.

When you skim a reading, you are trying to discover the topic and the claim. Start by reading the first one or two paragraphs and the last paragraph. If the reading is a relatively short newspaper article, such as the following sample essay, this may be enough to give you a general idea of the writer's topic and point of view. If the reading is longer and more complex, you will also need to examine the first sentence or two of each paragraph to get a better sense of the writer's ideas.

### SAMPLE ARGUMENT FOR ANALYSIS

For practice, let's skim the first reading in this chapter. To organize your impressions from skimming the reading, it's a good idea to write down some of them in your journal.

# Binge Drinking Must Be Stopped

*Henry Wechsler*

"Binge" drinking is a problem that plagues many colleges and universities across America. Fueled by an "alcohol culture," students will drink to excess at apartment parties or fraternity houses just off campus. But the disturbing fact is that thousands of them die each year as a result of alcohol abuse. And, as argued in the essay below, too many college administrators are apparently turning a blind eye to the problem. Dr. Henry Wechsler is a social psychologist with a long-term commitment to research on alcohol and drug abuse among young people. A lecturer in the Department of Society, Human Development and Health at the Harvard School of Public Health, he is the principal investigator of the College Alcohol Study. Since its inception in 1992, the study has surveyed over 50,000 students at 120 colleges in 40 states, producing dozens of publications that have focused national attention on college binge drinking and its harmful effects. Dr. Wechsler is the author of 18 books and monographs including most recently *Dying to Drink* (2003). This essay was originally published in the *Boston Globe* in 1997 and has been updated by the author for this edition of *Dialogues*.

1    A recent study conducted for the National Institute on Alcohol Abuse and Alcoholism estimated that over 1800 college students 18–24 years of age died from alcohol related injuries in the past year. We should be saddened and outraged by these tragic deaths of young men and women just starting to fulfill their life's promise.

2    These deaths are an extreme and unfortunate consequence of a style of drinking that is deeply entrenched and widespread in American colleges. Binge drinking is a reality of college life in America and perhaps the central focus of fraternity house life.

3    Since the Harvard School of Public Health study on college binge drinking was released in 1994, colleges have been deluged with reports on alcohol abuse. Even before our results became public, it was inconceivable that college administrators were unaware of the existence of alcohol problems at their institutions.

4    A quick ride in a security van on a Thursday, Friday, or Saturday night could provide all the information needed. A conversation with the chief of security could easily reveal where the binge drinking takes place and which students, fraternities, and alcohol outlets are violating college rules or local ordinances.

5    An incoming freshman learns during the first week of school where the alcohol and parties are and often has a binge drinking experience even before purchasing a textbook. If students can find it so easily, so can college administrators. It is not that complicated: Drunken parties are usually at certain fraternity houses and housing complexes just off campus. The beer that fuels these parties is bought in the liquor stores offering cut rate prices for large purchases. Heavy drinking also takes place in the many bars encircling most campuses where large quantities of alcohol are sold cheaply.

6    If we know so much about the problem, why is it that we have not been able to do much about it? First, because colleges, like problem drinkers, do not recognize that they have a problem. And those that do think that they have solved it through half-measures. It has been there for so long that they have adapted to it. They are lulled into complacency as long as the problem does not seem to increase or a tragedy does not occur.

7    Second, the solutions that are offered are usually only partial: a lecture, an awareness day, a new regulation in the dorms. The root of the problem is seldom touched. The focus is on the students, and not on the suppliers and marketers of the alcohol. The supply of large quantities of cheap alcohol is viewed as outside the purview of college officials. "It's off campus" is a euphemism for "that's not my job." The bar or liquor store may be off campus, but it is controlled by licensing boards that city officials and colleges can substantially influence. The fraternity house may be off campus and not owned by the college, but it is affiliated with and depends on the college for its existence. Many colleges and universities simply wink at the activities of the fraternities and claim no responsibility.

8    Third, when new policies are established, they are often assumed to be in effect without proper verification. It is easy to say there is no drinking allowed in a dormitory or a fraternity, but enforcement is necessary to put the policy into effect. Legally, no alcohol can be sold to people under age 21, but 86 percent of college students drink.

9    We can no longer be shocked at what is happening on many college campuses and in many fraternities. This is no longer a time merely to form a committee to study the situation. It is time to act.

10    Action needs to be taken on many fronts: the college president's office, the fraternity and sorority system, the athletics department, community licensing boards, and foremost, those students who are sick of the drinking they see around them.

11    Parents who pay for college tuitions should demand a safe environment for their children. Binge drinking need not remain an integral part of college life. University presidents must make it their responsibility to produce change.

After skimming "Binge Drinking Must Be Stopped," you might record the following (we indicate in parentheses the paragraphs in which we found our ideas):

> Wechsler starts off with a reference to a study that reports on the large number of college student deaths as the result of alcohol-related injuries. He says we should be saddened and outraged by this. Then he suggests that binge drinking has become very common on college campuses, particularly in fraternities (*paragraphs 1 and 2*). Wechsler believes parents should insist that colleges provide a safe environment for their children by finding solutions for binge drinking. University presidents must take responsibility for solving this problem (*paragraph 11*).

By skimming the article, you now have some sense of what the reading will be about and the writer's position. Before beginning a closer reading of the text, you will want to take one additional step to prepare yourself to be an active and responsive reader: Consider your experience with the topic.

## Consider Your Own Experience

Your next step in the reading process is to consider your own experience. Critical reading brings your own perspective, experience, education, and personal values to your reading. Sometimes you begin with very little knowledge about the subject of your reading. It may be a topic that you haven't given much thought or one that is unfamiliar and new. Other times you may start with some of your own ideas and opinions about the subject. By taking the time to consider what you know and how your own experiences and values relate to the author's ideas, you can add a dimension to your reading that enables you to question, ana-lyze, and understand the writer's ideas more effectively. You will be a more active critical reader because you can respond to the writer's ideas with ideas of your own.

Before beginning a close reading, take the time to reflect on these questions:

- ■ What do I know about this subject?
- ■ What have I heard or read about it recently?
- ■ What attitudes or opinions do I have about the subject?

Exploring what you already know or think about a subject can have several bene-fits: You can use your knowledge to better understand the situation or issue described in the reading; you can compare your own experience with that of the writer; you can for-mulate questions to keep in mind as you read; and you can become more aware of your own opinions about the subject. For instance, you may be reading an article about the benefits of the proposed plan for improving your state's welfare system. If you have some knowledge about this proposal from reading news stories or hearing discussions about it, you will begin your reading with some understanding of the issue. If you have had actual experience with the welfare system or know of others' experiences, you can provide examples of your own to challenge or support those of the writer. If you have taken the time to consider questions you have about the proposed plan, you will be actively seeking answers as you read. And, by exploring your own views on the subject before you read, you will find that the ideas in the article will enrich, inform, and pos-sibly change your opinion.

After previewing and skimming the reading, John, a freshman composition student, wrote the following reflection on the topic of binge drinking in his journal:

> It would be hard to be a student at college and not notice the heavy drinking that goes on every weekend. Some people just can't have fun unless they drink too much. It's a fact of college life—for some people. And if you live in a small college community, sometimes that's all there is to do on Saturday night. I've seen some kids really ruin their lives with too much partying. They forget why they came to college in the first place—or maybe that is why they came. But not everybody drinks to excess. Most of us just like to get a little buzz and socialize and have fun. Most of us will go just so far and stop, but there's always a few who can't seem to stop until they pass out or puke their guts out on the sidewalk. Yeah, we've all been told the dangers of drinking too much, but some people aren't mature enough to see that they're hurting them-selves. Binge drinking happens every weekend around here. It's not a pretty sight, but I'm not sure how the college president or anybody else could stop it. College stu-dents have always partied to relieve tension and to socialize. It's been going on for years. Why is college drinking suddenly such a big issue? And, if the drinking takes place outside of campus, how can the college stop it? If students want to get alcohol, even if they're underage, they'll find a way. Why should the college tell us whether we can drink or not?

John clearly has considerable experience with the topic and some strong opinions of his own. By considering them before he begins a close reading of the article, he is ready to explore and challenge the ideas he encounters in the reading.

# Annotate the Reading

Annotating the text is the next stage of critical reading to help you become a thoughtful and careful reader. *Annotating* is responding to the ideas in the reading right on the pages of your text. (If you don't own the publication the essay appears in, make a photocopy.) There are many different ways to annotate a reading, but many readers use the following methods:

- Highlight or underline passages that you consider significant.
- Write questions in the margins that respond to the writer's ideas or that you wish to follow up with further investigation.
- Circle words or phrases that need to be defined or made clearer.
- Add comments or brief examples of your own that support or challenge the writer's.
- Draw lines between related ideas.
- Note the writer's use of transitions and qualifiers that subtly shade meaning.
- Point out with arrows or asterisks particularly persuasive examples.
- Mark difficult-to-understand sections of the text that need a closer look.

Annotation is a way to create an active dialogue between you and the writer by responding in writing to individual points in the reading. Your annotations become a personal record of your thoughts, questions, objections, comments, and agreements with the writer. Annotation can help you read like a critic because it makes you slow down and pay attention to each idea as you read. As an additional benefit, your written comments in the margin will serve as a reminder of your response to the ideas in the essay when you read it again. Figure 2.1 on pages 33–35 is an example of some of the ways you might annotate "Binge Drinking Must Be Stopped."

## Binge Drinking Must Be Stopped

1    A recent study conducted for the National Institute on Alcohol Abuse and Alcoholism estimated that over 1800 college students 18–24 years of age died from alcohol related injuries in the past year. We should be saddened and outraged by these tragic deaths of young men and women just starting to fulfill their life's promise.

*Does everyone at college drink?*

2    These deaths are an extreme and unfortunate consequence of a style of drinking that is deeply entrenched and widespread in American colleges. Binge drinking is a reality of college life in America and perhaps the central focus of fraternity house life.

*claim*

3    Since the Harvard School of Public Health study on college binge drinking was released in 1994, colleges have been (deluged) with reports on alcohol abuse. Even before our results became public, it was inconceivable that college administrators were unaware of the existence of alcohol problems at their institutions.

*find more info on this*
*flooded*

4     A quick ride in a security van on a Thursday, Friday, or Saturday night could provide all the information needed. A conversation with the chief of security could easily reveal where the binge drinking takes place and which students, fraternities, and alcohol outlets are violating college rules or local ordinances.

*Is this the job of a college administrator?*

5     An incoming freshman learns during the first week of school where the alcohol and parties are and often has a binge drinking experience even before purchasing a textbook. If students can find it so easily, so can college administrators. It is not that complicated: Drunken parties are usually at certain fraternity houses and housing complexes just off campus. The beer that fuels these parties is bought in the liquor stores offering cut rate prices for large purchases. Heavy drinking also takes place in the many bars encircling most campuses where large quantities of alcohol are sold cheaply.

*qualifier*
*How does he know this?*

6     If we know so much about the problem, why is it that we have not been able to do much about it? First, because colleges, like problem drinkers, do not recognize that they have a problem. And those that do think that they have solved it through half-measures. It has been there for so long that they have adapted to it. They are lulled into complacency as long as the problem does not seem to increase or a tragedy does not occur.

*who is "we"?*

*Is this contradicted by the next ¶ ?*

7     Second, the solutions that are offered are usually only partial: a lecture, an awareness day, a new regulation in the dorms. The root of the problem is seldom touched. The focus is on the students, and not on the suppliers and marketers of the alcohol. The supply of large quantities of cheap alcohol is viewed as outside the purview of college officials. "It's off campus" is a euphemism for "that's not my job." The bar or liquor store may be off campus, but it is controlled by licensing boards that city officials and colleges can substantially influence. The fraternity house may be off campus and not owned by the college, but it is affiliated with and depends on the college for its existence. Many colleges and universities simply wink at the activities of the fraternities and claim no responsibility.

*Don't colleges try to do something about binge drinking?*

*Agreed. These don't change behaviour much.*

*less offensive substitute word*

*What does he mean?*

8     Third, when new policies are established, they are often assumed to be in effect without proper verification. It is easy to say there is no drinking allowed in a dormitory or a fraternity, but enforcement is necessary to put the policy into effect. Legally, no alcohol can be sold to people under age 21, but 86 percent of college students drink.

*Impressive statistic*

9     We can no longer be shocked at what is happening on many college campuses and in many fraternities. This is no longer a time merely to form a committee to study the situation. It is time to act.

*Who is "we"? Has it changed?*

10    Action needs to be taken on many fronts: the college president's office, the fraternity and sorority system, the athletics
department, community licensing boards, and foremost, those
students who are sick of the drinking they see around them.

*His solution. What should they do?*

11    Parents who pay for college tuitions should demand a safe
environment for their children. Binge drinking need not remain
an integral part of college life. University presidents must make
it their responsibility to produce change.

*Who is responsible? Don't the drinkers have some responsibility?*

*essential*

*Are college students "children"?*

**Figure 2.1**

## Summarize the Reading

Before you can begin to analyze and evaluate what you read, it's important to understand clearly what the writer is saying. *Summarizing* is a type of writing used to capture the essential meaning of a reading by focusing only on the writer's main points. When you summarize, you "tell back," in a straightforward way, the writer's main ideas. Although summaries can vary in length depending on the length of the original reading, all summaries share these qualities:

■ **A summary is considerably shorter than the original.** Because a summary is concerned only with the writer's main ideas, supporting details and examples are usually omitted. The length of a summary will vary depending on your purpose and the length and content of the original.

■ **A summary is written in your own words.** Although it may be necessary to use certain of the writer's words for which there are no substitutes, a summary is written in your own words. If you find it necessary to include a short phrase from the original, then quotation marks must be used to set it off. (In Chapter 9, we discuss ways to use summary in a researched argument paper and the need to document the ideas in your summary with a citation.)

■ **A summary is objective.** When you summarize, your job is to "tell back" the writer's main ideas with no comments or personal opinions of your own. Of course, once you have completed your summary, you are free to respond to it in any way you wish.

■ **A summary is accurate.** It's a good idea to reread several times before you attempt to summarize a reading because it's important that you truly understand what the writer means. Sometimes it takes many tries to capture that exact meaning.

■ **A summary is thorough.** Even though a summary is, as we've explained, much shorter than the original, a good summary contains each of the writer's main points.

Summarizing is an important step in critical reading because you need to understand a writer's ideas thoroughly before you can explain them, in writing, to others. Don't be discouraged when you first try to summarize a reading. Over time and with practice you will feel more comfortable writing summaries.

A good method to begin summarizing a reading is to write a one-sentence summary of the ideas in each paragraph. (Brief paragraphs that elaborate the same point can be summarized together.) By considering each paragraph separately, you will be sure to cover all the main ideas in the reading and be able to see at a glance how the ideas in the essay are connected to each other and how the writer has chosen to sequence them.

Let's go back to the essay "Binge Drinking Must Be Stopped" and try a one-sentence summary of each paragraph (we combine short paragraphs that are about the same idea):

*Paragraphs 1:* According to a recent study, some 1800 college students 18–24 years of age died from alcohol related injuries this past year—a tragic reality.

*Paragraph 2:* Colleges should be aware of the problem of excessive drinking among their students because studies have been released about it.

*Paragraph 3:* By speaking with law enforcement professionals in their own communities, colleges could become aware of where alcohol laws are being broken.

*Paragraph 4:* Freshmen learn where to find alcohol when they first arrive on campus: fraternities, student housing, and bars close to campus.

*Paragraph 5:* Colleges aren't doing anything about the problem because they have accepted it and don't want to admit it exists.

*Paragraph 6:* Because the cause of the problem is the availability of alcohol off campus, colleges don't think it is their responsibility to act even though they could exercise a strong influence over the places that sell alcohol to students.

*Paragraph 7:* Colleges don't check to see whether their own alcohol policies are being enforced.

*Paragraphs 8 and 9:* Rather than just talk about this problem, we need to do something about it at many different levels within the college and the community.

*Paragraph 10:* College presidents need to take responsibility for reducing the practice of excessive drinking at their colleges to provide a safe place for students.

Your one-sentence summary of each paragraph should reveal the essential parts of the essay: the claim and the main reasons the writer uses to support the claim. Once you have identified these important elements, you are ready to begin your summary. It might look something like this (note that we've added the name of the writer and the title of the article):

In his essay "Binge Drinking Must Be Stopped," Henry Wechsler expresses his concern about the common practice of excessive drinking on college campuses. He suggests that colleges are failing in their responsibility to deal with this problem adequately. Although colleges should be informed about the problem, they won't acknowledge its seriousness. Because it doesn't happen on their campuses, they don't feel that it is their responsibility. Wechsler thinks that colleges could exercise their influence off campus in ways that would help to solve the problem. And, even when colleges do have alcohol policies to restrict drinking, they don't check to see if their policies are being enforced. The problem of binge drinking needs to be dealt with now at many different levels within the college and the community. Wechsler thinks that college presidents need to take responsibility for dealing with binge drinking so that it is no longer an important part of college life.

In looking over this summary, you'll notice that we begin with a general sentence that presents the writer's topic and claim. Then, after reviewing our one-sentence paragraph summaries, we have chosen the writer's main reasons to include in the rest of our paragraph. We have tried to eliminate any ideas that are repeated in more than one paragraph, so we can focus on only the major points.

Summarizing a reading means taking all the separate ideas the writer presents, deciding which ones are important, and weaving them together to create a whole. Our next step in the critical reading process is to consider the ways in which the writer has presented those ideas.

## Analyze and Evaluate the Reading

To *analyze* something means to break it down into its separate parts, examine those parts closely, and evaluate their significance and how they work together as a whole. You already began this process when you summarized the main idea in each paragraph of your reading. But analysis goes beyond identifying the ideas in the essay. When we analyze, we consider how each part of the essay functions. We are discovering and evaluating the assumptions and intentions of the writer, which lie below the surface of the writing and which we consider separately from the meaning of the essay itself. Analysis helps us consider how successfully and effectively the writer has argued.

Although there is no set formula for analyzing an argument, we can offer some specific questions you should explore when reading an essay that is meant to persuade you:

- What are the writer's assumptions? What does the writer take for granted about the readers' values, beliefs, or knowledge? What does the writer assume about the subject of the essay or the facts involved?
- What kind of audience is the writer addressing?
- What are the writer's purpose and intention?
- How well does the writer accomplish those purposes?
- What kinds of evidence has the writer used—personal experience or scientific data or outside authorities?
- How convincing is the evidence presented? Is it relevant? Is it reliable? Is it specific enough? Is it sufficient? Is it slanted or dated?
- Does the writer's logic seem reasonable?
- Did the writer address opposing views?
- Is the writer persuasive?

For the sake of illustration, let's apply these questions to our reading:

- *What are the writer's assumptions?*
  The writer assumes that the estimated number of alcohol-related student deaths indicates a widespread problem of binge drinking on college campuses. He thinks that colleges have a responsibility to control the behavior of their students. He assumes that college students will continue to binge drink without any such controls.

■ *What kind of audience is the writer addressing?*

He seems to be addressing college administrators, parents of college students, and readers who have a special interest in college life.

■ *What are the writer's purpose and intention?*

He wants to make his readers aware that a problem exists and that colleges are not effectively dealing with it.

■ *How well does the writer accomplish this purpose?*

He makes a strong argument that colleges refuse to acknowledge that there's a problem.

■ *What kinds of evidence has the writer used?*

He refers to a recent study for the National Institute on Alcohol Abuse and Alcoholism" as well as others by the Harvard School of Public Health, and he uses examples of student hangouts that he has heard about but not experienced personally. He seems familiar with college programs on alcohol awareness. He implies that he consulted with the campus security chief for some of his information.

■ *How convincing is the evidence?*

Wechsler mentions a scientific study in paragraph 1 with figures and then again in paragraph 3; but he does not offer much in the way of details concerning the second study. While Wechsler could provide more solid evidence that the problem is widespread, his examples of places where students can find alcohol seem convincing.

■ *Does the writer's logic seem reasonable?*

Wechsler effectively links the evidence he presents to his claim that excessive drinking on college campuses is being ignored by college administrators.

■ *Did the writer address opposing views?*

No. We never hear how college administrators respond to this criticism. We also don't know if college students agree with the description of their behavior.

■ *Is the writer persuasive?*

The writer is persuasive if we assume that the problem is widespread and that colleges can have a major impact on students' behavior when they are not on campus.

# Argue with the Reading

Asking questions and challenging assumptions are important ways to read critically. Although you may not feel qualified to pass judgment on a writer's views, especially if the writer is a professional or an expert on a particular subject, you should keep in mind that as a part of the writer's audience, you have every right to determine whether an argument is sound, logical, and convincing. Your questions about and objections to the writer's ideas will help you evaluate the effectiveness of his or her argument and form your own judgment about the issue.

You may wish to record some of these thoughts in your annotations in the margins of the text. However, a good strategy for beginning writers is to respond at greater length in a journal. You might start by jotting down any points in the essay that contradict your own experience or personal views. Note anything you are skeptical about. Write down any questions you have about the claims, reasons, or evidence. If some point or conclusion seems forced or unfounded, record it and briefly explain why. The more skeptical and questioning you are, the more closely you are reading the text and analyzing its ideas. In particular, be on the lookout for logical fallacies, those instances in which the writer—whether unintentionally or purposefully—distorts or exaggerates evidence or relies on faulty logic to make a point. We discuss these fallacies extensively later in this chapter.

Likewise, make note of the features of the text that impress you—powerful points, interesting wording, original insights, clever or amusing phrases or allusions, well-chosen references, or the general structure of the essay. If you have heard or read different views on the issue, you might wish to record them as well.

As an example, let's consider some questions, challenges, and features that might have impressed you in our sample essay:

- Wechsler claims that binge drinking is a common practice at colleges across America. Is that true? Does binge drinking take place at all colleges or only on certain campuses? Do all students engage in this practice, or is it more common among certain age groups, gender, fraternity members as opposed to nonmembers, residential students? Do college students drink more than noncollege students in the same age group?
- The statistic about the number of student deaths (paragraph 1) and percentage of college students who drink (paragraph 8) is convincing.
- Colleges exist to educate students. Are they responsible for monitoring students' behavior when they are not attending classes or socializing off campus? Is it realistic to expect colleges to do this?
- Are colleges really denying that the problem exists? Don't they have counseling services to help students with drinking problems? What else can they do?
- Wechsler's points about the influence that colleges have in their communities (paragraph 7) are persuasive.
- Mentioning the concerns of students who don't drink and the parents of college students is a clever strategy Wechsler uses to expand his audience and pressure colleges to act.

## Create a Debate and Dialogue Between Two or More Readings

Few of us would expect to be experts on tennis or golf after watching one match or tournament. We know that it takes time and effort to really begin to understand even the fundamentals of a sport. Reading a single article on a particular subject is the first step in becoming educated about the issues at stake, but a single essay provides us with only one perspective on that subject. As we continue to read about the subject, each new article will offer a new perspective and new evidence to support that view. The more we read, the more complex and thorough our knowledge about the subject becomes. Creating a dialogue between two or more readings is the next step in the process of critical reading.

When you annotate a reading in the earlier stages of critical reading, you begin a dialogue between yourself and the writer. When you create a dialogue between two or more readings, you go one step further: You look at the ideas you find in them to see how they compare and contrast with each other, how they are interrelated, and how the information from one reading informs you as you read the next. By creating a dialogue between the ideas you encounter in several readings, you will be able to consider multiple viewpoints about the same subject.

## SAMPLE ARGUMENT FOR ANALYSIS

Begin reading this second selection on binge drinking by following the steps we've outlined in this chapter:

1. Preview the information about the author, where the article first appeared, the date of publication, and the title.
2. Skim the reading to discover the writer's topic and claim.
3. Consider your own experience, values, and knowledge about the subject.
4. Annotate the reading.
5. Summarize the essay.
6. Analyze and evaluate the effectiveness of the reading.
7. Argue with the reading.

# Stop Babysitting College Students
*Froma Harrop*

> Froma Harrop presents another viewpoint on the subject of binge drinking and college students in the following essay, which appeared in the *Tampa Tribune.* Harrop, an editorial writer and columnist for the *Providence Journal,* argues that college students should be the ones held responsible for their behavior, not businesses and educational institutions.

1  Anyone suspicious that the American university experience has become a four-year extension of childhood need look no farther than the colleges' latest response to the binge-drinking "problem." Now, in a grown-up world, college administrators would tell students who down four or five stiff drinks in a row that they are jerks.

2  If they commit violent acts as a result, the police get called. If they drive after drinking, they go to the slammer. If they die from alcohol poisoning, they have nothing but their own stupidity to blame.

3  But if they can drink responsibly, then let them have a good time.

4  Forget about hearing any such counsel, for that would turn students into self-directing adults. Better to blame the problem on all-purpose "cultural attitudes" and "societal pressures" abetted by the villainous alcohol industry.

5  Thus, demands grow for better policing of off-campus liquor outlets. That is, turn local businesses into babysitters. There are calls to ban sponsorship of college events by companies selling alcohol or the marketing of such beverages on campus. That is, protect

their charges from evil influences and trample on free speech. (What should colleges do with the frequent references in Western literature to the glories of drink? Rabelais, for example, said, "There are more old drunkards than old physicians.")

6    One former college official has suggested that universities stop serving champagne at parents' weekend brunches or at fundraising events. Remove the bad example for the sake of the children. (Somehow it is hard to believe that a college with any sense of self-preservation would insist that its big-check writers remain cold sober.)

7    The truth is, most Americans can drink without a problem. Careful use of alcohol relaxes and warms the drinker with a sense of well-being. Winston Churchill and Franklin Roosevelt saved Western civilization without ever missing a cocktail hour. Students have long enjoyed their own drinking traditions. Brahms' Academic Overture, the stately piece heard over and over again at college commencements, took its melody from a student drinking song.

8    Where is there a campus drinking crisis, anyway? Six college students have supposedly died this year from excessive drinking. These cases are lamentable, but many more college students died from sports-related injuries or car accidents.

9    An even more interesting question is: How many noncollege people in their late teens or early 20s have died from alcohol poisoning? Take note that no one is memorizing this particular statistic—even though the majority of high school students do not go on to college. That number is not etched on our national worry list for the following strange reason: Our society considers the 19-year-old who has a job an adult, while universities see the 19-year-old pre-law student as a child. Working people who cause trouble because they drink are punished. College students are given others to blame.

10    College administrators should know that, from a purely practical point of view, playing hide-the-bottle does no good when dealing with an alcoholic. Indeed, anyone who has hung around Alcoholics Anonymous or Al-Anon can immediately identify such behavior as "enabling." Rather than allow the problem drinker to sink into the mire of his addiction until he can no longer stand it and takes steps to straighten out, the enabler tries to save him. Rest assured that students interested in getting smashed for the night will find the booze.

11    Let us end here with yet another proposition: that binge drinking is more about binge than drinking. It would seem that someone who gulps five glasses of Jim Beam in five minutes is not looking for a pleasant high. Binge drinking is a stunt that has more in common with diving off bridges or swallowing goldfish than the quest for inebriation.

12    What any increase in binge drinking probably indicates is that the students really don't know how to drink. Binging may just be the latest evidence of decline in our nation's table arts. Instead of savoring wine and spirits in the course of a civilized meal, young people are administering them. The colleges' response is to put condoms on bottles.

## Construct a Debate

Now that you have a good understanding of Froma Harrop's views on college students' binge drinking, you are ready to consider the ideas in both the essays you read. Our first step will be to consider the differences between these two writers by constructing a debate.

From your summaries of the readings, select the main ideas that seem directly opposed to each other. To highlight those differences, create two columns, one for each writer. Here are a few of the ideas Wechsler and Harrop debate in their essays:

| *Wechsler* | *Harrop* |
|---|---|
| Binge drinking is a major problem on college campuses: A student has died. | Binge drinking is not a major problem on campuses: Few students have died. |
| Colleges have a responsibility to take action about this problem. | Students are responsible for their own drinking. |
| Colleges should prevent off-campus suppliers of alcohol from selling it to college students. | Colleges should not "police" off-campus suppliers of alcohol. |
| Colleges should provide a safe environment for students. | College students are adults and should take care of themselves. |
| Binge drinking continues because colleges aren't treating it as an important problem. | Binge drinking happens because some college students haven't learned to drink responsibly. |

These are just a sampling of the many ideas that might be debated by these writers. You should be able to come up with several more.

By considering differences, you can see at a glance the ways in which these writers oppose each other. Your next step is to find the ideas they have in common. This may take more searching, but it's an important step in creating a dialogue between them. To get you started, we'll list a few of the ideas we found. See if you can come up with a few more:

1. Both writers acknowledge that drinking takes place on college campuses.
2. Both writers indicate that binge drinking can be a problem and that students have died as a result.
3. Both writers agree that colleges are aware that binge drinking takes place off campus.

Now that you have found both differences and common ideas, you are ready to create a dialogue. When you create a dialogue between two readings, you find ways for the writers to speak to each other that recognize their differences and points of agreement.

Your dialogue will reveal how the ideas in both readings interrelate. Let's try to create a dialogue using some of the ideas we found:

**Wechsler:** Binge drinking is a serious problem on college campuses. It's an activity that has become commonplace.

**Harrop:** I agree that college students engage in binge drinking, but six deaths this year don't necessarily indicate that this is a crisis.

**Wechsler:** Just because more students haven't died doesn't mean that it isn't a dangerous activity and should be ignored. Colleges need to take steps to ensure that more students aren't harmed by this common practice.

**Harrop:** It's unfortunate that students have died, but why should we think it is the college's responsibility to police student drinking? College students are adults and should suffer the consequences of their behavior. It's their choice whether to drink and how much.

**Wechsler:** Colleges are responsible for their students. They need to find ways to prevent students from getting alcohol. They are responsible to the parents who pay the tuition and to the other students who have to tolerate excessive drinking among their peers.

**Harrop:** Practically speaking, colleges can't prevent students from drinking. Students who want to drink will find a way because they are adults with drinking problems, not children in need of supervision.

Complete this dialogue by finding additional ways in which the writers' ideas speak to each other.

As you can see, the dialogue helps us explore the readings in far greater depth than if we had read both essays in isolation. Each writer's ideas help us to evaluate the ideas of the other. By interrelating them in a dialogue, we can better appreciate how the perspective of each writer changes the way similar facts and information are interpreted. For instance, Henry Wechsler is outraged by the estimated 1800 alcohol-related student deaths. In contrast, Froma Harrop does not find the deaths of six college students from excessive drinking an alarming statistic when she compares it with the number of college students who have died from other accidental causes. It is up to us as readers to decide which writer's interpretation is more persuasive.

## SAMPLE ARGUMENTS FOR ANALYSIS

To practice creating your own dialogue between readings, read the following two letters to the editor, which appeared in two newspapers before and after Henry Wechsler's article. Read them critically, going through the steps we outlined in this chapter, and add them to the dialogue already created between Wechsler and Harrop. We think you'll find that your understanding of the issue will increase and that you'll feel more confident about forming your own position on the question of college binge drinking.

## Letter from the *Washington Post*

To the Editor:

1    When we saw the headline "Party Hardly" and the revolting picture of four bare-chested, probably underage fraternity brothers guzzling cheap beer, we thought, "Finally! Your paper is tackling an issue that affects every college student." Much to our chagrin, however, the article wasted two pages of newsprint glorifying drunkenness and poor study habits.

2    Perhaps you need to be aware of some ugly facts before your next article on college drinking: One out of every four student deaths is related to alcohol use (research shows that as many as 360,000 of the nation's 12 million undergraduates will die as a result of

alcohol abuse); alcohol is a factor in 66 percent of student suicides and 60 percent of all sexually transmitted diseases; studies show that between 33 percent and 59 percent of drinking college students drive while intoxicated at least once a year (with as many as 30 percent driving impaired three to 10 times per year); and alcohol consumption was a factor in at least half of the cases of a study of college women who had been raped by an acquaintance.

3    Alcohol affects not only those who drink it: Those students who do not drink are affected by their classmates or roommates who do. Students at schools with high levels of binge drinking are three times more likely to be pushed, hit or sexually assaulted than are students at schools with less drinking. Students who live with people who drink heavily often are kept awake by obnoxious behavior or the sound of their roommates vomiting in the trash can.

4    The shame does not lie solely with your paper, however. *The Princeton Review,* which ranks "party schools" based on how much students use alcohol and drugs, how few hours students study every day and the popularity of fraternities and sororities, should focus on what most feel is the real purpose of a college education: to learn—not to learn how to party.

*Kathryn Stewart*
*Corina Sole*

# Letter from the *Times-Picayune*

To the Editor:

1    The entire nation is justifiably concerned about recent tragic deaths caused by alcohol abuse on our college campuses. College students everywhere know where to procure alcohol and where to consume it without being "hassled."

2    Public dialogue asks if institutions are doing enough to control the situation. Unfortunately, it must be stated that colleges and universities are doing all they can.

3    A typical university fosters an alcohol awareness program, provides the services of a substance abuse coordinator, disciplines students for infractions and provides an atmosphere in which young people can grow responsibly.

4    There is more that must be done. Parents at one time held their sons and daughters accountable for the company they kept. A student who deliberately associates with a group known for its excesses, or who joins an organization suspended or expelled by the institution, is choosing bad company. Peer pressure does the rest.

5    The courts restrict the ability of colleges to discipline students for off-campus behavior unless the activity in question has a fairly direct relationship with institutional mission.

6    They require due process, including confrontation by witnesses, for any disciplinary action. Peer pressures in the college-age group are so strong that testimony of witnesses is frequently difficult to obtain.

7    Until we return to a system in which colleges can function, at least in part, in loco parentis (in place of the parent), other agencies of society will have to step in.

8    To be fully effective, a college would need the ability to impose severe sanctions, including dismissal, on the base of reasonable proof of misbehavior or association with bad elements. Advocates of unrestrained constitutional rights will have difficulty with this, but the student enters a contractual relationship with a college to pursue an education.

9    The educators, not the legal system, should do the educating. Colleges exist to form good citizens, conscious of their own rights and the rights of others. Colleges and universities should be evaluated on the basis of the results of their educational work.

*James C. Carter, S.J.*
Chancellor,
Loyola University,
New Orleans

# Deliberate About the Readings

As we explained in Chapter 1, deliberation is a way to arrive at your own position on a particular issue. You can't begin deliberation until you have really listened to and reflected on the complexities each issue involves. Once you have engaged in all the steps in the process of critical reading, you are ready to deliberate.

In your deliberation, first consider each of the writer's claims and main points. Then, thinking like a critic, find a way to respond that defines your own position on the issue. Using the four readings in this chapter, a deliberation in your journal about college binge drinking might look like this:

All the writers see binge drinking as a problem, although they differ about where they place the blame and how they plan to solve the problem. Wechsler thinks that binge drinking among college students occurs because colleges are indifferent to it and refuse to recognize its seriousness. He urges colleges to use their influence and power to prevent students from obtaining alcohol. He doesn't seem to think that the students who engage in binge drinking have a lot of control over their behavior. Carter, Sole, and Stewart all agree with Wechsler about the seriousness of the problem; however, they disagree about where to place the blame. Carter thinks that colleges are doing all they can and should be given more legal power to discipline students who binge drink. Sole and Stewart suggest that the media is to blame by endorsing values that encourage students to drink and party rather than concentrate on their studies. Only Harrop places the blame squarely on the shoulders of the binge drinkers themselves. She feels strongly that students need to be treated as adults with drinking problems and suffer the consequences of their actions.

After reading these writings, I am convinced that binge drinking is a problem worthy of our attention. The statistics that Wechsler, Stewart, and Sole cite are convincing and impressive. I also know from my own experience that many students drink excessively, and I think that six deaths are too many for us to ignore. I also think that binge drinking is a problem that affects the entire college community, not just the drinkers, as Stewart and Sole point out. However, I tend to agree with Harrop that students must be held responsible for their own actions. I disagree with Carter that schools should act like parents. College is about becoming an adult in all areas of our lives, not just academics.

Any solution to the problem of binge drinking needs to include the students who abuse alcohol. Unless those students also see their drinking habits as a problem, nothing the college or legal system can impose will affect their behavior. Perhaps a combination of actions, including broader and stronger efforts to educate students about alcohol abuse, greater enforcement and harsher penalties for underage drinking by the legal system, and efforts by colleges to restrict alcohol availability in the community and on the campus, would make a significant dent in this problem.

Now try writing your own deliberation, in which you consider the points you find most important in each reading, to arrive at your own position on the issue of binge drinking.

# Look for Logical Fallacies

When you read the arguments of others, you need to pay attention to the writer's strategies, assertions, and logic to decide if the argument is reasonable. Like the cross-examining attorney in a court case, you must examine the logical connections between the claim, the reasons, and the evidence to reveal the strengths and weaknesses of the writer's argument.

Sometimes writers make errors in logic. Such errors are called **logical fallacies**, a term derived from the Latin *fallere,* meaning "to deceive." Used unintentionally, these fallacies deceive writers into feeling that their arguments are more persuasive than they are. Even though an argument may be well developed and contain convincing evidence, a fallacy creates a flaw in the logic of an argument, thereby weakening its structure and persuasiveness.

## Preview: Logical Fallacies

- Ad hominem argument
- Ad misericordiam argument
- Ad populum argument
- Bandwagon appeal
- Begging the question
- Circular reasoning
- Dicto simpliciter
- False analogy
- False dilemma
- Faulty use of authority
- Hasty generalization
- Non sequitur
- Post hoc, ergo propter hoc
- Red herring
- Slippery slope
- Stacking the deck
- Straw man

Not all logical fallacies are unintentional. Sometimes a fallacy is deliberately employed—for example, when the writer's goal has more to do with persuading than with arriving at the truth. Every day we are confronted with fallacies in media commercials and advertisements. Likewise, every election year the airwaves are full of candidates' bloated claims and pronouncements rife with logical fallacies of all kinds.

Recognizing logical fallacies when they occur in a reading is an important step in assessing the effectiveness of the writer's argument. This final section of our chapter will acquaint you with some of the most common logical fallacies.

## Ad Hominem Argument

From the Latin "to the man," the **ad hominem** argument is a personal attack on an opponent rather than on the opponent's views. Certainly the integrity of an opponent may be important to readers. Nonetheless, writers are usually more persuasive and credible when they focus on issues rather than character flaws. If, for instance, you are reading a paper against the use of animals in medical research and the writer refers to the opposition as "cold-hearted scientists only interested in fame and fortune," you might question whether the writer objects to the scientists' views or to their personal prosperity. Name-calling and character assassination should make you suspicious of the writer's real motives or balanced judgment. Personal criticisms, even if true, can be overemphasized and, therefore, undercut the writer's credibility.

However, there may be cases in which an ad hominem argument is a legitimate rhetorical tool. When the special interests or associations of an individual or group appear to have a direct impact on their position on an issue, it is fair to raise questions about their lack of objectivity on that basis. For example, the organizer of a petition to build a state-supported recycling center may seem reasonably suspect if it is revealed that he owns the land on which the proposed recycling center would be built. While the property owner may be motivated by sincere environmental concerns, the direct relationship between his position and his personal life makes this fair game for a challenge.

### Examples of Ad Hominem Arguments

- How could Tom accuse her of being careless? He's such a slob.
- Of course he doesn't see anything wrong with violent movies. The guy's a warmonger.
- We cannot expect Ms. Lucas to know what it means to feel oppressed; she is the president of a large bank.

## Ad Misericordiam Argument

Its name also derived from Latin, the **ad misericordiam** argument is the appeal "to pity." This appeal to our emotions need not be fallacious or faulty. A writer, having argued several solid points logically, may make an emotional appeal for extra support. Your local Humane Society, for instance, might ask you to donate money so it can expand its facilities for abandoned animals. To convince you, the society might point out how, over the last few years, the number of strays and unwanted pets has tripled. And because of budget constraints, the society has been forced to appeal to the public. It may claim that a donation of $25 would house and feed a stray animal for a month. Any amount you give, they explain, will ultimately aid the construction of a new pet "dormitory" wing. To bolster the appeal, the Humane Society literature might then describe how the adorable puppy and kitten in the enclosed photo will have to be put to death unless the overcrowding of the society's facilities is relieved by donations such as yours.

When an argument is based solely on the exploitation of the reader's pity, however, the issue gets lost. There's an old joke about a man who murdered his parents and appealed to the court for leniency because he was an orphan. It's funny because it ludicrously illustrates how pity has nothing to do with murder. Let's take a more realistic example. If you were a lawyer whose client was charged with bank embezzlement, you would not get very far basing your defense solely on the fact that the defendant was abused as a child. Yes, you may touch the hearts of the jurors, even move them to pity. Yet that would not exonerate your client. The abuse the defendant suffered as a child, as woeful as it is, has nothing to do with his or her crime as an adult. Any intelligent prosecutor would point out the attempt to manipulate the court with a sob story while distracting it from more important factors such as justice.

## Examples of Ad Misericordiam Arguments

- It makes no difference if he was guilty of Nazi war crimes. The man is 85 years old and in frail health, so he should not be made to stand trial.
- Paula is 14 years old and lives on welfare with her mother; she suffers serious depression and functions like a child half her age. She should not be sent to adult court, where she will be tried for armed robbery, so she can spend her formative years behind bars.

## Ad Populum Argument

From the Latin "to the people," an **ad populum** argument is just that—an argument aimed at appealing to the supposed prejudices and emotions of the masses. Writers attempt to manipulate readers by using emotional and provocative language to add appeal to their claims. The problem with the ad populum argument, however, is that such language sometimes functions as a smoke screen hiding the lack of ideas in the argument. You'll find examples of this fallacy on the editorial pages of your local newspaper—for example, the letter from parents raising a furor because they don't want their child or the children of their friends and neighbors taught by teachers with foreign accents; or the columnist who makes the ad populum case against capital punishment by inflating the number of innocent people wrongfully executed by the state; or the writer who argues that if gays and lesbians are allowed to serve in the military, our national defense will be jeopardized by "sex maniacs."

## Examples of Ad Populum Arguments

- High school students don't learn anything these days. Today's teachers are academically underprepared.
- If you want to see the crime rate drop, tell Hollywood to stop making movies that glorify violence.
- Doctors oppose health reform because it will reduce their large incomes.

## Bandwagon Appeal

This familiar strategy makes the claim that everybody is doing this and thinking that. If we don't want to be left out, we had better get on the **bandwagon** and do and think the same things. The basic appeal in this argument is that of belonging to the group, behaving like the majority. It plays on our fears of being different, of being excluded. Of course, the appeal is fallacious inasmuch as we are asked to "get with it" without weighing the evidence of what is being promoted: "Smart shoppers shop at Sears"; "America reads Danielle Steel."

## Examples of Bandwagon Appeals

- Everybody's going to the System of a Down concert.
- Nobody will go along with that proposal.
- The majority of the American people want a constitutional amendment outlawing flag burning.

## Begging the Question

Similar to circular reasoning, **begging the question** passes off as true an assumption that needs to be proven. For instance, to say that the defendant is innocent because he passed a polygraph test begs the question: Does passing a polygraph test mean somebody is innocent? Sometimes the begged question is itself loaded in a bigger question: "Are you ever going to act like you are equal and pay for one of our dates?" The begged question here is whether paying the costs of a date is a measure of sexual equality.

## Examples of Begging the Question

- That foolish law should be repealed.
- She is compassionate because she's a woman.
- If you haven't written short stories, you shouldn't be criticizing them.

## Circular Reasoning

**Circular reasoning** is another common fallacy into which many writers fall. In it, the conclusion of a deductive argument is hidden in the premise of that argument. Thus, the argument goes around in a circle. For instance: "Steroids are dangerous because they ruin your health." This translates: Steroids are dangerous because they are dangerous. Sometimes the circularity gets camouflaged in a tangle of words: "The high cost of living in today's America is a direct consequence of the exorbitant prices manufacturers and retailers are placing on their products and services." Cut away the excess, and this translates: The high cost of living is due to the high cost of living. Repetition of key terms or ideas is not evidence. Nor does it prove anything. Instead of simply restating your premise, find solid evidence to support it.

## Examples of Circular Reasoning

- People who are happy with their work are cheerful because they enjoy what they're doing.
- Smoking is bad for you because it ruins your health.
- Bank robbers should be punished because they broke the law.

## Dicto Simpliciter

The fallacy known as **dicto simpliciter** comes from the Latin *dicto simpliciter ad dictum secundum quid,* which roughly translates as "from a general truth to a specific case regardless of the qualifications of the latter." In its briefer form, it means "spoken simply" and refers to a sweeping generalization that doesn't always apply. A dicto simpliciter argument makes the logical fallacy of exploiting an overly simplistic or unqualified "rule of thumb" while disregarding exceptions to that rule. For example, it's generally understood that birds fly. We know that at the local zoo Kiki the kiwi is a bird and is housed in the aviary. But to conclude that because she's a bird Kiki can therefore fly is fallacious reasoning. And the reason is that the kiwi bird is an exception—one of the few types of birds that are flightless.

## Examples of Dicto Simpliciter Arguments

- If torture can save the lives of those who would be killed by terrorists, then the government should employ torture as a preemptive measure of protection.
- Exercise is good for people. Now that Bob is out of the hospital, he should get back to the treadmill.
- Guns kill. So we cannot allow the average citizen to possess a weapon.

Here's another more familiar matter where dicto simpliciter arguments might be heard. It is generally accepted that men are physically stronger than women. However, it would be a fallacious claim that women shouldn't be allowed in military combat since they aren't strong enough to carry weapons. This statement is a logical fallacy since it does not account for the exceptions to the rule—women who are stronger than the average. In other words, this argument exploits a stereotype.

## False Analogy

An analogy compares two things that are alike in one or more ways. In any form of writing, analogies are very useful, as they expand meaning and demonstrate imagination. In arguments, they can be wonderful tools for persuasion. Unfortunately, they can also lead the writer astray and make his or her argument vulnerable to attack.

The problem with **false analogies** arises when the two things compared do not match up feature for feature, and ideas being compared do not logically connect or are pressed beyond legitimacy. The result is a false analogy. For instance, a candidate for a high-powered job may ask to be employed because of his extraordinary heroics during the Iraq War. He may even claim that being a CEO is like fighting a battle: He needs to be brave, tough in mind and body, and willing to take and deal out punishment. Although the argument might sound appealing, running a company involves more than combat skills. Certainly it is important for a corporate executive to be strong and tough-minded. However, an office full of five-star generals might not be expert at dealing with economic recession or product liability. The fallacy is an imperfect analogy: Business and soldiering overlap minimally.

A sound analogy will clarify a difficult or unfamiliar concept by comparing it with something easily understood or familiar.

## Examples of False Analogy

- The Ship of State is about to wreck on the rocks of recession; we need a new pilot.
- This whole gun control issue is polarizing the nation the way slavery did people living above and below the Mason-Dixon line. Do we want another Civil War?
- Letting emerging nations have nuclear weapons is like giving loaded guns to children.

## False Dilemma

A **false dilemma** involves the simplification of complex issues into an either/or choice. For example, "Either we legalize abortion or we send young women to back-alley butchers," "Love America or leave it," "Either we keep gun ownership legal or only criminals will have guns." Such sloganizing ultimatums, although full of dramatic impact, unfortunately appeal to people's ignorance and prejudices.

## Examples of False Dilemma

- English should be the official language of the United States, and anybody who doesn't like it can leave.
- Movies today are full of either violence or sex.
- Either we put warning labels on records and compact discs, or we'll see more and more teenage girls having babies.

## Faulty Use of Authority

The **faulty use of authority** occurs when someone who is an expert in one area is used as an authority for another unrelated area. For instance, the opinions of a four-star general about the use of force against an uncooperative foreign tyrant carry great weight in a discussion of U.S. foreign policy options. However, the opinions of that same individual about the Supreme Court's ruling on the question of assisted suicide are less compelling. His military expertise does not guarantee that his views on euthanasia are particularly valuable.

Advertisers frequently resort to the faulty use of authority to promote their products. Celebrities are asked to endorse products they may have no special knowledge about or any interest in aside from the sizable check they will receive for their services. Another example occurs when well-known popular figures rely on their achievements in one area to lend credibility to their views in another. For instance, the late Benjamin Spock, famous for his work on child development, became a spokesperson for the nuclear disarmament movement. Because of his reputation, people were willing to listen more closely to his views than to others who were less well known, yet his expertise in child-rearing gave him no more authority in this area than any other well-educated person. While Dr. Spock may, indeed, have been knowledgeable about nuclear arms, his expertise in that area would have to be demonstrated before he could be used as an effective authority on the subject.

## Examples of Faulty Use of Authority

- You should buy these vitamins because Larry King recommended them on television last night.
- The American Bar Association states that secondhand smoke is a serious cancer threat to nonsmokers.
- Americans shouldn't find hunting objectionable because one of our most popular presidents, Theodore Roosevelt, was an avid hunter.

## Hasty Generalization

As the name indicates, the **hasty generalization** occurs when a writer arrives at a conclusion based on too little evidence. It's one of the most frequently found fallacies. If the local newspaper's restaurant critic is served underdone chicken at Buster's Diner during her first and only visit, she would be making a hasty generalization to conclude that Buster's serves terrible food. Although this may be true, one visit is not enough to draw that conclusion. If, however, after three visits she is still dissatisfied with the food, she is entitled to warn her readers about eating at Buster's.

Hasty generalizations can also occur when the writer relies on evidence that is not factual or substantiated. A generalization can only be as sound as its supporting evidence. Writers should provide multiple and credible examples to support their points. Be wary of sweeping, uncritical statements and words such as *always, all, none, never, only,* and *most.* Note whether the writer qualifies the claim with words that are limiting, such as *many, some, often,* and *seldom.*

### Examples of Hasty Generalizations

- That shopping mall is unsafe because there was a robbery there two weeks ago.
- I'm failing organic chemistry because the teaching assistant doesn't speak English well.
- This book was written by a Stanford professor, so it must be good.

## Non Sequitur

From the Latin for "does not follow," a **non sequitur** draws a conclusion that does not follow logically from the premise. For instance, suppose you heard a classmate make the following claim: "Ms. Marshall is such a good teacher; it's hard to believe she wears such ugly clothes." The statement would be fallacious because the ability to teach has nothing to do with taste in clothing. Some of the worst teachers might be the best dressers. Although you might want to believe a good teacher would be a good dresser, there is no reason to think so. Writers must establish a clear connection between the premise and the conclusion. And unless one is made through well-reasoned explanations, readers will not accept the cause-and-effect relationship.

Political campaigns are notorious for non sequiturs: "Candidate Jones will be a great senator because she's been married for twenty years." Or, "Don't vote for Candidate Jones because she is rich and lives in an expensive neighborhood." Whether the voters decide to vote for Candidate Jones should not depend on the length of her marriage or the neighborhood in which she lives—neither qualifies her for or disqualifies her from public office. The non sequiturs attempt to suggest a relationship between her ability to be a successful senator and unrelated facts about her life.

## Examples of Non Sequitur

■ Mr. Thompson has such bad breath that it's a wonder he sings so well.
■ She's so pretty; she must not be smart.
■ I supported his candidacy for president because his campaign was so efficiently run.

### Post Hoc, Ergo Propter Hoc

The Latin **post hoc, ergo propter hoc** is translated as "after this, therefore because of this." A post hoc, ergo propter hoc argument is one that establishes a questionable cause-and-effect relationship between events. In other words, because event *Y* follows event *X*, event *X* causes event *Y*. For instance, you would be making a post hoc argument if you claimed, "Every time my brother Bill accompanies me to Jacobs Field, the Cleveland Indians lose." The reasoning here is fallacious because we all know that although the Indians lose whenever Bill joins you at Jacobs Field, his presence does not cause the team to lose. Experience tells us that there simply is no link between the two events. The only explanation is coincidence.

Our conversations are littered with these dubious claims: "Every time I plan a pool party, it rains"; "Whenever I drive to Chicago, I get a flat tire"; "Every movie that Harry recommends turns out to be a dud." What they underscore is our pessimism or dismay, rather than any belief in the truth of such statements.

It's not surprising that post hoc reasoning is often found in arguments made by people prone to superstition—people looking for big, simple explanations. You would be committing such a fallacy if, for instance, you claimed that you got a C on your math test because a black cat crossed your path that morning or because you broke a mirror the night before. Post hoc fallacies are also practiced by those bent on proving conspiracies. Following the assassination of President Kennedy in 1963, there was considerable effort by some to link the deaths of many people involved in the investigation to a government cover-up, even though the evidence was scanty. Today, we hear Democrats protest that America goes to war every time Republicans are in office and Republicans protest that America gets poorer when Democrats are in office.

## Examples of Post Hoc, Ergo Propter Hoc Arguments

■ Just two weeks after they raised the speed limit, three people were killed on that road.
■ I saw Ralph in the courthouse; he must have been arrested.
■ It's no wonder the crime rate has shot up. The state legislature voted to lower the drinking age.

You might also have heard people argue that since the women's liberation movement, the number of latchkey children has risen sharply. The claim essentially says that the women's movement is directly responsible for the rise in working mothers over the last 30 years. While it is true that the women's movement has made it more acceptable for mothers to return to the workforce, the prime reason is particular to the individual. For some, it is simple economics; for others, personal fulfillment; for others still, a combination of the two. The feminist movement is one among many factors linked with women in the workforce and the consequent rise in latchkey children.

## Red Herring

A **red herring**, as the name suggests, is evidence that is fallaciously used to distract the audience from the true issues of an argument. The term is derived from the practice of using the scent of a red herring to throw hunting dogs off the trail of their real prey. In modern life, this fallacy is more often used to confuse the audience by providing irrelevant information or evidence. For instance, when the head coach of a major league team was accused of using team funds on personal expenses, he defended himself by pointing to the team's winning record under his leadership. While the team had undeniably performed well during this period, his response was irrelevant to the charges made against him. He had hoped to distract his accusers from the real issue, which involved his lack of honesty and abuse of power. A red herring may distract the audience momentarily, but once it is discovered, it indicates that the individual has little or no effective reasons or evidence to support his or her position.

## Examples of Red Herrings

- Even though that hockey player was convicted of vehicular homicide, he shouldn't go to jail because he is such a great athlete.
- Susan didn't hire John for the job because his wife is always late for meetings.
- The teacher gave me an F in the course because she doesn't like me.

## Slippery Slope

The **slippery slope** presumes one event will inevitably lead to a chain of other events that end in a catastrophe—as one slip on a mountaintop will cause a climber to tumble down and bring with him or her all those in tow. This domino-effect reasoning is fallacious because it depends more on presumption than hard evidence: "Censorship of obscene material will spell the end to freedom of the press"; "A ban on ethnic slurs will mean no more freedom of speech"; "If assault rifles are outlawed, handguns will be next." America's involvement in Vietnam was the result of a slippery slope argument: "If Vietnam falls to the Communists, all of Southeast Asia, and eventually India and its neighbors, will fall under the sway of communism." Even though Vietnam did fall, the result has not been the widespread rise of communism in the region; on the contrary, communism has fallen on hard times.

## Examples of Slippery Slope Arguments

■ Legalized abortion is a step toward creating an antilife society.
■ A ban on ethnic slurs will mean no more freedom of speech.
■ If we let them build those condos, the lake will end up polluted, the wildlife will die off, and the landscape will be scarred forever.

## Stacking the Deck

When writers give only the evidence that supports their premise, while disregarding or withholding contrary evidence, they are **stacking the deck**. (Science students may know this as "data beautification," the habit of recording only those results that match what an experiment is expected to predict.) A meat-packing manufacturer may advertise that its all-beef hot dogs "now contain 10 percent less fat." Although that may sound like good news, what we are not being told is that the hot dogs still contain 30 percent fat.

This stacking-the-deck fallacy is common not only in advertising but also in debates of controversial matters. The faculty of a college, for instance, may petition for the firing of its president for failing to grant needed raises while an expensive new football stadium is being built. The complaint would not be fair, however, if the faculty ignored mentioning that the stadium funds were specifically earmarked for athletic improvement by a billion-aire benefactor. Also, if the complaint left unrecognized the many accomplishments of the president, such as the successful capital campaign, the plans for a new library, and the influx of notable scholars, it would be an example of stacking the deck.

As you progress through the chapters in this book, you will find that thinking like a critic is the key to understanding and responding to arguments. It will make you a stronger reader and a more effective writer. In the next chapter, we explore ways that you can think like a writer to find and develop topics for your own argument essays.

## Examples of Stacking the Deck

■ Parents should realize that private schools simply encourage elitism in young people.
■ We cannot take four more years of her in office, given the way she voted against the death penalty.
■ Dickens's *Bleak House* is six hundred pages of boring prose.

## Straw Man

A **straw man** literally refers to a straw-stuffed dummy in the shape of a man and dressed in clothes: a scarecrow, for instance, or an effigy for burning or target practice. Metaphorically, the term refers to something less than a real person, or a weak or ineffec-tive substitute. As a rhetorical term, the straw man (or straw person) refers to a strategy of refuting another person's actual position by substituting an exaggerated or distorted version of that position. What makes it a fallacy is that the user declares the opponent's conclusion to be wrong because of flaws in another, lesser argument: The straw man user presents a fictitious or misrepresented version of the opponent's argument, and refutes that. In short, it's a setup of the opponent, a deliberate misstatement or overstatement of his or her position. And it is easier to refute somebody whose real ideas have been pushed to the extreme—reduced to a dismissible straw man.

It's no surprise that the straw man argument is a familiar strategy in politics, as candidates will attack opponents on positions often much weaker than their best arguments. Consider, for example, this statement: "Senator Jane Smith claims that we should not fund the superbomber program. Do we really want her to leave our country defenseless?" In reality, Smith may be opposed to the superbomber program for technical, economic, or even strategic reasons, or she may be in favor of an alternative defense system. However, like a red herring, the opponent tries to refute Senator Smith's position by attacking a position that Smith doesn't hold—that she wants to leave the country defenseless. In short, the arguer arrives at a conclusion that easily dismisses the "straw man" he has set up while disregarding Smith's real arguments.

## Examples of Straw Man Arguments

- Home schooling is dangerous because it keeps kids isolated from society.
- Discrimination in hiring is *not* unfair. An employer has to discriminate between competent and incompetent, good and bad workers. Otherwise, we'd be hiring people least qualified for the job.
- People who are opposed to urbanization just want to go back to living in caves.

## EXERCISES

1. In your journal, list examples of logical fallacies you find in essays, news articles, editorials, advertising, junk mail, and other persuasive materials that you confront on a daily basis. Based on the information you and other group members collect, draw some hypotheses about which fallacies are most prevalent today and why. If your instructor asks you to do so, convert those hypotheses into an outline of an argument essay for your campus newspaper.

2. Explain the faulty logic of the following statements. Of what fallacy (or fallacies) is each an example?
   a. When did you stop hiring other people to take your exams for you?
   b. He's too smart to play football; besides, he broke his leg ten years ago.
   c. If we don't stop the publication of this X-rated material now, it won't be long before our children will be reading it at school.
   d. Karen must be depressed; she wore dark clothes all weekend.

e. How can you accuse me of being late? You're such a slowpoke.

f. Rap music isn't music because it's just noise and words.

g. He's at least 6 feet 6 inches tall, so he must be a terrific basketball player.

h. WGBB is the most popular radio station on campus because it has more listeners than any other station.

i. Indians living on reservations get the necessities of life at government expense, so they have no worries.

j. Take Tummy Tops laxatives instead of Mellow Malt, because Tummy Tops contains calcium while Mellow Malt has aluminum and magnesium.

k. Lite Cheese Popcorn contains 34 percent fewer calories!

l. Any decent person will agree that Nazism has no place in modern society.

# 3

# Finding Arguments:
# Thinking Like a Writer

When confronted with an issue we feel strongly about, most of us have no trouble offering an energetically delivered opinion. Yet when we are asked to *write* an argument, we feel paralyzed. To express our ideas in written form forces us to commit ourselves to some position or to endorse a particular action. We have to take a risk and make a public statement about what we think and feel and believe. Our written words can be scrutinized. That makes us vulnerable, and nobody likes to feel exposed.

It is helpful to think of writing an argument as one way to explore our ideas about a subject or issue. As such, writing can be a means of growth and discovery. Investigating new ideas can be intimidating, but it's also exciting. This chapter will demonstrate how writers begin the process of researching ideas to write about in argument essays. As novelist E. M. Forster explained, "How will I know what I think until I've seen what I've said?"

Exploration, of course, takes time. We are not recommending a writing process that begins an hour before a paper is due; rather, we are recommending what successful writers do: Take time to think your writing through. This means starting assignments early, working through all the stages, and allowing time to revise and polish your work before you submit it. Learning to write well is the same as learning to perform any other skilled activity. You have to practice your strokes or your scales to be a good tennis player or pianist; likewise, you have to practice your craft to be a good writer. As you gain more experience, some of the stages of the writing process will go more quickly for you on most projects. Even when you become a polished logician, however, you may find yourself writing about a topic that requires you to work out the assumptions in your argument slowly and painstakingly. That's okay. All writers do that.

## The Writing Process

Many rhetorical theorists have tried to describe the writing process, but that's a little like describing snowflakes: Each one is different. Each person has a different way of writing, especially depending on the job. Think about it. You can dash off a note to your roommate in a second; if you're writing a job application letter, you'll probably take a great deal more time. If you have only 20 minutes to answer an essay question on a history exam, you'll get it done somehow; but give you an entire semester to write a term paper on the same subject, and you will probably spend several weeks (if not months) doing the job. The scope and length of the assignment dictate a different writing process.

What most people studying the writing process agree on is that almost everyone goes through four distinct stages when writing: prewriting, drafting, rewriting, and editing.

## Prewriting

When something prompts you to write (your instructor gives you an assignment, your boss tells you to write a report, a letter requires an answer, you feel strongly about a controversy and want to write a letter to the editor), you spend time either mentally or physically preparing to respond. You may make notes, go to the library, interview someone, or just stare out the window. This is the *prewriting* stage in which you're letting the ideas you'll use begin to incubate, to take form. In this chapter, we provide strategies you can use to make this early stage of writing work for you.

## Drafting

In the second stage, you begin, however haltingly, to put words to paper. Some people make an outline; others write a bare-bones rough draft in an attempt to get some ideas down on paper. Many people like to start by sketching out their conclusions so that they can see where their writing must take them. Others prefer the linear, start-with-the-introduction system that moves them through the task. The first goal in the drafting stage is to get the framework of the writing in place so you can start adding material to fill it out. At some point in the process you also take your potential readers into account in order to get some idea of their expectations and receptivity.

## Rewriting

Once you have a rough draft framed, you're ready to do the hard work of writing: *rewriting*. At this stage, you may move parts of your paper around, or make a new out-line, or add or cut material to fill in gaps or eliminate imbalances. You will have your readers much more clearly in mind because your goal is to persuade them; what you know about their background, experiences, and values will help you decide on a final shape for your paper, even if it means throwing away a lot of what went into the rough draft. (A bad paper that's finished is still a bad paper; that's why you need to allow time for flexibility. Writers who are pressed for time sometimes have to polish something that's not good and hope their readers will not notice, a technique that does not usually work.) All writing is rewriting. So at this stage, most good writers turn to other writers for feedback—a sense of what prospective readers will think of their writing. In a class-room, this is done by exchanging drafts with classmates or having conferences with your instructor.

## Editing

To maximize your chance of persuading readers, your writing needs to be as readable as possible. That's why, after you've rewritten it, you need to work on your sentence structure so that words "flow" smoothly. Or you may need to change words here and there to heighten their impact. If others have read your paper and offered feedback, you may wish to act on some of their suggestions for improvement. You always need to edit and proof-read what you've written so that careless errors don't distract your readers from getting the message you're trying to convey.

   In a nutshell, that's the writing process. Now let's look at how you might exploit the features of that process when you start writing arguments.

# Finding Topics to Argue

Every writer knows the experience of being blocked—of having a topic but not knowing what to say about it, or of having only one point to make about an issue. Even worse is having an assignment but no topic. To help generate ideas, writers need to tap both internal and external resources.

## In Your Immediate Vicinity

The world around you is full of arguments; you just need to take a moment to see them. Look at the front page and editorial pages of your campus newspaper, for instance. What's going on? Look at billboards and bulletin boards. What are people having meetings about? What changes are coming up? Listen to the conversations of people on the bus, or waiting in line at the bookstore, or in the library. What's up? What have you been reading for a class that gets you thinking? You might want to know how a theory for the origin of the universe was derived, or what the results of a recent study of employment success for former welfare recipients were based on, or even why two experts in the field of early childhood learning draw different conclusions from the same evidence. The reading you do for your own enjoyment may also provide some interesting ideas. A science fiction novel may make you wonder about the plausibility of alien life. Reading a murder mystery may make you think about the value of forensic anthropology. Look through the magazines in your room, or at the ads on television, or at the junk mail that fills your mailbox. Even casually reading magazines and newspapers on a daily or weekly basis will turn up issues and controversies. What claims are people making? What are people asking you to do, or think, or wear, or look like, or support? These are sources of potential arguments; all you have to do is become aware of them. As Thoreau put it, "Only that day dawns to which we are awake."

## In Your Larger Worlds

Don't limit yourself to campus. Often there are debates and discussions going on in your workplace, in your place of worship, on your block, in your town. You belong to a number of communities; each has its issues of interest, and in those issues you can find plenty to write about. And those environments aren't the only places you'll find sources for arguments; the world turns on proposals, positions, and controversies. It's almost impossible to turn on the radio or television today without seeing someone presenting an opinion. Your computer (or the one available on your campus) can connect you to a global community engaged in debate and dialogue on every issue imaginable. On the Internet, you can participate in a number of discussions about controversial issues through listservs, Usenet newsgroups, blogs, and chat rooms. Make a list of the issues that interest you. What are the headlines in the newspaper? What's Congress voting on? What are the hot spots around the globe (or in the larger universe)? Don't stick to the familiar; there is much experimental territory just waiting to be explored.

## Keeping a Journal

You've probably noticed that we encourage recording ideas and observations in a journal, a technique used by many professional writers. The journal doesn't have to be fancy; the cheap supermarket variety works just as well as the $2,000 laptop. (If you're comfortable at a keyboard, a USB flash drive makes a great notebook and fits in your shirt pocket, too—although you might want to keep a backup copy.)

Writers use journals as portable file cabinets of ideas. In a journal, we record anything in language that interests us, not just materials for current projects. We may copy down a word or phrase or sentence we hear that we like, or photocopy and staple in a piece by a writer we admire, or even add things that infuriate or amuse us. A journal becomes a super-market of ideas and strategies, but there's something very positive about the simple act of copying words. Somehow, physically writing or typing them makes them yours; you learn something about technique in doing the physical work of copying. (That's why we don't recommend making too many photocopies; you don't mentally store the information in the same way you do when you copy a passage yourself.)

For the novice argument writer, a journal is invaluable. You can use yours to include notes on possible topics; examples of good introductions and conclusions; catchy words, phrases, and titles; examples of logical fallacies—just about anything a writer might need. A journal is also particularly helpful for creating *dialogues,* the voices and opin-ions of others who may hold views that are different from your own on particular issues. By keeping a record or notes on what people have to say in newspapers, magazine arti-cles, television talk shows, and casual conversation about various controversial issues, you'll have a ready resource to consult when you begin to deliberate about your position on a particular issue.

When you begin keeping the journal, set yourself a formal goal: for example, adding 100 words a day or writing five days out of the week. Then *stick to it.* Journals don't fill themselves. It takes discipline to keep a journal, and discipline is a characteristic of good writers. If you don't do the groundwork, your creativity won't break through. Throughout this text, we've scattered suggestions and exercises for using journals; if you want to mas-ter the power of argument fully, we encourage you to *do* the exercises. Don't just read them. Write!

## Developing Argumentative Topics

Topics alone aren't arguments, and many inexperienced writers have trouble making the jump from subject to argument. For example, you may be interested in heavy metal music. That's a subject—a big one. What can you argue about it? You could ask your-self, "What are the facts about heavy metal? When did it start? How can it be defined? What differentiates it from the mainstream rock played on most commercial radio sta-tions? How has it evolved over the last 40 years? Why are some groups played, it seems, once an hour, and others almost totally ignored?" You can ask functional ques-tions, such as "Who were the most influential figures in heavy metal music? Is heavy metal as relevant as it had been?" You might ask aesthetic questions about the impor-tance of melody or lyrics or harmony, or ethical questions such as whether the music in-dustry should put parental advisory labels on albums. You could even consider moral questions such as whether heavy metal music videos encourage sexism or violence. In recognizing the multiple possibilities of issues, you may find you have more to say on a topic than you think.

## Getting Started

Sometimes getting started can be the most difficult step in the writing process. Where do I begin? What should I include? What ideas will work best? How shall I organize it all? You may have a hundred ideas in your head about the topic or—even worse—none at all. When this happens, there are a number of tried-and-true techniques that professional writers use to redirect those anxious questions and concerns into productive writing. While you may not need to use all the strategies each time you begin to write, you'll find that trying out each one of them will help you discover what works best for you.

## Brainstorming

Brainstorming can help you get your ideas on paper in an informal and unstructured way. When you brainstorm, you write down as many ideas as you can about your subject, usually in short phrases, questions, or single words. Don't worry about placing them in any special order or even about making complete sense. The one rule to observe while you're brainstorming is not to judge the ideas that pop into your head and spill out onto your paper. When you give yourself permission to write down anything that seems related to your subject, you'll be surprised at the number of ideas that will occur to you. By not rejecting anything, you'll find that one idea will naturally lead to another. Even an idea that you may throw out later can lead you to an idea that may be a real gem. And the more ideas you record in your brainstorm, the more choices you will have to consider later as you sift through this record of your thoughts and decide what is and is not useful.

After reading the essays in Chapter 2 of this book, John, our first-year composition student, decided to write his first paper on college binge drinking. The topic was in the news because a student at another college in his state had died as the result of excessive drinking at a fraternity party. John began his prewriting preparation by brainstorming about the subject. Here's what he came up with:

| | |
|---|---|
| binge drinking | want to forget all about the week |
| drinking until you feel sick | makes us feel grown up |
| getting together with friends for a good time | nothing better to do on Saturday night |
| partying after a tough week at school | why does the college care? |
| so many bars, so little time | people can really hurt themselves |
| half the people underage | prevention—how? |
| whose responsibility is it? | part of the college experience |
| am I responsible for my friends? | ignore it—will it go away? |
| could I get arrested? | trying to act cool |
| nobody checks anyway | what starts as fun can lead to death |
| feeling terrible the next morning | definition of an adult |
| smelling like a beer can | do other cultures experience this? |
| role of the college administration | why drink to excess? |
| rite of passage | |
| impact of peer pressure | |

As you can see, John had many different ideas about binge drinking, and the more he brainstormed, the more he discovered what they were. After looking over his brainstorm, John chose a few of the ideas that especially interested him to explore further.

John was lucky to have a subject before he began brainstorming. But what happens if you don't have a particular topic in mind or your instructor doesn't assign one? You may find it difficult to come up with a topic, and you're not alone. Students often comment that the hardest part of writing is deciding what to write about.

# Finding Ideas Worth Writing About

Let's suppose you're not assigned a specific paper topic and are left on your own to come up with an issue worth arguing about. That can be daunting, of course. When asked where he gets the ideas for his stories, best-selling author Stephen King's joke response was "Utica"—as if there were an idea shop in that New York town. Other writers respond with the tongue-in-cheek claim that there's a post office box in, say, Madison, Wisconsin, where you can write for ideas, but to qualify you need to be published. The point is that ideas for fiction as well as nonfiction are all around us. You just have to know where to look.

Again, one of the most useful prewriting strategies for coming up with an idea is brainstorming—just as you might do if you had a topic to expand upon. Take out a piece of paper and jot down whatever comes to mind in response to these questions:

- What issues in print or TV news interest you?
- What issues make you angry?
- What problems in your dorm/on campus/in your town/in your country concern you?
- What political issue concerns you most?
- What aspects about the environment worry you?
- If you were a professor/dean/college president/mayor/governor/senator/president, what would be the first thing you'd do?
- What policies/practices/regulations/laws would you like to see changed?
- What do you talk about or argue over with friends or classmates?
- What ideas from books or articles have challenged your thinking?
- What books/movies/music/fashions/art do you like, and why?
- What television shows do you like/hate, and why?
- What personalities in politics/show business/the media/academia do you have strong feelings about?

Here's a quick brainstorming list one student developed:

*Issues That Interest Me*

1. The war on terrorism
2. Excessive salaries for athletes
3. People who protest movie violence but oppose bans on assault rifles
4. The benefits of stem cell research
5. Reality TV

6. Social messages in rap music
7. Environmentally unfriendly vehicles
8. Immigration policies
9. Bullying in cyberspace
10. Movies

Another strategy is to brainstorm these items with a group of classmates. Begin by choosing a subject in the day's news, then play free-association with it. Say the subject is *sports* and you begin saying the word. The next student then says the first word that comes to mind; then the next student responds with a new word, et cetera, et cetera. For instance: sports; baseball; St. Louis Cardinals; World Series; the latest player trades. And maybe eventually you and the group will generate ideas worth debating—the need for better coaching; salary caps; the use of steroids; team loyalty, or the lack thereof; the designated hitter rule.

Once you have brainstormed a list, organize the issues according to categories—for example, sports, politics, social issues, environment, the media, television, education, and so on. Then transfer the list to your journal. Now, whenever an assignment comes up, you'll have a database of ideas worth writing about.

Next try to focus these ideas by deciding the following:

■ Which subjects do I know something about?
■ Have I had personal experiences with any particular subject?
■ How do I feel about the subject? (angry? glad? sad? neutral?)
■ What is my stand on the subject? Should I defend it? argue against it? Do I feel strongly enough to make suggestions for changes?
■ Would this be a subject I'd want to do more research on?
■ Who would be my audience—friends? instructor? parents? And how much does he, she, or they know about the topic?

In subsequent chapters, we'll discuss how to frame an argument on a topic, the ways of approaching your audience, the kinds of evidence to present, and so forth. But at this point, we're simply interested in helping you come up with a checklist of arguable subjects worth writing about. Whatever you come up with in your checklist, each topic should have three basic things:

1. It should be interesting.
2. It should appeal to readers.
3. It should have a specific slant.

## Clustering

Some writers find that visualizing their ideas on a page helps them explore their subject in new ways. Clustering[1] is a technique you can use to do that. It involves choosing a key word, phrase, or even a short sentence, and placing it in the center of a blank page with a

---

[1]Clustering is a technique explored by Gabriele L. Rico in her book *Writing the Natural Way: Using Right Brain Techniques to Release Your Expressive Powers* (Los Angeles: J. P. Tarcher, 1983).

circle around it. Next you try to think of ideas, words, or other short phrases that you can associate or relate to your key word or phrase. As you do, write them in the blank area surrounding the center and circle them and draw lines linking them to your center circled word or phrase. As you accumulate more and more clusters, the words and phrases within them will generate ideas on their own; these can be linked to the words that inspired them. When you have exhausted your cluster, you will have a complex network of ideas that should provide many ways to begin to explore your subject. By choosing any one or a combination of these words or ideas as a starting point, you can move to freewriting to find ways of developing these ideas further.

Figure 3.1 shows how John used clustering to find new ways of thinking about binge drinking, the topic he had chosen for his paper. When John examined his cluster, he found a map of the many ideas he might explore further:

■ Should colleges play the role of in loco parentis and regulate student drinking or is drinking a matter of personal responsibility?
■ What role does peer pressure play in binge drinking?
■ Are print ads and television commercials for beer partly responsible for binge drinking among young people?
■ Is the extent of binge drinking on college campuses exaggerated or overstated?
■ If a student violates campus drinking rules, what should the consequences be?

John's cluster revealed the complexity of the issue and became a starting point for him to investigate the subject in greater depth.

## Freewriting

The next step is freewriting, which goes one step beyond brainstorming and which helps get a focus on the subject while developing things to say about it. Instead of simply listing phrases, questions, and words related to your subject, freewriting involves writing freely, and without stopping, whatever thoughts and ideas you have about your subject, without worrying about sentence structure, spelling, or grammar. As in brainstorming, when you freewrite, it's important not to censor your ideas. Your aim is to discover what you know about your subject, and the best way you can do that is by giving your mind permission to go wherever it pleases. Freewriting isn't intended to be a finished part of your paper; instead, it's a way to generate the ideas and focus that you can use later as you begin to draft the paper itself.

Freewriting can begin with anything: your topic, a particularly interesting idea you've read about, or an experience that you can connect with your subject. If you have used brainstorming or clustering before freewriting, these activities can provide you with a key word or phrase to get you started. For instance, John found a good idea from his brainstorm to begin his freewriting:

> Getting together with friends for a good time. That's what everyone looks forward to every weekend. Put away the books, get out of the dorm, and party. Four, five, sometimes more drinks. Feeling no pain. Binge drinking just seems to happen. It isn't something

**Figure 3.1**   Sample Cluster

you plan to do. When you're having a good time, you don't think about how terrible you're going to feel the next day or about all the stupid things you're doing. It's easy to get alcohol in town. Nobody ever checks for proof, and if they do you just go to another place down the street. It's so easy to get a phony ID anyway. And the crowds are so large, no one looks carefully. If college students want to drink, who's to say they can't? We're old enough to vote, die for our country, sign a contract. Why not drinking? And how are you ever going to learn to drink if you don't do it? College students drink for lots of reasons. Why? Well, it gets them in a party mood. It's fun. It makes us feel like adults. It's so cool. Everyone does it. There's nothing wrong with drinking, but is it a problem if you drink too much? Every weekend. They let it get out of control. Drunk driving, alcohol poisoning, stupid accidents. Binge drinking is drinking gone overboard. You can get in a car accident and end up killing or maiming yourself, another person. Even a friend. Then how would I feel? That's all I can think of right now.

John used his freewriting to think on paper. While he didn't come up with any conclusions about how he felt about binge drinking, he did produce a number of ideas that he explored later, when he worked on the first draft of his paper:

■ College students binge drink for many reasons.
■ Binge drinking can be a problem.

■ Drinking is related to feeling adult.

■ Binge drinking is not a planned behavior, but it can get to be a habit.

One of the best reasons for using freewriting before you begin the first draft of your paper is to avoid the most intimidating sight a writer can see: a blank page. Unfortunately, sometimes that blank page is the result of a blank mind and undue concern about how your writing and ideas will appear to others. When you freewrite, you write for yourself alone. It is a way to make your ideas flow. Freewriting generates ideas that will help you begin to think about your subject before worrying about polishing your writing for an audience.

## Asking Questions

Once you have a subject in mind, a good strategy for generating ideas is to make a list of questions you have about the subject. Your questions can cover areas in which you need more information, as well as questions you might like to answer as you think and write about your topic. For instance, John tried this strategy for his topic of college binge drinking and came up with the following questions:

Why do college students binge drink?

How many college students actually binge drink?

Is binge drinking a result of peer pressure?

Do students binge drink to show they are adults?

Do most college students find binge drinking acceptable?

Is binge drinking strictly a college student activity or do other age and economic groups do this as well?

Do college students stop binge drinking once they leave college?

Who should be responsible for binge drinking? the drinkers? the college? the law?

Why do college administrations feel that they must respond to the problem of drinking if it's off campus?

Do colleges have a legal responsibility to protect their students?

Are the alcohol prevention programs on campus effective?

How often does binge drinking result in fatal accidents?

It's easy to see how one question can lead to another. By choosing one question or several related ones, John had real direction for exploring his topic and focusing his paper as he began his research and his first draft.

## Engaging in Dialogue with Others

Talking to other people is a great source of ideas. None of the techniques we've discussed so far have to be solitary activities. By sharing your ideas and listening to the responses of others, you will find a wealth of new ideas and perspectives. In fact, you'll be engaging in the kind of *dialogue* we discussed in Chapter 1. You can do this in a number of ways: either participate in small peer groups in your class or in larger class discussions; speak individually with your instructor; seek out members of your community, on campus or outside your school; share ideas with others electronically through Internet chat rooms, e-mail, or listservs; or talk with family and friends. As Larry King and other talk show hosts prove every day, people love to talk. So, take advantage of it—and take notes.

# Refining Topics

Once you have found—through the strategies we've discussed—subjects that strike you as interesting, you have to begin narrowing down your topic to a manageable size. The next step, then, is to look over your list and reduce it to those topics that are legitimately arguable. (See Chapter 1 for a refresher.)

## Reducing Your Options

Your first step is to determine whether your subject is manageable. You don't want a subject that is too broad or unwieldy or that requires prohibitive amounts of research. For example, you would not want to argue that "welfare needs to be reformed." You could write a book about that if you had time to do all the research. To write a short paper, you have to narrow your subject. "The only people who should be eligible for welfare support should be disabled people and mothers of preschool children" is a manageable reduction of your first idea, and one that you can handle in an average-length paper (see Figure 3.2). The more narrow your topic, the more you restrict your research and tighten the focus of your argument.

## Avoiding Overspecialized Topics

However, don't pick a topic that requires extensive specialized knowledge, such as how to reduce the trade deficit or the problems inherent in thermonuclear fusion. The issue you choose should be one you know a little something about and, to keep you interested, about which you have strong convictions. Also, it should be an issue you are willing to spend a reasonable amount of time exploring on your own online, in interviews, or perhaps in the library. Aside from writing a convincing argument, a parallel goal of any project you research is to become better informed and more appreciative of the complexity of the issue. Therefore, select a topic on which you wish to be well informed and that you are willing to investigate and reflect on.

**Figure 3.2** "Reducing Your Options" Diagram

## Formulating a Working Claim

Once you have decided on your topic and used some of the strategies we've discussed, you are ready to create a working claim. As we explained in Chapter 1, the claim is the heart of your essay. It functions as a thesis statement. It states what you believe or what action you'd like your readers to take. In Chapter 1, we provided examples of the different ways you can state your claim. However, at this early stage of your writing, it would be difficult to create a claim that would be perfect for the paper you have yet to research and write. It's too early in the game to commit yourself. After all, your research may yield some surprising results, and you want to be open to all sides of the issue. At best, you can create a working claim—that is, a statement of your opinion or position on your topic that you can use temporarily to help you focus and organize your paper and limit your research.

After John, our first-year composition student, considered his subject of binge drinking by brainstorming, clustering, freewriting, asking questions about the topic, and engaging in dialogue with others, he realized what an enormous and complex topic it was and that he needed to narrow it. He began by asking questions about binge drinking. How prevalent is binge drinking? Who should be responsible for the regulation of student drinking? Are students themselves solely responsible? Should a college or university act in loco parentis? What are the consequences of ignoring the problem of binge drinking? What is the role of peer pressure in binge drinking? How can binge drinking be discouraged or controlled? What role does advertising play? Can binge drinking be fatal?

As John thought about the answers to these questions, he began to narrow the focus of his broad topic to one that he could explore in a paper of reasonable length. He decided that he would focus only on the issue of how to control or eliminate binge drinking on college campuses.

John's next step was to formulate a *working claim* for his paper on binge drinking. When he sat down to create his working claim, he examined and reflected on his topic and decided on the following *working claim*:

> Binge drinking is a serious problem on college campuses, and if we continue to ignore it or treat it as normal and acceptable student behavior, no one will ever find an effective way to eliminate it.

By creating a working claim early in his writing process, John benefited in a number of ways. He clearly took a position about his topic and expressed his point of view. While he had the opportunity to change his viewpoint as he thought further about his topic, his working claim served as a baseline. John's working claim also helped him organize the reasons he needed to support his position.

Let's take a look at John's working claim to see how it is organized. His claim can be divided into three parts:

1. Binge drinking is a problem on college campuses.
2. It is ignored or simply accepted as normal student behavior.
3. No one has yet found an effective way to solve this problem.

All these statements are arguable because, as we discussed in Chapter 1, they are based on judgment and interpretation, not on indisputable facts or personal opinion. As he developed his paper, John needed to decide on reasons to effectively convince his readers that these three parts of his working claim are true.

In addition, John's working claim helped him decide what he needed to investigate further. As John researched and became more knowledgeable about his topic, he revised his working claim to better reflect what he had learned. But at this stage of his paper, his working claim provided him with several specific areas that he needed to investigate in order to argue persuasively about them:

1. Is binge drinking really a problem on college campuses? How significant is it?
2. How is binge drinking ignored and by whom?
3. Is binge drinking regarded as normal student behavior and by whom?
4. What has been done to eliminate binge drinking?
5. What are some ways this problem can be dealt with?

In Chapter 9, we look at a number of ways available to John to research his topic. By using the questions suggested by his working claim as a guide, John had plenty of avenues to explore.

Thinking like a writer will help you make the jump from simply having an opinion on a subject to finding ways to express that opinion in an argument essay. In the next chapter, we look at the way in which audience influences and affects the choices we make about what to include in an argument essay and how to present our arguments.

## SAMPLE STUDENT ARGUMENT FOR ANALYSIS

Stephanie Bower, a student majoring in English Literature, was interested in the subject of television news reporting. She realized what a complicated and multifaceted topic it is and that she needed to focus on a particular aspect of broadcast news. She began refining her topic by asking questions about TV news reporting. What does the viewing audience expect of television news? What is the responsibility of news broadcast? Are the when, where, why, what, and how enough? What are the qualities of a newscast that satisfy my expectations for good news coverage? Which news programming do I find inadequate? What differences exist between national and local news coverage? What is the state of reporting on my local news channels? What are the strengths and weaknesses of those channels? What role does advertising play in a broadcast? How can local television news be improved? What are critics of the television news industry saying about the caliber of local news? What would I discover if I were to examine the quality of local news on a minute-by-minute basis? What recommendations could be made to improve the news?

As Stephanie thought about the answers, she realized that although each question poses an interesting issue to explore, she had to narrow the topic to one that she could cover in a paper of reasonable length. She thought back to some recent local news stories that had interested her, discovering to her dismay how complicated social issues had been pressed into just a few seconds. Worse, she was stunned to discover that extended coverage was given to a story about an abandoned dog. Reflecting on this, Stephanie realized she had material for a specific topic: local news—what was wrong with it, and how it might be improved. The box diagram in Figure 3.3 reflects her thought process as she narrowed down her topic.

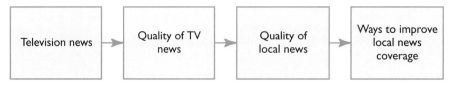

**Figure 3.3** Stephanie's "Reducing Options" Diagram

Her working claim, then, both limited the range of her topic and very clearly expressed her point of view about it:

> Local television news is known for its bare-bones coverage and journalistic mediocrity. Now, competing with the convenience of Internet news sources and the far more in-depth coverage available in newspapers, local television news must reconsider its responsibilities and its approach.

---

Bower 1

Stephanie Bower

Professor Van Zandt

English 111

4 December 2009

What's the Rush?

Speed Yields Mediocrity in Local Television News

Down to the second, time is a factor in television. Though national television news has outlets for lengthy reports and analysis in hour-long news magazines like *Dateline* and panel discussions like *Meet the Press*, local news is rendered almost exclusively in a "short story" format. Most local TV news stories are just twenty or thirty seconds long. These stories succeed in stating the basic facts, but they simply do not have time to do more. Though television newscasts operate in minutes and seconds, the brevity of local news stories is not just a natural feature of the medium. Rather, these stories are often the result of local news stations that lack resources and reporters, or that lack effort and enterprise. Because of these limitations and shortcomings, local television news has developed a reputation for journalistic mediocrity. With dozens of quality online news sources available for consumption at your convenience, local television news faces more competition than ever. Local newscasts must reconsider their responsibilities and their approach. Otherwise, mediocrity will result in obsolescence.

2    Local television news is still a popular source of information about public affairs. People want news that is relevant to their specific communities—stories about local schools, ballot issues, town elections, and art events, the restaurant scene, historic sites, zoning issues, and known personalities. Local stations have the potential to reach large regional audiences looking for coverage of the stories affecting their towns and cities. Yet local news is known for its focus on sensational crime coverage and "soft" news, which focuses on human interest stories, sports, and entertainment. Increased cable news viewership and the rise of the Internet as a news source have caused some decline in local news viewership, making the business that much more competitive (Belt and Just). News directors may feel pressure "to produce the cheapest type of news that they think will draw and hold viewers—namely, low effort stories featuring crime, lifestyle, and entertainment" (Belt and Just 195). Yet these kinds of stories offer little real informational value to viewers. Not all news stories demand a great deal of time and depth, but many stories require more than the twenty or thirty seconds they are allotted during a local newscast. A news story that runs for one minute and thirty seconds can tell viewers the who, what, when, where, and how of a story, but it cannot delve into an analysis of a situation or its contextual significance.

3    Why don't more stations air high quality, in-depth local news coverage? The answer seems to come down to money. In the world of corporate-owned and advertiser-dependent media, it becomes unclear whether local journalism outlets are impartial civic informers or cogs in the machinery of big business. During sweeps weeks, local stations engage in a high-stakes war to see who wins the important time slots. Stations suddenly run in-depth "Special Reports," such as a 2008 special investigation on WHDH-TV, Boston's NBC affiliate station, into how much taxpayer money was being wasted because of lights left on overnight in state buildings. But despite the success of this story, many local market stations do not spend time or money on the equipment, resources, and manpower required to do investigative or in-depth reporting on a regular basis. Deborah Potter, executive director of NewsLab, cites severely understaffed local news teams as a primary cause of low-quality coverage. She says the majority of local station budgets are spent on equipment and anchor salaries, and there is simply not enough left over to

pay for reporters and photographers to go out in the field. Potter says this shortage is the reason why there is "so little enterprise, so much cheap-to-cover crime, and so little depth on the air. Most television reporters have a simple mission every day: Get out there and scratch the surface" ("The Body Count").

4    Because there are not enough reporters working to fill the time with hard news, stations become dependent on news wires and video feeds. It is cheaper to pull video of President Obama travelling overseas from the satellite feeds than to send a photographer and reporter out in the field to cover a local story, and it is faster to rephrase a story taken from the news wires than to research and report on an original story. Stories taken from the news wires and satellite video feeds account for many of the "quick-hit" twenty- or twenty-five-second pieces aired during local newscasts. These stories may contain legitimate news, but they are typically not stories covering local news topics.

5    Health-related stories are popular with viewers and are frequently included in local news lineups. Yet the quick-hit format of the stories is particularly troublesome in this arena. Elizabeth Jensen writes that local newscasts frequently feature health information, but their reports are "brief, often lack necessary perspective . . . and occasionally contain 'egregious errors' with potentially serious consequences." Jensen cites a large study which showed that the median length of health stories in local newscasts was just thirty-three seconds, and of these only 27% included an interview with someone in the health profession. She writes that local news tends to cover the "sexy" stories—high profile diseases of the moment, such as West Nile virus, avian flu, and H1N1 ("swine flu")—far more often than the things that are more likely to affect people's health, like diabetes or heart disease. These are certainly topical news stories; however, the amount of coverage these stories receive coupled with a lack of time and depth may create unnecessary alarm.

6    On October 7, 2009, I examined the story line-ups for the local 5 p.m. newscast on WHDH-TV, Boston's NBC affiliate. Excluding commercials, the full air-time available for this newscast was twenty-two minutes. Of this, one minute and twenty-five seconds was spent on graphics and teases for upcoming stories. Five minutes was given to weather, one minute and fifteen seconds was given to sports, and one minute was given to entertainment. Two minutes and fifteen seconds was spent on national news. Local news accounted for nine minutes of coverage. Of this, four minutes and fifty seconds was devoted to the lead story

Bower 4

about a grisly murder in New Hampshire. Yet even the time given to this story—by far the longest piece of news coverage—was shorter than the total time devoted to weather. The other local news stories were between fifteen seconds and one minute and forty-five seconds long.

Local news stories can often do little more than highlight key facts and perhaps include a sound bite or two. For example, one of the local stories was about 100 firefighters who would be getting their jobs back because of state stimulus funds. The story was thirty seconds long—long enough to state the plain facts, but not long enough to provide context on the layoffs, how the decision was made to use state stimulus funds for their rehire, information on why this was a necessary use of funds, or even to add a human element by speaking to any of the rehired firefighters.

Stations often select stories that can be told quickly and that require little background or context. In the precious minutes the station has to cover the local news, they often spend two to five minutes on national or international news stories—stories that will be covered again during the station's national nightly newscast. Because it is a video-driven medium, television news will often fill precious chunks of time with stories because of a novelty video clip. For example, on September 25, 2009, WHDH devoted one minute and forty-five seconds of the newscast to a story about a moose wandering through a local neighborhood. They had a great video clip of the moose in someone's backyard—but this was one of the longest local stories in the half-hour newscast.

Local news occasionally devotes time to entertainment stories, particularly if the story benefits the affiliate station and its network. For example, WHDH devoted over a minute of its September 25 newscast to the September 26 premiere of *Saturday Night Live*, airing on WHDH's parent network NBC. This kind of promotional entertainment coverage benefits the network, but it draws even more time away from quality local news coverage.

Because of the time constraints imposed on television news, it can never provide the in-depth coverage available in newspapers or online news sites, despite the countless graphics and brandings promising "I-teams" and "in-depth coverage." Dane Claussen notes that "the entire transcript of a half-hour local television news broadcast will fit onto less than one page of a newspaper" ("Cognitive Dissonance"). Stephanie Ebbert, City Hall

Bureau Chief at the *Boston Globe*, says that local TV news is best-suited for "quick-hit" news:

> For more sophisticated, involved coverage, the consumer really has to turn to either a lengthier discussion of an event on a TV news magazine, or to radio or print media, which devote more resources to individual stories. That's not to say it can't be done on TV; it simply often isn't. The very subtleties that make some stories interesting and newsworthy are often difficult to crystallize in a minute and a half or to make friendly to viewers who are believed to be so very impatient. (personal interview)

Ebbert questions the idea that modern Americans, with their busy lifestyles and MTV-influenced visual perceptions, cannot pay attention long enough to ingest longer, more sophisticated TV news stories.

11   Todd Belt and Marion Just conducted a five-year, in-depth study of fifty local markets to determine the relationship between what a local news station covers and its level of commercial success. Are viewers as turned off by stories on public affairs and issues as news directors fear? Do they need fast-paced, attention-grabbing stories, as the industry seems to believe? Their study suggests that this is not the case. Belt and Just found that "audiences preferred news stories that reflected journalistic enterprise—station initiated investigations or on the spot reporting instead of merely reporting the news from other sources (Belt and Just 202-04)" Stations that included this kind of reportage fared better financially overall. They write, "Journalistic enterprise is one of the factors that leads to larger audiences and, therefore, greater advertising. . . . Stations that practice low effort journalism risk getting trapped in a downward spiral of declining ratings" (Belt and Just 202-04). The findings suggest that news producers are incorrect in their stubborn belief that audiences prefer soft news and investigative journalism is not worth the cost or effort.

12   If more time were given to news, it would have to taken from coverage of something else. So what has to go? Stations could take the time back from the promotional graphics that devour precious seconds with useless visuals, or they could have less repetition of stories in back-to-back newscasts. Another option is to take the time from the twenty-second "quick hit" wire stories, particularly those that cover national news. Of course these stories are news and they are of interest to

Bower 6

viewers, but if viewers want the national news tidbits, then isn't national network news the place to find them?

13    Another possible solution is to take the time back from the "Coming up next!" news teases designed to lure viewers to stay through the commercial break. Deborah Potter says that many viewers are turned off by local news because "they're annoyed by the tricks and gimmicks stations use to try to make them watch." Local news stations often run one-and-a-half to two minutes of tease video per half-hour newscast. This time, in addition to the time spent on promotional station graphics, branding slogans and music, adds up to a significant amount of seconds and minutes that could be spent expanding on news stories. Teases may work, and it is valuable for busy viewers to know what is coming up in case a story may be of particular interest to them. But stations should not underestimate their audiences by assuming they need to be continually wooed into watching a half hour of news. The story is what the viewers really want. Teases have no journalistic value and take time away from reporters and their pieces.

14    Today's news consumer has tremendous options for where, when, and how to get the news. There are dozens of high quality news sources online, and younger people in particular are comfortable with and trust these sources. Local television news has to offer something unique—coverage that is community-based, high-quality, and relevant. Eric Klinenberg calls the Internet "the ideal medium for deepening coverage with interactive links to video, text, and graphics" (58). Yet most news organizations do not yet have a model for earning the kind of profits online that they earn through television advertising, and TV is still the flagship enterprise for local news.

15    Local news affiliates may not have the financial resources or tremendous market sizes of their parent networks, but they still provide the important service of informing communities about their local schools, citizens, governments, and breaking news. Surely, it must be frustrating for professional television journalists to abandon insightful analysis and instead package the facts into a minute and thirty seconds of lead, soundbite, and tag. Research indicates that viewers want in-depth local news stories that are relevant to their lives and their communities. The question is whether local news stations will risk altering standard formats to give reporters the space to tell these stories.

Bower 7

Works Cited

Belt, Todd L., and Marion R. Just. "The Local News Story: Is Quality a Choice?"
        *Political Communication* 25 (2008): 194-95. Print.

"The Body Count." *American Journalism Review* 24.6 (2002): 60. Print.

Bradley, Samuel D., et al. "Wait! Don't Turn That Dial! More Excitement to Come!
        The Effects of Story Length and Production Pacing in Local Television
        News. . . ." *Journal of Broadcasting & Electronic Media* (2005): 3-22. Print.

Claussen, Dane S. "Cognitive Dissonance, Media Illiteracy, and Public Opinion on the
        News." *American Behavioral Scientist* 48 (2004): 212. Print.

Ebbert, Stephanie. Personal interview. 12 Dec. 2004.

Jensen, Elizabeth. "Study Laments Anemic Reporting." *Television Week* 13 Mar.
        2006: n. pag. Print.

Klinenberg, Eric. "Convergence: News Production in a Digital Age." *Annals of the
        American Academy of Political and Social Science* 597 (2005): 48-64. Print.

Potter, Deborah. "Stemming the Losses: How Can TV News Win Back Viewers?"
        *American Journalism Review* 22.10 (2000): 49. Print.

## QUESTIONS FOR DISCUSSION AND WRITING

1. Where does Stephanie Bower state her claim? Do you agree with Stephanie's working claim here? Did you have a strong opinion about local TV news before you read Stephanie's piece? Did reading her paper change your mind, or reinforce your thinking?

2. Did Stephanie sufficiently narrow her topic? Is her evidence convincing? Considering that some of her evidence is from leading critics of the world of journalism, did she make their information accessible to you and relevant to her claim?

3. Examine two instances in which Stephanie cites quotations from experts in the field to develop her argument. Comment on the way she incorporated the quotations into the text. Was it done successfully or awkwardly?

4. What two factors, according to Stephanie, account for mediocrity in local news? Do you agree? disagree?

5. What are some of the brandings such as "I-Team" or "Storm Center" or "in-depth coverage" your local stations use? How do these brandings affect you? Do they earn your respect, your curiosity, or even your disdain? Explain your reaction.

6. What suggestions does Stephanie offer to improve the quality of local TV news? Which suggestions do you think could be realistically implemented? Which are obstacles too great to control in your opinion?

7. In your journal, select a local TV newscast, one that is broadcast nightly at the same time. Watch it every day if you can, or at least three times. Like Stephanie, break down the content of the newscast recording the length of time in minutes and seconds of the story, the topic of the story, and the depth of the story. Evaluate the content.

8. How do you respond to Stephanie's question, "Is journalism an impartial civic informer or a big business?" To shape your answer, use some of the evidence Stephanie presented in her paper and find some of your own.

## EXERCISES

1. Get together with a small group of students in your class and brainstorm possible topics for an argument essay concerning a controversial issue on your campus or in your community. Try to think of at least ten topics that are current and that most people in your group find interesting and arguable.

2. Make a visit to the periodicals section of your college library and look through current issues of periodicals and newspapers on the shelves to find out what issues and subjects are being debated in America and around the world. Find one or more topics that interest you and make copies of those articles for further reading and response in your journal.

3. Take some time to explore the Internet by doing a keyword search using a Web search engine. In your journal, describe the results of your search. How many different sites devoted to your topic did you locate? What did you find surprising about the comments and opinions expressed by the participants?

4. Engage in a dialogue with other students, family members, friends, or people in the community who might have some interest and opinions on a potential topic. In your journal, record and respond to their diverse views.

5. Choose a topic that you might wish to investigate for an argument essay and use some of the strategies suggested in this chapter to get started: brainstorm, cluster, freewrite, question.

6. Formulate a list of questions about your potential topic.

7. After you have followed some of the strategies for exploring your topic, formulate a working claim. In your journal, identify which parts of your claim will need to be supported by reasons in your essay. Which parts of your claim will need to be investigated further?

# 4

# Addressing Audiences: Thinking Like a Reader

As we've discussed in previous chapters, the purpose of writing an argument is to prompt your listeners to consider seriously your point of view and, thus, win your listeners' respect through the logic and skill of your thinking. When used productively, argument is a way to resolve conflict and achieve common ground among adversaries. Thus, one of the primary ways to measure the success of your argument is to gauge how effectively it reaches and appeals to your audience. Knowing something about your audience will enable you to use your knowledge to make your arguments most effective.

Creating an argument would be a simple task if you could be guaranteed an audience of readers just like yourself. If everyone shared your cultural, educational, religious, and practical experiences, persuading them to accept your point of view would require very little effort. Clearly, however, this is not the case. A quick look around your classroom will reveal the many differences that make argument a challenging activity. Is everyone the same age? race? gender? ethnicity? Do you all listen to the same music? dress alike? live in the same neighborhood? vote for the same candidates? attend the same place of worship? Unless you attend a very unusual school, the answer to most of these questions will be a resounding "no." People are different; what interests you may bore the person behind you, whereas what puts you to sleep may inspire someone else to passionate activism. And what you see on the surface isn't the whole story about your classmates, either. That rough-looking guy who works as a mechanic may write poetry in his spare time; that conservatively dressed woman may spend her weekends touring the countryside on a motorcycle. It's too easy to make assumptions about people's values and beliefs just by looking at them. If you want to persuade these people, you're going to have to assess them very carefully.

Knowing your audience will help you determine almost every aspect of the presentation of your case:

- the kind of language you use;
- the writing style (casual or formal, humorous or serious, technical or philosophical);
- the particular slant you take (appealing to the reader's reason, emotions, ethics, or a combination of these);
- what emphasis to give the argument;
- the type of evidence you offer;
- the kinds of authorities you cite.

Also, this knowledge will let you better anticipate any objections to your position. In short, knowing your audience lets you adjust the shape of your argument the way you would refocus a camera after each photo you shoot.

If, for instance, you're writing for your economics professor, you would use technical vocabulary you would not use with your English professor. Likewise, in a newspaper article condemning alcohol abusers, you would have to keep in mind that some of your readers or their family members might be recovering alcoholics; they may take exception to your opinions. A travel piece for an upscale international magazine would need to have a completely different slant and voice than an article for the travel section of a small local newspaper.

Knowing your audience might make the difference between a convincing argument and a failing argument. Suppose, for instance, you decide to write an editorial for the student newspaper opposing a recently announced tuition hike. Chances are you would have a sympathetic audience in the student body because you share age, educational status, and interests. Most students do not like the idea of a higher tuition bill. That commonality might justify the blunt language and emotional slant of your appeal. It might even allow a few sarcastic comments directed at the administration. That same argument addressed to your school's board of trustees, however, would probably not win a round of applause. With them it would be wiser to adopt a more formal tone in painting a sympathetic picture of your financial strain; it's always smart to demonstrate an understanding of the opposition's needs, maybe even a compromise solution. In this case, your appeal to the trustees would be more credible if you acknowledged the university's plight while recommending alternative money-saving measures such as a new fundraising program.

Or suppose you write an article with a religious thrust arguing against capital punishment. You argue that even in the case of confessed murderers, state execution is an immoral practice running counter to Christian doctrine; for supporting evidence you offer direct quotations from the New Testament. Were you to submit your article to a religious publication, your reliance on the authority of the scriptures would probably appeal to the editors. However, were you to submit that same article to the "My Turn" column for *Newsweek,* chances are it would be turned down, no matter how well written. The editors aren't necessarily an ungodly lot, but *Newsweek,* like most other large-circulation magazines, is published for an audience made up of people of every religious persuasion, as well as agnostics and atheists. *Newsweek* editors are not in the business of publishing material that excludes a large segment of its audience. Knowing your readers works in two ways: It helps you decide what materials to put into your argument, and it helps you decide where to publish your argument, whether it be on an electronic bulletin board, in a local paper, or on the op-ed page of the *Wall Street Journal.*

## The Target Audience

The essays in this book come from a variety of publications, many of them magazines addressed to the "general" American readership. Others, however, come from publications directed to men or women, the political right or left, or from publications for people of particular ethnic, racial, and cultural identities. They are written for *target audiences.* When writers have a "target" audience in mind, particularly readers who share the same interests, opinions, and prejudices, they can take shortcuts with little risk of alienating anybody, because writers and readers have so many things in common. Consider the following excerpts concerning the use of animal testing in scientific research:

Contrary to prevailing misperception, in vitro tests need not replace existing in vivo test procedures in order to be useful. They can contribute to chemical-safety evaluation right now. In vitro tests, for example, can be incorporated into the earliest stages of the risk-assessment process; they can be used to identify chemicals having the lowest probability of toxicity so that animals need be exposed only to less noxious chemicals.

It is clear from the technical terminology (e.g., *in vitro, in vivo, toxicity*), professional jargon *(test procedures, chemical-safety evaluation, risk-assessment process)*, and the formal, detached tone that the piece was intended for a scientifically educated readership. Not surprisingly, the article, "Alternatives to Animals in Toxicity Testing," was authored by two research scientists, Alan M. Goldberg and John M. Frazier, and published in *Scientific American* (August 1989). Contrast it with another approach to the topic:

> Almost 30 years ago, Queen had been a child herself, not quite two years old, living in Thailand under the care of her mother and another female elephant, the two who had tended to her needs every day since her birth. They taught her how to use her trunk, in work and play, and had given her a sense of family loyalty. But then Queen was captured, and her life was changed irrevocably by men with whips and guns. One man herded Queen by whipping and shouting at her while another shot her mother, who struggled after her baby until more bullets pulled her down forever.

What distinguishes this excerpt is the emotional appeal. This is not the kind of article you would find in *Scientific American* or most other scientific journals. Nor would you expect to see this kind of emotional appeal in a newsmagazine such as *Newsweek* or *Time,* or a general interest publication such as the Sunday magazine of many newspapers. The excerpt comes from an animal rights newsletter published by PETA, People for the Ethical Treatment of Animals. Given that particular audience, the writer safely assumes immediate audience sympathy with the plight of elephants. There is no need for the author to qualify or apologize for such sentimentalizing statements as "Queen had been a child herself" and "They taught her how to use her trunk, in work and play, and had given her a sense of family loyalty." In fact, given the context, the author is probably more interested in reminding readers of a shared cause rather than winning converts to the cause of animal rights.

Sometimes targeting a sympathetic audience is intended to move people to action–to get people to attend a rally or to contribute money to a cause or to vote for a particular political candidate. During the 2004 presidential campaign, fund-raising letters went out asking for donations to one particular candidate who pledged to fight the high cost of health care. In one of several Web logs ("blogs") supporting that candidate, the pharmaceutical industry was portrayed as a "greedy goliath" that was no different than "illegal drug cartels, extorting money from hapless consumers." As used in this blog, the strategy in appealing to a target audience is to streamline the issue into an "us-versus-them" conflict–in this case, the consumer as innocent victim and the manufacturers as bad guys. The blogger went on to argue that drug manufacturers inflate their prices astronomically, citing as evidence how company CEOs enjoy incomes in the tens of millions of dollars. "The pharmaceutical industry exists for the sole purpose of preying upon Americans who are sick, unhealthy, in discomfort and injured," said the blogger. "Their goal is to insure [sic] that only your symptoms are treated." Crackling with charged language, the blog invited voters to join the effort to change a system that exploited the taxpaying consumer and bloated company profits.

While pharmaceutical companies may indeed inflate the cost of their products, the campaign blog was a one-way argument, addressed to people already sympathetic to the cause. But the blog lacked perspectives from the other side. Nothing was said about the billions of dollars spent by pharmaceutical companies to develop and bring to market a new drug, or the fact that only a small percentage of drugs that reach the market ever turns a profit. Nor was there mention of the fact that the FDA is funded by the pharmaceutical companies and not taxpayer dollars, or the fact that the time frame for turning a profit is a limited number of years, after which patents expire, allowing the generic makers to market the same product at reduced costs. In short, the function of the campaign letters and blogs was not to plumb the depths of the issue and offer a balanced argument. On the contrary, most of the target audience was already sold on the cause. The basic intention was to convert conviction into money and votes. And the means was charged, motivational rhetoric.

## The General Audience

Unless you're convinced that your readers are in total agreement with you or share your philosophical or professional interests, you may have some trouble picturing just whom you are persuading. It's tempting to say you're writing for a "general" audience; but, as we said at the beginning of this chapter, general audiences may include very different people with different backgrounds, expectations, and standards. Writing for such audiences, then, may put additional pressure on you.

In reality, of course, most of your college writing will be for your professors. This can be a little confusing because you may find yourself trying to determine just what audience your professor represents. You may even wonder why professors expect you to explain material with which they are familiar. You may feel that defining technical terms to your psychology instructor who covered them in class the week before, or summarizing a poem that you know your English professor can probably recite, is a waste of time. But they have a good reason: They assume the role of an uninformed audience to let you show how much *you* know.

Of course, if you are arguing controversial issues you may find yourself in the awkward position of trying to second-guess your instructor's stand on an issue. You may even be tempted to tone down your presentation so as not to risk offense and, thus, an undesirable grade. However, most instructors try not to let their biases affect their evaluation of a student's work. Their main concern is how well a student argues a position.

For some assignments, your instructor may specify an audience for you: members of the city council, the readers of the campus newspaper, Rush Limbaugh's radio listeners, and so on. But if no audience is specified, one of your earliest decisions about writing should be in choosing an audience. If you pick "readers of *The National Review*," for instance, you'll know you're writing for mostly male, conservative, middle-aged, middle-class whites; the expectations of these readers are very different than for readers of *Jet* or *Vibe*. If you are constrained to (or want the challenge of) writing for the so-called general audience, construct a mental picture of who those people are so you'll be able to shape your argument accordingly. Here are some of the characteristics we think you might include in your definition.

The "general" audience includes those people who read *Newsweek, Time,* and your local newspaper. That means people whose average age is about 35, whose educational level is high school plus two years of college, who make up the vast middle class of America, who politically stand in the middle of the road, and whose racial and ethnic origins span the world. You can assume that they read the daily newspaper and/or online news sites, watch the television news, and are generally informed about what is going on in the country. You can assume a good comprehension of language nuances and a sense of humor. They are people who recognize who Shakespeare was, though they may not be able to quote passages or name ten of his plays. Nor will they necessarily be experts in the latest theory of black holes or be able to explain how photo emulsions work. However, you can expect them to be open to technical explanations and willing to listen to arguments on birth control, gun control, weight control, and the issues of women and gays in the military. More importantly, you can look upon your audience as people willing to hear what you have to say.

# Guidelines for Knowing Your Audience

Before sitting down to write, think about your audience. Ask yourself the following questions: Will I be addressing other college students, or people from another generation? Will my audience be of a particular political persuasion, or strongly identified with a specific cultural background? How might the age of my readers and their educational background influence the way they think about a given issue? On what criteria will they make their decisions about this issue? A good example of profiling your audience was evident in the 2008 presidential election. On the one hand, the Republicans gambled that "experience" was the chief criteria for voters. The Democrats, on the other hand, focused on a need for "change." As the election results showed, the Democrats had assessed their audience more accurately than did the Republicans.

As the example above illustrates, an effective argument essay takes into account the values, beliefs, interests, and experiences of its audience. If you simply choose to argue what you feel is important without regard to your audience, the only person you persuade may be yourself! An effective argument tries to establish common ground with the audience. While this may be difficult at times, recognizing what you have in common with your audience will enable you to argue most persuasively.

Before you can do this, however, you will need to create a profile of your audience. You may find the audience checklist on page 84 helpful in assessing an audience. If you like visual prompts, write the answers to these questions on a card or a slip of paper that you can hang over your desk or display in a window on your computer screen while you're working on your argument. Looking at these questions and answers occasionally will remind you to direct your arguments on your particular audience.

## Using Debate and Dialogue

Debate and dialogue, two of the methods of developing arguments discussed in Chapter 1, can also be used to sharpen your awareness of audience. For an example of how this can happen, let's revisit John, our first-year composition student who had decided to write his argument essay on the topic of binge drinking. After reading critically in his subject area (Chapter 2) and formulating a working claim (Chapter 3), John turned his attention to the question of audience. He found that using debate and dialogue helped him answer some of

## Audience Checklist

1. Who are the readers I will be addressing?
   a. What age group?
   b. Are they male, female, or both?
   c. What educational background?
   d. What socioeconomic status?
   e. What are their political, religious, occupational, or other affiliations?
   f. What values, assumptions, and prejudices do they have about life?
2. Where do my readers stand on the issue?
   a. Do they know anything about it?
   b. If so, how might they have learned about it?
   c. How do they interpret the issue?
   d. How does the issue affect them personally?
   e. Are they hostile to my stand on the issue?
3. How do I want my readers to view the issue?
   a. If they are hostile to my view, how can I persuade them to listen to me?
   b. If they are neutral, how can I persuade them to consider my viewpoint?
   c. If they are sympathetic to my views, what new light can I shed on the issue? How can I reinspire them to take action?
4. What do I have in common with my readers?
   a. What beliefs and values do we share?
   b. What concerns about the issue do we have in common?
   c. What common life experiences have we had?
   d. How can I make my readers aware of our connection?

the questions in the audience checklist and provided essential information about how his audience might respond to his ideas.

John decided that his audience would be a general one composed of people of all ages. He anticipated that most people in his audience would not endorse excessive drinking, but with such a diverse group of people he was unsure exactly what reasons would fuel their opposition and how strongly they would agree or disagree with his reasons. John found that using two strategies, first, a "Yes, but..." exchange and, second, an imaginary dialogue between different perspectives, helped to answer questions 2 and 3 on the audience checklist: Where do my readers stand on the issue? and How do I want my readers to view the issue? He used the answers to these questions to develop ways to engage his readers in the essay.

Working with classmates in small peer groups, John found that a "Yes, but..." exchange revealed specific points that his audience might use to oppose his reasons. For instance, John began with the following statement:

College administrators have a responsibility to deter binge drinking by their students.

He received several responses from his peer group:

Yes, college administrators have a responsibility to their students, but that responsibility should be limited to academic matters.

Yes, binge drinking by students should be a concern to college administrators, but college administrators shouldn't interfere with the private lives or habits of their students.

Yes, college administrators should try to deter binge drinking by students, but they will be ineffective unless they receive support from the community and parents.

Although each of John's classmates agreed that college administrators had a valid interest in student binge drinking, there was considerable disagreement over how far that interest should extend and how effective any action taken by administrators would be. The "Yes, but..." exchange gave John greater insight into the ways others might respond to his ideas. As he developed his argument, he was able to acknowledge and address such concerns by his potential audience.

In a similar fashion, John used dialogue to gain insight into question 4 on the audience checklist: What do I have in common with my readers? In particular, John wanted to discover any concerns and values he and his readers might share about binge drinking. To create a dialogue, John interviewed several of his classmates, his teachers, members of his family, and a few individuals from the community; he also read articles by health professionals concerned with alcohol abuse and young adults. His goal was to listen to a wide spectrum of views on the subject and to keep an open mind. He used his journal to record comments and his own impressions. What emerged from this dialogue were several areas of shared concerns: Most agreed that binge drinking was an unhealthy practice that should be discouraged, and while there were many different suggestions about the measures that should be taken to eliminate it, all agreed that the students who engaged in binge drinking must ultimately accept responsibility for ending it. No solution would work, all agreed, unless the drinkers themselves were willing to stop. John found this information helpful because he knew that his audience would be more willing to listen to his argument if he could identify these shared values and concerns.

By engaging in both debate and dialogue, John gained knowledge that enabled him to appeal to his audience more effectively.

## Adapting to Your Readers' Attitudes

Writing for a general audience is a challenge because in that faceless mass are three kinds of readers you'll be addressing:

1. People who agree with you
2. People who are neutral–those who are unconvinced or uninformed on the issue
3. People who don't share your views, and who might be hostile to them

Each of these different subgroups will have different expectations of you and give you different obligations to meet if you are to present a convincing argument. Even readers sympathetic to your cause might not be familiar with specialized vocabulary, the latest developments around the issue, or some of the more subtle arguments from the opposition. Those hostile to your cause might be so committed to their own viewpoints that they might not take the time to discover that you share common concerns. And those neutral to the cause might simply need to be filled in on the issue and its background. If you're going to persuade your readers, you'll have to tailor your approach to suit their attitudes.

When addressing an audience, whether general or one of a particular persuasion, you must try to put yourself in its place. You must try to imagine the different needs and expectations these readers bring to your writing, always asking yourself what new information you can pass on and what new ways of viewing you can find for addressing the issue you're arguing. Depending on whether you anticipate a neutral, friendly, or unfriendly group of readers, let's look at some of the strategies you might use.

## Addressing a Neutral Audience

Some writers think a neutral audience is the easiest to write for, but many others find this the most challenging group of readers. After all, they're *neutral*; you don't know which way they're leaning, or what may make them commit to your position. Your best role is the conveyor of knowledge: The information you bring, and the ways in which you present it, are the means by which you hope to persuade a neutral audience. Here are some of the ways to convey that information.

### Fill in the Background

There are some issues about which few people are neutral: abortion, capital punishment, drug legalization, same-sex marriage, gun control. However, there are other issues about which some readers have not given a thought. For instance, if you're part of a farming community, your concern about preserving good farmland might make you feel concerned about unchecked industrial development in your area. To make a convincing case for readers from, say, Chicago or New York City, you first would have to explain the shortage of prime agricultural land. On the other hand, were you a writer from a large town, you might need to explain to readers from rural Vermont or Iowa why you think they should be concerned over mandatory recycling in large cities. In both cases, your task would be to provide your readers with the information they need to evaluate the issue by relating some of the history and background behind the controversy. All the while, you need to encourage them to weigh the evidence with an open mind.

### Present a Balanced Picture

Part of educating a neutral audience about your position involves presenting a balanced picture of the issue by presenting multiple perspectives about the issue, not just one. Even though you are trying to help your readers understand why your position has value, you will be more persuasive if you treat *all* views fairly, including opposing views. You should clearly and accurately lay out the key arguments of all sides; then demonstrate why your position is superior. Your readers need to feel that you have looked at the total picture and reached your position after carefully weighing all views, a process you hope your readers will engage in as well. Let your readers make their decisions based on their own analysis of the information you have provided. Don't be guilty of stacking the deck, a logical fallacy we discussed in Chapter 2. Not representing the other sides at all, or representing them unfairly and inaccurately, can leave you open to criticisms of distortion, and it may make your readers feel that you're misleading them.

### Personalize the Issues

One sure way of gaining readers' attention is to speak their language—that is, address their personal needs, hopes, and fears. (It's what skillful politicians do all the time on the campaign trail.) If you want to engage your readers' attention, demonstrate how the problem will affect them personally. On the matter of farmland, explain why if nothing is done to prevent its loss, the prices of corn and beans will triple over the next three years. On the recycling issue, explain how unrestricted trash dumping will mean that city dwellers will try to dump more trash in rural areas. However, although personalizing the issue is an effective way to make your readers aware of the importance of your issue, you should avoid creating an ad misericordiam argument. To be fully credible, you should be certain that the reasons and evidence you present to your readers are anchored in fact rather than emotion.

### Show Respect

When you're an informed person talking about an issue to people with less knowledge than you, there's a dangerous tendency to speak down to them. Think how you feel when someone "talks down" to you. Do you like it? How persuasive do you think you can be if your readers think you're talking down to them? Don't condescend or patronize them. Try not to simplify a complex issue so much that it is reduced to a false dilemma: "If we don't increase school taxes immediately, our children will no longer receive a quality education." Don't assume that your audience is so ill informed that it cannot envision a middle ground between the two alternatives. On the contrary, treat your readers as people who want to know what you know about the issue and who want you to demonstrate to them clearly and accurately why you think they should agree with you. Invite them into the discussion, encouraging them with sound reasons and strong evidence to consider the merits of your side. Although your audience may not be as informed as you, they are willing to listen and deserve respect.

## Addressing a Friendly Audience

Writing an argument for the already converted is much easier than writing for a neutral audience or one that is hostile. In a sense, half the battle is won because no minds have to be changed. You need not brace yourself for opposing views or refutations. Your role is simply to provide readers with new information and to renew enthusiasm for and commitment to your shared position. Nonetheless, we do have some suggestions for keeping your argument fair and balanced.

### Avoid Appealing to Prejudices

One of the risks of addressing a sympathetic audience is appealing to prejudices rather than reasons and facts. Although it might be tempting to mock those who don't agree with you or to demean their views, don't. Stooping to that level only diminishes your own authority and undermines your credibility. Two of the logical fallacies we discussed in Chapter 2 address this problem. The first, an ad hominem argument, is a personal attack on those who disagree with your position. Unfortunately, this approach will reflect negatively on *you*. Use reason and hard evidence instead of insults and ridicule to underscore the weakness of other arguments while you make your readers aware of your mutual concerns. The second fallacy is an ad populum argument and involves using the presumed prejudices of your audience members to manipulate their responses to your argument. Once again, this approach will make you appear unreasonable and biased and may backfire if your audience does not share your prejudices. Instead, encourage your readers to respect different viewpoints, recognizing the merits of their arguments even though you ultimately disagree. It's simply a more reasonable approach, one that allows you and your readers to share informed agreement, and it will win the respect of friends and foes alike.

### Offer New Information About the Issue

Even when your readers agree with you, they may need to have their memories refreshed regarding the history of the issue. In addition, you should provide readers with important new information on the issue. Such new developments might involve recent judicial decisions, newly enacted legislation, or new scientific data that could serve to strengthen your position and their agreement or require a reconsideration of your views. Unless you are absolutely up-to-date about the progress of your issue, you will appear to be either ill informed or deliberately withholding information, seriously undermining your credibility with your audience, even a friendly one. Your willingness to share and educate your audience will enhance the persuasiveness of your views.

## Addressing an Unfriendly Audience

As difficult as it may be to accept, some readers will be totally at odds with your views, even hostile to them. Writing for such a readership, of course, is especially challenging—far more than for neutral readers. So how do you present your argument to people you have little chance of winning over?

### The Rogerian Approach: Seek Common Ground and Show Empathy

One sure fire strategy in writing for an unfriendly audience is the so-called Rogerian approach—a strategy that evolved in the 1970s out of the writings of Carl Rogers. Considered one of the most influential American psychologists of the past century, Rogers made contributions to the fields of psychotherapy, counseling, education, and conflict resolution. In his humanistic approach to these fields, he stressed the importance of the individual and the need for empathy.

In the Rogerian approach to argumentation, your goal is to find ways to connect with your audience through empathy and common experiences rather than going on the attack or trying to persuade the other side that you are right and they are wrong. Your strategy is to validate your own point of view by making concessions to the other side, saying that you understand and respect the opinion of the opposition.

The classical approach to argument was laid out by the Greek philosopher, Aristotle, who said that one should appeal to an audience on the three basic levels: reason or logic (*logos*); emotions (*pathos*); and ethical and moral sense (*ethos*). What distinguishes the Rogerian argument from the classical is the stronger emphasis on the emotional and ethical appeals rather than strictly logical ones. In other words, the Rogerian approach—to unfriendly audiences in particular—is to build an emotional or psychological bridge, a common ground through empathy. While the Rogerian approach doesn't actually concede to the opposition or even agree with them, it does cite some of the opposition points as valid. In other words, the Rogerian argument shows respect for contrary views, even recognizing the logic of their argument. At the same time, the arguer states his or her own stance on the issue, thus preventing unnecessary conflict and a deadlock. And, if handled properly, instead of an "I win/you lose" outcome, both sides emerge as winners in the end.

For example, let's say that you are trying to persuade a group of senior citizens in your community to support a tax increase to fund local schools. After analyzing your audience, you conclude that many seniors are living on limited incomes and are more concerned about the financial burden of additional taxes than the school system–something that is no longer a priority in their lives. This factor alone might make them an unfriendly audience, one not easily receptive to your position. Thus a good strategy to begin your argument might be to let them know that you are well acquainted with the difficulties of living on limited means. You might even refer to relatives or friends who are in a similarly difficult financial position. By letting the members of your audience know that you empathize with and understand their hardships, they will be more willing to listen to you. And in this way you have established an emotional and psychological bond.

Next, you could remind your audience of the beliefs and values you have in common. While it is unlikely that senior citizens still have children attending school, they nonetheless may value education and understand its importance. You let them know that you share this value, one that underlies your support for additional public school funding. This, then, is your common ground. And your thesis is that a tax increase would ensure that today's kids receive same quality of education that existed when the seniors themselves had young children. A tax increase today might benefit their grandchildren.

In so recognizing the concerns of your readers as legitimate and worthy of attention, you demonstrate that you are aware of and respect their views. But this means learning what their concerns are. In our example, it would be wise first to read up on specific reasons why seniors would choose not to support a tax increase for public school programs. Perhaps there's an imbalance in how the tax revenues would be applied. Perhaps some senior programs need to be funded also. Perhaps the proposed tax hike is too high. By doing some research and addressing those concerns, you will make your audience aware that you understand its opposition. In the end, this may make your readers more receptive to your argument.

In summary, the Rogerian argument begins by establishing a common ground with an audience–beliefs, opinions, and common values. Showing respect, the writer demonstrates a good understanding of the audience's views. Then in the core of the argument, the writer objectively states his or her own position. Without sounding dismissive or superior, the writer explains how his or her position is valid while explaining how that differs form the audience's stand. Finally, the writer states the thesis, making some concessions while inviting the audience to give a little also. In the end, the author demonstrates how adopting his or her perspective to some degree benefits both sides.

### Convey a Positive Attitude

Whether or not they know it, an unfriendly audience will benefit from seeing the issue from another side. In a Rogerian approach, try to view yourself as someone shedding a different light on the problem. View the opposition as people who are potentially interested in learning something new. Without being defensive, arrogant, or apologetic,

## Review: Addressing Audiences

**A Neutral Audience**
- Fill in the background
- Present a balanced picture
- Personalize the issues
- Show respect for your readers

**A Friendly Audience**
- Avoid appealing to prejudices
- Offer new information about the issue

**An Unfriendly Audience**
- Seek common ground
- Show empathy
- Convey a positive attitude
- Remember the Golden Rule

**To Improve Your Credibility with Your Audience, Avoid These Fallacies**

| | |
|---|---|
| **Ad hominem argument** | Leveling a personal attack against an opponent. A reliance on ad hominem arguments undercuts your credibility and may make you appear mean-spirited and desperate. Focus instead on the substance of an opponent's claim. |
| **Ad misericordiam argument** | Attempting to exploit the audience's emotions rather than appealing to logic and reason. Avoid using arguments that rely only on wrenching the reader's heart strings rather than logic and real evidence. |
| **Ad populum argument** | Appealing to the audience's presumed prejudices rather than proven facts. Even if you know the prejudices of your audience, such an appeal at best only persuades those already convinced. Rely on the force of logic and supporting evidence rather than bias and stereotyping. |
| **Stacking the deck** | Presenting only evidence that supports your points and withholding contrary evidence. Instead, acknowledge that conflicting evidence exists and respond to it. |
| **False dilemma** | Presenting an issue as an either-or choice and ignoring the possibility of a middle ground. Treat your audience as intelligent equals who are aware that at least several thoughtful alternatives are likely to exist. |

make your claim, enumerate your reasons, and lay out the evidence for your readers to evaluate on their own. Regard them as intelligent people capable of drawing their own conclusions. You may not win converts, but you might at least lead some to recognize the merits of your opinions. You might even convince a few people to reconsider their views.

### Remember the Golden Rule

Even though they may not agree with you, treat the opposition with respect. Look upon them as reasonable people who just happen to disagree with you. Demonstrate your understanding of their side of the issue. Show that you have made the effort to research the opposition. Give credit where credit is due. If some of their counterpoints make sense, say so. In short, treat those from the other side and their views as you would want to be treated. You may just win a few converts.

## SAMPLE ARGUMENTS FOR ANALYSIS

How a writer appeals to his or her audience can have a positive or a negative effect on the way the writer's message is received. The following three articles—two by professionals and one by a student—are all concerned with the deleterious effects of cigarette smoking. Each writer is concerned with the efficacy and/or legitimacy of various regulations on smoking and the resulting treatment of smokers. Under its powers to regulate tobacco, the Food and Drug Administration in 2009 banned candy and fruit-flavored cigarettes, but not mentholated cigarettes. In "Let's Ban All Flavors of Cigarettes," Derrick Z. Jackson questions why menthol, which makes up 30 percent of the $87 billion U.S. cigarette market, was not included in the ban. The next piece, "The Bogus 'Science' of Secondhand Smoke," attacks claims by anti-smoking lobbies that even the smallest quantities of secondhand smoke can set the cancer process in motion. No apologist for the smoking industry, scientist Gio Batta Gori challenges the so-called scientific evidence used to support this claim. And our student piece by Denise Cavallaro questions the decision-making apparatus of her relatives and contemporaries who smoke despite statistics and numbers that show what a deadly decision they are making. For the first essay, by Derrick Z. Jackson, we have used annotations to illustrate some of the strategies he uses to appeal to his audience and the assumptions he makes about them. As a class exercise, read each of these essays and then consider the following questions:

1. Locate the claim or thesis statement and summarize the main ideas in each essay.
2. What kind of audience is each writer addressing? neutral? friendly? hostile? What evidence can you find to support this?
3. Which writers attempt to present a balanced picture to the audience? Provide examples.
4. Do the writers convey a positive attitude toward the audience? Do any of the writers antagonize the audience? How is this done?
5. Have these writers committed any of the logical fallacies we've discussed? Where do these errors occur, and how would you correct them?
6. How well does each writer establish common ground with the audience?
7. What is the purpose of each essay? How effectively does each writer accomplish this purpose?

# Let's Ban All Flavors of Cigarettes

*Derrick Jackson*

Derrick Z. Jackson is a journalist and regular columnist and associate editor for the *Boston Globe*. A graduate of the University of Wisconsin-Milwaukee and post-graduate journalism fellow at Harvard University, he is the recipient of various honorary degrees. He also teaches journalism courses at Simmons College in Boston. This article appeared in his column on September 30, 2009.

## Let's Ban All Flavors of Cigarettes

1   It was a good first step by the Food and Drug Administration to ban candy- and fruit-flavored cigarettes this month under its new powers to regulate tobacco. The next and much bigger step is ending Menthol Madness.

2   As cancer-stick observers know, Big Tobacco really did not mind closing the candy store on cigarettes flavored like Hershey's or Life Savers. They were not even one percent of the market. Menthol is by far the most prominent cigarette flavoring of all. But it was exempted from an immediate ban in the smoking-prevention act signed by President Obama in June.

*charged language*
*Assumes reader appreciates allusion to Big Brother*

3   The reason is simple: Menthol cigarettes are nearly 30 percent of the $87 billion U.S. cigarette market. Menthol masks the harshness of smoking with its cooling effect and minty taste. The tobacco lobby and political allies bemoaned the impact of a menthol ban on jobs and government coffers. In 2007, tobacco sales generated $26 billion in state and federal tax revenues.

*Assumes reader shares cynicism about tobacco industry's motives*
*Though liberal author? not afraid to criticize Obama*

4   When Obama signed the prevention act, he proclaimed that the tobacco industry's "millions upon millions in lobbying and advertising" on its "lies" to deny the deadly effects of smoking have "finally failed."

5   That is a lie as long as the menthol exemption exists. The exemption means that government coffers remain more important than the coffins for the annual 443,000 lives lost to tobacco. The concern over tax revenues still overrides the $193 billion in annual health-related economic costs from smoking—a figure provided by the Centers for Disease Control.

*Assumes politically savvy reader*

6   The FDA can still ban menthol. Public health-minded politicians negotiated an explicit provision in the prevention act that commits the FDA to study menthol within one year. Any serious study should clearly result in a ban.

7   Medical journal studies over the last four years have found that smokers of menthol cigarettes are significantly more likely to have difficulty quitting smoking and that tobacco

*Assumes reader is comfortable with medical journals and medical data*

companies have deliberately manipulated menthol levels (as they did with nicotine) to lure younger smokers with "milder" taste. While menthol cigarettes are nearly 30 percent of the overall U.S. market, 44 percent of smokers ages 12 to 17 reported smoking menthol brands.

8    The menthol exemption also leaves dangling in political midair explosive charges of racism. Menthol cigarettes are vastly disproportionately popular among African-Americans, with 80 percent of black smokers preferring menthol. According to the government, 30 percent of all cancer deaths are tied to cigarette smoking and African-Americans are 21 percent more likely to have lung cancer than white Americans. Smoking is tied to heart disease and strokes, and African-American men are twice as likely as white men to have strokes.

*Uses facts and reason not emotion*

9    This was enough for seven former US health secretaries to protest the exemption. One of them, Joseph Califano, told the *New York Times* that the exemption was "clearly putting black children in the back of the bus." This week, the American Legacy Foundation, established in the tobacco settlement with the states, urged the FDA to ban menthol along with the other flavors. "Literally many hundreds of tobacco industry documents conclusively establish that the tobacco industry has for decades systematically developed and marketed menthol products," the foundation said, " . . . to lure youth and younger tobacco users by masking the harsh flavor."

*Assumes literate reader who recognizes these references*

10    But with at least a year to go before possible banning, Big Tobacco is systematically hooking as many new smokers as possible. Martin Orlowsky, the CEO of Lorillard, which makes the top-selling menthol Newport, said this month, "We will continue to leverage the very strong brand equity position Newport has, particularly in key markets where the opportunity—that is, menthol opportunity—is greatest."

*strong language*

*sketches opposition plans*

11    As to where those "key markets" are, Reynolds American CEO Susan Ivey said in 2006, "If you look at the demographics of menthol, it is very urban. It has always had a strong African-American component. It's always had actually a strong Caucasian component. What has changed a lot in the last five years is a lot of additional Hispanic in that demographic. . . . we would see that menthol would have additional opportunity."

12    The FDA cannot close that window of opportunity too soon.

*strong call to action*

# The Bogus 'Science' of Secondhand Smoke

*Gio Batta Gori*

Gio Batta Gori, an epidemiologist and toxicologist, is a spokesman and consultant for the tobacco industry. He is a former deputy director of the National Cancer Institute's Division of Cancer Cause and Prevention and the recipient of the U.S. Public Health Service Superior Service Award in 1976 for his efforts to define less hazardous cigarettes. This article appeared on washingtonpost.com, January 30, 2007.

1   Smoking cigarettes is a clear health risk, as most everyone knows. But lately, people have begun to worry about the health risks of secondhand smoke. Some policymakers and activists are even claiming that the government should crack down on secondhand smoke exposure, given what "the science" indicates about such exposure.

2   Last July, introducing his office's latest report on secondhand smoke, then-U.S. Surgeon General Richard Carmona asserted that "there is no risk-free level of secondhand smoke exposure," that "breathing secondhand smoke for even a short time can damage cells and set the cancer process in motion," and that children exposed to secondhand smoke will "eventually... develop cardiovascular disease and cancers over time."

3   Such claims are certainly alarming. But do the studies Carmona references support his claims, and are their findings as sound as he suggests?

4   Lung cancer and cardiovascular diseases develop at advancing ages. Estimating the risk of those diseases posed by secondhand smoke requires knowing the sum of momentary secondhand smoke doses that nonsmokers have internalized over their lifetimes. Such lifetime summations of instant doses are obviously impossible, because concentrations of secondhand smoke in the air, individual rates of inhalation, and metabolic transformations vary from moment to moment, year after year, location to location.

5   In an effort to circumvent this capital obstacle, all secondhand smoke studies have estimated risk using a misleading marker of "lifetime exposure." Yet, instant exposures also vary uncontrollably over time, so lifetime summations of exposure could not be, and were not, measured.

6   Typically, the studies asked 60–70 year-old self-declared nonsmokers to recall how many cigarettes, cigars, or pipes might have been smoked in their presence during their lifetimes, how thick the smoke might have been in the rooms, whether the windows were open, and similar vagaries. Obtained mostly during brief phone interviews, answers were then recorded as precise measures of lifetime individual exposures.

7   In reality, it is impossible to summarize accurately from momentary and vague recalls, and with an absurd expectation of precision, the total exposure to secondhand smoke over more than a half-century of a person's lifetime. No measure of cumulative lifetime secondhand smoke exposure was ever possible, so the epidemiologic studies estimated risk based not only on an improper marker of exposure, but also on exposure data that are illusory.

8   Adding confusion, people with lung cancer or cardiovascular disease are prone to amplify their recall of secondhand smoke exposure. Others will fib about being nonsmokers

and will contaminate the results. More than two dozen causes of lung cancer are reported in the professional literature, and over 200 for cardiovascular diseases; their likely intrusions have never been credibly measured and controlled in secondhand smoke studies. Thus, the claimed risks are doubly deceptive because of interferences that could not be calculated and corrected.

9      In addition, results are not consistently reproducible. The majority of studies do not report a statistically significant change in risk from secondhand smoke exposure, some studies show an increase in risk, and, astoundingly, some show a reduction of risk.

10     Some prominent anti-smokers have been quietly forthcoming on what "the science" does and does not show. Asked to quantify secondhand smoke risks at a 2006 hearing at the UK House of Lords, Oxford epidemiologist Sir Richard Peto, a leader of the secondhand smoke crusade, replied, "I am sorry not to be more helpful; you want numbers and I could give you numbers . . . , but what does one make of them? . . . These hazards cannot be directly measured."

11     It has been fashionable to ignore the weakness of "the science" on secondhand smoke, perhaps in the belief that claiming "the science is settled" will lead to policies and public attitudes that will reduce the prevalence of smoking. But such a Faustian bargain is an ominous precedent in public health and political ethics. Consider how minimally such policies as smoking bans in bars and restaurants really reduce the prevalence of smoking, and yet how odious and socially unfair such prohibitions are.

12     By any sensible account, the anachronism of tobacco use should eventually vanish in an advancing civilization. Why must we promote this process under the tyranny of deception?

13     Presumably, we are grown-up people, with a civilized sense of fair play, and dedicated to disciplined and rational discourse. We are fortunate enough to live in a free country that is respectful of individual choices and rights, including the right to honest public policies. Still, while much is voiced about the merits of forceful advocacy, not enough is said about the fundamental requisite of advancing public health with sustainable evidence, rather than by dangerous, wanton conjectures.

14     A frank discussion is needed to restore straight thinking in the legitimate uses of "the science" of epidemiology—uses that go well beyond secondhand smoke issues. Today, health rights command high priority on many agendas, as they should. It is not admissible to presume that people expect those rights to be served less than truthfully.

---

# Smoking: Offended by the Numbers

*Danise Cavallaro*

Danise Cavallaro is a former English major, and it's clear from her word choice, tone, and the slant she takes that she is addressing her peers. As she mentions in her essay, many college students smoke, even if only at parties. In this essay, updated for this edition of *Dialogues*, Cavallaro wonders why anyone would ever want to smoke at all.

Danise Cavallaro
Professor Mitrani
English 102
13 October 2009

Smoking: Offended by the Numbers

I majored in English because I hate mathematics and numbers. I hate these numbers too, but at least they are non-mathematically interesting: 11; 445; 1,200; 50,000.

- Eleven is the number of chemical compounds found in cigarettes that have been proven to cause cancer.
- Four hundred forty-five is the number of people per day who are diagnosed with smoking-related lung cancer.
- One thousand two hundred is the number of people who die every day from tobacco.
- Fifty thousand is the number of people who die every year from secondhand smoke-related diseases ("Facts").

I thought that I would defy the rules of journalism and write out those numbers in longhand because they seem awfully small on the page when I looked at them numerically. I thought if they looked bigger on the page, they might hold a little more meaning. They're even larger when they're not written in longhand. Yankee Stadium, filled, holds just over 52,000 people. That's roughly all the people who die from secondhand smoke per year, plus about five-and-a-half days' worth of the daily death toll from firsthand smoke. That's not even counting the nearly 5 million people worldwide who die each year from a smoking-related disease—which would be 96 sold-out Yankee Stadiums. Now go back to thinking about just one Yankee Stadium. If you were at a baseball game, who would you be there with? Your parents or your family? Your boyfriend or girlfriend, your best friends, your roommate from college? Don't forget about yourself. Now imagine each of them hooked up on an oxygen tank, struggling to do something as simple as breathe, unable to pull enough air into their lungs to cheer a run or a tag-out at home. They're living, still very much medically alive, but think of their quality of life: struggling to breathe, severely limited activity, and feigned happiness at most things.

In my now 28 years of being alive, I have never once felt the urge to light a cigarette. However, I have a lot of friends and family who have. I'm still struggling to understand what makes cigarettes appealing. Kissing my ex fresh after he squashed his cigarette underneath his heel tasted similar to what I'd imagine licking an ashtray would be like. My best friend lives in Manhattan, complains to no end

Cavallaro 2

about how expensive things are, but has no problem forking over $9-$11 for a pack of cigarettes. Her parents give her a hard time about it every time she's home; and she usually retorts with, "At least my cigarettes are safer than the unfiltered ones you rolled in the Army!" This argument in no way rationalizes her decisions, which contribute to raising the risks of her contracting lung cancer and emphysema. My uncle watched my grandfather slowly lose a two-year battle with lung cancer caused by working with asbestos and smoking unfiltered cigarettes for more than 40 years, but he would take smoke breaks while visiting him in the hospital. He still smokes today. It makes me sick.

4      With all this firsthand knowledge, such as the statistics I cited above, along with the deluge of widely available facts and help (Are we not living in the Information Age?) and as smart as these select people are, how could anyone not be motivated to quit by the numbers alone? The anti-smoking ad campaigns are not strong enough (though the chemical additives put into tobacco are very powerful), and, for whatever silly economic reason, cigarettes are marketed as cool. People still buy them even though they're a waste of money, and smoke them even though they carry a high mortality rate, all in the name of being able to exercise their rights as autonomous Americans.

5      I wonder if smokers still think in that hard-headed "never going to happen to me" American way when they're gasping for breath as they walk up the stairs. It's no secret that nicotine is an extremely addictive drug, and one of the hardest to give up. As with many things, if quitting were easy more people would do it. Mount Everest would be as popular as Disneyland if it were merely a hill.

6      To help lower those numbers in America, I propose a national anti-smoking campaign similar to "Scared Straight," a program for would-be juvenile offenders that worked well by showing exactly what the troubled youths would become if they kept to the path they were on. The popular anti-tobacco website, "thetruth.com," famous for its silently-shocking TV commercials depicting nonviolent boycotts of tobacco companies, is a good start. Certainly, more can be done. It starts with the youth of today.

7      Bring in a cancer-ravaged lung to a high school health class. Consider the postmortem donation as a gift to science—the science of staying alive. Black and white X-rays of lungs filled with shadowy malignant growths don't shock and revolt nearly as much as once-live flesh does, or ever will. While nicotine-yellowed teeth are becoming increasingly easier to whiten with do-it-yourself kits, it's impossible to peek at the inside of your own lungs to see the damage that's been done. Please

Cavallaro 3

plaster huge pictures of cancer- or emphysema-ravaged lungs across billboards along I-95. The media must realize that not being politically correct and therefore not afraid to shock or offend, may actually save lives. Grossing out the populace could be a highly effective tool—statistics and numbers printed on paper hardly look menacing, but disintegrating lung tissue is guaranteed to shock.

8      Within the past few years, the media have broadcast more edgy anti-smoking campaigns. Television commercials depict people regrettably living with tobacco-related tracheotomies, amputations, and late-stage cancers. The folks they show are openly remorseful, are suffering and are acutely aware of the chosen circumstances that brought them to their current situation. Unfortunately, the commercials show victims who are middle-aged or older. Nine in ten tobacco users start before they reach their 18th birthday, so this portrayed demographic may not resonate with youth (kidshealth.org).

9      One of the many problems with adolescent smoking is that the more deadly side effects are not felt until many years after high school, when smoking is less of a faux-cool habit and more of a way of life. Asthma, while not to be scoffed at, is a condition that is treatable and seldom lethal. Lung cancer, the most common cause of cancer death among men and women, is not optimistically treatable and is highly lethal. However, lung cancer is also the most preventable. Therefore, I propose banning the depiction of smoking in movies and television geared towards young adults. Adolescents, an extremely malleable age group, are obviously influenced by the media and seek to imitate the clothing, hairstyles, music, and lifestyles portrayed by the media. Remove the idea that smoking is an acceptable way of life, and it will reduce the numbers of people for whom smoking will become a way of life. America needs to be more honest with this easily influenced age group.

10      I also propose making cigarettes more expensive, as teenagers are famous for being broke. The harder it is for youth (or anyone) to afford this deadly habit, the less likely that it could actually become a habit. Given that the current recession has caused a lot of Americans to rethink their necessities, perhaps a $12 or $15 pack of cigarettes would help adjust priorities.

11      The problem with all this is, again, the numbers. America was founded on tobacco fields, funded by the trade of dried tobacco leaf between England and the Native Americans. Even a giant cornerstone of our economy rests on cigarettes. The biggest tobacco companies in the world have branched out and now own major corporations that supply nearly everything consumable. In his book *Ashes to Ashes: America's Hundred-Year Cigarette War, the Public Health and the Unabashed*

Cavallaro 4

*Triumph of Philip Morris*, Richard Kluger details how Philip Morris not only dominated the cigarette industry but has managed through its acquisitions of other companies—from beer to frozen vegetables—in the 1980s to insulate itself from an attack on its tobacco engine. To take down Philip Morris would be to upset an economic juggernaut to which many other companies on the NASDAQ are inexorably linked. It would be catastrophic to this country's economy. The "economic downturn" beginning in 2008 was hailed as the closest this country has been to a full-out Depression since the 1930s, and removing just Philip Morris from our economy would no doubt send America to shambles. Let's look at another huge facet of our economy—health care. Wouldn't it be nice to save over $150 billion each year in health care costs directly attributable to smoking? What could be done with all those newfound numbers?

12          It may be quite impossible to financially overturn the tobacco companies while it appears that addicted individuals might keep their cigarette plants a-humming forever. For example, my aforementioned best friend has a pack-per-week habit, which increases during midterms, finals, and immediately following bad dates. One pack of cigarettes a week, at $10 a pack, amounts to $520 per year. That's a lot of money for a law school student with no job—most of a month's rent, half a year's worth of cell phone bills, and a lot of delicious dinners at a good restaurant. I know many people who smoke a pack a day, which amounts to over $3,000 a year, even if they buy cheaper brands. The numbers add up, and it can be a hard choice where to apply your numbers.

13          Be selfish, America. Keep your numbers to yourself.

Cavallaro 5

## Works Cited

"Facts." American Legacy Foundation, 2009. Web. 22 Oct. 2009.

Izenberg, Neil, MD. "Smoking Stinks!" *Kindshealth.org*. N.d. Web. 1 Oct. 2009.

Kluger, Richard. *Ashes to Ashes: America's Hundred-Year Cigarette War, the Public Health and the Unabashed Triumph of Philip Morris*. New York: Knopf, 1996. Print.

# Choosing Your Words

Whether addressing friends, foes, or the undecided, you must take care that your readers fully understand your case. In part, this is accomplished by choosing your words carefully and by accurately defining any technical, unfamiliar, foreign, or abstract terms. Here are a few specific tips to follow to inform your readers without turning them off.

## Distinguishing Denotation and Connotation

Many words, even the most common, carry special suggestions or associations, **connotations,** that differ from the precise dictionary definitions, **denotations.** For example, if you looked up the word *house* in the dictionary, one of the synonyms you'd find is *shelter.* Yet if you told people you live in a shelter, they would think that you live in a facility for the homeless or some kind of animal sanctuary. That is because *shelter* implies a covering or structure that protects those within from the elements or from danger. In other words, the term is not neutral, as is the word *house.* Likewise, dictionary synonyms for *horse* include *steed* and *nag,* but the former implies an elegant and high-spirited riding animal, while the latter suggests one that is old and worn out.

The denotations of words may be the same, but their connotations will almost always differ. And the reason is that dictionary denotations are essentially neutral and emotion-free, while connotations are most often associated with attitudes or charged feelings that can influence readers' responses. Therefore, it is important to be aware of the shades of differences when choosing your words. Consider the different meanings the connotations of the bracketed choices lend these statements:

By the time I got home I was _____ [sleepy, exhausted, weary, beat, dead].

My boyfriend drives around in a red _____ [car, vehicle, buggy, clunker, jalopy].

I could hear him _____ [shout, yell, bellow, scream, shriek].

Connotations can also be personal and, thus, powerful tools for shaping readers' responses to what you say. Consider the word *pig.* The dictionary definition, or denotation, would read something like this: "A domestic farm animal with a long, broad snout and a thick, fat body covered with coarse bristles." However, the connotation of *pig* is far more provocative, for it suggests someone who looks or acts like a pig; someone who is greedy or filthy; someone who is sexually immoral. (Most dictionaries list the connotations of words, although some connotations might only be found in a dictionary of slang—e.g., *The New Dictionary of American Slang,* edited by Robert L. Chapman, or *Slang!* by Paul Dickson.)

There is nothing wrong with using a word because of its connotations, but you must be aware that connotations will have an emotional impact on readers. You don't want to say something unplanned. You don't want to offend readers by using words loaded with unintentional associations. For instance, you wouldn't suggest to advertisers that they "should be more creative when hawking their products" unless you intended to insult them. Although the term *hawking* refers to selling, it is unflattering and misleading because it connotes somebody moving up and down the streets peddling goods by shouting. Linguistically, the word comes from the same root as the word *huckster,* which refers to an aggressive merchant known for haggling and questionable practices.

Connotatively loaded language can be used to create favorable as well as unfavorable reactions. If you are arguing against the use of animals in medical research, you will get a stronger response if you decry the sacrifice of "puppies and kittens" rather than the cooler, scientific, and less charged "laboratory animals."

You can understand why politicians, newspaper columnists, and anyone advocating a cause use connotative language. The loaded word is like a bullet for a writer making a strong argument. Consider the connotative impact of the italicized terms in the following excerpts taken from essays in this text:

> "When you agreed to buy the drink and the muffin you did not take into account the plastic-cup *shakedown*. (Michael Lewis, "The Case Against Tipping, page 20)

> The *menthol exemption* also leaves dangling in political *midair explosive charges* of racism. (Derrick Jackson, "Let's Ban All Flavors of Cigarettes," page 93)

> "The English language has been *hacked and torn apart* in the effort to promote equality, but the result is a disconnection from reality." (Shannon O'Neill, "Literature Hacked and Torn Apart: Censorship in Public Schools," page 276)

Each of the italicized words was selected not for its denotations but its negative connotations. In the first example, Michael Lewis could have simply said "take into account the plastic cup" or said "take into account the plastic tipping cup." Instead he added the word "shakedown" which implies a criminal act of intimidation or extortion on the part of the coffee establishment. Similarly, Derrick Jackson suggests that claims against "menthol exemption" may be "midair explosive charges" of racial discrimination, evoking powerful images of bombs (a punning use of "charges") going off in protest against the government's allowing the cigarettes industry to continue marketing potentially deadly menthol products to African-Americans.

## Being Specific

To help readers better understand your argument, you need to use words that are precise enough to convey your exact meaning. If you simply say, "The weather last weekend was *terrible*," your readers are left to come up with their own interpretations of what the weather was like. Was it hot and muggy? cold and rainy? overcast and very windy? some of each? Chances are your readers won't come up with the same weather conditions you had in mind. However, if you said, "Last weekend it rained day and night and never got above 40 degrees," readers will have a more precise idea of the weekend's weather. And you will have accomplished your purpose of saying just what you meant.

The terms *general* and *specific* are opposites just as *abstract* and *concrete* are opposites. General words do not name individual things but classes or groups of things: animals, trees, women. Specific words refer to individuals in a group: your pet canary, the oak tree outside your bedroom window, the point guard. Of course, general and specific are themselves relative terms. Depending on the context or your frame of reference, a word that is specific in one context may be general in another. For instance, there is no need to warn a vegetarian that a restaurant serves veal Oscar and beef Wellington when simply *meat* will do. In other words, there are degrees of specificity appropriate to the situation. The following list illustrates just such a sliding scale, moving downward from the more general to the more specific.

| General | animal | person | book | clothing | food | machine |
|---------|--------|--------|------|----------|------|---------|
|  | feline | female | novel | footwear | seafood | vehicle |
|  | cat | singer | American | shoes | fish | fighter jet |
| Specific | Daisy, my pet | Mary J.Blige | *The Great Gatsby* | her Nikes | tuna | F-17 |

General words are useful in ordinary conversation when the people you're addressing understand your meaning and usually don't ask for clarification. The same is true in writing when you are addressing an audience familiar with your subject. In such instances, you can get away with occasional broad statements. For example, if you are running for class president, your campaign speeches would not require a great number of specifics as much as general statements of promise and principles:

> If elected, I intend to do what I can to ensure a comfortable classroom environment for each student at this college.

But when your audience is unfamiliar with your subject or when the context requires concrete details, generalities and abstract terms fall flat, leaving people wondering just exactly what you are trying to communicate. Let's say, for instance, you write a note to your dean explaining why you'd like to change the room where your English class meets. You wouldn't get very far on this appeal:

> Room 107 Richards is too small and uncomfortable for our class.

However, if you offer some specifics evoking a sense of the room's unpleasantness, you'd make a more persuasive case for changing the room:

> Room 107 Richards has 20 fixed seats for 27 students, leaving those who come in late to sit on windowsills or the floor. Worse still is the air quality. The radiators are fixed on high and the windows don't open. By the end of the hour, it must be 90 degrees in there, leaving everybody sweaty and wilted including Prof. Hazzard.

What distinguishes this paragraph is the use of concrete details: "20 fixed seats for 27 students"; latecomers forced to "sit on windowsills or on the floor"; radiators "fixed on high"; "the windows don't open"; "90 degrees"; and everybody was left "sweaty and wilted including Prof. Hazzard." But more than simply conjuring up a vivid impression of the room's shortcomings, these specifics add substance to your argument for a room change.

**Concrete language** is specific language–words that have definite meaning. Concrete language names persons, places, and things: *Barack Obama, Mary Shelley, New Zealand, Venice Boulevard, book, toothpaste*. Concrete terms conjure up vivid pictures in the minds of readers because they refer to particular things or qualities that can be perceived by the five senses–that is, they can be seen, smelled, tasted, felt, and heard. Abstract words, in contrast, refer to qualities that do not have a definitive concrete meaning. They denote intangible qualities that cannot be perceived directly by the senses but are inferred from the senses—*powerful, foolish, talented, responsible, worthy.* Abstract words also denote concepts and ideas—*patriotism, beauty, victory, sorrow.* Although abstract terms can be useful depending on the context, writing that relies heavily on abstractions will fail to communicate clear meaning. Notice in the pairs below how concrete and specific details convert vague statements into vivid ones:

| | |
|---|---|
| **Abstract** | He was very nicely dressed. |
| **Concrete** | He wore a dark gray Armani suit, white pinstriped shirt, and red paisley tie. |
| **Abstract** | Jim felt uncomfortable at Jean's celebration party. |
| **Concrete** | Jim's envy of Jean's promotion made him feel guilty. |
| **Abstract** | That was an incredible accident. |
| **Concrete** | A trailer truck jackknifed in the fog, causing seven cars to plow into each other, killing two, injuring eight, and leaving debris for a quarter mile along Route 17. |

**Abstract language** is also relative. It depends on circumstances and the experience of the person using them. A *cold* December morning to someone living in Florida might mean temperatures in the forties or fifties. To residents of North Dakota, *cold* would designate air at subzero temperatures. It all depends on one's point of view. A *fair trial* might mean one thing to the prosecutor of a case, yet something completely different to the defense attorney. Likewise, what might be *offensive* language to your grandmother would probably not faze an average college student.

When employing abstract language, you need to be aware that readers may not share your point of view. Consequently, you should be careful to clarify your terms or simply select concrete alternatives. Below is an excerpt from a student paper as it appeared in the first draft. As you can see, it is lacking in details and specifics and has a rather dull impact.

**Vague:** Last year my mother nearly died from medicine when she went to the hospital. The bad reaction sent her into a coma for weeks, requiring life-support systems around the clock. Thankfully, she came out of the coma and was released, but somebody should have at least asked what, if any, allergies she had.

Although the paragraph reads smoothly, it communicates very little of the dramatic crisis being described. Without specific details and concrete words, the reader misses both the trauma and the seriousness of the hospital staff's neglect, thus dulling the argument for stronger safeguards. What follows is the same paragraph revised with the intent of making it more concrete.

**Revised:** Last year my mother nearly died from a codeine-based painkiller when she was rushed to the emergency room at Emerson Hospital. The severe allergic reaction sent her into a coma for six weeks, requiring daily blood transfusions, thrice weekly kidney dialysis, continuous intravenous medicines, a tracheotomy, and round-the-clock intensive care. Thankfully, she came out of the coma and was released, but the ER staff was negligent in not determining from her or her medical records that she was allergic to codeine.

## Using Figurative Language

Words have their literal meaning, but they also can mean something beyond dictionary definitions, as we have seen. The sentence "Mrs. Jones is an angel" does not mean that Mrs. Jones is literally a supernatural winged creature, but a very kind and pleasant woman. What makes the literally impossible meaningful here is figurative language.

**Figurative language** (or a **figure of speech**) is comparative language. It is language that represents something in terms of something else–in figures, symbols, or likeness (Mrs. Jones and an angel). It functions to make the ordinary appear extraordinary and the unfamiliar appear familiar. It also adds richness and complexity to abstractions. Here, for instance, is a rather bland literal statement: "Yesterday it was 96 degrees and very humid." Here's that same sentence rendered in figurative language: "Yesterday the air was like warm glue." What this version does is equate yesterday's humid air to glue on a feature shared by each—stickiness. And the result is more interesting than the original statement.

The comparison of humid air to glue is linked by the words *like*. This example represents one of the most common figures of speech, the simile. Derived from the Latin *similis*, the term means similar. A simile makes an explicit comparison between dissimilar things (humid air and glue). It says that *A* is like *B* in one or more respects. The connectives used in similes are most often the words *like, as,* and *than:*

- A school of minnows shot by me like pelting rain.
- His arms are as big as hams.
- They're meaner than junkyard dogs.

When the connectives *like, as,* or *than* are omitted, then we have another common figure of speech, the **metaphor.** The term is from the Greek *meta* (over) + *pherin* ("to carry or ferry") meaning to carry over meaning from one thing to another. Instead of saying that A is like B, a metaphor equates them–A *is* B. For example, Mrs. Jones and an angel are said to be one and the same, although we all know that literally the two are separate entities.

- This calculus problem is a real pain in the neck.
- The crime in this city is a cancer out of control.
- The space shuttle was a flaming arrow in the sky.

Sometimes writers will carelessly combine metaphors that don't go with each other. Known as **mixed metaphors,** these often produce ludicrous results. For example:

- The heat of his expression froze them in their tracks.
- The experience left a bad taste in her eyes.
- The arm of the law has two strikes against it.

When a metaphor has lost its figurative value, it is called a **dead metaphor**: the *mouth* of a river, the *eye* of a needle, the *face* of a clock. Originally these expressions functioned as figures of speech, but their usage has become so common in our language that many have become **clichés** ("golden opportunity," "dirt cheap," "a clinging vine"). More will be said about clichés below, but our best advice is to avoid them. Because they have lost their freshness, they're unimaginative and they dull your writing.

Another common figure of speech is **personification,** in which human or animal characteristics or qualities are attributed to inanimate things or ideas. We hear it all the time: Trees *bow* in the wind; fear *grips* the heart; high pressure areas *sit* on the northeast. Such language is effective in making abstract concepts concrete and vivid and possibly more interesting:

■ Graft and corruption walk hand in hand in this town.

■ The state's new tax law threatens to gobble up our savings.

■ Nature will give a sigh of relief the day they close down that factory.

As with other figures of speech, personification must be used appropriately and with restraint. If it's overdone, it ends up calling undue attention to itself while leaving readers baffled:

Drugs have slouched their way into our schoolyards and playgrounds, laughing up their sleeves at the law and whispering vicious lies to innocent children.

For the sake of sounding literary, drugs here are personified as pushers slouching, laughing, and whispering. But such an exaggeration runs the risk of being rejected by readers as pretentious. If this happens, the vital message may well be lost. One must also be careful not to take shortcuts. Like dead metaphors, many once-imaginative personifications have become clichés: "justice is blind," "virtue triumphed," "walking death." While such may be handy catch phrases, they are trite and would probably be dismissed by critical readers as lazy writing.

Another figure of speech worth mentioning is the **euphemism,** which is a polite way of saying something blunt or offensive. Instead of toilets, restaurants have *restrooms*. Instead of a salesperson, furniture stores send us *mattress technicians*. Instead of false teeth, people in advertising wear *dentures*. The problem with euphemisms is that they conceal the true meaning of something. The result can be a kind of double-talk—language inflated for the sake of deceiving the listener. Business and government are notorious for such practices. When workers are laid off, corporations talk about *restructuring* or *downsizing*. A few years ago, the federal government announced *a revenue enhancement* when it really meant that taxes were going up; likewise, the Environmental Protection Agency referred to acid rain as *poorly buffered precipitation*; and when the CIA ordered a *nondiscernible microbinoculator,* it got a poison dart. Not only are such concoctions pretentious, they are dishonest. Fancy-sounding language camouflages hard truths.

Fancy-sounding language also has no place in good writing. When euphemisms are overdone, the result is a lot of verbiage and little meaning. Consider the example below before the euphemisms and pretentious language are reduced:

**Overdone:** In the event that gaming industry establishments be rendered legal, law enforcement official spokespersons have identified a potential crisis situation as the result of influence exerted by the regional career-offender cartel.

Readers may have to review this a few times before they understand what's being said. Even if they don't give up, a reader's job is not to rewrite your words. Writing with clarity and brevity shows respect for your audience. Here is the same paragraph with its pretentious wordiness and euphemisms edited down:

**Revised:** Should casino gambling be legalized, police fear organized crime may take over.

Of course, not all euphemisms are double-talk concoctions. Some may be necessary to avoid sounding insensitive or causing pain. To show respect in a sympathy card to bereaved survivors, it might be more appropriate to use the expression *passed away* instead of the blunt *died*. Recently, terms such as *handicapped* or *cripple* have given way to less derogatory replacements such as *a person with disabilities.* Likewise, we hear *a person with AIDS* instead of *AIDS victim,* which reduces the person to a disease or a label.

As with metaphors and personification, some euphemisms have passed into the language and become artifacts, making their usage potentially stale. People over age sixty-five are no longer "old" or "elderly," they're *senior citizens;* slums are *substandard housing;* the poor are *socially disadvantaged.* Although such euphemisms grew out of noble intentions, they tend to abstract reality. A Jules Feiffer cartoon from a few years ago captured the problem well. It showed a man talking to himself:

> I used to think I was poor. Then they told me I wasn't poor, I was needy. They told me it was self-defeating to think of myself as needy, I was deprived. Then they told me underprivileged was overused. I was disadvantaged. I still don't have a dime. But I have a great vocabulary.

Although euphemisms were created to take the bite off reality, they can also take the bite out of your writing if not used appropriately. As Feiffer implies, sometimes it's better to say it like it is; depending on the context, "poor" simply might have more bite than some sanitized cliché. Similarly, some old people resent being called "seniors" not just because the term is an overused label, but because it abstracts the condition of old age. Our advice regarding euphemisms is to know when they are appropriate and to use them sparingly. Good writing simply means knowing when the right expression will get the response you want.

## Avoiding Clichés

A cliché (or trite expression) is a phrase that is old and overused to the point of being unoriginal and stale. At one time, clichés were fresh and potent; overuse has left them flat. In speech, we may resort to clichés for quick meaning. However, clichés can dull your writing and make you seem lazy for choosing a phrase on tap rather than trying to think of more original and colorful wording. Consider these familiar examples:

apple of his eye
bigger than both of us
climbing the walls
dead as a doornail
head over heels
last but not least
mind over matter
ripe old age
short but sweet
white as a ghost

The problem with clichés is that they fail to communicate anything unique. To say you were "climbing the walls," for example, is an expression that could fit a wide variety of contradictory meanings. Out of context, it could mean that you were in a state of high anxiety, anger, frustration, excitement, fear, happiness, or unhappiness. Even in context, the expression is dull. Furthermore, because such clichés are ready made and instantly handy, they blot out the exact detail you intended to convey to your reader.

Clichés are the refuge of writers who don't make the effort to come up with fresh and original expressions. To avoid them, we recommend being alert for any phrases you have heard many times before and coming up with fresh substitutes. Consider the brief paragraph below, which is full of clichés marked in italics, and its revision:

**Trite:** *In this day and age*, a university ought to be concerned with ensuring that its women students take courses that will strengthen their understanding of their own past achievements and future *hopes and dreams*. At the same time, any school *worth its salt* should be *ready and able* to provide *hands-on experience*, activities, and courses that reflect a commitment to diversity and inclusiveness. Education must *seize the opportunity* of leading us *onward and upward* so that we don't slide back to the male-only curriculum emphasis of the *days of old*.

**Revised:** A university today ought to be concerned with ensuring that its women students take courses that will strengthen their understanding of their own past achievements and future possibilities. At the same time, any decent school should provide experience, activities, and courses that reflect a commitment to diversity and inclusiveness. Education must lead us forward so that we don't revert to the male-only curriculum emphasis of the past.

## Defining Technical Terms

Special or technical vocabulary that is not clear from the context can function as an instant roadblock to freely flowing communication between you and your readers—sympathetic to your views or not. You cannot expect a novice in political science to know the meaning of *hegemony* or a nonmedical person to know exactly what you mean by *nephrological necrosis*. To avoid alienating nonexpert readers, you'll have to define such uncommon terms.

You can do so without being obtrusive or disrupting the flow of your writing with "time-outs" here and there to define terms. Notice how smoothly definitions have been slipped into the following passages:

In fact, the phenomenon is known as recidivism—that is, a convict re-offends after having been released from confinement. (Arthur Allen, "Prayer in Prison: Religion as Rehabilitation")

In contemporary discussions of religion and public affairs, the master concept has been secularization. The term itself derives from the Latin word saeculum, meaning "peroid of time" or "age" or "generation." The idea of the secular directs our attention to the place and time of this world rather than to things religious and beyond time. It supposes a demarcation between the sacred and the profane. (Hugh Heclo, "The Wall That Never Was")

Katharine Phillips, a psychiatrist at the Brown University School of Medicine, has specialized in "body dysmorphic disorder," a psychiatric illness in which patients become obsessively preoccupied with perceived flaws in their appearances—receding hairlines, facial imperfections, small penises, inadequate musculature. (Stephen S. Hall, "The Bully in the Mirror")

## Clarifying Familiar Terms

Even some familiar terms can lead to misunderstanding because they are used in so many different ways with so many different meanings: *liberal, Native American, lifestyle, decent, active.* It all depends on who is using the word. For instance, to an environmentalist the expression *big business* might connote profit-hungry and sinister industrial conglomerates that pollute the elements; to a conservative, however, the phrase might mean the commercial and industrial establishment that drives our economy. Likewise, a *liberal* does not mean the same thing to a Democrat as it does to a Republican. Even if you're writing for a sympathetic audience, be as precise as you can about familiar terms. Remember the advice of novelist George Eliot: "We have all got to remain calm, and call things by the same names other people call them by."

## Stipulating Definitions

For a word that doesn't have a fixed or standard meaning, writers often offer a *stipulative* definition that explains what they mean by the term. For instance, *Merriam-Webster's Dictionary* offers two standard definitions of *consumerism*: 1) the "promotion of the consumer's interests"; and 2) "the theory that an increasing consumption of goods is economically desirable; *also* : a preoccupation with and an inclination toward the buying of consumer goods." But in the essay, "Spent: America After Consumerism" (page 308), author Amitai Etzioni offers this stipulative definition: "Consumerism: the obsession with acquisition." The term "obsession" takes the standard definition a few steps further into darker, disturbing connotations that beyond basic "consumption" or preoccupation with goods. Drawing from Abraham Maslow's "hierarchy of human needs," Etzioni says that once fundamental creature comforts ("safety, shelter, food, clothing, health care, education" have been sated, people get satisfaction "from affection, self-esteem, and, finally, self-actualization." However, Etzioni decries the current trend to satisfy these higher needs by the acquisition of more and more goods, including pricey brand names that many people can barely afford. This is when "consumerism becomes a social disease." It is this stipulative meaning that drives his discussion in the essay.

Writers also offer stipulative definitions for terms that are used for the first time. This is done to communicate a new concept. Oftentimes the invented term is unusual but catchy. In the same Etzioni essay, the author invents the term "megalogues"—a term coined from the prefix "mega-" meaning "very large"(literally *million*) and suffix "-logues" to mean "*discourse*"–as in *monologue* or *dialogue*. Etzioni stipulates the term to mean a dominant social discussion involving "millions of members of a society exchanging views with one another at workplaces, during family gatherings, in the media, and at public events." He further stipulates that "megalogues" are "often contentious and passionate, and . . . tend to lead to changes in a society's culture and its members' behavior." Past examples are women's rights and minority; more recent examples ware the rights for gays to marry and the legitimacy of the 2003 invasion of Iraq.

Sometimes authors will take common words and invent a new term that stipulates a hybrid definition. One such example is "child-man" in the essay "Child-Man in the Promised Land" (page 367). Here social critic Kay S. Hymowitz argues that adolescence in males today has been extended. Forty years ago, most men got married and started families by the time they were in their mid-twenties. Today, however, the average age of marriage and family is dramatically older. And the reason is that today's single young men are in no hurry to grow up. These are what Hymowitz calls the "child-men"—males who prefer hanging out in "semi-hormonal adolescence and … self-reliance." This new hybrid group of single young males (or SYM) consists of single twentysomething college-educated males who prefer "to hang out in a playground of drinking, hooking up, playing Halo 3, and, in many cases, underachieving." She goes on to say they share interests in "stupid fun," anti-social behavior, and "gross-out humor." They're drawn to high-tech gadgets and video games; they prefer "battling cyborgs, exploding toilets, and the NFL" to serious drams; and they're very much at home on the Internet. While the media and marketplace encourage this restless "Peter Pan" syndrome, Hymowitz is concerned that today's "child man" not only avoids marriage but "any deep attachments." In fact, she says, they fear commitment. "[T]hey can't stand to think of themselves as permanently attached to one woman."

Stipulating your terms is like making a contract with your reader: You set down in black and white the important terms and their limits. The result is that you eliminate any misunderstanding and reduce your own vulnerability. And that can make the difference between a weak and a potent argument.

## Avoiding Overdefinition

Where do you stop explaining and begin assuming your reader knows what you mean? What terms are "technical" or "specialized" or "important" enough to warrant definition? You certainly don't want to define terms unnecessarily or to oversimplify. In so doing, you run the risk of dulling the thrust of your claims while insulting the intelligence of your readers. Just how to strike a balance is a matter of good judgment about the needs and capabilities of your audience.

A good rule of thumb is to assume that your readers are almost as knowledgeable as you. This way, you minimize the risk of patronizing them. Another rule of thumb is the synonym test. If you can think of a word or short phrase that is an exact synonym for some specialized or important term in your argument, you probably don't need to define it. However, if you need a long phrase or sentence to paraphrase the term, you may want to work in a definition; it could be needed. And don't introduce your definitions with clauses like "As I'm sure you know" or "You don't need to be told that. . . . " If the audience didn't need to know it, you wouldn't be telling them, and if they do know what the terms mean, you may insult their intelligence with such condescending introductions.

## Using Sarcasm and Humor Sparingly

Although we caution you against using sarcasm or humor too often, there are times when they can be very effective techniques of persuasion. Writers will often bring out their barbs for the sake of drawing blood from the opposition and snickers from the sympathetic. But artful sarcasm must be done with care. Too strong, and you run the risk of trivializing the issue or alienating your audience with a bad joke. Too vague or esoteric, and nobody will catch the joke. It's probably safest to use these touches when you are writing for a sympathetic audience; they're most likely to appreciate your wit. There is no rule of thumb here. Like any writer, you'll have to decide when to use these techniques and how to work them in artfully.

## Review: To Choose Your Words Carefully...
- Consider both denotative and connotative meanings.
- Be as specific and concrete as your context requires.
- Use figurative language to add richness and complexity.
- Check figurative language for precision and clarity.
- Be alert for clichés and unnecessary euphemisms.
- Define technical terms that are not clear from the context.
- Define familiar terms and terms with multiple meanings.

## EXERCISES

1. Let's say you were assigned to write a position paper defending the construction of a nuclear power plant in your state. What special appeals would you make were you to address your paper to the governor? to residents living next to the site where the proposed plant is to be built? to prospective construction workers and general contractors? to local environmentalists?

2. Choose one of the following claims, then list in sentence form three reasons supporting the argument. When you've finished, list in sentence form three reasons in opposition to the claim:
   a. Snowboarders are a menace to skiers.
   b. To save lives, a 55-mile-per-hour speed limit should be enforced nationwide.
   c. Condoms should be advertised on television.
   d. Students with drug convictions should be denied federally subsidized student aid.

3. Let's assume you have made up your mind on gun control. Write a brief letter to the editor of your local newspaper stating your views on the issue. In your letter, fairly and accurately represent arguments of the opposition while pointing out any logical weaknesses, flaws, impracticalities, and other problems you see. What different emphasis would your letter have were it to appear in a gun owner's newsletter? in a pro-gun control newsletter?

4. Write a letter to your parents explaining why you need an extra hundred dollars of spending money this month.

5. Each of the sentences below will take on a different meaning depending on the connotations of the words in brackets. Explain how each choice colors the writer's attitude and the reader's reaction to the statement.
   a. Sally's style of dress is really [weird, exotic, unusual].
   b. If a factory is [polluting, stinking up, fouling] the air over your house, you have a right to sue.
   c. Anyone who thinks that such words have no effect is [unaware, ignorant, unconscious] of political history.

    d. The anti-immigration passion being stirred up in this country has become [popular, trendy, common].

    e. It was clear from the way she [stomped, marched, stepped] out of the room how she felt about the decision.

6. Identify the figures of speech used in the following sentences from essays in this book. In each example, note the two things being compared and explain why you think the comparisons are appropriate or not:

    a. "But such a Faustian bargain is an ominous precedent in public health and political ethics." (Gio Batta Gori, "The Bogus 'Science' of Secondary Smoke")

    b. "Biographies have metamorphosed into demonographies whose authors don't just portray their subjects' warts and all, but set out to dig up as much dirt as possible, as if the story of a person's life is contained in the warts, only the warts, and nothing but the warts." (Deborah Tannen, "Taking a 'War of Words' Too Literally")

    c. "Many colleges and universities simply wink at the activities of the fraternities and claim no responsibility." (Henry Wechsler, "Binge Drinking Must Be Stopped")

    d. "And so in 1990 it was decided to put a tasteful and discreet cup on the counter. It's a way for our customers to say thanks to our partners.'" (Michael Lewis, "The Case Against Tipping")

    e. "Just as planes and ships disappear mysteriously into the Bermuda Triangle, so do the selves of girls go down in droves," (Mary Pipher, "Saplings in a Storm")

    f. "Natural selection cannot push the buttons of behavior directly; it affects our behavior by endowing us with emotions that coax us toward adaptive choices." (Steven Pinker, "Why They Kill Their Newborns")

    g. "Cops like Parks say that racial profiling is a sensible, statistically based tool." (Randall Kennedy, "You Can't Judge a Crook by His Color")

    h. "As cancer-stick observers know Big Tobacco did not mind closing the candy store on cigarettes flavored like Hershey's or Life Savers." (Derrick Jackson, "Ban All Flavors of Cigarettes")

    i. "If unchecked, we could find ourselves in a time when it's acceptable for books, like 'witches,' to be burned." (Shannon O'Neill, "Literature Hacked and Torn Apart: Censorship in Public Schools")

7. Rewrite the following paragraph to eliminate the clichés and trite expressions.

It is not that we don't care about what goes on up in space; it's that the vast majority of red-blooded Americans are hard put to see what these untold billions of dollars can do. While great strides have been made in space research, we ask ourselves: Is life any safer? Are material goods all the more abundant? Are we living to a ripe old age because of these vast expenditures? Beyond the shadow of a doubt, the answer is a resounding no. Those in Congress with a vested interest need to be brought back to reality, for the nation's pressing problems of crime, homelessness, and unemployment are right here on Mother Earth. Nothing is sacred including the budget for NASA, which should follow the footsteps of other programs and be slashed across the board. Yes, that will be a rude awakening to some who will have to bite the bullet, but there are just so many tax dollars to go around. And in the total scheme of things, wasting it on exploring the depths of outer space is not the way it should be.

# 5

# Shaping Arguments: Thinking Like an Architect

Just as there is no best way to build a house, there is no best way to structure an argument. Some essays take an inductive approach. Such an essay begins with a specific circumstance and then presents reasons and evidence in support of or in opposition to that circumstance. Other essays adopt a deductive approach, which begin with an idea or philosophical principle, move to a specific circumstance, then conclude with why that circumstance is right and should be maintained, or wrong and should be changed. Some essays express their conclusions in the opening paragraphs. Others build up to them in the last paragraph. Still others make use of narrative in part or as a whole—that is, a story or series of episodes or anecdotes structured on a time line. The effect is to dramatize the criteria of the author's argument rather than to argue them explicitly from point to point. As an architect designing a blueprint will tell you, the structure of a building depends on the site, the construction crew, and the prospective owners. Arguments are the same. Depending on your topic, your goals, and your readers, you'll write very different kinds of arguments.

Although no two arguments look alike, every argument has three basic structural parts: a beginning, a middle, and an end. This isn't a simplistic definition. As in architecture, each part of a structure is there for a purpose; leave out one of the parts, and the whole collapses. So let's look at those parts and the jobs they do.

## Components of an Argument

What follows is an organizational pattern for argument papers—a pattern to which, with some variations, most of the essays in this book conform. We offer it to help you plan your own argument papers. Although this model provides the structure, framework, and components of most arguments, it is not a formula written in stone. You should not feel bound to follow it every time you construct an argument. In fact, you might find it more effective to move blocks of writing around or to omit material. For instance, on issues unfamiliar to your readers, it might make sense to begin with background information so the context of your discussion will be understood. With familiar issues, it might be more persuasive to open with responses to opposing views. On especially controversial topics, you might wish to reserve your responses for the main body of the paper. Or, for dramatic effect, you might decide to save your responses until the very end, thereby emphasizing your consideration of other perspectives. As a writer, you're free to modify this model any way you like; or you may want to try different models in different drafts of your paper to see which arrangement works best in each case. As with building houses, your choices in building arguments are numerous.

## The Beginning

The beginning of your argument accomplishes, in a small space, three important goals:

- It introduces you, the writer. Here your audience meets you—senses your tone, your attitude toward your subject, and the general style of the piece.
- It appeals to your readers' reason, emotions, and/or sense of ethics. This can be done in a simple value statement, an anecdote, or some high-impact statistics intended to raise your readers' interest and concern.
- It identifies the topic and indicates your stand.

Depending on the issue and the audience, the beginning of an argument can be several paragraphs in length. In most arguments, the beginning will end with a clear statement of the claim you are making—your thesis.

Although "Once upon a time ..." is probably the most remembered introduction, it's not always the most effective; more ingenuity on your part is needed to "hook" your readers. For example, in *The Village Voice,* columnist Nat Hentoff began a column calling for eliminating duplication in the U.S. military by saying that he had telephoned the Pentagon press office for a comment on the subject. "Oh," said the officer with whom he spoke, "You want the *other* press office." As Hentoff remarked, he could have ended the column at that point; instead, he went on to develop his idea, confident that this introductory example would make his readers sympathetic to his point.

Composing good beginnings requires hard work. That's why many writers keep a journal in which they copy the strategies of writers they admire; that's how we happened to have a copy of Hentoff's introduction. As beginning arguers, you may want to develop your own repertoire of start-up strategies by copying strategies you admire into your own argument journal.

## The Middle

The middle portion of your argument is where you do the argumentative work: presenting your information, responding to other views, making your case. If you think of it in terms of building construction, here's where you pour a foundation and lay the framework; put in all the walls, floors, and systems; and have the building inspector examine your work. There are a number of substages.

### Provide Background Information

Before you can begin presenting your reasons, you want to be sure that your audience has the information necessary to understand the issue. Background information should answer any of the following questions depending on your topic:

- How significant is the issue? How many people are affected by it? Who are the people most affected?
- What facts, statistics, or information do your readers need to know to follow your reasons?
- What terminology or key words need to be defined so your readers will understand your meaning?

- What factors have caused the problem or situation to develop?
- What will be the consequences if the situation is not corrected?

If handled correctly, this part of your essay can be the most persuasive and convincing because it lets your readers know why you are concerned and the reasons behind that concern. Moreover, it gives your readers the opportunity to share your concern. For example, in "Let's Ban All Flavors of Cigarettes," Derrick Z. Jackson begins his essay with the claim that the Food and Drug Administration's recent ban of fruit-flavored cigarettes is a good but negligible start toward prevention compared to a ban that would include mentholated cigarettes. He wonders cynically if the government is more interested in state and federal tax revenue. His statistics are grimly persuasive: fruit-flavored cigarettes represent less than 1 percent of the market compared to menthol which makes up 30 percent of the $87 billion market, generating over $25 billion in tax revenue.

### Respond to Other Points of View

As we discussed in Chapter 4, it is important to let your audience know that you have seriously deliberated other points of view before reaching your own position. By doing this, you appear informed and open-minded. In this part of your essay, you should briefly review a number of viewpoints that are different from your own. If you've engaged in debate and dialogue, as we suggested in Chapter 1, you should be aware of opposing views and common concerns. Now is your opportunity to identify them and respond. You might even acknowledge the sincerity of those holding contrary views and cite the merits of their positions. Such acknowledgments help establish your authority as a writer. They will also help you define your own position more specifically for your readers by contrasting it with others.

### Present Reasons in Support of Your Claim

The reasons supporting your claim comprise the heart of your essay and, therefore, its largest portion. Here you explain those reasons and present supporting evidence—facts, statistics, data, testimony of authorities, examples—to convince your readers to agree with your position or take a particular course of action. Depending on the issue, this part of your essay usually takes several paragraphs, with each reason clearly delineated for your readers.

### Anticipate Possible Objections to Your Reasons

Even with a friendly audience, readers will have questions and concerns about your reasons. If you ignore these objections and leave them unanswered, you will weaken the effectiveness of your argument. Therefore, it is always wise to anticipate possible objections so you can respond to them in a constructive fashion that will strengthen and clarify your ideas. The kind of objections you anticipate, of course, will depend on your familiarity with your audience—their interests, values, beliefs, experiences, and so on. If you have carefully analyzed your audience, as suggested in Chapter 4, you will be more aware of the objections likely to surface in response to your reasons. Raising objections and

> ## Review: The Structure of an Argument
>
> **The Beginning ...**
> - Introduces you as a writer
> - States the problem
> - Establishes your position and appeal
> - Presents your claim (thesis)
>
> **The Middle ...**
> - Provides background information
> - Responds to other points of view
> - Presents arguments supporting the claim
> - Anticipates possible objections
>
> **The End ...**
> - Summarizes your position and implications
> - Invites readers to share your conclusion and/or take action

responding to them will once again demonstrate your awareness of alternative viewpoints. It will also give you an opportunity to strengthen your reasons and increase your credibility.

## The End

The end is usually a short paragraph or two in which you conclude your argument. Essentially, your ending summarizes your argument by reaffirming your stand on the issue. It might also make an appeal to your readers to take action. Some writers include an anecdote, a passionate summation, or even a quiet but resonant sentence. Lincoln's "Gettysburg Address," for example, ends with the quiet "government of the people, by the people, and for the people," which is one of the most memorable phrases in American political history. Looking over the essays in this book, you will find that no two end quite alike. As a writer, you have many choices; experimentation is usually the best way to decide what will work for you. Many writers copy effective conclusions into their journals so they can refresh their memories when writing their own arguments.

## SAMPLE ARGUMENT FOR ANALYSIS

To illustrate this three-part argument structure, we have included two sample argument essays for you to read. The first is "Indian Bones" by Clara Spotted Elk, a consultant for Native American interests. Although it is quite brief, the essay, published in the *New York Times,* contains all the essential components of an argument essay. It is followed by an analysis of its key structural features.

# Indian Bones

*Clara Spotted Elk*

1   Millions of American Indians lived in this country when Columbus first landed on our shores. After the western expansion, only about 250,000 Indians survived. What happened to the remains of those people who were decimated by the advance of the white man? Many are gathering dust in American museums.

2   In 1985, I and some Northern Cheyenne chiefs visited the attic of the Smithsonian's Natural History Museum in Washington to review the inventory of their Cheyenne collection. After a chance inquiry, a curator pulled out a drawer in one of the scores of cabinets that line the attic. There were the jumbled bones of an Indian. "A Kiowa," he said.

3   Subsequently, we found that 18,500 Indian remains—some consisting of a handful of bones, but mostly full skeletons—are unceremoniously stored in the Smithsonian's nooks and crannies. Other museums, individuals and federal agencies such as the National Park Service also collect the bones of Indian warriors, women, and children. Some are on display as roadside tourist attractions. It is estimated that another 600,000 Indian remains are secreted away in locations across the country.

4   The museum community and forensic scientists vigorously defend these grisly collections. With few exceptions, they refuse to return remains to the tribes that wish to rebury them, even when grave robbing has been documented. They want to maintain adequate numbers of "specimens" for analysis and say they are dedicated to "the permanent curation of Indian skeletal remains."

5   Indian people are tired of being "specimens." The Northern Cheyenne word for ourselves is "tsistsistas"—human beings. Like people the world over, one of our greatest responsibilities is the proper care of the dead.

6   We are outraged that our religious views are not accepted by the scientific community and that the graves of our ancestors are desecrated. Many tribes are willing to accommodate some degree of study for a limited period of time—provided that it would help Indian people or mankind in general. But how many "specimens" are needed? We will not accept grave robbing and the continued hoarding of our ancestors' remains.

7   Would this nefarious collecting be tolerated if it were discovered that it affected other ethnic groups? (Incidentally, the Smithsonian also collects skeletons of blacks.) What would happen if the Smithsonian had 18,500 Holocaust victims in the attic? There would be a tremendous outcry in this country. Why is there no outcry about the Indian collection?

8   Indians are not exotic creatures for study. We are human beings who practice living religions. Our religion should be placed not only on a par with science when it comes to determining the disposition of our ancestors but on a par with every other religion practiced in this country.

9   To that end, Sen. Daniel K. Inouye will soon reintroduce the "Bones Bill" to aid Indians in retrieving the remains of their ancestors from museums. As in the past, the "Bones Bill" will most likely be staunchly resisted by the collectors of Indian skeletons—armed with slick lobbyists, lots of money and cloaked in the mystique of science.

10    Scientists have attempted to defuse this issue by characterizing their opponents as radical Indians, out of touch with the culture and with little appreciation of science. Armed
only with a moral obligation to our ancestors, the Indians who support the bill have few
resources and little money.

11    But, in my view, the issue should concern all Americans—for it raises very disturbing
questions. American Indians want only to reclaim and rebury their dead. Is this too much
to ask?

# Analyzing the Structure

Now let's examine this essay according to the organizational features discussed so far.

## The Beginning

Paragraph 1 clearly introduces the nature of the problem: The remains of the Indians
"decimated by the advance of the white man" have wrongfully ended up "gathering
dust in American museums." It isn't until paragraph 6 that Spotted Elk spells out her
position: "We are outraged that our religious views are not accepted by the scientific
community and that the graves of our ancestors are desecrated." (Because this essay
was written for newspaper publication, the paragraphs are shorter than they might be
in a formal essay; you may not want to delay your thesis until the sixth paragraph in
a longer essay.) Notice, too, that in the introduction the author's persona begins to
assert itself in the brief and pointed summation of the American Indians' fate. When
Spotted Elk mentions the staggering decline in the population of her ancestors, we
sense a note of controlled but righteous anger in her voice. Citation of the gruesome
facts of history also appeals to the reader's ethical sense by prompting reflection on
the Indians' demise.

## The Middle

■ **Background Information**    Paragraphs 2 and 3 establish the context of the author's complaint. Paragraph 2 is personal testimony to the problem—how she and
other Native Americans viewed unceremonious "jumbled bones" in the museum
drawer and were stunned by the representative insensitivity of their host curator,
who treated the human remains as if they were a fossil. Paragraph 3 projects the
problem to progressively larger contexts and magnitudes—from the single Kiowa
in a drawer to the 18,500 in the Smithsonian at large; from that institution's collection to the estimated 600,000 remains in other museums, federal agencies and institutions, and "roadside tourist attractions." The broader scope of the problem is
underscored here.

■ **Response to Other Points of View**    In paragraph 4, Spotted Elk tersely sums up the
opposing position of the "museum community and forensic scientists": ". . . they
refuse to return remains to the tribes." She also states their reasoning: "They want to
maintain adequate numbers of 'specimens' for analysis and say they are dedicated to
the 'permanent curation of Indian skeletal remains.'"

■ **Reasons in Support of the Claim**   Paragraphs 5 through 9 constitute the heart of Spotted Elk's argument. Here she most forcefully argues her objections and offers her reasons with supporting details: Indians resent being treated as specimens and want to bury their dead as do other religious people (paragraphs 5 and 6). She follows with a concession that many Indians would accommodate some degree of anthropological study for a period of time, but do not approve of the huge permanent collections that now fill museums.

In paragraph 7, the author continues to support her claim that American Indians have been discriminated against with regard to the disposition of ancestral remains. She writes that there would be a public outcry if the remains of other ethnic groups such as Holocaust victims were hoarded. Her proposal for change appears in paragraph 8: "Our religion should be placed not only on a par with science when it comes to determining the disposition of our ancestors but on a par with every other religion practiced in this country." This is the logical consequence of the problem she has addressed to this point. That proposal logically leads into paragraph 9, where she mentions efforts by Senator Daniel Inouye to see the "Bones Bill" passed into law. Throughout, Spotted Elk uses emotional words and phrases—*grisly, unceremoniously, slick lobbyists, cloaked in mystique*—to reinforce her points.

■ **Anticipation of Possible Objections**   In paragraph 10, the author addresses objections of the opposition, in this case those "[s]cientists [who] have attempted to defuse this issue by characterizing their opponents as radical Indians, out of touch with the culture and with little appreciation of science." She refutes all three charges (of being "radical," as well as out of touch with Indian culture and science) with the phrase "[a]rmed only with a moral obligation to our ancestors"—a phrase that reaffirms her strong connection with her culture. On the contrary, it is science that is out of touch with the "living religion" of Native Americans.

## The End

The final paragraph brings closure to the argument. Briefly the author reaffirms her argument that Native Americans "want only to reclaim and rebury their dead." The question that makes up the final line of the essay is more than rhetorical, for it reminds us of the point introduced back in paragraph 5—that American Indians are no different than any other religious people with regard to the disposition of their ancestors. A powerful question brings the essay's conclusion into sharp focus.

As we stated in the beginning of this chapter, there is no best structure for an argument essay. As you develop your own essay, you may find it more effective to move certain structural features to locations that serve your purposes better. For instance, you may find that background information is more persuasive when you include it as support for a particular reason rather than provide it prior to your reasons. Possible objections might be raised along with each reason instead of saved for later. Ron Karpati's essay, "I Am the Enemy," provides a good example of a different approach to structuring an argument essay. Read the essay to see if you can pick out the structural elements he included and how he organized them. Following the essay, we've provided a brief analysis of its organization.

# I Am the Enemy
*Ron Karpati*

> Ron Karpati, a pediatrician and medical researcher of childhood illnesses, defends the use of animals in medical research. This article first appeared in *Newsweek*'s "My Turn" column.

1  I am the enemy! One of those vilified, inhumane physician-scientists involved in animal research. How strange, for I have never thought of myself as an evil person. I became a pediatrician because of my love for children and my desire to keep them healthy. During medical school and residency, however, I saw many children die of leukemia, prematurity and traumatic injury—circumstances against which medicine has made tremendous progress, but still has far to go. More important, I also saw children, alive and healthy, thanks to advances in medical science such as infant respirators, potent antibiotics, new surgical techniques and the entire field of organ transplantation. My desire to tip the scales in favor of the healthy, happy children drew me to medical 2  research.

My accusers claim that I inflict torture on animals for the sole purpose of career advancement. My experiments supposedly have no relevance to medicine and are easily replaced by computer simulation. Meanwhile, an apathetic public barely watches, convinced that the issue has no significance, and publicity-conscious politicians increasingly 3  give way to the demands of the activists.

We in medical research have also been unconscionably apathetic. We have allowed the most extreme animal-rights protesters to seize the initiative and frame the issue as one of "animal fraud." We have been complacent in our belief that a knowledgeable public would sense the importance of animal research to the public health. Perhaps we have been mistaken in not responding to the emotional tone of the argument created by those sad posters of animals by waving equally sad posters of children dying of leukemia or 4  cystic fibrosis.

Much is made of the pain inflicted on these animals in the name of medical science. The animal-rights activists contend that this is evidence of our malevolent and sadistic nature. A more reasonable argument, however, can be advanced in our defense. Life is often cruel, both to animals and human beings. Teenagers get thrown from the back of a pickup truck and suffer severe head injuries. Toddlers, barely able to walk, find themselves at the bottom of a swimming pool while a parent checks the mail. Physicians hoping to alleviate the pain and suffering these tragedies cause have but three choices: create an animal model of the injury or disease and use that model to understand the process and test new therapies; experiment on human beings—some experiments will succeed, most will fail—or finally, leave medical knowledge static, hoping that accidental discoveries will 5  lead us to the advances.

Some animal-rights activists would suggest a fourth choice, claiming that computer models can simulate animal experiments, thus making the actual experiments unnecessary.

Computers can simulate, reasonably well, the effects of well-understood principles on complex systems, as in the application of the laws of physics to airplane and automobile design. However, when the principles themselves are in question, as is the case with the complex biological systems under study, computer modeling alone is of little value.

6      One of the terrifying effects of the effort to restrict the use of animals in medical research is that the impact will not be felt for years and decades: drugs that might have been discovered will not be; surgical techniques that might have been developed will not be, and fundamental biological processes that might have been understood will remain mysteries. There is the danger that politically expedient solutions will be found to placate a vocal minority, while the consequences of these decisions will not be apparent until long after the decisions are made and the decision making forgotten.

7      Fortunately, most of us enjoy good health, and the trauma of watching one's child die has become a rare experience. Yet our good fortune should not make us unappreciative of the health we enjoy or the advances that make it possible. Vaccines, antibiotics, insulin and drugs to treat heart disease, hypertension and stroke are all based on animal research. Most complex surgical procedures, such as coronary-artery bypass and organ transplantation, are initially developed in animals. Presently undergoing animal studies are techniques to insert genes in humans in order to replace the defective ones found to be the cause of so much disease. These studies will effectively end if animal research is severely restricted.

8      In America today, death has become an event isolated from our daily existence—out of the sight and thoughts of most of us. As a doctor who has watched many children die, and their parents grieve, I am particularly angered by people capable of so much compassion for a dog or a cat, but with seemingly so little for a dying human being. These people seem so insulated from the reality of human life and death and what it means.

9      Make no mistake, however: I am not advocating the needlessly cruel treatment of animals. To the extent that the animal-rights movement has made us more aware of the needs of these animals, and made us search harder for suitable alternatives, they have made a significant contribution. But if the more radical members of this movement are successful in limiting further research, their efforts will bring about a tragedy that will cost many lives. The real question is whether an apathetic majority can be aroused to protect its future against a vocal, but misdirected, minority.

# Analyzing the Structure

## The Beginning

In paragraph 1, Karpati introduces himself as a scientist and a pediatrician with a personal and professional interest in his topic. While his first sentence proclaims, "I am the enemy," Karpati almost immediately lets his readers know that he is only an enemy to those who oppose his work; he describes himself as a caring doctor who wishes to help children stay healthy. His second sentence informs the reader that his topic will be the use of animals as research subjects; in the next sentences, he strongly implies that advances in medicine are the results of research using animals. His claim, stated in paragraph 3, is that such research is important to public health. By using the example of ill or injured children who might benefit from this work, Karpati makes a strong emotional appeal to his readers.

## The Middle
### Background Information

This information appears in several places in the essay. Paragraph 1 includes a list of advances in medicine that have come about, the reader assumes, through animal research. Later, in paragraph 7, Karpati lists specific drugs and surgical procedures that have resulted from using animals as research subjects. However, Karpati seems more interested in informing readers how he, a scientist who uses animals to conduct his research, is characterized negatively by animal-rights supporters.

### Response to Other Points of View

Because Karpati's essay is largely a defense of his position, he focuses heavily on the views of those who oppose him. In paragraph 2, he briefly summarizes the accusations of animal-rights supporters. In paragraph 3, he suggests that these objections are voiced by extremists. He also says that he is aware of the reasons why others wish to eliminate animal research. In paragraph 4, he acknowledges that "pain [is] inflicted on these animals in the name of medical science." He agrees with the opposition that "life is often cruel"; yet his examples imply that human suffering is more compelling to physicians than is the suffering of animals. In paragraph 9, he refers back to this point and lauds the animal-rights movement in making researchers more sensitive to the issue of animal suffering.

### Reasons in Support of the Claim

In paragraphs 4 through 8, Karpati presents his reasons to support his claim that medical research using animals should be continued for the benefit of human health. In paragraphs 4 and 5, he explains that the alternatives to animal research—experimenting on human subjects, relying on accidental discoveries, or using computer simulation—are not satisfactory. In paragraph 6, he warns that the impact of restricting animal research will have a far-reaching and negative impact on medical science. Paragraph 7 cites how animal research has contributed to the healthy lives that most of his readers take for granted. Finally, in paragraph 8, he reasserts the importance of human life over the well-being of animals.

### Possible Objections to Reasons

Karpati includes several objections to his reasons. For instance, in paragraphs 4 and 5, he anticipates that his readers might wonder why humans and computers can't be substituted for animals in research. He responds that experiments on humans will largely fail and computer simulations cannot duplicate complex biological processes.

## The End

In the last paragraph, Karpati summarizes his main point: The efforts of radical members of the animal-rights movement to limit the use of animals in research "will bring about a tragedy that will cost many lives." He makes a strong appeal to his readers to take action to prevent just that from happening.

## Blueprints for Arguments

Our analysis of Karpati's essay gives some idea of its general organization, but it does not reflect subdivisions or how the various parts are logically connected. That can be done by making an outline. Think of an outline as a blueprint of the argument you're building: It reveals structure and framework but leaves out the materials that cover the frame.

Opinions differ as to the value of making outlines before writing an essay. Some writers need to make formal outlines to organize their thoughts. Others simply scratch down a few key ideas. Still others write essays spontaneously without any preliminary writing. For the beginning writer, an outline is a valuable aid because it demonstrates at a glance how the various parts of an essay are connected, whether the organization is logical and complete, whether the evidence is sequenced properly, and whether there are any omissions or lack of proportion. Your outline need not be elaborate. You might simply jot down your key reasons in a hierarchy from strongest to weakest:

Introduction

Reason 1

Reason 2

Reason 3

Reason 4

Conclusion

This blueprint might be useful if you want to capture your readers' attention immediately with your most powerful appeal. Or you might use a reverse hierarchy, beginning with your weakest argument and proceeding to your strongest, in order to achieve a climactic effect. The outline will help you build your case.

You might prefer, as do some writers, to construct an outline after, rather than before, writing a rough draft. This lets you create a draft without restricting the free flow of ideas and helps you rewrite by determining where you need to fill in, cut out, or reorganize. You may discover where your line of reasoning is not logical; you may also reconsider whether you should arrange your reasons from the most important to the least or vice versa in order to create a more persuasive effect. Ultimately, outlining after the first draft can prove useful in producing subsequent drafts and a polished final effort. Outlines are also useful when evaluating somebody else's writing. Reducing the argument of the opposition to the bare bones exposes holes in the reasoning process, scanty evidence, and logical fallacies.

## The Formal Outline

Some instructors like students to submit *formal outlines* with their papers to show that they have checked their structure carefully. This kind of outlining has several rules to follow:

- Identify main ideas with capital Roman numerals.
- Identify subsections of main ideas with capital letters, indented one set of spaces from the main ideas.

- Identify support for subsections with Arabic numerals indented two sets of spaces from the main ideas.
- Identify the parts of the support with lowercase Roman numerals, indented three sets of spaces from the main ideas.
- Identify further subdivisions with lowercase letters and then italic numbers, each indented one set of spaces to the right of the previous subdivision.
- Make sure all items have at least two points; it's considered improper informal outlining to have only one point under any subdivision.

To demonstrate what a formal outline can look like, we have outlined Clara Spotted Elk's essay, "Indian Bones":

   I.  Hoarding of Indian remains
      A.  At Smithsonian
         1.  Single Kiowa at Smithsonian
         2.  18,500 others
      B.  In other locations
  II.  Authorities' defense of collections
      A.  Refusal to return grave-robbed remains
      B.  Maintenance of "specimens"
 III.  Indians' response
      A.  Outrage
         1.  Desire to be seen as humans
         2.  Desire to have religion accepted by science
         3.  Nonacceptance of desecration of graves
         4.  Resentment of lack of outcry by public
      B.  Accommodation
         1.  Limitation in time
         2.  Service to Indians and mankind
      C.  Demand equality with other religions
 IV.  "Bones Bill" legislation
      A.  Resistance from scientific community
         1.  Slick lobbyists
         2.  Money
         3.  Scientific mystique
         4.  Characterization of Indians
            i.  Radicals
           ii.  Out of touch with culture
          iii.  Little appreciation of science
      B.  Indian counter-resistance
         1.  Few resources
         2.  Little money
         3.  Moral obligation to ancestors

Keep in mind that an outline should not force your writing to conform to a rigid pattern and, thus, turn your essay into something stilted and uninspired. Follow the model as a map, taking detours when necessary or inspired.

# Two Basic Types of Arguments

Consider the following claims for arguments:

1. Watching television helps to eliminate some traditional family rituals.
2. Pornography poses a threat to women.
3. The rising sea level is a real threat to our way of life.
4. Bilingual education programs fail to help non-English-speaking children become part of mainstream society.
5. Hate crime legislation is intended to allow certain people to have more protection under the law than others.
6. Cigarette advertising should be banned from billboards everywhere.
7. Wall Street should be more tightly regulated.
8. Americans by law should be required to vote.
9. The Ten Commandments ought to be posted in public places, schools, and government offices.
10. Pass/fail grades have to be eliminated across the board if academic standards are to be maintained.

Looking over these statements, you might notice some patterns. The verbs in the first five are all in the present tense: *helps, poses, is, fail, is intended to.* However, each of the last five statements includes "should" words: *should, should not, ought to be, have to be.* These **obligation verbs** are found in almost all claims proposing solutions to a problem. What distinguishes the first group from the second is more than the form of the verb. The first five claims are statements of the writer's stand on a controversial issue. The second group are proposals for what *should* be. Of course, not every kind of argument will fit our classification scheme. However, essentially every argument in this book—and the ones you'll most likely write and read in your careers—falls into one of these two categories or a combination of each, for often a writer states his or her position on an issue, then follows it with proposals for changes. Later in this chapter, we will discuss proposals. For the moment, let's take a look at position arguments.

## Position Arguments

A *position argument* scrutinizes one side of a controversial issue. In such an argument, the writer not only establishes his or her stand but also argues vigorously in defense of it. Position arguments are less likely to point to a solution to a problem. Instead, they are philosophical in nature—the kinds of arguments on which political and social principles are founded, laws are written, and business and government policies are established. Position papers also tend to address themselves to the ethical and moral aspects of a controversy. If, for instance, you were opposed to the university's policy of mandatory testing for the AIDS virus, you might write a position paper protesting your school's infringement of individual rights and invasion of privacy.

As indicated by the present tense of the verbs in the first five claims, the position argument deals with the status quo—the way things are, the current state of affairs. Such an argument reminds the audience that something *currently* is good or bad, better or worse, right or wrong. Like all arguments, they tend to be aimed at changing the audience's feelings about an issue—abortion, animal research, health care, the death penalty, and so on. That is why many position papers tend to direct their appeals to the reader's sense of ethics rather than to reason.

By contrast, proposal arguments identify a problem and recommend a solution. That's why their claims contain verbs that *obligate* the readers to take some action. In this sense, they are practical rather than philosophical. For instance, if you were concerned about the spread of AIDS among college students, you might write a paper proposing that condom machines be installed in all dormitories. When you offer a proposal, you're trying to affect the future.

### Features to Look for in Position Arguments

What follows are some key features of position arguments. As a checklist, they can help you evaluate someone's stand on an issue and help guide you in writing your own position papers.

**The writer deals with a controversial issue.** The best kind of position paper is one that focuses on a debatable issue, one in which there is clear disagreement: the war on terrorism, abortion, capital punishment, gay marriage, health care, euthanasia, civil liberties, gun control, separation of church and state, censorship, sex in advertising, freedom of speech, homelessness, gun control. These are issues about which people have many different perspectives.

**The writer clearly states a position.** Readers should not be confused about where an author stands on an issue. Although the actual issue may be complex, the claim should be stated emphatically and straightforwardly. Don't waffle: "Using the death penalty in some situations and with some rights of appeal probably doesn't do much to lower crime anyway"; far better is an emphatic "Capital punishment is no deterrent to crime." In formulating your claim, be certain that your word choice is not ambiguous. Otherwise the argument will be muddled and, ultimately, unconvincing.

**The writer recognizes other positions and potential objections.** For every argument there are bound to be numerous other perspectives. Such is the nature of controversy. As a writer representing a position, you cannot assume that your readers are fully aware of or understand all the disagreement surrounding the issue. Nor can you make a persuasive case without anticipating challenges. So, in your argument, spell out accurately and fairly the main points of the opposition and objections that might arise. We offer six reasons for doing this:

1. *You reduce your own vulnerability.* You don't want to appear ill-informed or naive on an issue. Therefore, it makes sense to acknowledge opposing points of view to show how well you've investigated the topic and how sensitive you are to it. Suppose, for instance, you are writing a paper arguing that "anyone who commits suicide is insane." To avoid criticism, you would have to be prepared to answer objections that fully rational people with terminal illnesses often choose to take their own lives so as to avoid a painful demise and curtail the suffering of loved ones. Even if you strongly disagree, recognizing views from the other side demonstrates that you are a person of responsibility and tolerance—two qualities for which most writers of argument strive.

2. *You distinguish your own position.* By citing opposing views, you distinguish your own position from that of others. This not only helps clarify the differences but also lays out the specific points of the opposition to be refuted or discredited. Some writers do this at the outset of their arguments. Consider, for instance, how Ron Karpati sums up the views of the opposition in the opening paragraphs of his essay "I Am the Enemy." (Page 120)

3. *You can respond to opposing views.* A good response can challenge an opponent's ideas and examine the basis for the disagreement—whether personal, ideological, or moral. For instance, when Michael Kelley, in "Arguing for Infanticide" (page 195), responds to Steven Pinker's "Why They Kill Their Newborns" (page 187), he points out that Pinker's very logical argument for neonaticide ignores the moral and ethical values of our society regarding the relationship between mothers and their children. Kelley does not suggest that Pinker's reasons are incorrect; instead he challenges the basis for Pinker's argument.

4. *You might also challenge an opponent's logic, demonstrating where the reasoning suffers from flaws in logic.* For instance, the argument that Ms. Shazadi must be a wonderful mother because she's a great office manager does not logically follow. While some qualities of a good manager might bear on successful motherhood, not all do. In fact, it can be argued that the very qualities that make a good manager—leadership, drive, ruthlessness, determination—might damage a parent-child relationship. This logical fallacy, called a false analogy, erroneously suggests that the two situations are comparable when they are not. An example of this can be found in William Lutz's "With These Words, I can Sell You Anything" (page 320) when he points out that a well-known manufacturer of cleaning products added an artificial lemon scent and called it "new and improved," even though the lemon scent did not add to the cleaning power of the product, just the smell.

5. *You might challenge the evidence supporting an argument.* If possible, try to point out unreliable, unrealistic, or irrelevant evidence offered by the opposition; question the truth of counterarguments; or point to distortions. The realtor who boasts oceanside property is vulnerable to challenge if the house in question is actually half a mile from the beach. Look for instances of stacking the deck. For example, a writer might argue that supporting the building of a new sports complex will benefit the community by providing new jobs. However, if she fails to mention that workers at the old sports facility will then lose their jobs, she is misleading the audience about the benefits of this change. Challenge the evidence by looking for hasty generalizations. For example, a business degree from State U. may indeed guarantee a well-paying job after graduation, but the writer will need more than a few personal anecdotes to convince the reader that this is the case.

6. *You can gain strength through concessions.* Admitting weaknesses in your own stand shows that you are realistic, that you don't suffer from an inflated view of the virtues of your position. It also lends credibility to your argument while helping you project yourself as fair-minded. A successful example of this strategy is Ron Karpati's acknowledgment in paragraph 9 of "I Am the Enemy" (page 121) that the animal-rights movement has sensitized scientists to the needs of animals.

**The writer offers a well-reasoned argument to support the position.** A position paper must do more than simply state your stand on an issue. It must try to persuade readers to accept your position as credible and convince them to adjust their thinking about the issue. Toward those ends, you should make every effort to demonstrate the best reasons for your beliefs and support the positions you hold. That means presenting honest and logically sound arguments.

Persuaders use three kinds of appeal: to *reason,* to *emotions,* and to readers' sense of *ethics.* You may have heard these described as the appeals of *logos, pathos,* and *ethos.* Although it is difficult to separate the emotional and ethical components from a logical argument, the persuasive powers of a position argument may mean the proper combination of these three appeals. Not all arguments will cover all three appeals. Some will target logic alone and offer as support statistics and facts. Others centering around moral, religious, or personal values will appeal to a reader's emotions as well as reason. Arguments based on emotion aim to reinforce and inspire followers to stand by their convictions. However, relying too heavily on an emotional appeal can result in an ad misericordiam argument, one that attempts to exploit the readers' pity. The most successful arguments are those that use multiple strategies to appeal to readers' hearts and minds.

When the issue centers on right-or-wrong or good-or-bad issues, position arguments make their appeals to the audience's ethical sense. In such papers, your strategy has two intentions: one, to convince the reader that you are a person of goodwill and moral character—thus enhancing your credibility—and, two, to suggest that any decent and moral readers will share your position.

**The writer's supporting evidence is convincing.** A position paper does not end with an incontrovertible proof such as the demonstration of a scientific law or mathematical theorem. No amount of logic can prove conclusively that your functional judgment is right or wrong; if that were the case, there would be few arguments. It is also impossible to prove that your aesthetic judgments are superior to another's or that a particular song, movie, or book is better than another. But your arguments have a greater chance of being persuasive if you can present convincing evidence that your argument is valid.

We'll say more about evidence in Chapter 6, but for now remember that a strong argument needs convincing evidence: facts, figures, personal observations, testimony of outside authorities, and specific examples. In general, the more facts supporting a position, the more reason there is for the reader to accept that position as valid. The same is true when refuting another position. An author needs to give reasons and hard evidence to disprove or discredit an opponent's stand.

**The writer projects a reasonable persona.** Whenever we read an argument, we cannot help but be aware of the person behind the words. Whether it's in the choice of expressions, the tenacity of opinion, the kinds of examples, the force of the argument, the nature of the appeal, or the humor or sarcasm, we hear the author's voice and form an impression of the person. That impression, which is projected by the voice and tone of the writing, is the writer's *persona.*

Persona is communicated in a variety of ways: diction or the choice of words (formal, colloquial, slang, jargon, charged terms); the sentence style (long or short, simple or

## Checklist for Writing a Position Argument

**Have you:**
- chosen a controversial issue?
- clearly stated a position?
- recognized other positions and possible objections?
- developed a well-reasoned argument?
- provided convincing supporting evidence?
- projected a reasonable persona?

complex); and the kinds of evidence offered (from cool scientific data to inflammatory examples). As in face-to-face debates, a full range of feelings can be projected by the tone of a written argument: anger, irony, jest, sarcasm, seriousness.

Persona is the vital bond linking the writer to the reader. In fact, the success or failure of an argument might be measured by the extent to which the reader accepts the persona. If you like the voice you hear, then you have already begun to identify with the writer and are more likely to share in the writer's assumptions and opinions. If, however, that persona strikes you as harsh, distant, or arrogant, you might have difficulty subscribing to the argument even if it makes logical sense.

A good position argument projects a reasonable persona, one that is sincere and willing to consider opposing views. Steer clear of ad hominem arguments, which make personal attacks on those with whom you disagree rather than on their views. Although readers may not be convinced enough to change their stand or behavior, a writer with a reasonable persona can at least capture their respect and consideration. Remember, the success of your argument will largely depend on your audience's willingness to listen.

*A word of warning.* Not every persona has to be reasonable or pleasant, although for a beginner this works best. If an arrogant persona is fortified by wit and intelligence, readers may find it stimulating, even charming. A persona—whether outrageous, humorous, or sarcastic—can be successful if executed with style and assurance. Some of the best arguments in Part Two of this book have biting edges.

When you read an argument with a memorable persona, jot down in your argument journal the details of how the writer created it; that way, you can turn back to this information when you're trying to create personas for the arguments you write.

## SAMPLE POSITION ARGUMENT FOR ANALYSIS

Below is an example of a position argument whose title suggests the issue and the author's stand on it: "Is Anything Private Anymore?" In a digital world where highly personal information appears in a multitude of databases and where security cameras are everywhere, the author wonders if privacy still exists. Written by Sean Flynn, this essay first appeared in *Parade* magazine in September 2007.

# "Is Anything Private Anymore?"
*Sean Flynn*

1   Kevin Bankston was a closet smoker who hid his habit by sneaking cigarettes outside his San Francisco office. He expected anonymity on a big city street. But in 2005, an online mapping service that provided ground-level photographs captured him smoking—and made the image available to anyone on the Internet. This year, Google's Street View project caught him again.

2   Coincidence? Absolutely. Yet Bankston's twice-documented smoking highlights a wider phenomenon: Privacy is a withering commodity for all of us.

3   What you buy, where you go, whom you call, the Web sites you visit, the e-mails you send—all of that information can be monitored and logged. "When you're out in public, it's becoming a near certainty that your image will be captured," says (the newly nonsmoking) Bankston.

4   Should you care? I've interviewed numerous people on all sides of the privacy debate to find out just how wary we should be.

5   One thing is clear: In today's world, maintaining a cocoon of privacy simply isn't practical. Need a mortgage or a car loan? A legitimate lender is going to verify a wealth of private information, including your name and address, date of birth, Social Security number and credit history. We all make daily trade-offs for convenience and thrift: Electronic tollbooths mean you don't have to wait in the cash-only lane, but your travel habits will be tracked. The Piggly Wiggly discount card saves you $206 on your annual grocery bill, but it counts how many doughnuts and six-packs you buy. MySpace posts make it easy to keep in touch with friends, but your comments live on.

6   So how do you live in a digital world and still maintain a semblance of privacy? Experts say it's crucial to recognize that those bits of data are permanent—a trail of electronic crumbs that is never swept away, available to anyone with the skills and inclination to sniff it out.

7   Privacy may not feel like much of an issue for those in their teens and 20s. They've grown up chronicling their lives on popular social networking sites like MySpace or Facebook for easy retrieval by friends and strangers alike. But some young people don't realize that what was funny to college buddies might not amuse a law-firm recruiter. Employers regularly research job applicants on the Internet. Some colleges are helping students prepare: Duke University hosts seminars on how to clean up a Facebook account. "You learn why posting pictures of you riding the mechanical bull at Shooters is a bad idea," says Sarah Ball, a senior whose own page is secure and clean.

8   Amy Polumbo, 22, restricted her page on Facebook to 100 or so people who knew her password. "It was a way for me to keep in touch with friends all over the country," she says. But after she was crowned Miss New Jersey in June, someone downloaded pictures of her and threatened blackmail. She thwarted the attempt by releasing the photos herself (they're quite innocent) but suffered weeks of embarrassment.

9   "I know how easy it is for someone to take advantage of you on the Internet," says Polumbo. "The Web is a place where people can destroy your reputation if you're not careful."

10     In fact, all kinds of transgressions now are easily retrievable. An employee at a New York City bank watched his reputation shrink when his colleagues pulled up an article from a small-town newspaper about his drunk-driving arrest two years earlier. Divorce lawyers have been issuing subpoenas for electronic tollbooth records to use in custody cases. (You say you're home at 6 p.m. to have dinner with the kids, but Fast Lane says you're getting off the Massachusetts Turnpike at 7 p.m.) Abbe L. Ross, a divorce lawyer in Boston, finds a gold mine in computers: financial data, e-mails, what Web sites a soon-to-be-ex spouse looks at and for how long. "I love to look through hard drives," she says.

11     Details about you already are stashed in enormous databases. Unless you pay cash for everything, data brokers almost certainly have compiled a profile of you that will be bought and sold dozens of times to marketers and direct-mail firms. "There's almost nothing they can't find out about you," says Jack Dunning, who worked in the junk-mail business for 35 years. Right now, there are roughly 50,000 such lists for sale in a $4 billion a year industry. Now junk mail is going digital: Companies can use personal profiles and records from Internet search engines to tailor advertising—both what you see and precisely when you see it—to individual consumers.

12     And new databases are being created all the time. Most of the major proposals for health-care reform, for example, include compiling medical records into easily and widely accessible digital files. In July, the FBI requested $5 million to pay the major phone companies to maintain logs of your calls—information the Feds can't legally stockpile themselves but might find useful later.

13     Surveillance cameras are increasingly ubiquitous in our post-9/11 world. Indeed, New York City plans to ring the financial district with them, as central London did several years ago.

14     Of course, there are upsides. London's network of cameras helped capture failed car bombers in June. And streamlined electronic medical records would make health care safer and more efficient.

15     Still, most experts say we need to be vigilant about the increasing encroachments on our privacy.

16     The ability to collect information and images has outpaced the security available to protect them. Since January 2005, nearly 160 million personal records have been stolen or inadvertently posted online.

17     And even if information stays secure, the big question remains: Who should be allowed to access these databases? The FBI might find evidence against a few bad guys in millions of phone records, but the government could track all of your calls too. (President Bush has acknowledged that the National Security Agency tapped phone calls, though whose and how many is unknown.)

18     Even more disturbing: All of those data files can be linked and cross-referenced. At the 2001 Super Bowl in Tampa, fans were scanned with cameras linked to facial-recognition software in a hunt for suspected terrorists. Some privacy advocates worry that police could videotape anti-war marches and create a library of digital faces or start mining Web pages for personal information.

19     Kevin Bankston was only caught smoking, but he's worried about larger implications: "The issue isn't whether you have anything to hide," he says. "The issue is whether the lack of privacy would give the government an inordinate amount of power over the populace. This is about maintaining the privacy necessary for us to flourish as a free society."

# Analysis of Sample Position Argument

**The writer deals with a controversial issue.**  Most people assume that personal privacy is an inherent right. But is that a realistic expectation in today's world? Few people realize that almost every electronic transaction, whether a bank deposit or store purchase, leaves a permanent digital record. Nor do they realize that every phone call, e-mail, grocery store purchase, or Facebook entry becomes part of huge data systems accessible to others. Controversy arises because such personal information can be used by businesses to track spending habits and, thus, target customers. Also controversial is how the government can keep tabs on its citizenry. That issue is even more controversial since some forms of surveillance—at airports, on highways, and in commercial and financial areas—are considered essential in the fight against terrorism. Of course, to many people, such surveillance constitutes an infringement on individual privacy and, thus, a diminishing of civil liberties. In his essay, Flynn clearly addresses the controversy that in our digital world it may be impossible to protect personal information.

**The writer clearly states a position.**  The title of Flynn's essay implies the author's stand: that personal privacy no longer exists. He begins with the anecdote of a closet smoker who thought that cigarette breaks outside his office gave him anonymity. But an "online mapping service . . . captured him smoking—and made the image available to anyone on the Internet." He concludes this anecdote with a blunt generalization, "Privacy is a withering commodity for all of us" (paragraph 2)—a clear statement of his position. Flynn reiterates his position following other examples of privacy violations—e.g., his statement regarding the ready availability of telephone and health records: "Still, most experts say we need to be vigilant about the increasing encroachments on our privacy" (paragraph 15). And in paragraph 16: "The ability to collect information and images has outpaced the security available to protect them." Clearly, he has surveyed the many ways privacy is compromised and concludes that it is rapidly eroding.

**The writer recognizes other positions and possible objections.**  Flynn creates a balanced essay by citing other points of view. At the end of paragraph 5, for example, he cites the consumer perks built into some everyday transactions: "We all make daily trade-offs for convenience and thrift: Electronic tollbooths mean you don't have to wait in the cash-only lane, but your travel habits will be tracked. The Piggly Wiggly discount card saved you $206 on your annual grocery bill, but it counts how many doughnuts and six-packs you buy. MySpace posts make it easy to keep in touch with friends, but your comments live on." Later, when discussing terrorism, he acknowledges "upsides": "London's network of cameras helped capture failed car bombers in June" (paragraph 14). And referring to "easily and widely accessible" health care files, he concedes, "streamlined electronic medical records would make health care safer and more efficient."

As the author explores the topic, his tone remains matter-of-fact and objective. His most emotionally potent comment comes at his conclusion when he refers back to the young smoker. Here his tone approaches a warning regarding surveillance in public places: "Kevin Bankston was only caught smoking. . . . This is about maintaining the privacy necessary for us to flourish as a free society."

**The writer offers well-developed reasons to support the position.** Flynn offers concrete, concise, and convincing evidence to support his position that personal privacy is greatly compromised today. He describes virulent threats and documents these with examples to which the general public can relate. One of his claims is that in today's world of commerce, it is almost impossible to maintain personal privacy—that nearly every transaction is recorded electronically and leaves a permanent trail available to anyone skilled "to sniff it out" (paragraph 6). And he gets specific: "Need a mortgage or a car loan? A legitimate lender is going to verify a wealth of private information, including your name and address, date of birth, Social Security number and credit history" (paragraph 5). Later, he argues that because of the enormous databases, "Companies can use personal profiles and records from Internet search engines to tailor advertising—both what you see and precisely when you see it—to individual consumers" (paragraph 11). For support, Flynn quotes an authority in the field of direct-mail and marketing: "'There's almost nothing they can't find out about you,' says Jack Dunning, who worked in the junk-mail business for 35 years."

Another threat Flynn names are the social networking sites that make personal information available to everyone, including potential employers as well as thieves and sexual predators. He supports his position with reference to students who naively chronicle their lives on MySpace or Facebook. Young people may not know that "employers regularly research job applicants on the Internet," Flynn writes. What may amuse college pals "might not amuse a law-firm recruiter" (paragraph 7). He further supports his position with more anecdotal evidence, a reference to the newly crowned Miss New Jersey, whose Facebook page contained photographs that were used as blackmail. Flynn even quotes her directly: "'The Web is a place where people can destroy your reputation if you're not careful'" (paragraph 9).

Another argument Flynn makes supporting his claim of a diminishing privacy is the ubiquitous use of surveillance cameras in public places. In paragraph 18, he offers the powerful example of the 2001 Super Bowl where "fans were scanned with cameras linked to facial-recognition software in a hunt for suspected terrorists." Flynn's logical concern is that "police could videotape anti-war marches and create a library of digital faces or start mining Web pages for personal information." Building on all his specific concerns, Flynn concludes with larger implications: that the increased lack of privacy could "'give the government an inordinate amount of power over the populace.'"

**The writer's supporting evidence is convincing.** Flynn's evidence is very convincing. He supports his position in a variety of ways, using anecdotes that the average person can identify with—references to smoker Kevin Bankston or young people using Facebook. He makes use of expert opinion, quoting, for instance, Jack Dunning, who worked for 35 years in the direct-mail business. Throughout the piece, he also cites numerous examples of our compromised privacy.

**The writer projects a reasonable persona.** Flynn's tone is reasonable and balanced, as his purpose is to alert the general public to the ways personal data is part of public or available records. His tone is friendly as his intention is not to alarm but to enhance awareness so that people can take sensible precautions. Thus, he gives numerous examples but does not inflate them or create a sense of panic.

# Proposal Arguments

Position arguments examine existing conditions. *Proposal arguments,* however, look to the future. They make recommendations for changes to the status quo—namely, policy, practice, or attitude. Essentially, what every proposal writer says is this: "Here is the problem, and this is what I think should be done about it." The hoped-for result is a new course of action or way of thinking.

Proposals are the most common kind of argument. We hear them all the time: "There ought to be a law against that"; "The government should do something about these conditions." We're always making proposals of some kind: "Van should work out more"; "You ought to see that movie"; "We should recycle more of our trash." As pointed out earlier in this chapter, because proposals are aimed at correcting problems, they almost always make their claims in obligation verbs such as *ought to, needs to be,* and *must.*

Sometimes proposal arguments take up local problems and make practical recommendations for immediate solutions. For instance, to reduce the long lines at the photocopy machines in your campus library, you might propose that the school invest in more copiers and station them throughout the building. Proposal arguments also seek to correct or improve conditions with more far-reaching consequences. If, for example, too many of your classmates smoke, you might write a proposal to your school's administration to remove all cigarette machines from campus buildings or to limit smoking areas on campus.

Still other proposals address perennial social issues in an effort to change public behavior and government policy. A group of physicians might recommend that marijuana be legalized for medical use. An organization of concerned parents might ask the federal government to ban toys that contain toxic or flammable materials. Everyone has ideas about things that should be changed; proposals are the means we use to make those changes happen.

### Features to Look for in Proposal Arguments

Proposals have two basic functions: (1) They inform readers that there is a problem; (2) they make recommendations about how to correct those problems. To help you sharpen your own critical ability to build and analyze proposal arguments, we offer some guidelines.

**The writer states the problem clearly.** Because a proposal argument seeks to change the reader's mind and/or behavior, you first must demonstrate that a problem exists. You do this for several reasons. Your audience may not be aware that the problem exists or they may have forgotten it or think that it has already been solved. Sympathetic audiences may need to be reinspired to take action. It is crucial, therefore, that proposals clearly define the problem and the undesirable or dangerous consequences if matters are not corrected.

For both uninformed and sympathetic audiences, writers often try to demonstrate how the problem personally affects the reader. An argument for greater measures against shoplifting can be more convincing when you illustrate how petty thefts inevitably lead to higher prices. A paper proposing the elimination of pesticides might interest the everyday gardener by demonstrating how carcinogenic chemicals can contaminate local drinking water. To make the problem even more convincing, the claim should be supported by solid evidence—statistics, historical data, examples, testimony of witnesses and experts, maybe even personal experience.

**The writer clearly proposes how to solve the problem.** After defining the problem clearly, you need to tell your readers how to solve it. This is the heart of the proposal, the writer's plan of action. Besides a detailed explanation of what should be done and how, the proposal should supply reliable supporting evidence for the plan: testimony of others, ideas from authorities, statistics from studies.

**The writer argues convincingly that this proposal will solve the problem.** Perhaps the first question readers ask is "How will this solution solve the problem?" Writers usually address this question by identifying the forces behind the problem and demonstrating how their plan will counter those forces. Suppose, for instance, you propose putting condom machines in all college dorms as a means of combating the spread of AIDS. To build a convincing case, you would have to summon evidence documenting how condoms significantly reduce the spread of AIDS. To make the connection between the problem and your solution even stronger, you might go on to explain how readily available machines leave students little excuse for unsafe sex. Students cannot complain that they jeopardized their health because they couldn't make it to a drugstore.

**The writer convincingly explains how the solution will work.** Generally readers next ask how the plan will be put into action. Writers usually answer by detailing how their plan will work. They emphasize their plan's advantages and how efficiently (or cheaply, safely, conveniently) it can be carried out. For the condom machine proposal, that might mean explaining how and where the machines will be installed and how students can be encouraged to use them. You might cite advantages of your proposal, such as the easy installation of the machines and the low price of the contents.

**The writer anticipates objections to the proposed solution.** Writers expect disagreement and objections to proposal arguments: Proposals are aimed at changing the status quo, and many people are opposed to or are fearful of change. If you want to persuade readers, especially hostile ones, you must show that you respect their sides of the argument too. Most proposal writers anticipate audience response to fortify their case and establish credibility. (See Chapter 4 for more discussion of audience response.)

**The writer explains why this solution is better than the alternatives.** Although you may believe that your solution to the problem is best, you cannot expect readers automatically to share that sentiment. Nor can you expect readers not to wonder about other solutions. Good proposal writers investigate other solutions that have been tried to solve this problem so they can weigh alternative possibilities and attempt to demonstrate the superiority of their plan and the disadvantages of others. If you are knowledgeable about ways the problem has been dealt with in the past, you might be

---

## Checklist for Writing a Proposal Argument

**Have you:**
- ■ stated the problem clearly?
- ■ proposed a solution clearly?
- ■ explained why the solution will work?
- ■ demonstrated how the solution will work?
- ■ addressed possible objections?
- ■ shown why the solution is better than alternatives?
- ■ projected a reasonable persona?

---

able to show how your plan combines the best features of other, less successful solutions. For instance, in the condom machine proposal you might explain to your readers that universities have attempted to make students more aware that unsafe sex promotes the spread of AIDS; however, without the easy availability of condom machines, students are more likely to continue to engage in unsafe sex. The promotion of AIDS awareness and the presence of condom machines might significantly reduce that problem.

**The writer projects a reasonable persona.** As in position arguments, your persona is an important factor in proposals, for it conveys your attitude toward the subject and the audience. Because a proposal is intended to win readers to your side, the best strategy is to project a persona that is fair-minded. Even if you dislike somebody else's views on an issue, projecting a reasonable and knowledgeable tone will have a more persuasive effect than a tone of belligerence.

If you are arguing for condom machines in dormitories, you would be wise to recognize that some people might object to the proposal because availability might be interpreted as encouragement of sexual behavior. So as not to offend or antagonize such readers, adopting a serious, straightforward tone might be the best mode of presenting the case.

## SAMPLE PROPOSAL ARGUMENT FOR ANALYSIS

The following argument was written by Amanda Collins, a first-year English composition student, whose assignment was to write a proposal argument. In her paper, she argues for the implementation of foreign language teaching in American elementary schools, focusing in particular on her own home town of East Bridgewater, Massachusetts. Read her essay and respond to the questions that follow. Note that she used research to support her ideas and documentation to acknowledge her sources. The style of documentation used in this paper is MLA, which we discuss in detail in the Documentation Guide.

Amanda Collins

Professor Ingram

ENG 1350

15 December 2009

Bring East Bridgewater Elementary

into the World

Introduction

1    According to a survey of ten European countries and Russia, the average age of students beginning foreign language instruction is eight (Bergentoft 13). In Sweden, ninety-nine percent of the students in primary school study English. One hundred percent of the students study English in secondary schools (Bergentoft 19). However, "across the United States, only about one in three elementary schools offers its students the opportunity to gain some measure of skill in another language" (Met 37). The United States falls drastically short of the standards being set by the rest of the world.

2    The Commonwealth of Massachusetts is no exception. According to a report from the Center for Applied Linguistics (CAL), only forty-four schools across the state offer foreign language programs in primary school (Branaman, Rhodes, and Holmes). Schools not offering foreign language study leave their students at a disadvantage. Foreign language needs to be considered as vital to a child's education as are math, science and reading. Parents would not be happy if their children began math or English studies in high school. So why shouldn't parents be outraged that second languages do not hold much significance in the Massachusetts curriculum? (Brown 166). East Bridgewater must take steps to change this and open Central Elementary School to foreign language learning.

3    The world is changing as are the skills one needs to succeed. Globalization brings us together. People around the world are connected to each other more than ever before, whether through international communication, travel, or commerce. In a world today that is constantly crossing borders "there is a need for linguistically and culturally competent Americans" (Brown 165). And learning languages is one way to reach such competency. America's students need to be prepared for entrance into this ever-merging world where they will compete with their international peers who are fluent in two or three languages. It is time to adopt a plan like those proven successful elsewhere in America and abroad. It's time to give East Bridgewater's students an advantage. In order to do this, East Bridgewater must live up to the school system's motto, "There is no better place to learn," and mandate foreign language education in the elementary curriculum for every child.

Collins 2

4    Although the Massachusetts Department of Education adopted a curriculum framework in August 1999 that includes foreign language in the requirements for elementary schools, it is still a recommendation, not yet a requirement (Massachusetts Dept. of Educ.). Massachusetts's new Curriculum Framework for World Languages states that "students should graduate from high school able to read, write, and converse in a world language in order to participate in the multilingual, interdependent communities of the twenty-first century . . . to develop proficiency, this framework recommends a sequence of language learning that starts in kindergarten and continues through grade twelve and beyond . . . the World Languages discipline is about making connections" (Massachusetts Dept. of Educ.). The framework places the same value on learning a foreign language as is placed on mathematics, reading and science. Despite the framework's passing, foreign language is not mandated in the elementary curriculum. There is a real need not only to finalize the benefits that students gain by learning languages at an early age, but also to work toward advancing our schools' curricula to include Foreign Language in Elementary School (FLES).
Why Should Children Learn Foreign Languages?

5    Language is an important aspect of the education of students of all ages. It is becoming more important for citizens to be well versed in a language other than their own. The United States was basically a self-sufficient and self-contained country before the World Wars. "Rapid and widespread political, economic, and military changes after World War II gave rise to issues that were global in scope, and many people became aware of the impact that events outside U.S. borders had on domestic affairs" (Smith 38). The United States was learning just how fundamental foreign languages are.

6    One reason is that transcontinental communications have become essential to everyday life in the world. With so much cross-cultural interaction, we must prepare American children to grow into adults capable of interacting with other cultures. The future of the United States depends on continued and constant communication with countries that speak languages other than our own. There are only about 45 other countries outside the United States where English is spoken. So, in order to maintain the status that this country now enjoys, we must train American children to comprehend changes in the global community. Students must learn foreign languages.

7    In 1999 a study titled *Exploring the Economics of Language* found that "multilingual societies have a competitive advantage over monolingual societies in

Collins 3

international trade" (Met 36). The study went on to point out that businesses that had people with the proper language skills to negotiate and carry out commerce with foreign enterprises were at a distinct advantage over those that lacked such talent. So it stands to reason that giving America's students the opportunity to learn a foreign language increases their chances of succeeding in the business world. Likewise, the country benefits because successful businesses on the world level only help the American economy. As Andrew Smith asserts, there is a need to "prepare our students to meet the challenges of our increasingly, sometimes dangerously, interconnected world. It is not likely that the United States will exert global leadership for long with a citizenry that is globally deaf, dumb, and blind" (41).

8          Besides the business industry, other jobs require expertise in a second language. The State Department, the Central Intelligence Agency, and the National Security Agency are among more than 70 government agencies that require proficiency in foreign languages (Met 36). The non-profit service industries need employees to interact with other cultures and speak other languages. The Red Cross, for example, not only aids victims in the United States but throughout the world. Additionally, the Internet and other electronic communications, though originally English-based, are becoming more linguistically diverse, making proficiency in other languages indispensable. Again, we must not deprive students of the opportunity to advance in such career paths; we must provide them language training to make possible career success.

Other Benefits to Learning a Language Early

9          While most people have the ability to learn a foreign language at any age, there are benefits to starting that process when students are young (Lipton 1115). In 1959 neurologist Wilder Penfield claimed that the brain was best able to learn a foreign language before the age of ten. Later research by scientists Chugani and Phelps resulted in the same conclusion: the ideal time to begin studying a foreign language is before puberty (Lipton 1114). Thompson et al. discovered in the year 2000 that the area of the brain associated with language learning grew the most rapidly from age six to thirteen and then slowed. Another researcher suggested that children learning a language before the age of twelve will develop a more authentic accent (Lipton 1114). So this scientific evidence makes a strong case that foreign language learning must begin at a young age. But there are other studies that make the case even stronger.

Collins 4

10        In 1987, a Connecticut test of twenty-six thousand students revealed that children who began foreign language education before grade four did significantly better on speaking, listening, reading, writing and cultural understanding tests than students who started language learning in seventh grade or after (Brown 165). This and other similar studies initiated further investigation into the academic benefits of early foreign language learning.

11        Numerous studies have been conducted to evaluate the ways in which learning a language will enhance the simultaneous learning of other subjects. "Learning [foreign] languages . . . provides a unique conduit to higher-order thinking skills. From the early stages of learning, students move from a representational knowledge base to comparison, synthesis, and hypothesis, all elements of higher-order thinking skills" (Brown 167). Students can gain better understanding of the grammar of their native language when they study the grammar of a foreign tongue, and students who can speak another language can develop stronger reading skills (Met 38). On the national level, there is a call for improved literacy, which is why it is important for parents and educators to recognize how FLES helps students learn to read and write (Bruce 608). FLES students scored higher on the 1985 Basic Skills Language Arts Test than non-FLES students. Foreign language study has helped improve standardized test scores in mathematics and reading for students from a variety of backgrounds. Bilingualism also improves "cognitive functioning, such as metalinguistic skills and divergent thinking" (Met 38). It has even been suggested that students gain more creativity. Foreign language study helps students become more academically successful overall.

12        Additionally, because the world is full of many cultures, studying a foreign language helps prepare students for the cultural understanding that is necessary for the acceptance of such diversity. Brown states, "no other subject matter in the elementary school prepares students for the realization that there are other languages and cultures beyond their own" (167). This in turn aids in teaching students geography, history, and social studies because they will have something to build on, knowing that the United States is not the only country of consequence. Researchers Carpenter and Torney found that younger students studying languages are more open to other cultures and develop more positive attitudes toward foreign cultures and languages (Lipton 1114). From brain functions to academics to character development, learning foreign languages in elementary school is proven to be profitable.

Collins 5

Optimal Solution for East Bridgewater

13    There is no doubt that East Bridgewater must adopt some version of a FLES program. Based on the current circumstances at the Central Elementary School, I recommend that the East Bridgewater School Committee adopt a Sequential FLES program in which students study a language no more than thirty minutes per session up to five times a week.

14    As for the specific language, that decision can be left up to the School Committee. However, it is suggested that only one language be taught for the first year, or at least until the program is underway and running smoothly. And it makes sense to recommend Spanish since that language is used more often than other foreign languages in the United States.

15    Language instruction should take place at least three times a week for thirty minutes. Each school day is six hours long, minus time for lunch and recess. In order to arrange for the addition of a language program, the length of other lessons per day would have to be shortened slightly, but never by more than ten minutes each. This should not be a problem. Foreign languages are as equally important to a child's education as math, reading or science, and, therefore, would advance students' education in the long run. Since it has been proven that the study of a second language enhances students' performances in other subjects, the amount of time shaved from each subject's session would be more than made up for in the students' overall success.

16    To fund this undertaking, East Bridgewater should apply to the Federal Language Assistance Program (FLAP). As of the year 2000, Springfield and Medford were the only two towns to receive FLAP grants. Funds are also available through Goals 2000: Educate America Act of 1994. Under the Improving America's Schools Act of 1994, Title VII grants are given out for foreign language assistance. In the year 2001, the Massachusetts Board of Education received two, and Newton, Malden, Medford, Salem, and Springfield Public Schools each received a grant. East Bridgewater has the opportunity to apply for all of these grants.

17    Meetings should be scheduled with parents to discuss the importance of foreign language education. Brochures outlining fundraising activities should be distributed. The costs of the meetings and printed materials would be minimal, and they would be more than paid for with the benefits of the program. When parents and communities join together, fundraisers can bring in large revenues. East Bridgewater can hold benefits similar to the concert and art auction held by parents in Athens, Georgia. These grants and locally raised money can also help defray the cost of adding teachers to the staff and carrying out the proper training.

Collins 6

Books and other teaching materials can be purchased from grant funds as well. There really is no shortage of money available. Once a town or district realizes the advantages of foreign language learning and expresses a desire to include it in their elementary school, the government and private agencies could offer funds to help get those programs underway.

18

Teaching foreign language to students is a necessity. Linguistic and national borders are becoming a thing of the past as the result of globalization. It is a school's responsibility and a student's right to have every opportunity afforded them to become globally aware and literate citizens. East Bridgewater's School Committee shares that responsibility as educators of this country's future leaders. Now is the time to act and close the gap on the foreign language deficiency that exists in East Bridgewater's Central Elementary School.

Collins 7

### Works Cited

Bergentoft, Rune. "Foreign Language Instruction: A Comparative Perspective." *Annals of the American Academy of Political and Social Science* 532 (1994): 8-34. Print.

Branaman, Lucinaa, Nancy Rhodes, and Annette Holmes. "National Directory of Early Foreign Language Programs." Center for Applied Linguistics. CAL, 1999. Web. 4 Dec. 2004.

Brown, Christine L. "Elementary School Foreign Language Programs in the United States." *Annals of the American Academy of Political and Social Science* 532 (1994): 164-76. Print.

Bruce, Anita. "Encouraging the Growth of Foreign Language Study." *Modern Language Journal* 86 (2002): 605-09. Print.

Caccavale, Therese. "Holliston Public Schools Foreign Language." Teacher Web, 16 Oct. 2009. Web. 7 Dec. 2009.

Lambert, Richard D. "Problems and Processes in U.S. Foreign Language Planning." *Annals of the American Academy of Political and Social Science* 532 (1994): 47-58. Print.

Collins 8

Lipton, Gladys C. "The FLES Advantage: FLES Programs in the Third Millennium."
 *French Review* 74 (2001): 1113-24. Print.
Massachusetts Dept. of Educ. "World Languages Curriculum Framework."
 Massachusetts Dept. of Educ., Jan. 1996. Web. 1 Dec. 2009.
Met, Myriam. "Why Language Learning Matters." *Educational Leadership* 59 (2001):
 36-40. Print.
Smith, Andrew F. "How Global Is the Curriculum?" *Educational Leadership* 60
 (2002): 38-41. Print.

**QUESTIONS FOR ANALYSIS AND DISCUSSION**

Briefly summarize the main points of Amanda Collins's essay. Then answer the following questions about the essay to see how it fulfills our guidelines for a proposal argument:

1. Where does Collins identify the problem? Explain how she demonstrates that the problem is significant. Does she explain how today's young students can be affected? Where does she do this?
2. What solution does Collins propose? Where is it stated?
3. Does Collins explain how her solution will work? Where does she do this? Does she provide enough detail to understand how it will work?
4. Has Collins anticipated objections to her solution? in which paragraphs? How does she respond to the objection?
5. Does Collins seem aware of other attempts to solve the problem? Where does she refer to them?
6. What attitude about her subject does Collins convey to her readers? Does she seem reasonable and balanced? Where exactly?

# Analyzing the Structure
## The Beginning

Amanda Collins has already divided her paper into four parts: "Introduction," "Why Should Children Learn Foreign Language?" "Other Benefits to Learning a Language Early," and "Optimal Solution for East Bridgewater." Her "Introduction" constitutes the beginning of the essay. The middle includes those paragraphs grouped under her next two parts ("Why Should Children Learn Foreign Language?" and "Other Benefits to Learning a Language Early"). The end corresponds to those paragraphs under "Optimal Solution for East Bridgewater."

In paragraph 1, Amanda introduces the problem: compared to several foreign countries, only about a third of American elementary schools offer foreign language teaching. And this creates a disadvantage not only for children who are preparing for a global world but for America. Then in paragraph 2, she tightens her focus to the state of Massachusetts, which, characteristic of the rest of the country, offers a paltry response: only 44 schools statewide offer foreign language programs at the primary level. She concludes that paragraph with a point-blank proposal that "East Bridgewater must take steps to change this and open Central Elementary School to foreign language learning."

We get a sense of Amanda from these introductory paragraphs. We hear both concern and sincerity in her tone. We also are clear on her positions. Equating foreign language learning with math and writing, she projects a sense of urgency if American young people are to grow up to function successfully in a world that is linguistically and culturally interconnected and competitive. She appeals to both reason and emotion when she states: "It is time to adopt a plan like those proven successful elsewhere in America and abroad. It's time to give East Bridgewater's students an advantage." She also appeals to a sense of ethics, reminding authorities of their responsibility and duty to live up to the school system's motto, "There is no better place to learn." And she concludes this part of the argument insisting that East Bridgewater mandate that foreign language be taught at Central Elementary so students can begin to share in the benefits to come.

## The Middle

The next eight paragraphs Amanda has divided into two sections: "Why Should Children Learn Foreign Language?" and "Other Benefits to Learning a Language Early." These represent the middle of Amanda's essays, where she makes her case, where she does the real arguing for her proposal.

**Background Information** Paragraphs 1, 2, and 4 set the context for Amanda's complaint and the basis for her proposal. In paragraph 1, she says how America "falls drastically short of the standards being set by the rest of the world." In the next paragraph she says that Massachusetts is characteristic of the larger problem with only 44 schools statewide—a small percentage—offering foreign language programs at the primary level. Paragraph 4 focuses on how despite an adopted curriculum that includes a foreign language requirement in Massachusetts schools, it has still not been mandated, leaving East Bridgewater students deprived.

**Reasons in Support of the Claim** Paragraphs 5 through 12 make up the heart of Amanda's essay. Here she supports her claim that it's important for children to learn foreign languages. And she offers several reasons. One key point is the competition in international business that American students will eventually face in the multilingual world of commerce. As evidence, she cites a source (paragraph 6) that claims how only 45 countries besides the United States speak English, implying that most of the rest of the 160 or so countries do not. So in a majority of the world's nations, commerce is conducted in foreign tongues.

She also refers to a study that supports her claim that "monolingual societies" are at a distinct disadvantage over those where other languages are spoken. She summons the support of Andrew Smith (paragraph 7) who also sees a need to prepare our children for an increasing global economy and culture. In the next paragraph, she points out that besides business, other careers require expertise in a second language—e.g., nonprofit organizations as well as some 70 government agencies, including the CIA, that require proficiency in foreign languages. She concludes that with the Internet and other electronic communications, once English-based, the world is becoming more linguistically diverse, making proficiency in other languages indispensable. Again, she argues, we must not deprive students the opportunity to advance in such career paths.

In paragraphs 9 through 12, Amanda offers other benefits to early language learning besides career success, thus bolstering her claim. Because children best learn foreign languages at a young age, she argues they will develop more authentic accents. Second, foreign language learning also helps children perform better in speaking, writing, and even mathematics. For support, she cites numerous studies, allowing her to conclude: "From brain functions, to academics, to character development, learning foreign languages in elementary school is proven to be profitable."

**Response to Other Points of View** Although Amanda cites no specific opposing views, she implies that America may be slow to develop language programs at the primary level because of a general apathy and/or the belief that speaking English is good enough. She hints at this when she mentions America's pre–World Wars sense of self-sufficiency and self-containment. And even though Americans had learned "how fundamental foreign languages" were following World War II, vigorous implementation, especially on the primary school level, has been lacking.

**Anticipates Possible Objections to Reasons** Amanda indirectly anticipates opposition to early language training: that if people need to learn a foreign language for their careers they can take courses as adults. With considerable supporting evidence, she argues that the earlier children learn foreign languages the better. And she cites scientific studies that confirm how young children absorb foreign languages faster and more efficiently than adolescents or adults.

## The End

The final five paragraphs constitute the end of Amanda's argument. Here she returns to the problem in East Bridgewater and offers specific proposals on implementing foreign language training in Central Elementary. She recommends a program of half-hour sessions three to five times a week; she suggests Spanish since it is the second most-spoken language in America; she suggests various means of funding the program; and she recommends that parents get involved. She concludes with reaffirmations of her argument that it is important for young students to learn foreign languages and that it is a school's responsibility to provide students that opportunity. Her final sentence rounds out her argument and nicely returns to the home front: "Now is the time to act and close the gap on the foreign language deficiency that exists in East Bridgewater's Central Elementary School."

## Narrative Arguments

Sometimes position and proposal arguments do not take on the familiar shapes as just discussed. Sometimes the author's position on an issue is implied rather than straight-forwardly stated. Sometimes instead of a well-reasoned argument bound by a hierarchy of supporting details, the evidence is incorporated in a dramatic illustration of the issue. So is the author's stand. What we're talking about is argument in the form of a *narrative.*

Instead of spelling out the claims and making explicit points, the narrative argument relies on a scene, a series of episodes, or a story to advocate a change of behavior or way of thinking. Whether true or hypothetical, a narrative may serve as the body of an argument or it may be used at the beginning as a springboard to the central claim and discussion. Either way, a narrative can be a powerful strategy for winning the sympathy of an audience by describing experiences that evoke emotional responses. Below is an argument aimed at getting people to protest a governmental proposal to remove grizzly bears from list of animals protected by the Endangered Species Act. It begins with a student's personal narrative, an account that is emotionally appealing and that leads into an explicit appeal.

> We'd been hiking for three hours east of Yellowstone's Slough Creek when our guide motioned us to stop. "Bears," he whispered. We heard a piercing sound— more like a wailing cry than a roar. We cut through some sage and over a rise when we saw a grizzly bear mother and two yearling cubs. From about a hundred yards we watched in hushed fascination as the adorable cubs romped and wrestled in the grass while the mother watched from a short distance. They were seemingly unaware of our presence and continued to cavort, one cub trying to engage the mother in play by nudging her with his nose. This went on for several minutes until the mother made a sound and stood erect, sniffing the air. She must have sensed danger because she bellowed for the cubs to follow. In a moment they tumbled down a ravine and out of sight.
>
> To see that mother grizzly and her young at such close range was not just a rare experience but an eye-opener. It was a reminder that these magnificent, elusive creatures are in a constant struggle to survive. They reproduce only every three years and spend at least that time rearing their cubs. They are vulnerable to hunters, traffic, and male grizzlies which will kill their own cubs in order to render nursing mothers fertile again. While their numbers have increased over the past decades, these bears are threatened once again.
>
> The current administration has recently proposed taking grizzlies off the Endangered Species list, thus stripping them of the kind of protection from hunters that could push them to the edge of extinction once again. We must do everything in our power to make people aware of the continuing struggle to save these iconic vestiges of frontier America.

The appeal here makes a case for protecting the grizzlies by re-creating an encounter with a mother bear and her cubs, thus invoking in the reader identification with the author's sympathy for the creatures. Even if the reader has never encountered grizzly bears in the wild, the narrative at least evokes in readers yearnings for such. To anyone who has ever visited a zoo or seen wildlife movies, the description of the cubs at play has a strong emotional appeal.

While this strategy—the use of a story—differs from the standard position and proposal argument, the narrative argument still has three basic parts—a beginning, middle and end—and, here, a paragraph for each. The first is the actual narrative, the "story" in which the author invites the reader to partake in the experience. Here we read the author's observations of the animals "cavorting"; the final sentence concludes with the animals' sensing danger and eventually departing. In essence, this opening paragraph is the author's invitation to share in the emotional experience of the encounter. The second paragraph shifts to an appreciation of that experience and an evaluation of the vulnerability of the animals. Here the author reminds us that these "magnificent" creatures are threatened by a variety of forces, and the author names specifics—hunters, vehicular traffic, and other grizzlies. The third paragraph states the specific problem that could further endanger the animals—the then-current administration's proposal to remove them from the Endangered Species list. And it concludes with a proposal for people who care to "do everything in ...[their] power to make people aware of the continuing struggle to save" the grizzlies.

A narrative can also constitute other peoples' experiences as in the third-person account below of a teenager's death by drug overdose. Like the above first-person narrative, the Web log entry that follows is constructed on a time line, moving from the deeper to the more recent past.

Megan B. started smoking marijuana and drinking alcohol at the age of thirteen. But when those didn't work for her she decided she needed to step it up a level. So by fourteen she began using cocaine as well as taking prescription drugs including Ritalin, Xanax, and Percocet. There was no need to go to a doctor for prescriptions. Friends got them from their parents' medicine cabinets. Like so many kids, she regarded prescription drugs as "safer" than other drugs. She figured that since people took them legally all the time, she'd be fine with them. By the time she was sixteen, she had graduated to heroin, sniffing it with friends to calm herself and get sleep. The stuff was easy to get and only a few dollars a bag. But then her heroin use started spiraling out of control. She missed curfews. She missed school; she didn't come home nights, saying she was staying at friends' homes. When her parents asked if she was taking drugs, she, of course, lied. For some time they believed her. Then two months before her seventeenth birthday, she died from an overdose. Her parents had missed the warning signs—the erratic behavior, her bouts of depression, restlessness, angry denials—discounting them as teenage rebelliousness. By the time they tried to intervene, to get professional help, Megan was dead.

What makes this narrative so effective is its objective tone, its matter-of-fact chronicling of Megan B.'s sad demise. Nowhere in the passage does the author take on an admonishing or threatening tone; nor does she cite a lot of dry statistics about drugs and young people's deaths. Instead, the author creates a growing sense of inevitability that climaxes in the stark final announcement, "By the time they tried to intervene, to get professional help, Megan was dead." The Internet has hundreds of websites with narratives of the accidental deaths of drug victims. Likewise, there are dedicated sites with stories of deaths due to drunk driving, guns, house poisons, suicide, and other tragedies.

### Features to Look for in Narrative Arguments

For a narrative argument to be successful, it should tell a story that clearly dramatizes a controversial issue. It should also meet some of the following basic criteria, which we offer as a checklist to evaluate your own or other writers' narratives.

**The writer's narrative illustrates a controversial issue.** Like either a position or proposal argument, the narrative should tell a story that dramatizes an experience or series of experiences relevant to a controversial issue.

**The narrative is a scene, a series of episodes, or a story that advocates a change of behavior or way of thinking.** A narrative is more than just the citation of personal evidence—yours or someone else's—in support of your stand on an issue. It is a running account of events, usually arranged in chronological order, that illustrate someone's experience with aspects of the issue being debated. Even if your audience is aware of the problem and may even be sympathetic, framing your argument as a narrative has the potential to invite the reader to identify personally with the character or characters in the discourse and, as a result, move them to action. A paper proposing stricter laws against drunk drivers, for instance, might be especially persuasive if it is cast as a real-life account of someone who experienced injury in an automobile accident caused by a drunk driver.

**The narrative should be credible.** Whether your narrative is based on your own personal experience or someone else's, it should have credibility if it is going to win the sympathy of an audience. If because of inaccuracies, contradictions, or unbelievable exaggeration the story strains for validity, your narrative will lose its power to persuade.

**The narrative should be representative.** No matter how credible, your narrative should be *representative* of the issue. Say, for instance, you were stopped for exceeding the speed limit by 30 miles per hour in a town you passed through infrequently. In your narrative, you describe how the police officer not only reprimanded you but also put you under arrest, escorting you to the police station where you were put in a jail cell overnight. No matter how harrowing that narrative may be, no matter how unpleasant the police reaction was, your case would be weak if you argued that the town's police force was out of control and should be investigated by the district attorney's office. Unless you had other evidence that police overreaction was standard in that town, your narrative would not be symptomatic of a real problem. In contrast, the tragic story of Megan B. whose drug abuse was not dealt with in time is representative of hundreds of young people who annually fall victim to drug overdoses.

**The narrative must avoid sentimentality.** Opening an argument with a strong narrative has the potential of snagging the readers' attention and sympathy from the start. But you should be careful not to let your appeal become too emotional or sink into melodrama, otherwise your argument will lose sympathy. Choose your words and present facts and details carefully. Avoid words and expressions that are emotionally too loaded, too forceful.

## SAMPLE NARRATIVE ARGUMENT

Narratives can have a greater impact on readers than other kinds of arguments because narratives appeal to values and emotions common to most people and, thus, have more persuasive power than cool logic and dry statistics. What follows is an appeal for people to be open-minded about physician-assisted suicide. It's an argument that is fashioned on a narrative and, thus, structured on a time line—and one that is particularly poignant since much of it chronicles the author's grappling with his own terminal medical condition. Jerry Fensterman is the former director of development for Fenway Community Health in Boston, Massachusetts. This article appeared as a guest editorial in the *Boston Globe* on January 31, 2006, a few months before his death.

## I See Why Others Choose to Die
*Jerry Fensterman*

1    The U.S. Supreme Court's recent decision to let stand Oregon's law permitting physician-assisted suicide is sure to fuel an ongoing national debate. Issues of life and death are deeply felt and inspire great passions. It would be wonderful, and unusual, if all those joining the fray would do so with the humility and gravity the matter deserves.

2    I am approaching 50, recently remarried, and the father of a terrific 13-year-old young man. By every measure I enjoy a wonderful life. Or at least I did until April 2004, when I was diagnosed with kidney cancer. Surgery was my only hope to prevent its spread and save my life. The discovery of a new lump in December 2004 after two surgeries signaled that metastasis was underway. My death sentence had been pronounced.

3    Life may be the most intense addiction on earth. From the moment I first heard the words "you have cancer" and again when I was told that it was spreading out of control, I recognized my addiction to life almost at the cellular level. I have tried since then, as I did before, to live life to the fullest. I also committed myself to doing everything within my power to extend my life.

4    Toward that end I am participating in my third clinical trial in a year. I have gained some small benefit from it. I am, however, one of the first people with my cancer to try this drug. Its median benefit seems to be only on the order of three months. So my expectations are modest. The side effects of these drugs are significant, as are the symptoms of the cancer's gallop through my body. All things considered, I believe I have earned my merit badge for "doing all one can in the face of death to stay alive."

5    That the experience has changed me is obvious. I have a few scars, have lost 50 pounds, and my hair is thinner. I rely on oxygen nearly all the time, can no longer perform the job I loved, and have difficulty eating. More profoundly, my universe has contracted. Simply leaving home has become an enormous task, and travel is essentially out of the question. I can no longer run, swim, golf, ski, and play with my son. I haven't yet learned how to set goals or make plans for a future that probably consists of weeks or months, not years. I am also nearing a point where I will not be able to take care of my most basic needs.

6    Mine has been a long, difficult, and certain march to death. Thus, I have had ample time to reflect on my life, get my affairs in order, say everything I want to the people I love, and seek rapprochement with friends I have hurt or lost touch with. The bad news is that my pain and suffering have been drawn out, the rewarding aspects of life have inexorably shrunk, and I have watched my condition place an increasingly great physical and emotional burden on the people closest to me. While they have cared for me with great love and selflessness, I cannot abide how my illness has caused them hardship, in some cases dominating their lives and delaying their healing.

7    Perhaps the biggest and most profound change I have undergone is that my addiction to life has been "cured." I've kicked the habit! I now know how a feeling, loving, rational person could choose death over life, could choose to relieve his suffering as well as that of his loved ones a few months earlier than would happen naturally.

8    I am not a religious person, but I consider myself and believe I have proved throughout my life to be a deeply moral person. Personally I would not now choose physician-assisted suicide if it were available. I do not know if I ever would. Yet now, I understand in a manner that I never could have before why an enlightened society should, with thoughtful safeguards, allow the incurably ill to choose a merciful death.

9    The Supreme Court's ruling will inflame the debate over physician-assisted suicide. Besides adding my voice to this debate, I ask you to carefully search your soul before locking into any position. If you oppose physician-assisted suicide, first try to walk a mile in the shoes of those to whom you would deny this choice. For as surely as I'm now wearing them, they could one day just as easily be on your feet or those of someone you care deeply about.

## Analysis of Sample Narrative Argument

Unlike the Megan B. and grizzly bear examples, Fensterman does not begin with a story and conclude with his claim. Instead, he opens with an acknowledgment of the U.S. Supreme Court's ruling to let stand the law permitting physician-assisted suicide. He then follows with seven paragraphs that personalize his coming to terms with his "death sentence." These paragraphs constitute the body of the piece and, like most narratives, the contents are structured on a time line. In this case, the narrative begins in April 2004 when the author was diagnosed with kidney cancer and then relates events occurring in the next year and a half. In his final two paragraphs, he refers back to the controversy, saying that he would not choose physician-assisted suicide at this time and does not know if he ever would. But he has learned through his own experience of terminal illness why the option should be available.

# Analyzing the Structure

## The Beginning

Paragraph 1 constitutes the beginning of Fensterman's narrative argument—where he names the controversy, which his following narrative dramatizes. Here he specifically cites the U.S. Supreme Court's recent ruling "to let stand Oregon's law permitting physician-assisted suicide." Acknowledging how this will only fuel the ongoing national debate, he asks, because the issue is a matter of life and death, that people enter it "with the humility and gravity the matter deserves," thus anticipating his own personal story.

## The Middle

Paragraphs 2 through 7 constitute Fensterman's personal narrative of his "death sentence." He immediately identifies himself as a 50-year-old recently remarried man and a father who "enjoys a wonderful life" and who clearly has a lot to live for. But in April 2004, he was diagnosed with cancer of the kidney. Over the next five paragraphs (3–7), he chronicles the events of the next two years. In December 2004, a new lump was discovered following two surgeries, signaling the cancer had spread. That "death sentence" announcement made Fensterman recognize his "addiction to life almost at the cellular level" (paragraph 3). As he says, since then he has dedicated himself to prolonging his life including participating in another clinical trial. But the benefits were short-lived and the side effects were significant—scars, weight loss, thinning of his hair. Worse, his universe "was contracted." He could no longer work, travel, "run, swim, golf, ski, and play" with his son. In paragraphs 6 and 7, as he approaches death, he says that he is reflecting on his life, getting his affairs in order, and contacting family members and friends. But what pains him the most is how his condition has become "an increasingly great physical and emotional burden on the people" to whom he is closest. And this hardship is what he "cannot abide" (paragraph 6). He concludes that he has become "cured" of his "addiction to life." As a result, he says he now understands "how a feeling, loving, rational person could choose death over life, could choose to relieve his suffering as well as that of his loved ones a few months earlier than would happen naturally" (paragraph 7).

## The End

The final two paragraphs (8 and 9) make up the end of Fensterman's piece. Here he returns to the present tense and to his request for open-mindedness. Even after all the anguish he has undergone and the hardship no doubt assumed by his loved ones, Fensterman surprisingly announces that he "would not now choose physician-assisted suicide if it were available." That statement makes even stronger his appeal that "an enlightened society . . . allow the incurably ill to choose a merciful death." At the end of paragraph 9, he shifts to a powerful personal appeal, asking those who might be opposed to physician-assisted suicide to "walk a mile in the shoes of those to whom you would deny this choice." And he concludes with a reminder that he is wearing shoes that could one day "be on your feet or those of someone you care deeply about."

# Analyzing the Narrative Features

**The writer's narrative dramatizes a controversial issue.** In the opening paragraph of Fensterman's piece, he cites the topic he will ultimately be addressing through his narrative argument, namely, the recent U.S. Supreme Court's decision to let stand Oregon's law permitting physician-assisted suicide. But his focus is a plea for open-minded debate, informed by an appreciation of the experience of a person suffering with a terminal illness. He recognizes that the passage of this law will provoke debate about the rightness or wrongness of physician-assisted suicide. But he wants to argue that one should be acutely aware of the feelings and circumstances of patients suffering a terminal illness before denying them the right to end their lives through physician-assisted suicide.

**The writer's narration is credible.** Fensterman's narrative is highly credible. In paragraph 2, he forthrightly identifies himself and his plight: "I am approaching 50, recently remarried, and the father of a terrific 13-year-old young man. By every measure I enjoy a wonderful life. Or at least I did until April 2004, when I was diagnosed with kidney cancer." He is an ordinary man, leading an ordinary life, and grateful for ordinary things. However, like everyone else's, his life is fragile, and it nearly crashed down around him when he was diagnosed with cancer. This is a situation everyone can identify with and one everyone secretly fears. At the same time, anyone who knows of the ravages of cancer or knows someone who has suffered from it can identify intensely with the piece.

**The writer's narrative is representative of the issue.** Fensterman's narrative could not be more representative of the issue. His reflection on the various stages of cancer diagnosis and treatment represent what so many people go through. In paragraph 3, he says that he recognizes that "Life may be the most intense addiction on earth. From the moment I first heard the words 'you have cancer' and again when I was told that it was spreading out of control, I recognized my addiction to life almost at the cellular level." He acknowledges the physical toll the disease takes: "I have a few scars, have lost 50 pounds, and my hair is thinner. I rely on oxygen nearly all the time, can no longer perform the tasks I love. . . . Simply leaving home has become an enormous task" (paragraph 5). The specific details reflect what many cancer victims feel. He also acknowledges the burden of his illness on those he loves: "While they have cared for me with great love and selflessness, I cannot abide how my illness has caused them hardship, in some cases dominating their lives and delaying their healing" (paragraph 6). Such a painful sentiment can be widely shared.

**The writer's narrative avoids sentimentality.** A subject such as imminent death is difficult to discuss without being emotional. Yet Fensterman manages to do just that while avoiding sentimentality. He is straightforward in his description of his own physical and emotional suffering. And in the proclamation that concludes the various stages he has gone through he dispassionately states, "Perhaps the biggest and most

## Checklist for Writing a Narrative Argument

- Does your narrative dramatize a controversial issue?
- Is your narrative credible?
- Is your narrative representative of the issue?
- Does your narrative avoid sentimentality?
- Does your narrative advocate a change of behavior or a way of thinking?

profound change I have undergone is that my addiction to life has been 'cured.' I've kicked the habit" (paragraph 7).

**The writer's narrative advocates a change of behavior or a way of thinking.** Clearly, Fensterman has used the story of his personal struggle with cancer to influence the debate over the appropriateness of physician-assisted suicide. Every aspect of his narrative does that—from the diagnosis of the disease (paragraph 2), to his awareness of the toll cancer treatment is taking on his body and on the family and friends he loves (paragraphs 4, 5, and 6), to his realization that "I now know how a feeling, loving, rational person could choose death over life, could choose to relieve his suffering as well as that of his loved ones a few months earlier than would happen naturally." Although he admits that he personally would not choose physician-assisted suicide, the entire point of his narrative is to illustrate that in the face of terminal suffering a person should have a choice. As he so powerfully concludes, "If you oppose physician-assisted suicide, first try to walk a mile in the shoes of those whom you would deny this choice. For as surely as I'm now wearing them, they could one day just as easily be on your feet or those of someone you care about deeply" (paragraph 9).

## EXERCISES

1. Look online or in current issues of a local or national newspaper for essays about controversial issues. Make a list in your journal of the strategies different writers use to begin their arguments. Bring your examples to class and work in a group to share your findings. Photocopy your examples so that each member has a "catalogue" of good introductions to consider.

2. Repeat exercise 1, but this time collect examples of conclusions from argument essays. Your goal here is to compile a catalogue of endings to consult.

3. Construct a formal outline for one of the essays other than "Indian Bones" in this chapter. Compare it with another student's. If there are places where your outlines differ, analyze how your readings are different.

4. Go back to the examples you found for exercise 1. Divide the essays you and the members of your group found into position and proposal arguments.

5. In your journal, respond to the ideas in Amanda Collins's, Sean Flynn's, or Jerry Fensterman's essay. With which of their reasons do you agree? How would you refute any of their reasons? Make a pro/con checklist that lists their reasons and points you might use to debate them.

6. Through the Internet or your library resources, do some reading on either Karpati's or Fensterman's subject to find out how others view the issue. Create a dialogue among the various positions on the issue and explore their points of view to find common or shared concerns or values. With this knowledge, deliberate about how you stand on the issue.

7. If you were to write an argument essay of your own on either subject, how would you begin your essay? Experiment with a few introductions. Next, write a first draft.

8. Write a narrative argument on some debatable issue with which you have had personal experience.

# Using Evidence:
# Thinking Like an Advocate

Because the United States is a democracy, a widespread conviction in our society holds that having opinions is our responsibility as citizens—a conviction supported by our fast-forward multimedia culture. You see opinions expressed on the nightly news every time a reporter sticks a microphone in the face of somebody on the street, or whenever Oprah Winfrey moves into the studio audience. It's the heart of talk radio and television programs. In newspapers and magazines, it comes in the form of "opinion polls" that tally up our positions on all sorts of weighty issues:

"Should the use of marijuana for medical purposes be legalized?"

"Is the economy this year in better shape than it was last year at this time?"

"Do you think that the American judicial system treats people equally whether they are rich or poor?"

"Is the U.S. government doing enough to prevent acts of domestic terrorism?"

"Do men and women have the same opportunities for promotions and raises in the workplace?"

"Should openly gay men and women be allowed to serve in the U.S. military?"

All this on-the-spot opinion-making encourages people to take an immediate stand on an issue, whether or not they have sufficient understanding and information about it. However, holding an opinion on a matter does not necessarily mean that you have investigated the issue or that you have carefully considered the views of others or that you have gathered enough information to support your position. If you want to make successful arguments, you need more than a gut reaction or simple reliance on yourself for the "truth."

This means thinking of yourself as an *advocate*—a prosecutor or defense attorney, if you like. You need a case to present to the jury of your readers, one that convinces them that your interpretation of an issue is plausible. Like an advocate, when you're constructing an argument you look for support to put before your readers: facts, statistics, people's experiences—in a word, *evidence*. The jury judges your argument both on the evidence you bring forth and on your interpretation of that evidence. So, like an advocate, to write successful arguments you need to understand and weigh the value of the *supporting evidence* for your case.

# How Much Evidence Is Enough?

Like any advocate, you need to decide *how much* evidence to present to your readers. Your decision will vary from case to case, although with more practice you'll find it easier to make a judgment. Common sense is a good predictor: If the evidence is enough to persuade you, it's probably enough to persuade like-minded readers. Unsympathetic readers may need more proof. The more unexpected or unorthodox your claim, the more evidence you need to convince skeptical readers. It's often as much a case of the *right* evidence as it is the *right amount* of evidence. One fact or statistic, if it touches on your readers' most valued standards and principles, may be enough to swing an argument for a particular group. Here's where outlining (Chapter 5) can help; an outline helps you make sure you present evidence for every assertion you make.

It's easier to gather too much evidence and winnow out the least effective than to have too little and try to expand it. One of our instructors used to call this the "Cecil B. DeMille strategy," after the great Hollywood producer. DeMille's theory was that if audiences were impressed by five dancers, they would be overwhelmed by five hundred—but just to be sure, he'd hire a thousand. That's a good strategy to have when writing arguments; you can always use a sentence such as "Of the 116 explosions in GMC trucks with side-mounted fuel tanks, four cases are most frequently cited" and then go on to discuss those four. You've let your readers know that another 112 are on record so they can weigh this fact when considering the four you examine in particular. You may never need a thousand pieces of evidence—or dancers—in an argument, but there's no harm in thinking big!

# Why Arguments Need Supporting Evidence

**Evidence** is composed of facts and their interpretations. As we said in Chapter 1, facts are pieces of information that can be verified—that is, statistics, examples, testimony, historical details. For instance, it is a fact that SAT verbal scores across the nation have gone up for the last ten years. One interpretation might be that students today are spending more time reading and less time watching television than students in the last decade. Another interpretation might be that secondary schools are putting more emphasis on language skills. A third might be that changes in the test or the prevalence of test-preparation courses has contributed to the higher scores.

In everyday conversation, we make claims without offering supporting evidence: "Poverty is the reason why there is so much crime"; "The president is doing a poor job handling the economy"; "Foreign cars are better than American cars." Although we may have good reasons to back up such statements, we're not often called upon to do so, at least not in casual conversation. In written arguments, however, presenting evidence is critical, and a failure to do so is glaring. Without supporting data and examples, an argument is hollow. It will bore the reader, fail to convince, and collapse under criticism. Moreover, you'll be in danger of making a hasty generalization by drawing a conclusion with too little evidence. Consider the following paragraph:

> Video games are a danger to the mental well-being of children. Some children play video games for hours on end, and the result is that their behavior and concentration are greatly affected. Many of them display bad behavior. Others have difficulty doing

other, more important things. Parents with young children should be stricter about what video games their children play and how long they play them.

Chances are this paragraph has not convinced you that video games are a threat to children. The sample lacks the details that might persuade you. For instance, exactly what kind of bad behavior do children display? And what specific video games out of the hundreds on the market are the real culprits? How is concentration actually affected? What "more important things" does the author mean? And how many hours of video consumption need occur before signs of dangerous behavior begin to manifest themselves?

Consider how much sharper and more persuasive the following rewrite is with the addition of specific details, facts, and examples:

> Video games may be fun for children, but they can have detrimental effects on their behavior. They encourage violent behavior. A steady dose of some of the more violent games clearly results in more aggressive behavior. One study by the Department of Psychology at State University has shown that after two hours of "Urban Guerrilla," 60 percent of the 12 boys and 20 percent of the 12 girls tested began to mimic the street-fighting gestures—punching, kicking, karate-chopping each other. The study has also shown that such games negatively affect concentration. Even half an hour after their game playing had lapsed, the boys had difficulty settling down to read or draw. Since my parents restricted my little brother's game playing to weekends, he concentrates when completing his homework and has fewer fights with his best friend.

The statistics from the academic study, as well as the concrete case of the writer's own brother, give readers something substantial to consider. Presenting supporting evidence puts meat on the bones of your argument. (In Chapter 9, we will go into greater depth about how to gather research evidence, particularly from the library and the Internet.)

# Forms of Evidence

We hope that when you begin to develop an argument, you utilize debate, dialogue, and deliberation, as we suggested in Chapter 1. As you do this, you need to expand and deepen your understanding of the issue by collecting useful evidence from both sides of the issue. Don't neglect this critical step: Remember, the bulk of your argument is composed of material supporting your claim.

Writers enlist four basic kinds of evidence to support their arguments: personal experience (theirs and others'), outside authorities, factual references and examples, and statistics. We'll examine each separately, but you'll probably want to use combinations of these kinds of evidence when building your arguments in order to convince a wide range of readers.

## Personal Experience—Yours and Others'

The power of personal testimony cannot be underestimated. Think of the number of movies that have failed at the box office in spite of huge and expensive ad campaigns simply because word of mouth trashed it. Or, conversely, think of the number of times you've read a book on the recommendation of friends—or taken a certain course or shopped at a particular store. You might have chosen the college you're attending based on the recommendation of someone you know. Many people find the word-of-mouth judgments that make up personal testimony the most persuasive kind of evidence.

In written arguments, the personal testimony of other people is used to affirm facts and support your claim. Essentially, their experiences provide you with eyewitness accounts of events that are not available to you. Such accounts may prove crucial in winning over an audience. Suppose you are writing about the rising abuse of alcohol among college students. In addition to statistics and hard facts, your argument can gain strength from quoting the experience of a first-year student who nearly died one night from alcohol poisoning. Or, in an essay decrying discrimination against minorities in hiring, consider the authenticity provided by an interview of neighborhood residents who felt they were passed over for a job because of race or ethnic identity.

Your own eyewitness testimony can be a powerful tool of persuasion. Suppose, for example, that you are writing a paper in which you argue that the big teaching hospital in the city provides far better care and has a lower death rate than the small rural hospital in your town. The hard facts and statistics on the quality of care and comparative mortality rates you provide will certainly have a stark persuasiveness. But consider the dramatic impact on those figures were you to recount how your own trip to the rural emergency room nearly cost you your life because of understaffing or the lack of critical but expensive diagnostic equipment.

Personal observation is useful and valuable in arguments. However, you should be careful not to draw hasty generalizations from such testimony. The fact that you and three of your friends are staunchly in favor of replacing letter grades with a pass/fail system does not support the claim that the entire student body at your school is in favor of the conversion. You need a much greater sample. Likewise, the dislike most people in your class feel for a certain professor does not justify the claim that the university tenure system should be abolished. On such complex issues, you need more than personal testimony to make a case.

You also have to remember the "multiple-perspective" rule. As any police officer can tell you, there are as many versions of the "truth" of an incident as there are people who saw it. The people involved in a car accident see it one way (or more), yet witnesses in a car heading in the other direction may interpret events differently, as will people in an apartment six stories above the street on which the accident took place. Your job is to sort out the different testimonies and make sense of them. Personal experience—yours and that of people you know—is valuable. However, on major issues you need statistics and data, as well as the evidence provided by outside authorities. But before we turn to outside authorities here is an example of a position argument based on personal experience.

This position argument, based on personal experience, is written by Kari Peterson, an English major at the University of Hawaii in Honolulu. Here she argues for healthcare reform, using her own personal experience to make a convincing case for needed changes in coverage so that people of student age, like her, can get proper care without going into stifling debt.

Kari Peterson
Professor Larson
English 101
1 December 2009

The Statistics Speak: A Real Person's
Argument for Universal Healthcare

1     The room's walls are antiseptic white. Everything is white—the cold tiles, the thin sheets, the drawn blinds on the only window in the small space. It's 2:35 in the morning or so the clock says. Time here feels fluid and neverending. My left arm throbs. No, it screams at me, echoing from the bicep through the shoulder and deep into my chest cavity. The catheter runs all the way to my heart like some strange alien. It hurts so badly that I wish it would just rip itself out in spectacular fashion as in movies. But this is a man-made alien, pumping me full of lifesaving antibiotics. These drugs have cruel tendencies also, making my stomach do repetitious back flips and my joints ache. I press the call button and beg for painkillers.

2     But the night nurse tells me she couldn't reach the physician. Later she asks if I know whether or not the morphine will be covered by my insurance carrier. I am ready to sell my soul at this point for relief. What's a few hundred dollars? The nurse asks, "Is Tylenol okay?" I try not to yell and tell her calmly no.

3     I am only twenty-two years old. I should be looking to the future, not prophesying its imminent end. That's hard to do when you're in a place where people so often go to die. This will be my reality for the next fourteen or more days. I may repeat it several times a year. Ironically, equally difficult is dealing with a hospitalization's aftermath of bureaucratic hassles and with a healthcare system unable or unwilling to offer the care I need.

4     I have Cystic Fibrosis. In the simplest of terms it is a congenital disease marked by recurring respiratory infection, pancreatic difficulties, a tendency towards the development of sinusitis and diabetes, and premature death. Unfortunately my condition is shared by 30,000 other Americans—most of whom are children and young adults because most CF patients do not survive into middle age. While I will always struggle with this disease, the healthcare system as it exists now is not sufficient or beneficial to me.

5     The United States is the only Western industrialized nation that has not implemented a universal healthcare system of some kind. On a per capita basis, United States citizens pay more than anyone else for healthcare. In terms of quality, the US is globally ranked an appalling 23rd in infant mortality and for overall

healthcare 37th, according to the World Health Organization. So why is our healthcare so expensive and yet so abysmal in relative quality? Privatized insurance is one of the major culprits.

6    I currently rely on private insurance for my medical coverage under my parents' carrier as their dependent. I am able to do so as long as I maintain a full-time student status or until I turn 25. My 25th birthday present will be the sudden anxiety of potentially losing my health insurance. I will be able to attain insurance if I am hired by a company that offers benefits and if I survive the usual 90-day probationary period that most employers implement. Alternatively, I may also purchase private insurance. My circumstance is mired in caveats and catch 22s. Most 90-day probationary periods do not allow for sick leave, and I am likely to become ill in that 3-month window.  I also may not be able to purchase private insurance because many providers have "pre-existing condition clauses" in their policies. These clauses are essentially a way of eliminating sick people from eating into company profits. Insurance carriers make more money if they don't have to render services and even more if they can jack up premiums simultaneously. Without health insurance, my medical costs are thousands of dollars per month even when I am "healthy." Every E.R. trip is a couple of thousand more, and hospital admissions can easily exceed twenty thousand when everything is totaled up. I would like for my parents to be able to keep our home.

7    Without insurance or an executive's income, I am left with one final option at my disposal. Assuming my health is poor enough to qualify, I can go on disability. It probably seems like such an obvious solution. From my vantage point, however, it looks like a bandage proposed as a remedy for a gunshot wound. To be eligible for disability, I would no longer be able to attend university or earn an annual income that exceeds $12,000 a year. My medications would be covered by Medicare, except for the two most critical for stabilizing my condition. Coincidentally, these are the two most expensive medications I take. Lastly there are emotional ramifications. No one wants to be labeled by the thing they hate most. No one wants to forget their life's ambitions. No one wants to be thought of as useless or worse. It's sad, but the prevailing attitude in America seems to be that somehow sick people are secondary citizens often deserving of their sad conditions.

8    The universal healthcare bill being proposed in the fall of 2009 would establish insurance legislation that prohibits "cherry picking"–i.e., the pre-existing condition clauses–as well as offer a public option to compete with the private sector. Universal healthcare does not mean that people would have to give up their

Peterson 3

current care if they are satisfied with it. In many ways, the bill functions as a simple means of breaking up the insurance monopoly. To compete with the government, insurance companies would have to lower premiums or simply offer high quality care. It will not put them out of business.

9     Finally, the ideology that is used as an arsenal against a universal healthcare system is so unequivocally un-American it must be addressed. The preamble to the United States Constitution states, "We the People of the United States, in Order to form a more perfect Union, establish Justice, insure domestic Tranquility, provide for the common defense, promote the general Welfare, and secure the Blessings of Liberty to ourselves and our Posterity."

10     Universal healthcare is not a handout to the undeserving. It is not unpatriotic. It is not unprecedented by the founding principles this nation holds true. It is, however, a matter of leveling the playing field and offering all persons equal opportunity to make the most of their destinies. It doesn't get any more American than that.

Peterson 4

Works Cited

"The World Health Organization's ranking of the world's health systems." 2007. Web. 2 Nov. 2009. <Theodora.http//www.geographic.org>

## Outside Authorities

Think of the number of times you've heard statements such as these:

"Scientists have found that . . ."

"Scholars inform us that . . ."

"According to his biographer, President Lincoln decided that . . ."

What these statements have in common is the appeal to outside authorities—people recognized as experts in a given field, people who can speak knowledgeably about a subject. Because authoritative opinions are such powerful tools of persuasion, you hear them all the time in advertisements. Automobile manufacturers quote the opinions of professional race car drivers; the makers of toothpaste cite dentists' claims; famous basketball players push brand-name sneakers all the time. Similarly, a good trial lawyer will almost always rely on forensic experts or other such authorities to help sway a jury.

Outside authorities can provide convincing evidence to support your ideas. However, there are times when expert opinion can be used inappropriately. This faulty use of authority can undermine the effectiveness of your argument. For the most part, experts usually try to be objective and fair-minded when asked for opinions. But, an expert with a vested interest in an issue might slant the testimony in his or her favor. The dentist who has just purchased a huge number of shares in a new toothpaste company would not be an unbiased expert. You wouldn't turn for an unbiased opinion on lung cancer to scientists working for tobacco companies, or ask an employee facing the loss of his or her job to comment on the advisability of layoffs. When you cite authorities, you should be careful to note any possibility of bias so your readers can fairly weigh the contributions. (This is often done through *attribution*; see Chapter 9.) Knowing that Professor Brown's research will benefit from construction of the supercollider doesn't make her enthusiasm for its other potential benefits less credible, but it does help your readers see her contributions to your argument in their proper context.

You should also check the credentials of those experts you are citing as evidence. Certainly claims supported by the research of reliable authorities in the field can add to the validity of your argument. But research is often debated, and evidence often disputed. So you should evaluate the credentials of the expert or experts who conducted the studies— what organizations, institutions, and universities they are affiliated with; their educational background; the books and/or journals where they may have published their results. It would also be wise to familiarize yourself with the actual research to be certain that it looks like valid and convincing support for your argument.

Another faulty use of authority is the use of an expert to provide evidence in a subject area in which he or she possesses no expertise. If you are going to cite authorities, you must make sure that they are competent; they should have expertise in their fields. You wouldn't turn to a professional beekeeper for opinions on laser surgery any more than you would quote a civil engineer on macroeconomic theory. And yet, just that is done all the time in advertising. Although it makes better sense to ask a veterinarian for a professional opinion about what to feed your pet, advertisers hire known actors to push dog food (as well as yogurt and skin cream). Of course, in advertising, celebrity sells. But that's not the case in most written arguments. It would not impress a critical reader to cite Tom Cruise's views on the use of fetal tissue or the greenhouse effect. Again, think about the profile of your audience. Whose expertise would they respect on your topic? Those are the experts to cite.

## Factual References and Examples

Facts do as much to inform as they do to persuade, as we mentioned in Chapter 1. If somebody wants to sell you something, they'll pour on the details. For instance, ask the used car salesperson about that black 2008 Ford Explorer in the lot and he or she will hold forth about what a "creampuff" it is: only 18,400 original miles, mint condition, five-speed transmission with overdrive, all-black leather interior, and loaded—AC, power brakes, cruise control, CD player, premium sound system, captain's chair, and so on. Or listen to how the cereal manufacturers inform you that their toasted Os now contain "all-natural oat bran, which has been found to prevent cancer." Information is not always neutral. The very selection process implies intent. By offering specific facts or examples about your claim, you can make a persuasive argument.

The strategy in using facts and examples is to get readers so absorbed in the information that they nearly forget they are being persuaded to buy or do something. So common is this strategy in television ads that some have been given the name "infomercials"—ads that give the impression of being a documentary on the benefits of a product. For instance, you might be familiar with the margarine commercial narrated by a man who announces that at 33 years of age he had a heart attack. He then recounts the advice of his doctor for avoiding coronary disease, beginning with the need for exercise and climaxing with the warning about cutting down on cholesterol. Not until the very end of the ad does the narrator inform us that, taking advantage of his second chance, the speaker has switched to a particular brand of margarine, which, of course, is cholesterol free.

In less blatant form, this "informational" strategy can be found in newspaper columns and editorials, where authors give the impression that they are simply presenting the facts surrounding particular issues when in reality they may be attempting to persuade readers to see things their way. For instance, suppose in an apparently objective commentary a writer discusses how history is replete with people wrongfully executed for first-degree murder. Throughout the piece, the author cites several specific cases in which it was learned too late that the defendant had been framed or that the real killer had confessed. On the surface, the piece may appear to be simply presenting historical facts, but the more subtle intention may be to convince people that capital punishment is morally wrong. The old tagline from *Dragnet,* "Just the facts, ma'am," isn't quite the whole picture. How those facts are used is also part of their persuasive impact.

Often facts and examples are used to establish cause-and-effect relationships. It's very important, when both writing and reading arguments, to test the links the facts forge. While one event may indeed follow another, you can't automatically assume a causal relationship. This can result in a logical fallacy, in this case post hoc, ergo propter hoc. For instance, it may rain the day after every launch of the space shuttle, but does that prove that shuttle launches affect the weather in Florida? Similarly, we are all familiar with politicians who claim credit for improvements in the economy that have little to do with the legislation they have proposed. They hope to gain votes by having the public believe that there is a direct causal relationship between their actions and the economic improvement. Often this strategy backfires when opponents point out the lack of any actual connection.

Sometimes even experts disagree; one might see the rise in prostate cancer rates for vasectomy patients as reason to abolish the surgery; another might point to other contributing causes (diet, lack of exercise, hormonal imbalance). If you don't have the expertise to determine which of the conflicting experts is correct, you'll probably decide based on the *weight of the evidence*—whichever side has the most people or the most plausible reasons supporting it. This, in fact, is how most juries decide cases.

## Statistics

People are impressed by numbers. Saying that 77 percent of the student body at your school supports a woman's right to choose is far more persuasive than saying that a lot of people on campus are pro-choice. **Statistics** have a special no-nonsense authority. Batting averages, medical statistics, polling results (election and otherwise), economic indicators, the stock market index, unemployment figures, scientific ratings, FBI statistics, percentages, demographic data—they all are reported in numbers. If they're accurate, statistics are difficult to argue against, though a skillful manipulator can use them to mislead.

The demand for statistics has made market research a huge business in America. During an election year, weekly and daily results on voters' opinions of candidates are released from various news organizations and TV networks, as well as independent polling companies such as the Harris and Gallup organizations. Most of the brand-name products you buy, the TV shows and movies you watch, or the CDs you listen to were made available after somebody did test studies on sample populations to determine the potential success of these items. Those same statistics are then used in promotional ads. Think of the number of times you've heard claims such as these:

"Nine out of ten doctors recommend Zappo aspirin over any other brand."

"Our new Speed King copier turns out 24 percent more copies per minute."

"Sixty-eight percent of those polled approve of women in military combat roles."

Of course, these claims bear further examination. If you polled only ten doctors, nine of whom recommended Zappo, that's not a big enough sample to imply that 90 percent of *all* doctors do. To avoid drawing a hasty generalization from too small a sample, avoid using sweeping words such as *all, always, never,* or *none.* Either be straightforward about the statistics supporting your claim or limit your claim with qualifiers such as *some, many, often,* or *few.* As Mark Twain once observed, "There are lies, damned lies, and statistics."

Numbers don't lie, but they can be manipulated. Sometimes, to sway an audience, claim makers will cite figures that are inaccurate or dated, or they will intentionally misuse accurate figures to make a case. If, for instance, somebody claims that 139 students and professors protested the invitation of a certain controversial guest to your campus, it would be a distortion of the truth not to mention that another 1,500 attended the talk and gave the speaker a standing ovation. Providing only those numbers or statistics that support the writer's claim and ignoring or concealing figures that might indicate otherwise is one way of stacking the deck. While this practice might deceive—at least temporarily—an uninformed audience, the writer risks damaging his or her credibility once the true figures are revealed.

Be on guard for the misleading use of statistics, a technique used all too frequently in advertising. The manufacturer that claims its flaked corn cereal is 100 percent cholesterol free misleads the public because no breakfast cereal of any brand contains cholesterol (which is found only in animal fats). French fries prepared in pure vegetable oil are also cholesterol free, but that doesn't mean that they're the best food for your health. Manufacturers that use terms like *cholesterol-free, light*, and *low fat* are trying to get you to buy their products without really revealing the basis for their nutritional claims. Although it's tempting to use such crowd-pleasing statistics, it's a good idea to avoid them in your own arguments because they are deceptive. If your readers discover your deception, your chances of persuading them to accept your position or proposal become unlikely.

# Different Interpretations of Evidence

As we already said, evidence consists of solid facts, scientific studies and data, historical analysis, statistics, quotations from accepted authorities, and pertinent examples, as well as personal narratives that your audience will find relevant and compelling.

But not all evidence is of equal worth or value; not all evidence makes an argument valid. And not all scientific facts have a single interpretation. This is why different people can look at the same scientific data and have completely different interpretations. Although they may not argue over facts or the data, they will strenuously debate the interpretations of facts. In fact, some of the most hotly contested issues in society and politics revolve around the interpretation of the evidence. And the reason that people disagree about interpretation is that people hold fundamental differences in underlying beliefs, values, and assumptions.

## Different Definitions

People will disagree based on different definitions of terms and concepts. If your parents say to be home at a "reasonable" hour, does that mean 11 P.M. or 2 A.M.? What might be deemed "reasonable" to your parents may not be the same to you, especially if you showed up at 3 A.M. But if they specified to be home no later than 1 A.M., then you have precision, which means a 3 A.M. arrival would not be "reasonable."

The point is that arguments over the definition of a subjective term such as "reasonable" will never resolve the argument. The same is true when critics declare that this book or movie is the "best of the year." There will always be dissenters, even people who may think the selection or award winner was far worse than its competition. Criteria differ from person to person. For instance, what is "violent" to a 16-year-old video game fan is not the same as what is violent to an acknowledged pacifist. What is pornography to some is erotic art to others. In fact, for decades the U.S. Supreme Court could not come up with a clear definition of *pornography* in order to determine laws and regulations and eventually gave up, deciding that any regulation of such—with the exception of child pornography, which is prohibited under law—was an infringement on rights of free speech. Such avoidance by the courts essentially freed itself from the decades-long trap of word play.

The point is that language is relative; it is difficult for people to agree completely on the definition of any complex word. And adding to their complexity are the different connotations of words—connotations that signal different emotional reactions in an audience. Consider such charged words as "evil," "racist," "liberal," "Nazi," "religious extremist," even "terrorist." Often arguments are made in which such terms are employed beyond their dictionary definitions for the purpose of arousing strong reactions. With the proper audience, the effect can be powerful.

## Different Interpretations of Tradition and Past Authority

It can be said that evidence sometimes lies in the eyes of the beholder. That is, what is evidence to some people may not be evidence to others. The reason is that writers often appeal to authority and traditions that for them have special weight. This is especially evident in arguments based on moral values and beliefs, such as those regarding the death penalty, euthanasia, abortion, same-sex marriages, and animal rights. Such appeals may be persuasive to those who believe in the authority of tradition, but not persuasive to others who don't share in those beliefs.

Sometimes people will claim that something is right because it has always been practiced. Consider, for instance, the following statements:

"When we were kids, we walked to school. So, you're not taking the car."

"Women have always taken their husband's last name in marriage, so why should we change now?"

"The ancient Greeks and Romans practiced euthanasia in order to end a patient's unnecessary suffering, so why shouldn't we?"

Each of these claims is a familiar appeal to tradition. Of course, such appeals raise the question that because something is an old practice does not necessarily mean it should be continued today. The logical fallacy is that behavior is never necessarily right simply because it has always been done.

Tradition is often used as evidence of a higher authority. But even such a fixed piece of evidence can actually be interpreted in different ways by different audiences as different sets of beliefs and assumptions may prevail. For instance, the dominant argument against gun control is the Second Amendment of the U.S. Constitution guarantee: "A well regulated militia, being necessary to the security of a free state, the right of the people to keep and bear arms, shall not be infringed." For the National Rifle Association and others, those words represent the highest legal authority in preserving and protecting the rights of law-abiding citizens to have guns in our American democracy. If your audience is highly traditional and interprets the Second Amendment straightforwardly, this is an argument to which they would be open. But another audience might reject that strict interpretation. That audience might not question people's right to bear arms but the interpretation of that amendment regarding the regulation of guns. While many people would agree that hunters, sportspeople, and collectors have the right to own guns, nearly everybody would argue that the Second Amendment does not give individuals the unlimited right to own any weapons they like. And that is where the debates become heated—on the question of just how much governmental restriction is too much. When tackling controversial issues, you must be aware of your audience's attitude toward your evidence.

Similarly, the First Amendment is often enlisted as the highest authority regarding an individual's right to free speech in America. But like gun control, that right is limited by the court's interpretation. In the eyes of the law, you cannot intentionally publish lies about a public figure, claiming, for instance, that a local politician sells illegal drugs on the side. Such a claim is libelous and an abridgment of your free-speech rights—and, of course, grounds for a lawsuit. Nor, in the eyes of the law, can you get away with crying "Fire!" in a crowded theater if there is no fire, because the ensuing panic could lead to injury.

While there are some restraints on the rights to free speech, the powerful First Amendment has been invoked to protect flag burning, nude dancing, Internet pornography, Nazi party parades, and Ku Klux Klan rants, to varying degrees of success. And although such claims may seem to undermine the guarantee by protecting dubious and malicious intentions, restriction of the principle could give way to even greater dangers—the tyrannical abuse by government. In several other free and democratic societies, censorship laws empower governments legally to prohibit certain kinds of speech that are protected by the U.S. Constitution.

Religious tradition is another powerful authority that is invoked in arguments about major social issues. References to Biblical or Koranic prohibitions are often presented as evidence against arguments in favor of certain public practices. For instance, consider same-sex marriages. Because of scriptural laws against homosexuality, many people argue that gay and lesbian couples should not be allowed to wed under the eyes of the law. The same is true regarding capital punishment. The Sixth Commandment from the Old Testament of the Bible says, "Thou shall not kill." For years, people opposed to legalized abortion have employed such "evidence." The same Sixth Commandment has also been referenced by others in opposition to capital punishment and euthanasia. But the problem with strict appeal to such authority for evidence is that, like tradition, interpretation of religious taboos can be ambiguous and contradictory. For instance, the Old Testament of the Bible also argues, "An eye for an eye, and a tooth for a tooth"—thus, "evidence" that can be enlisted in an argument in favor of the death penalty. Once again, familiarity with your audience should help you determine just the kind of authority and tradition you enlist as evidence. If, for instance, you knew you were addressing religiously conservative readers, summoning the moral import of the scriptures could be very persuasive on some of these public issues.

## Different Interpretations of Scientific Data

As we said earlier, scientific data is a persuasive form of evidence. In fact, in most arguments scientific evidence is universally perceived as valid and acceptable. But not everybody interprets scientific evidence in the same way, nor do they draw the same conclusions. For example, one of the most talked about issues of our times is global warming. Over the last several decades, scientific data point to rising average temperatures of the earth's atmosphere and oceans. The data also cite the rise in carbon dioxide in the atmosphere, one of the components of the so-called "greenhouse gas." These are the hard facts. Many scientists have looked at the data and determined that there is a direct relationship—namely, that the rise in $CO_2$ has caused the rise in oceanic and atmospheric temperatures; they blame the effect on human consumption of fossil fuels. These scientists warn that unless something drastic is done, the world's weather will change for the worse for many populated areas, while polar caps will continue to melt and raise sea levels to catastrophic proportions, leading to global coastal flooding.

However, not everybody draws the same conclusion from the data. Not everybody blames the global warming phenomenon on human activity. Nor do they warn of catastrophic climate changes and serious effects on life. Nor do they offer the same political responses. In the following article, scientist Siegfried Frederick Singer responds to the alarms of many, including former vice president Al Gore, narrator of the Academy Award-winning movie, *An Inconvenient Truth*, and author of the book of the same title, and winner of the 2008 Nobel Peace Prize for his work on behalf of the environment.

# The Great Global Warming Swindle

*S. Fred Singer*

Singer, an atmospheric physicist, is a research fellow at the Independent Institute, is Professor Emeritus of Environmental Sciences at the University of Virginia, and is a former founding director of the U.S. Weather Satellite Service. He is author of *Hot Talk, Cold Science: Global Warming's Unfinished Debate* (The Independent Institute, 1997). This article appeared on May 22, 2007, in the *San Francisco Examiner.*

1   Al Gore's *An Inconvenient Truth* has met its match: a devastating documentary recently shown on British television, which has now been viewed by millions of people on the Internet. Despite its flamboyant title, *The Great Global Warming Swindle* is based on sound science and interviews with real climate scientists, including me. *An Inconvenient Truth*, on the other hand, is mostly an emotional presentation from a single politician.

2   The scientific arguments presented in *The Great Global Warming Swindle* can be stated quite briefly:

3   1. There is *no* proof that the current warming is caused by the rise of greenhouse gases from human activity. Ice core records from the past 650,000 years show that temperature increases have *preceded—not resulted from—*increases in $CO_2$ by hundreds of years, suggesting that the warming of the oceans is an important *source* of the rise in atmospheric $CO_2$. As the dominant greenhouse gas, water vapor is far, far more important than $CO_2$. Dire predictions of future warming are based almost entirely on computer climate models, yet these models do not accurately understand the role of water vapor—and, in any case, water vapor is not within our control. Plus, computer models cannot account for the observed cooling of much of the past century (1940–75), nor for the observed *patterns* of warming—what we call the "fingerprints." For example, the Antarctic is cooling while models predict warming. And where the models call for the middle atmosphere to warm faster than the surface, the observations show the exact opposite.

4       The best evidence supporting natural causes of temperature fluctuations are the changes in cloudiness, which correspond strongly with regular variations in solar activity. The current warming is likely part of a natural cycle of climate warming and cooling that's been traced back almost a million years. It accounts for the Medieval Warm Period around 1100 A.D., when the Vikings settled Greenland and grew crops, and the Little Ice Age, from about 1400 to 1850 A.D., which brought severe winters and cold summers to Europe, with failed harvests, starvation, disease, and general misery. Attempts have been made to claim that the current warming is "unusual" using spurious analysis of tree rings and other proxy data. Advocates have tried to deny the existence of these historic climate swings and claim that the current warming is "unusual" by using spurious analysis of tree rings and other proxy data, resulting in the famous "hockey–stick" temperature graph. The hockey-stick graph has now been thoroughly discredited.

5   2. If the cause of warming is mostly natural, then there is little we can do about it. We cannot control the inconstant sun, the likely origin of most climate variability. None of the schemes for greenhouse gas reduction currently bandied about will do any good; they are all irrelevant, useless, and wildly expensive:

- Control of $CO_2$ emissions, whether by rationing or elaborate cap-and-trade schemes
- Uneconomic "alternative" energy, such as ethanol and the impractical "hydrogen economy"
- Massive installations of wind turbines and solar collectors
- Proposed projects for the sequestration of $CO_2$ from smokestacks or even from the atmosphere

6   Ironically, *even if* $CO_2$ were responsible for the observed warming trend, all these schemes would be ineffective—unless we could persuade every nation, including China, to cut fuel use by 80 percent!

7   3. Finally, no one can show that a warmer climate would produce negative impacts overall. The much-feared rise in sea levels does not seem to depend on short-term temperature changes, as the rate of sea-level increases has been steady since the last ice age, 10,000 years ago. In fact, many economists argue that the opposite is more likely—that warming produces a net benefit, that it increases incomes and standards of living. Why do we assume that the present climate is the optimum? Surely, the chance of this must be vanishingly small, and the economic history of past climate warmings bear this out.

8 But the main message of *The Great Global Warming Swindle* is much broader. Why should we devote our scarce resources to what is essentially a non-problem, and ignore the real problems the world faces: hunger, disease, denial of human rights—not to mention the threats of terrorism and nuclear wars? And are we really prepared to deal with natural disasters; pandemics that can wipe out most of the human race, or even the impact of an asteroid, such as the one that wiped out the dinosaurs? Yet politicians and the elites throughout much of the world prefer to squander our limited resources to fashionable issues, rather than concentrate on real problems. Just consider the scary predictions emanating from supposedly responsible world figures: the chief scientist of Great Britain tells us that unless we insulate our houses and use more efficient light bulbs, the Antarctic will be the only habitable continent by 2100, with a few surviving breeding couples propagating the human race. Seriously!

9   I imagine that in the not-too-distant future all the hype will have died down, particularly if the climate should decide to cool—as it did during much of the past century; we should take note here that it has not warmed since 1998. Future generations will look back on the current madness and wonder what it was all about. They will have movies like *An Inconvenient Truth* and documentaries like *The Great Global Warming Swindle* to remind them.

---

Having read the Singer piece, you can see that the effectiveness of *The Great Global Warming Swindle* rests entirely on a challenge to the validity of the evidence used by those who claim that global warming is caused by greenhouse gases, or emissions due to the burning of fossil fuels. First, Singer discredits these arguments in a general sense, pointing out that they are based on emotion and fear, not on sound science. He then breaks his argument into three parts. In the first, Singer points out that 650,000 years of evidence point to the fact that temperature increases have preceded—not resulted from—increases in $CO_2$ by hundreds of years. He says scientific evidence shows that the warming of oceans accounts for the rise in atmospheric $CO_2$. Singer also questions the validity of computer models, the cornerstone of the evidence offered by the global-warming contingent. He points out that computer models do not take into account the role of warming oceans and their impact on water vapor. He notes the role of solar activity and explains how it accounts for the "Medieval Warm Period" around 1100 A.D. as well as the "Little Ice Age" beginning three hundred years later.

In his second argument, he points out that since global warming is natural, little can be done about it. Arguments to develop alternative fuels are expensive and a large drain on the economy. Finally, he says that the fight against global warming diverts resources that should be used to fight bigger issues such as terrorism, nuclear threats, disease, hunger, and human rights.

Regardless of your own stand on the global warming issue, Singer's essay is an effective example of how evidence is clearly and instructively presented. Refer back to it when you need a model for your own presentation of evidence.

## Some Tips About Supporting Evidence

Because, as argument writers, you'll be using evidence on a routine basis, it will help you to develop a systematic approach to testing the evidence you want to use. Here are some questions to ask yourself about the evidence you enlist in an argument.

### Do You Have a Sufficient Number of Examples to Support Your Claim?

You don't want to jump to conclusions based on too little evidence. Suppose you want to make the case that electric cars would be better for the environment than motor vehicles. If all you offer as evidence is the fact that electric vehicles don't pollute the air, your argument would be somewhat thin. Your argument would be much more convincing if you

### Preview: To Evaluate Supporting Evidence, Ask ...

- Is the evidence sufficient?
- Is the evidence detailed enough?
- Is the evidence relevant?
- Does the evidence fit the claim?
- Is the evidence up-to-date and verifiable?
- Is the evidence appropriate for the audience?
- Is the evidence biased?
- Is the evidence balanced and fairly presented?

offered the following evidence: that in addition to zero emission at the tailpipe—which is good for the atmosphere—electric cars do not use engine fluids or internal combustion parts, all of which constitute wastes that contaminate our landfills and water supplies. Furthermore, because electric vehicles don't use gasoline or oil, the hazards associated with storage of such fluids are eliminated.

Likewise, you should avoid making hasty generalizations based on your own experience as evidence. For instance, if your Acme Airlines flight to Chattanooga was delayed last week, you shouldn't conclude that Acme Airlines always leaves late. However, were you to consult airline industry records to demonstrate that over the last six months 47 percent of the frequent flyers interviewed complained that Acme flights left late, you would have a persuasive case.

## Is Your Evidence Detailed Enough?

The more specific the details, the more persuasive your argument. Instead of generalizations, cite figures, dates, and facts; instead of paraphrases, offer quotations from experts. Remember that your readers are subconsciously saying, "Show me! Prove it!" If you want to tell people how to bake bread, you wouldn't write, "Mix some flour with some yeast and water"; you'd say, "Dissolve one packet of yeast in 1 cup of warm water and let it sit for ten minutes. Then slowly mix in 3 cups of sifted whole wheat flour." Or, as in our electric car example above, instead of simply asserting that there would be none of the fluid or solid wastes associated with internal combustion vehicles, specify that in electric vehicles there would be no motor oil, engine coolants, transmission fluid or filters, spark plugs, ignition wires, and gaskets to end up in landfills. What your readers want are specifics—and that's what you should give them.

## Is Your Evidence Relevant to the Claim You Make or Conclusion You Reach?

Select evidence based on how well it supports the point you are arguing, not on how interesting, novel, or humorous it is or how hard you had to work to find it. Recall that using evidence that is unrelated or irrelevant is a logical fallacy called a non sequitur. For instance, if you are arguing about whether John Lennon was the most influential songwriter in rock-and-roll history, you wouldn't mention that he had two sons or that he owned dairy cattle; those are facts, but they have nothing to do with the influence of his lyrics. Historian Barbara Tuchman relates that in writing *The Guns of August*, she discovered that the Kaiser bought his wife the same birthday present every year: 12 hats of his choosing, which he required her to wear. Tuchman tried to use this detail in Chapter 1, then in Chapter 2, and so on, but was finally obligated to relegate the detail to a stack of notecards marked "Unused." It just didn't fit, even though for her it summarized his stubborn selfishness. (She did work it into a later essay, which is why we know about it.) Learn her lesson: Irrelevant evidence distracts an audience and weakens an argument's persuasive power.

## Does Your Conclusion (or Claim) Exceed the Evidence?

Don't make generalizations about entire groups when your evidence points to select members. Baseball may be the national pastime, but it would be unwise to claim that *all* Americans love baseball. Experience tells you that some Americans prefer football or basketball, while others don't like any sports. Claims that are out of proportion to the evidence can result in a fallacy called the **bandwagon appeal.** The bandwagon appeal suggests to the audience that they should agree with the writer because everyone else does, rather than because the writer has supplied compelling evidence to support the reasons and claim. This is a favorite strategy of advertisers, who work to convince us that we should buy a certain product because everyone else is doing so. While this strategy is in itself fallacious, these salespeople are often unable to produce adequate evidence to support their sweeping claims of nationwide popularity for their product.

## Is Your Evidence Up-to-Date and Verifiable?

You want to be sure that the evidence you enlist isn't so dated or vague that it fails to support your claim. For instance, figures demonstrating an increase in the rate of teen pregnancy will not persuade your audience if the numbers are ten years old. Similarly, it wouldn't be accurate to say that Candidate Nakamura fails to support the American worker because 15 years ago he purchased a foreign car. His recent and current actions are far more relevant.

When you're citing evidence, your readers will expect you to be specific enough for them to verify what you say. A writer supporting animal rights may cite the example of rabbits whose eyes were burned by pharmacological testing, but such tests have been outlawed in the United States for many years. Another writer may point to medical research that appears to abuse its human subjects, but not name the researchers, the place where the testing took place, or the year in which it occurred. The readers have no way of verifying the claim and may become suspicious of the entire argument because the factual claims are so difficult to confirm.

## Is Your Evidence Appropriate for Your Audience?

As discussed in Chapter 3, before you write, it is important to spend some time identifying the audience you will address in your argument. Knowing your audience helps you determine the slant of your argument as well as your language and voice. Likewise, it will influence the evidence you choose to present, the sources of information you use, and the kind of authorities or experts in the field you cite to support your point of view. And that evidence could help make the difference between a convincing argument and one that fails.

Imagine that you are writing an argument against the use of steroids by college students. If you are writing a paper for your biology professor and are discussing the damaging effect of steroids on the body, you would use highly technical evidence—evidence most likely from medical journals aimed at scientists and medical professionals or from your biology textbook. If, however, you are writing an article for your college newspaper, your audience would be your peers, young adults both male and female who may be experimenting or tempted to experiment with steroids. Your focus might be on issues of peer pressure to look good or to succeed in athletics. Therefore the evidence you select might include quotations from known health professionals published in psychology journals or specialized websites, or from newspaper articles addressing the impact of steroids on one's mental and emotional health. Such evidence would not be highly technical.

Let's take another example. Assume that you decided to write a paper arguing that healthier food should be served in your student cafeteria. If you were addressing your peers, the evidence you cite might come from general publications devoted to nutrition or you might quote one of the many health and diet gurus published widely today. Your evidence would be geared to convince your peers that a healthier diet would lead to healthier and trimmer bodies and possibly better frames of mind. In contrast, if your goal was to convince the university's trustees, your argument would focus on the obligation of the university to provide a healthy diet. You might argue that doing so not only enhances the well-being of the student body but also the reputation of the university. And this enhancement translates into more student applications for admission. To support these arguments you would use evidence based on your own personal experience as well as experiences of your peers. Additionally, evidence taken from publications geared to university administrators would be convincing.

Keep in mind that whether your audience is a peer group, a professor, or a college administrator, you must document your evidence—you must let your reader know where you got your support material. You must document the source of any idea you *summarize* or *paraphrase or quote* directly from. The most widely used forms of documentation used in colleges and universities are the Modern Language Association (MLA) style, used widely in the humanities, and the American Psychological Association (APA) style, used widely in the social sciences. These are explained in greater detail in Chapter 9, Researching Arguments.

## Is Your Evidence Slanted?

Sometimes writers select evidence that supports their case while ignoring evidence that does not. Often referred to as stacking the deck, this practice makes for an unfair argument, and one that could be disastrous for the arguer. Even though some of your evidence has merit, your argument will be dismissed if your audience discovers that you slanted or suppressed evidence.

For example, suppose you heard a friend make the following statements: "If I were you, I'd avoid taking a course with Professor Gorman at all costs. He gives surprise quizzes, he assigns 50 pages a night, and he refuses to grade on a curve." Even if these reasons are true, that may not be the whole truth. Suppose you learned that Professor Gorman is, in fact, a very dynamic and talented teacher whose classes successfully stimulate the learning process. By holding back that information, your friend's argument is suspect.

Sometimes writers will take advantage of their readers' lack of information on a topic and offer evidence that really doesn't support their claims. Recently several newspapers reported that a study written up in the *Archives of Internal Medicine* proved that eating nuts prevents heart attacks. According to the study, some thirty thousand Seventh-Day Adventists were asked to rate the frequency with which they ate certain foods. Those claiming to eat nuts five or more times a week reported fewer heart attacks. What the newspapers failed to report was that most Seventh-Day Adventists are vegetarians, and that those who ate more nuts also ate fewer dairy products (which are high in cholesterol and saturated fat, both of which contribute to heart disease) and eggs (also high in cholesterol) than others in the study. Newspapers have failed to report that all the subsequent pro-nut publicity was distributed by a nut growers' association.[1]

It is to your benefit to present all relevant evidence so that you clearly weigh both sides of an issue. As we discussed in Chapter 4, you want to demonstrate to your readers that you have made an effort to consider other perspectives and that your conclusions are fair and balanced. Otherwise your argument might not be taken seriously. Let's return to the argument that electric cars are more beneficial to the environment than cars with

---

[1] Mirkin, Gabe, and Diana Rich. *Fat Free Flavor Full*. Boston: Little, Brown, 1995, 51.

internal combustion engines. Your key evidence is the fact that electric cars do not use petroleum products and various motor parts that contribute to the pollution of air, land, and waterways. If you left your argument at that, you would be guilty of suppressing an important concern regarding electric vehicles: the disposal of the great amounts of lead in the huge electric vehicles' lead-acid batteries and even the lighter lead-carbon alternatives. Failure to acknowledge that opposing point reduces your credibility as a writer. Readers would wonder either about your attempt at deception or about your ignorance. Either way, they would dismiss your argument.

A much better strategy would be to confront this concern and then try to overcome it. While acknowledging that lead is a dangerous pollutant, you could point out that more than 95 percent of battery lead is recycled. You could also point out that progress is being made to improve battery technology and create alternatives such as lithium ion batteries used in recent concept cars.[2] The result is a balanced presentation that makes your own case stronger.

## To Test Your Evidence for Logical Fallacies, Ask These Questions

| | |
|---|---|
| **Stacking the deck** | Did I present evidence that only supports my point of view? Have I withheld evidence that might contradict it? |
| **Non sequitur** | Is my evidence related and relevant to the reasons or claim it is supporting? |
| **Hasty generalization** | Have I provided sufficient evidence to support my conclusions? |
| **Dicto simpliciter** | Does my evidence cover exceptions to any generalizations that I've made? |
| **Red herring** | Does all of my evidence pertain to the true issue? Have I tried to distract my audience's attention with irrelevant concerns? |
| **Bandwagon appeal** | Can my evidence stand on its own? Have I argued that my audience should support my ideas because they reflect a popular viewpoint? |
| **Faulty use of authority** | Are the authorities I cite actually experts in my subject area? Could my authorities be biased because of their background or their professional or political associations? |

---

[2]Jim Motavalli, "Axion's New Lead-Carbon Batteries May Help Usher In Electric Cars," thedailygreen.com//living-green/blogs, April 14, 2009.

In summary, using evidence means putting yourself in an advocate's place. You'll probably do this while building your argument, and certainly when you revise; then you should see yourself as an advocate for the other side and scrutinize your evidence as if you were going to challenge it in court. As a reader, you need to keep that Missouri "show me!" attitude in mind at all times. A little healthy skepticism will help you test the information you're asked to believe. The next chapter will help you do so.

## SAMPLE ARGUMENT FOR ANALYSIS

The following is a paper written by a student, Arthur Allen. In it, Allen considers the high rate of recidivism in America—that is, convicts committing more crimes after they've been released from prison. In his paper, he argues that religion might be a better form of rehabilitation than just more harsh punishment. Read the essay carefully and take notes about it in your argument journal. Then, either individually or in your peer group, answer the questions that follow. Notice the style is MLA, which is discussed in the documentation guide.

---

Allen 1

Arthur Allen

Professor Capobianco

English 097

2 March 2009

Prayer in Prison: Religion as Rehabilitation

1    Prisons don't work if the prisoners are released only to commit more crimes. Unfortunately, that happens all too frequently. In fact, the phenomenon is known as recidivism—that is, a convict re-offends after having been released from confinement. The challenge faced within prisons across America is how best to minimize recidivism in order to ensure that the convicts do not commit more crimes. There are two main schools of thought regarding the prevention of recidivism: increasing the harshness of the punishment (most often by increasing time in prison) or offering convicts rehabilitation programs.

2    The Canadian crime-reduction research group Canada Safety Council found that "there is little evidence that harsh penalties are the best way to prevent further offences" ("Crime"). The council cites studies in Australia, Canada, and America, all pointing to this conclusion. In fact, the group finds that "long prison sentences without other remedial programs may actually increase the chances of re-offending after release" ("Crime"). However, a seemingly more effective method of reducing recidivism, while largely controversial, is rehabilitation, more often than not using a religious basis.

Allen 2

3    The obvious concern with religion-based rehabilitation is the perceived clash with the Constitution, which prohibits the government from making any "law respecting an establishment of religion or forbidding free exercise thereof" (O'Connor 531). There are no questions, however, about its effectiveness: In Texas, about 40% of parolees who do not participate in any form of rehabilitation program return to prison within three years; in the same amount of time, less than 5% of those who participated in a rehabilitation program were rearrested (Bradley). Other implementations of these types of programs have been comparably successful in Louisiana (Van Wel) as well as in Iowa, Kansas and Minnesota (Alter).

4    One of the major rehabilitation programs nationally is the Interchange Freedom Initiative (IFI) Program, a third-party rehabilitation program based on offering religion to inmates. Sam Dye, director of the Interchange program in Iowa, says,

> The only true lasting change that is worth anything is change that comes from the inside out, change from the heart. You can coerce a person, from the outside, to do what you want them to do; but once that external pressure is gone, typically people go back to act the way they did before. So if you really want to change a person, you have to get a hold of their heart. (Bradley)

This seems to make sense: The prisoner must be changed from the inside out in order to keep that prisoner from committing a future crime. That is to say, prisoners will not change simply because they have been told they were wrong or because they were punished severely. Recidivism occurs when there is no change in the status quo of the life of the criminal. If a person is pushed to the point where he or she needs to sell drugs and rob stores in order to pay the bills, a harsh prison life will not change that situation.

5    However, the question surrounding rehabilitation programs is not about their effectiveness but about their constitutionality. Les Nester, a lawyer and critic of the IFI program, says, "the concerns would be that the state is actually promoting and advancing Christianity. If you look at the programming, it is very sectarian, very evangelical programming . . . . I think the IFI program is a brainwash tactic" (Neary). He argues that because the state government is promoting the use of rehabilitation programs that use Christianity as a way to rehabilitate criminals, the state is

Allen 3

declaring affiliation with a specific religion. However, the IFI is not purely a Christian program. It incorporates many faiths, including Judaism and Islam, in its treatment of prisoners. One graduate of the program states, "I think Islam has everything to do with my growth and development and my transformation that I have accomplished, in the sense that Islam taught me for the first time what it is to take responsibility for my actions" (Neary).

6       The argument for inclusion of any religion rather then exclusion of all religions is summed up succinctly in an article by William Bennett, who "states, "The First Amendment does not require the government to be neutral on the subject of religion. It requires it to be neutral only on any one particular form of religion" (Bennett 54). In other words, while the government should not show favoritism toward one particular religion, it also does not have the obligation of pretending religion does not exist. Thus, this distinction allows the government to sponsor religious programs in the context of furthering the social good (reduction of crime) as long as it does not promote one religious program over another.

7       In another article, John Swomley argues that the government could not give funding to one religious group without giving funding to all religious groups; this argument then implies that the government could not provide any funding to religious rehabilitation programs in prisons if it did not give funding to all 300-plus religious groups (Swomley 62). This argument is backwards: The government is free to give money to any religious group it sees fit. It is prohibited, however, from denying one group funding in the same situation where it would grant another group that same funding. To say that the government is responsible for giving "all or none" to religious groups would be like saying the government is required to either employ all races in government positions or employ none of them. If a religion-based rehabilitation program wants to operate, it should not be denied fund but should be funded equally as all other religion-based rehabilitation programs representing different faiths.

8       Furthermore, civil liberties groups have actually held back from suing the IFI program because it provides a number of unique services including a support community both for convicts in prison and for those who have been released. As one graduate of the IFI program puts it, "Now I have someone I can call, even in the middle of the night. And when I start feeling bad . . . who you gonna call? You call your brother, he uses drugs. You call your sister, she's using drugs. Mom's upset with you. Dad's gone. Whereas, with IFI, I was given a family." In other words, because it is a third-party nonprofit program, the IFI is not only able to reach prisoners in a

Allen 4

way government officials can't by offering spiritual growth and continuity, but also it provides follow-through support after prison by offering a new family to which the convicts feel a sense of loyalty and responsibility (Bradley).

As an alternative to harsher punishments, rehabilitation is clearly superior. When prison is the necessary evil in a person's life, the harshness of it will make little difference. The change must truly come from the inside out. And faith-based rehabilitation programs have proven successful.

Allen 5

## Works Cited

Alter, Alexandra. "Study Touts Faith-Based Prison Rehabilitation Program." The Pew Forum on Religion and Public Life. Pew Forum, 19 June 2003. Web. 28 Feb. 2009.

Bennett, William. "America's Indentity Is Rooted in Religion." *Religion in America: Opposing Viewpoints*. Ed. William Dudley et al. San Diego: Greenhaven p, 2001. Print.

Bradley, Barbra. *God Pods*. NPR News. Iowa, 2001. Radio.

"Crime, Punishment, Safety." *Canada Safety Council.* Canada Safety Council, 2009. Web. 27 Feb. 2009.

Neary, Lynn. *Sing Sing Studies*. NPR News, Washington DC. 1998. Radio.

O'Connor, Karen, and Larry J. Sabato. *American Government: Continuity and Change.* New York: Pearson Education, 2004. Print.

Swomley, John. "TK." Religion in America: Opposing Viewpoints. Ed. William Dudley et al. San Diego: Greenhaven P, 2001. Print.

Van Wel, Alex. "US Prison Rehabilitation through Faith." BBC News. BBC, 2 Oct. 2002. Web. 27 Feb. 2009.

**QUESTIONS FOR ANALYSIS AND DISCUSSION**

1. What claim (Chapter 1) is Allen arguing? What are the reasons for his claim? What do you think the pros and cons he listed in developing this argument might have been?

2. Who is Allen's target audience? What clues does he give you? What values and prejudices might the readership hold?

3. What different forms of evidence (personal, outside authorities, factual references, statistics) does Allen provide? Which form(s) of evidence does he rely on most?

4. Evaluate the supporting evidence that Allen provides. Is it relevant? Is it detailed enough? Does it seem dated and verifiable? Does his claim exceed his evidence? Does his evidence strike you as slanted? If you were his reader, would you be persuaded by his reasons? What changes (if any) in evidence would you recommend to help him make his argument more persuasive?

5. Use debate, dialogue, and deliberation to respond to Allen's essay in your journal. See Chapter 1 to review this process.

   a. Create a dialogue to help you understand and respond productively to Allen's ideas.

   b. Given what you've learned through debate and dialogue, write at least a page in which you deliberate about the conflicting issues that Allen raises in his essay. How does your understanding of Allen's position change or modify your own viewpoint? Is there a way to reconcile conflicting concerns about this subject?

# Establishing Claims: Thinking Like a Skeptic

Y ou have decided the issue you're going to argue. With the aid of debate and dialogue, you've sharpened your ideas and considered alternative perspectives and common concerns. You've thought about your audience and determined what you have in common, where you might agree, and where you might disagree. After deliberating, you have formulated a working claim, and you have gathered solid evidence to support it. Now it's time to establish the logical structure of your argument and decide how best to arrange this material to persuade your readers.

If you've ever tried handing in a paper made up of slapped-together evidence and first-draft organization, you've probably discovered a blueprint for disaster. Perhaps you didn't test your work, didn't revise it, or didn't think about how it would appeal to a reader. You assumed that because *you* understood how the parts fit together, your readers would as well. To help you detect and correct these problems, this chapter focuses on thinking like a *skeptic*— a skeptical building inspector, to be exact—because a skeptical attitude works best.

To construct a persuasive argument, one that has a chance of convincing your readers, you have to pay careful attention to the logical structure you are building. You can't take anything for granted; you have to question every step you take, every joist and joint. You have to ask yourself if you're using the right material for the right purpose, the right tool at the right time. In other words, you have to think like a building inspector examining a half-built two-story house—one whose builder is notoriously crafty at compromising quality. A healthy skepticism—and a logical system—help uncover flaws before they create a disaster.

## The Toulmin Model

Stephen Toulmin, a British philosopher and logician, analyzed hundreds of arguments from various fields of politics and law.[1] He concluded that nearly every argument has certain patterns and parts. The best arguments, Toulmin found, are those addressed to a skeptical audience, one eager to question the reasoning where it seems faulty, to demand support for wobbly assumptions, and to raise opposing reasons.

The slightly retooled version of the Toulmin model we describe below encourages you to become a skeptical audience. It also gives you the tools to write persuasive arguments aimed to win over a skeptical reader. It provides useful everyday terms to help you unearth, weigh, and, if necessary, fix an argument's logical structures. It lets you verify that the major premises in your argument or those of your opposition are clear and accurate, helps you

---

[1]Toulmin, Stephen. *The Uses of Argument.* Cambridge: Cambridge UP, 1958.

determine whether repairs to your claims are needed and whether counterarguments are addressed. It shows you where supporting evidence may be needed and helps you avoid logical fallacies. And, since Toulmin's terms are designed to be broadly practical, they allow you to present your case to a wide variety of readers.

# Toulmin's Terms

According to Toulmin, a fully developed argument has six parts. They are the *claim*, the *grounds*, the *warrant*, the *backing*, the *qualifiers*, and the *rebuttals*.

## The Claim

The **claim** is the assertion you are trying to prove—the same term as discussed in Chapter 1. It is the position you take in your argument, often as a proposal with which you are asking your reader to agree. In a well-constructed argument, each part makes its ultimate claim, its conclusion, seem inevitable. For example, *you should stay home from school if you have the flu.* This sounds like a reasonable claim, but some people may challenge it. You need to explain why your audience should agree with you.

## The Grounds

Just as every argument contains a claim, every claim needs supporting evidence. The **grounds** are the hard data—statistics, research studies, facts, and examples that bolster your claim and that your audience accepts without requiring further proof. Grounds are the "truth" on which you base your claim. For example, *The influenza virus is highly contagious. According to the Centers for Disease Control, every year, an average of 36,000 people die in the United States from complications connected to the flu.* While some readers may accept the grounds as enough proof to accept your claim, others will require more information. This is where the warrant comes in.

## The Warrant

The claim is usually stated explicitly. However, underlying the claim are a number of assumptions and principles that are also critical to the success of your argument. These are the **warrants** that implicitly support your argument by connecting your claim to the grounds. They enable your audience to follow the reasoning in your argument. They explain why the hard evidence supports your claim. So the success of your argument depends on whether the audience accepts these often half-buried assumptions, commonly held values, legal or moral principles, laws of nature, commonsense knowledge, or shared beliefs. Warrants tend to be based on values shared by the population. They may be true or mere presumptions based on emotion, rather than hard facts. For example, *The flu is easily passed from person to person, and it is inconsiderate to make other people sick. The responsible thing to do is to stay home until you feel better.*

Let's look at a few more examples. We are all familiar with the advertiser that promises that its shampoo will eliminate dandruff. The basic **claim** here is that you should shampoo your hair with this manufacturer's product. And as **grounds** the manufacturer says that studies have shown that 60 percent of those people who use their shampoo no longer have dandruff. One underlying **warrant** here is that people don't want dandruff—a commonly held assumption that you share with your audience. Another is that we assume 60 percent to be a sufficient proportion to accept the claim. Because warrants are based on commonly held values or patterns of reasoning, they are not easily detected. Here's another example:

> **Claim:** Cigarette smoking is harmful to your health.
> **Grounds:** The U.S. Surgeon General has warned that cigarettes cause a number of diseases including cancer, heart trouble, and injury to fetuses in pregnant women.
> **Warrant:** The Surgeon General is a medical authority we can trust.

At times, warrants can be a challenge to determine since they are often based on unstated but commonly held assumptions. And that is why it is important to find them. More on that below.

## The Backing

Because your warrant is an assumption, you cannot be certain that it will always be accepted by your readers. So you must provide reasons to back it up. These reasons, called **backing,** indicate that the warrant is reliable in a particular argument, though it doesn't have to be true in all cases at all times. For example, *The flu can lead to other serious conditions such as pneumonia. In fact, over 200,000 people end up hospitalized because of flu-related complications. It is better to stay home when you have the flu, rather than risk getting even more sick and missing more time at work or school.* The backing provides additional support to the warrant by addressing other facets of the claim. In this case, the risk of complications.

## The Qualifiers

**Qualifiers** provide a way to indicate when, why, and how your claim and warrant are reliable. They're words or phrases such as *often, probably, possibly, almost always;* verbs like *may* and *might, can* and *could;* or adjectives and adverbs that yoke your claim to some condition. The subtlest kind of qualifier is an adjective that acknowledges that your claim is true to a degree: *Complications from the flu often make it harder to go back to school. Usually it takes longer for you to feel better.* The qualifiers *often* and *harder* and *usually* imply that the statement is conditional and not absolute. They allow for exceptions.

You need to consider a few guidelines about using qualifiers; like antibiotics, they're too powerful to use unwisely. Using too few qualifiers can indicate that you're exaggerating your argument's validity. As we've mentioned in previous chapters, common fallacies, such as *hasty generalizations,* are often potentially valid arguments that go astray by not qualifying their claims enough, if at all. Using *no* qualifiers can result in a claim that is too general and sweeping. Although many students think a qualified claim is a weak claim, in fact, the qualified claim is often the most persuasive. Few truths are *completely* true; few claims are *always* right. A well-qualified claim, then, shows that the writer respects both the difficulty of the issue and the intelligence of the reader.

Nevertheless, qualifiers alone cannot substitute for reasoning your way to the tough, subtle distinctions on which the most persuasive arguments depend. An example could be "Innocent people have an inviolable right to life." It's wisely qualified with the word "innocent" since just saying "People have an inviolable right to life" wouldn't hold up. Hitler, after all, was human. Did he too have "an inviolable right to life"? But even *innocent* is not qualification enough. It raises too many tough, troubling questions. "Innocent" of what? "Innocent" by whose judgment, and why? What if killing a few innocent people were the only way to end a war that is killing *many* innocent people?

Using a lot of qualifiers, therefore, is no guarantee that your argument is carefully reasoned. In fact, strongly qualifying your argument's claim may be a sign that you doubt your argument's validity. But such doubt can itself be encouraging. Misusing or overusing qualifiers can indicate that your instinct of anxiety is right—that you've discovered better reasons to doubt your initial argument than to defend it. In fact, acknowledging the appeal of a flawed claim—and describing how you only discovered its flaws once you tried trumpeting its strengths—is an effective way of earning the reader's respect. It shows you to be an honest arguer capable of learning from errors—and thus worth learning *from*.

Deciding what to state and what to imply is a large part of writing any good argument. Just as a building's cross-beams don't have to be visible to be working, not everything important in an argument has to be stated. For example, if someone were to claim that winters in Minnesota are "mostly long and cold," we probably wouldn't stop the flow of argument to ask him to define the qualifier *mostly*. We'd instead keep the qualifier in mind, and let the Minnesotan's definition of "mostly" emerge, implied, from the rest of the story. Similarly, it's sometimes wise to leave your argument's qualifiers implied.

Still, it's often better to risk belaboring the obvious. To minimize the chances that your reader will misunderstand (or altogether miss) your meaning, qualify your claims as clearly and explicitly as possible. "Reading" the argument you're writing like a skeptical reader will help you decide which qualifiers are needed, where they are needed, and how explicitly they need to be stated.

## The Rebuttals

Reading your argument skeptically also allows you to participate, answer, and even pre-empt rebuttals. **Rebuttals** represent the exceptions to the claim. There are many different kinds of rebuttals, and any persuasive argument ought to acknowledge and incorporate the most important ones. Rebuttals are like large-scale qualifiers. They acknowledge and explain the conditions or situations in which your claim would not be true—while still proving how your claim *is* true under other conditions. It's wise, then, to anticipate such rebuttals by regularly acknowledging all your argument's limits. This acknowledgment will prompt you to craft your claims more carefully. For example, look at the claim that you should stay home from school if you have the flu. One could argue that if you are coughing and sneezing, you *probably* will give the flu to people sitting around you. Then again, you might not. You might sit in the back of the room, away from other people. Or you could take medication that reduces your sneezing. A challenger might argue that while it is inconsiderate to expose classmates to the flu, if one has an exam that one thinks cannot be missed or face failure, it may be in one's personal best interest to go to class. You would need to persuasively convince your reader that your claim holds true despite these challenges. You might anticipate the challenge and write: *Rather than expose your classmates to dangerous strains of flu, such as H1N1, go to your student health service and request a letter explaining your absence. This will protect your classmates and allow you the time to get better so that you can focus on the test later.*

Let's look at another example. Say that a sportswriter argues that allowing big-market baseball teams to monopolize talent ruins competition by perpetuating dynasties. Your rebuttal might be to cite the overlooked grounds of ignored evidence—grounds that complicate, if not contradict, the writer's claim: "Then why have small-market teams won four of the last ten World Series?" Had the sportswriter anticipated and integrated this rebuttal, she could have improved the argument—from her warrant on up. Her argument could have taken into account this rebuttal in the form of more careful qualifications. "While the rule of money doesn't guarantee that the richer teams will always win the World Series, it does make it more difficult for hard-pressed teams to compete for available talent." This is now, of course, a less sweeping claim—and, therefore, more precise and persuasive.

Of course, no writer can anticipate their readers' every rebuttal, nor should the writer even try. But you should test your argument by trying to rebut it yourself or working with classmates in small groups. Then revise your arguments with those rebuttals in mind.

## Review: Six Parts of an Argument

| | |
|---|---|
| **Claim** | The assertion you are trying to prove |
| **Grounds** | The supporting evidence for the claim |
| **Warrant** | A generalization that explains why the evidence supports the claim |
| **Backing** | The reasons that show the warrant is reliable |
| **Qualifiers** | The words that show when, how, and why your claim is reliable |
| **Rebuttal** | The exceptions to the claim |

# Finding Warrants

Finding your warrants in order to explicate your argument can help you in several ways: You persuade your reader more effectively, detect flaws in your own argument, and identify the cause of otherwise confusing debates more quickly.

For example, let's say you want to argue the claim that all students in American schools should be taught in English rather than in the students' native or family languages. The grounds supporting this claim are results of research showing a high correlation between English fluency and socioeconomic success.

For your audience to accept the connection between your claim and your grounds, you and they must agree on several warrants that underlie it. (Remember that warrants are underlying assumptions or common knowledge.) The first might be the assumption that schools prepare students for socioeconomic success in U.S. society. Since one of the purposes of an education is to develop skills such as reading, writing, and thinking critically, skills that are considered basic requirements for success, most of your audience would likely accept this assumption. Therefore, it can be left implied and unstated.

The second warrant implied by your claim may not be as readily acceptable to your audience as the one above and will need to be explicitly supported in your essay: that our English language skills affect whether we are successful. The third warrant, implied by the second, is that individuals who are not fluent in English will not be successful members of society. These warrants will need considerable backing to show that they are reliable. How do English language skills enable individuals to attain socioeconomic success? How are individuals who lack fluency in English adversely affected? You will want to provide additional backing in the form of evidence, examples, and statistics to demonstrate that English language skills have a significant impact on an individual's chances for social and economic success.

Your fourth and final warrant is particularly important because it establishes a critical link between your claim that all students should be taught in English and the need for fluency to succeed. This warrant assumes nonnative speaking students will achieve greater fluency in English in the English-only classroom. You will need additional backing to prove this warrant, especially when you take into account possible rebuttals. For instance, what about students who enter U.S. schools with no English skills at all? How can they learn the required curriculum with no fluency in English? Will English-only classrooms fail to teach them language skills as well as subject matter? Will this approach alienate them from the American educational system and, thus, from success in our society? Making your responses to these rebuttals explicit will strengthen your argument.

Using Toulmin's approach to analyze your argument allows you to dig beneath the surface of your claim to find the underlying assumptions that form its foundation. It also allows your audience to see that even if they disagree with your claim, they may agree with many of the principles and assumptions that support it. Revealing this common ground, however hidden it lies, can provide opportunities to begin a dialogue that emerges from the recognition of shared values and beliefs. For instance, take the notoriously divisive issue of capital punishment. Those who support capital punishment say, in essence, "A human life is so precious that anyone who is guilty of depriving another of it should forfeit his or her own life." Those who oppose capital punishment say, in effect, "Human life is so precious that we have no right to deprive another of it no matter what the cause." By digging down to the warrants that underlie these positions, we may be surprised to find that the two sides have much in common: a respect for and appreciation of the value of human life. This discovery, of course, is no guarantee that we can reconcile dramatically opposing views on a particular issue. But the recognition of commonality might provide a first step toward increasing understanding—if not consensus—between opposing sides.

Digging deeply to excavate your warrants can also help you avoid two common logical fallacies: post hoc, ergo propter hoc and slippery slope arguments. A post hoc, ergo propter hoc fallacy occurs when the writer mistakenly draws a causal relationship between two or more events or situations that are unrelated or simply coincidental. Similarly, a slippery slope argument is based on an assumption that a particular outcome is inevitable if certain events happen or if a situation is allowed to continue. In both cases, the writer fails to identify and support the underlying warrants that would create a convincing logical link.

## SAMPLE ARGUMENTS FOR ANALYSIS

Now let's turn to two sample arguments to see how our version of the Toulmin model can help you test your own arguments more effectively. The first piece, originally published in the *New York Times Magazine,* provides a very logical but highly

## To Avoid Errors in Logic, Check for These Logical Fallacies

| | |
|---|---|
| **Post hoc, ergo propter hoc** | Be certain to demonstrate a cause-effect relationship between events by uncovering all warrants that underlie your claim. |
| **Slippery slope argument** | Make explicit the chain of events that link a situation to its possible outcome. Provide proof that this progression will inevitably occur. |

## Warrants

Notice the many layers of warrants that can underlie a single claim:

| | |
|---|---|
| **Claim** | All students in American public schools should be taught in English-only classrooms. |
| **Grounds** | Research shows high correlation between English fluency and socioeconomic success in America. |
| **Warrant** | Schools prepare students for success in our society. |
| **Warrant** | Success in American society can be determined by our English language skills. |
| **Warrant** | Individuals who are not fluent in English will not succeed in our society. |
| **Warrant** | Teaching classes only in the English language will ensure that students will be fluent in English. |

provocative argument about a crime that always receives considerable media attention: infanticide. The second article appeared a few days later in the *New York Times*. And while these essays relate events that happened several years ago, the issue of infanticide is still a national problem. In fact, statistically, the U.S. ranks high on the list of countries whose inhabitants kill their babies. For infants under the age of 1 year, the American homicide rate is 11th in the world. The author of the first essay, Steven Pinker, wrote this piece while director of the Center for Cognitive Neuroscience at Massachusetts Institute of Technology. Pinker is currently the Johnstone Family Professor of Psychology in the Department of Psychology at Harvard University. He is the author of *How the Mind Works* (1997) and most recently *The Stuff of Thought* (2007). Following Pinker's essay is a point-by-point counterargument (page 195) by Michael Kelley.

# Why They Kill Their Newborns
*Steven Pinker*

1    Killing your baby. What could be more depraved? For a woman to destroy the fruit of her womb would seem like an ultimate violation of the natural order. But every year, hundreds of women commit neonaticide: They kill their newborns or let them die. Most neonaticides remain undiscovered, but every once in a while a janitor follows a trail of blood to a tiny body in a trash bin, or a woman faints and doctors find the remains of a placenta inside her.

2    Two cases have recently riveted the American public. Last November, Amy Grossberg and Brian Peterson, 18-year-old college sweethearts, delivered their baby in a motel room and, according to prosecutors, killed him and left his body in a dumpster. They will go on trial for murder next year and, if convicted, could be sentenced to death. In June, another 18-year-old, Melissa Drexler, arrived at her high-school prom, locked herself in a bathroom stall, gave birth to a boy and left him dead in a garbage can. Everyone knows what happened next: she touched herself up and returned to the dance floor. In September, a grand jury indicted her for murder.

3    How could they do it? Nothing melts the heart like a helpless baby. Even a biologist's cold calculations tell us that nurturing an offspring that carries our genes is the whole point of our existence. Neonaticide, many think, could be only a product of pathology. The psychiatrists uncover childhood trauma. The defense lawyers argue temporary psychosis. The pundits blame a throwaway society, permissive sex education and, of course, rock lyrics.

4    But it's hard to maintain that neonaticide is an illness when we learn that it has been practiced and accepted in most cultures throughout history. And that neonaticidal women do not commonly show signs of psychopathology. In a classic 1970 study of statistics of child killing, a psychiatrist, Phillip Resnick, found that mothers who kill their *older* children are frequently psychotic, depressed or suicidal, but mothers who kill their newborns are usually not. (It was this difference that led Resnick to argue that the category infanticide be split into neonaticide, the killing of a baby on the day of its birth, and filicide, the killing of a child older than one day.)

5    Killing a baby is an immoral act, and we often express our outrage at the immoral by calling it a sickness. But normal human motives are not always moral, and neonaticide does not have to be a product of malfunctioning neural circuitry or a dysfunctional upbringing. We can try to understand what would lead a mother to kill her newborn, remembering that to understand is not necessarily to forgive.

6    Martin Daly and Margo Wilson, both psychologists, argue that a capacity for neonaticide is built into the biological design of our parental emotions. Mammals are extreme among animals in the amount of time, energy and food they invest in their young, and humans are extreme among mammals. Parental investment is a limited resource, and mammalian mothers must "decide" whether to allot it to their newborn or to their current and future offspring. If a newborn is sickly, or if its survival is not promising, they may cut their losses and favor the healthiest in the litter or try again later on.

7      In most cultures, neonaticide is a form of this triage. Until very recently in human evolutionary history, mothers nursed their children for two to four years before becoming fertile again. Many children died, especially in the perilous first year. Most women saw no more than two or three of their children survive to adulthood, and many did not see any survive. To become a grandmother, a woman had to make hard choices. In most societies documented by anthropologists, including those of hunter-gatherers (our best glimpse into our ancestors' way of life), a woman lets a newborn die when its prospects for survival to adulthood are poor. The forecast might be based on abnormal signs in the infant, or on bad circumstances for successful motherhood at the time—she might be burdened with older children, beset by war or famine or without a husband or social support. Moreover, she might be young enough to try again.

8      We are all descendants of women who made the difficult decisions that allowed them to become grandmothers in that unforgiving world, and we inherited that brain circuitry that led to those decisions. Daly and Wilson have shown that the statistics on neonaticide in contemporary North America parallel those in the anthropological literature. The women who sacrifice their offspring tend to be young, poor, unmarried and socially isolated.

9      Natural selection cannot push the buttons of behavior directly; it affects our behavior by endowing us with emotions that coax us toward adaptive choices. New mothers have always faced a choice between a definite tragedy now and the possibility of an even greater tragedy months or years later, and that choice is not to be taken lightly. Even today, the typical rumination of a depressed new mother—how will I cope with this burden?—is a legitimate concern. The emotional response called bonding is also far more complex than the popular view, in which a woman is imprinted with a lifelong attachment to her baby if they interact in a critical period immediately following the baby's birth. A new mother will first coolly assess the infant and her current situation and only in the next few days begin to see it as a unique and wonderful individual. Her love will gradually deepen in ensuing years, in a trajectory that tracks the increasing biological value of a child (the chance that it will live to produce grandchildren) as the child proceeds through the mine field of early development.

10     Even when a mother in a hunter-gatherer society hardens her heart to sacrifice a newborn, her heart has not turned to stone. Anthropologists who interview these women (or their relatives, since the event is often too painful for the woman to discuss) discover that the women see the death as an unavoidable tragedy, grieve at the time and remember the child with pain all their lives. Even the supposedly callous Melissa Drexler agonized over a name for her dead son and wept at his funeral. (Initial reports that, after giving birth, she requested a Metallica song from the deejay and danced with her boyfriend turned out to be false.)

11     Many cultural practices are designed to distance people's emotions from a newborn until its survival seems probable. Full personhood is often not automatically granted at birth, as we see in our rituals of christening and the Jewish bris. And yet the recent neonaticides will seem puzzling. These are middle-class girls whose babies would have been kept far from starvation by the girl's parents or by any of thousands of eager adoptive couples. But our emotions, fashioned by the slow hand of natural selection, respond to the signals of the long-vanished tribal environment in which we spent 99 percent of our evolutionary history. Being young and single are two bad omens for successful motherhood, and the girl who conceals her pregnancy and procrastinates over its consequences will soon be disquieted by a third omen. She will give birth in circumstances that are particularly unpromising for a human mother: alone.

12    In hunter-gatherer societies, births are virtually always assisted because human anatomy makes birth (especially the first one) long, difficult and risky. Older women act as midwives, emotional supports and experienced appraisers who help decide whether the infant should live. Wenda Trevathan, an anthropologist and trained midwife, has studied pelvises of human fossils and concluded that childbirth has been physically torturous, and therefore probably assisted, for millions of years. Maternal feelings may be adapted to a world in which a promising newborn is heralded with waves of cooing and clucking and congratulating. Those reassuring signals are absent from a secret birth in a motel room or a bathroom stall.

13    So what is the mental state of a teenage mother who has kept her pregnancy secret? She is immature enough to have hoped that her pregnancy would go away by itself, her maternal feelings have been set at zero and she suddenly realizes she is in big trouble.

14    Sometimes she continues to procrastinate. In September, 17-year-old Shanta Clark gave birth to a premature boy and kept him hidden in her bedroom closet, as if he were E.T., for 17 days. She fed him before and after she went to school until her mother discovered him. The weak cry of the preemie kept him from being discovered earlier. (In other cases, girls have panicked over the crying and, in stifling the cry, killed the baby.)

15    Most observers sense the desperation that drives a woman to neonaticide. Prosecutors sometimes don't prosecute; juries rarely convict; those found guilty almost never go to jail. Barbara Kirwin, a forensic psychologist, reports that in nearly 300 cases of women charged with neonaticide in the United States and Britain, no woman spent more than a night in jail. In Europe, the laws of several countries prescribed less-severe penalties for neonaticide than for adult homicides. The fascination with the Grossberg-Peterson case comes from the unusual threat of the death penalty. Even those in favor of capital punishment might shudder at the thought of two reportedly nice kids being strapped to gurneys and put to death.

16    But our compassion hinges on the child, not just on the mother. Killers of older children, no matter how desperate, evoke little mercy. Susan Smith, the South Carolina woman who sent her two sons, 14 months and 3 years old, to watery deaths, is in jail, unmourned, serving a life sentence. The leniency shown to neonaticidal mothers forces us to think the unthinkable and ask if we, like many societies and like the mothers themselves, are not completely sure whether a neonate is a full person.

17    It seems obvious that we need a clear boundary to confer personhood on a human being and grant it a right to life. Otherwise, we approach a slippery slope that ends in the disposal of inconvenient people or in grotesque deliberations on the value of individual lives. But the endless abortion debate shows how hard it is to locate the boundary. Anti-abortionists draw the line at conception, but that implies we should shed tears every time an invisible conceptus fails to implant in the uterus—and, to carry the argument to its logical conclusion, that we should prosecute for murder anyone who uses an IUD. Those in favor of abortion draw the line at viability, but viability is a fuzzy gradient that depends on how great a risk of an impaired child the parents are willing to tolerate. The only thing both sides agree on is that the line must be drawn at some point before birth.

18    Neonaticide forces us to examine even that boundary. To a biologist, birth is as arbitrary a milestone as any other. Many mammals bear offspring that see and walk as soon as they hit the ground. But the incomplete 9-month-old human fetus must be evicted from the womb before its oversized head gets too big to fit through its mother's pelvis. The usual

primate assembly process spills into the first years in the world. And that complicates our definition of personhood.

19     What makes a living being a person with a right not to be killed? Animal-rights extremists would seem to have the easiest argument to make: that all sentient beings have a right to life. But champions of that argument must conclude that delousing a child is akin to mass murder; the rest of us must look for an argument that draws a small circle. Perhaps only the members of our own species, Homo sapiens, have a right to life? But that is simply chauvinism; a person of one race could just as easily say that people of another race have no right to life.

20     No, the right to life must come, the moral philosophers say, from morally significant traits that we humans happen to possess. One such trait is having a unique sequence of experiences that defines us as individuals and connects us to other people. Other traits include an ability to reflect upon ourselves as a continuous locus of consciousness, to form and savor plans for the future, to dread death and to express the choice not to die. And there's the rub: our immature neonates don't possess these traits any more than mice do.

21     Several moral philosophers have concluded that neonates are not persons, and thus neonaticide should not be classified as murder. Michael Tooley has gone so far as to say that neonaticide ought to be permitted during an interval after birth. Most philosophers (to say nothing of nonphilosophers) recoil from that last step, but the very fact that there can be a debate about the personhood of neonates, but no debate about the personhood of older children, makes it clearer why we feel more sympathy for an Amy Grossberg than for a Susan Smith.

22     So how do you provide grounds for outlawing neonaticide? The facts don't make it easy. Some philosophers suggest that people intuitively see neonates as so similar to older babies that you couldn't allow neonaticide without coarsening the way people treat children and other people in general. Again, the facts say otherwise. Studies in both modern and hunter-gatherer societies have found that neonaticidal women don't kill anyone but their newborns, and when they give birth later under better conditions, they can be devoted, loving mothers.

23     The laws of biology were not kind to Amy Grossberg and Melissa Drexler, and they are not kind to us as we struggle to make moral sense of the teenagers' actions. One predicament is that our moral system needs a crisp inauguration of personhood, but the assembly process for Homo sapiens is gradual, piecemeal and uncertain. Another problem is that the emotional circuitry of mothers has evolved to cope with this uncertain process, so the baby killers turn out to be not moral monsters but nice, normal (and sometimes religious) young women. These are dilemmas we will probably never resolve, and any policy will leave us with uncomfortable cases. We will most likely muddle through, keeping birth as a conspicuous legal boundary but showing mercy to the anguished girls who feel they had no choice but to run afoul of it.

## An Analysis Based on the Toulmin Model

Clearly Steven Pinker has taken a controversial stance on a disturbing social issue. In fact, in light of civilized society's attitudes toward the sacredness of the mother-infant bond, his position is one that many people might find shocking and repugnant. How could he propose that neonaticide, the murder of one's newborn infant, be viewed as an acceptable form of behavior, one that we have inherited from our evolutionary ancestors? As Pinker readily admits in the first three paragraphs, neonaticide seems alien to most of the values we as civilized people cherish. Nevertheless, Pinker argues that while it may be regarded as immoral, neonaticide is not necessarily the act of a mentally deranged woman, but rather a difficult decision guided by an instinct for survival handed down to a mother by generations of women before her. While he does not condone or endorse this practice, Pinker urges his readers to try to understand a context that might drive women to commit such an act.

No matter how repugnant an idea may be, it cannot be repudiated unless it is understood. Therefore it is important to be detached and put aside emotion when confronted with ideas that are unacceptable. Genocide, child slavery, and child prostitution, for example, are topics most people would rather avoid. But to understand the forces underlying these practices, and to eradicate them, one must be knowledgeable about them. This might require digesting material that is disturbing and contrary to all the values held by a civilized society.

So, while your first reaction to Pinker's ideas may be to dismiss them as outrageous and unworthy of serious consideration, a close analysis of his argument using the Toulmin method may demonstrate how carefully Pinker has crafted his argument to challenge many of our assumptions about human behavior and, in particular, motherhood.

## Claims and Grounds

Pinker presents the first part of his claim in paragraph 4 of his essay: Neonaticide is not an abnormal behavior but one that has been practiced "in most cultures throughout history." This statement seems to contradict the popular notion of neonaticide. Because our society regards neonaticide as an immoral act, many people likely assume that it is a rare occurrence. However, Pinker anticipates this assumption in paragraph 1 by reminding us that neonaticide *does* occur in our own society. It is, he claims, more common than we realize, since most murders of newborn babies go undetected. Only "every once in a while" do we discover that this act has taken place because some physical evidence is found. While Pinker offers no grounds for his assertion that "every year, hundreds of women commit neonaticide," his audience's familiarity with newspaper accounts of newborns abandoned in dumpsters and public restrooms lends credibility to his statement. This point is important because it establishes a link between contemporary women's behavior and the practices of our "long-vanished tribal environment."

Pinker develops this idea further in paragraphs 6 through 8 by suggesting that this behavior has been programmed into our "biological design" through human evolutionary development. He provides the grounds to support this part of his claim by citing two scholarly sources: Philip Resnick's study of child-killing statistics, which indicates that women who kill their newborn babies are typically not mentally ill, and research by Martin Daly and Margo Wilson that suggests neonaticide may be an intrinsic part of our "biological design," a necessity for human beings with limited resources to invest in their offspring. Relying on these grounds, Pinker goes on to argue in paragraph 9 that neonaticide is an "adaptive choice," one that is preferable to nurturing an infant whose continued survival is in doubt because of either the physical condition of the child or environmental difficulties for the mother.

So far, then, we have found two of the essential parts of the Toulmin model in Pinker's essay:

| | |
|---|---|
| **Claim** | Neonaticide is not a pathologic behavior but can be, rather, the result of evolutionary development. |
| **Grounds** | Various anthropological studies indicate that neonaticide is a common and accepted practice in many contemporary societies; studies by psychologists argue that neonaticide is a normal part of our parenting emotions; research by psychologists demonstrates that women who commit neonaticide are not mentally ill. |

## Warrants, Backing, and Rebuttals

Now let's move on to Pinker's warrants, which work to support his claim. Pinker never directly states, yet he strongly implies as a *warrant,* that "biology is destiny." It is clear from his claim and the grounds used to support it that Pinker believes the biological impulses of a new mother who commits neonaticide may overwhelm her civilized sense of what is morally or even emotionally right. Human beings, according to Pinker, are at the mercy of their neurological programming. Pinker offers *backing* for this *warrant* in paragraph 10 when he relates interviews by anthropologists with women who have killed their newborn babies and who appear to grieve sincerely for their children, regarding their actions as "an unavoidable tragedy." These women, according to Pinker, were compelled to make a difficult choice, which each did in spite of her maternal feelings toward the newborn. Pinker reinforces this point later in the essay when he states in paragraph 23 that "the laws of biology were not kind to Amy Grossberg and Melissa Drexler," two young women who killed their infants just after birth. Pinker strongly implies that biological forces were at work when these women made their decisions.

Pinker's warrant provides plenty of opportunity for *rebuttal* because even if the reader accepts the idea that human beings, despite the teachings of civilized society, are still subject to the dictates of more primitive and instinctive urges, Pinker asserts that the urge to kill one's baby is stronger than, say, the maternal instinct to nurture that infant. We have all heard of situations in which a mother has risked or sacrificed her own life to save that of her child. Why, we might ask, wouldn't this emotion dominate the behavior of a new mother? Pinker acknowledges this rebuttal in paragraph 11 when he points out that the neonaticides we read about in newspapers are often committed by middle-class girls who have the resources to support a child or the option to give the baby up for adoption.

Pinker responds to this rebuttal in two ways: First, he reiterates his claim that the internal forces of our evolutionary background are stronger than the individual's own sense of right and wrong. These young women are responding to the "signals of the long-vanished tribal environment in which we spent 99 percent of our evolutionary history." Moreover, Pinker goes on to suggest, neonaticide is triggered by environmental and social factors, specifically the age, marital status, and isolation of the new mother, that work to suppress more positive maternal responses. As he explains in paragraph 12, maternal feelings are more likely to emerge in an atmosphere of "cooing and clucking and congratulating" than in a "motel room or bathroom stall."

Pinker goes on to support his argument with several additional layers of warrants: If human behavior is controlled by deeply ingrained biological forces, then we can't be held legally responsible for these actions. In other words, while we may deeply deplore the act of neonaticide, we cannot fault these women for acting on an impulse they may not completely understand or feel able to control. In paragraph 15, Pinker provides backing for this claim by observing that few women in the United States are actually incarcerated for this crime and several European countries treat neonaticide less severely than other forms of homicide. Thus, although the killing of one's baby generates strong moral outrage in our society, we treat it less severely than most other offenses in the same category.

Logically, then, the next question must be "Why is this the case?" When older children are murdered by their mothers, as in Pinker's example of Susan Smith in paragraph 16, we waste little sympathy on the plight of the mother. We can agree with Pinker that "our compassion hinges on the child." Why do we react, according to Pinker, in a very different way to the death of a newborn? Pinker has very carefully brought us to his next warrant, which even he admits is the "unthinkable": Our reaction to the killing of a newborn and the killing of an older child is different because a newborn is not yet a "full person."

Pinker provides backing for his warrant in paragraphs 18 through 20. In paragraph 18, he points out a fact most readers would agree with: Unlike other mammals, human babies are helpless at birth. They are "incomplete." It will take an infant several years to achieve the level of physical development that some mammals enjoy at birth. Thus, a newborn baby cannot claim its rights as a person based on its physical completeness. Then, Pinker asks, on what basis can a newborn be seen as possessing "a right not to be killed"? By what traits do we define a person with a right to life? In paragraph 20, Pinker calls on the *backing* of "moral philosophers" who describe the traits human beings must possess to be considered fully human. Pinker concludes that newborn babies "don't possess these traits any more than mice do."

Anticipating that most readers will have a strong negative response to these ideas, Pinker acknowledges several rebuttals to this warrant. In paragraph 17, he recognizes that neither side of the abortion debate would agree with his assertion that birth should not be a marker to determine when a human being is given a right to life. To anti-abortionists, who maintain that "personhood" begins at conception, Pinker responds that if we adopt this viewpoint, the destruction of any fertilized human egg would be considered murder. To those in favor of abortion rights, who consider personhood to begin when the baby is capable of living outside the protection of the mother's body, Pinker counters that this depends on the condition of the infant and the willingness of the parents to accept the risks inherent in a premature birth. In paragraph 19, Pinker also rejects the position that all life deserves to be preserved. If this were practiced, Pinker reasons, then "delousing a child is akin to mass murder." Pinker's stance forces us to reexamine how we define a "person" and how we can determine at what point the right to live unharmed begins.

We can briefly summarize Pinker's warrants and backing as follows:

**Warrant 1**     Biology is destiny. We are at the mercy of our neurological programming, which has been handed down from our evolutionary ancestors.

**Backing**     Examples of women who grieve for the newborns they killed; references to Melissa Drexler and Amy Grossberg, who killed their newborn infants.

| | |
|---|---|
| **Warrant 2** | If human behavior is controlled by deeply ingrained biological forces, then women can't be held legally responsible for following their natural impulses. |
| **Backing** | Examples of lenient criminal treatment of women who commit neonaticide; examples of less severe penalties for women who kill newborns, as opposed to those given for the murder of older children or adults. |
| **Warrant 3** | A newborn infant is not a full person. Neonates do not yet possess those human qualities that bestow on them the right to life. |
| **Backing** | A description of a newborn infant's physical helplessness; a definition of a "full person" according to some moral philosophers; a comparison of the intellectual and moral awareness of a newborn infant with that of a mouse. |

## Qualifiers

Throughout his essay, Pinker is careful to use *qualifiers* that limit and clarify his claim. There are many examples of these; we will point out a few that appear early in the essay along with our emphasis and comments:

| | |
|---|---|
| **Paragraph 4** | "But it's *hard* [difficult but not impossible] to maintain that neonaticide is an illness when we learn that it has been practiced and accepted in *most* [but not all] cultures throughout history. And that neonaticidal women do not *commonly* [typical but not in all cases] show signs of psychopathology." |
| **Paragraph 5** | "But normal human motives are *not always* [happens some of the time] moral, and neonaticide *does not have to be* [but it could be] a product of malfunctioning neural circuitry or a dysfunctional upbringing." |

By using qualifiers, Pinker demonstrates his awareness that his claim may not always be true under all circumstances and accounts for the differing experiences of his audience.

As we stated at the beginning of this chapter, to construct a persuasive argument, you must pay careful attention to the logical structure you are building. As the Toulmin method illustrates, unless your claim is supported by a firm foundation (your warrants) and well buttressed by convincing grounds and backing, your structure will not withstand the rebuttals that will test its strength.

Pinker's view on neonaticide is disturbing, to say the least. For his essay to be persuasive, the reader must be willing to accept each of his warrants and the backing he uses to support them. Four days after Pinker's essay appeared in the *New York Times,* the following article was published in the *Washington Post.* As you read the article, notice how author Michael Kelley, a senior writer at the *National Journal,* attacks Pinker's claim by questioning each of his warrants and their backing. Calling Pinker's premise one of the "most thoroughly dishonest constructs anyone has ever attempted to pass off as science," Kelley also levels severe criticism at one of Pinker's sources, Michael Tooley. Kelley comments that Pinker's citation of Tooley's radical views, even though he may not directly agree with them, makes him "guilty by association." Kelley's accusation demonstrates why you should choose your sources carefully. Your audience will associate your views with the company they keep.

# Arguing for Infanticide
*Michael Kelley*

1   Of all the arguments advanced against the legalization of abortion, the one that always struck me as the most questionable is the most consequential: that the widespread acceptance of abortion would lead to a profound moral shift in our culture, a great devaluing of human life. This seemed to me dubious on general principle: Projections of this sort almost always turn out to be wrong because they fail to grasp that, in matters of human behavior, there is not really any such thing as a trendline. People change to meet new realities and thereby change reality.

2   Thus, for the environmental hysterics of the 1970s, the nuclear freezers of the 1980s and the Perovian budget doomsayers of the 1990s, the end that was nigh never came. So, with abortions, why should a tolerance for ending human life under one, very limited, set of conditions necessarily lead to an acceptance of ending human life under other, broader terms?

3   This time, it seems, the pessimists were right. On Sunday, Nov. 2, an article in the *New York Times,* the closest thing we have to the voice of the intellectual establishment, came out for killing babies. I am afraid that I am sensationalizing only slightly. The article by Steven Pinker in the *Times Magazine* did not go quite so far as to openly recommend the murder of infants, and printing the article did not constitute the *Times'* endorsement of the idea. But close enough, close enough.

4   What Pinker, a professor of psychology at the Massachusetts Institute of Technology, wrote and what the *Times* treated as a legitimate argument, was a thoroughly sympathetic treatment of this modest proposal: Mothers who kill their newborn infants should not be judged as harshly as people who take human life in its later stages because newborn infants are not persons in the full sense of the word, and therefore do not enjoy a right to life. Who says that life begins at birth?

5   "To a biologist, birth is as arbitrary a milestone as any other," Pinker breezily writes. "No, the right to life must come, the moral philosophers say, from morally significant traits that we humans happen to possess. One such trait is having a unique sequence of experiences that defines us as individuals and connects us to other people. Other traits include an ability to reflect upon ourselves as a continuous locus of consciousness, to form and savor plans for the future, to dread death and to express the choice not to die. And there's the rub: our immature neonates don't possess these traits any more than mice do."

6   Pinker notes that "several moral philosophers have concluded that neonates are not persons, and thus neonaticide should not be classified as murder," and he suggests his

acceptance of this view, arguing that "the facts don't make it easy" to legitimately outlaw the killing of infants.

7    Pinker's casually authoritative mention of "the facts" is important, because Pinker is no mere ranter from the crackpot fringe but a scientist. He is, in fact, a respected explicator of the entirely mainstream and currently hot theory of evolutionary psychology, and the author of *How the Mind Works,* a widely read and widely celebrated book on the subject.

8    How the mind works, says Pinker, is that people are more or less hard-wired to behave as they do by the cumulative effects of the human experience. First cousins to the old Marxist economic determinists, the evolutionary psychologists are behavioral determinists. They believe in a sort of Popeye's theory of human behavior: I do what I do because I yam what I yam because I wuz what I wuz.

9    This view is radical; it seeks to supplant both traditional Judeo-Christian morality and liberal humanism with a new "scientific" philosophy that denies the idea that all humans are possessed of a quality that sets them apart from the lower species, and that this quality gives humans the capacity and responsibility to choose freely between right and wrong. And it is monstrous. And, judging from the writings of Pinker and his fellow determinists on the subject of infanticide, it may be the most thoroughly dishonest construct anyone has ever attempted to pass off as science.

10    Pinker's argument was a euphemized one. The more blunt argument is made by Michael Tooley, a philosophy professor at the University of Colorado, whom Pinker quotes. In this 1972 essay "Abortion and Infanticide," Tooley makes what he calls "an extremely plausible answer" to the question: "What makes it morally permissible to destroy a baby, but wrong to kill an adult?" Simple enough: Personhood does not begin at birth. Rather, "an organism possesses a serious right to life only if it possesses the concept of a self as a continuing subject of experiences and other mental states, and believes that it is itself such a continuing entity."

11    Some would permit the killing of infants "up to the time an organism learned how to use certain expressions," but Tooley finds this cumbersome and would simply establish "some period of time, such as a week after birth, as the interval during which infanticide will be permitted."

12    And Tooley does not bother with Pinker's pretense that what is under discussion here is only a rare act of desperation, the killing of an unwanted child by a frightened, troubled mother. No, no, no. If it is moral to kill a baby for one, it is moral for all. Indeed, the systematic, professionalized use of infanticide would be a great benefit to humanity. "Most people would prefer to raise children who do not suffer from gross deformities or from severe physical, emotional, or intellectual handicaps," writes eugenicist Tooley. "If it could be shown that there is no moral objection to infanticide the happiness of society could be significantly and justifiably increased."

13    To defend such an unnatural idea, the determinists argue that infanticide is in fact natural: In Pinker's words, "it has been practiced and accepted in most cultures throughout history." This surprising claim is critical to the argument that the act of a mother killing a child is a programmed response to signals that the child might not fare well in life (because of poverty, illegitimacy or other factors). And it is a lie.

14    In fact, although millions of mothers give birth every year under the sort of adverse conditions that Pinker says trigger the "natural" urge to kill the baby, infanticide is

extremely rare in all modern societies, and is universally treated as a greatly aberrant act, the very definition of a moral horror. The only cultures that Pinker can point to in which infanticide is widely "practiced and accepted" are those that are outside the mores of Western civilization: ancient cultures and the remnants of ancient cultures today, tribal hunter-gatherer societies.

15    And so goes the entire argument, a great chain of dishonesty, palpable untruth piled upon palpable untruth. "A new mother," asserts Pinker, "will first coolly assess the infant and her situation and only in the next few days begin to see it as a unique and wonderful individual." Yes, that was my wife all over: cool as a cucumber as she assessed whether to keep her first-born child or toss him out the window. As George Orwell said once of another vast lie, "You have to be an intellectual to believe such nonsense. No ordinary man could be such a fool."

### QUESTIONS FOR ANALYSIS AND DISCUSSION

1.  Briefly outline the basic Toulmin components of Kelley's argument: What is his claim? What grounds does he use to support it? Then find and identify Kelley's warrants and the backing he provides to demonstrate their reliability.

2.  To what aspects of Pinker's claim and warrants does Kelley object? On what grounds does he object?

3.  Pinker limits his discussion of neonaticide to the behavior of "depressed new mothers" (paragraph 9). Does Kelley ignore this distinction in his response to Pinker? How does Kelley shift the discussion from Pinker's "anguished girls" (paragraph 23) to "millions of mothers" (paragraph 14 in Kelley)? Do you think this is a fair interpretation of Pinker's intent?

4.  Kelley begins his essay with a reference to the legalization of abortion. On what basis does he suggest a link between the "widespread acceptance of abortion" and Pinker's theories about neonaticide?

5.  In paragraph 3 of his essay, Kelley states that Pinker "did not go quite so far as to openly recommend the murder of infants." Discuss the implications of Kelley's use of the qualifiers *quite* and *openly*. What do you think he intends to imply about Pinker's objectives?

6.  In paragraph 10, what does Kelley mean by describing Pinker's argument as "euphemized"? What connection does Kelley make between Pinker's views and the theories expressed by Michael Tooley in his 1972 essay? Does your analysis of Pinker's claim and warrants lead you to believe that Pinker endorses Tooley's theories, as Kelley asserts?

7.  In your journal, discuss your own response to Kelley's essay. Which reasons do you find particularly persuasive? With which reasons do you disagree, and why?

8.  In paragraph 9, Kelley criticizes Pinker's attempt to take a "scientific" approach to a serious moral issue by suggesting that humans lack "the capacity and responsibility to choose freely between right and wrong." In your journal, consider how Pinker might respond to that statement. Would he agree with Kelley's interpretation of his ideas? How would Pinker suggest that society should deal with the problem of neonaticide?

## SAMPLE STUDENT ARGUMENT FOR ANALYSIS

The previous two essays focused on parental love becoming grossly dysfunctional as the possible result of tragic neurological wiring. What follows is a paper about the effects of parental love on children of divorce. Given the fact that half of all children will see their parents' marriage terminate by the time they turn 18, divorce has become an American way of life. While society may shake its collective head at such a statistic, lamenting the loss of the traditional family, not all children of divorce see it as a problem. In the following essay, Lowell Putnam explores the effect of his parents' divorce on his development, arguing that divorce should not be a taboo topic and that children of broken homes are not always damaged.

Putnam wrote this essay when he was a college freshman. When he is not living on campus, he splits his time between his mother's home in New York and his father's home in Massachusetts.

Read through Putnam's essay and make notes in your journal. Notice whether and how its parts work together—and, if possible, where some of the parts may need to be reworked. Then respond to the questions that follow.

---

Putnam 1

Lowell Putnam
Professor Ramos
English 201
5 March 2007

Did I Miss Something?

1    The subject of divorce turns heads in our society. It is responsible for bitten tongues, lowered voices, and an almost pious reverence saved only for life-threatening illness or uncontrolled catastrophe. Having grown up in a "broken home," I am always shocked to be treated as a victim of some social disease. When a class assignment required that I write an essay concerning my feelings about or my personal experiences with divorce, my first reaction was complete surprise. An essay on aspects of my life affected by divorce seems completely superfluous because I cannot differentiate between the "normal" part of my youth and the supposed angst and confusion that apparently come with all divorces. The separation of my parents over sixteen years ago (when I was three years old) has either saturated every last pore of my developmental epidermis to a point where I cannot sense it or it has not affected me at all. Eugene Ehrlich's *Highly Selective Dictionary for the Extraordinarily Literate* (1997) defines divorce as a "breach"; however, I cannot sense any schism in my life resulting from the event to which other people seem to attribute so much importance. My parents' divorce is a ubiquitous part of who I am, and the only "breach" that could arrive from my present familial arrangement would be to tear me away from what I consider my normal living conditions.

Putnam 2

2    Though there is no doubt in my mind that many unfortunate people have had their lives torn apart by the divorce of their parents, I do not feel any real sense of regret for my situation. In my opinion, the paramount role of a parent is to love his or her child. Providing food, shelter, education, and video games are of course other necessary elements of successful child rearing, but these secondary concerns stem from the most fundamental ideal of parenting, which is love. A loving parent will be a successful one even if he or she cannot afford to furnish his or her child with the best clothes or the most sophisticated gourmet delicacies. With love as the driving force in a parent's mind, he or she will almost invariably make the correct decisions. When my mother and father found that they were no longer in love with each other after nine years of marriage, their love for me forced them to take the precipitous step to separate. The safest environment for me was to be with one happy parent at a time, instead of two miserable ones all the time. The sacrifice that they both made to relinquish control over me for half the year was at least as painful for them as it was for me (probably even more so), but in the end I was not deprived of a parent's love, but merely of one parent's presence for a few weeks at a time. My father and mother's love for me has not dwindled even slightly over the past fifteen years, and I can hardly imagine a more well-adjusted and contented family.

3    As I reread the first section of this essay, I realize that it is perhaps too optimistic and cheerful regarding my life as a child of divorced parents. In all truthfulness, there have been some decidedly negative ramifications stemming from our family separation. My first memory is actually of a fight between my mother and father. I vaguely remember standing in the end of the upstairs hallway of our Philadelphia house when I was about three years old, and seeing shadows moving back and forth in the light coming from under the door of my father's study, accompanied by raised voices. It would be naïve of me to say that I have not been at all affected by divorce, since it has permeated my most primal and basic memories; however, I am grateful that I can only recall one such incident, instead of having parental conflicts become so quotidian that they leave no mark whatsoever on my mind. Also, I find that having to divide my time equally between both parents leads to alienation from either side of my family. Invariably, at every holiday occasion, there is one half of my family (either my mother's side or my father's) that has to explain that "Lowell is with his [mother/father] this year," while aunts, cousins, and grandparents collectively arch eyebrows or avert eyes. Again, though, I should not be hasty to lament my distance from loved ones, since there are many families with "normal" marriages where the children never even meet their cousins, let alone get to spend every other Thanksgiving with them. Though

Putnam 3

divorce has certainly thrown some proverbial monkey wrenches into some proverbial gears, in general my otherwise strong familial ties have overshadowed any minor blemishes.

4  Perhaps one of the most important reasons for my absence of "trauma" (for lack of a better word) stemming from my parents' divorce is that I am by no means alone in my trials and tribulations. The foreboding statistic that sixty percent of marriages end in divorce is no myth to me, indeed many of my friends come from similar situations. The argument could be made that "birds of a feather flock together" and that my friends and I form a tight support network for each other, but I strongly doubt that any of us need or look for that kind of buttress. The fact of the matter is that divorce happens a lot in today's society, and as a result our culture has evolved to accommodate these new family arrangements, making the overall conditions more hospitable for me and my broken brothers and shattered sisters.

5  I am well aware that divorce can often lead to issues of abandonment and familial proximity among children of separated parents, but in my case I see very little evidence to support the claim that my parents should have stayed married "for the sake of the child." In many ways, my life is enriched by the division of my time with my father and my time with my mother. I get to live in New York City for half of the year, and in a small suburb of Boston for the other half. I have friends who envy me, since I get "the best of both worlds." I never get double-teamed by parents during arguments, and I cherish my time with each one more since it only lasts half the year.

6  In my opinion, there is no such thing as a perfect life or a "normal" life, and any small blips on our karmic radar screen have to be dealt with appropriately but without any trepidation or self-pity. Do I miss my father when I live with my mother (and vice versa)? Of course I do. However, I know young boys and girls who have lost parents to illness or accidental injury, so my pitiable position is relative. As I look back on the last nineteen years from the relative independence of college, I can safely say that my childhood has not been at all marred by having two different houses to call home.

## QUESTIONS FOR ANALYSIS AND DISCUSSION

1. Identify Putnam's claim. Where does he state it in his essay? From your experience, do you agree with him? Do you agree that people discuss divorce "in an almost pious reverence saved only for life-threatening illness"?

2. On what grounds does Putnam base his claim? Find specific evidence he presents to support his claim. Do you find it convincing and supportive?

3. Do you agree with Putnam's definition of what makes a good parent?

4. Putnam has several warrants, some of them stated explicitly and some implied. In paragraph 2, he states: "A loving parent will be a successful one even if he or she cannot afford to furnish his or her child with the best clothes or the most sophisticated gourmet delicacies." Do you agree with his warrant? On what commonly shared values or beliefs does he base this warrant? Are there any aspects of his warrant with which you disagree? What backing does Putnam provide to support his warrant? Is it sufficient?

5. What other warrants underlie Putnam's claim? In a small peer group, identify several layers of warrants and discuss whether these need additional backing to be convincing.

6. Notice the qualifier Putnam uses in paragraph 3 when he says, "In all truthfulness, there have been *some* decidedly negative ramifications stemming from our family separation" (emphasis added). What limitations does this qualifying statement put on his argument? Does this limitation weaken his argument at all?

7. Does Putnam acknowledge and address anticipated rebuttals to his argument? Can you locate any in his essay? What rebuttals can you make in response to his argument?

8. If you are a child of divorced parents, write about the experience as it affected your emotional and psychological outlook. How did it impact your life growing up, and how did it affect your adult view of marriage? Answer the same questions if your parents remained married, considering in your response how your life may have been different if your parents had divorced while you were young.

9. In your peer group, discuss the effects of divorce on children. Further develop Putnam's idea that it is just another way of life. Compare notes with classmates to assemble a complete list. Based on this list, develop your own argument about the effects of divorce on children.

# Using Visual Arguments:
# Thinking Like an Illustrator

Ours is a visual world. From the first cave paintings of prehistoric France to the complicated photomosaic posters that adorn dormitory walls today, we are inspired, compelled, and persuaded by visual stimuli. Everywhere we look images vie for our attention—magazine ads, T-shirt logos, movie billboards, artwork, traffic signs, political cartoons, statues, and storefront windows. Glanced at only briefly, visuals communicate information and ideas. They project commonly held values, ideals, and fantasies. They relay opinion, inspire reaction, and influence emotion. And because competition for our attention today is so great and the time available for communication is so scarce, images must compete to make an impression or risk being lost in a blur of visual information.

Because the goal of a calculated visual is to persuade, coax, intimidate, or otherwise subliminally influence its viewer, it is important that its audience can discern the strategies or technique it employs. In other words, to be a literate reader of visuals, one must be a literate reader of arguments.

Consider the instant messages projected by brand names, company logos, or even the American flag. Such images may influence us consciously and unconsciously. Some visual images, such as advertisements, may target our emotions, while others, such as graphics, may appeal to our intellect. Just as we approach writing with the tools of critical analysis, we should carefully consider the many ways visuals influence us.

## Common Forms of Visual Arguments

Visual arguments come in many different forms and use many different media. Artists, photographers, advertisers, cartoonists, and designers approach their work with the same intentions that authors of written material do—they want to share a point of view, present an idea, inspire, or evoke a reaction. Think back to when you had your high school yearbook photo taken. The photographer didn't simply sit you down and start snapping pictures. More likely, the photographer told you how to sit, tilt your head, and where to gaze. You selected your clothing for the picture carefully and probably spent extra time on your hair that day. Lighting, shadow, and setting were also thoughtfully considered. You and your photographer crafted an image of how you wanted the world to see you—an image of importance because it would be forever recorded in your yearbook, as well as distributed to family and friends as the remembrance of a milestone in your life. In effect, you were creating a visual argument.

While there are many different kinds of visual arguments, the most common ones take the form of artwork, advertisements, editorial cartoons, and news photos. These visuals often do not rely on an image alone to tell their story, although it is certainly possible for a thoughtfully designed visual to do so. More often, however, advertisements are accompanied by ad copy, editorial cartoons feature comments or statements, and news photos are placed near the stories they enhance.

Ancillary visuals—that is, tables, graphs, and charts—have great potential for enhancing written arguments and influencing the audience. They provide snapshots of information and provide factual support to written information. We will discuss these types of visuals, and how you can use them to enhance your own written arguments, later in this chapter. But first, let us examine some powerful visual images and the ways they capture our attention, impact our sensibilities, and evoke our responses.

## Analyzing Visual Arguments

As critical readers of written arguments, we do not take the author simply at face value. We consider the author's purpose and intent, audience, style, tone, and supporting evidence. We must apply these same analytical tools to "read" visual arguments effectively. As with written language, understanding the persuasive power of "visual language" requires a close examination and interpretation of the premise, claims, details, supporting evidence, and stylistic touches embedded in any visual piece. We should ask ourselves the following four questions when examining visual arguments:

- Who is the target *audience?*
- What are the *claims* made in the images?
- What shared history or cultural *assumptions*—or warrants—does the image make?
- What is the supporting *evidence?*

Like works of art, visuals often employ color, shape, line, texture, depth, and point of view to create their effect. Therefore, to understand how visuals work and to analyze the way visuals persuade, we must also ask questions about specific aspects of form and design. For example, some questions to ask about print images such as those in newspaper and magazine ads include:

- What in the frame catches your attention immediately?
- What is the central image? What is the background image? foreground images? What are the surrounding images? What is significant in the placement of these images? their relationship to one another?
- What verbal information is included? How is it made prominent? How does it relate to the other graphics or images?
- What specific details (people, objects, locale) are emphasized? Which are exaggerated or idealized?
- What is the effect of color and lighting?
- What emotional effect is created by the images—pleasure? longing? anxiety? nostalgia?
- Do the graphics and images make you want to know more about the subject or product?

■ What special significance might objects in the image have?
■ Is there any symbolism embedded in the images?

Considering these questions helps us to survey a visual argument critically and enables us to formulate reasoned assessments of its message and intent. In the next pages of this chapter, we will analyze in greater detail some visual arguments presented in art, advertising, editorial cartoons, and photographs. Part Two of this book continues the investigation of visual arguments as they connect to the topics of each chapter.

## Art

The French artist Georges Braque (1882–1963) once said, "In art, there can be no effect without twisting the truth." While not all artists would agree with him, Braque, who with Pablo Picasso originated the cubist style, "saw" things from a different perspective than the rest of us, and he expressed his vision in his paintings. All art is an interpretation of what the artist sees. It is filtered through the eyes of the artist and influenced by his or her own perceptions.

Throughout history, artists have applied their craft to advance religious, social, and political visual arguments. Portraits of kings and queens present how the monarchs wanted their people to see them, with symbolic tools of power such as scepters, crowns, and rich vestments. Art in churches and cathedrals was used as a means of visual instruction for people who could not read. Much of modern art reveals impressions, feelings, and emotions without remaining faithful to the actual thing depicted. While entire books are written about the meaning and function of art, let's examine how one particular artist, Pablo Picasso (1881–1973), created a visual argument.

### Pablo Picasso's *Guernica*

Pablo Picasso, with fellow artist Georges Braque, invented a style of painting known as **cubism.** Cubism is based on the idea that the eye observes things from continually changing viewpoints, as fragments of a whole. Cubism aims to represent the essential reality of forms from multiple perspectives and angles. Thus, cubist paintings don't show reality as we see it. Rather, they depict pieces of people, places, and things in an unstable field of vision.

Picasso's painting *Guernica* (Figure 8.1, page 205) represents the essence of cubism. During the Spanish Civil War, the German air force bombed the town of Guernica, the cultural center of the Basque region in northern Spain and a Loyalist stronghold. In only a few minutes on April 26, 1937, hundreds of men, women, and children were massacred in the deadly air strike. Two months later, Picasso expressed his outrage at the attack in a mural he titled simply, *Guernica.*

The mural is Picasso's statement about the horror and devastation of war. The painting is dynamic and full of action, yet its figures seem flat and static. It is balanced while still presenting distorted images and impressions. It is ordered while still evoking a sense of chaos and panic. To better understand Picasso's "statement," let's apply some of the questions about visual arguments described earlier in the chapter to this painting.

© 2009 Estate of Pablo Picasso/Artists Rights Society (ARS), New York.

**Figure 8.1**   *Pablo Picasso, Guernica, 1937*

## Who Is Picasso's Target Audience?

Knowing the history of the painting can help us understand whom Picasso was trying to reach. In January 1937, Picasso was commissioned to paint a mural for the 1937 *Exposition Internationale des Arts et Techniques dans la Vie Moderne,* an art exhibition to open in France in May of that same year. Although he had never been a political person, the atrocity of Guernica in April compelled him to express his anger and appeal to the world.

Before the mural went on display, some politicians tried to replace it with a less "offensive" piece of art. When the picture was unveiled at the opening of the expo, it was received poorly. One critic described it as "the work of a madman." Picasso had hoped that his work would shock people. He wanted the outside world to care about what happened at Guernica. However, Picasso may have misjudged his first audience. In 1937, Europe was on the brink of world war. Many people were in denial that the war could touch them and preferred to ignore the possibility that it was imminent. It was this audience who first viewed *Guernica*—an audience that didn't want to see a mural about war, an audience that was trying to avoid the inevitable. Years later, the mural would become one of the most critically acclaimed works of art of the twentieth century.

## What Claims Is Picasso Making in the Images?

Picasso's painting comprises many images that make up an entire scene. It depicts simultaneously events that happened over a period of time. The overall claim is that war itself is horrible. The smaller claims address the injustice of Guernica more directly. A mother wails in grief over her dead infant, a reminder that the bombing of Guernica was a massacre of innocents. Picasso also chose to paint his mural in black and white, giving it the aura of a newspaper, especially in the body of the horse. He could be saying, "This is news" or "This is a current event that you should think about."

It should be mentioned that Picasso created many versions of the images in the mural, carefully considering their position, placement, and expression, sometimes drawing eight or nine versions of a single subject. He thoughtfully considered how the images would convey his message before he painted them in the mural.

## What Shared History or Cultural Assumptions Does Picasso Make?

The assumptions in any argument are the principles or beliefs that the audience takes for granted. These assumptions implicitly connect the claim to the evidence. By naming his mural *Guernica*, Picasso knew that people would make an immediate connection between the chaos on the wall and the events of April 26, 1937. He also assumed that the people viewing the painting would be upset by it. In addition, there are symbols in the painting that would have been recognized by people at the time—such as the figure of the bull in the upper-left-hand corner of the mural, a long-time symbol for Spain.

### What Is Picasso's Supporting Evidence?

Although Picasso was illustrating a real event, cubism allowed him to paint "truth" rather than "reality." If Picasso was trying to depict the horror of Guernica, and by extension, the terror and chaos of war, all the components of his mural serve as supporting evidence. The wailing figures, panicked faces, the darkness contrasted by jumbled images of light all project the horror of war. Even the horse looks terrified. Overall, *Guernica* captures the emotional cacophony of war. Picasso wasn't just trying to say, "War is hell." He was also trying to impress upon his audience that such atrocities should never happen again. In essence, Picasso was making an appeal for peace by showing its opposite, the carnage of war.

#### QUESTIONS FOR ANALYSIS AND DISCUSSION

Referring to the more specific questions regarding visual arguments discussed earlier in the chapter, apply them to Picasso's painting.

1. What images in the painting catch your attention, and why?
2. What is the central image? Is there a central image? What appears in the foreground? What is significant about the placement of the images? How do they relate to one another?
3. What verbal information, if any, is included, and why? (Remember that Picasso did title his painting *Guernica*. What might have happened if he had named it something more abstract?)
4. What specific details are emphasized? What is exaggerated or idealized?
5. What is the effect of color and light?
6. Does the image make you want to know more?
7. What symbolism is embedded in the image?

## Norman Rockwell's *Freedom of Speech*

Picasso's mural was designed to be displayed in a large hall at the World Exposition and later, presumably, in a museum. Other artists had less grand aspirations for their work. Norman Rockwell (1894–1978) was an artist who featured most of his work on the covers of magazines, most notably the *Saturday Evening Post,* a publication he considered "the greatest show window in America." In 47 years, Rockwell contributed 321 paintings to the magazine and became an American icon.

On January 6, 1941, President Franklin Delano Roosevelt addressed Congress, delivering his famous "Four Freedoms" speech. Against the background of the Nazi domination of Europe and the Japanese oppression of China, Roosevelt described the four essential human freedoms—freedom of speech, freedom of worship, freedom from want, and freedom from fear. Viewing these freedoms as the fundamental basis on which our society was formed, Roosevelt called upon Americans to uphold these liberties at all costs. Two years later, Rockwell, inspired by Roosevelt's speech, created his famous series of paintings on these "Four Freedoms," reproduced in four consecutive issues of the *Saturday Evening*

*Post.* So popular were the images that they were used by the U.S. government to sell war bonds, to inspire public support for the war effort, and to remind people of the ideals for which they were fighting. The paintings serve as an example of how art can sometimes extend into advertising.

Let's take a closer look at one of the four paintings, *Freedom of Speech* (Figure 8.2 below). When the war department adopted the painting for the war bond effort, it added two slogans to the image. The command "Save Freedom of Speech" was printed at the top of the painting in large, capital letters and, in even larger typeface, "Buy War Bonds" was printed at the bottom. As we analyze this painting, we will also make references to its later use as part of the effort to sell war bonds.

**Figure 8.2** *Norman Rockwell,* Freedom of Speech, *1943*

Before he took a brush to his canvas, Rockwell consciously or unconsciously asked himself some of the same questions writers do when they stare at a blank piece of paper while preparing to create a written argument. After determining that he would use the American small-town vehicle of democracy, the town meeting, as the means to express the theme of freedom of speech, he then painted his "argument."

### Who Is Rockwell's Audience?

The *Saturday Evening Post* was widely read in America in the 1930s and 1940s. Rockwell would have wanted his work to appeal to a wide audience, readers of the magazine. If we examine the people in the painting—presumably based on Rockwell's Arlington, Vermont, friends and neighbors—we can deduce the kind of audience the artist was hoping to touch: small-town citizens from a middle-income, working-class environment. Like the language of an argument written for a "general audience," the figures represent what Rockwell considered all-American townsfolk.

The venue is a meetinghouse or town hall because people are sitting on benches. The figures represent a generational cross-section of men and women, from the elderly white-haired man to the left of the central standing figure to the young woman behind him. Style of dress reinforces the notion of class diversity, from the standing man in work clothes to the two men dressed in white shirts, ties, and suit jackets. The formality of the seated figures also opens audience identity to life beyond a small, rural community. That is, some of the men's formal attire and the woman in a stylish hat broaden the depiction to include white-collar urban America. While diversity in age and class is suggested, diversity of race is not. There are no Asians, African Americans, or other nonwhites in the scene. This exclusion might be a reflection of the times and, perhaps, the popular notion of what constituted small-town America 70 years ago. While such exclusion would be unacceptable today, it should be noted that in the years following this painting's completion, Rockwell used his considerable talent and fame to champion the civil rights struggle.

### What Is Rockwell's Claim?

When the government adopted Rockwell's painting for their World War II effort campaign to sell war bonds, they added the caption: "Save Freedom of Speech. Buy War Bonds." When we consider the poster as an advertising piece, this essentially becomes the poster's claim. And we know the artist's intention, to illustrate the theme of freedom of speech. Rockwell's challenge was in how he makes his claim—how he dramatizes it on canvas. Just as a writer uses words to persuade, the artist makes his claim in symbolic details of the brush.

It has been said that Norman Rockwell's paintings appeal to a dreamy-eyed American nostalgia and at the same time project a world where the simple acts of common folk express high American ideals. In this painting, we have one of the sacred liberties dramatized by a working-class man raised to the figure of a political spokesperson in the assembly of others. Clearly expressing his opinion as freely as anybody else, he becomes both the illustration and defender of the democratic principles of freedom and equality.

## What Are Rockwell's Assumptions?

As with written arguments, the success of a visual argument depends on whether the audience accepts the assumptions (the values, legal or moral principles, commonsense knowledge, or shared beliefs) projected in the image. One assumption underlying Rockwell's illustration is that freedom of speech is desirable for Americans regardless of gender, class, or position in society. We know this instantly from the facial expressions and body language of the figures in the canvas. For example, the face of the man standing seems more prominent because it is painted against a dark blank background and is brighter than any others, immediately capturing our attention. His face tilts upward with a look of pride, lit as if by the inspiration of the ideals he represents—freedom of expression. One might even see suggestions of divine inspiration on his face as it rises in the light and against the night-blackened window in the background. The lighting and man's posture are reminiscent of religious paintings of past centuries. Additionally, the man's body is angular and rough, while his facial characteristics strongly resemble those of a young Abraham Lincoln—which suggests a subtle fusion of the patriotic with the divine. The implied message is that freedom of speech is a divine right.

As for the surrounding audience, we take special note of the two men looking up at the speaker. The older man appears impressed and looks on with a warm smile of approval, while the other man on the right gazes up expectantly. In fact, the entire audience supports the standing man with reasonable, friendly, and respectful gazes. The speaker is "Everyman." And he has the support and respect of his community. Rockwell's audience, subscribers of the *Saturday Evening Post,* saw themselves in this image—an image that mirrored the values of honest, decent, middle America.

## What Is Rockwell's Supporting Evidence?

The key supporting image in Rockwell's painting is the sharp contrast between the standing man and those sitting around him. Not only is he the only one on his feet, but he is the only working-class person clearly depicted. He stands out from the others in the room; and it is significant that they look up to him—a dramatic illustration of what it means to give the common man his say. Were the scene reversed—with the central figure formally dressed and those looking up approvingly attired in work clothes—we would have a completely different message: that is, a representative of the upper class perhaps "explaining" higher concepts to a less-educated people. The message would be all wrong. In the painting, class barriers are transcended as the "common man" has risen to speak his mind with a face full of conviction, while upper-class people look on in support. That's the American ideal in action.

Because this is a painting instead of a newspaper photograph, every detail is selected purposely and, thus, is open to interpretation. One such detail is the fold of papers sticking out of the man's jacket pocket. What might those papers represent? And what's the point of such a detail? What associations might we make with it? There are words printed on the paper, but we cannot read them, so we're left to speculate. The only other paper in the painting is in the hand of the man on the right. The words "report" and "town" are visible. So, we might conclude that the speaker's pocket contains the same pamphlet, perhaps a summary report of the evening's agenda or possibly a resolution to be voted on. Whatever the documentation, the man clearly doesn't need it because his remarks transcend whatever is on that paper. And here lies more evidence of Rockwell's claim and celebration of the unaided articulation of one man's views out of many—the essence of freedom of speech.

Referring to the more specific questions regarding visual arguments discussed earlier in the chapter, apply them to Rockwell's painting.

1. What images in the painting catch your attention, and why?
2. What is the central image? Is there a central image? What appears in the foreground? What is significant about the placement of the images? How do they relate to one another?
3. What verbal information, if any, is included, and why?
4. What specific details are emphasized? What is exaggerated or idealized?
5. What is the effect of color and light?
6. Does the image make you want to know more?
7. What symbolism is embedded in the image?

# Advertisements

Norman Rockwell sought to embody a concept through his art; and, as a result, his painting tries to prompt reflection and self-awareness. In other words, his visuals serve to open the mind to a new discovery or idea. Advertising also selects and crafts visual images. However, advertising has a different objective. Its goal is not to stimulate expansive and enlightened thought but to direct the viewer to a single basic response: buy this product!

Images have clout, and none are so obvious or so craftily designed as those from the world of advertising. Advertising images are everywhere—television, newspapers, the Internet, magazines, the sides of buses, and on highway billboards. Each year, companies collectively spend more than $150 billion on print ads and television commercials (more than the gross national product of many countries). Advertisements comprise at least a quarter of each television hour and form the bulk of most newspapers and magazines. Tapping into our most basic emotions, their appeal goes right to the quick of our fantasies: happiness, material wealth, eternal youth, social acceptance, sexual fulfillment, and power.

Yet, most of us are so accustomed to the onslaught of such images that we see them without looking and hear them without listening. But if we stopped to examine how the images work, we might be amazed at their powerful and complex psychological force. And we might be surprised at how much effort goes into the crafting of such images—an effort solely intended to make us spend our money.

Like a written argument, every print ad or commercial has an *audience, claims, assumptions,* and *evidence.* Sometimes these elements are obvious; sometimes they are understated; sometimes they are implied. They may boast testimonials by average folk or celebrities, or cite hard scientific evidence. And sometimes they simply manipulate our desire to be happy or socially accepted. But common to every ad and commercial, no matter what the medium, is the *claim* that you should buy this product.

Print ads are potentially complex mixtures of images, graphics, and text. So in analyzing an ad, you should be aware of the use of photography, the placement of those images, and the use of text, company logos, and other graphics such as illustrations, drawings, sidebar boxes, and so on. You should also keep in mind that every aspect of the image has been thought about and carefully designed. Let's take a look at how a recent magazine ad for Toyota uses some of these elements including social appeal, the use of color and light, and setting to convince us to buy the Toyota Prius hybrid car.

## Toyota Prius Ad

When analyzing a print ad, we should try to determine what first captures our attention. In the Toyota Prius ad (Figure 8.3 on page 213), it is the bold, white outline of a car. The instant suggestion is a compact vehicle with a simple and streamlined design. The outline format barely intrudes upon our view of the beach scene; and, ironically, we're not even shown the actual vehicle the ad is selling. Second, we note a smiling, ethnically diverse couple. The man and woman are not in contact with one another but with the outline of the vehicle, suggesting that in their relationship they share positive interest in the car outline they are leaning on. Their attire is sporty and casual; and their smiles are relaxed and content. We wonder: Are they potential buyers? Did they design the car? Are they simply feeling good about what the car represents? But the small print at the bottom identifies them as "Toyota Associates," perhaps meaning that they had something to do with the design or production of the Prius.

The third component we notice is the beach itself. The soft lighting signals approaching dusk; the sand, sand dunes, sea, and sky are quiet, pristine, and undisturbed. We see a simple and unblemished image of nature. The fourth aspect we note is the text. The slogan, "WE SEE BEYOND CARS" is rendered in a large font, bold print; the lower expository text is in a smaller font; and the last segment of the ad identifying the couple is smaller still. The last item our eye moves to is in the upper right hand corner: Toyota and the url: toyota.com/beyondcars.

One of the most striking aspects of this ad is how it doesn't look like any other car ad. We are accustomed to images that show the actual vehicles—images that highlight particular features that manufacturers want consumers to associate with their cars: power, speed, ruggedness, luxury, handling, durability, et cetera. This ad defies those traditional approaches. Instead, we see a clean-cut twosome—who may or may not be romantically involved—leaning against the outline of a car we cannot see, though we know from the text it is a Prius. The message is that the Prius is an idea as much as it is a car. And driving this zero-emissions vehicle isn't just about transportation; it's about being part of a movement that will preserve the environment. The pristine environment, which the Prius will protect, is what shines through in this ad. In short, the Prius is desirable because it is barely there.

**Figure 8.3**

### Who is the Audience for the Ad?

The ad attracts viewers not unlike the young couple in the ad—young to middle aged men and women who are technologically savvy, educated, and concerned over the environment. In fact, the ad assumes that protection of the environment takes precedence over the luxury of a polluting, powerful, gas-guzzling vehicle. The appeal is to individuals seeking alternatives to the typically over engineered powerhouse machines. In its understated approach, the ad also assumes that viewers appreciate nuance and subtlety. In fact, the ad does not talk about the car, but rather about Toyota's mission to protect the environment. In so doing, viewers are invited to explore the relationship between the visuals and the text.

### What Is the Claim?

Because advertisers are vying for our attention, they must project their claim as efficiently as possible in order to discourage us from turning the page. The stated or implied claim of all advertising is that the product will make life better for us. Of course, most ads aren't so bold in their claims. But the promise is there by inference. The claim of this ad is that if you want to save the environment from the fallout of fossil-fuel consumption, you should buy a Prius. Further, by purchasing one, you become part of a community of responsible, "with-it" and technologically savvy people.

Lastly, the ad claims in its slogan, "WE SEE BEYOND CARS." Combined with the minimalist outline of the Prius and the undisturbed beauty of the beach, that slogan suggests that there is something beyond cars that you the consumer are really interested in: preserving the beauty and purity of nature. Beyond advertising a car, the ad makes the claim that you can be part of a transcendent movement, the green movement, simply by purchasing a Prius and helping make the world a better place. The ad claims that Toyota is devoted to protecting the environment, in fact, announcing that it spends $23 million per day on research. Such a claim re-brands Toyota not just as a manufacturer of cars but as a key player in the preservation of the environment.

### What Is the Evidence?

The evidence for the desirability of the Toyota Prius is in the visuals and the text. If one goes to the website toyota.com/beyondcars, one sees a minimalist visual in the same style as this ad which presents evidence about Toyota's presence in the U.S. car market, its research funding and Toyota car production, and sales.

### What Are the Assumptions?

The creators of this ad made several assumptions about us, the audience: (1) that we are familiar with the traditional car ads that showcase their vehicles; (2) that a significant segment of the car-buying public is environmentally conscious and looking for ways to save it; (3) that a company associated with protecting the environment via hybrid cars is admirable; and (4) that the audience cares less about a vehicle's power, glamour, or speed and more about the environmental impact of the vehicle. In short, the ad assumes people are as interested in supporting a cause as they are in buying a car.

## Sample Ads for Analysis

Apply the principles of critical analysis described in the above section on advertising, as well as the elements of form and design discussed earlier in the chapter, to the ads that appear in the following pages.

© The Clorox Pet Products Company. Reprinted with permission.

**Figure 8.4**

## Fresh Step Cat Litter

### QUESTIONS FOR ANALYSIS AND DISCUSSION ————————

1. What first caught your eye in this ad? In what order do you look at other elements in the ad? Do you think the advertiser intends you to look at each component of the ad in a particular order? Why?
2. What is the visual joke in this ad? Consider the cat's posture, body language, facial expression, and relationship to the setting. What do the furniture, wall decorations, and other decorative touches say about the occupant? Do you find the ad visually pleasing? (Consider the size and placement of the cat, the background, and graphics.)
3. Who might be the target audience for this ad? Consider gender, age group, socioeconomic level, lifestyle, and self-image. Defend your answers using specifics in the ad.
4. There is a minimal amount of text here. How does the wording relate to the visuals? With reference to the copy, what is the implied argument in the copy? Explain the claim in the text. What are the warrants?

**Figure 8.5**

Victoria's Dirty Secret

### QUESTIONS FOR ANALYSIS AND DISCUSSION

1. In what ways does the model look like the typical Victoria's Secret model? Be specific. In what ways does this model differ? Consider her attire, the wings, hair styling, expression, body posture, shoes, and so on. If you see any differences, how would you explain them? How do the similarities and/or differences contribute to the ad's criticism of the catalogue production of Victoria's Secret?
2. Consider the chain saw. What is the effect of having the model holding a sketched chain saw instead of a real one? And what do you make of the style of the drawing? Why not have a more realistic drawing than this roughly drawn one?
3. After reading the text of the ad, consider some of the characteristics of its argument. What is the basic claim? Locate specific evidence. Are opposing points of view presented? Where specifically?
4. Is this ad a proposal or a position argument? Explain your answer.
5. Visual arguments should inspire or provoke a reaction. On a scale of one to ten, how persuasive is this ad? Are you inspired to take action—specifically to contact Leslie H. Wexner, CEO of Victoria's Secret's parent company? Does it inspire you to get involved with ForestEthics' campaign?
6. Consider the small photograph insert. What is depicted, and how well does it illustrate the argument being made in the ad? How does it relate to the image of the model? Explain in detail.

# Editorial or Political Cartoons

Editorial cartoons have been a part of American life for over a century. They are a mainstay feature on the editorial pages in most newspapers—those pages reserved for columnists, contributing editors, and illustrators to present their views in words and pen and ink. As in the nineteenth century when they first started to appear, such editorial cartoons are political in nature, holding up political and social issues for public scrutiny and sometimes ridicule.

A stand-alone editorial cartoon—as opposed to a strip of multiple frames—is a powerful and terse form of communication that combines pen-and-ink drawings with dialogue balloons and captions. They're not just visual jokes, but visual humor that comments on social/political issues while drawing on viewers' experience and knowledge.

The editorial cartoon is the story of a moment in the flow of familiar current events. And the key words here are *moment* and *familiar*. Although a cartoon captures a split instant in time, it also infers what came before and, perhaps, what may happen next—either in the next moment or in some indefinite future. And usually the cartoon depicts a specific moment in time. One of the most famous cartoons of the last 50 years is the late

Bill Mauldin's Pulitzer Prize–winning drawing of the figure of Abraham Lincoln with his head in his hands. It appeared the morning after the assassination of President John Kennedy in 1963. There was no caption nor was there a need for one. The image represented the profound grief of a nation that had lost its leader to an assassin's bullet. But to capture the enormity of the event, Mauldin brilliantly chose to represent a woeful America by using the figure of Abraham Lincoln as depicted in the sculpture of the Lincoln Memorial in Washington, D.C. In so doing, the message implied that so profound was the loss that it even reduced to tears the marble figure of a man considered to be our greatest president, himself assassinated a century before.

For a cartoon to be effective, it must make the issue clear at a glance and it must establish where it stands on the argument. In the Mauldin illustration, we instantly recognize Lincoln and identify with the emotions. We need not be told the circumstances, since by the time the cartoon appeared the next day, all the world knew the horrible news that the president had been assassinated. To convey less obvious issues and figures at a glance, cartoonists resort to images that are instantly recognizable, that we don't have to work hard to grasp. Locales are determined by giveaway props: An airplane out the window suggests an airport; a cactus and cattle skull, a desert; an overstuffed armchair and TV, the standard living room. Likewise, human emotions are instantly conveyed: pleasure is a huge toothy grin; fury is steam blowing out of a figure's ears; love is two figures making goo-goo eyes with floating hearts overhead. People themselves may have exaggerated features to emphasize a point or emotion.

In his essay "What Is a Cartoon?" Mort Gerberg says that editorial cartoons rely on such visual clichés to convey their messages instantly. That is, they employ stock figures for their representation—images instantly recognizable from cultural stereotypes like the fat-cat tycoon, the mobster thug, and the sexy female movie star. And these come to us in familiar outfits and props that give away their identities and profession. The cartoon judge has a black robe and gavel; the prisoner wears striped overalls and a ball and chain; the physician dons a smock and holds a stethoscope; the doomsayer is a scrawny long-haired guy carrying a sign saying, "The end is near." These are visual clichés known by the culture at large, and we instantly recognize them.

The visual cliché may be what catches our eye in the editorial cartoon, but the message lies in what the cartoonist does with it. As Gerberg observes, "The message is in twisting it, in turning the cliché around."

## Mike Luckovich's "Let's Be Responsible" Cartoon

Consider Mike Luckovich's cartoon (from the *Atlanta Journal-Constitution*) in Figure 8.6 that addresses the issue of texting while driving. The visual cliché is a group of friends gathering in a very ordinary bar. We know that from the familiar props: the ubiquitous signage identifying the setting as a bar, the single dangling light fixture, bottles of alcohol, draft pulls, and the broad back of the bartender. Even the patrons are familiar figures—four casually dressed, slightly unkempt, individuals who look neither prosperous nor polished but slightly down on their luck. Note the dark-haired young man wears a T-shirt with a cartoon figure on it; another male sports unconventionally messy hair and the suggestion of beads around his neck. The woman has over-styled blond hair, and the bald man wears a plain white shirt. The twist, of course, is that instead of

**Figure 8.6**

clasping a martini or a beer, the patrons of this bar are all regarding their cell phones. There is not a drink on the table, (though we can assume that they have had or will be having considerable alcohol since they are concerned about who will be driving.) Maybe not.

The issue, of course, is the debate about driving while texting. The cartoon addresses the numerous deadly accidents caused by drivers who were texting rather than paying attention to the road, thus causing accidents which fill the news. A public debate still rages about outlawing texting while driving, fueled by the increased number of text messages being sent as well as the number of resulting accidents. (In June 2008, 75 billion text messages were sent. A year later, 135.2 billion text messages were sent.) According to a recent *New York Times*/CBS news poll (NYTimes.com/polls), nearly all Americans say sending a text message while driving should be illegal; and half of all Americans say texting behind the wheel should be punished at least as harshly as drunk driving. This concern is reflected in some legislation: it is now illegal in at least 15 states to text while driving, and the federal government is exerting pressure to ban it in all states.

The cartoon's joke is in the twist—the gap between the familiar and the unexpected. The familiar is the bar scene; the unexpected is the fact that the patrons are not holding alcoholic drinks but texting devices. What is important is a sober texter not a sober driver. Thus, the caption: "Let's be responsible. On the drive back, who's the designated texter?"

## What Is the Cartoon's Claim?

The claim in this cartoon is that driving while texting is as dangerous and possibly more dangerous than driving while drinking. This claim is implicit in the satirical image of the bar patrons holding their cell phones and concentrating on texting. And it is implicit in the comment, "Let's be responsible. On the drive back, who's the designated texter?"

## What Are the Cartoon's Assumptions?

This cartoon makes the assumption that people are preoccupied with texting and that they recognize that texting while driving is irresponsible and dangerous. It also presumes that readers are aware of the spate of serious accidents caused by "texters" and that they equate such behavior with drunk driving. Furthermore, the cartoon assumes familiarity with the campaign to designate a sober driver if other passengers are drinking. Part of the humor of the cartoon is based on the substitution of texting devices for alcohol.

## What Is the Cartoon's Evidence?

The cartoon presents the ironic and humorous notion that its bar patrons are not even thinking about drinks. None are present. Instead, they are preoccupied with text messaging. This is the vice they go to the bar to indulge. They are so consumed with texting, that they want to be certain they can continue on the drive home. The implication is that they will not be able to restrain themselves from texting and must appoint a "designated texter" so texting will not be interrupted.

### QUESTIONS FOR ANALYSIS AND DISCUSSION

Apply the principles of critical analysis described in the above section on editorial cartoons, as well as the elements of form and design discussed earlier in the chapter, to the cartoons. First take a look at Figure 8.7, Cartoon by Pat Bagley.

1. What is the claim or claims embodied in the visual elements of this political cartoon? What constitutes the evidence of the claim or claims? Cite the specific pieces of evidence.
2. Consider the audience for this cartoon. What groups of citizens would be most likely to have a strong reaction? Does the cartoon suggest a solution to the problems depicted? Are the problems interrelated?
3. What is the tone of the cartoon? Would you describe it as comical? satirical? facetious? overstated? amusing? disturbing?
4. This cartoon originally appeared on the editorial page in the *Salt Lake City Tribune*. Is the cartoon particular to the Salt Lake City area? Why or why not? What could you change in the piece so that it applied to a different city or area?
5. What is the grill-like tray on the top of the cars? And what is the bumper extension jutting off each car? How do they fit into the ad? What is the significance of the insignia on the vehicle on the lower right corner that says "SUV2020"?

"BACK IN AUGHT-FIVE WE HAD TO CHOOSE BETWEEN HIGHWAYS AND EDUCATION.."

**Figure 8.7**   *Cartoon by Pat Bagley*

6. What might "back in aught-five we had to choose" most likely refer to?
7. Based on the cartoonist's "argument," what do you think he is advocating? Is he for or against highway improvement? for or against education? Can you tell? Does it matter?

### QUESTIONS FOR ANALYSIS AND DISCUSSION

Refer to Figure 8.8, cartoon by Daryl Cagle.

1. What is happening in this cartoon? Whom does the first kid "hate"? Does the cartoon make more sense when we know that it appeared shortly after September 11, 2001? Why or why not?
2. Consider the comment made by the middle kid in the cartoon, who agrees at first, but then asks a clarifying question. Is this significant? Why doesn't the first kid ask the same thing?
3. What is the cartoonist's claim in this cartoon? What evidence does he provide? Explain.
4. Although this cartoon was drawn in the context of the events following September 11, 2001, would it have been equally effective ten years ago? ten years into the future? Would the previous cartoon be as timeless? Explain.

**Figure 8.8**   *Cartoon by Daryl Cagle*

# News Photographs

Although editorial cartoons can stand on their own, they are frequently featured on editorial pages in newspapers that include commentary on the topic they depict. Photographs are another vehicle used to augment commentary in newspapers, journals, and magazines. Indeed, sometimes the photograph *tells* the story better than words ever could, because it has the ability to touch our deepest emotions instantly.

At first glance, you may think that photos are simply snapshots of an event or moment. But most photographs presented in leading newspapers and journals are the result of effort and planning. Photojournalists are constantly making editorial decisions when they take a picture. They think about where to take the photo, the right moment, whom to include, the angle, the lighting, the depth of field, and the ISO selected. They consider the subject matter and how it might affect an audience. In some cases, they think about why they are taking the picture and what argument they want to present on film. Some of the most compelling photographs in history come from photojournalists capturing one moment. These photos are not posed, but they still tell a story. Some famous photos include the shot of a sailor kissing a nurse in New York City's Times Square when victory was declared at the end of World War II. Or, who can forget the Pulitzer Prize–winning photo of firefighter Chris Fields carrying the lifeless body of 1-year-old Baylee Almon from the wreckage of the federal office building after the Oklahoma City bombing? While we might not recall the names of the people involved, the image itself remains stamped on our memory.

As a unit, the news story and the photo work together to tell a story. The best photos often tell a story without using any words. But knowing the context in which the photo was taken is important as well. At the very least, the date and location establish the circumstances. Consider Figure 8.9, a photograph of the aftermath of a home foreclosure, taken by Larry Downing in Waco, Texas, for Reuters. A young girl jumps rope on the sidewalk next to her family's belongings after she, her parents, and her four brothers and sisters received a court order of eviction that was carried out by McLennan County Deputy Constables. The photograph, one of the Reuters news photo Images of the Year 2009, speaks to the human toll of home foreclosure, especially on families with young children. Anyone who has read a newspaper or watched a newscast last year knows the high number of foreclosures that came with the weakening real estate market and a declining economy. According to the United States Foreclosure Report, by the third quarter of 2009 1 in every 136 homes was in some stage of foreclosure. And the emotional toll is heavy. Losing one's home can result in chronic anxiety, depression, and feelings of failure—all sources of strain on

**Figure 8.9**

personal and family relationships. This photograph captures some of the painful consequences of foreclosure on both a social and emotional level. The image also powerfully conveys the injustice of the process that leaves a family's worldly possessions on the sidewalk, including the children. At the same time, while capturing the pain and humiliation of dispossession, central is the innocence of a child who can jump rope during this cataclysmic event. One wonders if her jump-roping is a product of her youthful innocence or a desperate distraction from what is happening to her and her family.

## Who Is the Target Audience?

This photograph was selected by the Reuters News Photo Service as one of the best Images of the Year 2009 because it was newsworthy, powerful, and artful. The photo targets a general audience likely to be concerned with social and economic issues and open to an exploration of the human consequences of such. The cost of foreclosure is not just the loss of a home but the loss of childhood innocence as well.

## What Is the Purpose of the Image?

The image captures a moment in time—one that the photographer felt was important to underscore. It shows a family's experience of foreclosure: their possessions suddenly mere rubble on the sidewalk; their small but cozy home no longer a shelter; the constables on the far left, overseeing this eviction; and, most importantly, the youngest victim, a young girl jumping rope in front of her former home. The purpose of the photograph is to document the human toll when a home is foreclosed.

## What Are the Claims Made in the Image?

This photograph puts flesh on a statistic from the rash of home foreclosures in the U.S. in the past few years. It dramatizes something of the human toll. Given this economic context, the viewer can draw a number of claims from the image. Foremost is that the home offers a family security and shelter. Rich or poor, being a home owner is part of the American Dream. Another claim is that foreclosure turns one's valued possessions into rubble. The jumble of chairs, mattresses, and stuffed plastic bags looks like stuff to be discarded. Almost washed out are three men at the far left in the photograph, most probably the officials conducting the eviction. The claim here might be that they are the heartless enforcers of a foreclosure. Most importantly, the viewer notes the young girl jump roping. She is the heart of the photograph. And what are the claims here? To some viewers the young girl might be the embodiment of youthful innocence. The claim could also be that she is too young to be fully aware of what is happening and can rebound with resilience. On the other hand, one could see the child jump roping as a desperate distraction. The claim, thus, would be that this event will rob this child of all that childhood should be about: security, family, and certainty.

## What Assumptions Does the Image Make?

The photographer assumes that most people will find this image arresting. Given the context, a crisis in housing, it is assumed that the photograph is emotionally charged.

## QUESTIONS FOR ANALYSIS AND DISCUSSION

Consider the photograph in Figure 8.10 taken by *Boston Globe* photojournalist Suzanne Kreiter. It shows two panhandlers on a Boston street. The photograph accompanied an article, "A Street to Call Home," which reports on how some homeless people panhandle on the very spot where they live.

**Figure 8.10**

1. This photograph accompanied an article about homelessness in an urban area of the Northeast. What assumptions about the audience does the photographer make?

2. What details in the photograph convey homelessness to the viewer? Consider objects, location, and background.

3. A close examination of the two main figures in this photograph makes a strong statement about their character. Consider their position, posture, relationship to one another, the direction of their gazes, the facial expressions, and their clothing, and describe the character of these individuals.

4. Would you describe these people as heroic? downtrodden? defiant? helpless victims? noble survivors? Explain why.

5. What argument about homelessness is embedded in this photograph? In other words, what is the claim?

6. Does the background of the photograph detract from or add to the meaning of the photograph?

7. How do you expect to see the homeless depicted? Is this expectation based on stereotype? Does this image of the homeless reinforce or contradict the stereotypical view of the homeless? Explain your answer. Does this photograph change your idea of urban poverty? Why or why not?

8. Do you see any similarities in style or content between this photograph and Norman Rockwell's "Freedom of Speech"?

# Ancillary Graphics: Tables, Charts, and Graphs

Art, advertisements, editorial cartoons, and news photos all present interesting visual ways to persuade, and knowing how they do this improves your critical thinking and analytical skills. Ancillary graphics, however, such as tables, charts, and graphs, are some visual tools you can use in your own persuasive essays. In Chapter 6, we discussed how numerical data and statistics are very persuasive in bolstering an argument. But a simple table, chart, or graph can convey information at a glance while conveying trends that support your argument. In fact, such visuals are preferable to long, complicated paragraphs that confuse the reader and may detract from your argument.

Ancillary graphics usually take the form of tables, charts, graphs (including line, bar, and pie graphs), and illustrations such as maps and line drawings (of a piece of equipment, for example).

## Numerical Tables

There are many ways of representing statistical data. As you know from courses you've taken in math or chemistry, the simplest presentation of numerical data is the table. Tables are useful in demonstrating relationships among data. They present numerical information arranged in rows or columns so that data elements may be referenced and compared. Tables also facilitate the interpretation of data without the expense of several paragraphs of description.

Suppose you are writing a paper in which you argue that part-time faculty at your institution teach more hours, but are underpaid and undersupported when it comes to benefits. Your research reveals that most part-time faculty receive less than $4,000 per course, and nearly one-third earn $3,000 or less per course—which is little more than the minimum wage. You also discover that the treatment of part-timers at your own school reflects a national trend—faced with rising enrollments and skyrocketing costs, colleges and universities have come to rely more on part-time instructors. Moreover, while they may carry heavier teaching loads, these part-time faculty do not receive the same benefits as professors. Your claim is that such lack of support is not only unfair to the instructors but also that it compromises the nature of higher education since low compensation drives instructors to take on other jobs to meet the cost of living.

Presenting this information in a table will allow you to demonstrate your point while saving space for your discussion. The tables below provide the results of a survey conducted by the Coalition on the Academic Work Force (CAW), describing how history faculty are facing this situation.

As the title indicates, the table reproduced in Figure 8.11 shows the percentage of history courses taught by full- and part-time faculty. The table intends to help readers understand how much institutions have come to depend on part-time instructors, especially graduate teaching assistants and part-time nontenure-track teachers—people who are paid the least and often denied the benefits enjoyed by full-time faculty. The horizontal rows break down faculty types into five discrete categories—from "Full-Time Tenure Track" at the top to "Graduate Teaching Assistants" at the bottom. The three vertical columns tabulate the percentages according to categories: "Intro Courses," "Other Courses," and "All Courses," which is the median—the calculated halfway point between the other two categories.

Reading from left to right along the first row, we see that 49 percent of the introductory history courses and 72 percent of the "other courses" were taught by full-time tenure-track faculty. This compares with 41 percent of the introductory courses taught by part-timers

**Percentage of History Courses Taught, by Faculty Type**

|  | Intro Courses | Other Courses | All Courses |
|---|---|---|---|
| **Full-Time Tenure Track** | 49% | 72% | 59% |
| **Full-Time Nontenure Track** | 9% | 5% | 7% |
| **Part-Time Tenure Track** | 1% | 1% | 1% |
| **Part-Time Nontenure Track** | 23% | 15% | 19% |
| **Graduate Teaching Assistants** | 17% | 8% | 13% |
| **Percentage of All Courses Taught** | 55% | 45% | |
| **Number of Courses Taught** | 5,825 | 4,759 | 10,584 |

Source: AHA Surveys.

**Figure 8.11**

(part-time tenure track [1%] + part-time nontenure-track faculty [23%] + graduate teaching assistants [17%]). The last column, which represents the median percentage of intro and other courses, tells us that part-timers taught 33 percent or a third of all history courses. That is a compelling figure when tabulated for comparison to full-time faculty.

The second table (Figure 8.12) presents the reported benefits for nontenure-track and part-time faculty. Here nine categories of benefits are tabulated according to three categories of faculty. (Presumably nearly 100 percent of history departments provide full-time tenure-track faculty the kinds of support and benefits listed.) The first line shows the comparative institutional support for travel to professional meetings for the three categories of instructors: 76.9 percent for full-time nontenure track, 46.4 for part-time faculty paid a fraction of full-time salary, and 15.2 for part-time faculty paid by the course.

The fifth line down tabulates the copaid health plan for the three categories of faculty. As we can see at a glance, 72 percent of the institutions with full-time nontenure-track faculty and 63 percent of the departments with part-time faculty paid a fraction of full-time salaries provide some kind of health plan copaid by the school and faculty member.

**History Departments, Benefits**

| | % for Full-Time Nontenure-Track Faculty | % for Part-Time Faculty (Paid by semester) | % for Part-Time Faculty (Paid by course) |
|---|---|---|---|
| **Support Travel to Prof. Mtgs.** | 76.9 | 46.4 | 15.2 |
| **Support Attendance at Prof. Mtgs.** | 41.0 | 28.6 | 22.9 |
| **Provide Regular Salary Increases** | 68.4 | 53.6 | 28.1 |
| **Access to Research Grants** | 52.1 | 39.3 | 13.3 |
| **Health Plan Paid by Both** | 72.17 | 62.96 | 12.99 |
| **Health Plan Paid by School** | 32.17 | 22.22 | 2.26 |
| **Health Plan Paid by Employee** | 1.74 | 7.41 | 3.95 |
| **Retirement Plan** | 73.91 | 55.56 | 10.17 |
| **Life Insurance** | 76.52 | 44.44 | 5.65 |

*Source*: AHA Surveys.

**Figure 8.12**

This compares with just 13 percent of institutions providing such a benefit to part-time faculty paid on a per-course basis. Similarly, 32 percent of the institutions with full-time nontenure-track faculty provided a health plan paid for by the school, as compared to 2.26 percent of those with faculty paid by the course. Reading across the other benefits categories reveals how much more generous institutions were to full-time nontenure-track faculty than to part-timers—including retirement plans and insurance.

As the above paragraphs demonstrate, explaining all this information in the body of your text can be complicated and confusing. And when you are trying to prepare a compelling argument, simplicity of style and clarity of text are essential. Using tables helps you clearly depict data while you move forward with your discussion.

## Line Graphs

Line graphs show the relationship between two or more sets of numerical data by plotting points in relation to two axes. The vertical axis is usually used to represent amounts, and the horizontal axis normally represents increments of time, although this is not always the case. Line graphs are probably easier for most people to read than tables, and they are especially useful when depicting trends or changes over time. Consider the graph in Figure 8.13 below.

This graph plots the comparative increase and decrease of full- and part-time faculty over a 30-year period (based on data from American Historical Association [AHA] surveys). The vertical or *y*-axis represents the percentage of part-time faculty, and the horizontal or *x*-axis represents the time starting from 1980. There are two lines

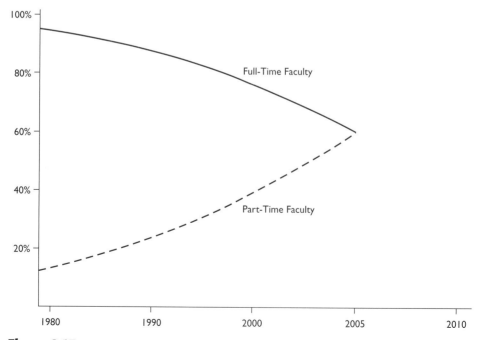

**Figure 8.13**

on the graph: The upper line represents the decreasing percentage of full-time history faculty of the colleges and universities surveyed, while the lower line represents the increase in part-time history faculty over the same 30-year period. The declining slope of the upper line instantly captures the decreasing dependence on full-time faculty, whereas the rising slope of the lower line illustrates the increasing dependence on part-time hires. Because the data are plotted on the same graph, we understand how the two are interrelated.

We also notice that neither line is straight but slightly curving. The upper line (full-time faculty) curves downward, while the lower line (part-time faculty) curves upward. Around the year 2005, these lines cross just below the 50th percentile level on the y-axis— that is, more than half the college history courses surveyed are currently being taught by part-timers. Also, if we extrapolate both lines toward the right along the curves they are defining, we will eventually arrive at some hypothetical future date when 100 percent of all history courses are taught by part-time faculty and none by full-timers. While we presume that most colleges and universities would not allow this to happen, the trend suggests just how the increased dependence on part-timers is changing the nature of higher education, as fewer courses are taught by full-time faculty. The graphs indeed make a persuasive argument.

## Bar Graphs

Bar graphs are often used to compare parts and enable readers to grasp complex data and the relationships among variables at a glance. A bar graph uses horizontal or vertical bars and is commonly used to show either quantities of the same item at different times, quantities of different items at the same time, or quantities of the different parts of an item that make up the whole. They are usually differentiated by contrasting colors, shades, or textures, with a legend explaining what these colors, shades, or textures mean.

The bar graph in Figure 8.14 shows the increase of part-time and adjunct faculty in history departments over a 29-year period as broken down by type of employment and gender (based on data from the AHA survey of the historical profession and unpublished data from AHA departmental surveys). As indicated, the graph demonstrates a dramatic increase in that time period. In 1980, only 4.3 percent of male and 2.0 percent of female history faculty were part-time—a total of 6.3 percent. Nearly three decades later, part-time male and female faculty increased to over 46 percent. This number could be even larger if graduate teaching assistants were included. As this graph shows, bar graphs take comparative amounts of data and transform them into instant no-nonsense images.

## Pie Charts

Pie charts present data as wedge-shaped sections of a circle or "pie." The total amount of all the pieces of the pie must equal 100 percent. They are an efficient way of demonstrating the relative proportion of the whole something occupies—an instant way to visualize "percentages" without thinking in numbers. But when using pie charts, it is best to include six or fewer slices. If more pieces than that are used, the chart becomes messy and its impact is muted. Figure 8.15 dramatically demonstrates the portion of all history courses in the CAW survey that were taught by part-time faculty, including graduate students.

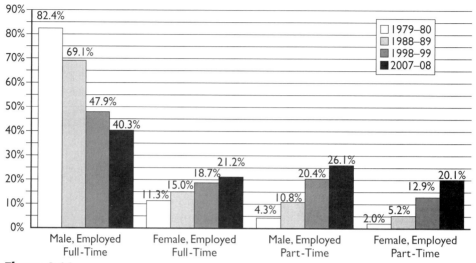

**Figure 8.14**

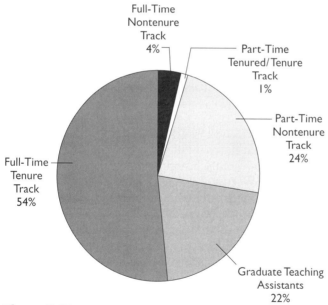

**Figure 8.15**

This pie chart clearly reveals that the combined wedges of graduate teaching assistants and part-time instructors form a substantial portion of the pie. In fact, they comprise almost half of the teaching population. This image quickly and powerfully demonstrates the point of your argument that part-time faculty make up a disproportionately large part of history faculty while receiving a disproportionately small percentage of the benefits. The chart allows readers to visualize the information as they read it. In the student sample in Chapter 9, Shannon O'Neill includes a pie chart along with an editorial cartoon to bolster her written argument, "Literature Hacked and Torn Apart: Censorship in Public Schools." (See page 276)

Used together, these visuals can play an invaluable role in bolstering a written argument on behalf of part-time faculty. Instead of blinding readers with reams of raw data, these visuals organize confusing numbers, and at-a-glance bring their significance to life. Comparative benefits and changing dependencies are transformed into memorable and easy-to-understand tables, graphs, and charts.

## Tips for Using Ancillary Graphics

While understanding the types of ancillary graphics at your disposal is important, it is also important to know how to use them properly. Here are a few guidelines to consider when using graphics in your persuasive essays:

- Include only the data you need to demonstrate your point.
- Make a reference to the chart or graphic in the body of your text.
- Try to keep the graphic on the same page as your discussion.
- Present only one type of information in each graph or chart.
- Label everything in your graph and provide legends where appropriate.
- Assign a figure number to each graphic for easy reference.
- Don't crowd your text too closely around the graphic.
- Remember to document the sources used to create the graphics.

As you begin to incorporate visuals into your own papers, consider the discussion provided earlier in this chapter regarding visual arguments. Consider why you wish to use the graphic and what you want it to do. Think about your audience's needs.

## SAMPLE STUDENT ARGUMENT FOR ANALYSIS

Lee Innes, a first-year business major, was interested in the subject of women in sports—an enormous topic that he needed to narrow down. He began by asking why male athletes dominate the world of sports. What the impact of sex-role stereotyping is on women's athletics? What is Title IX and what is its impact on college athletics? Is scholarship money unfairly distributed to male athletes? In what major sports do women excel? In what major sports do women receive the most attention or the highest salaries or the most product endorsement fees? Why is it that tennis, volleyball, and soccer are among the sports in which women receive the most attention? Why does a sport like women's beach volleyball attract a large and enthusiastic audience?

Although each question presented an interesting issue to explore, he decided to narrow the focus to one that he could cover in a paper of reasonable length. While anticipating the 2008 Summer Olympics in Beijing, he thought back on the 2004 summer games in Greece, an event he had followed closely. He recalled feeling conflicted as he watched the women's beach volleyball. The athletic skill and strength of the women was dazzling. But their athletic feats attracted less attention than their scant bikinis. Reflecting on this, Lee realized he had a narrowly defined a specific topic: women's volleyball uniforms. His essay would consider the controversial issue of women as sexual spectacles in the

Olympics—in particular, if the selection of their uniforms was a case of sexism in sport. He arrived at a *working* claim that both limited the range of his topic and very clearly expressed his point of view about it:

> Women in all sports, including Olympic beach volleyball, should be judged and promoted on their skill as athletes not on how they look in bikinis.

This claim helped him concentrate his research on those areas pertinent to his ideas. In addition to referencing expert views from magazines, newspapers, and websites. Lee bolstered his claim—and argument—by including a photo of a woman in Olympic uniform and a comparative schematic of men's versus women's uniforms. The visuals clearly enhanced his written argument.

---

Innes  1

Lee Innes
Professor Khoury
Writing 122
19 February, 2010

A Double Standard of Olympic Proportions

1  As the London Olympics of 2012 loom on the horizon, I find myself considering the pressing issues facing this international event. After losing our bid to host these games in 2012, how will we perform? Will America prove to be an athletic force? Will performance-enhancing drugs taint the games again? Will the French judges ever favor anyone but the French? And will the women's volleyball team still sport skimpy bikini uniforms?

2  Admittedly, the last question may carry less weight than the others, but as a stereotypical red-blooded heterosexual male, I certainly appreciated the aesthetic value of the volleyball competition in 2008 in Beijing. However, the display—and it indeed seemed to be just that—troubled me on a more visceral level. If I had been reading a popular magazine targeting young males, *Maxim* or *FHM* for example, ogling young women in bikinis would have felt fine. But this was the Olympics, and these women were representing my country—the United States—in an athletic competition.

3  So to be honest, as both an athlete and an American, I cringed each time one of the women paused to adjust her "uniform." How could these women concentrate on winning Olympic gold with the constant threat of a wedgie on international television? Just what were these women thinking when they picked this uniform, I wondered? How could I take their sporting event seriously when it was so obvious that they didn't take *themselves* seriously? And how could they objectify themselves in this way as they represented not only U.S. athletes, but in many ways, female athletes in particular?

4    When I shared this observation with a friend who played college volleyball herself, I was surprised to learn that not only did the women of the U.S. Volleyball Team *not* pick those uniforms; they were *forced* to wear them by the Olympic committee. At the time, I was shocked—both by the idea that an official sports organization would require such a uniform, and by the fact that women had not reacted with more outrage.

5    In 1998, the International Volleyball Federation (FIVB), based in Switzerland, decided volleyball uniforms should be standardized. It was this organization that chose the bikini uniform worn by the Olympic athletes. Interestingly, there was only one woman on the committee when they designed and implemented the uniform. Kristine Drakich, in a 1997 interview with the Canadian Association for the Advancement of Women and Sport and Physical Activity, commented that she was the only female athlete representative for the International Volleyball Federation's Beach Volleyball World Council at that time. The council, she observed, was "an intimidating place for anybody . . . this is a place with about 50 members, all men, except for my position" (Robertson). One can surmise that a predominantly male committee was responsible for voting in favor of adopting the bikini uniform for women for beach volleyball competition. (It makes one wonder if Hugh Heffner sat in on the meetings.)

6    Perhaps more at issue and culturally significant is that the men's beach volleyball uniform was nowhere near as revealing. The men's uniform featured a tank top and lose fitting shorts. The women's uniform, in addition to the bikini top, sports a brief with a waistline that falls below the belly button. And the women's uniform bottoms must be two and a half inches wide on the sides, providing very little coverage, even for the toned glutes of these women. That's only *five* inches wide.

7    Surprisingly, the women's uniform provoked little public outcry, and not for lack of publicity. Jeanne Moos reported on the decision in a *CNN Online* article: "Women's volleyball uniforms will be standardized in order to banish t-shirts and shorts." Moos expressed her own viewpoint bluntly, "Beach volleyball has now joined go-go girl dancing as perhaps the only two professions where a bikini is the required uniform." Yet the announcement of the FIVB's decision created little more than a ripple of controversy. Even men noticed the inequality. Blogger Sean P. Aune observed that photos of beach volleyball players were "little more than soft-porn." "There is no doubt these women work just as hard as any other athletes to get where they are, and all you ever see or hear about them is just these blasted outfits. How many people know that Misty May-Treanor and Kerri Walsh are on a run of

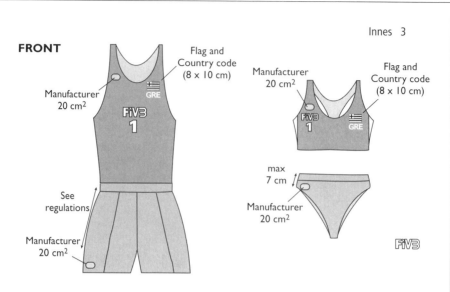

Innes 3

**FRONT**

Flag and Country code (8 x 10 cm)

GRE

Manufacturer 20 cm²

FiVB

1

Manufacturer 20 cm²

Flag and Country code (8 x 10 cm)

FiVB

1

GRE

See regulations

max 7 cm

Manufacturer 20 cm²

Manufacturer 20 cm²

FiVB

**Figure 1** Men's Volleyball uniform is shown on the left, and women's volleyball uniform on the right.

nearly 100 consecutive wins as a team? Does that matter? Oh who cares, slap some more butt shots up there!" Aune also noted that the country of origin of each player is written across their rear ends. Something I hadn't noticed before.

Opponents of the uniform seemed to become more vocal as the extensive television coverage of the Olympic beach volleyball matches brought the issue to the public eye. Jeneé Osterheldt reported in the August 20, 2004, *Kansas City Star* that the required uniform was upsetting some sports officials and players. "[Female] players can't cover up, even if they want to. . . . Donna Lopiano, executive director of the Women's Sports Foundation, [says] 'It's like telling a swimmer she has to wear a bikini instead of a high-performance suit, when the material has been shown to increase speed. Elasticized attire on leg muscles, especially larger muscles like the thigh, has been proven to reduce fatigue. If you are looking for performance enhancement, you wouldn't choose bikini bottoms'" (Osterheldt).

But Lopiano's statement addressed what seems to be an irrelevant detail to the IFVB board. Official commentary on the "performance enhancement" of the uniforms is absent from the literature. It would appear that performance has little, if anything, to do with the decision at all. The uniforms, it seems, were designed not for functionality but for marketing purposes. In a *Business Week* article addressing the "comeback" of beach volleyball as a legitimate sport, Leonard Armato, the

Innes   4

marketing man responsible for getting volleyball on NBC as an athletic event, was quoted admitting, "[Beach volleyball is] an incredibly sexy sport. We're not embarrassed that the women [wear] bikinis (Kher mouch)."

10      Based on ticket sales for beach volleyball, it seems like the IFVB had the right idea.

11      Even when the IFVB rendered its initial decision in 1999, few players complained, and even those who did seemed to lack spirit. "I'm kind of bummed—I like my tights," said the sport's perhaps most famous player, Gabrielle Reece, to a CNN reporter at the time. Reece, who was known for wearing black Lycra tights rather than a bikini suit while playing, added "You take one step, that bathing suit goes straight up. You're always yanking and fiddling" (Moos).

**Figure 2**   Player giving hand signal that she will block on both sides.

12      "Bummed" doesn't exactly express the feminist fury one might expect. If the Williams sisters of tennis fame have taught us anything, women like to choose what to wear, and they will often select uniforms that are both performance enhancing and flattering. If they choose to be sexy, that's one thing. But to be ordered to wear a sexy uniform with no alternatives, one would expect more protests than were reported in media outlets. It also seems like female viewers aren't all that upset—they seem to accept this as a part of a male-dominated sports culture. *Fanhouse* reporter

Stephanie Stradley observed that "King Kaufman at *Salon* wondered [in an online essay] why women wear bikinis and the men wear shirts, [well] duh, so men will watch."

13    All of which then leads me to my next question: If the women aren't complaining, is there anything wrong here? As we approach the next summer Olympiad, is it permissible for me to enjoy both the view, so to speak, as well as the competition? It would appear to be the case. Michael Noble commented in his article "Can't Wait for the Next Olympixxx" in the Canadian newspaper *Townie,*

> Of course there is a sexual element to all sports, male and female, and there always has been. Tight pants, skirts, shorts and bathing suits can be found throughout the Olympic lineup. In proper and respectful sports though, admiring the bodies within these suits is kept on a "wink-wink, nudge-nudge" level. They know what you're looking at, but they don't make new rules to accentuate it.

> Volleyball has taken a different route. Instead of a nudge and a wink, it's a point and a yell—"Hey everyone, take a look at this ass!" Clearly women's sports are changing. At one time, female athletes were all portrayed as manly "butches." Today they're shown as suped-up sex machines. You've come a long way, baby.

14    However, one could also argue that such media attention helps out both the sport and the athletes. Since their victory in Athens seven years ago, Kerri Walsh and Misty May have enjoyed tremendous popularity. One could argue that their cute bikinis certainly didn't hurt their careers. Donning bikinis long before their foray into Olympic glory, the pair was in a Visa ad during the 2004 Super Bowl, playing beach volleyball in the snow and ice. Their likenesses have been displayed on McDonald's wrappers and boxes. And after their Olympic win, they were featured on the front page of practically every sports section of every newspaper in the country. Even the *Wall Street Journal* ran a photo.

15    Reflection on the issue at hand—is it fair that a group of men have mandated what most female athletes seem to agree is a less than ideal uniform— seems to have no satisfactory answer. A look at the uniforms in the *2009 Beach Volleyball Handbook* leads one to presume that little will change in London. Despite the lack of vocal protest, I am still left with the gnawing feeling that something is amiss. Perhaps Andrea Lewis, a writer for the Progressive Media Project, summarizes it best: "The games are a great showcase for athletic talents of both genders, but it's still an Olympian task for women to be treated equally."

Innes 6

Works Cited

Aune, Sean P. "Olympic Beach Volley Ball Uniforms. SeanPAune.com, 13 Aug. 2008.
    Web. 2 Feb. 2010.

Hruby, Patrick. "A Day at the Beach." *Washington Times* 20 Aug. 2004. Web.
    6 Feb. 2010.

Khermouch, Gerry. "Son of a Beach Volleyball." *Business Week* 20 Apr. 2002. Print.

Lewis, Andrea. "Women Athletes Shined at Olympic Games." *Progressive Media
    Project,* 30 Aug. 2004. Web. 5 Feb. 2010.

Moos, Jeanne. "Bikini Blues–Beach Volleyball Makes the Swimsuit Standard." *CNN
    Online.* CNN, 13 Jan. 1999. Web. 5 Feb. 2010.

Moore, David Leon. "Beach Volleyball's Dynamic Duo." *USATODAY.com.* USA Today,
    13 Aug. 2004. Web. 8 Feb. 2010.

Osterheldt, Jeneé. "Olympic Athletes Prance Chic to Cheek." *Kansas City Star*
    20 Aug. 2004, late ed.: A1. Print.

Robertson, Sheila. "Insight Into an Activist." ACTION Canadian Association for the
    Advancement of Women and Sport and Physical Activity. CAAWS, n.d. Web.
    4 Feb. 2010.

Stradley Stephanie. "In Beach Volleyball, Why Do Men Wear Shirts and Women Wear
    Bikinis?" *Olympics Fanhouse.* AOL, 14 Aug. 2008. Web. 7 Feb. 2010.

**QUESTIONS FOR ANALYSIS AND DISCUSSION**

1. Do you agree with Lee Innes's working claim here? What are your thoughts about the role of male and female athletic attire? about the use of attire to promote or popularize a sporting event? In your journal, respond to Innes's ideas by exploring your own views on the media's promotion of women athletes and whether or not the promotion is based on talent or appearance.

2. Consider the effectiveness of the author's use of the visuals—the photograph of the female player's bikini and the comparative uniform schematics for men and women. Do the illustrations bolster Innes's argument? Do the visuals convince you of an inequity if not sexual exploitation in uniform guidelines? Explain your answers.

3. Even if you didn't watch the 2008 Olympic women's beach volleyball competition or don't follow the sport, do you think that most fans are concerned with what Innes and others see as sexual exploitation? Do you think that the media will ever respond to Innes's concern? Why or why not?

4. What do you make of the fact that few female athletes complained that they had to wear bikinis? Does that weaken Innes's argument? Or do you see that lack of concern as legitimate disinterest? Or as suggested by the article, do you think that the lack of complaints suggests more deeply rooted gender issues in our culture?

5. In the last paragraph, Innes wonders if there's really a problem in what female athletes wear. What specific counterarguments to his position does he cite? In spite of these, why is he still left with a "gnawing sense that something isn't right here"? Do you agree? Are you also convinced as Andrea Lewis claims that rendering equal treatment for woman athletes is "an Olympian task"?

6. In your journal, write an entry as if done by a member of the Women's Olympic Volleyball Team after the first day of competition. In it, explore how she felt about her uniform.

# Researching Arguments: Thinking Like an Investigator

Most arguments derive their success from the evidence they contain, so good argumentative writers learn to find evidence in many sources and present the best evidence to support their claims. In the academic world, much of that evidence is gathered through *research,* either conducted in a lab or field or through examination of the previously published work of other investigators and scholars. The research paper you may be asked to write challenges you to learn how more experienced writers find and present evidence that meets the standards of the academic community.

In the previous chapters, we've stressed the importance of finding evidence that will impress readers of your argument's merits. To review, researched evidence plays an important role in convincing readers of the following:

- Expert, unbiased authorities agree with your position in whole or in part, adding to your credibility.
- Your position or proposal is based on facts, statistics, and real-life examples, not mere personal opinion.
- You understand different viewpoints about your subject as well as your own.
- Your sources of information are verifiable because researched evidence is always accompanied by documentation.

A good analogy to use, once again, is that of the lawyer presenting a case to a jury. When you write a researched argument, you're making a case to a group of people who will make a decision about a subject. Not only do you present your arguments in the case but also you call on witnesses to offer evidence and expert opinion, which you then interpret and clarify for the jury. In a researched argument, your sources are your witnesses.

Writing an argumentative research paper isn't different from writing any other kind of argument, except in scale. An argument research paper is not a different species from the essays you have been writing; but it is usually longer than nonresearched papers; and the formal presentation (including documentation) must be addressed in more detail.

## Sources of Information

There are two basic kinds of research sources, and depending partly on the type of issue you've picked to research, one may prove more helpful than the other. The first is *primary sources,* which include firsthand accounts of events (interviews, diaries, court records, letters, manuscripts). The second is *secondary sources,* which interpret, comment on, critique, explain, or evaluate events or primary sources. Secondary sources include most reference works and any books or articles that expand on primary sources. Depending on whether you choose a local or a more global issue to write about, you may decide to focus more on primary or more on secondary sources; but in most research, you'll want to consider both.

## Primary Sources

If you choose a topic of local concern, your chief challenge will be finding enough research material. Very current controversies or issues won't yet have books written about them, so you may have to rely more heavily on electronic databases, which you can access through a computer, or interviews and other primary research methods to find information. If you choose a local issue to argue, consider the following questions.

- Which experts on campus or in the community might you interview for the pros and cons of the debated issue? an administrator at your college? a professor? the town manager? Think of at least two local experts who could provide an overview of the issue from different perspectives.
- What local resources—such as a local newspaper, radio station, TV station, or political group—are available for gathering print or broadcast information? If one of your topics is a campus issue, for example, the student newspaper, student committees or groups, university online discussion groups, or the student government body might be places to search for information.

Once you determine the several possible sources of information, your next step is to set up interviews or make arrangements to read or view related materials. Most students find that experts are eager to talk about local issues and are willing to be interviewed. However, you'll need plenty of time to gather background information, phone for interviews, prepare questions, and write up your notes afterward. If you're depending on primary research for the bulk of your information, get started as soon as the paper is assigned.

### Preparing for Interviews

A few common courtesies apply when preparing for interviews. First, be ready to discuss the purpose of your interview when setting up an appointment. Second, go into the interview with a list of questions that shows you have already thought about the issue. Be on time and have a notebook and pen or recorder, especially if you decide to quote people directly. But first ask their permission to do so.

### Conducting Interviews

Be prepared to jot down only key words or ideas during the interview, reserving time afterward to take more detailed notes. Keep the interview on track by asking focused questions if the interviewee wanders while responding. When leaving, ask if it would be okay to call should you have follow-up questions.

### Writing Up Interviews

As soon as possible after the interview, review your notes (or recording) and flesh out the details of the conversation. Think about what you learned. How does the information you gathered relate to your main topic or question? Did you learn anything that surprised or intrigued you? What questions remain? Record the date of your interview; you will need to document your source when you write the paper.

## Preparing Interview Questions

Consider the following guidelines as you prepare questions for an interview:

- Find out as much information as you can about the issue and about the expert's stand on the issue before the interview. Then you won't waste interview time on generating details you could have found in the newspaper or on the local TV news.
- Ask open-ended questions that allow the authority to respond freely, rather than questions requiring only yes or no answers.
- Prepare more questions than you think you need and rank them in order of priority according to your purpose. Using the most important points as a guide, sequence the list in a logical progression.

## Secondary Sources

Many primary sources—published interviews, public documents, results of experiments, and first-person accounts of historical events, for example—are available in your library, which is also a vast repository of secondary source material. If your topic is regional, national, or international in scope, you'll want to consider both of these kinds of sources. For example, if your topic is proposed changes to the Social Security system, you might find information in the *Congressional Record* on committee deliberations, a primary source, and also read articles on the op-ed page of the *New York Times* for interpretive commentary, a secondary source.

# A Search Strategy

Because the sheer amount of information in the library can be daunting, plan how you will find information before you start your search. Always consult a reference librarian if you get stuck in planning your search or if you can't find the information you need.

## Preview: A Search Strategy

- Choose your topic.
- Get an overview of your topic.
- Compile a working bibliography.
- Locate sources.
- Evaluate sources.
- Take notes.

## Choosing Your Topic

Your argument journal may remind you of potential topics, and Chapter 3 covered how to develop a topic. But what if you still can't think of one? You might try browsing through two print sources that contain information on current issues:

> *Facts on File* (1940 to the present). A weekly digest of current news.
>
> *Editorials on File* (1970 to the present). Selected editorials from U.S. and Canadian newspapers reprinted in their entirety.

Or go online to the *Political Junkie* website, which will provide you with ideas from the latest news stories in national and regional newspapers and magazines, columnists' viewpoints on current issues, up-to-the-minute reports on public figures, and links to the websites of numerous political and social organizations. You can access this site at http://www.politicaljunkie.com. Also, think about which subjects you find interesting from the essays in Part Two of this book. These four sources should give you a wealth of ideas to draw on.

## Getting an Overview of Your Topic

If you don't know a lot about your topic, encyclopedias can give you general background information. Just as important, encyclopedia articles often end with bibliographies on their subjects—bibliographies prepared by experts in the field. Using such bibliographies can save you hours in the library.

Your library no doubt houses in print generalized and specialized encyclopedias. Your library also should allow you access to online general and specialized encyclopedia databases related to your topic. What follows are a few of the dozens of major online encyclopedias that you may find helpful:

> ***Some General and Specialized Online Encyclopedias***
> *Academic American Encyclopedia*
> *New Encyclopedia Britannica*
> *Cambridge Histories Outline*
> *Encyclopedia of Life Sciences*
> *Gale Encyclopedia of Medicine*
> *International Encyclopedia of Social and Behavioral Sciences*
> *Oxford Art Online*
> *Oxford Encyclopedia of American Literature*
> *Oxford Encyclopedia of British Literature*
> *Oxford Music Online*

This is just a brief listing of the many encyclopedias available in areas that range widely. It is worth discussing the value of online encyclopedias, such as the ever popular *Wikipedia* (en.wikipedia.org). *Wikipedia* has been described as a sort of "collective brain" of information that is provided by anyone who wants to share knowledge about a subject. Hundreds of thousands of people have contributed to *Wikipedia* entries, and thousands more have edited and amended them. *Wikipedia*'s strengths include its currency, the vast quantity of information available, and the fact that entries may be amended and challenged. Within seconds of breaking news, *Wikipedia*'s entries will reflect new information, provided someone wishes to add it. Many entries will feature source material at the end of the page. Review these sources with the same critical eye that you evaluate the *Wikipedia* entry. While the information on *Wikipedia* is expected to be correct, it is not guaranteed; and be aware that there is no central editorial authority who confirms the accuracy of the entries. Likewise, source material may sometimes be questionable. Our recommendation is to use *Wikipedia* as a resource, but not the *only* resource in your research arsenal. Note any challenges or disputes to the entry (which will appear in a block above the entry), and use the information only if you feel confident that the information is accurate.

## Compiling a Working Bibliography

Because you don't know at the beginning of your search which sources will prove most relevant to your narrowed topic, keep track of every source you consult. Record complete publication information about each source in your notebook, on index cards, or on printouts of online sources. The list that follows describes the information you'll need for particular kinds of sources.

### *For a Book*

- Authors' and/or editors' names
- Full title, including subtitle
- Place of publication (city, state, country)
- Date of publication (from the copyright page)
- Name of publisher
- Volume or edition numbers
- Library call number

### *For an Article*

- Authors' names
- Title and subtitle of article
- Title of periodical (magazine, journal, newspaper)
- Volume number and issue number, if any
- Date of the issue
- All page numbers on which the article appears
- Library location

### *For an Electronic Source*

- Authors' names, if given
- Title of material accessed
- Name of periodical (if applicable)
- Volume and issue numbers (if applicable)
- Date of material, if given
- Page numbers or numbers of paragraphs (if indicated)
- Title of the database
- Publication medium (e.g., CD-ROM, diskette, microfiche, online)
- Name of the vendor, if relevant

■ Electronic publication date
■ Date of your access to the material
■ Path specification for online media (e.g., FTP information; directory; file name). APA also asks for DOI (digital object identifier), instead of a URL.

Note that for electronic sources, which come in many different formats, you should record all the information that would allow another researcher to retrieve the documents you used. This will vary from source to source, but it's important to give as much information as you can.

Your instructor may ask you to prepare an *annotated bibliography,* in which you briefly summarize the main ideas in each source and note its potential usefulness. You will also want to evaluate each source for accuracy, currency, or bias.

# Sample Entries for an Annotated Bibliography

Shannon O'Neill, a journalism major, decided to write her argument essay on book banning in the public schools. Here are some sample entries from her annotated bibliography. (Shannon O'Neill's paper can be found on pages 276–282 in the Documentation Guide.)

**Barnhisel, Greg, ed.** *Media and Messages: Strategies and Readings in Public Rhetoric.* **New York: Longman, 2005.** This book contains many useful essays, editorials, and articles examining contemporary issues in the media and presents a balanced view of a large variety of topics. Barnhisel draws useful summaries and conclusions based on information in each chapter. The book is unbiased because it presents criticisms from all angles. In my paper, I used an article and an editorial because they give interesting perspectives on censorship of the written word; one focused on student newspapers; the other criticized censorship as the result of "politically correctness." Both pieces oppose censorship. While the text as a whole is balanced, there aren't any useful pieces advocating for censorship of the written word; rather, they focused on censorship of the visual media or Internet.

**"Challenging a Book in Your School."** *Gateways to a Better Education.* **1998. 5 Oct. 2009** http://www.gtbe.org. This website is for a national organization that promotes the spread of Christian values. While it does not advocate censorship or removal of specific works, it encourages parents to challenge their children's curriculum and take an active part in deciding what should or should not be taught in public schools—all with a Christian agenda. This site is clearly biased, but it is an important and useful source for the presentation of the religious argument for book censorship.

**"Challenged and Banned Books." American Library Association. 2009. 5 Oct. 2009** http://www.ala.org/ala/oif/bannedbooksweek/challengedbanned/challengedbanned. htm#web. This organization's website is extremely useful because it gives background information on the banning and censoring of books and lists recently and frequently banned books and authors. It also gives statistics on reasons for challenges, which I used for a pie chart. The site could be considered biased, though, because it encourages the idea of free speech and discourages censorship based on the premise of the First Amendment. It also encourages people to read banned books and coined Banned Book Week, which celebrates books that have been banned or challenged.

A working bibliography (as opposed to an annotated bibliography) would include the complete publication information for each source, but not the evaluation of its usefulness to the paper.

# Locating Sources

Your college library offers a range of methods and materials for finding the precise information you need. Here is a brief guide to locating periodicals, books, and electronic sources.

## Finding Periodicals

Instead of going to the periodicals room and leafing page by page through magazines, journals, and newspapers for information pertinent to your topic, use periodical indexes to locate articles you need. Your library will have these indexes available in print, CD-ROM, or online databases. The form you choose will depend on what is available and how current your information must be. When deciding whether to use the printed or electronic versions, carefully note the dates of the material the indexes reference. For example, you cannot use the CD-ROM version of *The Readers' Guide to Periodical Literature* to find a source from 1979. However, for a more current source (from 1983 to the present), use the CD-ROM version since it provides abstracts of articles. They will allow you to decide whether locating the full article is worth your time and effort. Here is a list of some of the periodical indexes often available in college libraries. If your library does not have these indexes, ask the reference librarian about the best way to find periodical articles in your library.

### Periodical Indexes
#### General
*Readers' Guide to Periodical Literature.* 1915 to present. Print. Indexes popular journals and magazines and some reviews of movies, plays, books, and television.

*Readers' Guide Abstracts.* 1983 to present. Same content as *Readers' Guide* but with abstracts.

*Newspaper Abstracts.* 1985 to present. Abstracts of articles in national and regional newspapers.

*New York Times.* 1851 to present. Extensive coverage of national and international news.

*Periodical Abstracts.* 1986 to present. Abstracts and full-text articles from more than 950 general periodicals.

*ABI/Inform.* August 1971 to present. About eight hundred thousand citations to articles in 1,400 periodicals. Good source for business-related topics. Complete text of articles from five hundred publications since 1991.

*LexisNexis Universe.* Full-text access to newspapers, magazines, directories, legal and financial publications, and medical journals.

#### Specialized
*Applied Science and Technology Index/Applied Science and Technology Abstracts.* 1913 to present. Covers all areas of science and technology.

*Art Index/Art Abstracts.* 1929 to present. Wide coverage of art and allied fields.

*Business Periodicals Index.* 1958 to present. Covers all areas of business.

*Education Index/Education Abstracts.* 1929 to present; June 1983 to present. Covers elementary, secondary, and higher education.

*PAIS International in Print/PAIS Database* (formerly *Public Affairs Information Service Bulletin*). 1915 to present. Excellent index to journals, books, and reports in economics, social conditions, government, and law.

*Ethnic Newswatch.* 1990 to present. Indexes news publications by various ethnic groups. Includes full texts of most articles.

*Social Sciences Index* (*International Index* 1907–1965; *Social Sciences and Humanities* 1965–1974; *Social Sciences Index* 1974 to present). 1907 to present. Indexes scholarly journals in political science, sociology, psychology, and related fields.

*Humanities Index.* (See *Social Sciences Index* entry for name changes.) 1907 to present. Covers scholarly journals in literature, history, philosophy, folklore, and other fields in the humanities.

*America: History and Life.* 1964 to present. Index and abstracts to articles in more than 2,000 journals. Covers the histories and cultures of the United States and Canada from prehistory to the present.

*SPORT Discus.* 1975 to present. Covers sports, physical education, physical fitness, and sports medicine.

*Social Issues Researcher (SIRS).* Full-text articles from newspapers, journals, and government publications related to the social sciences.

*Congressional Universe.* Offers a legislative perspective on congressional bills, hearings, public laws, and information on members of Congress.

*Sociofile.* 1974 to present. Coverage includes family and socialization, culture, social differentiation, social problems, and social psychology.

*Essay and General Literature Index.* 1900 to present. Indexes essays and chapters in collected works. Emphasis is on social sciences and humanities.

## Finding Books

Your library catalogue—whether in print (card), electronic, or microform format—indexes the books your library holds. Books are listed in three basic ways: by author, title, and general subject. If the catalogue is electronic, you can also use keyword searches to locate books. On a computer terminal, you type in a word related to your topic, and the catalogue lists all the sources that include that word.

To make keyword searching more efficient, you can often combine two or more search terms. For example, if you know that you want information on "violence" and can narrow that to "violence and music not rap music," the catalogue will give you a much shorter list of sources than if you had typed only "violence," a very broad topic. This is called Boolean searching, and the typical ways you can combine terms are to use "and" to combine search terms; "or" to substitute search terms (e.g., "violent crime" or "assault"); and "not" to exclude terms. For example, suppose you are looking for information on cigarette smoking by teenagers. In a Boolean search, you could use the search phrase: "teenager or youth and smoking not marijuana."

If you are searching by subject rather than author or title, it's useful to know that libraries organize subject headings according to the *Library of Congress Subject Headings*

*(LCSH).* These are large red books, usually located near the library's catalogue. You will save time and be more successful if you look up your subject in the *LCSH.* For example, if you search the catalogue using the term "movies," you won't find a single source. If you look up "movies" in the *LCSH,* it will tell you that the subject heading is "motion pictures." Type in "motion pictures," and you'll find the sources you need.

Listed below are other useful sources of information.

### Biographies

There are so many different biographical sources it is difficult to know which one has the information you need. The following titles will save you a lot of time:

*Biography and Genealogy Master Index.* (Spans from B.C. to the present.) Index to more than one million biographical sources.

*Biographical Index.* 1947 to present. International and all occupations. Guide to sources in books, periodicals, letters, diaries, etc.

*Contemporary Authors.* 1962 to present. Contains biographical information about authors and lists of their works.

### Almanacs

*World Almanac and Book of Facts.* 1968 to present. Facts about government, business, society, etc. International in scope.

*Statistical Abstract of the United States.* 1879 to present. Published by the U.S. Bureau of the Census. Good source for statistics about all aspects of the United States including economics, education, society, and politics.

*Statistical Masterfile.* 1984 to present. State and national government statistics and private and international.

### Reviews, Editorials

*Book Review Digest.* 1905 to present. Index to book reviews with excerpts from the reviews.

*Book Review Index.* 1965 to present. Indexes to more books than the above but doesn't have excerpts from reviews.

### Bibliographies

Look for bibliographies in journal articles, books, encyclopedia articles, biographical sources, etc.

## Finding Internet Sources

The Internet offers countless possibilities for research using government documents, newspapers and electronic journals, websites, business publications, and much more. You may have access to the Internet through campus computer labs, your own computer, or your handheld device.

To make your search easier and more efficient, you can rely on several of the powerful search engine databases available for exploring the Internet. Search engine databases are built by computer robot programs called "spiders" that "crawl" the web. Each of the search engines we've listed below uses keyword searches to find material on your topic. These words can specify your topic, supply the title of a book or article about your topic, name a person associated with your topic, and so on. It's important to try out a number of keyword combinations when you are searching for resources. For instance, if your topic is assisted suicide, you might also search under "euthanasia" and "physician-assisted suicide." By adding additional terms such as "terminal illness," "legalization," and "patient's rights," you may be able to both narrow your search and find material filed under different topic headings that are related to your subject. And you'll get a more accurate response if you use quotation marks around key search phrases.

Here is a list of the more popular search engines. You'll find them useful for locating information on the Internet:

*Google   http://www.google.com*
This search engine is the first line for searching and the most popular. It will give you a lot of options, including blog posts, wiki pages, group discussion threads, and various document formats such as PDFs. Keywords can be used for subject searches or to find a phrase that appears in the sources. You may also supply the name of a person or a title to prompt your search. It will search for each of your keywords separately or as a unit. You can also limit or expand the time parameters of your search from the current date to up to two years. A word of caution: Information found on *Google* may not always be appropriate or credible, and advertisers pay to appear higher up in the search results. Thus, you may receive some recommendations that have little or nothing to do with your search. (See section below on evaluating sources.)

*Yahoo!   http://www.yahoo.com*
*Yahoo!* works just like *Google*. It will also expand your search by linking you to two other search engines if you request them.

*Exalead.com   http://www.exalead.com/search*
Although not as useful for academic research as are *Google* and *Yahoo!* this search engine provides thumbnail preview pages.

*About.com   http://www.about.com*
Although not as useful for academic research as are *Google, Dogpile*, and *Yahoo!* this search engine connects users to a network of experts or "guides" who offer practical solutions to common problems spanning a wide field of topics.

In addition to the traditional search engines, there are others that conduct "meta searches"; that is, they allow you to leverage the power of many popular search engines at the same time. Combined, these engines cover more of the Internet than a single search engine can cover. Here is a list of some of the most popular and powerful meta-search engines:

*Dogpile   http://www.dogpile.com*
This is a popular meta-search engine that combines the power of several other major search engines including *Google, Yahoo! Search, Bing, Ask.com*, and *LookSmart*. It displays results from each different search engine.

*Ixquick.com   http://ixquick.com*
This meta-search engine ranks results based on the number of "top 10" rankings a site receives from the various search engines.

*Zworks.com   http://zworks.com*
Like *Ixquick*, when you use *Zworks* you are searching many popular search engines at the same time. Combined, these engines cover more databases on the Internet than any one search engine covers.

*Wikipedia   http://wikipedia.org*
*Wikipedia* is an online multilingual encyclopedia (see description on page 244). It is not a search engine, but it can provide you with both information and links to more information. *Wikipedia* covers a vast range of topics with articles that are useful and current and that offer links to related pages and additional information. Because entries are created by anyone who registers and are constantly being revised, material is subject to error and misinformation.

When you are using any search engine, be sure to check the instructions so you can use it as effectively as possible. Also, don't rely on only one search engine. Use several to give yourself access to the broadest range of materials.

Three additional websites that may help you if you are searching for information related to government, politics, legislation, or statistics are the following:

**Library of Congress   http://www.loc.gov**
This website provides information about the U.S. Congress and the legislative process. It will search for past legislative bills by topic, bill number, or title; allow you to read the *Congressional Record* from the current and past years' Congresses; find committee reports by topic or committee name; and provide full-text access to current bills under consideration in the House of Representatives and the Senate.

**U.S. Census Bureau   http://www.census.gov**
You can find facts, figures, and statistics derived from the last census at this site. There is also some information about world population.

**White House   http://www.whitehouse.gov**
At this site, you can find current and past White House press briefings and news releases, as well as a full range of statistics and information produced by federal agencies for public use.

Remember that the Internet is constantly changing, so no book will be completely up to date on how to access its information. Check to see if your college has workshops or courses on using the Internet—it's an important research tool, and it's worth your time to learn how to navigate in cyberspace.

# Evaluating Sources

The first examination of your sources is a preliminary assessment to help you decide whether the material is *relevant* and *reliable* for your purposes.

## Print Sources
You can often sense a print source's relevance by skimming its preface, introduction, table of contents, conclusion, and index (for books) or abstract and headings (for articles) to see whether your topic appears and how often. Many students mark their bibliography cards

with numbers (1 = most relevant, 2 = somewhat relevant, 3 = not very relevant) to help them remember which sources they most want to examine. If a source contains no relevant material, mark the bibliography card "unusable" but don't discard it; if you refine your topic or claim later, you may want to go back to that source.

The reliability of a printed source is judged in a number of ways:

■ Check the date: Is it recent or timely for your topic?
■ Look at the citations: Is the author's evidence recent or timely?
■ Is the author an expert in the field? To find out, use the biographical sources listed earlier in this chapter or find book reviews in the reference section.
■ Where does the author work? A source's credentials may influence your readers. You may also find out what biases the author may have; for example, if the author is the founder of Scientists Against Animal Research, you'll have a good idea about his or her personal beliefs on that subject.

## Electronic Sources

Using Internet material presents special challenges in determining the value of a source. Unlike most printed journal and newspaper articles and books, online materials are not necessarily reviewed by editors or professional colleagues to determine whether facts are correct and conclusions reliable. Anyone with the technical skills can develop a website and post opinions for the world to read. So it's difficult to determine whether such information is worth using. But here are a few suggestions that will help you determine if a source is credible:

■ **Domain address** Each Internet host computer is assigned a domain indicating the type of organization that created the site. This domain indicator appears at the end of the address. Most sites will be labeled one of the following:

*edu* for an educational site
*gov* for a government site
*com* for a commercial site
*org* for an organizational site

While we can't vouch for the quality of all the material at these different domains, it is more likely that sites affiliated with an educational institution or a government office will provide information that has been carefully researched and prepared. Although commercial and organizational sites may also provide valid information, it is important to check carefully for bias or misinformation that might be made available to further the interests of the business or organization.

■ **Author of the site** Try to identity the author or authors of the material published at the site. Is the author a professional or an authority in a field relevant to the topic? The director of a public health clinic may have opinions worth considering on the medical use of marijuana; he may or may not have the same level of credibility in a discussion about punishment for juvenile criminals.

■ **Identity of the organization** If the site is maintained by an organization, find out what interests the organization represents. Who created the organization? A government-appointed committee investigating public support of family planning will have a very different agenda from a committee organized by private interest groups. While both groups may be scrupulously honest in their presentation of the facts, each may interpret those facts with a particular bias. Your awareness of their "slant" will help you decide how to use the information. The reference section of most libraries can provide directories of associations and organizations.

■ **Date of posting** Check the date when the site was posted. Has the site been updated recently? If not, is the material still current and relevant?

■ **Quality of references** Are sources provided to support the information posted on the site? Most credible sites will document their facts, research studies, and statistics. Many articles and essays will be followed by a bibliography. It's always a good idea to double-check these references to determine whether the information is accurate. The absence of any references to support statements of fact and statistics may indicate that the site is unreliable.

■ **Quality of material** Look for indications that the material has been written or assembled by an educated, well-informed individual who offers a balanced and thoughtful perspective on the issue. Is the written text free of obvious grammatical mistakes, spelling errors, problems with sentence structure, and so on? Does the author indicate awareness and respect for other views even while disagreeing with them? Is the coverage of material thorough and well supported? Although poorly written websites can indicate low reliability, don't be fooled by slick, attractive presentations. You need to investigate beneath the surface to determine whether the content of the site meets academic standards of fairness and thoroughness.

■ **Intended use** Consider how you will use the material at the site. If you are looking for reliable statistics and factual information, then checking the author's credentials and the status of the organization or company will be important to maintaining your own credibility. However, sometimes personal examples and experiences of individuals who are not professionally qualified may still be of value. For example, a student writing a paper on Alzheimer's disease came across a site in which an Alzheimer's patient kept a diary of the progression of her illness. Even though she was not qualified to give expert medical opinion on the disease itself, her diary provided a unique insight into the feelings and perceptions of someone experiencing the loss of her intellectual capabilities. In her paper, the student writer was able to incorporate some of this compelling personal testimony.

Let's see how this advice works in practice. Shannon O'Neill decided to do an Internet search to find background information for her argument essay on book banning in the public schools. (Sample entries from her annotated bibliography appear earlier in this chapter.) Using several search engines and a keyword search, Shannon had no trouble finding a large number of sites concerned with this subject. However, before relying on the information at the sites, Shannon had to determine which sites were reliable. To do this, she examined several features of each site, as recommended above.

The first site Shannon found was *The Online Books Page: Banned Books Online* at http://onlinebooks.library.upenn.edu/banned-books.html. Using the criteria from the list we've provided, Shannon made the following evaluation of the site (see Figure 9.1):

■ **Domain address** As Shannon noted, the domain address identified the website as being based at the University of Pennsylvania, a well-known and reputable school.

■ **Author of the site** At the end of the site, the author identified himself by name. Using the home page link "About Us" under "The Inside Story" (see Figure 9.1), Shannon found information about the author who identified himself as a computer scientist who works in a library at the University of Pennsylvania and who received a PhD in computer science at Carnegie Mellon University. But since this description didn't indicate any special expertise on the subject of banned books, Shannon returned to the home page and clicked on the link "Banned Books."

■ **Identity of the organization** That link provided on the home page allowed Shannon to gather more information about *The Online Books Page* and its author. Shannon

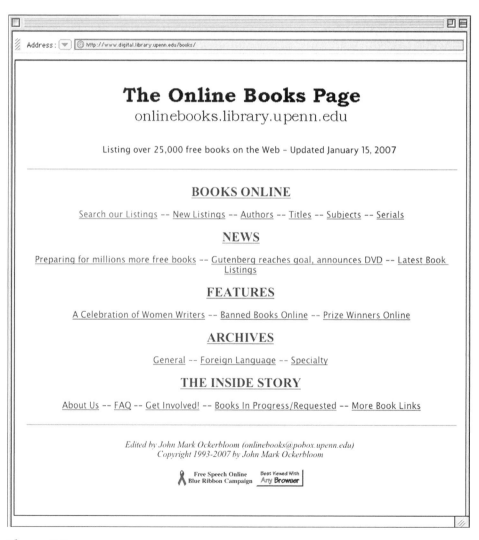

**Figure 9.1**

found a number of links that provided her with considerable information on banned books including classics by Geoffrey Chaucer and John Milton. Another link specified the criteria used to determine which books were placed on the banned book list. Still other links provided further background information about the goals of the site and its association with the Library of Congress. This information and the support of well-known and credible organizations and projects made Shannon feel confident about the value of this site.

■ **Date of posting** Shannon noted that the material on the website was current, having last been updated in the very month in which she was doing her research. The site itself contained information about both recent attempts to limit public library Internet access and historical accounts of book banning.

■ **Quality of references** The author provided frequent references to other websites on banned books, as well as to printed books on censorship. Checking through the Internet and the college library, Shannon confirmed that these references were used reliably and even decided to incorporate some of them into her research.

■ **Quality of material** Shannon found the text well written and the entire site organized and thorough. To evaluate whether the author's perspective was balanced, Shannon checked to see if books from the full range of the political spectrum were included in the list. She discovered that the list included a group of diverse books, from the Bible to the Qur'an to works of nineteenth-century poetry to contemporary books that had been criminalized under "hate speech" laws in other countries. Although it was clear to Shannon that the author of the site did not approve of book banning, this bias did not seem to distort the information he provided.

■ **Intended use** Shannon was interested in finding out the titles of books that were banned, those responsible for the banning, and the reasons behind the decisions. She found *The Online Books Page* very useful. Shannon was particularly impressed by its range of titles. The site's list covered classic and historical works, as well as more modern ones. The explanations that accompanied each listing briefly explained the circumstances surrounding the book's censorship and provided specific dates and information about it.

After carefully evaluating *The Online Books Page: Banned Books Online,* Shannon concluded that it was a reliable source that might supply her with valuable information for her argument essay.

Shannon found three other websites that were also concerned with the issue of banned books. However, after using the criteria outlined above to evaluate the three, Shannon decided not to use them. Here are some of the reasons why:

■ **Domain address** Two of the sites had addresses that indicated that they had no association with any educational institution, government, business, or organization; the websites were developed by individuals for their own personal use. Shannon decided that the materials on these sites were more likely to reflect personal opinion than careful research. The third site was maintained by an organization that Shannon decided to investigate further.

■ **Author of the site** By using the links provided in each site, Shannon discovered that one author was a student writing a paper for an Internet course; another was an individual who supplied some personal information about his life (as well as family photographs) but nothing that indicated expertise on book banning; and the third was identified as a news editor for a newspaper published in California. Shannon needed more information before she could conclude that any of these authors was a reliable source.

■ **Identity of the organization** Only the site authored by the newspaper editor indicated an association with an organization. Using links in the site, Shannon found that he was affiliated with a religious group that strongly advocated the elimination of different races and religions in American life. After reading several articles on the group's website, Shannon concluded that the material contained strong political and racial bias that made her question the reliability of the newspaper editor.

■ **Date of posting** None of the sites had been updated within the past year. Although Shannon was interested in both historical and current information on book banning, she was concerned that the authors had made no attempts to keep the information in the sites current and timely.

■ **Quality of references** Only one site contained a list of related readings, and none of the sites used references to support statements of fact or opinion.

■ **Quality of material** Shannon immediately noticed the poor writing quality of the student paper. It was filled with misspellings and grammatical errors and was poorly organized. The second site demonstrated better quality writing, but the author did not develop or support his ideas sufficiently. For instance, he based much of his claim on an "informal survey" without specifying the details of how the survey was conducted. The site authored by the newspaper editor did not reflect respect for other viewpoints or any attempt to present a balanced perspective on the issue of book banning.

■ **Intended use** Shannon wanted to be sure that the information she used in her argument essay was accurate. The absence of information about two of the authors and the political affiliations of the third caused her to doubt that any of these sites could be relied on for accuracy.

As Shannon discovered, the Internet can offer a wide array of source material to research, but it does take additional effort to determine which sources will meet the standards required for academic research. If you remember to think like an investigator and examine your findings carefully, you'll discover reliable and valuable information and ideas for your argument essays.

# Taking Notes

There are as many different styles of note taking as there are writers. Some people like to use index cards, recording one idea on each card. This is useful because you can easily shift cards around as you change your outline; you don't have to recopy material as often. Other students take notes in a journal or on sheets of paper so they can make notes or copy bibliographic references in the margins. If you decide to use note cards, we offer two words of advice: First, mark every note card in some way to identify the source. You might want to use the author's name, an abbreviation of the title, or a numbering system tying your note cards and bibliography together. Don't neglect this or you'll find yourself desperately searching for a reference at 2 a.m. on the day your paper is due, with no way to track it down. Second, on each note card indicate whether it's a summary, paraphrase, or direct quote; some people use different colored cards, pens, or highlighters to distinguish the three kinds of notes. Other people use the initials *S, P,* and *Q* to mark the cards. This designation proves useful when deciding how and when to *document* your sources (see the Documentation Guide).

Most research notes fall into one of three categories: summary, paraphrase, and quotation.

You may also make use of online note-taking. The Internet offers several sites that help students to take, manage, and store their notes and documents—including images and audio data—securely online. Most of these services offer easy systems for organizing notes according to categories just as you would with index cards or file folders as well as search engines for finding old notes. You can also create as many folders as you like, while assigning as many notes as desired to each folder. Because these services are Web applications rather than desktop programs, you can access material from any computer.

Some of these services require a fee; one is NoodleTools http://www.noodletools.com which offers students innovative software that searches, accesses, records, and organizes information using online note cards. It also formats your bibliography in MLA or APA style. (NoodleTools is included in Pearson Longman's MyCompLab. If this book was packaged with an access code to MyCompLab, you will have free access to NoodleTools.) In spite of the fee, NoodleTools is an excellent resource that might be worth the money for all the conveniences offered. Other online services are free, such as mynoteit.com, *Google Docs*, WordPress.com, and Yahoo! Notepad, which is accessible upon opening a free e-mail account with Yahoo!

A word of caution: You can lose track of sources if the particular research link goes down. To avoid such pitfalls, always make copies of your information on CDs, discs, and/or data sticks. You should also make hard copies and print notes with particularly important information.

## Summary

*Summary* is most useful for recording an author's main idea without the background or supporting evidence. To summarize accurately, condense an extended idea into a sentence or more in your own words. Your goal is to record the *essence* of the idea as accurately as possible in your own words.

Here's Shannon's summary of a passage from one of her sources:

**Original**

In Mark Twain's lifetime, his books *Tom Sawyer* and *Huckleberry Finn* were excluded from the juvenile sections of the Brooklyn Public Library (among other libraries), and banned from the library in Concord, MA, home of Henry Thoreau. In recent years, some high schools have dropped *Huckleberry Finn* from their reading lists, or have been sued by parents who want the book dropped. In Tempe, Arizona, a parent's lawsuit attempted to get the local high school to remove the book from a required reading list and *went as far as a federal appeals court* in 1998. (The court's *decision in the case*, which affirmed Tempe High's right to teach the book, has some interesting comments about education and racial tensions.) The Tempe suit, and recent others, were concerned with the use of the word "nigger," a word that also got *Uncle Tom's Cabin* challenged in Waukegan, Illinois. (From Ockerbloom, John Mark. *The Online Books Page: Banned Books Online*. http://digital.library.upenn. edu/books/banned-books.html.)

**Shannon's Summary**

Mark Twain's *Huckleberry Finn* is one of the most infamously banned books, as some say it promotes racism by using the "n" word. In 1998, parents in Arizona filed a lawsuit attempting to remove the book from a high school reading list, and the suit went all the way to the federal appeals court. The court's decision returned the book to the reading list.

For more on writing summaries, see Chapter 2.

## Paraphrase

*Paraphrasing* is useful when you want to preserve an author's line of reasoning or specific ideas but don't want or need to use the original words. When you paraphrase, you restate the original as accurately as possible using your own words and sentence structure.

Here is an excerpt from another source that Shannon used in her paper:

**Original**

Textbook publishers are sensitive to the often right-wing committees and boards of education that purchase books for large states like Texas and California, and will also delete references to evolution or the scientifically hypothesized age of the Earth. (From Barnhisel, Greg, ed. *Media and Messages: Strategies and Readings in Public Rhetoric*, p. 422.)

**Shannon's Paraphrase**

When they prepare their book lists, publishers put their business at risk if they forget that states with large, expensive, book-consuming school systems—Texas, for example—often have unyielding opinions about a number of sensitive topics. Evolution, for example, is not discussed in some of the science textbooks students use in school—an inappropriate move that denies students exposure to an important scientific theory.

## Quotation

*Direct quotation* should be used only when the author's words are particularly memorable or succinct, or when the author presents factual or numerical evidence that can't be easily paraphrased. You must copy the author's *exact* wording, spelling, capitalization, and punctuation *as you find it* (even if it contains an obvious mistake). Proofread every direct quotation at least twice; it's easier than you think to leave something out, change a verb tense, or add a word or two. If you want to add words for grammatical completeness or clarity, put them in square brackets such as these [ ]. If you want to eliminate words, mark the omission with three spaced periods, called *ellipsis points* (if the omission comes at the end of a sentence, the ellipsis is typed with four spaced periods). If you find a source you are certain to quote from, it might be worthwhile to photocopy it to avoid errors when rewriting the words.

Here is an example of the effective use of quotation, based on another of Shannon's sources:

**Original**

Congress shall make no law respecting an establishment of religion, or prohibiting the free exercise thereof; or abridging the freedom of speech, or of the press; or the right of the people peaceably to assemble, and to petition the Government for a redress of grievances. ("About the First Amendment." *First Amendment Center.* http://www. firstamendmentcenter.org/about.aspx?item=about_firstamd.)

**Shannon's Effective Use of Quotation**

According to the First Amendment, citizens of the United States are guaranteed the right to freedom of speech, which also includes the freedoms of thought and expression: "Congress shall make no law respecting an establishment of religion, or prohibiting the free exercise thereof; or abridging the freedom of speech, or of the press [. . .]."

# Drafting Your Paper

Sometimes the sheer size of a researched argument paper can be intimidating. As a result, some writers suffer from "writer's block" at the outset. Here are strategies for starting your draft.

1. **Write a five-minute summary.** Write a quick, one- or two-paragraph description of what your final paper will say—that is, a thumbnail sketch of the paper to clarify in your own mind how it will come together. The summary doesn't have to be formal; some people don't even use complete sentences. Almost always, these summaries dispel writer's block and get your creativity flowing.
2. **Divide the paper into sections.** Dividing the paper into sections makes the task of writing a long paper more manageable. Most writers divide a paper, as we did in Chapter 5, into beginning, middle, and end, and further subdivide the middle.
3. **First, draft the sections you're confident about.** Drafting first the sections you feel most confident about builds momentum for drafting other parts of the paper. As reported by many students, this strategy might also lead you to alter the slant or emphasis of the final paper, thereby resulting in a better outcome.
4. **Use a simple code to indicate sources.** Using a simple code to indicate sources will save you a great deal of time in revising your paper. As you write your draft, you may not want to interrupt the flow of your ideas to copy quotations or summaries from note cards; instead, you can insert into your draft the author's or source's name and a quick reference to the content so that you'll know on a later draft what you intended to include. Here's an example of how Shannon used coded references in her first draft:

Attempts to ban books in public schools is on the rise. [People, Attacks 6] John Steinbeck's *Of Mice and Men* is a frequent target of protest for parents. [Mitchell, NYT B17]

Here you can see Shannon's code at work as she refers to notes from a report published by People for the American Way and an article from page B17 of the *New York*

*Times.* Later, she will have to incorporate these sources into her first draft and provide parenthetical citations; for the time being, she simply lists in shorthand the evidence to support her general statements.

## Incorporating Your Research

Because the effort made in finding sources and taking notes is so time-consuming, some writers think that their work will be "wasted" if they don't somehow cram all the notes they've taken into their final papers. Unfortunately, the results of such cramming often look less like a paper and more like note cards stapled together with an occasional sentence wedged between to provide transitions. Every successful writer ends up gathering more research data than is needed for a paper. But it's better to have a lot of material to choose from than not enough to make a persuasive case. The five tests at the end of Chapter 6 (sufficiency, detail, relevance, avoidance of excess, and appropriateness) should help you determine which notes to incorporate into the final draft. Here, too, the flexibility of having one note per card may help because you can shuffle and change the sequence of sources to see which order of presentation will have the most impact on your readers. If you are working on a computer, you may mark and move blocks of text around as you judge the arrangement of your evidence. The first arrangement may not always be the best, so allow yourself some flexibility.

When incorporating sources into your paper, you don't want the "seams" to show between your own writing and the summaries, paraphrases, and quotations from your sources. So it's worth the effort to write sentences and phrases that smoothly introduce sources into the text. Consider two examples:

**Awkward**     The Anaheim school board decided to ban *Beloved,* and this was "not an example of censorship, but an isolated incident."

**Revised**     The school board in the Anaheim, California, school system stated that their decision to ban *Beloved* was "not an example of censorship, but an isolated incident."

Remember that while *you,* the writer, may understand how a particular source supports your points, your *readers* may miss the connections unless you provide them. Again we fall back on the analogy of making a case to a jury: A good attorney not only presents a witness's testimony but also helps the jury understand what that testimony means.

## Attribution

Many students fail to understand the importance of introducing their sources when incorporating them into a paper. This introduction is called **attribution,** and it is an important part of the process of documentation. Attribution shows your readers that your evidence comes from identifiable, reliable sources. When the attribution contains the name of a book or the author's professional affiliation or other credentials, it also suggests to your readers how reliable the source may be. For instance, if you present a statistic on divorce and attribute it to the book *How to Pick Up Women,* your readers are less likely to respect that statistic than if it came from the U.S. Census Bureau. Likewise, if you cite evidence that eating rutabagas prevents colon cancer, your readers will treat the evidence differently if it comes from an unbiased researcher at the Mayo Clinic rather than from one at the

American Rutabaga Institute. In neither case is the evidence less likely to be true, but the attribution in both cases makes the difference in plausibility.

Many students have only one phrase in their repertoires for attribution: "According to. . . ." This works, but it is not very informative. By choosing a more connotative argumentative verb, as you do when you state a position or proposal, you can signal to your readers the source's attitude toward the statement. For instance, consider this sentence:

Senator Smith _____ that the change is needed.

Using the list of attribution verbs below, look at how selecting a verb can determine the way your audience regards Smith's position (not all these verbs will work in this sentence structure).

## Attribution Verbs

**Source Is Neutral**

| | | |
|---|---|---|
| comments | observes | says |
| describes | points out | sees |
| explains | records | thinks |
| illustrates | reports | writes |
| notes | | |

**Source Implies or Suggests but Doesn't Actually Say**

| | | |
|---|---|---|
| analyzes | asks | assesses |
| concludes | considers | finds |
| predicts | proposes | reveals |
| shows | speculates | suggests |
| supposes | infers | implies |

**Source Argues**

| | | |
|---|---|---|
| alleges | claims | contends |
| defends | disagrees | holds |
| insists | maintains | argues |

**Source Agrees with Someone/Something Else**

| | | |
|---|---|---|
| admits | agrees | concedes |
| concurs | grants | allows |

**Source Is Uneasy or Disagrees**

| | | |
|---|---|---|
| belittles | bemoans | complains |
| condemns | deplores | deprecates |
| derides | laments | warns |

If you're not sure of the connotations of any of these verbs, or you're not sure that the sentence you created works with a particular choice, consult an unabridged dictionary or your instructor. Clumsy attribution can distract readers in the same way typos and grammatical errors can; so you want to make your attributions as smooth as possible. (For placement of a bibliographic reference after attributed material, see the next section on documentation.)

## Revising and Editing Your Paper

After you have worked your source material into a draft, it's time to look at your writing skeptically, as your readers will. Start by testing all the parts of your argument. This may not be easy to do because you've been living with this topic for some time and may have lost your objectivity and ability to see the gaps. (If you're working in writing groups, ask another member to read your paper and offer you some feedback on it.) Then change, delete, add, or reorganize material to make your case more effectively.

To help you revise your argument, we recommend making an outline of the draft *as you've written it*—not as you intended to write it. This will serve as an X-ray of the paper, helping you detect any holes or imbalances. Moreover, it will show you the actual order in which points are presented so that you can consider reorganizing or changing your argumentative strategy. The strategies explained in Chapters 6 and 7 for assessing evidence and considering claims ought to help you at this stage; apply them as stringently to your own writing as you would to an essay you're reading.

If you made notes in your journal about connections you wanted to make in your final paper, now is the time to include those connections if, in fact, they still fit. You might also consider other kinds of evidence to include. Can you think of personal experiences—yours or others'—to support the evidence of your outside authorities? Have you found facts and statistics to buttress the opinions you present? What are your readers' criteria for judging an issue? Have you presented claims that meet those criteria and phrased them in that manner? It's also time to make sure that all transitions between points are included and are accurate. For instance, if you switch points around, make sure that the point you call "second" is actually the second, not the third or fourth. Also, check that you've included documentation for all your sources and that you have bibliographic note cards or other records of documentation information to prepare the notes in your final copy. Then polish your prose so that your sentences are smooth, your paragraphs are complete, and your grammar and punctuation are precise. Many students let down their efforts when they sense their papers are nearing completion; as a result, their final grades suffer. The revising and editing stage requires sharp attention. Don't undercut all your hard research efforts by presenting your argument in anything but its best form.

## Preparing and Proofreading Your Final Manuscript

Once you have polished the draft to your satisfaction, it is time to attend to the presentation of your paper. Flawless presentation is important in research, not only because of the appreciation it will win from your instructor and readers, but also because it will reinforce your credibility with your readers. A sloppy paper with typographical or grammatical errors, missing documentation, or illegible print makes your readers think that your argument might be sloppy as well. A well-prepared paper suggests to your readers that you have taken care to ensure that everything is correct—not only the presentation, but the content as well. This good impression may make readers more inclined to accept your arguments.

Most instructors expect research papers to be neatly and legibly typed with clear titles, double spacing, standard margins (1-inch) and type sizes (10- or 12-point), and minimal handwritten corrections. Your last name and the page number should appear in the upper-right-hand corner of every page after the title page. For English courses, the standard guide to manuscript format is the *MLA Handbook for Writers of Research Papers*, 7th edition. MLA requirements are spelled out in most college composition handbooks and illustrated in Shannon's final paper (see the Documentation Guide). Before you submit your paper, proofread it carefully for typographical errors, misspellings, omitted words, and other minor errors. If possible, let several hours elapse before your final proofreading so you can see what you've actually typed instead of what you *think* you typed.

## Plagiarism

**Plagiarism** is a crime in the academic community. The scholarly world operates by exchanging information and acknowledging its sources. If you fail to acknowledge your sources or let it appear that someone else's work is your own, you are sabotaging the exchange of scholarly information. You're blocking the channels. And plagiarism has very serious consequences: It can earn you a failing grade on an assignment or for a course, a suspension or even expulsion from school, and/or a permanent notation on the transcript that future employers and graduate schools will see.

Plagiarism falls into two categories: intentional and accidental. Intentional plagiarism includes copying a phrase, a sentence, or a longer passage from a source and passing it off as your own; summarizing or paraphrasing someone else's ideas without acknowledgment; and buying or borrowing a paper written by someone else and submitting it as your own. Accidental plagiarism includes forgetting to place quotation marks around someone else's words and not acknowledging a source because you were ignorant of the need to document it. Carelessness and ignorance are not defenses against plagiarism.

Many questions about plagiarism involve the tricky subject of *common knowledge*—that is, standard information in a field of study as well as commonsense observations and proverbial wisdom. Standard information includes the major facts in a discipline—for example, the chemical formula for water is $H_2O$ or the Seneca Falls Convention for Women's Rights took place in 1848. If most of your sources accept such a fact without acknowledgment, you can assume it is common knowledge to readers in that field. However, if you're dealing with lesser-known facts (the numbers of soldiers at the Battle of Hastings), interpretations of those facts (assessments of the importance of the Seneca Falls meeting), or a specialist's observation (a scholar's analysis of Susan B. Anthony's rhetoric), you'll need to provide documentation.

Commonsense information, such as the notions that politicians are concerned with getting votes and that icy roads make driving dangerous, need not be documented. Proverbs and clichés don't need documentation either, although proverbs taken from recognized poems or literary works do. (Thus, "A stitch in time" needs no documentation, but "To be or not to be" should carry a reference to *Hamlet*.)

Here are four simple rules to help you avoid plagiarism:

1. *Take your research notes carefully.* Write down (or print out) a full bibliographical reference for each source (the forms appear in the Documentation Guide). Also, note whether you are quoting, paraphrasing, or summarizing what you find in your source (see earlier discussion in this chapter). If your notes are clear and thorough, you'll never have to worry about which words and ideas are yours and which come from your sources.

2. *Always introduce your source carefully so that your audience knows to whom they're listening.* Proper attribution is a signal to your readers that you're switching from your own work to someone else's. It also is a signal to you to check that a source is represented accurately (with no exaggeration) and that a bibliographic citation appears in your list of Works Cited or References.

3. *When in doubt, document.* While it is possible to overdocument, it is not an intellectual crime to do so. Rather, it reveals a lack of self-confidence in your own argument or your determination to prove to your instructor and readers that you've seen every source ever published on your subject. However, overdocumenting is a less serious academic sin than plagiarizing!

4. *Enter the documentation right after the use of the source; it doesn't "carry over" between paragraphs or pages.* It is tempting, especially when using one source for an extended period, to leave all the documentation until the end of a large passage of text (which might be several paragraphs or several pages in length). But even if you weave attribution skillfully throughout the whole passage, the convention in academics is that you document a source in each paragraph in which you use it. If another source intervenes, it is twice as important that the main source be documented on every use. So if you use the same article in four successive paragraphs, each of those paragraphs must have some parenthetical source reference. With skillful attribution, the parenthetical reference can be reduced to a simple page number, which won't interrupt the flow of your text.

To understand how plagiarism works, let's look at some of the ways writers might handle, or mishandle, this passage from Dennis Baron's article "English in a Multicultural Society," which appeared in the Spring 1991 issue of *Social Policy*. Here's the original passage from page 8:

> The notion of a national language sometimes wears the disguise of inclusion: we must all speak English to participate meaningfully in the democratic process. Sometimes it argues unity: we must speak one language to understand one another and share both culture and country. Those who insist on English often equate bilingualism with lack of patriotism. Their intention to legislate official English often masks racism and certainly fails to appreciate cultural difference; it is a thinly veiled measure to disenfranchise anyone not like "us."

**Plagiarized Use**

Supporters of U.S. English argue we must all speak one language to understand one another and share both culture and country. But Dennis Baron argues that "[t]heir intention to legislate official English often masks racism and certainly fails to appreciate cultural difference" (8). English-only legislation really intends to exclude anyone who is not like "us."

This is plagiarism because the writer has copied Baron's words in the first sentence and paraphrased them in the last, but made it appear as though only the middle sentence was actually taken from Baron's article.

**Plagiarized Use**

Calls for a national language sometimes wear the disguise of inclusion, according to linguist Dennis Baron. When U.S. English argues that we must all speak English to participate meaningfully in the democratic process, or that we must speak one language to understand one another and share both culture and country, Baron says they are masking racism and failing to appreciate cultural difference (8).

Here the plagiarism comes in presenting Baron's actual words without quotation marks, so it looks as if the writer is paraphrasing rather than quoting. Even with the attribution and the citation of the source, this paragraph is still an example of plagiarism because the direct quotations appear as the writer's paraphrase.

**Acceptable Use**

Linguist Dennis Baron argues that supporters of official English legislation use the reasons of inclusion, unity, and patriotism to justify these laws, but that their efforts may hide racist and culturally intolerant positions. Baron says that sometimes English-only laws are "thinly veiled measure[s] to disenfranchise anyone not like 'us'" (8).

Here the source is properly handled. The writer paraphrases most of the original text in the first sentence, then skillfully incorporates a direct quotation in the second (note the use of square brackets to make the noun agree in number with the verb, and the conversion of double quotation marks from the original into single quotation marks in the quote). The attribution clearly says that both points are taken from Baron, but the quotation marks show where Baron's own words, rather than the writer's, are used.

# Documentation Guide:

## MLA and APA Styles

The two most common systems of documentation used in colleges and universities are the Modern Language Association (MLA) style, used widely in the humanities, and the American Psychological Association (APA) style, used widely in the social sciences. We will explain them in detail in this chapter. (Some of your courses may also require you to use the Council of Science Editors, or CSE, style; *The Chicago Manual of Style,* which you might know as Turabian style; or a journalistic style guide such as *The Associated Press Style Book.*) Your instructor will tell you which rules to follow.

## Where Does the Documentation Go?

Both MLA and APA styles call for parenthetical citations within the paper and a source list at the end of the paper. In both styles, you use a brief reference or attribution to your source in parentheses within the body of the paper and a full bibliographical citation in a list of Works Cited (MLA) or References (APA). (These are the equivalents of what you probably called a "Bibliography" in high school.) Documenting your sources, if performed properly, will help you avoid plagiarism. The shape that citations take in the two systems, however, is a little different, so make sure you observe the forms carefully.

## Documentation Style

Let's look at how both systems handle documentation for some of the most commonly used information sources. Suppose you want to quote from Matt Bai's article "The New Boss," which appeared in the January 30, 2005, issue of the *New York Times Magazine.* Here's how it would appear in your list of sources or bibliography:

> **MLA**　Bai, Matt. "The New Boss." *The New York Times Magazine* 30 Jan. 2005: 38+. Print.

> **APA**　Bai, M. (2005, January 30). The new boss. *The New York Times Magazine*, pp. 38–45, 62, 68, 71.

As you can see, each style orders information differently.

Likewise, both styles use a parenthetical reference in the paper to show where the evidence comes from, but again they do it differently.

> **MLA**　One author talks about giving "added value" to employers, some of whom have come to view him, warily, as a partner (Bai 42).

If the author's name appears in your attribution, only the page number needs to go in the parentheses:

**MLA**   Matt Bai talks about giving "added value" to employers, some of whom have come to view him, warily, as a partner (42).

Both references tell your readers that they can find this source in your Works Cited list, alphabetized by the last name *Bai*. If you had more than one reference to Bai in your Works Cited list, then you would add a shortened form of the title in the parentheses so readers would know to which Bai article you were referring (Bai, "New Boss" 42).

The APA style references for the same situations would be

**APA**   One author talks about giving "added value" to employers, some of whom have come to view him, warily, as a partner (Bai, 2005, p. 42).

or

**APA**   Bai (2005) talks about giving "added value" to employers, some of whom have come to view him, warily, as a partner (p. 42).

When you use more than one work by an author in your paper, APA style distinguishes them by date of publication. For example, if you cited two Bai articles from 2005, the earlier one would be designated 2005a, and the second as 2005b.

Using parenthetical citations for electronic sources can be much trickier because such sources typically have no page numbers. If your source uses paragraph numbers, provide the paragraph number preceded by *par.* or *para.* If you need to include the author's name or a brief title, place a comma after the name or title. If another type of designation is used in the source to delineate its parts (such as *screens* or *Part II*), write out the word used for that part:

**MLA**   Between 2000 and 2004, the message delivered by political advertisements changed dramatically (Edwards, par. 15).

**APA**   Between 2000 and 2004, the message delivered by political advertisements changed dramatically (Edwards, 2005, para. 15).

If your source has no numbering, no page or paragraph numbers should appear in your parenthetical reference unless your instructor indicates that you should do otherwise. Some instructors ask students to number the paragraphs of electronic sources to make references easier to locate.

## A Brief Guide to MLA and APA Styles

The handbooks for MLA and APA documentation are available in most college libraries. If you don't find the information you need in this brief guide, look for these books or websites:

**MLA**   *MLA Handbook for Writers of Research Papers.* 7th ed. New York: MLA, 2009. Print.

The website of the Modern Language Association is http://www.mla.org.

**APA**    *Publication Manual of the American Psychological Association* (6th ed.). (2009). Washington, DC: American Psychological Association.

The American Psychological Association does not provide a guide to documentation on its website; however, the Purdue University Online Writing Lab provides a useful guide to APA documentation: http://owl.english.purdue.edu/handouts/research/r_apa.html.

## Books

**MLA**    Author. *Title*. Edition. City of Publication: Publisher, Year. Medium of Publication.

**APA**    Author. (Year of Publication). *Title*. City of Publication, State: Publisher.

### One Author

**MLA**    Krakauer, Jon. *Where Men Win Glory: The Odyssey of Pat Tillman*. New York: Random, 2009. Print.

**APA**    Krakauer, J. (2009) *Where men win glory: The odyssey of Pat Tillman*. New York, NY: Random House.

MLA uses the author's full first name plus middle initial, whereas APA uses the initial of the first name (unless more initials are needed to distinguish among people with the same initials). APA capitalizes only first words and proper nouns in titles and subtitles; MLA capitalizes all words except prepositions, conjunctions, and articles. MLA lists only the city; APA lists the city but also includes the state. MLA shortens certain publishers' names, whereas APA just drops unnecessary words such as *Co., Inc.*, and *Publishers*. Lastly, MLA includes the medium of the publication consulted, which is "Print" in this case.

### Two or More Authors

**MLA**    Reinhart, Carmen M., and Kenneth S. Rogoff. *This Time Is Different: Eight Centuries of Financial Folly*. Princeton: Princeton UP, 2009. Print.

**APA**    Reinhart, C. M., & Rogoff, K. S. (2009). *This time is different: Eight centuries of financial folly*. Princeton, NJ: Princeton University Press.

In MLA style, only the first author's name is given in inverted form. In APA style, the ampersand (&) is used to join authors' names. The ampersand is also used in parenthetical references in text, for example "(Reinhart & Rogoff, 2009, p. 63)," but not in attributions, for example, "According to Pyles and Algeo." In MLA style, for works with more than three authors you may replace all but the first author's name by the abbreviation *et al.* In APA style, list the names of up to six authors, and use the abbreviation *et al.* to indicate the remaining authors.

### More Than One Book by an Author

**MLA**    Gladwell, Malcolm. *Outliers.* New York: Little, 2008. Print.

        ---. *What the Dog Saw and Other Adventures.* New York: Little, 2009. Print.

In MLA style, if you cite more than one work by a particular author, the individual works are listed in alphabetical order. For the second and any additional entries, type three hyphens and a period instead of the author's name; then skip a space and type the title in italics.

In APA style, when you cite more than one work by an author, the author's name is repeated for each work. The order of the entries is based on the publication dates of the titles, with the earliest-published given first, instead of alphabetical order. If two works by one author are published in the same year, alphabetization is done by title and the letters *a*, *b*, etc., are placed immediately after the year.

### Book with an Editor

**MLA**    Haynes, Kenneth, ed. *Geoffrey Hill: Collected Critical Writings.* New York: Oxford UP, 2008. Print.

**APA**    Haynes, K. (Ed.). (2008). *Geoffrey Hill: Collected critical writings.* New York, NY: Oxford University Press.

### Essay in a Collection or Anthology

**MLA**    Fisher, M. F. K. "Gare de Lyon." *Americans in Paris: A Literary Anthology.* Ed. Adam Gopnik. New York: Library of America, 2004. 581-91. Print.

**APA**    Fisher, M. F. K. (2004). Gare de Lyon. In A. Gopnik (Ed.), *Americans in Paris: A literary anthology* (pp. 581–591). New York, NY: Library of America.

### Book in a Later Edition

**MLA**    Janaro, Richard, and Thelma Altshuler. *The Art of Being Human.* 9th ed. New York: Longman, 2009.

**APA**    Janaro, R., & Altshuler, T. (2009). *The art of being human* (9th ed). New York, NY: Longman.

### Multivolume Work

**MLA**    Doyle, Arthur Conan. *The New Annotated Sherlock Holmes.* Ed. Leslie S. Klinger. 2 vols. New York: Norton, 2004. Print.

**APA**    Doyle, A. C. (2004). *The new annotated Sherlock Holmes* (L. S. Klinger, Ed.). (Vols. 1–2). New York, NY: Norton.

### Book with a Group or Corporate Author

**MLA**     American Medical Association. *Handbook of First Aid and Emergency Care.* New York, Random, 2009. Print.

**APA**     American Medical Association. (2009). *Handbook of first aid and emergency care.* New York, NY: Random House.

Begin the entry with the corporate or group name alphabetized by the first letter of the main word (not including *a, an,* or *the*).

### Article from a Reference Work

**MLA**     Bragg, Michael B. "Aircraft Deicing." *The McGraw-Hill Concise Encyclopedia of Science and Technology.* 6th ed. 2009. Print.

**APA**     Bragg, M. (2009). Aircraft deicing. In *The McGraw-Hill concise encyclopedia of science and technology* (Vol. 1, pp. 339–342). New York, NY: McGraw-Hill.

If the reference book is widely available (such as a major encyclopedia or bibliography), a short bibliographic form as shown here is acceptable in MLA; APA recommends including more information rather than less. For a less widely known reference book, MLA recommends using the form for a book, multiple-authored book, or series, depending on what the book is.

### Editor's Preparation of a Previous Work

**MLA**     Lovecraft, H. P. *Tales.* Ed. Peter Straub. New York: Library of America, 2005. Print.

**APA**     Lovecraft, H. P. (2005). *Tales* (P. Straub, Ed.). New York, NY: Library of America.

### Translated Work

**MLA**     Pamuk, Orhan. *The Museum of Innocence.* Trans. Maureen Freely. New York: Knopf, 2009. Print.

**APA**     Pamuk, O. (2009). *The museum of innocence* (M. Freely, Trans.). New York, NY: Alfred A. Knopf. (Original work published 2008)

In APA style, the date of the translation is placed after the author's name. The date of the original publication of the work appears in parentheses at the end of the citation. This text would be cited in a paper as (Pamuk, 2008/2009).

### Anonymous Work

**MLA**     *The Chicago Manual of Style: The Essential Guide for Writers, Editors, and Publishers.* 16th ed. Chicago: U of Chicago P, 2010. Print.

**APA**     *The Chicago manual of style: The essential guide for writers, editors, and publishers* (16th ed.). (2010). Chicago, IL: University of Chicago Press.

## Periodicals

MLA format and APA format for articles in journals, periodicals, magazines, newspapers, and so on, are similar to the formats for books. One of the few differences concerns the volume number of each issue. Volume numbers for magazines or journals found in a library or acquired by subscription (these usually appear six times a year or less frequently) should be included in your entry. If a journal appears monthly or more frequently, or can be acquired on newsstands, you can usually omit the volume number. If the journal has continuous pagination (i.e., if the January issue ends on page 88 and the February issue begins on page 89), you don't need to include the month or season of the issue in your citation. If the journal starts over with page 1 in each issue, then you must include the month or season in your citation.

Magazines and newspapers (unlike scholarly journals) often carry articles on discontinuous pages (e.g., pages 35–37 and then 114–115). MLA permits the use of the form "35+" instead of giving all the pages on which such articles appear. With APA style, all page numbers must be noted.

**MLA**    Author. "Article Title." *Journal or Magazine Title* volume number (Date): inclusive pages. Medium of publication.

**APA**    Author. (Date). Article title. *Journal or Magazine Title, volume number,* inclusive pages.

### Scholarly Journal

**MLA**    Spandler, Helen, and Tim Calton. "Psychosis and Human Rights: Conflicts in Mental Health Policy and Practice." *Social Policy and Society* 8. (2009), 245-256. Print.

**APA**    Spandler, H., & Calton, T. (2009). Psychosis and human rights: Conflicts in mental health policy and practice. *Social Policy and Society, 8*(1), 245–256.

### Magazine Article

**MLA**    Wallace, Amy. "An Epidemic of Fear." *Wired* Nov. 2009: 128+. Print.

**APA**    Wallace, A. (2009, November). An epidemic of fear. *Wired,* 128–135, 166, 168, 170.

This is the form for a magazine that appears monthly. For a magazine that appears bimonthly or weekly, provide the complete date.

**MLA**    Mahr, Krista. "A Tough Catch." *Time* 16 Nov. 2009: 38-43. Print.

**APA**    Mahr, K. (2009, November 16). A tough catch. *Time,* 38–43.

### Review

**MLA**    Vaill, Amanda. "Brooklyn Bohemians." Rev. of *February House*, by Sherill Tippins. *New York Times Book Review* 6 Feb. 2005: 8. Print.

**APA**    Vaill, A. (2005, February 6). Brooklyn bohemians [Review of the book *February house*, by S. Tippins]. *The New York Times Book Review,* p. 8.

When newspapers designate sections with identifying letters (e.g., *A*, *B*), that information is included in the reference. With MLA style, "4+" indicates that the review begins on page 4 and continues on other nonadjacent pages in the newspaper. APA includes initial articles such as "The" in a newspaper title; MLA omits them. If the reviewer's name does not appear, begin with "Rev. of *Title*" in the MLA system or "[Review of the book *Title*]" in the APA system. If the reviewer's name does not appear but the review has a title, begin with the title of the review in both systems.

## Newspaper Article

**MLA**  Begley, Sharon. "Reversing Partial Blindness." *Wall Street Journal* 1 Feb. 2005: D1. Print.

**APA**  Begley, S. (2005, February 1). Reversing partial blindness. *The Wall Street Journal*, p. D1.

## Newspaper Editorial

**MLA**  Judge, Michael. "Epitaph on a Tyrant." Editorial. *Wall Street Journal* 7 Feb. 2005: A19. Print.

**APA**  Judge, M. (2005, February 7). Epitaph on a tyrant [Editorial]. *The Wall Street Journal*, p. A19.

## Letter to the Editor of a Magazine or Newspaper

**MLA**  Rafferty, Heather A. Letter. "The Other 'CIA.'" *Weekly Standard* 7 Feb. 2005: 5. Print.

**APA**  Rafferty, H. (2005, February 7). The other "CIA" [Letter to the editor]. *The Weekly Standard*, p. 5.

If the newspaper or magazine doesn't give a title to the letter, for MLA style use the word *Letter* followed by a period after the author's name. Do not underline the word or enclose it in quotation marks. For APA style, skip that information and use the rest of the citation form.

## Internet Sources
### Web Page

**MLA**  Redford, Robert. "Common Sense for the Clean Energy and Climate Debate." *OnEarth*. Natural Resources Defense Council, 11 Nov. 2009. Web. 12 Nov. 2009.

**APA**  Redford, R. (2009, November 11). Common sense for the clean energy and climate debate. Retrieved from http://www.onearth.org/node/1603

For MLA, begin with the name of the individual who created the website. Follow with the title of the work in quotation marks (if you are citing a smaller work within a larger site), then the title of the entire website in italics. Then write the name of the organization associated with the site, if available; the date of publication, if available; the medium of publication, which is the "Web" in this case, and the date of access.

MLA does not require a URL in the citation. However, if your source is difficult to locate, you can provide the complete URL in angle brackets after the date of access. If the URL is long, you can break it onto the next line after a single or double slash.

For APA, begin with the last name of the author followed by initials and period. Follow with the date of publication or latest update. Use "(n.d.)" if no date is available.

If there is no author, begin with the title of the site, and then the date of publication or update. Close with the electronic address, whether it is the URL or DOI (digital object identifier).

### Online Magazine Article

**MLA**    Upbin, Bruce, and Dan Bigman. "The Carbon Question." *Forbes Magazine.* Forbes.com, 15 Oct. 2009. Web. 12 Nov. 2009.

**APA**    Upbin, B., & Bigman, D. (2009, October 15). The carbon question. *Forbes Magazine.* Retrieved from *http://www.forbes.com/forbes/2009/1102/opinions-steve-forbes-climate-change-lets-get-real.html*

MLA gives the date of access for electronic sources, and this date of access appears right after *Web*. APA provides the date of publication and lists this date after the author.

### Online Article in Electronic Journal

**MLA**    Knypstra, Syste. "Teaching statistics in an Activity Encouraging Format." *Journal of Statistics Education,* 17.2 (2009): n. pag. Web. 23 Oct. 2009.

**APA**    Knypstra, S. (2009). Teaching statistics in an activity encouraging format. *Journal of Statistics Education, 17*(2). Retrieved from www.amstat.org/publications/jse/v17n2/knypstra.html

### Online Article Retrieved from a Database

**MLA**    Thompson, Ayanna. "Introduction: Shakespeare, Race, and Performance." *Shakespeare Bulletin* 27.3 (2009): 359-61. *Project Muse.* Web. 7 Nov. 2009.

**APA**    Thompson, A. Introduction: Shakespeare, race, and performance. *Shakespeare Bulletin, 27*(3), 359–361. doi: 10.1353/shb.0.0109

To document material from a database in MLA, italicize the database service, indicate the medium of publication, i.e., Web, and the date of access. For APA, provide the DOI (digital object identifier) if available. Otherwise, you can list the database after *Retrieved from*.

### Online Book

**MLA**    Bacon, Jono. *The Art of Community: Building the New Age of Participation.* Sebastopol: O'Reilly, 2009. *Art of Community.* Web. 4 Nov. 2009.

**APA**    Bacon, J. (2009). *The art of community: Building the new age of participation.* Retrieved from http://www.artofcommunityonline.org/get/

### CD-ROM

**MLA**    "Electrometer." *The McGraw-Hill Encyclopedia of Science and Technology.* 9th ed. CD-ROM. New York: McGraw, 2002.

**APA**    Electrometer. (2002). In *The McGraw-Hill encyclopedia of science and technology (9th ed.).* [CD-ROM]. New York, NY: McGraw-Hill.

### E-Mail

**MLA**    Mendez, Michael R. "Re: Solar power." E-mail to Edgar V. Atamian. 13 Sept. 2009.

In APA, electronic correspondence via e-mail typically does not appear in the reference list. It is cited only in an in-text reference: (M. Mendez, personal communication, September 13, 2009).

## Miscellaneous Sources

### Film, Filmstrip, Slide Program, Videotape, DVD

**MLA**    Nair, Mira. *Amelia*. Perf. Hilary Swank, Richard Gere, and Ewan McGregor. Fox Searchlight Pictures, 2009. Film.

**APA**    Forster, M. (Director). (2004). *Finding neverland* [Motion picture]. United States: Miramax.

To cite a filmstrip, slide program, videotape, or DVD in MLA style, include the name of the medium after the distributor and year of release. If you are citing the work as a whole rather than the work of one of the creative artists involved in the project, start with the title instead. For instance:

**MLA**    *Harry Potter and the Half-Blood Prince*. Dir. David Yates. Warner Bros., 2009. DVD.

**APA**    Heyman, D. (Producer), & Yates, D. (Director). (2009). *Harry Potter and the half-blood prince* [Motion picture]. United States: Warner Bros.

### Television or Radio Program

**MLA**    Burns, Ken, dir. *The National Parks: America's Best Idea*. PBS. KCTS, Seattle. 28 Sept. 2-Oct. 2009. Television.

**APA**    Burns, K., and Duncan, D. (Producers). (2009) *The National Parks: America's Best Idea*. [Television series]. Seattle: KCTS.

In MLA, include the network as well as the call letters and city of the local station, if available. Then, add the broadcast date and medium of reception. For a radio broadcast, substitute *Radio*.

In APA, list the producer for an entire television series. To cite an individual episode in a series, list the writer and director instead, and substitute "Television series episode."

### Interview

**MLA**    Pennington, Linda Beth. Personal interview. 20 Apr. 2003.

In APA, personal communications including interviews do not appear in the reference list. They are cited only in an in-text reference: (L. Pennington, personal interview, April 20, 2009).

The APA doesn't offer forms for "nonrecoverable" materials such as personal letters, e-mail messages, lectures, and speeches, and these sources are not included in reference listings. However, in college writing assignments, most instructors will ask you to include them.

You may, therefore, have to design a hybrid citation form based on the standard forms. Remember that the APA encourages you to provide more, rather than less, information in your citations. The MLA has forms for almost any kind of communication, even nonrecoverable ones. Consult the *MLA Handbook for Writers of Research Papers,* 7th edition, to find additional forms.

## SAMPLE RESEARCH PAPERS

Following are two sample student research papers, the first in MLA format and the second in APA format. As you read them, notice the margins and other format requirements of the two styles, such as the use of running heads, the placement of titles, and the different citation forms. We have added marginal annotations to highlight special features and to demonstrate the structural elements of the arguments.

As these research papers demonstrate, the researched argument is different from the other arguments you've written only in quantity and format, not in quality. You must still make a claim and find evidence to support it, tailor your presentation to your readers, and use a logical structure that considers the various sides of an issue. As you progress in your academic life and, later, in your professional life, you will find that variations on the researched argument can become successful senior projects, theses, sales proposals, journal articles, grant proposals, and even books—so mastering the skills of argumentative writing will serve you well.

Shannon O'Neill

Professor Martinez

English 111

13 November 2009

Literature Hacked and Torn Apart:

Censorship in Public Schools

During the 2008 Summer Olympic Games in Beijing, international journalists covering the event found their access to certain Web sites restricted by the Chinese government—something that the country's citizens deal with every day. But even in America, where we wouldn't dream of a government that told us what sites we could not browse, an industry of censorship is lurking in the fine print: the banning of books in public schools.

According to the First Amendment, citizens of the United States are guaranteed the right to freedom of speech, which also includes the freedom of expression: "Congress shall make no law respecting an establishment of religion, or prohibiting the free exercise thereof; or abridging the freedom of speech, or of the press . . . ." Although rooted in the Constitution, these rights are considered inconvenient by some who would censor the voices of others in order to promote a private agenda.

Greg Barnhisel of Duquesne University observes that book banning is nothing new. Since the advent of the printing press, "society has bemoaned how information or entertainment corrupts the youth and coarsens the intellectual atmosphere." He says that in the early 1800s, "parents fretted about the craze for rebellious Romantic writers like Byron and Goethe that resulted in a rash of faddish suicides of young men imitating the melancholy heroes of literature" (465).

Two centuries later, parents are still the loudest advocates for book censorship. Taking the authority of schools into their own hands, they arrogantly assert that what they think is best for *their* children to read is what is best for *all* children. According to the American Library Association's (ALA) Web site, 10,220 challenges to books were reported between 1990 and 2008. They estimate, however, that for every challenge that is reported, four or five are not. Seventy percent of those challenges were to literature in schools or school libraries, and parents were the initiators fifty-seven percent of the time. The reasons for the challenges ranged from homosexuality to a religious viewpoint.

Gateways to a Better Education, a national organization devoted to promoting Christian values in public schools, envisions them as "learning

---

*Side annotations:*

1" margin on each side and bottom

Heading appears on first page

Double-space between title and first line and throughout

Introduces general topic and position

Ellipsis indicates words omitted from quotation

Use of authority

Narrows topic to book banning

Gives sense of history

Identifies opposition and cites statistics

communities enriched by the appropriate and lawful expression of Christian values and ideas." Their Web site continues, "We are making the case that implementing our vision is culturally appropriate, academically legitimate, legally permitted, and morally imperative. ("Our Mission")" But their case is "imperative" only if you share their vision of using the classroom to advocate Christian beliefs. If unchecked, such efforts can blur the separation of church and state, imposing religious ideals on students and parents who may not share those beliefs.

In an article on the group's Web site, Gateways spokesperson Eric Buehrer asserts that parents and teachers have the moral obligation to censor the material presented to students: "There are many educators who believe that when parents question something being taught in the classroom, it's meddling. When parents ask to have something removed . . . it's censorship! But, is it? To hear certain groups tell it, you'd conclude that Hitler is alive and well and lurking in the wings of Hooterville High School." While Beuhrer does not advocate the banning of a specific book in his article, he supports and encourages parents who wish to challenge books on a local level.

Denying students access to literature that does not support one individual's religious or moral beliefs is detrimental to the learning process. By questioning the authority of schools, parents are questioning the art of learning itself. Books should be selected based on established academic principles and not on the fulfillment of religious or moral agendas. Censors have criticized many classic, exemplary literary works. John Mark Ockerbloom of "*The Online Books Page*" reports that Mark Twain's *Adventures of Huckleberry Finn,* an infamously banned book, is controversial because it contains the "n" word. In 1998, parents in Arizona filed a lawsuit attempting to remove the book from a high school reading list, and the suit went all the way to the federal appeals court. The court's decision returned the book to the reading list.

Sometimes, in their zeal to protect young readers from offense, even well-intended people miss the point. Literature is created in a context, reflecting the fears and prejudices of the time. Twain did not intend to ridicule African Americans. To the contrary, his work reflected the dialect and prejudice of the book's period. Reading the book, we join Huck Finn on a moral journey that leads him to question and finally reject the accepted—and hypocritical—social institutions of his time. Today we consider the "n" word brutal and insulting, but without it, the book would be less effective in helping us understand our sad history of racism and tolerance for slavery. Excising the word to avoid offense is an odd sort of denial, a way to pretend that people of the time spoke respectfully to those whom they

*Annotations (right margin):*

Last name and page number at right-hand corner of each page

Cites specific opposition group and its position

Claim

Quotes opposition

Reasons support author's claim

Specific evidence

Acknowledges possible objections

Specific evidence

O'Neill 3

Responds to objections

brutalized. When we remove the word, we are reaching back in time and altering the record of what people said.

Acknowledges specific objections

The human body is often the target of challenges and bans. Robert Lipsyte's novel *One Fat Summer,* about an overweight boy who gains self-confidence, was removed from a seventh-grade class in New York because one parent complained about its mention of adolescent sexuality. The teachers in the district, however, praised the book for addressing the difficulties of growing up, and claimed that students enjoyed reading it (Vinciguerra). In fighting to have the book removed, the critic confronted reality and ignored it, asserting in effect that adolescents are unaware of sex—a preposterous notion. Where students benefited from the book's lessons, others peeked beneath the covers and saw something dangerous.

Responds to objections

Similarly, *It's Perfectly Normal,* by Robie H. Harris, has made the ALA's top ten list of most frequently challenged books three times since 2003, topping the list once. The association's Web site gives "homosexuality, nudity, sex education, religious viewpoint, abortion, and being unsuited to age group" as the reasons. The message sent by parents who criticize this book is that what their kids are going through during puberty is *not* normal, but is shameful and embarrassing.

Specific evidence

*My Sisters Keeper,* by Jodi Picoult, in which a young girl sues her parents over the right to control her own body when they want her to donate an organ to her dying sister, was banned in 2008 in a Michigan school district ("Book Is Banned"). Perhaps parents were threatened by the novel's strong-willed protagonist. Clearly the message being sent is that anything that has to do with our bodies is off limits and inappropriate.

Also under attack are books that have encouraged kids to read—J. K. Rowling's *Harry Potter* series. Number two on the ALA's list of the most frequently challenged books of 2003, the series has also climbed the ladder of success. The fifth in the series, *Harry Potter and the Order of the Phoenix,* had the largest first printing of any work of fiction—8.5 million copies (Rutten). The ALA states that the series has been challenged because of "Satanism."

Specific evidence

Acknowledges opposition with direct quotation

An article on the Christian Web site "*Surf-in-the-Spirit*" cites the Bible and claims that the Harry Potter series persuades children to enjoy the "ungodly practice" of magic. The author asserts that the books promote Satan's goals, which are to "destroy [our children's] lives and condemn their souls. He will surely succeed if parents fall into the trap of believing that these books 'are only a story' and are just innocent evil. . . . This is the worst kind of evil, because it has deceived so many . . . into accepting it" (Smith). People have the right to believe that wizardry is

O'Neill 4

Satan's work, but banning the popular series is yet another way of imposing personal beliefs on those who may have a different opinion about magic.

Parenthetical reference

Conservatives are not alone in promoting censorship; liberals share the affliction. The art of deciding what is politically correct has become its own industry. The English language has been hacked and torn apart in the effort to promote equality, but the result is a disconnection from reality. It seems like nothing is acceptable enough for literature, since both political spectrums endure a conflicting battle.

Response to opposition

Acknowledges other sources of censorship liberals

In her essay "Cut on the Bias," education scholar Diane Ravitch says that the educational publishing industry adheres to specific guidelines that prevent the exposure of controversial words or topics, notably those involving gender, race, religion, or sex. Ravitch compiled a list of over five hundred words that have been banned by publishers, including "landlord," "senior citizen," "yacht," and "actress" (428). "Founding Fathers" is avoided because it is supposedly sexist, and a story about animals living in a rotted tree trunk was criticized because it could be offensive to people who live in low-income apartments (Barnhisel 422). It cannot be denied that the country's Founding Fathers were men; the sad fact is that during the establishment of the United States, women were not *considered* capable of running a revolution. Ravitch correctly asserts that the enforcement of politically correct—but historically inaccurate—language promotes denial and ignorance: "Bowdlerization is not only dishonest, it leads to the dumbing down of language

Use of authority

Fig.1. "This is acceptable!" cartoon. From Mike Cramer, 26 July 1993. *Illinois Issues. edu.* Illinois Issues. 26 July 1993. Web. 6 Feb. 2005.

Supports claim with editorial cartoon

Specific evidence

and ideas. And . . . I'm convinced: The widespread censorship of language and ideas in education caused by the demands of advocacy groups will not end unless it is regularly exposed to public review and ridicule" (429).

Quotes authority

Claim with evidence

But for some, censoring books is not enough; they want to destroy them. In 2004, officials at a high school in New York ripped certain pages, deemed inappropriate because of sexuality, from tenth-grade students' copies of Susan Kaysen's *Girl, Interrupted* (Staino). The destruction of books is insulting to anyone who has any respect for literature. In Wisconsin in 2009, a fight between a town library and a group of locals ensued over eighty-two "sexually explicit" books in the young-adult section. When the library refused to move the books in question to the adult section, four disgruntled men filed a suit, asked for financial damages, and called for a novel about a homosexual teenager to be publicly burned because it was "explicitly vulgar, racial and anti-Christian" and it "damaged" their "mental and emotional well-being" (Hanna).

Specific evidence

Students at a high school in Florida came close to being denied access to literature that would not only teach them about life in Afghanistan and the impact of war, but also about redemption and forgiveness (Denis). *The Kite Runner*, a highly acclaimed novel by Khaled Hosseini, made the ALA's top ten list of most frequently challenged books of 2008. Their Web site explains that the blame was placed on having "offensive language" and being "sexually explicit" and "unsuited to age group." That year, a parent from the Florida school questioned the novel's appropriateness, but the school board voted to keep the book in the curriculum ("Board Rejects" 2). A sophomore from the school said of the book, "This is . . . the real word. This is what goes on in other countries and it really opens your eyes . . ." (Denis).

Long quotation (more than four lines); left margin indented 1 inch (10 spaces double-space)

Appallingly, students' writing is subject to censorship as well. Jill Rosen explains in her article "High School Confidential" that:

> Yanked newspaper stories, disappointed student journalists and resolute administrators are an unfortunately common part of the high-school experi-ence. Censorship occurs so consistently, so ubiquitously that it's almost clichéd, no more eyebrow-raising than the cafeteria serving mystery meat or a nerd getting books smacked out of his arms in the hallway. (498)

Rosen claims that school administrators can do this because of the Supreme Court's 1988 decision in *Hazelwood School District vs. Kuhlmeier*. Before that case,

O'Neill 6

"papers operated under the premise that a student's right to free speech should only be limited in cases where it could disrupt school or invade the rights of others" (498).

Cites authority to support claim

Barnhisel states that censorship is an especially complicated issue in a country as diverse as the United States: "For every George W. Bush fighting for 'family values'. . . there is a Madonna . . . seeking to expand the bounds of what's permissible." He says that standards are "handled by thousands of different people and groups with thousands of different agendas and values and hundreds of ways of enforcing their desires" (471).

Cites authority to support claim

If we ban everything that might offend anyone, what is left to write? Books that discuss diversity, our bodies, and the struggles of minorities expose children to life's truths. Senseless and gratuitous violence is woven into television shows, video games, and movies to enhance their popularity, but literature chosen by educators with the intention of making students think is at the center of a crossfire.

Cites evidence to support claim

Censorship denies reality and creates false worlds in which certain words or actions do not exist. U.S Supreme Court Justice Louis D. Brandeis put it perfectly that "Fear of serious injury alone cannot justify oppression of free speech. . . . Men feared witches and burnt women. It is the function of speech to free men from the bondage of irrational fears" ("Schools and Censorship").

Should parents be concerned about what their children are reading? Of course. The issue is not about parental supervision; it is about efforts to censor reading material to advance a narrow and not necessarily shared agenda. If unchecked, we could find ourselves in a time when it's acceptable for books, like "witches," to be burned.

O'Neill 7

## Works Cited

*ALA.org.* American Library Association, 2009. Web. 5 Oct. 2009.

Barnhisel, Greg, ed. *Media and Messages: Strategies and Readings in Public Rhetoric.* New York: Longman, 2005. Print.

"Board Rejects Book Ban." *Brechner Report* 33.4 (2009): 2. Web. 14 Oct. 2009.

"Book Is Banned by Clawson School District." *WXYZ.com.* Scripps TV Station Group, 18 Dec. 2008. Web. 10 Oct. 2009.

Buchanan, Brian J., ed. "About the First Amendment." *Firstamendment center.org.* First Amendment Center, n.d. Web. 12 Oct. 2009.

Buehrer, Eric. "Challenging a Book in Your School." *Gtbe.org.* Gateways to a Better Education, 1998. Web. 5 Oct. 2009.

Denis, Alex. "Parent's Complaint May Get Novel Banned in Schools." *WJHG.com.* Gray Television, 17 Nov. 2008. Web. 8 Oct. 2009.

Hanna, Jason. "Library Fight Riles Up City, Leads to Book-Burning Demand." *CNN.com.* Cable News Network, 22 July 2009. Web. 8 Oct. 2009.

Ockerbloom, John Mark, ed. "Banned Books Online." *The Online Books Page.* U Pennsylvania, 2009. Web. 10 Oct. 2009.

"Our Mission." *Gtbe.org.* Gateways to a Better Education, 2006. Web. 6 Oct. 2009.

Ravitch, Diane. "Cut on the Bias." Barnhisel. 428-429.

Rosen, Jill. "High School Confidential." Barnhisel. 496-503.

Rutten, Tim. "It's All Hillary and Harry." *Los Angeles Times.* Los Angeles Times, 18 June 2003. Web. 6 Oct. 2009.

"Schools and Censorship: Banned Books." *Pfaw.org.* People for the American Way, n.d. Web. 11 Oct. 2009.

Smith, Kathy A. "Harry Potter: Seduction into the Dark World of the Occult, Part One." *Surf-in-the-Spirit.* Fill the Void Ministries, 2000. Web. 6 Oct. 2009.

Staino, Rocco. "NY High School Interrupts 'Girl, Interrupted.'" *School Library Journal.* Reed Business Information, 12 Dec. 2008. Web. 8 Oct. 2009.

Twain, Mark. *Adventures of Huckleberry Finn.* Ed. Susan K. Harris. Boston: Houghton Mifflin, 2000. Print.

Vinciguerra, Thomas. "A 1977 Novel Comes under Scrutiny." *New York Times* 8 June 1997, LI ed., sec. 1:3:8. Print.

List is alphabetical by author's last name. Use title if no author. Double-space throughout

Title of books, journals, and newspapers are underlined

Websites are constantly updated. Include date of access.

Website with individual author

1/2"

Running head: TAPPED OUT                                                    1

Abbreviated title and number appear on each page, including the title page.

Tapped Out: Bottled Water's Detrimental Side
Dan Hoskins
Roger Williams University
Professor Goodfellow
ENG 102
November 20, 2009

If your instructor requires an abstract of your paper, locate it onthe second page of your paper.

Tapped Out: Bottled Water's Detrimental Side

Less than a generation ago, getting a drink of water was as simple as turning on the kitchen faucet. Over the last two decades, however, bottled water has emerged as a healthier and environmentally friendly alternative. Whether this perception is accurate is a matter currently being scrutinized. But it can be argued that bottled water is not, in fact, more pure than tap water. Furthermore, the disposal of the bottles poses a threat to the environment. Therefore steps should be taken to discourage the use of bottled water.

The rise in the use of bottled water can be attributed to a national health movement that began in the late 1970s. The bottled water conglomerate Nestle Waters claims on its Web site that bottled water products emerged in the late 1970s as "the refreshing alternative to sugary drinks" (Nestle-Waters NA, 2009).

Federal and state legislation passed in the late 1970s and 1980s to ensure the purity of public water sources reflected a growing sense that tap water was polluted and unsafe. In *H20: The Guide to Quality Bottled Water,* Arthur von Wiesenberger (1988) cites acts such as the Resource Conservation and Recovery Act of 1976 and California's Safe Drinking Water and Toxic Enforcement Act of 1986 as significant initiatives aimed at cleaning up public water supplies. While these acts did contribute to the protection of public water, Wiesenberger claims that they also created the impression that tap water was inherently unsafe, thus paving the way for bottled water as a healthy alternative.

Since the passage of such legislation, bottled water consumption has risen. According to *The Washington Post,* bottled water has replaced juice as America's third most popular drink of choice behind soda and milk (Mui, 2009). Now a staple of the American household, bottled water has over the last 20 years become a multibillion dollar industry, as shown in Figure 1 (Fiberwater, 2009).

This industry has grown primarily on the idea that bottled water is safer and healthier than tap water. The difference in price between bottled water and tap water implies a gap in quality: if it cost more, it must be better, right? Generally, bottled water sells for about one to four dollars per gallon. By comparison, tap water costs 0.003 dollars per gallon (San Francisco Public Utility Commission, 2004). Also suggestive of superiority are marketing images of refreshing streams or picturesque mountain ranges, promoting images of natural wholesomeness and environmental friendliness. In spite of such images, bottled water companies stretch the truth.

Double-space between title and first line and throughout paper.

States proposal

1" margins

Quotes authority

Author is not cited in text, so name and date appear in parentheses

Cites supporting evidence with price comparision

TAPPED OUT                                                                                          3

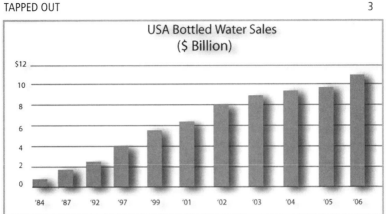

Includes
graph of
statistical data
as supporting
evidence

*Figure 1.*  Bottled water: The brightest star in the beverage universe. Adapted from
Fiberwater.com (2009, October 25).

Governmental agencies regulate both tap and bottled water. The
Environmental Protection Agency (EPA) (as well as state and local governments)
controls tap water consumption, while the Food and Drug Administration (FDA)
handles the safety of bottled water. But it is clear that the EPA, which controls tap
water, is a stronger regulatory body than the FDA, which, unfortunately, is limited to
inspecting only products that are sold over state borders. Since bottled water
conglomerates have distilleries in different states, many a bottled water can slip
through the cracks of inspection. Tap water, on the other hand, has no such luxury
and thus is held to higher standards than bottled water (San Francisco Public Utility
Commission, 2004).

Use of authority
as support

Obviously, a difference in inspectors does not necessarily mean that bottled
water is contaminated. However, the Web site *Food and Water Watch* (2009) cites a
Natural Resources Defense Council investigation of bottled waters that found many
to contain bacteria not allowed under the safety guidelines of most United States
legislatures. The article, "Bottled Water: Illusions of Purity," states that the
investigation tested "more than 1,000 bottles of water of 103 brands" to find that
"nearly one in five brands contained, in at least one sample, more bacteria than
allowed under microbiological-purity guidelines adopted by some states, the
industry, and the European Union" (Food and Water Watch, 2009).

Use of authority
as support

In case contaminants in the water are not bad enough, there's the second
part of the *bottled* water equation: the bottle. Bottle plastics often contain harmful

chemicals, such as phthalates, that can contaminate the contents. According to "Bottled Water: Illusions of Purity," when heated, "Phthalates can cause reproductive difficulties, liver problems and increased risk of cancer" (Food and Water Watch, 2009).

Use of authority as support

Another false charge is that tap water contains dangerous levels of lead. Most often cited as the source is the piping through which the water travels. However, frequent EPA field testing shows that the lead content in tap water is not potentially harmful. Bottled water, on the other hand, it has been shown, can carry harmful compounds such as phthalate in both its water and the bottle carrying it.

Presents other position

Refutes other position

Even more damaging than bottled water's effects on the human body are the cumulative effects on the environment by the production and disposal of billions of water bottles. In "Message in a Bottle: What a Waste," M. F. Epstein notes the large number of discarded water bottles littering Boston's Charles River. He writes that while picking up trash along the river, "the 112 bottles that I picked up are a minute portion of the 3 billion plastic bottles of water that Americans buy and discard annually" (Epstein, 2009).

Cites supporting evidence with statistics

If this one section of Boston can have such an epidemic of bottle littering, one can only imagine the impact on a global scale. While bottled water does use recyclable plastic, the San Francisco Public Utility Commission points out that "not all of the containers are recycled and a portion inevitably end up in the land fill" (2004).

The improper disposal of bottles is one detrimental effect on the environment. Another is the bottle's actual production. While the plastic used is of high quality and can be recycled, an article on the Web site lighterfootsteps.com, "Five Reasons Not to Drink Bottled Water," claims that the 1.5 million tons of plastic used for bottled water each year "requires up to 47 million gallons of oil per year to produce" (Baskind, 2008). Many brands, such as Fiji, claim their water comes from an exotic location where the water is natural and untouched by human hands. While this claim may be a promotional gimmick, the actual transport of bottled water over thousands of miles from those exotic locations, if a reality, is detrimental in itself. A great deal of carbon dioxide and other greenhouse gasses are released in the process.

Reasons supporting proposal

A number of solutions exist for stopping the rising tide of bottled water and its impact on our health and the environment. The simplest and most obvious, of course, is to stop buying bottled water. On an individual level, we each can make a difference by refraining from purchasing the product and by helping to recycle and pick up discarded bottles when we see them.

TAPPED OUT                                                                                   5

Reusable aluminum containers, which allow for portable water without the threat of waste, can be purchased at most retailers. If consumers still feel threatened by the rumors surrounding tap water, these aluminum containers can be refilled with water from a household filter. Currently, there are many different types of filters on the market, some of which can be attached to a sink faucet. Aluminum containers and household filters create the same benefits of bottled water—portability and pureness—without the littering.

Of course, this personal boycott may only have minor results. But there are larger solutions that can stop bottled water use on a national level. Many Web sites and environmental advocates suggest federal legislation aimed at limiting the sale of bottled water. Short of a national ban, which is highly improbable, the only governmental option to discourage consumption is to legislate a sales tax on bottles.

But how do we address the other problems posed by bottled water—the litter of plastic bottles and carbon emissions? To accomplish these, something larger than expanded FDA regulations would be needed. In conjunction with a sales tax on bottled water there should be a national campaign against bottled water similar to campaigns against tobacco use.

Since a number of Web sites, books, and newspaper articles are already discrediting America's dependency on bottled water, this process may have already begun informally. Furthermore, there is at least one film, *Tapped,* that speaks out against the use of bottled water. Some Web sites have propagated a "No Bottled Water Pledge" with signers pledging themselves to end the use of bottled water.

Is there hope for significant change? Is a campaign against bottled water enough to make Americans forgo the convenience and overcome the notion that tap water is unhealthy? Recent reports suggest there is. While an article in *The Washington Post* suggests decreased sales of bottled water is a result of the current economic recession, other articles note this trend is caused by a backlash against bottled water itself. Robinson-Jacobs (2008) suggests that one of the reasons bottled water sales are suffering is because "Environmentalists are making inroads in their efforts to get consumers back to the tap."

Bottled water sales originally grew out of fears about tap water and an inclination to become healthier. If these motivations to become healthier drove Americans away from the tap, they can certainly drive them back there. Most Americans who drink bottled water are unaware of the negative consequences. But as this message is distributed, bottled water sales are more than likely going to

*Proposes solution to problem*

*Acknowledges weakness of proposal*

*Implementation of proposal*

*Cites other solutions to problem*

*Cites authorities*

*Cites solution to problem*

TAPPED OUT                                                                                           6

decrease. As such, it is important to do our part by spreading the word that bottled

water is not good for our health or our environment.

**Cites solution to problem**
        One Web site, fakeplasticfish.com, goes so far to suggest that readers write

to President Obama asking him to set an example as our nation's leader and stop

his consumption of bottled water. The Web site has even dug up some rather

unglamorous shots of him drinking bottled water at a press conference (Terry, 2009).

An Obama-supported boycott on bottled water could be quite effective in

diminishing bottled water sales.

**Conclusion**
        However, whether you are the president of the United States or just a lowly

undergraduate student like myself, you too can aid in the fight against bottled

water. Remember that tap water, while dirt cheap, is not necessarily dirty. Keeping

these ideas in mind, small steps can be taken to help protect our health.

---

TAPPED OUT                                                                                           7

References

**Begin first line of each citation at left margin.**
Baskind, C. (2008, May 11). Five reasons not to drink bottled water.

        Lighter Footsteps. Retrieved from http://lighterfootstep.com/2008

        /05/five-reasons-not-to-drink-bottled-water/

**Indent all subsequent lines five spaces from left margin.**
Robinson-Jacobs, K. (2008, October 31). Bottled water sales growth slow

        to trickle. *Dallas Morning News*. Retrieved from http://www

        .dallasnews.com/

Epstein, M. F. (2009, October 7). Message in a bottle: What a waste. *The*

        *Boston Globe*. Retrieved from http://www.boston.com

Fiberwater. (2009, October 25). Bottled water: The brightest star in the

        beverage universe. Retrieved from http://www.fiberwater.com

        /industry_bwi.php

**Capitalize the first letter of titles and subtitles.**
Food and Water Watch. (2009, October 24). Bottled water: Illusions of

        purity. Retrieved from http://www.foodandwaterwatch.org/water

        /bottled/bottled-water-illusions-of-purity

TAPPED OUT                                                                8

Mui, Y. Q. (2009, August 13). Bottled water boom appears tapped out.
       *Washington Post*. Retrieved from http://www.washingtonpost
       .com

Nestle-Waters NA. (2009, October 25). *History of bottled water*. Retrieved
       from http://www.nestle-watersna.com/popup.aspx?w=600&h=
       400&f=/NR/rdonlyres/E40D0A10-2D3F-415A-A8E4-7503B9DBBF27
       /693/timeline.swf

San Francisco Public Utility Commission. (2004, April). Bottled water vs.
       tap water: Making a healthy choice. Retrieved from http://www
       .dph.sf.ca.us/phes/water/FactSheets/bottled_water.pdf

Terry, B. (2009, July 9). Bottled water problem: It's not just the bottle. Fake
       Plastic Fish. Retrieved from http://fakeplasticfish.com/2009/07
       /bottled-water-problem-its-not-just/

Wiesenberger, A. von. (1988). *H20: The guide to quality bottled water*.
       Santa Barbara, CA: Woodbridge Press.

# PART TWO

# The Readings

# Advertising and Consumerism

The clock radio wakes us, blaring advertisements for vitamins, banks, and automobiles. Our coffee cups announce the brand we drink, and the logos on our clothing reveal the psychology of our fashion choices. As we wait for the bus or drive our cars, billboards display lounging vacationers in exotic locations. As we read a magazine, clothing ads tell us what we should wear, cigarette ads depict a life of clean refreshment, and alcohol ads warn us to drink their product responsibly. We open the newspaper and shuffle through pages of department store advertisements. And as we sit down at our desks to work, the Internet browser flashes a banner for a camcorder, and it's not even 9:00 a.m.!

Every single day of our lives, we are bombarded with advertising images and messages. Advertising is so pervasive, few of us really notice it or consider its enormous influence on our lives. This chapter examines the many different ways advertising weaves its web of influence—how it hooks consumers, how it creates feelings of need, and how it manipulates us through words and symbols convincing us to buy.

While most of us know advertising is everywhere, we may not be aware of how marketers target us. Hours of market research on the demographic structure, geographic area, age, gender, and cultural background of a consumer group are devoted to each and every product before it hits the shelf. Marketers really get to know us, and what they know may surprise us. The language marketers use to appeal to consumers focuses on images and fantasies. Advertisers often twist words that carry no true meanings yet still convince us that their product is better or more desirable. And they use images to manipulate our most basic instincts to get us to believe that we need their product.

Advertising is effective because it taps into our psychology. With so many products and services offering similar products, advertisers have a limited amount of time to convince us that their product is not only better, but also that we truly need it to be happy. Consumer psychology addresses why we want what we want. The essays in this chapter encourage us to take a closer look at our consumer habits and the cultural and social forces that drive our desire to acquire more things.

## Targeting a New World
*Joseph Turow*

Advertisers do not pitch their marketing campaigns to a universal audience. Rather, they target specific audiences to market specific products. This "divide and conquer" approach is called target marketing. In the following article, communications professor Joseph Turow explores how the techniques of target marketing exploit and even encourage rips in the American social fabric.*

### BEFORE YOU READ

The following piece discusses how marketers use target marketing, based on demographic profiling, to sell specific products to particular groups of people. How would you describe the consumer target group to which you belong? What values define your group, and why?

### AS YOU READ

How can exploiting Americans' social and cultural divisions help advertisers market their products? Is there anything unethical about this approach?

1   "Advertisers will have their choice of horizontal demographic groups and vertical psychographic program types."

2   "Our judgment as to the enhanced quality of our subscriber base has been confirmed by the advertisers."

3   "Unfortunately, most media plans are based on exposure opportunities. This is particularly true for television because G.R.P. analysis is usually based on television ratings and ratings do not measure actual exposure."

4   Most Americans would likely have a hard time conceiving the meaning of these quotations. The words would clearly be understood as English, but the jargon would seem quite mysterious. They might be surprised to learn that they have heard a specialized language that advertisers use about them. Rooted in various kinds of research, the language has a straightforward purpose. The aim is to package individuals, or groups of people, in ways that make them useful targets for the advertisers of certain products through certain types of media.

5   Clearly, the way the advertising industry talks about us is not the way we talk about ourselves. Yet when we look at the advertisements that emerge from the cauldron of marketing strategies and strange terminology, we see pictures of our surroundings that we can understand, even recognize. The pictures remind us that the advertising industry does far more than sell goods and services through the mass media. With budgets that add up to hundreds of billions of dollars, the industry exceeds the church and the school in its ability

---

*Joseph Turow, *Breaking Up America: Advertisers and the New Media World* (excerpt), 1998.

to promote images about our place in society—where we belong, why, and how we should act toward others.

6    A revolutionary shift is taking place in the way advertisers talk about America and the way they create ads and shape media to reflect that talk. The shift has been influenced by, and has been influencing, major changes in the audiovisual options available to the home. But it most importantly has been driven by, and has been driving, a profound sense of division in American society.

7    The era we are entering is one in which advertisers will work with media firms to create the electronic equivalents of gated communities. Marketers are aware that the U.S. population sees itself marked by enormous economic and cultural tensions. Marketers don't feel, though, that it benefits them to encourage Americans to deal with these tensions head-on through a media brew of discussion, entertainment, and argumentation aimed at broadly diverse audiences. Rather, new approaches to marketing make it increasingly worthwhile for even the largest media companies to separate audiences into different worlds according to distinctions that ad people feel make the audiences feel secure and comfortable. The impact of these activities on Americans' views of themselves and others will be profound, enduring, and often disturbing.

8    The changes have begun only recently. The hallmark is the way marketers and media practitioners have been approaching the development of new audiovisual technology. Before the late 1970s, most people in the United States could view without charge three commercial broadcast stations, a public (non-commercial) TV station, and possibly an independent commercial station (one not affiliated with a network). By the mid-1990s, several independent broadcast TV stations, scores of cable and satellite television channels, videocassettes, video games, home computer programs, online computer services, and the beginnings of two-way ("interactive") television had become available to major segments of the population with an interest and a budget to match.

9    People in the advertising industry are working to integrate the new media channels into the broader world of print and electronic media to maximize the entire system's potential for selling. They see these developments as signifying not just the breakup of the traditional broadcast network domain, but as indicating a breakdown in social cohesion, as well. Advertisers' most public talk about America—in trade magazine interviews, trade magazine ads, convention speeches, and interviews for this book—consistently features a nation that is breaking up. Their vision is of a fractured population of self-indulgent, frenetic, and suspicious individuals who increasingly reach out only to people like themselves.

10    Advertising practitioners do not view these distinctions along primarily racial or ethnic lines, though race and ethnicity certainly play a part, provoking turf battles among marketers. Rather, the new portraits of society that advertisers and media personnel invoke involve the blending of income, generation, marital status, and gender into a soup of geographical and psychological profiles they call "lifestyles."

11    At the business level, what is driving all this is a major shift in the balance between targeting and mass marketing in U.S. media. Mass marketing involves aiming a home-based medium or outdoor event at people irrespective of their background or patterns of activities (their lifestyles). Targeting, by contrast, involves the intentional pursuit of specific segments of society—groups and even individuals. The Underground [radio]

Network, the Comedy Central cable channel, and *Details* magazine are far more targeted than the ABC Television Network, the Sony Jumbotron Screen on Times Square, and the Super Bowl. Yet even these examples of targeting are far from close to the pinpointing of audiences that many ad people expect is possible.

12   The ultimate aim of this new wave of marketing is to reach different groups with specific messages about how certain products tie into their lifestyles. Target-minded media firms are helping advertisers do that by building *primary media communities*. These are formed when viewers or readers feel that a magazine, TV channel, newspaper, radio station, or other medium reaches people like them, resonates with their personal beliefs, and helps them chart their position in the larger world. For advertisers, tying into those communities means gaining consumer loyalties that are nearly impossible to establish in today's mass market.

13   Nickelodeon and MTV were pioneer attempts to establish this sort of ad-sponsored communion on cable television. While they started as cable channels, they have become something more. Owned by media giant Viacom, they are lifestyle parades that invite their target audiences (relatively upscale children and young adults, respectively) into a sense of belonging that goes far beyond the coaxial wire into books, magazines, videotapes, and outdoor events that Viacom controls or licenses.

14   The idea of these sorts of "programming services" is to cultivate a must-see, must-read, must-share mentality that makes the audience feel part of a family, attached to the program hosts, other viewers, and sponsors. It is a strategy that extends across a wide spectrum of marketing vehicles, from cable TV to catalogs, from direct mailings to online computer services, from outdoor events to in-store clubs. In all these areas, national advertisers make it clear that they prefer to conduct their targeting with the huge media firms they had gotten to know in earlier years. But the giants don't always let their offspring operate on huge production budgets. To keep costs low enough to satisfy advertisers' demands for efficient targeting, much of ad-supported cable television is based on recycled materials created or distributed by media conglomerates. What makes MTV, ESPN, Nickelodeon, A&E, and other such "program services" distinctive is not the uniqueness of the programs but the special character created by their *formats*: the flow of their programs, packaged to attract the right audience at a price that will draw advertisers.

15   But media firms have come to believe that simply attracting groups to specialized formats is often not enough. Urging people who do not fit the desired lifestyle profile *not* to be part of the audience is sometimes also an aim, since it makes the community more pure and thereby more efficient for advertisers. So in a highly competitive media environment, cable companies aiming to lure desirable types to specialized formats felt the need to create "signature" materials that both drew the "right" people and signaled the "wrong" people that they ought to go away. It is no accident that the producers of certain signature programs acknowledge that they chase away irrelevant viewers as much as they attract desirable ones.

16   An even more effective form of targeting, ad people believe, is a type that goes beyond chasing undesirables away. It simply excludes them in the first place. Using computer models based on zip codes and a variety of databases, it is economically feasible to tailor materials for small groups, even individuals. That is already taking place in the direct mail, telemarketing, and magazine industries. With certain forms of interactive television, it is

technologically quite possible to send some TV programs and commercials only to neighborhoods, census blocks, and households that advertisers want to reach. Media firms are working toward a time when people will be able to choose the news, information, and entertainment they want when they want it. Advertisers who back these developments will be able to offer different product messages—and variable discounts—to individuals based on what they know about them.

17    Clearly, not all these technologies are widespread. Clearly, too, there is a lot of hype around them. Many companies that stand to benefit from the spread of target marketing have doubtless exaggerated the short time it will take to get there and the low costs that will confront advertisers once they do. Moreover, as will be seen, some marketers have been slower than others to buy into the usefulness of a media system that encourages the partitioning of people with different lifestyles.

18    Nevertheless, the trajectory is clear. A desire to label people so that they may be separated into primary media communities is transforming the way television is programmed, the way newspapers are "zoned," the way magazines are printed, and the way cultural events are produced and promoted. Most critically, advertisers' interest in exploiting lifestyle differences is woven into the basic assumptions about media models including the Internet.

19    For me and you—individual readers and viewers—this segmentation and targeting can portend terrific things. If we can afford to pay, or if we're important to sponsors who will pick up the tab, we will be able to receive immediately the news, information, and entertainment we order. In a world pressing us with high-speed concerns, we will surely welcome media and sponsors that offer to surround us with exactly what we want when we want it. As an entirety, though, society in the United States will lose out.

20    One of the consequences of turning the U.S. into a pastiche of market-driven labels is that such a multitude of categories makes it impossible for a person to directly overlap with more than a tiny portion of them. If primary media communities continue to take hold, their large numbers will diminish the chance that individuals who identify with certain social categories will even have an opportunity to learn about others. Off-putting signature programs such as *Jersey Girls* may make the situation worse, causing individuals annoyed by the shows or what they read about them to feel alienated from groups that appear to enjoy them. If you are told over and over again that different kinds of people are not part of your world, you will be less and less likely to want to deal with those people.

21    The creation of customized media materials will likely take this lifestyle segregation further. It will allow, even encourage, individuals to live in their own personally constructed worlds, separated from people and issues they don't care about or don't want to be bothered with. The desire to do that may accelerate when, as is the case in the late-twentieth-century United States, seemingly intractable antagonisms based on age, income, ethnicity, geography, and more result from competition over jobs and political muscle. In these circumstances, market segmentation and targeting may accelerate an erosion of the tolerance and mutual dependence between diverse groups that enable a society to work. Ironically, the one common message across media will be that a common center for sharing ideas and feelings is more and more difficult to find—or even to care about.

**QUESTIONS FOR ANALYSIS AND DISCUSSION**

1. Turow uses three quotations to begin his essay. How do these quotations contribute to the points he makes in his article? Are they an effective way to reach his audience? Explain.
2. How does packaging individuals, or groups of people, make them "useful targets" for advertisers? Give some examples of ways advertisers "package" people or groups of people.
3. According to Turow, what social impact does target marketing have on America? Do you agree with his perspective? Explain.
4. Evaluate Turow's tone in this essay. What phrases or words reveal his tone? Who is his audience? How does this tone connect to his intended audience?
5. What point is the author trying to make in this article? What is his own particular opinion of targeted marketing? Cite examples from the text in your response.
6. Why would producers of certain television programs actually want to "chase away" certain viewers? How can audience exclusion help improve a target market for advertisers? Is this practice damaging to our society? Why or why not?

# Which One of These Sneakers Is Me?
*Douglas Rushkoff*

Brand-name products target groups of consumers—Pepsi and Levi's appeal to large, diverse populations, while Fendi or Gucci appeal to very elite ones. Brands depend on image—the image the brand promotes and the image the consumer believes will be projected by the product. For many teens, brands can announce membership in a particular group, value systems, personality, and personal style. As writer and cultural columnist Douglas Rushkoff explains in the next essay, today's youth are more consumer and media savvy than previous generations, forcing retailers to rethink how they brand and market goods to this group. But while teens like to think that they are hip to advertising gimmicks, marketers are one step ahead of the game—a game that teens are likely to lose as they strive to "brand" themselves.*

**BEFORE YOU READ**

When you were in junior and senior high school, did you have particular brands to which you were most loyal? What cultural and social influences, if any, contributed to your desire for a particular brand?

---

*Douglas Rushkoff, *The London Times*, April 30, 2000.

**AS YOU READ**

What can a brand tell you about the person who uses it? Do brands "define" people? How do brands "identify" people as members of a particular group or lifestyle?

1   I was in one of those sports "superstores" the other day, hoping to find a pair of trainers for myself. As I faced the giant wall of shoes, each model categorized by either sports affiliation, basketball star, economic class, racial heritage or consumer niche, I noticed a young boy standing next to me, maybe 13 years old, in even greater awe of the towering selection of footwear.

2   His jaw was dropped and his eyes were glazed over—a psycho-physical response to the overwhelming sensory data in a self-contained consumer environment. It's a phenomenon known to retail architects as "Gruen Transfer," named for the gentleman who invented the shopping mall, where this mental paralysis is most commonly observed. Having finished several years of research on this exact mind state, I knew to proceed with caution. I slowly made my way to the boy's side and gently asked him, "what is going through your mind right now?"

3   He responded without hesitation, "I don't know which of these trainers is 'me.'" The boy proceeded to explain his dilemma. He thought of Nike as the most utilitarian and scientifically advanced shoe, but had heard something about third world laborers and was afraid that wearing this brand might label him as too anti-Green. He then considered a skateboard shoe, Airwalk, by an "indie" manufacturer (the trainer equivalent of a micro-brewery) but had recently learned that this company was almost as big as Nike. The truly hip brands of skate shoe were too esoteric for his current profile at school—he'd look like he was "trying." This left the "retro" brands, like Puma, Converse and Adidas, none of which he felt any real affinity, since he wasn't even alive in the 70's when they were truly and non-ironically popular.

4   With no clear choice and, more importantly, no other way to conceive of his own identity, the boy stood there, paralyzed in the modern youth equivalent of an existential crisis. Which brand am I, anyway?

5   Believe it or not, there are dozens, perhaps hundreds of youth culture marketers who have already begun clipping out this article. They work for hip, new advertising agencies and cultural research firms who trade in the psychology of our children and the anthropology of their culture. The object of their labors is to create precisely the state of confusion and vulnerability experienced by the young shopper at the shoe wall—and then turn this state to their advantage. It is a science, though not a pretty one.

6   Marketers spend millions developing strategies to identify children's predilections and then capitalize on their vulnerabilities. Young people are fooled for a while, but then develop defense mechanisms, such as media-savvy attitudes or ironic dispositions. Then marketers research these defenses, develop new countermeasures, and on it goes.

7   The battle in which our children are engaged seems to pass beneath our radar screens, in a language we don't understand. But we see the confusion and despair that results. How did we get in this predicament, and is there a way out? Is it your imagination, you wonder, or have things really gotten worse? Alas, things seem to have gotten worse. Ironically, this is because things had gotten so much better.

8    In olden times—back when those of us who read the newspaper grew up—media was a one-way affair. Advertisers enjoyed a captive audience, and could quite authoritatively provoke our angst and stoke our aspirations. Interactivity changed all this. The remote control gave viewers the ability to break the captive spell of television programming whenever they wished, without having to get up and go all the way up to the set. Young people proved particularly adept at "channel surfing," both because they grew up using the new tool, and because they felt little compunction to endure the tension-provoking narratives of storytellers who did not have their best interests at heart. It was as if young people knew that the stuff on television was called "programming" for a reason, and developed shortened attention spans for the purpose of keeping themselves from falling into the spell of advertisers. The remote control allowed young people to deconstruct TV.

9    The next weapon in the child's arsenal was the video game joystick. For the first time, viewers had control over the very pixels on their monitors. The television image was demystified. Then, the computer mouse and keyboard transformed the TV receiver into a portal. Today's young people grew up in a world where a screen could as easily be used for expressing oneself as consuming the media of others. Now the media was up-for-grabs, and the ethic, from hackers to camcorder owners, was "do it yourself."

10   Likewise, as computer interfaces were made more complex and opaque—think Windows—the do-it-yourself ethic of the Internet was undone. The original Internet was a place to share ideas and converse with others. Children actually had to use the keyboard! Now, the Internet encourages them to click numbly through packaged content. Web sites are designed to keep young people from using the keyboard, except to enter in their parents' credit card information.

11   But young people had been changed by their exposure to new media. They constituted a new "psychographic," as advertisers like to call it, so new kinds of messaging had to be developed that appealed to their new sensibility.

12   Anthropologists—the same breed of scientists that used to scope out enemy populations before military conquests—engaged in focus groups, conducted "trend-watching" on the streets, in order to study the emotional needs and subtle behaviors of young people. They came to understand, for example, how children had abandoned narrative structures for fear of the way stories were used to coerce them. Children tended to construct narratives for themselves by collecting things instead, like cards, bottlecaps called "pogs," or keychains and plush toys. They also came to understand how young people despised advertising—especially when it did not acknowledge their media-savvy intelligence.

13   Thus, Pokemon was born—a TV show, video game, and product line where the object is to collect as many trading cards as possible. The innovation here, among many, is the marketer's conflation of TV show and advertisement into one piece of media. The show is an advertisement. The story, such as it is, concerns a boy who must collect little monsters in order to develop his own character. Likewise, the Pokemon video game engages the player in a quest for those monsters. Finally, the card game itself (for the few children who actually play it) involves collecting better monsters—not by playing, but by buying more cards. The more cards you buy, the better you can play.

14   Kids feel the tug, but in a way they can't quite identify as advertising. Their compulsion to create a story for themselves—in a world where stories are dangerous—makes them vulnerable to this sort of attack. In marketers terms, Pokemon is "leveraged" media,

with "cross-promotion" on "complementary platforms." This is ad-speak for an assault on multiple fronts.

15    Moreover, the time a child spends in the Pokemon craze amounts to a remedial lesson in how to consume. Pokemon teaches them how to want things that they can't or won't actually play with. In fact, it teaches them how to buy things they don't even want. While a child might want one particular card, he needs to purchase them in packages whose contents are not revealed. He must buy blind and repeatedly until he gets the object of his desire.

16    Meanwhile, older kids have attempted to opt out of aspiration altogether. The "15–24" demographic, considered by marketers the most difficult to wrangle into submission, have adopted a series of postures they hoped would make them impervious to marketing techniques. They take pride in their ability to recognize when they are being pandered to, and watch TV for the sole purpose of calling out when they are being manipulated.

17    But now advertisers are making commercials just for them. Soft drink advertisements satirize one another before rewarding the cynical viewer: "image is nothing," they say. The technique might best be called "wink" advertising, for its ability to engender a young person's loyalty by pretending to disarm itself. "Get it?" the ad means to ask. If you're cool, you do.

18    New magazine advertisements for jeans, such as those created by Diesel, take this even one step further. The ads juxtapose imagery that actually makes no sense—ice cream billboards in North Korea, for example. The strategy is brilliant. For a media-savvy young person to feel good about himself, he needs to feel he "gets" the joke. But what does he do with an ad where there's obviously something to get that he can't figure out? He has no choice but to admit that the brand is even cooler than he is. An ad's ability to confound its audience is the new credential for a brand's authenticity.

19    Like the boy at the wall of shoes, kids today analyze each purchase they make, painstakingly aware of how much effort has gone into seducing them. As a result, they see their choices of what to watch and what to buy as exerting some influence over the world around them. After all, their buying patterns have become the center of so much attention!

20    But however media-savvy kids get, they will always lose this particular game. For they have accepted the language of brands as their cultural currency, and the stakes in their purchasing decisions as something real. For no matter how much control kids get over the media they watch, they are still utterly powerless when it comes to the manufacturing of brands. Even a consumer revolt merely reinforces one's role as a consumer, not an autonomous or creative being.

21    The more they interact with brands, the more they brand themselves.

## QUESTIONS FOR ANALYSIS AND DISCUSSION

1.  How does Rushkoff support his argument? Evaluate his use of supporting sources. Are there any gaps in his article? If so, identify areas where his essay could be stronger. If not, identify some of the essay's particular strengths.
2.  How would you define your personal style and the image you wish to project? What products and/or brands contribute to that image? Explain.
3.  In paragraph 7, Rushkoff notes that things have gotten worse because they have gotten better. What does he mean by this statement? Explain.

4. Look up the phrase "Gruen transfer" on the Internet. Were you aware of this angle of marketing practice? Does it change the way you think about how products are sold to you? Explain.

5. In order to stay in business, marketers have had to rethink how they sell products to the youth market. How have they changed to keep pace with the youth market? Explain.

6. In his conclusion, Rushkoff predicts that even media-savvy kids will still "lose" the game. Why will they fail? Explain.

## Branded World: The Success of the Nike Logo
*Michael Levine*

In the last essay, a teenager is faced with a daunting challenge—choosing a sneaker brand that was "him." Sneakers are well known for their use of logos to distinguish brands from each other. The young man worries that choosing the wrong brand will make him look like he is "trying" or is a member of the wrong group. Clearly, he believes the expression "the clothes make the man." To him, a logo is a reflection of his identity and of the image he wishes to project.

Logos are graphic designs that represent and help market a particular brand or company. Some logos are instantly recognizable, needing no words to explain what they represent. A good example of a logo with international recognition is the image of the Olympic rings. Other logos may be more obscure and specific to particular countries or demographic groups. Chances are most senior citizens wouldn't recognize the Lugz logo or know what product was associated with it. Sometimes a logo can simply be the initial or name of the brand. Chanel is famous for its interlocking C design, and Kate Spade's name serves as her logo. Spade's logo is distinctive because of the font face used to spell her name, which is written in lowercase letters. The next piece, by public relations guru Michael Levine, examines why the brand Nike is such a successful logo.*

### BEFORE YOU READ

What makes you want to buy a product? Is it peer influence, cultural pressure, or social status? Do generational marketing techniques influence you?

### AS YOU READ

Consider the influence of athlete endorsement for products: from sports equipment and apparel to soft drinks, watches, and automobiles. What image does the athlete project about the product? How much does the brand's logo factor into the product promotion? Do athletes sell products, or do athletes wearing brand logos sell products? Explain.

---

*Michael Levine, A Branded World: *Adventures in Public Relations and the Creation of Superbrands* (excerpt), 2003.

1 There are few branding tales as epic and impressive as that of Nike. Before Phil Knight made the swoosh a universally known symbol, a soft shoe you wore to play sports or run in was called a sneaker. There weren't separate sneakers for basketball, running, walking, cross training, and tennis; there were just sneakers. They were made by companies like Keds and PF Fliers, and they were usually worn by children. Professional athletes wore shoes made for their individual sports, which were either not available to the general public or were not identifiable by brand. A few companies, like Adidas, were making "tennis shoes," which adults wore when they played a sport on the weekends.

2 Now, there are "athletic shoes." They are very specific to their tasks and can be found in stores like Foot Locker and Sports Authority, classified by usage: Cross-trainers are not the same as shoes for walking, which are different from running shoes, which are not to be confused with basketball shoes. And much of that distinction can be attributed to Nike and the awe-inspiring job it has done in defining not only its own brand but the very category of product the brand helped to create.

3 "The way you build a brand is by creating a new category you can be first in," says branding guru Al Ries. "I have yet to hear anybody ever refer to Nike as a sneaker. It's only the older people who used to buy Keds who refer to Nike as a sneaker. There is an enormous difference between an athletic shoe and a sneaker. You can look at the two and say they look alike, they smell alike, they sound alike. I say no: Your typical inner-city kid isn't going to wear Keds and call it a sneaker. They want a Nike; it's a different deal." How did Nike transform the category of sports footwear into the massive $14 billion business it is today? And how did it manage to grab an astounding 45 percent of the market by the year 2000? Was it just such an obviously superior product that the public couldn't help but notice and respond to? Or was the branding of Nike so well considered and crafty that it outshone all the rest of the brands in its category, using every possible branding tactic almost perfectly?

4 Once it was associated with the active, aggressive, powerful brand Nike had assigned itself, the swoosh become an incredibly articulate mark . . .

5 I am inclined to state that the latter was the prevailing condition. Nike took what was, for its category, a revolutionary product (the waffle sole) and transformed what could have been a niche product into something that every kid in the street playing basketball had to have. Beyond that, however, Nike expanded its brand into other market segments, appealing to adults, to women, to nonathletes. And it extended its brand into products other than shoes: apparel, signature hats, shirts, shorts, and many other products that bore the suddenly familiar Nike symbol.

6 "[Nike] figured out a very simple brand visually, and they didn't deviate from it at all. They kept that message very well defined," says Howard Rubenstein, president of Rubenstein Associates, a New York publicity firm. "If you just glance at [Nike's] logo, you know what the message is."

7 The swoosh, Nike's squiggly symbol, has no intrinsic meaning in our lexicon; before the company developed it, it did not exist as a symbol communicating anything. But once it was associated with the active, aggressive, powerful brand Nike had assigned itself, the swoosh become an incredibly articulate mark, communicating the continued thrust forward of anyone who had the wherewithal to don a piece of apparel that bore the symbol.

8    Still, the swoosh wasn't the only way that Nike differentiated itself from other athletic shoe companies, and it certainly wasn't the main tool in developing that brand's identity. More than anything else, the company was probably best known in its early years for its associations with well-known sports celebrities, who never, ever appeared in public without a swoosh on at least one visible article of clothing.

9    Tiger Woods, Derek Jeter, and especially Michael Jordan were routinely seen wearing the Nike logo, and while they never necessarily said a word in a Nike advertisement, it was clear their endorsement was meant to relay a message to consumers: "Be like (fill in the extremely famous sports celebrity). Wear Nike." The copy might have read "Just Do It," but the message was loud and clear.

10   "Nike was successful in making that [swoosh] synonymous with performance," says *Variety* publisher Charlie Koones. "Not just the performance of their shoe, but performance on a larger scale." By allying themselves with great athletes, by building a bit of a jock attitude. It's interesting to ask yourself what is the feeling that comes out of your brand promise."

11   The road for Nike has not been entirely bump free, however. Allegations that the company's products were manufactured overseas in sweatshops have dogged the brand, and there have been declines in the athletic shoe market generally in the past few years. But Nike continues on, and even if its brand is a tiny bit diminished, it is still head and shoulders above the rest of the industry.

12   "At one time, I think Nike truly was a genuine brand," says Duane Knapp, author of *The Brand Mindset*. "In others words, they were perceived by the customer as one of a kind. Maybe in some customers' minds, that's true today. They're not perfect. At this point in time, you'd have to ask their customers what's the difference between Nike and Adidas. It really doesn't matter what the executives think; it matters what the customers think. When Phil Knight invented the waffle sole, they were a genuine brand. Now that they've gotten into different things, my feeling is they've probably moved from right to left on that continuum in the customer's mind. They are not a one-of-a-kind brand anymore. That doesn't mean they're a bad brand. But every brand is moving toward being a commodity unless the company does something continually, every single day, and that is where the public relations comes in."

13   Nike's position in the athletic shoe and apparel industry is without peer, but it is true that the brand is not as strong as it once was, partially due to increased competition and partially because nothing could stay that hot. Allegations that the company used overseas sweatshops to assemble $120 athletic shoes didn't help.

14   Through it all, Nike's public relations professionals emphasized that the company was doing its best to improve conditions in its worldwide facilities, and, as it addressed the problem, it continued to thrive. While the situation is not yet completely resolved, it has not crippled Nike by any stretch of the imagination.

15   Knapp brings up two important points: First, the company has to have a strong sense of its identity from the consumer's point of view. The image company executives have is irrelevant if the consumer sees the product and the brand in a different light. Second, the brand identity and brand integrity must be reinforced in the consumer's mind every day. Not once a week, not whenever there's a sales downturn: every day. If the mission of the company is not to satisfy the customer's expectations and exceed them every time, the brand might never become a true household name, and it certainly won't last for decades like Coca-Cola, Disney, and McDonald's—and even those brands have had major stumbling points.

**QUESTIONS FOR ANALYSIS AND DISCUSSION**

1. Levine notes that Nike's swoosh logo has no "intrinsic meaning" beyond what it has come to represent: Nike products. Examine the clothing you are wearing and the personal items within 10 feet of you right now. How many items bear a logo? What are they? Do they have any "intrinsic meaning"? Explain.
2. What brands do you tend to purchase and why? Are there particular logos that are associated with the brands you prefer? Explain.
3. Are you more likely to purchase a product with a prominent or prestigious logo than a "no-name" brand? Why or why not?
4. What is your college or university's logo? Is it a shield? A phrase? A mascot? How does the symbol chosen by your school reflect its values and identity? Explain.
5. Levine quotes Duane Knapp on the shifting of the Nike brand, "At one time, I think Nike truly was a genuine brand." Why does Knapp feel that Nike is not a "genuine" brand anymore? What changed? Do you agree with his assessment?

# The $100 Christmas
## Bill McKibben

For many of us, the December holidays are a time of gift lists and hurried shopping. Christmas sales begin the day after Thanksgiving and stores stay open until midnight on Christmas Eve, hoping to get the last dollar out of holiday shoppers. Many department stores generate almost one-third of their annual revenue during the holiday season. But is the spirit of giving getting out of hand? Has it been corrupted by advertisers weaving the "powerful dark magic" of greed? In the next essay, author Bill McKibben describes how his church promoted the radical idea that people spend only $100 on gifts per family during the holidays. And he proposes that other churches, mosques, and synagogues consider making the same recommendation.[*]

**BEFORE YOU READ**

How do you approach the holiday season? Do you anticipate it with excitement? stress? depression? Do you plan, decorate, and shop? Are your memories warm, lonely, comforting, happy? Explain.

**AS YOU READ**

How is McKibben's proposal both conservative and radical at the same time?

---

[*]Bill McKibben, *Mother Jones*, 1997.

1    I know what I'll be doing on Christmas Eve. My wife, my 4-year-old daughter, my dad, my brother, and I will snowshoe out into the woods in late afternoon, ready to choose a hemlock or a balsam fir and saw it down—I've had my eye on three or four likely candidates all year. We'll bring it home, shake off the snow, decorate it, and then head for church, where the Sunday school class I help teach will gamely perform this year's pageant. (Last year, along with the usual shepherds and wise people, it featured a lost star talking on a cell phone.) And then it's home to hang stockings, stoke the fire, and off to bed. As traditional as it gets, except that there's no sprawling pile of presents under the tree.

2    Several years ago, a few of us in the northern New York and Vermont conference of the United Methodist Church started a campaign for what we called "Hundred Dollar Holidays." The church leadership voted to urge parishioners not to spend more than $100 per family on presents, to rely instead on simple homemade gifts and on presents of services—a back rub, stacking a cord of firewood. That first year I made walking sticks for everyone. Last year I made spicy chicken sausage. My mother has embraced the idea by making calendars illustrated with snapshots she's taken.

3    The $100 figure was a useful anchor against the constant seductions of the advertisers, a way to explain to children why they weren't getting everything on their list. So far, our daughter, Sophie, does fine at Christmas. Her stocking is exciting to her, the tree is exciting; skating on the pond is exciting. It's worth mentioning, however, that we don't have a television, so she may not understand the degree of her impoverishment. This holiday idea may sound modest. It is modest. And yet at the same time it's pretty radical. Christmas, it turns out, is a bulwark of the nation's economy. Many businesses—bookstores, for instance, where I make my living—do one-third of their volume in the months just before December 25th. And so it hits a nerve to question whether it all makes sense, whether we should celebrate the birth of a man who said we should give all that we have to the poor by showering each other with motorized tie racks.

4    It's radical for another reason, too. If you believe that our consumer addiction represents our deepest problem—the force that keeps us from reaching out to others, from building a fair society, the force that drives so much of our environmental degradation—then Christmas is the nadir. Sure, advertising works its powerful dark magic year-round. But on Christmas morning, with everyone piling downstairs to mounds of presents, consumption is made literally sacred. Here, under a tree with roots going far back into prehistory, here next to a crèche with a figure of the infant child of God, we press stuff on each other, stuff that becomes powerfully connected in our heads to love, to family, and even to salvation. The 12 days of Christmas—and in many homes the eight nights of Hanukkah—are a cram course in consumption, a kind of brainwashing.

5    When we began the $100 campaign, merchants, who wrote letters to the local papers, made it clear to us what a threatening idea it was. Newspaper columnists thought it was pretty extreme, too—one said church people should stick to religion and leave the economy alone. Another said that while our message had merit, it would do too much damage to business.

6    And he was right, or at least not wrong. If we all backed out of Christmas excess this year, we would sink many a gift shop; if we threw less lavish office parties, caterers would suffer—and florists and liquor wholesalers and on down the feeding chain. But we have to start somewhere, if we're ever to climb down from the unsustainable heights we've reached, and Christmas might as well be it.

7    When we first began to spread this idea about celebrating Christmas in a new way, we were earnest and sober. Big-time Christmas was an environmental disgrace—all that wrapping paper, all those batteries. The money could be so much better spent: The price of one silk necktie could feed a village for a day; the cost of a big-screen television could vaccinate more than 60 kids. And struggling to create a proper Christmas drives poor families into debt. Where I live, which is a poor and cold place, January finds many people cutting back on heat to pay off their bills. Those were all good reasons to scale back. But as we continued our campaign, we found we weren't really interested in changing Christmas because we wanted fewer batteries. We wanted more joy. We felt cheated by the Christmases we were having—so rushed, so busy, so full of mercantile fantasy and catalog hype that we couldn't relax and enjoy the season.

8    Our growing need to emphasize joy over guilt says a great deal about the chances for Christian radicalism, for religious radicalism in general. At its truest, religion represents the one force in our society that can postulate some goal other than accumulation. In an I-dolatrous culture, religion can play a subversive role. Churches, mosques, and synagogues almost alone among our official institutions can say, It's not the economy, stupid. It's your life. It's learning that there's some other center to the universe.

9    Having that other center can change the way we see the world around us. It's why devoted clergy and laypeople occasionally work small miracles in inner cities and prisons; it's why alcoholics talk about a Higher Power. If we're too big, then perhaps the solution lies in somehow making ourselves a little smaller.

10    You may be too late for this Christmas. You may already have bought your pile of stuff, or perhaps it's too late to broach the subject with relatives who will gather with you for the holidays, bearing (and therefore expecting) great stacks of loot. Our local Methodist ministers begin in September, preaching a skit sermon about the coming holiday. Many in our church community now participate. So do some of our neighbors and friends around the country. None of us are under any illusions; we know that turning the focus of Christmas back to Christ is a long and patient effort, one that works against every force that consumer culture can muster. But to judge from our own holidays in recent years, it's well worth the effort. I know what we'll be doing Christmas morning: After we open our stockings and exchange our few homemade gifts, we'll go out for a hike. Following the advice of St. Francis of Assisi, who said that even the birds deserve to celebrate this happy day, we'll spread seed hither and yon—and for one morning the chickadees and the jays will have it easy. And then we'll head back inside to the warm and fragrant kitchen and start basting the turkey, shaping the rolls, mashing the potatoes.

## QUESTIONS FOR ANALYSIS AND DISCUSSION

1. Is a $100 holiday possible in your family? realistic? good in principle but impossible in practice? Is it fair? Explain.
2. McKibben defines the current materialistic traditions of Christmas and Hanukkah as the result of advertisers who have exploited the spirit of these holidays and brainwashed consumers. "The 12 days of Christmas—and in many homes the eight nights of Hanukkah—are a cram course in consumption. . . ." Do you agree? Why or why not?

3. McKibben states that his daughter, Sophie, is happy with her modest gifts because she finds the entire holiday experience exciting. He comments, though, that "it's worth mentioning, however, that we don't have a television, so she may not understand the degree of her impoverishment." What connection is McKibben making between television and our desire for things? Does he have a point?

4. How did merchants react to the proposal of a $100 holiday? Why is one columnist's comment that "church people should stick to religion and leave the economy alone" ironic? Explain.

## Spent: America after Consumerism
### Amitai Etzioni

In this next essay, author and sociology professor Amitai Etzioni explores the role of self-regulation in the current economic crisis. Etzioni argues that we are guided by the normative values of our society. Therefore, if we internalize our consumer habits to value thrift over consumption, everyone benefits. American consumerism afflicts every class, and every economic bracket. Etzioni argues that consumerism is unhealthy and even immoral. But can we all really turn our backs on decades of conspicuous consumer habits?*

### BEFORE YOU READ

What do you purchase and why? Do you buy basic necessities—the things you need to live—or do buy things for other reasons, such as to enhance your self-image, enjoy the newest gadget, or fit into your peer group? What social factors influence your buying decisions?

### AS YOU READ

What role do the "normative values of a culture" play in how we approach our buying decisions as a general population?" Explain.

1    Much of the debate over how to address the economic crisis has focused on a single word: regulation. And it's easy to understand why. Bad behavior by a variety of businesses landed us in this mess—so it seems rather obvious that the way to avoid future economic meltdowns is to create, and vigorously enforce, new rules proscribing such behavior. But the truth is quite a bit more complicated. The world economy consists of billions of transactions every day. There can never be enough inspectors, accountants, customs officers, and police to ensure that all or even most of these transactions are properly carried out. Moreover, those charged with enforcing regulations are themselves

*Amitai Etzioni, *The New Republic*, June 17, 2009.

not immune to corruption, and, hence, they too must be supervised and held accountable to others—who also have to be somehow regulated. The upshot is that regulation cannot be the linchpin of attempts to reform our economy. What is needed instead is something far more sweeping: for people to internalize a different sense of how one ought to behave, and act on it because they believe it is right.

2    That may sound far-fetched. It is commonly believed that people conduct themselves in a moral manner mainly because they fear the punishment that will be meted out if they engage in anti-social behavior. But this position does not stand up to close inspection. Most areas of behavior are extralegal; we frequently do what is expected because we care or love. This is evident in the ways we attend to our children (beyond a very low requirement set by law), treat our spouses, do volunteer work, and participate in public life. What's more, in many of those areas that are covered by law, the likelihood of being caught is actually quite low, and the penalties are often surprisingly mild. For instance, only about 1 in 100 tax returns gets audited, and most cheaters are merely asked to pay back what they "missed," plus some interest. Nevertheless, most Americans pay the taxes due. Alan Lewis's classic study The Psychology of Taxation concluded that people don't just pay taxes because they fear the government; they do it because they consider the burden fairly shared and the monies legitimately spent. In short, the normative values of a culture matter. Regulation is needed when culture fails, but it cannot alone serve as the mainstay of good conduct.

3    So what kind of transformation in our normative culture is called for? What needs to be eradicated, or at least greatly tempered, is consumerism: the obsession with acquisition that has become the organizing principle of American life. This is not the same thing as capitalism, nor is it the same thing as consumption. To explain the difference, it is useful to draw on Abraham Maslow's hierarchy of human needs. At the bottom of this hierarchy are basic creature comforts; once these are sated, more satisfaction is drawn from affection, self-esteem, and, finally, self-actualization. As long as consumption is focused on satisfying basic human needs—safety, shelter, food, clothing, health care, education—it is not consumerism. But, when the acquisition of goods and services is used to satisfy the higher needs, consumption turns into consumerism—and consumerism becomes a social disease.

4    The link to the economic crisis should be obvious. A culture in which the urge to consume dominates the psychology of citizens is a culture in which people will do most anything to acquire the means to consume—working slavish hours, behaving rapaciously in their business pursuits, and even bending the rules in order to maximize their earnings. They will also buy homes beyond their means and think nothing of running up credit-card debt. It therefore seems safe to say that consumerism is, as much as anything else, responsible for the current economic mess. But it is not enough to establish that which people ought not to do, to end the obsession with making and consuming evermore than the next person. Consumerism will not just magically disappear from its central place in our culture. It needs to be supplanted by something.

5    A shift away from consumerism, and toward this something else, would obviously be a dramatic change for American society. But such grand cultural changes are far from unprecedented. Profound transformations in the definition of "the good life" have occurred throughout human history. Before the spirit of capitalism swept across much of the world, neither work nor commerce were highly valued pursuits—indeed, they were often delegated

to scorned minorities such as Jews. For centuries in aristocratic Europe and Japan, making war was a highly admired profession. In China, philosophy, poetry, and brush painting were respected during the heyday of the literati. Religion was once the dominant source of normative culture; then, following the Enlightenment, secular humanism was viewed in some parts of the world as the foundation of society. In recent years, there has been a significant increase in the influence of religious values in places like Russia and, of course, the Middle East. (Details can be found in John Micklethwait and Adrian Wooldridge's new book, *God is Back*—although, for many, he never left.) It is true that not all these changes have elevated the human condition. The point is merely that such change, especially during times of crisis, is possible.

6    To accomplish this kind of radical change, it is neither necessary nor desirable to imitate devotees of the 1960s counterculture, early socialists, or followers of ascetic religious orders, all of whom have resisted consumerism by rejecting the whole capitalist project. On the contrary, capitalism should be allowed to thrive, albeit within clear and well-enforced limits. This position does not call for a life of sackcloth and ashes, nor of altruism. And it does not call on poor people or poor nations to be content with their fate and learn to love their misery; clearly, the capitalist economy must be strong enough to provide for the basic creature comforts of all people. But it does call for a new balance between consumption and other human pursuits.

7    There is strong evidence that when consumption is used to try to address higher needs—that is, needs beyond basic creature comforts—it is ultimately Sisyphean. Several studies have shown that, across many nations with annual incomes above $20,000, there is no correlation between increased income and increased happiness. In the United States since World War II, per capita income has tripled, but levels of life satisfaction remain about the same, while the people of Japan, despite experiencing a sixfold increase in income since 1958, have seen their levels of contentment stay largely stagnant. Studies also indicate that many members of capitalist societies feel unsatisfied, if not outright deprived, however much they earn and consume, because others make and spend even more: Relative rather than absolute deprivation is what counts. This is a problem since, by definition, most people cannot consume more than most others. True, it is sometimes hard to tell a basic good from a status good, and a status good can turn into a basic one (air conditioning, for instance). However, it is not a matter of cultural snobbery to note that no one needs inflatable Santas or plastic flamingos on their front lawn or, for that matter, lawns that are strikingly green even in the scorching heat of summer. No one needs a flat-screen television, not to mention diamonds as a token of love or a master's painting as a source of self-esteem.

8    Consumerism, it must be noted, afflicts not merely the upper class in affluent societies but also the middle class and many in the working class. Large numbers of people across society believe that they work merely to make ends meet, but an examination of their shopping lists and closets reveals that they spend good parts of their income on status goods such as brand-name clothing, the "right" kind of car, and other assorted items that they don't really need.

9    This mentality may seem so integral to American culture that resisting it is doomed to futility. But the current economic downturn may provide an opening of sorts. The crisis has caused people to spend less on luxury goods, such as diamonds and flashy cars; scale back

on lavish celebrations for holidays, birthdays, weddings, and bar mitzvahs; and agree to caps on executive compensation. Some workers have accepted fewer hours, lower salaries, and unpaid furloughs.

10    So far, much of this scaling-back has been involuntary, the result of economic necessity. What is needed next is to help people realize that limiting consumption is not a reflection of failure. Rather, it represents liberation from an obsession—a chance to abandon consumerism and focus on . . . well, what exactly? What should replace the worship of consumer goods?

11    The kind of culture that would best serve a Maslowian hierarchy of needs is hardly one that would kill the goose that lays the golden eggs—the economy that can provide the goods needed for basic creature comforts. Nor one that merely mocks the use of consumer goods to respond to higher needs. It must be a culture that extols sources of human flourishing besides acquisition. The two most obvious candidates to fill this role are communitarian pursuits and transcendental ones.

12    Communitarianism refers to investing time and energy in relations with the other, including family, friends, and members of one's community. The term also encompasses service to the common good, such as volunteering, national service, and politics. Communitarian life is not centered around altruism but around mutuality, in the sense that deeper and thicker involvement with the other is rewarding to both the recipient and the giver. Indeed, numerous studies show that communitarian pursuits breed deep contentment. A study of 50-year-old men shows that those with friendships are far less likely to experience heart disease. Another shows that life satisfaction in older adults is higher for those who participate in community service.

13    Transcendental pursuits refer to spiritual activities broadly understood, including religious, contemplative, and artistic ones. The lifestyle of the Chinese literati, centered around poetry, philosophy, and brush painting, was a case in point, but a limited one because this lifestyle was practiced by an elite social stratum and based in part on exploitation of other groups. In modern society, transcendental pursuits have often been emphasized by bohemians, beginning artists, and others involved in lifelong learning who consume modestly. Here again, however, these people make up only a small fraction of society. Clearly, for a culture to buy out of consumerism and move to satisfying higher human needs with transcendental projects, the option to participate in these pursuits must be available on a wider scale.

14    All this may seem abstract, not to mention utopian. But one can see a precedent of sorts for a society that emphasizes communitarian and transcendental pursuits among retired people, who spend the final decades of their lives painting not for a market or galleries but as a form of self-expression, socializing with each other, volunteering, and, in some cases, taking classes. Of course, these citizens already put in the work that enables them to lead this kind of life. For other ages to participate before retirement, they will have to shorten their workweek and workday, refuse to take work home, turn off their BlackBerrys, and otherwise downgrade the centrality of labor to their lives. This is, in effect, what the French, with their 35-hour workweeks, tried to do, as did other countries in "old" Europe. Mainstream American economists—who argue that a modern economy cannot survive unless people consume evermore and hence produce and work evermore— have long scoffed at these societies and urged them to modernize. To some extent, they

did, especially the Brits. Now it seems that maybe these countries were onto something after all.

15    A society that downplayed consumerism in favor of other organizing principles would not just limit the threat of economic meltdown and feature a generally happier populace; it would have other advantages as well. Such a society would, for example, use fewer material resources and, therefore, be much more compatible with protecting the environment. It would also exhibit higher levels of social justice.

16    Social justice entails redistribution of wealth, taking from those disproportionally endowed and giving to those who are underprivileged through no fault of their own—for reasons ranging from past injustices and their lingering contemporary effects to technological changes to globalization to genetic differences. The reason these redistributions have been surprisingly limited in free societies is that those who command the "extra" assets tend also to be those who are politically powerful. Promoting social justice by organizing those with less and forcing those in power to yield has had limited success in democratic countries and led to massive bloodshed in others. So the question arises: Are there other ways to reduce the resistance of elites to redistribution?

17    The answer is found when elites derive their main source of contentment not from acquiring more goods and services, but from activities that are neither labor nor capital intensive and, hence, do not require great amounts of money. Communitarian activities require social skills and communication skills as well as time and personal energy—but, as a rule, minimal material or financial outlays. The same holds for transcendental activities such as prayer, meditation, music, art, sports, adult education, and so on. True, consumerism has turned many of these pursuits into expensive endeavors. But one can break out of this mentality and find that it is possible to engage in most transcendental activities quite profoundly using minimal goods and services. One does not need designer clothes to enjoy the sunset or shoes with fancy labels to benefit from a hike. Chess played with plastic pieces is the same game as the one played with carved mahogany or marble pieces. And I'm quite sure that the Lord does not listen better to prayers read from a leatherbound Bible than those read from a plain one, printed on recycled paper. (Among several books that depict how this kind of culture can flourish is *Seven Pleasures* by Willard Spiegelman.) In short, those who embrace this lifestyle will find that they can achieve a high level of contentment even if they give up a considerable segment of the surplus wealth they command.

18    As for actually putting this vision into practice: The main way societies will determine whether the current crisis will serve as an event that leads to cultural transformation or merely constitute an interlude in the consumerism project is through a process I call "moral megalogues." Societies are constantly engaged in mass dialogues over what is right and wrong. Typically, only one or two topics dominate these megalogues at any given time. Key recent issues have included the legitimacy of the 2003 invasion of Iraq and whether gay couples should be allowed to marry. In earlier decades, women's rights and minority rights were topics of such discussions. Megalogues involve millions of members of a society exchanging views with one another at workplaces, during family gatherings, in the media, and at public events. They are often contentious and passionate, and, while they have no clear beginning or endpoint, they tend to lead to changes in a society's culture and its members' behavior.

19    The megalogue about the relationship between consumerism and human flourishing is now flickering but has yet to become a leading topic—like regulation. Public intellectuals, pundits, and politicians are those best-positioned to focus a megalogue on this subject and, above all, to set the proper scope for the discussion. The main challenge is not to pass some laws, but, rather, to ask people to reconsider what a good life entails.

20    Having a national conversation about this admittedly abstract question is merely a start, though. If a new shared understanding surrounding consumption is to evolve, education will have a crucial role to play. Schools, which often claim to focus solely on academics, are actually major avenues through which changes in societal values are fostered. For instance, many schools deeply impress on young children that they ought to respect the environment, not discriminate on racial or ethnic grounds, and resolve differences in a peaceful manner. There is no reason these schools cannot push back against consumerism while promoting communitarian and transcendental values as well. School uniforms (to counter conspicuous consumption) and an emphasis on community service are just two ways to work these ideas into the culture of public education.

21    For adults, changes in the workplace could go a long way toward promoting these values. Limits on overtime, except under special conditions (such as natural disasters); shorter workweeks; more part- and flex-time jobs; increased freedom to work from home; allowing employees to dress down and thereby avoid squandering money on suits and other expensive clothes—all these relatively small initiatives would encourage Americans to spend more time on things besides work.

22    Finally, legislation has a role to play. Taxes can discourage the purchase of ever-larger houses, cause people to favor public transportation over cars, and encourage the use of commercial aviation rather than private jets. Government could also strike a blow against consumerism by instituting caps on executive pay.

23    Is all this an idle, abstract hypothesis? Not necessarily. Plenty of religious Americans have already embraced versions of these values to some extent or other. And those whose secular beliefs lead them to community service are in the same boat. One such idealist named Barack Obama chose to be a community organizer in Chicago rather than pursue a more lucrative career.

24    I certainly do not expect that most people will move away from a consumerist mindset overnight. Some may keep one foot in the old value system even as they test the waters of the new one, just like those who wear a blazer with jeans. Still others may merely cut back on conspicuous consumption without guilt or fear of social censure. Societies shift direction gradually. All that is needed is for more and more people to turn the current economic crisis into a liberation from the obsession with consumer goods and the uberwork it requires— and, bit by bit, begin to rethink their definition of what it means to live a good life.

## QUESTIONS FOR ANALYSIS AND DISCUSSION

1.  What are the limitations of regulation in terms of addressing our "current economic woes"? What solution does Etzioni offer? Explain.
2.  Etzioni admits that the eradication of consumerism is "far fetched." In your opinion, just how unlikely is it? What factors will influence it? What trends do you see emerging in the current economy, and what predictions

can you make? Connect your observations to Etzioni's points made in this
essay.

3. What is the difference between consumption and consumerism? Why is one
acceptable, and one morally questionable? Explain.

4. What connection, if any, exists between consumerism and happiness?
Respond to the statement "money cannot buy happiness" with your own
viewpoint.

5. What is a "moral megalogue"? What role would a megalogue play in addressing American consumerism?

6. Summarize Etzioni's argument in one paragraph. Then, respond to his argument in a paragraph of your own.

## The Design Imperative
*Robert Horning*

Fashion and design have reached unprecedented heights. Never has so much been so
available to so many people. Designer products are no longer relegated to the very
rich—even a student can own a designer toilet brush that proclaims to the world the
owner's good taste and fashion sense. But are consumers in control, or are we all under the influence of one big marketing pitch? In the next article, *PopMatters* feature editor and columnist Robert Horning examines how all this choice controls our lives.*

### BEFORE YOU READ

Consider the differences between items that are advertised as things we "need"
and the items we really need but are not advertised. How do marketers get us to
believe we need a product?

### AS YOU READ

In this essay, Rob Horning notes that every consumer choice we make contributes
to the beast of "plentitude"—our quest for more and better stuff that tells the world
who we are. Think about the stuff you own and what it says about you. What "design" choices do you make—from ringtones to computers to shoes and lip balm?

1    How to interpret consumer behavior remains a definitive ideological question. Where
some see duped consumers compelled to trod the so-called hedonic treadmill and
chase after ever more frivolous novelties, others see empowered individuals, gratefully
coloring their lives with newfound variety, discovering fresh ways to please and express
themselves through the rich tapestry of goods.

---

*Robert Horning, *PopMatters*, January 29, 2008.

2    If consumerism's apologists are to be believed, customizing our identity with the niceties of industrial design is one of the paramount blessings our shopping-fixated culture bestows. As self-described "dynamist" Virginia Postrel argues in *The Substance of Style: How the Rise of Aesthetic Value Is Remaking Commerce, Culture, and Consciousness*, our most utilitarian choices are now also informed by our aesthetic preferences, which makes them alleged opportunities for pleasure, because presumably nothing can be as pleasing as the narcissistic preening of our own identities (Harper Perennial, 2004).

3    Thanks to this "variety revolution," once mundane products like toilet brushes, spatulas, and ice cube trays are now complemented by design so flamboyant that it's unmistakable even to the untrained consumer's eye, affording them an a-ha moment in which they can think to themselves, with some satisfaction, "Wow, that toilet brush is cool." No longer a prole with a dirty toilet, one becomes a fledgling design critic and a curator of the tastefully appointed museum that used to be a one-bedroom apartment.

4    But there's nothing particularly new or revolutionary about design-oriented consumerism. During the Renaissance, Baldassare Castiglione espoused the influential ideal of sprezzatura, the paradoxical art of seeming like you pay no attention to the impression you're making while simultaneously making it seem like you've thought of everything. This aristocratic impulse to carefully stylize and design one's life eventually began to trickle down, evolving into what we know as fashion.

5    In the mid 18th-century, Lord Chesterfield would advise his son, "If you are not in fashion, you are nobody." Then, according to historian Neil McKendrick, the prevalence of fashion spawned a full-blown late-18th-century consumer revolution, which transformed a tradition-bound people into novelty-seeking mavens (*The Birth of a Consumer Society: The Commercialization of 18th Century England*, 1982). He cites excited proto-Postrels commenting approvingly on the sudden democratizing of such luxuries as mirrors, manufactured toys, and distinctive dishware.

6    Fueling this, though, as McKendrick argues, was the distinctly undemocratic impulse of social emulation, of trying to imitate one's betters, and the "compulsive power of fashion," to which commercial interests "pandered." Alarmed moralists saw in this emulation the destruction of the "natural" social order; mercantilists believed the profligate importing of overseas luxuries would ruin the economy. But these objections were swept away, McKendrick suggests, by the English population's particular susceptibility to the allure of fashion.

7    Because the infrastructure of a popular press and a transportation system were in place to spread ideas, and because income was sufficiently distributed throughout the different classes and the structure of society was just open enough to give license to dream about social mobility, it made sense to try and display one's belongings as evidence of one's aspirations and proof of one's worthiness. As the possibility of emulative spending was recognized by nascent consumers and manufacturers alike, the economy centered around industrially designed goods began to rapidly proliferate. Entrepreneurs began to manufacture stuff—lots and lots of it. The consumer society, as we know it, was born.

8    Above all, the consumer revolution depended on the sudden availability of things, which allowed ordinary people to buy ready-made objects that once were inherited or self-produced. The ability to pick and choose among branded novelties to a previously unimagined degree gave birth to the peculiarly modern pleasure of shopping, in which purchasing

power supplies immediate satisfaction to the impulse to create that once people had to actually make things to fulfill.

9    This mountain of stuff is what Rich Gold, an eclectic avant-garde performance artist cum industrial designer cum computer scientist, refers to as "the Plenitude" in his whimsical, PowerPoint presentation of a book by the same name (*The Plenitude: Creativity, Innovation, and Making Stuff*, MIT Press, 2007). At first, Gold's slim volume seems like the typical celebration of innovation geared for the management crowd, with a series of bullet-pointed tips on how to foster creativity in a corporate environment. And he certainly writes for the attention-challenged business-book reader, making sure to present information in lists, to repeat it several times, and to couple it with illustrations that allow a reader to skip the text itself, if need be. But if one actually bothers to read it, it quickly becomes clear that Gold is far more subversive than it at first appears, making some striking points about the origins of the cult of design and how it manages to reproduce itself.

10    A veteran of several art collectives himself, Gold notes his having been influenced by DeBord and the Situationists, but clearly he has read his Baudrillard, as well. Gold's plenitude concept owes a great deal to Baudrillard's concept of "the system of objects," an all-embracing network of goods through which we come to know ourselves and our position within society. "Material goods are not the objects of consumption," he claims. Instead, "consumption is the virtual totality of all objects and messages presently constituted in a more or less coherent discourse. Consumption, insofar as it is meaningful, is a systematic act of the manipulation of signs" (*The System of Objects*, Verso, 1996). Gold points to the shirt as an example: whereas before the consumer society existed, you would have a shirt specifically made for you by the local shirtmaker and would care deeply about it, as it may be the only one you would have owned. Now we take our shirts for granted, and they signify not ourselves but our allegiance to the Plenitude.

11    As a system, the Plenitude bears with its own ideology, which Gold is careful to elaborate delicately, in terms that won't alienate the business mind. Most significant of these is the notion of copyright. As Gold points out, this makes creativity and distinctive design mandatory. Under an illustration of Mickey Mouse ears, he inscribes this slogan, "We must make new things by law. It's illegal to tell the same story again." Then he elaborates: "Variation is built into the legal system of the culture and lies at the heart of the Plenitude. At this point it's a reflex for us to seek out the new, the different, the creative, the innovative. That's what we like and that's what we buy." We are institutionally trapped in the prison-house of design. Not only that, but between the lines of this statement, though, is the implication that our predilection for novelty has been induced in us, a point reinforced by Gold's calling the toy store the "most frightening place in the mall" because its purpose is "to incorporate our young into the Plenitude."

12    Just as everything manufactured must manifest some essential "creative" difference, the same logic comes to apply when we attempt to produce our own identities, using the consumer goods our culture supplies as the only viable tools for the job. Ignoring the possibilities of design inherent in things becomes tantamount to neglecting to develop our own self-worth.

13    Gold credits the imperative to design with having "created most of the bounty around us," and regards design as a product's way of saying "I care about you." And he extends the anthropomorphizing to argue the good design occurs when "engineers open

themselves up and let the stuff around them rant on about what it wants to be." In other words, rather than design serving us, we become so enmeshed in the network of things and so reliant on the symbolic language of goods that we end up entirely alienated from the material culture we have created and believe ourselves to exist to serve it, to further its ends. "Stuff desires to be better stuff," he proclaims, humbly submitting himself to be the doll whisperer.

14    Once we regard industrial design as an autonomous function of goods themselves, nothing exists to check it and the constrictive code of conspicuous consumerism it represents from colonizing even more of our everyday lives. If the design cult had its way, we wouldn't even be able to carry a coffee mug without wondering if it's cool enough to be seen walking down the street with it in hand. Nothing is to be free of the anxiety that comes with wondering whether someone will mutter "Cool" when they see it.

15    When design and customization options are associated with a particular good, you can no longer avail yourself of the usefulness of a thing without venturing a bit of your identity at the same time. It's akin to what I've always imagined living in the East Village or Williamsburg, New York hipster neighborhoods, would be like, where you can't go out to do your laundry or go to the grocery store without feeling the pressure to look cool. The tyranny of design makes it so you can't simply own a functional car that gets you places; because of the rich associations marketers have imbued in autos, every aspect of your vehicle says something to the world about the personality you wish to project.

16    You can't simply take advantage of the usefulness of a cell phone without opening up a Pandora's box of personalization options; not only must you be worrying about which phone to get, you need to consider what color it should be, which picture to use as a background, what ringtone to have it play, what banner slogan to have it display. There's no escaping the conundrum. As Baudrillard notes, "The code is totalitarian; no one escapes it: our individual flights do not negate the fact that each day we participate in its collective elaboration." Or as another philosopher put it (okay, Rush drummer Neil Peart), "If you choose not to decide, you still have made a choice."

17    So despite the plethora of options it affords us, modern design isn't about improving our quality of life; its purpose is to create differentiation that allows retailers who harness it, like Target, to secure a competitive advantage and make concrete profit out of the intangible insecurities of consumers like us, who are without any alternatives for buoying their self-esteem—the ubiquity of design makes any gesture for recognition we might make ultimately reducible to a pose, a scheme, a design. Social symbolism may very well be a zero-sum game, and inescapable industrial design may have sapped the symbolic potency out of what non-commercial aspects of culture remain.

18    We're left with no viable way to communicate any of our intentions without tacitly assenting to the tyranny of design, without seeming to confess that industrial designers have already found a material way of saying what we mean better than we can say ourselves. So while we are taught to revel in creativity, all we can express is novelty; no matter what we attempt, the message ends up, "Look at me, I'm original." And all the while Gold's Plentitude becomes more mystifyingly diverse and unfathomable, as rich and complex as we humans used to be.

19    The early consumer society was haunted by this, too: In 1825, pamphleteer William Cobbett was complaining about the "constant anxiety to make a show" that went along

with the dissemination of manufactured goods. "What a mass of materials for producing that general and dreadful convulsion that must, first or last, come and blow this funding and jobbing and enslaving and starving system to atoms!" (from *Rural Rides*, 1830).

20      But that dreadful convulsion has not come; instead we have adapted entirely to the system, even as it has eradicated the possibility of any genuine gestures of individuality. Gold notes that "the Plenitude's 'diversity' is overwhelming and it drowns out beauty, drowns out anybody trying to say anything." We are consigned to communicating through design, but it's an impoverished language that can only say one thing: "That's cool." Design ceases to serve our needs, and the superficial qualities of useful things end up cannibalizing their functionality. The palpability of the design interferes, distracts from the activity an item is supposed to be helping you do. The activity becomes subordinate to the tools. You become the tool.

## QUESTIONS FOR ANALYSIS AND DISCUSSION

1. According to Horning, what is "Plentitude" and how does it control our lives? Evaluate how Horning supports this assertion. How do you think advertising agencies would respond to his argument? Explain.
2. What factors contributed to the "consumer revolution"? What circumstances are necessary for consumerism to take root and flourish? Explain. How effective are the author's references to history in framing his argument?
3. Respond to the statement "stuff desires to be better stuff." What does this statement mean, and how does it apply to consumer culture?
4. Horning quotes Neil Peart, drummer for the band Rush who said, "If you choose not to decide, you still have made a choice." What does Peart mean? How can not making a choice, in fact, be one?
5. Horning observes that we each desire to be "original" by conveying our originality through the things we buy and the consumer choices we make. How does our desire to be original play into the concept of "plentitude"? What is the irony behind our desire to be original in a society driven by mass marketed goods? Explain.
6. Evaluate Horning's argument. What position does he take on consumerism and consumer culture? Identify areas of his essay that made sense to you. Did you disagree with any of his points? Explain.

## Reading The Visual

### Bump

*Adbusters* magazine is a nonprofit, reader-supported, 120,000-circulation journal that provides critical commentary on consumer culture and corporate marketing agendas. Articles and issues from the magazine have been featured on MTV and PBS, the *Wall Street Journal*, *Wired*, and in hundreds of other newspapers, magazines, and television and radio shows around the world. Articles in *Adbuster* are "dedicated to examining the relationship between human beings and their physical and mental environment," striving to create a "world in which the economy and ecology resonate in balance." This "ad" appeared in both their magazine and on their website, at www.adbusters.org.

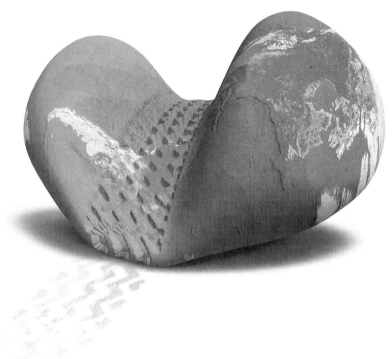

# What was that bump?

QUESTIONS FOR ANALYSIS AND DISCUSSION

1. What message is *Adbusters* trying to convey with this ad? Explain.
2. What is your impression of this ad? Does it appeal to you? Why or why not? Who do you think is the intended audience?
3. Visit the http://adbusters.org/spoofads/ website and view some of the other "ads" they have posted online. Select one and explain how *Adbusters* twists the original ad to make a point.

# With These Words, I Can Sell You Anything
*William Lutz*

Words such as "help" and "virtually" and phrases such as "new and improved" and "acts fast" seem like innocuous weaponry in the arsenal of advertising. But not to William Lutz, and English professor who analyzes how such words are used in ads—how they misrepresent, mislead, and deceive consumers. In this essay, he alerts us to the special power of "weasel words"—those familiar and sneaky little critters that "appear to say one thing when in fact they say the opposite, or nothing at all." The real danger, Lutz argues, is how such language debases reality and the values of the consumer.[*]

## BEFORE YOU READ

Consider the phrase "like magic" as it might be used in an ad—for example, "Zappo dish detergent works like magic." What does the phrase suggest at a quick glance? What does it mean upon detailed analysis? Make a list of other such words used in advertising to make "big promises."

## AS YOU READ

A "weasel word" is a word so hollow it has no meaning. As you read Lutz's article, consider your own reaction to such words when you hear them. Have they ever motivated you to make a purchase?

1    One problem advertisers have when they try to convince you that the product they are pushing is really different from other, similar products is that their claims are subject to some laws. Not a lot of laws, but there are some designed to prevent fraudulent or untruthful claims in advertising. Even during the happy years of nonregulation under President Ronald Reagan, the FTC did crack down on the more blatant abuses in advertising claims. Generally speaking, advertisers have to be careful in what they say in their ads, in the claims they make for the products they advertise. Parity claims are safe because they are legal and supported by a number of court decisions. But beyond parity claims there are weasel words.

2    Advertisers use weasel words to appear to be making a claim for a product when in fact they are making no claim at all. Weasel words get their name from the way weasels eat the eggs they find in the nests of other animals. A weasel will make a small hole in the egg, suck out the insides, then place the egg back in the nest. Only when the egg is examined closely is it found to be hollow. That's the way it is with weasel words in advertising: Examine weasel words closely and you'll find that they're as hollow as any egg sucked by a weasel. Weasel words appear to say one thing when in fact they say the opposite, or nothing at all.

---

[*]William Lutz, *Doublespeak* (excerpt), 1989.

## "Help"—The Number One Weasel Word

3 The biggest weasel word used in advertising doublespeak is "help." Now "help" only means to aid or assist, nothing more. It does not mean to conquer, stop, eliminate, solve, heal, cure, or anything else. But once the ad says "help," it can say just about anything after that because "help" qualifies everything coming after it. The trick is that the claim that comes after the weasel word is usually so strong and so dramatic that you forget the word "help" and concentrate only on the dramatic claim. You read into the ad a message that the ad does not contain. More importantly, the advertiser is not responsible for the claim that you read into the ad, even though the advertiser wrote the ad so you would read that claim into it.

4     The next time you see an ad for a cold medicine that promises that it "helps relieve cold symptoms fast," don't rush out to buy it. Ask yourself what this claim is really saying. Remember, "helps" means only that the medicine will aid or assist. What will it aid or assist in doing? Why, "relieve" your cold "symptoms." "Relieve" only means to ease, alleviate, or mitigate, not to stop, end, or cure. Nor does the claim say how much relieving this medicine will do. Nowhere does this ad claim it *will cure anything*. In fact, the ad doesn't even claim it will *do* anything at all. The *ad only claims* that it will aid in relieving (not curing) your cold symptoms, which are probably a runny nose, watery eyes, and a headache. In other words, this medicine probably contains a standard decongestant and some aspirin. By the way, what does "fast" mean? Ten minutes, one hour, one day? What is fast to one person can be very slow to another. Fast is another weasel word.

5     Ad claims using "help" are among the most popular ads. One says, "Helps keep you young looking," but then a lot of things will help keep you young looking, including exercise, rest, good nutrition, and a facelift. More importantly, this ad doesn't say the product will keep you young, only "young *looking*." Someone may look young to one person and old to another.

6     A toothpaste ad says, "Helps prevent cavities," but it doesn't say it will actually prevent cavities. Brushing your teeth regularly, avoiding sugars in foods, and flossing daily will also help prevent cavities. A liquid cleaner ad says, "Helps keep your home germ free," but it doesn't say it actually kills germs, nor does it even specify which germs it might kill.

7     "Help" is such a useful weasel word that it is often combined with other action-verb weasel words such as "fight" and "control." Consider the claim, "Helps control dandruff symptoms with regular use." What does it really say? It will assist in controlling (not eliminating, stopping, ending, or curing) the symptoms of dandruff, not the cause of dandruff nor the dandruff itself. What are the symptoms of dandruff? The ad deliberately leaves that undefined, but assume that the symptoms referred to in the ad are the flaking and itching commonly associated with dandruff. But just shampooing with *any* shampoo will temporarily eliminate these symptoms, so this shampoo isn't any different from any other. Finally, in order to benefit from this product, you must use it regularly. What is "regular use"—daily, weekly, hourly? Using another shampoo "regularly" will have the same effect. Nowhere does this advertising claim say this particular shampoo stops, eliminates, or cures dandruff. In fact, this claim says nothing at all, thanks to all the weasel words.

8    Look at ads in magazines and newspapers, listen to ads on radio and television, and you'll find the word "help" in ads for all kinds of products. How often do you read or hear such phrases as "helps stop . . . ," "helps overcome . . . ," "helps eliminate . . . ," "helps you feel . . . ," or "helps you look . . . "? If you start looking for this weasel word in advertising, you'll be amazed at how often it occurs. Analyze the claims in the ads using "help," and you will discover that these ads are really saying nothing.

9    There are plenty of other weasel words used in advertising. In fact, there are so many that to list them all would fill the rest of this book. But, in order to identify the doublespeak of advertising and understand the real meaning of an ad, you have to be aware of the most popular weasel words in advertising today.

## Virtually Spotless

10 One of the most powerful weasel words is "virtually," a word so innocent that most people don't pay any attention to it when it is used in an advertising claim. But watch out. "Virtually" is used in advertising claims that appear to make specific, definite promises when there is no promise. After all, what does "virtually" mean? It means "in essence of effect, although not in fact." Look at that definition again. "Virtually" means *not in fact*. It does *not* mean "almost" or "just about the same as," or anything else. And before you dismiss all this concern over such a small word, remember that small words can have big consequences.

11    In 1971 a federal court rendered its decision on a case brought by a woman who became pregnant while taking birth control pills. She sued the manufacturer, Eli Lilly and Company, for breach of warranty. The woman lost her case. Basing its ruling on a statement in the pamphlet accompanying the pills, which stated that, "When taken as directed, the tablets offer virtually 100 percent protection," the court ruled that there was no warranty, expressed or implied, that the pills were absolutely effective. In its ruling, the court pointed out that, according to *Webster's Third New International Dictionary,* "virtually" means "almost entirely" and clearly does not mean "absolute" (*Whittington* v. *Eli Lilly and Company,* 333 F. Supp. 98). In other words, the Eli Lilly company was really saying that its birth control pill, even when taken as directed, *did not in fact* provide 100 percent protection against pregnancy. But Eli Lilly didn't want to put it that way because then many women might not have bought Lilly's birth control pills.

12    The next time you see the ad that says that this dishwasher detergent "leaves dishes virtually spotless," just remember how advertisers twist the meaning of the weasel word "virtually." You can have lots of spots on your dishes after using this detergent and the ad claim will still be true, because what this claim really means is that this detergent does not *in fact* leave your dishes spotless. Whenever you see or hear an ad claim that uses the word "virtually," just translate that claim into its real meaning. So the television set that is "virtually trouble free" becomes the television set that is not in fact trouble free, the "virtually foolproof operation" of any appliance becomes an operation that is in fact not foolproof, and the product that "virtually never needs service" becomes the product that is not in fact service free.

## New and Improved

13 If "new" is the most frequently used word on a product package, "improved" is the second most frequent. In fact, the two words are almost always used together. It seems just about everything sold these days is "new and improved." The next time you're in the supermarket, try counting the number of times you see these words on products. But you'd better do it while you're walking down just one aisle, otherwise you'll need a calculator to keep track of your counting.

14 Just what do these words mean? The use of the word "new" is restricted by regulations, so an advertiser can't just use the word on a product or in an ad without meeting certain requirements. For example, a product is considered new for about six months during a national advertising campaign. If the product is being advertised only in a limited test market area, the word can be used longer, and in some instances has been used for as long as two years.

15 What makes a product "new"? Some products have been around for a long time, yet every once in a while you discover that they are being advertised as "new." Well, an advertiser can call a product new if there has been "a material functional change" in the product. What is "a material functional change," you ask? Good question. In fact it's such a good question it's being asked all the time. It's up to the manufacturer to prove that the product has undergone such a change. And if the manufacturer isn't challenged on the claim, then there's no one to stop it. Moreover, the change does not have to be an improvement in the product. One manufacturer added an artificial lemon scent to a cleaning product and called it "new and improved," even though the product did not clean any better than without the lemon scent. The manufacturer defended the use of the word "new" on the grounds that the artificial scent changed the chemical formula of the product and therefore constituted "a material functional change."

16 Which brings up the word "improved." When used in advertising, "improved" does not mean "made better." It only means "changed" or "different from before." So, if the detergent maker puts a plastic pour spout on the box of detergent, the product has been "improved," and away we go with a whole new advertising campaign. Or, if the cereal maker adds more fruit or a different kind of fruit to the cereal, there's an improved product. Now you know why manufacturers are constantly making little changes in their products. Whole new advertising campaigns, designed to convince you that the product has been changed for the better, are based on small changes in superficial aspects of a product. The next time you see an ad for an "improved" product, ask yourself what was wrong with the old one. Ask yourself just how "improved" the product is. Finally, you might check to see whether the "improved" version costs more than the unimproved one. After all, someone has to pay for the millions of dollars spent advertising the improved product.

17 Of course, advertisers really like to run ads that claim a product is "new and improved." While what constitutes a "new" product may be subject to some regulation, "improved" is a subjective judgment. A manufacturer changes the shape of its stick deodorant, but the shape doesn't improve the function of the deodorant. That is, changing the shape doesn't affect the deodorizing ability of the deodorant, so the manufacturer calls it "improved." Another manufacturer adds ammonia to its liquid cleaner and calls it "new and improved." Since adding ammonia does affect the cleaning ability of the product, there has

been a "material functional change" in the product, and the manufacturer can now call its cleaner "new," and "improved" as well. Now the weasel words, "new and improved" are plastered all over the package and are the basis for a multimillion-dollar ad campaign. But after six months the word "new" will have to go, until someone can dream up another change in the product. Perhaps it will be adding color to the liquid, or changing the shape of the package, or maybe adding a new dripless pour spout, or perhaps a _____. The "improvements" are endless, and so are the new advertising claims and campaigns.

18    "New" is just too useful and powerful a word in advertising for advertisers to pass it up easily. So they use weasel words that say "new" without really saying it. One of their favorites is "introducing," as in, "Introducing improved Tide," or "Introducing the stain remover." The first is simply saying, here's our improved soap; the second, here's our new advertising campaign for our detergent. Another favorite is "now," as in "Now there's Sinex," which simply means that Sinex is available. Then there are phrases like "Today's Chevrolet," "Presenting Dristan," and "A fresh way to start the day." The list is really endless because advertisers are always finding new ways to say "new" without really saying it. If there is a second edition of this book, I just call it the "new and improved" edition. Wouldn't you really rather have a "new and improved" edition of this book rather than a "second" edition?

## Acts Fast

19  "Acts" and "works" are two popular weasel words in advertising because they bring action to the product and to the advertising claim. When you see the ad for the cough syrup that "Acts on the cough control center," ask yourself what this cough syrup is claiming to do. Well, it's just claiming to "act," to do something, to perform an action. What is it that the cough syrup does? The ad doesn't say. It only claims to perform an action or do something on your "cough control center." By the way, what and where is our "cough control center"? I don't remember learning about that part of the body in human biology class.

20      Ads that use such phrases as "acts fast," "acts against," "acts to prevent," and the like are saying essentially nothing, because "act" is a word empty of any specific meaning. The ads are always careful not to specify exactly what "act" the product performs. Just because a brand of aspirin claims to "act fast" for headache relief doesn't mean this aspirin is any better than any other aspirin. What is the "act" that this aspirin performs? You're never told. Maybe it just dissolves quickly. Since aspirin is a parity product, all aspirin is the same and therefore functions the same.

## Works Like Anything Else

21 If you don't find the word "acts" in an ad, you will probably find the weasel word "works." In fact, the two words are almost interchangeable in advertising. Watch out for ads that say a product "works against," "works like," "works for," or "works longer." As with "acts," "works" is the same meaningless verb used to make you think that this product really does something, and maybe even something special or unique. But "works," like "acts," is basically a word empty of any specific meaning.

## Like Magic

22 Whenever advertisers want you to stop thinking about the product and to start thinking about something bigger, better, or more attractive than the product, they use that very popular weasel word, "like." The word "like" is the advertiser's equivalent of a magician's use of misdirection. "Like" gets you to ignore the product and concentrate on the claim the advertiser is making about it. "For skin like peaches and cream" claims the ad for a skin cream. What is this ad really claiming? It doesn't say this cream will give you peaches-and-cream skin. There is no verb in this claim, so it doesn't even mention using the product. How is skin ever like "peaches and cream"? Remember, ads must be read literally and exactly, according to the dictionary definition of words. (Remember "virtually" in the Eli Lilly case.) The ad is making absolutely no promise or claim whatsoever for this skin cream. If you think this cream will give you soft, smooth, youthful-looking skin, you are the one who has read that meaning into the ad.

23 The wine that claims "It's like taking a trip to France" wants you to think about a romantic evening in Paris as you walk along the boulevard after a wonderful meal in an intimate little bistro. Of course, you don't really believe that a wine can take you to France, but the goal of the ad is to get you to think pleasant, romantic thoughts about France and not about how the wine tastes or how expensive it may be. That little word "like" has taken you away from crushed grapes into a world of your own imaginative making. Who knows, maybe the next time you buy wine, you'll think those pleasant thoughts when you see this brand of wine, and you'll buy it. Or, maybe you weren't even thinking about buying wine at all, but now you just might pick up a bottle the next time you're shopping. Ah, the power of "like" in advertising.

24 How about the most famous "like" claim of all, "Winston tastes good like a cigarette should"? Ignoring the grammatical error here, you might want to know what this claim is saying. Whether a cigarette tastes good or bad is a subjective judgment because what tastes good to one person may well taste horrible to another. Not everyone likes fried snails, even if they are called escargot. (*De gustibus non est disputandum*, which was probably the Roman rule for advertising as well as for defending the games in the Coliseum.) There are many people who say all cigarettes taste terrible, other people who say only some cigarettes taste all right, and still others who say all cigarettes taste good. Who's right? Everyone, because taste is a matter of personal judgment.

25 Moreover, note the use of the conditional, "should." The complete claim is, "Winston tastes good like a cigarette should taste." But should cigarettes taste good? Again, this is a matter of personal judgment and probably depends mostly on one's experiences with smoking. So, the Winston ad is simply saying that Winston cigarettes are just like any other cigarette: Some people like them and some people don't. On that statement, R. J. Reynolds conducted a very successful multimillion-dollar advertising campaign that helped keep Winston the number-two-selling cigarette in the United States, close behind number one, Marlboro.

## Can't It Be Up to the Claim?

26 Analyzing ads for doublespeak requires that you pay attention to every word in the ad and determine what each word really means. Advertisers try to wrap their claims in language that sounds concrete, specific, and objective, when in fact the language of advertising is

anything but. Your job is to read carefully and listen critically so that when the announcer says that "Crest can be of significant value . . . ," you know immediately that this claim says absolutely nothing. Where is the doublespeak in this ad? Start with the second word.

27    Once again, you have to look at what words really mean, not what you think they mean or what the advertiser wants you to think they mean. The ad for Crest only says that using Crest "can be" of "significant value." What really throws you off in this ad is the brilliant use of "significant." It draws your attention to the word "value" and makes you forget that the ad only claims that Crest "can be." The ad doesn't say that Crest is of value, only that it is "able" or "possible" to be of value, because that's all that "can" means.

28    It's so easy to miss the importance of those little words, "can be." Almost as easy as missing the importance of the words "up to" in an ad. These words are very popular in sales ads. You know, the ones that say, "Up to 50 percent Off!" Now, what does that claim mean? Not much, because the store or manufacturer has to reduce the price of only a few items by 50 percent. Everything else can be reduced a lot less, or not even reduced. Moreover, don't you want to know 50 percent off of what? Is it 50 percent off the "manufacturer's suggested list price," which is the highest possible price? Was the price artificially inflated and then reduced? In other ads, "up to" expresses an ideal situation. The medicine that works "up to ten times faster," the battery that lasts "up to twice as long," and the soap that gets you "up to twice as clean" all are based on ideal situations for using these products, situations in which you can be sure you will never find yourself.

## Unfinished Words

29 Unfinished words are a kind of "up to" claim in advertising. The claim that a battery lasts "up to twice as long" usually doesn't finish the comparison—twice as long as what? A birthday candle? A tank of gas? A cheap battery made in a country not noted for its technological achievements? The implication is that the battery lasts twice as long as batteries made by other battery makers, or twice as long as earlier model batteries made by the advertiser, but the ad doesn't really make these claims. You read these claims into the ad, aided by the visual images the advertiser so carefully provides.

30    Unfinished words depend on you to finish them, to provide the words the advertisers so thoughtfully left out of the ad. Pall Mall cigarettes were once advertised as "A longer, finer and milder smoke." The question is, longer, finer, and milder than what? The aspirin that claims it contains "Twice as much of the pain reliever doctors recommend most" doesn't tell you what pain reliever it contains twice as much of. (By the way, it's aspirin. That's right; it just contains twice the amount of aspirin. And how much is twice the amount? Twice of what amount?) Panadol boasts that "nobody reduces fever faster," but, since Panadol is a parity product, this claim simply means that Panadol isn't any better than any other product in its parity class. "You can be sure if it's Westinghouse," you're told, but just exactly what it is you can be sure of is never mentioned. "Magnavox gives you more" doesn't tell you what you get more of. More value? More television? More than they gave you before? It sounds nice, but it means nothing, until you fill in the claim with your own words, the words the advertisers didn't use. Since each of us fills in the claim differently, the ad and the product can become all things to all people, and not promise a single thing.

31    Unfinished words abound in advertising because they appear to promise so much. More importantly, they can be joined with powerful visual images on television to appear to be making significant promises about a product's effectiveness without really making any promises. In a television ad, the aspirin product that claims fast relief can show a person with a headache taking the product and then, in what appears to be a matter of minutes, claiming complete relief. This visual image is far more powerful than any claim made in unfinished words. Indeed, the visual image completes the unfinished words for you, filling in with pictures what the words leave out. And you thought that ads didn't affect you. What brand of aspirin do you use?

32    Some years ago, Ford's advertisements proclaimed "Ford LTD—700 percent quieter." Now, what do you think Ford was claiming with these unfinished words? What was the Ford LTD quieter than? A Cadillac? A Mercedes Benz? A BMW? Well, when the FTC asked Ford to substantiate this unfinished claim, Ford replied that it meant that the inside of the LTD was 700 percent quieter than the outside. How did you finish those unfinished words when you first read them? Did you even come close to Ford's meaning?

## Combining Weasel Words

33  A lot of ads don't fall neatly into one category or another because they use a variety of different devices and words. Different weasel words are often combined to make an ad claim. The claim, "Coffee-Mate gives coffee more body, more flavor," uses Unfinished Words ("more" than what?) and also uses words that have no specific meaning ("body" and "flavor"). Along with "taste" (remember the Winston ad and its claim to taste good), "body" and "flavor" mean nothing because their meaning is entirely subjective. To you, "body" in coffee might mean thick, black, almost bitter coffee, while I might take it to mean a light brown, delicate coffee. Now, if you think you understood that last sentence, read it again, because it said nothing of objective value; it was filled with weasel words of no specific meaning: "thick," "black," "bitter," "light brown," and "delicate." Each of those words has no specific, objective meaning, because each of us can interpret them differently.

34    Try this slogan: "Looks, smells, tastes like ground-roast coffee." So, are you now going to buy Taster's Choice instant coffee because of this ad? "Looks," "smells," and "tastes" are all words with no specific meaning and depend on your interpretation of them for any meaning. Then there's that great weasel word "like," which simply suggests a comparison but does not make the actual connection between the product and the quality. Besides, do you know what "ground-roast" coffee is? I don't, but it sure sounds good. So, out of seven words in this ad, four are definite weasel words, two are quite meaningless, and only one has any clear meaning.

35    Remember the Anacin ad—"Twice as much of the pain reliever doctors recommend most"? There's a whole lot of weaseling going on in this ad. First, what's the pain reliever they're talking about in this ad? Aspirin, of course. In fact, any time you see or hear an ad using those words "pain reliever," you can automatically substitute the word "aspirin" for them. (Makers of acetaminophen and ibuprofen pain relievers are careful in their advertising to identify their products as nonaspirin products.) So, now we know that Anacin has aspirin in it. Moreover, we know that Anacin has twice as much aspirin in it, but we don't

know twice as much as what. Does it have twice as much aspirin as an ordinary aspirin tablet? If so, what is an ordinary aspirin tablet, and how much aspirin does it contain? Twice as much as Excedrin or Bufferin? Twice as much as a chocolate chip cookie? Remember those Unfinished Words and how they lead you on without saying anything.

36    Finally, what about those doctors who are doing all that recommending? Who are they? How many of them are there? What kind of doctors are they? What are their qualifications? Who asked them about recommending pain relievers? What other pain relievers did they recommend? And there are a whole lot more questions about this "poll" of doctors to which I'd like to know the answers, but you get the point. Sometimes, when I call my doctor, she tells me to take two aspirin and call her office in the morning. Is that where Anacin got this ad?

## Read the Label, or the Brochure

37  Weasel words aren't just found on television, on the radio, or in newspaper and magazine ads. Just about any language associated with a product will contain the doublespeak of advertising. Remember the Eli Lilly case and the doublespeak on the information sheet that came with the birth control pills. Here's another example.

38    [Several years ago], the Estée Lauder cosmetics company announced a new product called "Night Repair." A small brochure distributed with the product stated that "Night Repair was scientifically formulated in Estée Lauder's U.S. laboratories as part of the Swiss Age-Controlling Skincare Program. Although only nature controls the aging process, this program helps control the signs of aging and encourages skin to look and feel younger." You might want to read these two sentences again, because they sound great but say nothing.

39    First, note that the product was "scientifically formulated" in the company's laboratories. What does that mean? What constitutes a scientific formulation? You wouldn't expect the company to say that the product was casually, mechanically, or carelessly formulated, or just thrown together one day when the people in the white coats didn't have anything better to do. But the word "scientifically" lends an air of precision and promise that just isn't there.

40    It is the second sentence, however, that's really weasely, both syntactically and semantically. The only factual part of this sentence is the introductory dependent clause—"only nature controls the aging process." Thus, the only fact in the ad is relegated to a dependent clause, a clause dependent on the main clause, which contains no factual or definite information at all and indeed purports to contradict the independent clause. The new "skincare program" (notice it's not a skin cream but a "program") does not claim to stop or even retard the aging process. What, then, does Night Repair do? According to this brochure, nothing. It only "helps," and the brochure does not say how much it helps. Moreover, it only "helps control," and then it only helps control the "signs of aging," not the aging itself. Also, it "encourages" skin not to be younger but only to "look and feel" younger. The brochure does not say younger than what. Of the sixteen words in the main clause of this second sentence, nine are weasel words. So, before you spend all that money for Night Repair, or any other cosmetic product, read the words carefully, and then decide if you're getting what you think you're paying for.

## Other Tricks of the Trade

41 Advertisers' use of doublespeak is endless. The best way advertisers can make something out of nothing is through words. Although there are a lot of visual images used on television and in magazines and newspapers, every advertiser wants to create that memorable line that will stick in the public consciousness. I am sure pure joy reigned in one advertising agency when a study found that children who were asked to spell the world "relief" promptly and proudly responded "r-o-l-a-i-d-s."

42 The variations, combinations, and permutations of doublespeak used in advertising go on and on, running from the use of rhetorical questions ("Wouldn't you really rather have a Buick?" "If you can't trust Prestone, who can you trust?") to flattering you with compliments ("The lady has taste." "We think a cigar smoker is someone special." "You've come a long way, baby."). You know, of course, how you're *supposed* to answer those questions, and you know that those compliments are just leading up to the sales pitches for the products. Before you dismiss such tricks of the trade as obvious, however, just remember that all of these statements and questions were part of very successful advertising campaigns.

43 A more subtle approach is the ad that proclaims a supposedly unique quality for a product, a quality that really isn't unique. "If it doesn't say Goodyear, it can't be Polyglas." Sounds good, doesn't it? Polyglas is available only from Goodyear because Goodyear copyrighted that trade name. Any other tire manufacturer could make exactly the same tire but could not call it "Polyglas," because that would be copyright infringement. "Polyglas" is simply Goodyear's name for its fiberglass-reinforced tire.

44 Since we like to think of ourselves as living in a technologically advanced country, science and technology have a great appeal in selling products. Advertisers are quick to use scientific doublespeak to push their products. There are all kinds of elixirs, additives, scientific potions, and mysterious mixtures added to all kinds of products. Gasoline contains "HTA," "F-130," "Platformate," and other chemical-sounding additives, but nowhere does an advertisement give any real information about the additive.

45 Shampoo, deodorant, mouthwash, cold medicine, sleeping pills, and any number of other products all seem to contain some special chemical ingredient that allows them to work wonders. "Certs contains a sparkling drop of Retsyn." So what? What's "Retsyn"? What's it do? What's so special about it? When they don't have a secret ingredient in their product, advertisers still find a way to claim scientific validity. There's "Sinarest. Created by a research scientist who actually gets sinus headaches." Sounds nice, but what kind of research does this scientist do? How do you know if she is any kind of expert on sinus medicine? Besides, this ad doesn't tell you a thing about the medicine itself and what it does.

## The World of Advertising

46 In the world of advertising, people wear "dentures," not false teeth; they suffer from "occasional irregularity," not constipation; they need deodorants for their "nervous wetness," not for sweat; they use "bathroom tissue," not toilet paper; and they don't dye their hair, they "tint" or "rinse" it. Advertisements offer "real counterfeit diamonds" without the slightest hint of embarrassment, or boast of goods made out of "genuine imitation leather" or "virgin vinyl."

## Advertising Doublespeak Quick Quiz

Now it's time to test your awareness of advertising doublespeak. The following is a list of statements from some recent ads. Your job is to figure out what each of these ads really says.

DOMINO'S PIZZA: "Because nobody delivers better."

SINUTAB: "It can stop the pain."

TUMS: "The stronger acid neutralizer."

MAXIMUM STRENGTH DRISTAN: "Strong medicine for tough sinus colds."

LISTERMINT: "Making your mouth a cleaner place."

CASCADE: "For virtually spotless dishes nothing beats Cascade."

NUPRIN: "Little. Yellow. Different. Better."

ANACIN: "Better relief."

SUDAFED: "Fast sinus relief that won't put you fast asleep."

ADVIL: "Better relief."

PONDS COLD CREAM: "Ponds cleans like no soap can."

MILLER LITE BEER: "Tastes great. Less filling."

PHILIPS MILK OF MAGNESIA: "Nobody treats you better than MOM (Philips Milk of Magnesia)."

BAYER: "The wonder drug that works wonders."

CRACKER BARREL: "Judged to be the best."

KNORR: "Where taste is everything."

ANUSOL: "Anusol is the word to remember for relief."

DIMETAPP: "It relieves kids as well as colds."

LIQUID DRÁNO: "The liquid strong enough to be called Dráno."

JOHNSON & JOHNSON BABY POWDER: "Like magic for your skin."

PURITAN: "Make it your oil for life."

PAM: "Pam, because how you cook is as important as what you cook."

TYLENOL GEL-CAPS: "It's not a capsule. It's better."

ALKA-SELTZER PLUS: "Fast, effective relief for winter colds."

47    In the world of advertising, the girdle becomes a "body shaper," "form persuader," "control garment," "controller," "outerwear enhancer," "body garment," or "anti-gravity panties," and is sold with such trade names as "The Instead," "The Free Spirit," and "The Body Briefer."

48    A study some years ago found the following words to be among the most popular used in U.S. television advertisements: "new," "improved," "better," "extra," "fresh," "clean," "beautiful," "free," "good," "great," and "light." At the same time, the following words were found to be among the most frequent on British television: "new," "good-better-best," "free," "fresh," "delicious," "full," "sure," "clean," "wonderful," and "special." While these words may occur most frequently in ads, and while ads may be filled with weasel words, you have to watch out for all the words used in advertising, not just the words mentioned here.

49    Every word in an ad is there for a reason; no word is wasted. Your job is to figure out exactly what each word is doing in an ad—what each word really means, not what the advertiser wants you to think it means. Remember, the ad is trying to get you to buy a product, so it will put the product in the best possible light, using any device, trick, or means legally allowed. Your own defense against advertising (besides taking up permanent residence on the moon) is to develop and use a strong critical reading, listening, and looking ability. Always ask yourself what the ad is really saying. When you see ads on television, don't be misled by the pictures, the visual images. What does the ad say about the product? What does the ad not say? What information is missing from the ad? Only by becoming an active, critical consumer of the doublespeak of advertising will you ever be able to cut through the doublespeak and discover what the ad is really saying.

## QUESTIONS FOR ANALYSIS AND DISCUSSION

1. How would a copywriter for an advertising agency respond to this article? Would he or she agree with the way Lutz characterizes all advertisements as trying to trick consumers with false claims into buying a product?

2. When you see the word "new" on a product, do you think twice about buying that product? What regulations restrict use of the word "new"? How can manufacturers make a product "new" to sidestep these regulations? Do these regulations serve the interests of the advertiser or the consumer?

3. Review Lutz's "Advertising Doublespeak Quick Quiz." Choose five items and analyze them using dictionary meanings to explain what the ads are really saying.

4. What tone does Lutz use throughout the article? Is his writing style humorous, informal, or academic? What strategies does he use to involve the reader in the piece?

5. In paragraph 43, Lutz describes how manufacturers claim for their products unique properties that are not in fact unique after all. Could these claims be considered circular reasoning? Explain.

## The Language of Advertising
*Charles A. O'Neill*

In this essay, marketing executive Charles A. O'Neill disputes William Lutz's criticism of advertising doublespeak. While admitting to some of the craftiness of his profession, O'Neill defends the huckster's language—both verbal and visual—against claims that it distorts reality. Examining some familiar television commercials and magazine ads, he explains why the language may be charming and seductive but far from brainwashing.[*]

### BEFORE YOU READ

O'Neill makes several generalizations that characterize the language of advertising. Think about ads you have recently seen or read and make a list of your own generalizations about the language of advertising.

### AS YOU READ

Does the fact that O'Neill is a professional advertising consultant influence your reception of his essay? Does it make his argument more or less persuasive?

1 His name was Joe Camel. On the billboards and in the magazine ads, he looked like a cartoonist's composite sketch of the Rolling Stones, lounging around in a celebrity waiting area at MTV headquarters in New York. He was poised, confident, leaning against a railing or playing pool with his friends. His personal geometry was always just right. He often wore a white suit, dark shirt, sunglasses. Cigarette in hand, wry smile on his lips, his attitude was distinctly confident, urbane.

2 He was very cool and powerful. So much so that more than 90 percent of 6-year-olds matched Joe Camel with a picture of a cigarette, making him as well known as Mickey Mouse.[1]

3 Good advertising, but bad public relations.

4 Finally, after extended sparring with the tobacco company about whether Joe really promoted smoking, the Federal Trade Commission brought the ads to an end. President Clinton spoke for the regulators when he said, "Let's stop pretending that a cartoon camel in a funny costume is trying to sell to adults, not children."

5 Joe's 23-year-old advertising campaign was stopped because it was obvious that he could turn kids into lung cancer patients. That's bad enough. But beneath the surface, the debate about Joe typifies something more interesting and broad-based: the rather uncomfortable, tentative acceptance of advertising in our society. We recognize the legitimacy—even the value—of advertising, but on some level we can't quite fully embrace it as a "normal" part of our experience.

---

[*]This essay first appeared in the textbook *Exploring Language* in 1998 and was updated in 2007.

6    At best, we view advertising as distracting. At worst, we view it as dangerous to our health and a pernicious threat to our social values. One notable report acknowledged the positive contribution of advertising (e.g., provides information, supports worthy causes, and encourages competition and innovation), then added, "In the competition to attract even larger audiences . . . communicators can find themselves pressured . . . to set aside high artistic and moral standards and lapse into superficiality, tawdriness, and moral squalor."[2]

7    How does advertising work? Why is it so powerful? Why does it raise such concern? What case can be made for and against the advertising business?

8    In order to understand advertising, you must accept that it is not about truth, virtue, love, or positive societal values. It is about money. It is about moving customers through the sales process. Sometimes the words and images are concrete; sometimes they are merely suggestive. Sometimes ads provide useful information; sometimes they convince us that we need to spend money to solve a problem we never knew we had. Ads are designed to be intrusive. We're not always pleased about the way they clutter our environment and violate our sense of private space. We're not always happy with the tactics they use to impose themselves upon us.

9    Whatever the product or creative strategy, advertisements derive their power from a purposeful, directed combination of images. These can take the form of text in a magazine or newspaper, images on television, interactive games on web pages, or mini-documentaries on YouTube. Whatever the means of expression, the combination of images is the language of advertising, a language unlike any other.

10   Everyone who grows up in the civilized world knows that advertising language is different from other languages. Read this aloud: "With Nice 'n Easy, it's color so natural, the closer he gets, the better you look." Many children would be unable to explain how this classic ad for Clairol's Nice 'n Easy hair coloring differs from "ordinary language," but they would say, "It sounds like an ad."

11   The language of advertising changes with the times. Styles and creative concepts come and go. But there are at least four distinct, general characteristics of the language of advertising that make it different from other languages. They lend advertising its persuasive power:

■ The language of advertising is edited and purposeful.
■ The language of advertising is rich and arresting; it is specifically intended to attract and hold our attention.
■ The language of advertising involves us; in effect, *we* complete the message.
■ The language of advertising is simple and direct. It holds no secrets from us.

## Edited and Purposeful

12   In his famous book, *Future Shock,* Alvin Toffler describes various types of messages we receive from the world around us each day. He observed that there is a difference between normal, "coded" messages and "engineered" messages. Much of normal, human experience is "uncoded." When a man walks down a street, for example, he sees where he is going and hears random sounds. These are mental images, but they are not messages "designed

by anyone to communicate anything, and the man's understanding of it does not depend directly on a social code—a set of agreed-upon signs and definitions."[3]

13    In contrast, the language of advertising is "coded." It exists in the context of our society. It is also carefully engineered and ruthlessly purposeful. When he wrote in the 1960s, Toffler estimated that the average adult was exposed to 560 advertising messages each day. Now, our homes are equipped with 400-channel, direct-broadcast satellite television, the Internet, video-streaming mobile devices, and other new forms of mass media. We're literally swimming in a sea of information. We're totally wired and wireless. We're overwhelmed by countless billboards in subway stations, stickers on light poles, 15-second spots on television, and an endless stream of spam and pop-up messages online.

## Demanding Attention

14 Among the hundreds of advertising messages in store for us each day, very few will actually command our conscious attention. The rest are screened out. The people who design and write ads know about this screening process; they anticipate and accept it as a premise of their business.

15    The classic, all-time favorite device used to breach the barrier is sex. There was a time, many years ago, when advertisers used some measure of subtlety and discretion in their application of sexual themes to their mass media work. No more. Sensuality has been replaced by in-your-face, unrestrained sexuality. One is about romance and connection; the other, physical connection and emotional distance.

16    A poster promotes clothing sold by the apparel company, French Connection group, United Kingdom: (FCUK). Large type tells us, "Apparently there are more important things in life than fashion. Yeah, right." This text is accompanied by a photo of two young people in what has become a standard set up: A boy. A girl. She is pretty, in a detached, vapid sort of way. He has not shaved for 48 hours. They are sharing physical space, but there is no sense of human contact or emotion. The company name appears on the lower right hand side of the poster. The headline is intended to be ironic: "Of course there are things that are more important than fashion, but right now, who cares?" The company maintains that they are "not trying to shock people." As absurd as it may seem, this is actually the truth. This company is not in the business of selling shock. They are selling clothes. They are making a lot of money selling clothes, because they know what motivates their teenaged customers—a desire to separate from their parents and declare their membership in the tribe of their peers.

17    Fortunately, advertisers use many other techniques to attract and hold the attention of the targeted consumer audience. The strategy may include strong creative execution, humor, or a plain, straightforward presentation of product features and customer benefits. Consider this random cross section of advertisements from popular media:

■ An ad for SalesForce.com used a photo of the Dalai Lama beneath the headline, "There is no software on the path to enlightenment." (What does this mean? "Salesforce.com provides computer services, so I won't have to buy software myself.")

■ An ad for Chevrolet HHR automobiles sports a headline, "We're innocent in every way like apple pie and Chevrolet—Mötley Crüe." (Another use of irony. Most

readers of Rolling Stone are unlikely to consider the band to be a paragon of innocence, and by extension, neither is the car.)

■ Some ads entertain us and are effective, even though they don't focus much on the
product. They work because we remember them. Geico is an automobile insurance
company, but they use angst-ridden cavemen and a cute little lizard—appropriately
enough, a Gecko—as characters in their ads.

■ Some ads tell us we have problems—real or imagined—that we'd better solve right
away. Do you have dry skin or "unsightly eyebrow hairs?" (Causing the hapless
reader to think, "I never really noticed, but now that they mention it. . . .").

18      Soft drink companies are in an advertising category of their own. In the archetypical
version of a soft drink TV spot, babies frolic with puppies in the sunlit foreground while
their youthful parents play touch football. On the porch, Grandma and Pops quietly smile
as they wait for all of this affection to transform the world into a place of warmth, harmony, and joy.

19      Dr. Pepper ads say "Be you!" and feature dancers prancing around singing songs
about "individuality." In Coke's ads, the singer Maya tells us this can of syrupy fizz is
"real." And Pepsi has Britney Spears singing "Pepsi: for those who think young!" The
message: If you are among the millions of people who see the commercial and buy the
product, you will become "different." You will find yourself transformed into a unique
("Be you," "individuality," "real"), hip ("young") person.[4]

20      These "slice of life" ads seduce us into feeling that if we drink the right combination
of sugar, preservatives, caramel coloring, and a few secret ingredients, we'll fulfill our
yearning for a world where folks from all nations, creeds, and sexual orientations live together in a state of perfect bliss. At least for the five minutes it takes to pour the stuff down
our parched, fast-food-filled throats. If you don't buy this version of the American Dream,
look around. You are sure to find a product that promises to help you gain prestige in whatever posse you do happen to run with.

21      When the connection is made, the results can be very powerful. Starbucks has proven
that a commodity product like coffee can be artfully changed from a mere beverage into an
emotional experience.

22      Ad campaigns and branding strategies do not often emerge like Botticelli's *Venus*
from the sea, flawless and fully grown. Most often, the creative strategy is developed only
after extensive research. "Who will be interested in our product? How old are they? Where
do they live? How much money do they earn? What problem will our product solve?" The
people at Starbucks did not decide to go to China on a whim. The people at French
Connection did not create their brand name simply to offend everyone who is old-
fashioned enough to think that some words don't belong on billboards, T-shirts, and store-
fronts.

## Involving

23 We have seen that the language of advertising is carefully engineered; we have discovered
a few of the devices it uses to get our attention. Coke and Pepsi have entranced us with visions of peace and love. An actress offers a winsome smile. Now that they have our attention,

advertisers present information intended to show us that their product fills a need and differs from the competition. Advertisers exploit and intensify product differences when they find them and invent them when they do not.

24    As soon as we see or hear an advertisement, our imagination is set in motion, and our individual fears and aspirations, quirks, and insecurities come out to play.

25    It was common not long ago for advertisers in the fashion industry to make use of gaunt, languid models. To some observers, these ads promoted "heroin chic." Perhaps only a few were substance abusers, but something was most certainly unusual about the models appearing in ads for Prada and Calvin Klein products. A young woman in a Prada ad projects no emotion whatsoever. Her posture suggests that she is in a trance or drug-induced stupor. In a Calvin Klein ad, a young man, like the woman from Prada, is gaunt beyond reason. He is shirtless. As if to draw more attention to his peculiar posture and "zero body fat" status, he is shown pinching the skin next to his navel. To some, this also suggests that he is preparing to insert a needle.

26    The fashion industry backed away from the heroin theme. Now the models look generally better fed. But they are, nonetheless, still lost in a world of ennui and isolation. In an ad by Andrew Mark NY, we see a young woman wearing little leather shorts. Her boyfriend's arm is wrapped around her, his thumb pushing ever-so-slightly below the waistband of her pants. What does he look like? He appears to be dazed. He is wearing jeans, an unzipped leather jacket. He hasn't shaved for a couple of days. We are left with the impression that either something has just happened here or is about to. It probably has something to do with sex.

27    Do these depictions of a decadent lifestyle exploit certain elements of our society—the young, insecure, or clueless? Or did these ads, and others of their ilk, simply reflect profound bad taste? Most advertising is about exploitation—the systematic, deliberate identification of our needs and wants, followed by the delivery of a carefully constructed promise that the product will satisfy them.

28    Advertisers make use of a variety of techniques and devices to engage us in the delivery of their messages. Some are subtle, making use of warm, entertaining, or comforting images or symbols. Others, as we've seen, are about as subtle as an action sequence from Quentin Tarantino's latest movie. Although it may seem hard to believe, advertising writers did not invent sex. They did not invent our tendency to admire and seek to identify ourselves with famous people. Once we have seen a famous person in an ad, we associate the product with the person. When we buy Coke, we're becoming a member of the Friends of Maya Club. The logic is faulty, but we fall for it just the same. Advertising works, not because Maya and Britney have discriminating taste, or the nameless waif in the clothing ad is a fashion diva, but because we participate in it.

## Keeping It Simple

29  Advertising language differs from other types of language in another important respect: it is simple by design. To measure the simplicity of an ad, calculate its Fog Index. Robert Gunning[5] developed this formula to determine the comparative ease with which any given piece of communication can be read. The resulting number is intended to correspond with grade level.

■ Calculate the number of words in an average sentence.

■ Count the number of words of three or more syllables in a typical 100-word passage, omitting words that are capitalized, combinations of two simple words, or verb forms made into three-syllable words by the addition of -ed or -es.

■ Add the two figures (the average number of words per sentence and the number of three-syllable words per 100 words), then multiply the result by .4.

30    Consider the text of this ad for Geico automobile insurance:

"The Gecko speaks out." (Headline)

"I love to entertain, but I'm here to save you money on car insurance. Get a FREE rate quote. 15 minutes could save you 15% or more." (Body copy)

1. Words per sentence:        10
2. Three syllable words/100:  2
3. Subtotal:                  12
4. Multiply by .4:            4.8

31    According to Gunning's scale, you should be able to comprehend this ad if you are just about to finish the 4th grade. Compare this to comic books, which typically weigh in at 6th grade level or *Atlantic Monthly*, at the 12th.

32    Why do advertisers favor simple language? The answer lies with the consumer. As a practical matter, we would not notice many of these messages if length or eloquence were counted among their virtues. Today's consumer cannot take the time to focus on anything for long, much less blatant advertising messages. Every aspect of modern life runs at an accelerated pace. Voice mail, text messaging, cellular phones, e-mail, the Internet—the world is always awake, always switched on, and hungry for more information. Time is dissected into increasingly smaller segments.

## Who Is Responsible?

33  Some critics view the advertising industry as a cranky, unwelcome child of commerce—a noisy, whining, brash truant who must somehow be kept in line but can't just yet be thrown out of the house. In reality, advertising mirrors the fears, quirks, and aspirations of the society that creates it (and is, in turn, sold by it). This alone exposes advertising to parody and ridicule. The overall level of acceptance and respect for advertising is also influenced by the varied quality of the ads themselves. Critics have declared advertising guilty of other failings as well:

1. Advertising encourages unhealthy habits.
2. Advertising feeds on human weaknesses and exaggerates the importance of material things, encouraging "impure" emotions and vanities.
3. Advertising sells daydreams—distracting, purposeless visions of lifestyles beyond the reach of the majority of the people who are most exposed to advertising.
4. Advertising warps our vision of reality, implanting in us groundless fears and insecurities.
5. Advertising downgrades the intelligence of the public.
6. Advertising debases English.
7. Advertising perpetuates racial and sexual stereotypes.

34      What can be said in advertising's defense? Does it encourage free-market competition and product innovation? Sure. But the real answer is simply this: Advertising is, at heart, only a reflection of society.

35      What can we say about the charge that advertising debases the intelligence of the public? Exactly how intelligent is "the public"? Sadly, evidence abounds that the public at large is not particularly intelligent after all. Americans now get 31 percent of their calories from junk food and alcoholic beverages.[6] Michael can't read. Jessica can't write. And the entire family spends the night in front of the television, watching people eat living insects in the latest installment of a "reality" show.

36      Ads are effective because they sell products. They would not succeed if they did not reflect the values and motivations of the real world. Advertising both reflects and shapes our perception of reality. Ivory Snow is pure. Federal Express won't let you down. Absolut is cool. Sasson is sexy. Mercedes represents quality. Our sense of what these brand names stand for may have as much to do with advertising as with the objective "truth."

37      Good, responsible advertising can serve as a positive influence for change, while fueling commerce. But the obverse is also true: Advertising, like any form of mass communication, can be a force for both "good" and "bad." It can just as readily reinforce or encourage irresponsible behavior, ageism, sexism, ethnocentrism, racism, homophobia, heterophobia—you name it—as it can encourage support for diversity and social progress.

38      As Pogo once famously said, "We have met the enemy, and he is us."[7]

NOTES

1.  Internet: http://www.joechemo.org.

2.  Pontifical Council for Social Communications, "Ethics in Advertising," published 2/22/97.

3.  Alvin Toffler, *Future Shock* (New York Random House, 1970) 146.

4.  Shannon O'Neill, a graduate student at the University of New Hampshire, contributed this example and others cited here.

5.  Curtis D. MacDougall, *Interpretive Reporting* (New York: Macmillan, 1968) 94.

6.  2000 study by the American Society for Clinical Nutrition (*Milwaukee Journal Sentinal,* 7/28/03).

7.  Walt Kelly, *Pogo* cartoon (1960s); referring to the Vietnam War.

## QUESTIONS FOR ANALYSIS AND DISCUSSION

1.  O'Neill opens his essay with a discussion of the controversial figure Joe Camel. What are your views on the Joe Camel controversy? Do you think the FTC and the former president were justified in expressing their concerns about the character? Should ads that target young people for products that are bad for them be outlawed? Explain.

2.  Do you think it is ethical for advertisers to create a sense of product difference when there really isn't any? Consider advertisements for products such as gasoline, beer, or coffee.

3.  In the last section of the essay, O'Neill anticipates potential objections to his defense of advertising. What are some of these objections? What effect does his anticipation of these objections have on the essay as a whole?

4.  O'Neill is an advertising professional. How does his writing style reflect the advertising techniques he describes? Cite examples to support your answer.

## Sample Ads and Study Questions

The following section features recently published magazine advertisements. Diverse in content and style, some ads use words to promote the product, while others depend on emotion, name recognition, visual appeal, or association. They present a variety of sales pitches and marketing techniques.

Corresponding to each ad is a list of questions to help you analyze how the ad works its appeal to promote a product. When studying the advertisements, approach each as a consumer, an artist, a social scientist, and a critic with an eye for detail.

**M&MS**

1. Who is featured in the picture? How does this ad play upon expectations already created by the product in past advertisements?
2. This ad is promoting a candy product. What connection, if any, do the characters have to the product? In your opinion, does the ad effectively market the product?
3. Who do you think is the target audience for this advertisement? How do you think a young adult would respond to it? a politician or government worker? a child? an older adult? Explain.
4. After viewing this ad, would you be more inclined to purchase the product it is advertising? Why or why not?
5. What do you need to know about pop culture to understand the ad and the characters depicted in it?

**PEOPLE IN NEED** ─────────────────────────────────────────

1. Examine this advertisement carefully. What is happening in this ad? What is being "sold"?
2. How do the desert setting and mountains and dry earth contribute to the image? Do these elements tap into audience expectations about what is happening in the ad? Are they confusing? eye-catching? Explain.
3. Would you know what this ad was "selling" if there were no company name mentioned in the ad? Explain.
4. If you were leafing through a magazine and saw this ad, would you stop to read it? Why or why not?
5. How does this ad make a point? What cultural and social issue does it raise? In your opinion, is it an effective way to raise awareness? money? Explain.

**FRIDAY MONKEY**

1. What is happening in this ad? How do the people in the ad "sell" the product? Does the product have any relationship to the people and what they are doing? Explain.
2. How would this ad be different if a woman were pictured in the center flanked by two men?
3. Who is the audience for this ad? How old do the women and man seem in the ad? How are they dressed? Does the ad appeal equally to men as well as women?
4. If you were leafing through a magazine and saw this ad, would you stop to examine it? Why or why not? In what sort of magazine would you expect to see this ad?
5. Review the tagline featured in the ad "Try everything once." What are the multiple interpretations of this line? Where does the tagline appear? Would the tagline work as well if it were placed in the upper left corner of the ad? Why or why not?

## UNITED COLORS OF BENETTON

1. Benetton is a clothing company. How does the image of the waterfowl connect with the product they sell? In your opinion, is this effective marketing? Why or why not?
2. What is the meaning of the red dot on the duck? Why is it there?
3. What is happening in this photo? Why do you think Benetton chose this photo to market their product line?
4. If you were reading a magazine or walking by a billboard and saw this ad, would you stop to look at it? Would the ad encourage you to buy Benetton clothing? Why or why not?

**TIDE**

1.  What is happening in this ad? What makes you stop and look at it? What happened first, and what will happen next?
2.  Who is the likely target audience for this ad? In what magazines would you expect to see it? Is it an effective ad? Explain.
3.  How does the tagline "Because stains love your clothes" connect with the product and what is happening in the ad?
4.  Would this ad be as effective if the coffee and shirt had their "mouths" closed rather than open? Explain.

**YOUR STRENGTH MAKES YOU UNIQUE.**
Don't be pressured, be yourself, don't let tobacco define you.

FREE YOURSELF  Tobacco Free Florida .com

## TOBACCO FREE FLORIDA

1. Would you know what this ad was promoting if the company name was not located at bottom-right section of the ad? Would there be any ambiguity about what was being "sold" in the advertisement? Explain.
2. Where would you expect to see an ad like this and why? If you were an advertising executive, where would you place this ad? How would you target your public? Explain.
3. This ad uses the tagline "YOUR STRENGTH MAKES YOU UNIQUE." How does the typeface work with the tagline and its message? Explain.
4. This ad promotes a nonprofit campaign that taps into teen's feeling of peer pressure to smoke. Visit the website www.tobaccofreeflorida.com/ that explains the project. After viewing the site and viewing some of the ads that comprise the campaign, explain why you think this ad and others on the site will or will not curtail teen smoking.

## WRITING ASSIGNMENTS

1. You are an advertising executive. Select one of the products featured in the sample ads section and write a new advertising campaign for it. Do you tap into popular consciousness? Do you use "weasel words"? How do you hook your audience, and how do you create a need for the product? Defend your campaign to your supervisors by explaining the motivation behind your creative decisions.

2. Write a paper in which you consider advertising strategies. Support your evaluation with examples of advertising campaigns with which you are familiar. Make an argument for or against particular campaigns. Are they appropriate? Do they exploit emotions? Are they opportunistic? You may draw support from the articles written by William Lutz, Rob Horning, and Charles A. O'Neill.

3. In his essay, William Lutz highlights some marketing ploys that he finds particularly annoying and ineffective. Identify some commercials or advertisements that especially annoyed you. Why exactly did they bother you? Try to locate any cultural, linguistic, social, or intellectual reasons behind your annoyance or distaste. How do these commercials compare to the marketing criticisms expressed in essays featured in this section?

4. Write an essay in which you explore the connection between social diversification, product targeting, and audience packaging. Explore some of the reasons why the "divide and conquer" method of marketing works, and if it is an ethical approach to advertising.

5. Teens and young adults covet certain brand-name clothing because they believe it promotes a particular image. What defines brand image? Is it something created by the company, or by the people who use the product? How does advertising influence the social view we hold of ourselves and the brands we use? Write an essay on the connection among advertising, image, and cultural values of what is "in," or popular, and what is not.

6. Robert Horning notes that the roots of materialism are deeply connected to human nature and our personal desire to express and define ourselves. If materialism is an important element of civilization, why do so many critics of consumerism imply that our desire for things is bad for our culture and our society?

7. *Adbusters* addresses the unethical ways advertisers manipulate consumers to "need" products. However, if we study ads long enough, we can determine for ourselves the ways we may be manipulated. Select several print or television advertisements and analyze how they manipulate consumers to increase their "quest for stuff." Is there anything wrong with this manipulation? Why or why not?

# 11

# Gender Matters

In the past century, we have witnessed enormous changes in the roles of women and men at home, in the workplace, and in society. Traditional ways of defining the self in terms of gender have been challenged and irrevocably altered. The essays in this chapter examine how these changes have affected men and women as they continue to redefine themselves, their relationships with each other, and their relationships with society.

Perceptions of gender begin at an early age, and it seems as if children face social and cultural pressures their parents' generation never experienced. Several essays in this chapter take a look at the way society influences our perceptions of gender and our expectations of ourselves and of the opposite sex. We live in a society obsessed with image—a society seemingly more driven by the cultivation of the body and how we clothe it than in personal achievement. In fact, so powerful is the influence of image that other terms of self-definition are difficult to identify. Men and women confront challenges related to body image and self-perception daily. From where does all the body-consciousness pressure come? Why are so many young people seemingly at war with their bodies? And how do cultural perceptions of beauty influence our view of what it means to be male or female?

Most college-age men and women were born after the "sexual revolution" and the feminist movements of the 1960s and 1970s. But it is these movements that have shaped the way men and women behave today and how they view themselves and each other, evaluate opportunity, and envision the future. Some people claim that things have become more complicated, and not for the better. Others take for granted a culture where a woman can pursue a business or medical career without facing tremendous obstacles, or a society in which a man staying at home to raise his children is considered normal. In addition to exploring cultural influences on gender, the chapter also addresses how feminism has—or has not—changed the way men and women perceive themselves and their role in the world.

## Saplings in the Storm
### *Mary Pipher*

With the onset of adolescence, children are faced with a multitude of gender-related issues. In addition to dealing with physical and emotional changes, many adolescents must try to adapt to shifting social roles. Changing social expectations can be overwhelming, says psychologist Mary Pipher, especially for girls. In this excerpt taken from the introduction to her best-selling book *Reviving Ophelia* (1995), Pipher's special area of interest is how American culture influences the mental health of its people. In this essay, she explains why she is concerned that girls may be losing their true selves in an effort to conform to what they believe society expects from them.*

## BEFORE YOU READ

Did the way you fit into your social groups change when you reached adolescence? If so, in what ways? What do you think accounts for such changes?

## AS YOU READ

According to Pipher, what social constraints do girls alone face with the onset of adolescence? Why do these cultural pressures exist?

1   When my cousin Polly was a girl, she was energy in motion. She danced, did cartwheels and splits, played football, basketball and baseball with the neighborhood boys, wrestled with my brothers, biked, climbed trees and rode horses. She was as lithe and as resilient as a willow branch and as unrestrained as a lion cub. Polly talked as much as she moved. She yelled out orders and advice, shrieked for joy when she won a bet or heard a good joke, laughed with her mouth wide open, argued with kids and grown-ups and insulted her foes in the language of a construction worker.

2   We formed the Marauders, a secret club that met over her garage. Polly was the Tom Sawyer of the club. She planned the initiations, led the spying expeditions and hikes to haunted houses. She showed us the rituals to become blood "brothers" and taught us card tricks and how to smoke.

3   Then Polly had her first period and started junior high. She tried to keep up her old ways, but she was called a tomboy and chided for not acting more ladylike. She was excluded by her boy pals and by the girls, who were moving into makeup and romances.

4   This left Polly confused and shaky. She had temper tantrums and withdrew from both the boys' and girls' groups. Later she quieted down and reentered as Becky Thatcher. She wore stylish clothes and watched from the sidelines as the boys acted and spoke. Once again she was accepted and popular. She glided smoothly through our small society. No one spoke of the changes or mourned the loss of our town's most dynamic citizen. I was the only one who felt that a tragedy had transpired.

5   Girls in what Freud called the latency period, roughly age six or seven through puberty, are anything but latent. I think of my daughter Sara during those years—performing chemistry experiments and magic tricks, playing her violin, starring in her own plays, rescuing wild animals and biking all over town. I think of her friend Tamara, who wrote a 300-page novel the summer of her sixth-grade year. I remember myself, reading every children's book in the library of my town. One week I planned to be a great doctor like Albert Schweitzer. The next week I wanted to write like Louisa May Alcott or dance in Paris like Isadora Duncan. I have never since had as much confidence or ambition.

*Mary Pipher, *Reviving Ophelia* (excerpt), 1995.

6    Most preadolescent girls are marvelous company because they are interested in everything—sports, nature, people, music and books. Almost all the heroines of girls' literature come from this age group—Anne of Green Gables, Heidi, Pippi Longstocking and Caddie Woodlawn. Girls this age bake pies, solve mysteries and go on quests. They can take care of themselves and are not yet burdened with caring for others. They have a brief respite from the female role and can be tomboys, a word that conveys courage, competency and irreverence.

7    They can be androgynous, having the ability to act adaptively in any situation regardless of gender role constraints. An androgynous person can comfort a baby or change a tire, cook a meal or chair a meeting. Research has shown that, since they are free to act without worrying if their behavior is feminine or masculine, androgynous adults are the most well-adjusted.

8    Girls between seven and eleven rarely come to therapy. They don't need it. I can count on my fingers the girls this age whom I have seen: Coreen, who was physically abused; Anna, whose parents were divorcing; and Brenda, whose father killed himself. These girls were courageous and resilient. Brenda said, "If my father didn't want to stick around, that's his loss." Coreen and Anna were angry, not with themselves, but rather at the grown-ups, whom they felt were making mistakes. It's amazing how little help these girls needed from me to heal and move on.

9    A horticulturist told me a revealing story. She led a tour of junior-high girls who were attending a math and science fair on her campus. She showed them side oats grama, bluestem, Indian grass and trees—redbud, maple, walnut and willow. The younger girls interrupted each other with their questions and tumbled forward to see, touch and smell everything. The older girls, the ninth-graders, were different. They hung back. They didn't touch plants or shout out questions. They stood primly to the side, looking bored and even a little disgusted by the enthusiasm of their younger classmates. My friend asked herself, What's happened to these girls? What's gone wrong? She told me, "I wanted to shake them, to say, 'Wake up, come back. Is anybody home at your house?'"

10    Recently I sat sunning on a bench outside my favorite ice-cream store. A mother and her teenage daughter stopped in front of me and waited for the light to change. I heard the mother say, "You have got to stop blackmailing your father and me. Every time you don't get what you want, you tell us that you want to run away from home or kill yourself. What's happened to you? You used to be able to handle not getting your way." The daughter stared straight ahead, barely acknowledging her mother's words. The light changed. I licked my ice-cream cone. Another mother approached the same light with her preadolescent daughter in tow. They were holding hands. The daughter said to her mother, "This is fun. Let's do this all afternoon."

11    Something dramatic happens to girls in early adolescence. Just as planes and ships disappear mysteriously into the Bermuda Triangle, so do the selves of girls go down in droves. They crash and burn in a social and developmental Bermuda Triangle. In early adolescence, studies show that girls' IQ scores drop and their math and science scores plummet. They lose their resiliency and optimism and become less curious and inclined to take risks. They lose their assertive, energetic and "tomboyish" personalities and become more deferential, self-critical and depressed. They report great unhappiness with their own bodies.

12    Psychology documents but does not explain the crashes. Girls who rushed to drink in experiences in enormous gulps sit quietly in the corner. Writers such as Sylvia Plath, Margaret Atwood and Olive Schreiner have described the wreckage. Diderot, in writing to his young friend Sophie Volland, described his observations harshly: "You all die at 15."

13    Fairy tales capture the essence of this phenomenon. Young women eat poisoned apples or prick their fingers with poisoned needles and fall asleep for a hundred years. They wander away from home, encounter great dangers, are rescued by princes and are transformed into passive and docile creatures.

14    The story of Ophelia, from Shakespeare's *Hamlet*, shows the destructive forces that affect young women. As a girl, Ophelia is happy and free, but with adolescence she loses herself. When she falls in love with Hamlet, she lives only for his approval. She has no inner direction; rather she struggles to meet the demands of Hamlet and her father. Her value is determined utterly by their approval. Ophelia is torn apart by her efforts to please. When Hamlet spurns her because she is an obedient daughter, she goes mad with grief. Dressed in elegant clothes that weigh her down, she drowns in a stream filled with flowers.

15    Girls know they are losing themselves. One girl said, "Everything good in me died in junior high." Wholeness is shattered by the chaos of adolescence. Girls become fragmented, their selves split into mysterious contradictions. They are sensitive and tenderhearted, mean and competitive, superficial and idealistic. They are confident in the morning and overwhelmed with anxiety by nightfall. They rush through their days with wild energy and then collapse into lethargy. They try on new roles every week—this week the good student, next week the delinquent and the next, the artist. And they expect their families to keep up with these changes.

16    My clients in early adolescence are elusive and slow to trust adults. They are easily offended by a glance, a clearing of the throat, a silence, a lack of sufficient enthusiasm or a sentence that doesn't meet their immediate needs. Their voices have gone underground—their speech is more tentative and less articulate. Their moods swing widely. One week they love their world and their families, the next they are critical of everyone. Much of their behavior is unreadable. Their problems are complicated and metaphorical—eating disorders, school phobias and self-inflicted injuries. I need to ask again and again in a dozen different ways, "What are you trying to tell me?"

17    Michelle, for example, was a beautiful, intelligent seventeen-year-old. Her mother brought her in after she became pregnant for the third time in three years. I tried to talk about why this was happening. She smiled a Mona Lisa smile to all my questions. "No, I don't care all that much for sex." "No, I didn't plan this. It just happened." When Michelle left a session, I felt like I'd been talking in the wrong language to someone far away.

18    Psychology has a long history of ignoring girls this age. Until recently adolescent girls haven't been studied by academics, and they have long baffled therapists. Because they are secretive with adults and full of contradictions, they are difficult to study. So much is happening internally that's not communicated on the surface.

19    Simone de Beauvoir believed adolescence is when girls realize that men have the power and that their only power comes from consenting to become submissive adored objects. They do not suffer from the penis envy Freud postulated, but from power envy.

20    She described the Bermuda Triangle this way: Girls who were the subjects of their own lives become the objects of other's lives. "Young girls slowly bury their childhood, put

away their independent and imperious selves and submissively enter adult existence." Adolescent girls experience a conflict between their autonomous selves and their need to be feminine, between their status as human beings and their vocation as females. De Beauvoir says, "Girls stop being and start seeming."

21    Girls become "female impersonators" who fit their whole selves into small, crowded spaces. Vibrant, confident girls become shy, doubting young women. Girls stop thinking, "Who am I? What do I want?" and start thinking, "What must I do to please others?" This gap between girls' true selves and cultural prescriptions for what is properly female creates enormous problems. To paraphrase a Stevie Smith poem about swimming in the sea, "they are not waving, they are drowning." And just when they most need help, they are unable to take their parents' hands.

22    This pressure disorients and depresses most girls. They sense the pressure to be someone they are not. They fight back, but they are fighting a "problem with no name." One girl put it this way: "I'm a perfectly good carrot that everyone is trying to turn into a rose. As a carrot, I have good color and a nice leafy top. When I'm carved into a rose, I turn brown and wither."

23    Adolescent girls are saplings in a hurricane. They are young and vulnerable trees that the winds blow with gale strength. Three factors make young women vulnerable to the hurricane. One is their developmental level. Everything is changing—body shape, hormones, skin and hair. Calmness is replaced by anxiety. Their way of thinking is changing. Far below the surface they are struggling with the most basic of human questions: What is my place in the universe, what is my meaning?

24    Second, American culture has always smacked girls on the head in early adolescence. This is when they move into a broader culture that is rife with girl-hurting "isms," such as sexism, capitalism and lookism, which is the evaluation of a person solely on the basis of appearance.

25    Third, American girls are expected to distance from parents just at the time when they most need their support. As they struggle with countless new pressures, they must relinquish the protection and closeness they've felt with their families in childhood. They turn to their none-too-constant peers for support.

26    Parents know only too well that something is happening to their daughters. Calm, considerate daughters grow moody, demanding and distant. Girls who loved to talk are sullen and secretive. Girls who liked to hug now bristle when touched. Mothers complain that they can do nothing right in the eyes of their daughters. Involved fathers bemoan their sudden banishment from their daughters' lives. But few parents realize how universal their experiences are. Their daughters are entering a new land, a dangerous place that parents can scarcely comprehend. Just when they most need a home base, they cut themselves loose without radio communications.

27    Most parents of adolescent girls have the goal of keeping their daughters safe while they grow up and explore the world. The parents' job is to protect. The daughters' job is to explore. Always these different tasks have created tension in parent-daughter relationships, but now it's even harder. Generally parents are more protective of their daughters than is corporate America. Parents aren't trying to make money off their daughters by selling them designer jeans or cigarettes, they just want them to be well adjusted. They don't see their daughters as sex objects or consumers but as real people with talents and interests.

But daughters turn away from their parents as they enter the new land. They befriend their peers, who are their fellow inhabitants of the strange country and who share a common language and set of customs. They often embrace the junk values of mass culture.

28    This turning away from parents is partly for developmental reasons. Early adolescence is a time of physical and psychological change, self-absorption, preoccupation with peer approval and identity formation. It's a time when girls focus inward on their own fascinating changes.

29    It's partly for cultural reasons. In America we define adulthood as a moving away from families into broader culture. Adolescence is the time for cutting bonds and breaking free. Adolescents may claim great independence from parents, but they are aware and ashamed of their parents' smallest deviation from the norm. They don't like to be seen with them and find their imperfections upsetting. A mother's haircut or a father's joke can ruin their day. Teenagers are furious at parents who say the wrong things or do not respond with perfect answers. Adolescents claim not to hear their parents, but with their friends they discuss endlessly all parental attitudes. With amazing acuity, they sense nuances, doubt, shades of ambiguity, discrepancy and hypocrisy.

30    Adolescents still have some of the magical thinking of childhood and believe that parents have the power to keep them safe and happy. They blame their parents for their misery, yet they make a point of not telling their parents how they think and feel; they have secrets, so things can get crazy. Most parents feel like failures during this time. They feel shut out, impotent and misunderstood. They often attribute the difficulties of this time to their daughters and their own failings. They don't understand that these problems go with the developmental stage, the culture and the times.

31    Parents experience an enormous sense of loss when their girls enter this new land. They miss the daughters who sang in the kitchen, who read them school papers, who accompanied them on fishing trips and to ball games. They miss the daughters who liked to bake cookies, play Pictionary and be kissed good-night. In place of their lively, affectionate daughters they have changelings—new girls who are sadder, angrier and more complicated. Everyone is grieving.

32    Fortunately adolescence is time-limited. By late high school most girls are stronger and the winds are dying down. Some of the worst problems—cliques, a total focus on looks and struggles with parents—are on the wane. But the way girls handle the problems of adolescence can have implications for their adult lives. Without some help, the loss of wholeness, self-confidence and self-direction can last well into adulthood. Many adult clients struggle with the same issues that overwhelmed them as adolescent girls. Thirty-year-old accountants and realtors, forty-year-old homemakers and doctors, and thirty-five-year-old nurses and schoolteachers ask the same questions and struggle with the same problems as their teenage daughters.

33    Even sadder are the women who are not struggling, who have forgotten that they have selves worth defending. They have repressed the pain of their adolescence, the betrayals of self in order to be pleasing. These women come to therapy with the goal of becoming even more pleasing to others. They come to lose weight, to save their marriages or to rescue their children. When I ask them about their own needs, they are confused by the question.

34    Women often know how everyone in their family thinks and feels except themselves. They are great at balancing the needs of their coworkers, husbands, children and friends,

but they forget to put themselves into the equation. They struggle with adolescent questions still unresolved: How important are looks and popularity? How do I care for myself and not be selfish? How can I be honest and still be loved? How can I achieve and not threaten others? How can I be sexual and not a sex object? How can I be responsive but not responsible for everyone?

35    Before I studied psychology, I studied cultural anthropology. I have always been interested in that place where culture and individual psychology intersect, in why cultures create certain personalities and not others, in how they pull for certain strengths in their members, in how certain talents are utilized while others atrophy from lack of attention. I'm interested in the role cultures play in the development of individual pathology.

36    For a student of culture and personality, adolescence is fascinating. It's an extraordinary time when individual, developmental and cultural factors combine in ways that shape adulthood. It's a time of marked internal development and massive cultural indoctrination.

37    An analysis of the culture cannot ignore individual differences in women. Some women blossom and grow under the most hostile conditions while others wither after the smallest storms. And yet we are more alike than different in the issues that face us. The important question is, Under what conditions do most young women flower and grow?

38    Adolescent clients intrigue me as they struggle to sort themselves out. But these last few years my office has been filled with girls—girls with eating disorders, alcohol problems, posttraumatic stress reactions to sexual or physical assaults, sexually transmitted diseases (STDs), self-inflicted injuries and strange phobias, and girls who have tried to kill themselves or run away. A health department survey showed that 40 percent of all girls in my midwestern city considered suicide last year. The Centers for Disease Control in Atlanta reports that the suicide rate among children age ten to fourteen rose 75 percent between 1979 and 1988. Something dramatic is happening to adolescent girls in America, something unnoticed by those not on the front lines.

39    At first I was surprised that girls were having more trouble now. After all, we have had a consciousness-raising women's movement since the sixties. Women are working in traditionally male professions and going out for sports. Some fathers help with the housework and child care. It seems that these changes would count for something. And of course they do, but in some ways the progress is confusing. The Equal Rights Amendment was not ratified, feminism is a pejorative term to many people and, while some women have high-powered jobs, most women work hard for low wages and do most of the "second shift" work. The lip service paid to equality makes the reality of discrimination even more confusing.

40    Many of the pressures girls have always faced are intensified in the 1990s. Many things contribute to this intensification: more divorced families, chemical addictions, casual sex and violence against women. Because of the media, which Clarence Page calls "electronic wallpaper," girls all live in one big town—a sleazy, dangerous tinsel town with lots of liquor stores and few protected spaces. Increasingly women have been sexualized and objectified, their bodies marketed to sell tractors and toothpaste. Soft-and hard-core pornography are everywhere. Sexual and physical assaults on girls are at an all-time high. Now girls are more vulnerable and fearful, more likely to have been traumatized and less free to roam about alone. This combination of old stresses and new is poison for our young women.

41    Parents have unprecedented stress as well. For the last half-century, parents worried about their sixteen-year-old daughters driving, but now, in a time of drive-by shootings and car-jackings, parents can be panicked. Parents have always worried about their daughters' sexual behavior, but now, in a time of date rapes, herpes and AIDS, they can be sex-phobic. Traditionally parents have wondered what their teens were doing, but now teens are much more likely to be doing things that can get them killed.

42    I am saying that girls are having more trouble now than they had thirty years ago, when I was a girl, and more trouble than even ten years ago. Something new is happening. Adolescence has always been hard, but it's harder now because of cultural changes in the last decade. The protected place in space and time that we once called childhood has grown shorter. There is an African saying, "It takes a village to raise a child." Most girls no longer have a village.

**QUESTIONS FOR ANALYSIS AND DISCUSSION**

1.  What does Pipher mean when she says that girls "disappear mysteriously into the Bermuda Triangle" in early adolescence? Why do you think she uses this analogy repeatedly?
2.  How do girls change with the onset of adolescence? To what extent are these changes physical and to what extent are they cultural? Do you think girls must make sacrifices to "fit in"? Explain.
3.  What is the benefit of androgyny to girls? Can the same benefits be applied to boys?
4.  Pipher's essay focuses on what happens to girls when they reach adolescence. Do you think she feels boys face similar issues? Do you think Pipher thinks society is harder on girls than on boys? Explain.
5.  Is audience important to the success of this essay? Why or why not? How could this essay apply to issues that face both men and women?
6.  Place Pipher's essay in different historical contexts. For example, do you think the problems she describes faced girls in the 1930s or the 1950s? Are the underlying social pressures facing teenage girls the same today? Explain.

# The Bully in the Mirror
*Stephen S. Hall*

The expression goes "vanity, thy name is woman," and most people think of body obsessive behavior as a female trait. Women still account for 90 percent of cosmetic surgical procedures, and roughly the same number is true for teenagers being treated for eating disorders. But boys are becoming just as obsessed with their bodies, say psychiatrists Harrison Pope, Katharine Phillips, and Roberto Olivardia. Their research reveals a disturbing trend—teenage boys are spending more time in the gym in quest of steroid-boosted buff bodies. This article, prepared by science writer Stephen S. Hall, describes how cultural messages reinforce this viewpoint, from the action heroes boys play with as children, to the images they view on television, to the peer pressure they receive at school. In America today, young men are constantly faced with "the bully in the mirror."*

**BEFORE YOU READ** ───────────────────────────

What is the "perfect" male physique? What does it look like? Is your image influenced by outside forces, such as the media, your gender, or your age? How do the real men you know compare to the image you have in your mind?

**AS YOU READ** ───────────────────────────

The young man featured in this article, Alexander, comments that people judge others on physical appearance. What do you want people to notice about you? How do your feelings compare to those Alexander expresses in this article?

1    On an insufferably muggy afternoon in July, with the thermometer pushing 90 degrees and ozone alerts filling the airwaves, Alexander Bregstein was in a foul mood. He was furious, in fact, for reasons that would become clear only later. Working on just three hours of sleep, and having spent the last eight hours minding a bunch of preschool kids in his summer job as a camp counselor, Alexander was itching to kick back and relax. So there he was, lying on his back in the weight room of his gym, head down on an incline bench, earphones pitching three-figure decibels of the rock band Finger Eleven into his ears as he gripped an 85-pound weight in each hand and then, after a brief pause to gather himself, muscled them into the air with focused bursts of energy. Each lift was accompanied by a sharp exhalation, like the quick, short stroke of a piston.

2    The first thing you need to know about Alexander is that he is 16 years old, bright, articulate and funny in that self-deprecating and almost wise teen-age way. However, about a year ago, Alexander made a conscious decision that those weren't the qualities he wanted people to recognize in him, at least not at first. He wanted people to see him first, and what they see these days are thick neck muscles, shoulders so massive that he can't scratch his back, a powerful bulge in his arms and a chest that has been deliberately chiseled for the two-button look—what Alexander now calls "my most endearing feature." He walks with a kind of cocky gravity-testing bounce in his step that derives in part from his muscular build but also from the confidence of knowing he looks good in his tank top and baggy shorts. As his spotter, Aaron Anavim, looked on, Alexander lifted the 85-pound weights three more times, arms quivering, face reddening with effort. Each dumbbell, I realized as I watched, weighed more than I did when I entered high school.

3    Another half-dozen teen-agers milled around the weight room, casting glances at themselves and one another in the mirror. They talked of looking "cut," with sharp definition to their muscles, and of developing "six-packs," crisp divisions of the abdominals, but of all the muscles that get a workout in rooms like these, the most important may be the ones that move the eyes in restless sweeping arcs of comparison and appraisal. "Once you're in

───────────────────────

*Stephen S. Hall, *New York Times*, August 22, 1999.

this game to manipulate your body," Alexander said, "you want to be the best," likening the friendly competition in the room to a form of "whipping out the ruler." While we talked between sets of Alexander's 90-minute routine, his eyes wandered to the mirror again and again, searching for flaws, looking for areas of improvement. "The more you lift," he admitted, "the more you look in the mirror."

4    In this weight room, in a gym in a northern New Jersey suburb, the gym rats have a nickname for Alexander: Mirror Boy. That's a vast improvement over the nicknames he endured at school not long ago. "I know it sounds kind of odd to have favorite insults," he told me with a wry smile, munching on a protein bar before moving on to his next set of lifts, "but Chunk Style always was kind of funny." And kind of appropriate. Until recently, Alexander carried nearly 210 pounds on a 5-foot-6 frame, and when I asked if he was teased about his weight, he practically dropped a dumbbell on my feet. "Oh! Oh, man, was I teased? Are you kidding?" he said in his rapid, agreeable patter. "When I was fat, people must have gone home and thought of nothing else except coming in with new material the next day. They must have had study groups just to make fun of people who were overweight." He even got an earful at home. "My parents—God bless them, but they would make comments all the time. My father would say, 'If you eat all that, you'll be as big as a house.' And I'm, like: 'Dad, it's a little late for that. What am I now? A mobile home?'"

5    The day of reckoning came during a spring-break vacation in Boca Raton, Fla. As his family was about to leave its hotel room to go to the beach, Alexander, then 15, stood in front of a mirror and just stared at the spectacle of his shirtless torso. "I remember the exact, like, moment in my mind," he said. "Everything about that room is burned into my head, every little thing. I can tell you where every lamp was, where my father was standing, my mother was sitting. We were about to go out, and I'm looking in this mirror—me, with my gut hanging over my bathing suit—and it was, like: Who would want to look at this? It's part of me, and I'm disgusted! That moment, I realized that nobody was giving me a chance to find out who I was because of the way I looked." And so Alexander decided to do something about it, something drastic.

6    There is a kind of timeless, archetypal trajectory to a teen-ager's battle with body image, but in most accounts the teen-ager is female and the issue is anorexia or bulimia. As any psychologist knows, however, and as any sufficiently evolved adult male could tell you, boys have body-image problems, too. Traditionally, they have felt pressure to look not thin, but rather strong and virile, which increasingly seems to mean looking bulked up and muscular, and that is why I was interested in talking to Alexander.

7    No one can quite cite any data, any scientific studies proving that things are different, but a number of psychologists with whom I spoke returned to the same point again and again: the cultural messages about an ideal male body, if not new, have grown more insistent, more aggressive, more widespread and more explicit in recent years.

8    Since roughly 90 percent of teen-agers who are treated for eating disorders are female, boys still have a way to go. Young girls have suffered greatly from insecurity about appearance and body image, and the scientific literature on anorexia and related body-image disorders depicts a widespread and serious health problem in adolescent females. But to hear some psychologists tell it, boys may be catching up in terms of insecurity and even psychological pathology. An avalanche of recent books on men and boys underlines the precarious nature of contemporary boyhood in America. A number of studies in the past decade—of men, not

boys—have suggested that "body-image disturbances," as researchers sometimes call them, may be more prevalent in men than previously believed and almost always begin in the teen-age years. Katharine Phillips, a psychiatrist at the Brown University School of Medicine, has specialized in "body dysmorphic disorder," a psychiatric illness in which patients become obsessively preoccupied with perceived flaws in their appearance—receding hairlines, facial imperfections, small penises, inadequate musculature. In a study of "30 cases of imagined ugliness," Phillips and colleagues described a surprisingly common condition in males whose symptoms include excessive checking of mirrors and attempts to camouflage imagined deformities, most often of the hair, nose and skin. The average age of onset, Phillips says, is 15.

9    Several years ago, Harrison G. Pope Jr., of Harvard Medical School, and his colleagues published a modest paper called "Muscle Dysmorphia: An Underrecognized Form of Body Dysmorphic Disorder" in a relatively obscure journal called *Psychosomatics*. The study described a group of men and women who had become "pathologically preoccupied" by their body image and were convinced that they looked small and puny, even though they were bulging with muscles. The paper got a lot of attention, and it led to an even more widely publicized study earlier this year from the same lab reporting how male action-figure toys like G.I. Joe and the "Star Wars" characters have bulked up over the years.

10    When you visit the office of Harrison (Skip) Pope, in a grim institutional building on the rolling grounds of McLean Hospital in Belmont, Mass., the first thing you notice are the calipers hanging on the wall—partly as *objets d'art*, but partly as a reminder that what we subjectively consider attractive can sometimes yield to objective measurement. Pope, after all, was one of the scientists who devised what might be called the Buff Equation, or: FFMI 5 W 3 (1 2 BF/100) 3 h 2 2 1 6.1 3 (1.8 2 H).

11    The formula is ostensibly used to calculate a person's Fat-free Mass Index; it has sniffed out presumed steroid use by Mr. America winners, professional bodybuilders and men whose unhealthy preoccupation with looking muscular has induced them to use drugs.

12    Pope is a wiry, compact psychiatrist who can squat 400 pounds in his spare time. ("You can reach me pretty much all day except from 11 A.M. to 2 P.M.," he told me, "when I'm at the gym.") I had gone to see him and his colleague Roberto Olivardia not only because they were the lead authors on the G.I. Joe study, but also because their studies of body-image disorders in slightly older postadolescent men may be the best indicator yet of where male body-image issues are headed.

13    Shortly after I arrived, Olivardia emptied a shopping bag full of male action dolls onto a coffee table in the office. The loot lay in a heap, a plastic orgy of superhero beefcake— three versions of G.I. Joe (Hasbro's original 1964 version plus two others) and one G.I. Joe Extreme, Luke Skywalker and Han Solo in their 1978 and later versions, Power Rangers, Batman, Superman, Iron Man and Wolverine from the X-Men. The inspiration for the whole study came from an adolescent girl. Pope's 13-year-old daughter, Courtney, was surfing the Web one night, working on a school project on how Barbie's body had radically changed over the years, and Pope thought to himself, there's got to be the male equivalent of that.

14    Once Pope and Olivardia gathered new and "vintage" action figures, they measured their waist, chest and biceps dimensions and projected them onto a 5-foot-10 male. Where the original G.I. Joe projected to a man of average height with a 32-inch waist, 44-inch chest and 12-inch biceps, the more recent figures have not only bulked up, but also show

much more definition. Batman has the equivalent of a 30-inch waist, 57-inch chest and 27-inch biceps. "If he was your height," Pope told me, holding up Wolverine, "he would have 32-inch biceps." Larger, that is, than any bodybuilder in history.

15    Now let it be said that measuring the styrene hamstrings of G.I. Joe does not represent 20th-century science at its most glorious. But Pope says it's a way to get at what he calls "evolving American cultural ideals of male body image." Those ideals, he maintains, create "cultural expectations" that may contribute to body-image disorders in men. "People misinterpreted our findings to assume that playing with toys, in and of itself, caused kids to develop into neurotic people as they grew up who abused anabolic steroids," Pope said. "Of course that was not our conclusion. We simply chose the toys because they were symptomatic of what we think is a much more general trend in our society."

16    Leaving such extreme pathology aside, the point remains that a boy's body image is shaped, if not determined, by the cruelest, most unforgiving and meanest group of judges imaginable: other boys. And even if you outgrow, physically and emotionally, the body image that oppressed you as an adolescent, it stays with you in adult life as a kind of subdermal emotional skin that can never be shed, only incorporated into the larger person you try to become.

17    It was during his sophomore year, getting "the daylights pounded out of him" in wrestling and gaining even more weight, that Alexander began what he calls, with justification, his "drastic transformation." He started by losing 30 pounds in one month. For a time, he consumed only 900 calories a day, and ultimately got down to 152 pounds. He began to lift weights seriously, every day for three months straight. He started to read magazines like *Flex* and *Men's Fitness*. He briefly dabbled with muscle-building supplements like creatine. He got buff, and then beyond buff.

18    By the time his junior year in high school began, Alexander had packaged his old self in a phenomenally new body, and it has had the desired effect. "My quality of social life changed dramatically when I changed my image," he said. He still maintained friendships with the guys in the computer lab, still programmed, still played Quake with dozens of others. But he worked out at the gym at least five times a week. He shifted his diet to heavy protein. He pushed himself to lift ever-heavier weights. Until an injury curtailed his season, he brought new strength to his wrestling. Still, he wasn't satisfied. When I asked him if he ever felt tempted to try steroids during his effort to remake his physical image, he denied using them, and I believe him. But he wasn't coy about the temptation.

19    "When someone offers you a shortcut," he replied, "and it's a shortcut you want so bad, you're willing to ignore what it might be doing to your insides. I wanted to look better. Who cares if it's going to clog up my kidneys? Who cares if it'll destroy my liver? There was so much peer pressure that I didn't care."

20    Alexander was especially pleased by the good shape he was in—although he didn't care for aerobics, his resting heart rate was low, he ran a mile under six minutes and seemed to have boundless energy. But fitness was only part of what he was after. As he put it: "No one's looking for a natural look, of being thin and in shape. It's more of looking toward a level beyond that." He added that "guys who work out, especially guys who have six-packs and are really cut up, are the ones girls go after."

21    To be honest, I was a little dubious about this until I spoke with an admittedly unscientific sampling of teen-age girls. It turned out that they not only agreed with the sentiment, but also spoke the same lingo. "If you're going swimming or something like that, girls like

the stomach best," said Elizabeth, a 14-year-old. "Girls like it if they have a six-pack, or if they're really ripped, as they say. That's the most important thing. And arms too."

22    "But not too much," added her friend Kate, also 14. "You don't like it if the muscles are too huge."

23    "It changes your perspective on them if they have a flabby stomach," Elizabeth continued. "And the chest is important too."

24    After Alexander finished his workout that hot July day, we stopped to get something to drink at the gym's cafe. "I feel pretty good right now," Alexander admitted, "and I was furious when I went in there." It turned out that the night before, he had a conversation with a girl that took a decidedly unsatisfying turn at the end.

25    At a time when the collective amount of American body fat is enough to stretch the jaws of Skip Pope's calipers from coast to coast, when so many adults amble about like fatted calves and so many children are little more than couch potatoes in training, it's hard to find fault with disciplined, drug-free efforts by teen-age boys to add a bit of muscle; weight lifting is not a sport with shortcuts, and it has become an essential adjunct to contemporary athletic performance. But there is a psychological side to all this heavy lifting that may be as unhealthy and undermining on the inside as it seems fit on the outside. And it resides not in that telltale mirror, but in how we see ourselves.

26    "I look in the mirror and I don't see what other people see," Alexander told me. "I look in the mirror, and I see my flaws. People go, 'Oh, you're narcissistic.' I go, 'No, I was looking at how uneven my pecs are,' although I know that in reality, they're, like, a nanometer off. And I have three friends who do exactly the same thing. They look and they go, 'Look how uneven I am, man!' And I go: 'What are you talking about! They look pretty even to me.' It's not narcissism—it's lack of self-esteem."

27    I'm not so worried about kids like Alexander—he clearly has demonstrated both the discipline to remake his appearance and the psychological distance not to take it, or himself, too seriously. But there will be many other boys out there who cannot hope to match the impossibly raised bar of idealized male body image without resorting to the physically corrosive effects of steroids or the psychologically corrosive effects of self-doubt. Either way, the majority of boys will be diminished by chasing after the golden few.

28    Moreover, this male preoccupation with appearance seems to herald a dubious, regressive form of equality—now boys can become as psychologically and physically debilitated by body-image concerns as girls have been for decades. After all, this vast expenditure of teen-age male energy, both psychic and kinetic, is based on the premise that members of the opposite sex are attracted to a retro, rough-hewn, muscular look, and it's a premise that psychologists who study boys have noticed, too. "While girls and women say one thing, some of them continue to do another," Pollack says. "Some of them are still intrigued by the old male images, and are attracted to them."

29    Because he's a perceptive kid, Alexander recognizes how feckless, how disturbing, how crazy this all is. "I tell you, it's definitely distressing," he said, "the fact that as much as girls get this anorexic thing and they're going through these image things with dolls and stuff, guys are definitely doing the same." True, he admitted, his social life has never been better. "But in a way it depresses me," he said, before heading off to a party, "that I had to do this for people to get to know me."

1.  Alexander states that he suffered from cruel comments about his weight for most of his life. Even his parents would make comments about his weight. What motivated Alexander to change his physique? Is it an extreme response, or a reasonable one? Does Alexander think he is better off now? Does Hall? Explain.

2.  Alexander comments that he had an epiphany in a hotel room when he was 15: "I realized that nobody was giving me a chance to find out who I was because of the way I looked." What is ironic about this statement? Is the "ripped" Alexander the real person? Explain.

3.  In your opinion, do the "jacked-up" muscles on action figures influence the way boys feel about their own bodies? If possible, go to a toy store or online and examine some of these figures. Do they reflect, as Pope claims, "evolving American cultural ideals of male body image"?

4.  What cultural messages tell boys that steroid use is permissible? Describe some of the ways children receive these messages.

5.  Analyze the author's use of statistics, facts, and supporting information to reinforce the points he makes in his essay. Do his conclusions seem reasonable based on the data he cites? Why or why not?

## Reading the Visual

### NEDA Ad and BOSS Ad

Adolescence can be a period of great self-consciousness and insecurity. Some young people—especially teenage girls—may suffer from eating disorders such as anorexia nervosa or bulimia due to distorted self-perception. The person they see in the mirror is drastically different from physical reality. In 2004, the National Eating Disorders Association (NEDA) launched the "Get Real" awareness campaign to portray how distorted the self-image of someone suffering from an eating disorder can be. The campaign ran ads in several fashion and popular magazines, including *InStyle* and *People*. This print ad was created for NEDA by Porter Novelli, a public relations firm known for health care promotional campaigns.

The second ad is for BOSS cologne, a popular men's fragrance. The ad, aimed at the youth market, implies that the wearer of this cologne is a desirable sex object wanted for his lean, muscled and athletically toned physique. Rather than depicting a normal male, the ad features an idealized Adonis-like man clearly excelling in the world of athletics.

## QUESTIONS FOR ANALYSIS AND DISCUSSION

1. These two ads are aimed at different genders. What does each ad assume about the viewer? How does each ad use social constructions of body image to promote its product? Explain.

2. What social and cultural influences could the BOSS ad have on young men? Do you think that men envision themselves to be like the man in the photograph if they use BOSS?

3. Both of these ads use untypical depictions of the body to get their point across. Evaluate how each tries to reach its audience and take action based on what viewers see.

4. If you were leafing through a magazine and saw either one of these ads, would you stop to read it or examine it? If so, why? What catches your eye?

5. What is happening in the NEDA photo? What is the young woman thinking? What does she see, and what do we, as the audience, see? Explain.

6. We have heard the expression "sex sells." How does sex "sell" BOSS cologne? Explain.

# What I Think About the Fashion World

*Liz Jones*

Are thin models part of a fashion conspiracy, or are they merely reflective of what the public wants to see? For many young women, the perfect beauty is defined by fashion models: tall, thin, long limbed, and with sculpted features. In a culture in which women are often measured by how they look, the pressure to be thin can be great. In this article, Liz Jones gives her perspective on the fashion industry's influence on female body image. Jones is the former editor of the British edition of *Marie Claire*, a women's fashion magazine. While editor of *Marie Claire*, she shocked the fashion world by featuring two covers, one featuring a thin Pamela Anderson and one with a voluptuous Sophie Dahl, then a size 12. Many fashion critics spoke out against Jones for using the magazine to "forward her own agenda," but consumers voted with their pocketbooks by buying more issues with the Dahl cover.*

## BEFORE YOU READ

Try to picture your version of the perfect female body. What does it look like? Is your image influenced by outside forces, such as the media, your gender, or your age? How do real women you know compare to the image in your mind?

## AS YOU READ

In your opinion, is the fashion industry's use of extremely thin models harmful? In your opinion, has mass media created unrealistic expectations of beauty? Explain.

1   For four weeks last month I sat in the front row of catwalk shows in London, Milan, Paris and New York watching painfully thin models walking up and down inches from my nose.

2   Kate Moss, the original "superwaif," was looking positively curvaceous compared to the current bunch of underweight teenagers.

3   For those used to the fashion industry there was nothing unusual about the shows at all. But for me it was the end; it was then that I decided to resign as editor of *Marie Claire* magazine.

4   I had reached the point where I had simply had enough of working in an industry that pretends to support women while it bombards them with impossible images of perfection day after day, undermining their self-confidence, their health and hard-earned cash.

5   My decision to quit was partly precipitated by the failure of a campaign I started a year ago to encourage magazines, designers and advertisers to use models with more realistic, representative body images. Then I could not have anticipated the extraordinarily hostile reaction to my fairly innocuous suggestions from fellow editors and designers. A year later

*Liz Jones, *YOU*, a supplement of *The London Daily Mail*, April 15, 2001.

I have come to realize the sheer terrorism of the fashion industry and accept that, alone, I cannot change things.

6    But in the spring last year I was full of optimism that we could change. I believed wholeheartedly that we could stop magazines and advertisers using underweight girls as fashion icons. I had already banned diets and slimming advice from our pages but after meeting Gisele, the Brazilian supermodel credited with bringing "curves to the catwalk," and discovering that she is a tiny size 8, I decided to challenge the status quo.

7    We decided to publish two covers for the same edition—one featuring Sophie Dahl, a size 12; the other, Pamela Anderson, a minute size 6—and we asked readers to choose between the skinny, cosmetically enhanced "perfection," or a more attainable, but still very beautiful curvy woman. Sophie Dahl won by an overwhelming majority.

8    But you would think that we had declared war. The reaction was staggering. Newspapers, radio and TV stations were largely behind us. They welcomed the opportunity to demystify the closed and cliquey world of fashion. Our covers were in the national press for weeks—even making headlines in the *New York Post*. I had requests from universities here and abroad wanting to include our experiment in their college courses. Documentaries were made in the U.S. and Germany. The response from readers was unprecedented. We received 4,000 letters in two weeks.

9    However, the very people from whom I had expected the most support—my fellow female editors—were unanimous in their disapproval.

10    I was invited to speak at the Body Image Summit set up by Tessa Jowell, Minister for Women, in June 2000 to debate the influence of media images on rising problems of anorexia and bulimia among women. One suggestion was that a group—consisting of editors, designers, young women readers and professionals who treat women with eating disorders—should get together on a regular basis to monitor the industry, bring in guidelines on using girls under a certain body size and weight and discuss ways the industry could evolve. My job was to gather these people: not one single other editor agreed to take part.

11    Instead most of them were hostile and aggressive. Jo Elvin, then editor of *New Woman*, accused *Marie Claire* of "discriminating against thin women." (As if there aren't enough role models in the media for thinness, from Jennifer Aniston to Gwyneth Paltrow to American supermodel Maggie Rizer.) Another fashion editor made the point that there had always been skinny women—look at Twiggy, for example. Jasper Conran absurdly suggested we should be looking at obesity as a serious health problem instead of anorexia and bulimia. I didn't bother to point out that people with obesity were not usually put on magazine covers as fashion icons.

12    The next day, after the summit, I received a fax, signed by nearly all the other editors of women's magazines and some model agencies, stating that they would not be following any initiative to expand the types of women featured in their magazines—one of the topics up for discussion at the summit was how to introduce more black and Asian women onto the pages of Britain's glossies.

13    When I read the list of names, I felt like giving up the fight there and then. I was isolated, sickened to my stomach that something so positive had been turned into a petty catfight by women I respected and admired. They were my peers, friends and colleagues I sat next to in the front row of the fashion shows. They were also the most important, influential group of women in the business, the only people who could change the fashion and beauty industry. Why were they so reluctant to even think about change?

14    Like me, they had sat at the summit while a group of teenage girls, black, Asian and white, some fat, some thin, had berated us all for what we were doing to their lives. I had found it moving to listen to these young women, brave enough to come and talk in front of all these scary high profile people. Anyway, to me, it made good business sense to listen to them and address their concerns: why alienate your readers? I could see those teenagers turning away from magazines because we seemed hopelessly outmoded, old fashioned, unattainable. But I was clearly alone.

15    The other editors seemed to revel in the chance to counter attack. Alexandra Shulman, editor of *Vogue*, denounced the whole campaign as a promotional tool for *Marie Claire* and said that suggestions of an agreement to set up a self-regulatory body within the industry was "totally out of order." Debbie Bee, then editor of *Nova*—a supposedly cutting edge fashion magazine for young women—asserted in her editorial the following month that magazines didn't cause anorexia as readers were intelligent enough to differentiate between an idealized model and real life.

16    Fiona McIntosh, editor of *Elle*, published a cover picture of Calista Flockhart with the caption, "I'm thin, so what?" She accused me of "betraying the editors' code." Frankly, I didn't even know there was a code; only one, surely, to put your readers first.

17    Some model agencies blacklisted the magazine. Storm, who represents Sophie Dahl and who you would have thought would have been happy that one of their models was being held up as an example of healthy gorgeousness, told us that we could no longer book any of their girls. Several publicists from Hollywood, reacting both to the cover and a feature called "Lollipop ladies" about women in Hollywood whose heads are too big for their tiny bodies, wrote to me saying their stars would not be gracing our covers.

18    I had clearly put my head too far above the parapet. I realized that far from being the influential trendsetters I had thought, magazine editors are more often ruled by fear—and advertisers. No one feels that they can afford to be different. They are happy to settle, instead, for free handbags and relentless glamour.

19    To be honest, it would have been very easy to give up then. Every time the contacts of a fashion shoot landed on my desk with a model whose ribs showed, whose bony shoulders and collar bone could have cut glass, whose legs were like sticks, we could have published them anyway and said, "Oh well, we tried." But we didn't. We threw them out, set up a reshoot, and eventually, slowly, agencies started to take us seriously and would only send girls with curves in all the right places.

20    I cannot deny the campaign got the magazine talked and written about. The choice of covers got the readers involved and made them have a little bit of power for a change; they got to choose who they wanted on the cover. The Sophie Dahl cover started to sell out, and readers would phone me, frantic, saying, "I could only buy the Pamela Anderson cover, but I want you to register my vote for Sophie." It could never have been a scientific exercise—subscribers to the magazine had to take pot luck; but still they would phone up saying, "No, I wanted Sophie!"

21    But I was dismayed by accusations that this was just another way to boost sales. I suffered from anorexia from the age of 11 until my late twenties and understand first hand the damaging effect of a daily diet of unrealistically tiny role models gracing the pages of the magazines that I was addicted to. Although it did not cause my illness, the images definitely perpetuated the hatred I had for my own body.

22    I agree with Debbie Bee of *Nova* that young women are intelligent enough to be able to tell the difference between a model and real life but the effects are often subliminal. One piece of research we did at *Marie Claire* was to ask a group of intelligent professional women about their bodies, then let them browse a selection of magazines for an hour, before asking them again. Their self-esteem had plummeted.

23    Never before have we been bombarded with so many images of perfection: more and more glossies on the shelves, web sites, digital satellite channels, more and more channels showing music videos 24 hours a day. New technology is also removing the images we see of women even further from reality. Just try finding a cover on the shelves this month where the star has not had her spots removed, the dark circles under her eyes eradicated, the wrinkles smoothed and her waist trimmed. It is common practice nowadays to "stretch" women whose legs aren't long enough. One men's magazine currently on the shelves, so the industry gossip has it, has put one star's head on another woman's body—apparently, her original breasts weren't "spherical enough."

24    So women have been conditioned to go to the gym and diet, or if they don't, to feel guilty about it, but that still won't achieve "cover girl" perfection because you can't be airbrushed in real life. I've seen the models close up: believe me, lots of them have varicose veins, spots, appendectomy scars and, yes, cellulite. Only the 16 year olds don't have fine lines.

25    So did I achieve anything with my campaign? I believe so. One newspaper conducted a survey of high street and designer shops and proved how women over size 12 were not being catered for. Stores are now providing a broader range of sizes.

26    In the subsequent issue, we published naked pictures of eight ordinary women, and asked readers to fill in a questionnaire telling us honestly how they feel about the women in the photographs, and about their own bodies. Interestingly, of the respondents so far, all the women say their boyfriends find the size 16 woman the most attractive. The results will be made into a Channel 4 documentary in the autumn.

27    In the next issue, my final edition as editor, we have on our cover three young women, all a size 12, curvy, imperfect, but very beautiful all the same. On the shoot, it was apparent that Suzanne, Myleene and Kym from Hear'Say were all happy in their own skin. For now. On the Popstars[1] program, Nasty Nigel had told the girls they should go on a diet. "Christmas is over," he said to Kym, "but the goose is still fat." How long before the girls start feeling paranoid about their bodies, under the constant pressure of fame, is anybody's guess.

28    In Britain an estimated 60,000 people, most of them young women, suffer from eating disorders while far greater numbers have an unhealthy relationship with food. Many of them take up smoking or eat diet pills to keep their weight below a certain level. Of all psychiatric disorders, anorexia has the most fatalities—it is very hard to recover from. I refuse to conform to an industry that could, literally, kill.

29    It's time for the industry—the photographers, the editors, the casting directors, designers and the advertisers—to wake up and allow women to just be themselves. From the phone calls and letters I received at *Marie Claire*, I know that women are fed up with feeling needlessly bad about their wobbly bits.

30    I only hope that my successor listens to them.

---

[1]The British equivalent to the television program "American Idol."

## QUESTIONS FOR ANALYSIS AND DISCUSSION

1. By running the two covers, Jones sought to discover whether women wanted perfection and aspiration or something more realistic and attainable. What did sales of the June 2000 cover reveal? Based on your own observations, how do you think American women would have reacted to the same experiment?
2. How did other fashion magazine editors react to Jones's *Marie Claire* covers? What do you think their reaction reveals about the fashion industry?
3. Debbie Bee of *Nova*, another British fashion magazine, argues that young women are "intelligent enough to be able to tell the difference between a model and real life." How does Jones test this theory? What does she discover?
4. Evaluate how well Jones supports her viewpoint in this essay. Does she provide supporting evidence? Is she biased? Does she provide a balanced perspective, or does she slant her data? Explain.
5. Jones is a former editor for a major fashion magazine. Does the fact that she held this position and was willing to risk her career for this issue influence your opinion of her essay or her points? Why or why not?

# Child-Man in the Promised Land
*Kay S. Hymowitz*

Many social critics agree that adolescence has been extended. Only forty years ago, many men and women were married and starting families by the time they were 24 years old. Today, however, the average age of marriage and family has been bumped back, in some cases *way* back. Today's single young men hang out in a hormonal limbo between adolescence and adulthood argues writer and social critic Kay S. Hymowitz. Men are in no hurry to grow up, and the trend has some interesting consequences.*

## BEFORE YOU READ

Why are young adults waiting longer than ever to get married and have children? What are your own plans for marriage and family? For life five to ten years after graduation?

## AS YOU READ

Is Hymowitz supportive or critical of "Child-Man" she describes? Identify areas in her essay that reveal her point of view on this topic.

1 It's 1965 and you're a 26-year-old white guy. You have a factory job, or maybe you work for an insurance broker. Either way, you're married, probably have been for a few years now; you met your wife in high school, where she was in your sister's class.

*Kay S. Hymowitz, *City Journal*, Winter 2008.

You've already got one kid, with another on the way. For now, you're renting an apartment in your parents' two-family house, but you're saving up for a three-bedroom ranch house in the next town. Yup, you're an adult!

2       Now meet the twenty-first-century you, also 26. You've finished college and work in a cubicle in a large Chicago financial-services firm. You live in an apartment with a few single guy friends. In your spare time, you play basketball with your buddies, download the latest indie songs from iTunes, have some fun with the Xbox 360, take a leisurely shower, massage some product into your hair and face—and then it's off to bars and parties, where you meet, and often bed, girls of widely varied hues and sizes. They come from everywhere: California, Tokyo, Alaska, Australia. Wife? Kids? House? Are you *kidding*?

3       Not so long ago, the average mid-twentysomething had achieved most of adulthood's milestones—high school degree, financial independence, marriage, and children. These days, he lingers—happily—in a new hybrid state of semi-hormonal adolescence and responsible self-reliance. Decades in unfolding, this limbo may not seem like news to many, but in fact it is to the early twenty-first century what adolescence was to the early twentieth: a momentous sociological development of profound economic and cultural import. Some call this new period "emerging adulthood," others "extended adolescence"; David Brooks recently took a stab with the "Odyssey Years," a "decade of wandering."

4       But while we grapple with the name, it's time to state what is now obvious to legions of frustrated young women: the limbo doesn't bring out the best in young men. With women, you could argue that adulthood is in fact emergent. Single women in their twenties and early thirties are joining an international New Girl Order, hyperachieving in both school and an increasingly female-friendly workplace, while packing leisure hours with shopping, traveling, and dining with friends [see "The New Girl Order," Autumn 2007]. Single Young Males, or SYMs, by contrast, often seem to hang out in a playground of drinking, hooking up, playing *Halo 3*, and, in many cases, underachieving. With them, adulthood looks as though it's receding.

5       Freud famously asked: "What do women want?" Notice that he didn't ask what men wanted—perhaps he thought that he'd figured that one out. But that's a question that ad people, media execs, and cultural entrepreneurs have pondered a lot in recent years. They're particularly interested in single young men, for two reasons: there are a lot more of them than before; and they tend to have some extra change. Consider: in 1970, 69 percent of 25-year-old and 85 percent of 30-year-old white men were married; in 2000, only 33 percent and 58 percent were, respectively. And the percentage of young guys tying the knot is declining as you read this. Census Bureau data show that the median age of marriage among men rose from 26.8 in 2000 to 27.5 in 2006—a dramatic demographic shift for such a short time period.

6       That adds up to tens of millions more young men blissfully free of mortgages, wives, and child-care bills. Historically, marketers have found this group an "elusive audience"— the phrase is permanently affixed to "men between 18 and 34" in adspeak—largely immune to the pleasures of magazines and television, as well as to shopping expeditions for the products advertised there. But by the mid-1990s, as SYM ranks swelled, marketers began to get their number. One signal moment came in April 1997, when *Maxim*, a popular British "lad magazine," hit American shores. *Maxim* strove to be the anti-*Playboy*-and-*Esquire*; bad-boy owner Felix Dennis sniffed at celebrity publishers with their tired formulas.

Instead, he later observed, the magazine's creators adopted the "astonishing methodology of asking our readers what they wanted . . . and then supplying it."

7   And what did those readers—male, unmarried, median age 26, median household income $60,000 or so—want? As the philosophers would say, duh. *Maxim* plastered covers and features with pouty-lipped, tousled-haired pinups in lacy underwear and, in case that didn't do the trick, block-lettered promises of sex! lust! naughty! And it worked. More than any men's magazine before or since, *Maxim* grabbed that elusive 18- to 34-year-old single-college-educated-guy market, and soon boasted about 2.5 million readers—more than *GQ, Esquire,* and *Men's Journal* combined.

8   Victoria's Secret cover art doesn't fully explain the SYM's attraction to *Maxim.* After all, plenty of down-market venues had the sort of bodacious covers bound to trigger the young male's reptilian brain. No, what set *Maxim* apart from other men's mags was its voice. It was the sound of guys hanging around the Animal House living room—where put-downs are high-fived; gadgets are cool; rock stars, sports heroes, and cyborg battles are awesome; jobs and Joni Mitchell suck; and babes are simply hot—or not. "Are there any cool jobs related to beer?" a reader's letter asks in a recent issue. Answer: brand manager, beer tester, and brewmaster.

9   *Maxim* asked the SYM what he wanted and learned that he didn't want to grow up. Whatever else you might say about *Playboy* or *Esquire,* they tried to project the image of a cultured and au courant fellow; as Hefner famously—and from today's cultural vantage point, risibly—wrote in an early *Playboy,* his ideal reader enjoyed "inviting a female acquaintance in for a quiet discussion of Picasso, Nietzsche, jazz, sex." Hearing this, the *Maxim* dude would want to hurl. He'd like to forget that he ever went to school.

10   *Maxim* happily obliges. The editors try to keep readers' minds from wandering with articles like "Confessions of a Strip Club Bouncer." But they rely heavily on picture-laden features promoting the latest skateboards, video games, camcorders, and other tech products, along with an occasional Q-and-A with, say, Kid Rock—all with the bare minimum of print required to distinguish a magazine from a shopping catalog or pinup calendar. *Playboy's* philosophy may not have been Aristotle, but it was an attempt, of sorts, to define the good life. The *Maxim* reader prefers lists, which make up in brevity what they lose in thought: "Ten Greatest Video Game Heroes of All Time," "The Five Unsexiest Women Alive," "Sixteen People Who Look Like They Absolutely Reek," and so on.

11   Still, *Maxim* is far from dumb, as its self-mockery proves. The *Maxim* child-man prides himself on his lack of pretense, his unapologetic guyness. The magazine's subtext seems to be: "We're just a bunch of horny, insensitive guys—so what?" What else to make of an article entitled "How to Make Your Girlfriend Think Her Cat's Death Was an Accident"? "The only thing worse than a show about doctors is a show about sappy chick doctors we're forced to watch or else our girlfriends won't have sex with us," the editors grumble about the popular (with women) *Grey's Anatomy.*

12   The *Maxim* child-man voice has gone mainstream, which may explain why the magazine's sales were flat enough for Dennis to sell it last summer. You're that 26-year-old who wants sophomoric fun and macho action? Now the culture has a groaning table of entertainment with your name on it. Start with the many movies available in every guy-friendly genre: sci-fi flicks like *Transformers,* action and crime movies like *American Gangster,* comedies like *Superbad,* and the seemingly endless line of films starring Adam Sandler,

Jim Carrey, and the "Frat Pack," as *USA Today* dubbed the group of young male comedians that includes Will Ferrell, Ben Stiller, Vince Vaughn, Owen and Luke Wilson, Jack Black, and Steve Carell.

13      With a talent for crude physical comedy, gleeful juvenility, and self-humiliation, the Frat Packers are the child-man counterparts to the more conventional leads, like George Clooney and Brad Pitt, whom women and Esquire editors love. In *Old School* (2003), three guys in their thirties decide to start a college fraternity. Frank the Tank (the moniker refers to his capacity for alcohol), played by Ferrell, flashes his saggy white derriere streaking through the college town; the scene is a child-man classic. In 2005's *The 40-Year-Old Virgin*, Carell plays a middle-aged nerd with a large action-figure collection but no action. In one guy-favorite scene, a beautician painfully waxes Carell's hirsute chest; as Carell pointed out later, this was a "guy thing, this sadistic nature that men have to see other men in non-life-threatening pain."

14      Even though the networks must be more restrained, television also has plenty of "stupid fun" (as *Maxim* calls a regular feature), gross-out humor, and even low-level sadism for child-man viewers. This state of affairs is newer than you might think. Apart from sports programming and *The Simpsons*, which came along in the early 1990s, there wasn't a lot to make young men pick up the remote. Most prime-time television appealed to women and families, whose sensibilities were as alien to dudes as finger bowls.

15      Today, the child-man can find entire networks devoted to his interests: Spike TV runs wrestling matches, *Star Trek* reruns, and the high-tech detective drama *CSI*; Blackbelt TV broadcasts martial arts around the clock; sci-fi is everywhere. Several years ago, the Cartoon Network spied the potential in the child-man market, too, and introduced Adult Swim, late-night programming with "adult" cartoons like *Family Guy* and *Futurama*, a cult favorite co-created by Matt Groening of *The Simpsons* fame. Adult Swim has cut into the male Letterman and Leno audience, luring gold-plated advertisers Saab, Apple, and Taco Bell; child-men, it should come as no surprise, eat lots of fast food.

16      One can also lay the success of cable giant Comedy Central at the child-man's sneakered foot. In its early-nineties infancy, Comedy Central had old movie comedies, some stand-up acts, and few viewers. The next several years brought some buzz with shows like *Politically Incorrect.* But it was in 1997—the same year that *Maxim* arrived in America—that the network struck gold with a cartoon series starring a group of foul-mouthed eight-year-old boys. With its cutting subversion of all that's sacred and polite, *South Park* was like a dog whistle that only SYMs could hear; the show became the highest-rated cable series in that age group.

17      In 1999, the network followed up with *The Man Show*, famous for its "Juggies" (half-naked women with exceptionally large, well, juggies), interviews with porn stars, drinking songs, and a jingle that advised, "Quit your job and light a fart / Yank your favorite private part." It was "like *Maxim* for TV," one network executive told Media Life. Comedy Central's viewers, almost two-thirds of them male, have made both *The Daily Show* and *The Colbert Report* cultural touchstones and launched the careers of stars like Bill Maher, Jimmy Kimmel, Dave Chapelle, and, most notably, Daily Show anchor Jon Stewart—who has already hosted the Academy Awards and is set to do so again, a perfect symbol of the mainstreaming of the SYM sensibility.

18      Nothing attests more to the SYM's growing economic and cultural might than video games do. Once upon a time, video games were for little boys and girls—well, mostly little

boys—who loved their Nintendos so much, the lament went, that they no longer played ball outside. Those boys have grown up to become child-man gamers, turning a niche industry into a $12 billion powerhouse. Men between the ages of 18 and 34 are now the biggest gamers; according to Nielsen Media, almost half—48.2 percent—of American males in that age bracket had used a console during the last quarter of 2006, and did so, on average, *two hours and 43 minutes per day.* (That's 13 minutes longer than 12- to 17-year-olds, who evidently have more responsibilities than today's twentysomethings.) Gaming—online games, as well as news and information about games—often registers as the top category in monthly surveys of Internet usage.

19    And the child-man's home sweet media home is the Internet, where no meddling censors or nervous advertisers deflect his desires. Some sites, like MensNewsDaily.com, are edgy news providers. Others, like AskMen.com, which claims 5 million visitors a month, post articles like "How to Score a Green Chick" in the best spirit of *Maxim*-style self-parody. "How is an SUV-driving, to-go-cup-using, walking environmental catastrophe like yourself supposed to hook up with them?" the article asks. Answer: Go to environmental meetings, yoga, or progressive bookstores ("but watch out for lesbians").

20    Other sites, like MenAreBetterThanWomen.com, TuckerMax.com, TheBestPageIn TheUniverse.com, and DrunkasaurusRex.com, walk *Maxim's* goofiness and good-natured woman-teasing over the line into nastiness. The men hanging out on these sites take pride in being "badasses" and view the other half bitterly. A misogynist is a "man who hates women as much as women hate each other," writes one poster at MenAreBetterThanWomen. Another rails about "classic woman 'trap' questions—Does this make me look fat? Which one of my friends would you sleep with if you had to? Do you really enjoy strip clubs?" The Fifth Amendment was created because its architects' wives "drove them ape-shit asking questions that they'd be better off simply refusing to answer."

21    That sound you hear is women not laughing. Oh, some women get a kick out of child-men and their frat/fart jokes; about 20 percent of *Maxim* readers are female, for instance, and presumably not all are doing research for the dating scene. But for many of the fairer sex, the child-man is either an irritating mystery or a source of heartbreak. In Internet chat rooms, in advice columns, at female water-cooler confabs, and in the pages of chick lit, the words "immature" and "men" seem united in perpetuity. Women complain about the "Peter Pan syndrome"—the phrase has been around since the early 1980s but it is resurgent—the "Mr. Not Readys," and the "Mr. Maybes." *Sex and the City* chronicled the frustrations of four thirtysomething women with immature, loutish, and uncommitted men for six popular seasons.

22    Naturally, women wonder: How did this perverse creature come to be? The most prevalent theory comes from feminist-influenced academics and cultural critics, who view dude media as symptoms of backlash, a masculinity crisis. Men feel threatened by female empowerment, these thinkers argue, and in their anxiety, they cling to outdated roles. The hyper-masculinity of *Maxim* et al. doesn't reflect any genuine male proclivities; rather, retrograde media "construct" it.

23    The fact that guys cheer on female heroines like Buffy the Vampire Slayer as much as they do Chuck Norris tells against this theory somewhat. But there's an ounce of truth to it. The men of the new media are in backlash mode, largely because they believe that feminists have stood in their way as media gatekeepers—that is, agents, editors, producers, and

the like—who don't understand or accept "men acting like men." They gleefully stick their thumbs in the eyes of politically correct tsk-tskers. In one *South Park* episode, the Sexual Harassment Panda, a mascot who teaches schoolkids the evils of sexual harassment, is fired after his little talks provoke a flood of inane lawsuits. In *Maxim*, readers can find articles like "How to Cure a Feminist," one of whose recommendations is to "pretend you share her beliefs" by asking questions like, "Has Gloria Steinem's marriage hurt the feminist agenda?"

24    Insofar as the new guy media reflect a backlash against feminism, they're part of the much larger story of men's long, uneasy relationship with bourgeois order. The SYM with a taste for *Maxim* or *South Park* may not like Gloria Steinem, but neither does he care for anyone who tells him to behave—teachers, nutritionists, prohibitionists, vegetarians, librarians, church ladies, counselors, and moralists of all stripes. In fact, men have always sought out an antisocial, even anarchic, edge in their popular culture. In a renowned essay, the critic Barbara Ehrenreich argued that the arrival of *Playboy* in 1953 represented the beginning of a male rebellion against the conformity of mid-century family life and of middle-class virtues like duty and self-discipline. "All woman wants is security," she quotes an early *Playboy* article complaining. "And she is perfectly willing to crush man's adventurous freedom-loving spirit to get it." Even the name of the magazine, Ehrenreich observed, "defied the convention of hard-won maturity."

25    Ehrenreich was right about the seditious impulse behind *Playboy*, but wrong about its novelty. Male resistance to bourgeois domesticity had been going on since the bourgeoisie went domestic. In *A Man's Place*, historian John Tosh locates the rebellion's roots in the early nineteenth century, when middle-class expectations for men began to shift away from the patriarchal aloofness of the bad old days. Under the newer bourgeois regime, the home was to be a haven in a heartless world, in which affection and intimacy were guiding virtues. But in Tosh's telling, it didn't take long before men vented frustrations with bourgeois domestication: they went looking for excitement and male camaraderie in empire building, in adventure novels by authors like Robert Louis Stevenson, and in going to "the club."

26    By the early twentieth century, the emerging mass market in the U.S. offered new outlets for the virile urges that sat awkwardly in the bourgeois parlor; hence titles like *Field and Stream* and *Man's Adventure*, as well as steamier fare like *Escapade* and *Caper*. When television sets came on the market in the late 1940s, it was the airing of heavyweight fights and football games that led Dad to make the big purchase; to this day, sports events—the battlefield made civilized—glue him to the Barcalounger when he should be folding the laundry.

27    But this history suggests an uncomfortable fact about the new SYM: he's immature because he can be. We can argue endlessly about whether "masculinity" is natural or constructed—whether men are innately promiscuous, restless, and slobby, or socialized to be that way—but there's no denying the lesson of today's media marketplace: give young men a choice between serious drama on the one hand, and Victoria's Secret models, battling cyborgs, exploding toilets, and the NFL on the other, and it's the models, cyborgs, toilets, and football by a mile. For whatever reason, adolescence appears to be the young man's default state, proving what anthropologists have discovered in cultures everywhere: it is marriage and children that turn boys into men. Now that the SYM can put off family into the hazily distant future, he can—and will—try to stay a child-man. Yesterday's paterfamilias or

Levittown dad may have sought to escape the duties of manhood through fantasies of adventures at sea, pinups, or sublimated war on the football field, but there was considerable social pressure for him to be a mensch. Not only is no one asking that today's twenty- or thirtysomething become a responsible husband and father—that is, grow up—but a freewheeling marketplace gives him everything that he needs to settle down in pig's heaven indefinitely.

28      And that heaven can get pretty piggish. Take Tucker Max, whose eponymous website is a great favorite among his peers. In a previous age, Max would have been what was known as a "catch." Good-looking, ambitious, he graduated from the University of Chicago and Duke Law. But in a universe where child-men can thrive, he has found it more to his liking—and remarkably easy—to pursue a different career path: professional "asshole." Max writes what he claims are "true stories about my nights out acting like an average twentysomething"—binge drinking (UrbanDictionary.com lists Tucker Max Drunk, or TMD, as a synonym for "falling down drunk"), fighting, leaving vomit and fecal detritus for others to clean up, and, above all, hooking up with "random" girls galore—sorority sisters, Vegas waitresses, Dallas lap dancers, and Junior Leaguers who're into erotic asphyxiation.

29      Throughout his adventures, Max—like a toddler stuck somewhere around the oedipal stage—remains fixated on his penis and his "dumps." He is utterly without conscience— "Female insecurity: it's the gift that keeps on giving," he writes about his efforts to undermine his prey's self-esteem in order to seduce them more easily. Think of Max as the final spawn of an aging and chromosomally challenged Hugh Hefner, and his website and bestselling book, *I Hope They Serve Beer in Hell,* as evidence of a male culture in profound decline. *Playboy*'s aspirations toward refinement still hinted at the call of the ego and a culture with limits on male restiveness; Max, the child-man who answers to no one except his fellow "assholes," is all id—and proud of it.

30      Now, you could argue that the motley crew of *Maxim*, Comedy Central, *Halo 3*, and even the noxious Tucker Max aren't much to worry about, and that extended adolescence is what the word implies: a temporary stage. Most guys have lots of other things going on, and even those who spend too much time on TuckerMax.com will eventually settle down. Men know the difference between entertainment and real life. At any rate, like gravity, growing up happens; nature has rules.

31      That's certainly a hope driving the sharpest of recent child-man entertainments, Judd Apatow's hit movie *Knocked Up*. What sets *Knocked Up* apart from, say, *Old School*, is that it invites the audience to enjoy the SYM's immaturity—his T-and-A obsessions, his slobby indolence—even while insisting on its feebleness. The potheaded 23-year-old Ben Stone accidentally impregnates Alison, a gorgeous stranger he was lucky enough to score at a bar. He is clueless about what to do when she decides to have the baby, not because he's a "badass"—actually, he has a big heart—but because he dwells among social retards. His roommates spend their time squabbling about who farted on whose pillow and when to launch their porn website. His father is useless, too: "I've been divorced three times," he tells Ben when his son asks for advice about his predicament. "Why are you asking me?" In the end, though, Ben understands that he needs to grow up. He gets a job and an apartment, and learns to love Alison and the baby. This is a comedy, after all.

32      It is also a fairy tale for guys. You wouldn't know how to become an adult even if you wanted to? Maybe a beautiful princess will come along and show you. But the important

question that Apatow's comedy deals with only obliquely is what extended living as a child-man does to a guy—and to the women he collides with along the way.

33    For the problem with child-men is that they're not very promising husbands and fathers. They suffer from a proverbial "fear of commitment," another way of saying that they can't stand to think of themselves as permanently attached to one woman. Sure, they have girlfriends; many are even willing to move in with them. But cohabiting can be just another Peter Pan delaying tactic. Women tend to see cohabiting as a potential path to marriage; men view it as another place to hang out or, as Barbara Dafoe Whitehead observes in *Why There Are No Good Men Left*, a way to "get the benefits of a wife without shouldering the reciprocal obligations of a husband."

34    Even men who do marry don't easily overcome child-manhood. Neal Pollack speaks for some of them in his 2007 memoir *Alternadad*. Pollack struggles with how to stay "hip"—smoking pot and going to rock concerts—once he becomes a father to Elijah, "the new roommate," as he calls him. Pollack makes peace with fatherhood because he finds that he can introduce his toddler to the best alternative bands, and also because he has so many opportunities to exercise the child-man's fascination with "poop." He is affectingly mad for his little boy. Yet his efforts to turn his son into a hip little Neal Pollack—"My son and I were moshing! Awesome!"—reflect the self-involvement of the child-man who resists others' claims on him.

35    *Knocked Up* evokes a more destructive self-involvement in a subplot involving Alison's miserably married sister Debbie and her husband, Pete, the father of her two little girls. Pete, who frequently disappears to play fantasy baseball, get high in Las Vegas, or just go to the movies on his own, chronically wields irony to distance himself from his family. "Care more!" his wife yells at him. "You're cool because you don't give a shit."

36    And that "coolness" points to what may be the deepest existential problem with the child-man—a tendency to avoid not just marriage but any deep attachments. This is British writer Nick Hornby's central insight in his novel *About a Boy*. The book's antihero, Will, is an SYM whose life is as empty of passion as of responsibility. He has no self apart from pop-culture effluvia, a fact that the author symbolizes by having the jobless 36-year-old live off the residuals of a popular Christmas song written by his late father. Hornby shows how the media-saturated limbo of contemporary guyhood makes it easy to fill your days without actually doing anything. "Sixty years ago, all the things Will relied on to get him through the day simply didn't exist," Hornby writes. "There was no daytime TV, there were no videos, there were no glossy magazines. . . . Now, though, it was easy [to do nothing]. There was almost too much to do."

37    Will's unemployment is part of a more general passionlessness. To pick up women, for instance, he pretends to have a son and joins a single-parent organization; the plight of the single mothers means nothing to him. For Will, women are simply fleshy devices that dispense sex, and sex is just another form of entertainment, a "fantastic carnal alternative to drink, drugs, and a great night out, but nothing much more than that."

38    As the title of his 2005 novel *Indecision* suggests, Benjamin Kunkel also shows how apathy infects the new SYM world. His hero, 28-year-old Dwight Wilmerding, suffers from "abulia"—chronic indecisiveness—so severe that he finds himself para-

lyzed by the Thanksgiving choices of turkey, cranberry sauce, and dressing. His parents are divorced, his most recent girlfriend has faded away, and he has lost his job. Like Will, Dwight is a quintessential slacker, unable to commit and unwilling to feel. The only woman he has loved is his sister, who explains the attraction: "I'm the one girl you actually got to know in the right way. It was gradual, it was inevitable." Like Hornby, Kunkel sees the easy availability of sex as a source of slacker apathy. In a world of serial relationships, SYMs "fail to sublimate their libidinal energies in the way that actually makes men attractive," Kunkel told a dismayed female interviewer in *Salon*. With no one to challenge them to deeper connections, they swim across life's surfaces.

39    The superficiality, indolence, and passionlessness evoked in Hornby's and Kunkel's novels haven't triggered any kind of cultural transformation. Kunkel's book briefly made a few regional bestseller lists, and Hornby sells well enough. But sales of "lad lit," as some call books with SYM heroes, can't hold a candle to those of its chick-lit counterpart. The SYM doesn't read much, remember, and he certainly doesn't read anything prescribing personal transformation. The child-man may be into self-mockery; self-reflection is something else entirely.

40    That's too bad. Men are "more unfinished as people," Kunkel has neatly observed. Young men especially need a culture that can help them define worthy aspirations. Adults don't emerge. They're made.

41    What messages do these magazines project about women, and how do they influence men's personal identities and how they relate to the opposite sex?

QUESTIONS FOR ANALYSIS AND DISCUSSION ──────────

1.  According to Hymowitz, what does the popularity of men's magazines such as *Maxim* and *FHM* reveal about men and masculinity today? Why are these magazines so popular? Do you think they would have found a market if they had been introduced 20 or 30 years ago? Why or why not?

2.  Evaluate Hymowitz's comparison of a man from 1965 and a man today. What differences exist? Why does she think things have not changed for the better? Do you agree? Explain.

3.  Hymowitz noted that psychologist Sigmund Freud famously asked, "What do women want?" Based on your personal experience and information provided in this essay, answer this question from your own perspective. If you are male, what do you think women want? If you are female, what do you think men want?

4.  How are men's magazines, television media, the Internet and the movie industry influencing men's personal self-image and how they relate to women, personal responsibility, and the world today? Explain.

5.  Based on the detail provided in this essay, provide a definition of the modern "child-man" in America today.

6.  What are the social and cultural implications of the "child-man" ethic? How could it affect both men and women today, and for the next generation? Explain.

# In the Combat Zone

*Leslie Marmon Silko*

Safety experts warn women not to walk alone at night, to park where it is well-lit, and to avoid areas that could conceal muggers or rapists. Self-defense classes for women stress avoidance tactics rather than ways to confront violence actively. This approach, says the Native American best-selling author Leslie Marmon Silko, creates a cultural consciousness of women as victims and targets. In this essay, Silko relates how her childhood hunting experiences helped empower her in a society that tends to view women as prey.*

## BEFORE YOU READ

Have you ever found yourself planning your activities based on personal safety? For example, did you do without something because you were afraid of going to the store at night by yourself? Or have you skipped taking a shortcut when it was dark out? If not, why don't you fear these situations?

## AS YOU READ

Note Silko's references to hunting throughout the essay. How does the theme of hunting unify the piece?

1    Women seldom discuss our wariness or the precautions we take after dark each time we leave the apartment, car, or office to go on the most brief errand. We take for granted that we are targeted as easy prey by muggers, rapists, and serial killers. This is our lot as women in the United States. We try to avoid going anywhere alone after dark, although economic necessity sends women out night after night. We do what must be done, but always we are alert, on guard and ready. We have to be aware of persons walking on the sidewalk behind us; we have to pay attention to others who board an elevator we're on. We try to avoid all staircases and deserted parking garages when we are alone. Constant vigilance requires considerable energy and concentration seldom required of men.

2    I used to assume that most men were aware of this fact of women's lives, but I was wrong. They may notice our reluctance to drive at night to the convenience store alone, but they don't know or don't want to know the experience of a woman out alone at night. Men who have been in combat know the feeling of being a predator's target, but it is difficult for men to admit that we women live our entire lives in a combat zone. Men have the power to end violence against women in the home, but they feel helpless to protect women from violent strangers. Because men feel guilt and anger at their inability to shoulder responsibility for the safety of their wives, sisters, and daughters, we don't often discuss random acts of violence against women.

---

*Leslie Marmon Silko, *In the Combat Zone*, 1996.

3    When we were children, my sisters and I used to go to Albuquerque with my father. Sometimes strangers would tell my father it was too bad that he had three girls and no sons. My father, who has always preferred the company of women, used to reply that he was glad to have girls and not boys, because he might not get along as well with boys. Furthermore, he'd say, "My girls can do anything your boys can do, and my girls can do it better." He had in mind, of course, shooting and hunting.

4    When I was six years old, my father took me along as he hunted deer; he showed me how to walk quietly, to move along and then to stop and listen carefully before taking another step. A year later, he traded a pistol for a little single shot .22 rifle just my size. He took me and my younger sisters down to the dump by the river and taught us how to shoot. We rummaged through the trash for bottles and glass jars; it was great fun to take aim at a pickle jar and watch it shatter. If the Rio San Jose had water running in it, we threw bottles for moving targets in the muddy current. My father told us that a .22 bullet can travel a mile, so we had to be careful where we aimed. The river was a good place because it was below the villages and away from the houses; the high clay riverbanks wouldn't let any bullets stray. Gun safety was drilled into us. We were cautioned about other children whose parents might not teach them properly; if we ever saw another child with a gun, we knew to get away. Guns were not toys. My father did not approve of BB guns because they were classified as toys. I had a .22 rifle when I was seven years old. If I felt like shooting, all I had to do was tell my parents where I was going, take my rifle and a box of 12 shells and go. I was never tempted to shoot at birds or animals because whatever was killed had to be eaten. Now, I realize how odd this must seem; a seven-year-old with a little .22 rifle and a box of ammunition, target shooting alone at the river. But that was how people lived at Laguna when I was growing up; children were given responsibility from an early age.

5    Laguna Pueblo people hunted deer for winter meat. When I was thirteen I carried George Pearl's saddle carbine, a .30–30, and hunted deer for the first time. When I was fourteen, I killed my first mule deer buck with one shot through the heart.

6    Guns were for target shooting and guns were for hunting, but also I knew that Grandma Lily carried a little purse gun with her whenever she drove alone to Albuquerque or Los Lunas. One night my mother and my grandmother were driving the fifty miles from Albuquerque to Laguna down Route 66 when three men in a car tried to force my grandmother's car off the highway. Route 66 was not so heavily traveled as Interstate 40 is now, and there were many long stretches of highway where no other car passed for minutes on end. Payrolls at the Jackpile Uranium Mine were large in the 1950s, and my mother or my grandmother had to bring home thousands from the bank in Albuquerque to cash the miners' checks on paydays.

7    After that night, my father bought my mother a pink nickel-plated snub-nose .22 revolver with a white bone grip. Grandma Lily carried a tiny Beretta as black as her prayer book. As my sisters and I got older, my father taught us to handle and shoot handguns, revolvers mostly, because back then, semiautomatic pistols were not as reliable—they frequently jammed. I will never forget the day my father told us three girls that we never had to let a man hit us or terrorize us because no matter how big and strong the man was, a gun in our hand equalized all differences of size and strength.

8    Much has been written about violence in the home and spousal abuse. I wish to focus instead on violence from strangers toward women because this form of violence terrifies

women more, despite the fact that most women are murdered by a spouse, relative, fellow employee, or next-door neighbor, not a stranger. Domestic violence kills many more women and children than strangers kill, but domestic violence also follows more predictable patterns and is more familiar—he comes home drunk and she knows what comes next. A good deal of the terror of a stranger's attack comes from its suddenness and unexpectedness. Attacks by strangers occur with enough frequency that battered women and children often cite their fears of such attacks as reasons for remaining in abusive domestic situations. They fear the violence they imagine strangers will inflict upon them more than they fear the abusive home. More than one feminist has pointed out that rapists and serial killers help keep the patriarchy in place.

9      An individual woman may be terrorized by her spouse, but women are not sufficiently terrorized that we avoid marriage. Yet many women I know, including myself, try to avoid going outside of their homes alone after dark. Big deal, you say; well yes, it is a big deal since most lectures, performances, and films are presented at night; so are dinners and other social events. Women out alone at night who are assaulted by strangers are put on trial by public opinion: Any woman out alone after dark is asking for trouble. Presently, for millions of women of all socioeconomic backgrounds, sundown is lockdown. We are prisoners of violent strangers.

10     Daylight doesn't necessarily make the streets safe for women. In the early 1980s, a rapist operated in Tucson in the afternoon near the University of Arizona campus. He often accosted two women at once, forced them into residential alleys, then raped each one with a knife to her throat and forced the other to watch. Afterward the women said that part of the horror of their attack was that all around them, everything appeared normal. They could see people inside their houses and cars going down the street—all around them life was going on as usual while their lives were being changed forever.

11     The afternoon rapist was not the only rapist in Tucson at that time; there was the prime-time rapist, the potbellied rapist, and the apologetic rapist all operating in Tucson in the 1980s. The prime-time rapist was actually two men who invaded comfortable foothills homes during television prime time when residents were preoccupied with television and eating dinner. The prime-time rapists terrorized entire families; they raped the women and sometimes they raped the men. Family members were forced to go to automatic bank machines, to bring back cash to end the ordeal. Potbelly rapist and apologetic rapist need little comment, except to note that the apologetic rapist was good looking, well educated, and smart enough to break out of jail for one last rape followed by profuse apologies and his capture in the University of Arizona library. Local papers recounted details about Tucson's last notorious rapist, the red bandanna rapist. In the late 1970s this rapist attacked more than twenty women over a three-year period, and Tucson police were powerless to stop him. Then one night, the rapist broke into a midtown home where the lone resident, a woman, shot him four times in the chest with a .38 caliber revolver.

12     In midtown Tucson, on a weekday afternoon, I was driving down Campbell Avenue to the pet store. Suddenly the vehicle behind me began to weave into my lane, so I beeped the horn politely. The vehicle swerved back to its lane, but then in my rearview mirror I saw the small late-model truck change lanes and begin to follow my car very closely. I drove a few blocks without looking in the rearview mirror, but in my sideview mirror I saw the compact truck was right behind me. OK. Some motorists stay upset for two or three blocks, some require ten

blocks or more to recover their senses. Stoplight after stoplight, when I glanced into the rearview mirror I saw the man—in his early thirties, tall, white, brown hair, and dark glasses. This guy must not have a job if he has the time to follow me for miles—oh, ohhh! No beast more dangerous in the U.S.A. than an unemployed white man.

13    At this point I had to make a decision: do I forget about the trip to the pet store and head for the police station downtown, four miles away? Why should I have to let this stranger dictate my schedule for the afternoon? The man might dare to follow me to the police station, but by the time I reach the front door of the station, he'd be gone. No crime was committed; no Arizona law forbids tailgating someone for miles or for turning into a parking lot behind them. What could the police do? I had no license plate number to report because Arizona requires only one license plate, on the rear bumper of the vehicle. Anyway, I was within a block of the pet store where I knew I could get help from the pet store owners. I would feel better about this incident if it was not allowed to ruin my trip to the pet store.

14    The guy was right on my rear bumper; if I'd had to stop suddenly for any reason, there'd have been a collision. I decide I will not stop even if he does ram into the rear of my car. I study this guy's face in my rearview mirror, six feet two inches tall, 175 pounds, medium complexion, short hair, trimmed moustache. He thinks he can intimidate me because I am a woman, five feet five inches tall, 140 pounds. But I am not afraid, I am furious. I refuse to be intimidated. I won't play his game. I can tell by the face I see in the mirror this guy has done this before; he enjoys using his truck to menace lone women.

15    I keep thinking he will quit, or he will figure that he's scared me enough; but he seems to sense that I am not afraid. It's true. I am not afraid because years ago my father taught my sisters and me that we did not have to be afraid. He'll give up when I turn into the parking lot outside the pet store, I think. But I watch in my rearview mirror; he's right on my rear bumper. As his truck turns into the parking lot behind my car, I reach over and open the glove compartment. I take out the holster with my .38 special and lay it on the car seat beside me.

16    I turned my car into a parking spot so quickly that I was facing my stalker who had momentarily stopped his truck and was watching me. I slid the .38 out of its holster onto my lap. I watched the stranger's face, trying to determine whether he would jump out of his truck with a baseball bat or gun and come after me. I felt calm. No pounding heart or rapid breathing. My early experience deer hunting had prepared me well. I did not panic because I felt I could stop him if he tried to harm me. I was in no hurry. I sat in the car and waited to see what choice my stalker would make. I looked directly at him without fear because I had my .38 and I was ready to use it. The expression on my face must have been unfamiliar to him; he was used to seeing terror in the eyes of the women he followed. The expression on my face communicated a warning: if he approached the car window, I'd kill him.

17    He took a last look at me and then sped away. I stayed in the car until his truck disappeared in the traffic of Campbell Avenue.

18    I walked into the pet store shaken. I had felt able to protect myself throughout the incident, but it left me emotionally drained and exhausted. The stranger had only pursued me—how much worse to be battered or raped.

19    Years before, I was unarmed the afternoon that two drunken deer hunters threatened to shoot me off my horse with razor-edged hunting crossbows. I was riding a colt on a national

park trail near my home in the Tucson Mountains. These young white men in their late twenties were complete strangers who might have shot me if the colt had not galloped away erratically bucking and leaping—a moving target too difficult for the drunken bow hunters to aim at. The colt brought me to my ranch house where I called the county sheriff's office and the park ranger. I live in a sparsely populated area where my nearest neighbor is a quarter-mile away. I was afraid the men might have followed me back to my house so I took the .44 magnum out from under my pillow and strapped it around my waist until the sheriff or park ranger arrived. Forty-five minutes later, the park ranger arrived—the deputy sheriff arrived fifteen minutes after him. The drunken bow hunters were apprehended on the national park and arrested for illegally hunting; their bows and arrows were seized as evidence for the duration of bow hunting season. In southern Arizona that is enough punishment; I didn't want to take a chance of stirring up additional animosity with these men because I lived alone then; I chose not to make a complaint about their threatening words and gestures. I did not feel that I backed away by not pressing charges; I feared that if I pressed assault charges against these men, they would feel that I was challenging them to all-out war. I did not want to have to kill either of them if they came after me, as I thought they might. With my marksmanship and my .243 caliber hunting rifle from the old days, I am confident that I could stop idiots like these. But to have to take the life of another person is a terrible experience I will always try to avoid.

20     It isn't height or weight or strength that make women easy targets; from infancy women are taught to be self-sacrificing, passive victims. I was taught differently. Women have the right to protect themselves from death or bodily harm. By becoming strong and potentially lethal individuals, women destroy the fantasy that we are sitting ducks for predatory strangers.

21     In a great many cultures, women are taught to depend upon others, not themselves, for protection from bodily harm. Women are not taught to defend themselves from strangers because fathers and husbands fear the consequences themselves. In the United States, women depend upon the courts and the police; but as many women have learned the hard way, the police cannot be outside your house twenty-four hours a day. I don't want more police. More police on the street will not protect women. A few policemen are rapists and killers of women themselves; their uniforms and squad cars give them an advantage. No, I will be responsible for my own safety, thank you.

22     Women need to decide who has the primary responsibility for the health and safety of their bodies. We don't trust the State to manage our reproductive organs, yet most of us blindly trust that the State will protect us (and our reproductive organs) from predatory strangers. One look at the rape and murder statistics for women (excluding domestic incidents) and it is clear that the government FAILS to protect women from the violence of strangers. Some may cry out for a "stronger" State, more police, mandatory sentences, and swifter executions. Over the years we have seen the U.S. prison population become the largest in the world, executions take place every week now, inner-city communities are occupied by the National Guard, and people of color are harassed by police, but guess what? A woman out alone, night or day, is confronted with more danger of random violence from strangers than ever before. As the U.S. economy continues "to downsize," and the good jobs disappear forever, our urban and rural landscapes will include more desperate, angry men with nothing to lose.

23    Only women can put a stop to the "open season" on women by strangers. Women are TAUGHT to be easy targets by their mothers, aunts, and grandmothers who themselves were taught that "a women doesn't kill" or "a woman doesn't learn how to use a weapon." Women must learn how to take aggressive action individually, apart from the police and the courts. . . . Those who object to firearms need trained companion dogs or collectives of six or more women to escort one another day and night. We must destroy the myth that women are born to be easy targets.

## QUESTIONS FOR ANALYSIS AND DISCUSSION

1. Why, according to Silko, do women live in a state of fear? What measures must they take to prevent personal harm? What effect does this mentality have on society as a whole?

2. How does a gun equalize the differences between men and women? Do you agree with Silko's father's comment that she and her sisters should never be afraid because a gun "equalized all differences of size and strength" (paragraph 7)?

3. Silko points out that "more than one feminist has pointed out that rapists and serial killers help keep the patriarchy in place" (paragraph 8). How do acts of violence against women maintain the "patriarchy"? What is the patriarchy?

4. Crime experts say that most rapes are motivated by a desire for power and not really for sex. Apply this fact to the rapists Silko describes in paragraphs 10 and 11.

5. In paragraph 21, Silko comments that in many cultures, "women are not taught to defend themselves from strangers because fathers and husbands fear the consequences themselves." What does she mean? Does this statement apply to American society? Explain.

6. How does Silko's story of her trip to the pet store support her argument? Explain.

7. Throughout the essay, Silko makes references to hunting. Explore the multi-faceted levels of this hunting theme.

# Where the Boys Aren't
## *Melana Zyla Vickers*

Before the 1970s, most college campuses—with the exception of women's colleges—were dominated by men. In 1972, Title IX, now known as the Patsy T. Mink Equal Opportunity in Education Act, ensured that "No person in the United States shall, on the basis of sex, be excluded from participation in, be denied the benefits of, or be subjected to discrimination under any education program or activity receiving Federal financial assistance." This act allowed women equal access to a college education. By the 1980s, a noticeable gender shift rippled through college campuses across the country. More women were enrolling in college than men. Where have the boys gone? In the next essay, columnist Melana Zyla Vickers explores the new gender gap on college campuses.*

What is the ratio of male to female students at your institution and in your classroom? Is it fairly equal? Do you notice a "gender gap" on campus?

Before Title IX, women could be excluded from college enrollment merely because they were female. Has a form of reverse gender discrimination emerged on college campuses? Can Title IX be applied in reverse to balance the gender distribution on campus?

1   Here's a thought that's unlikely to occur to twelfth-grade girls as their college acceptances begin to trickle in: After they get to campus in the fall, one in four of them will be mathematically unable to find a male peer to go out with.

2   At colleges across the country, 58 women will enroll as freshmen for every 42 men. And as the class of 2010 proceeds toward graduation, the male numbers will dwindle. Because more men than women drop out, the ratio after four years will be 60-40, according to projections by the Department of Education.

3   The problem isn't new—women bachelor's degree-earners first outstripped men in 1982. But the gap, which remained modest for some time, is widening. More and more girls are graduating from high school and following through on their college ambitions, while boys are failing to keep pace and, by some measures, losing ground.

4   Underperformance in education is no longer a problem confined to black males, Hispanic males, or even poor whites. In 2004, the nation's middle-income, white undergraduate population was 57 percent female. Even among white undergraduates with family incomes of $70,000 and higher, the balance tipped in 2000 to 52 percent female. And white boys are the only demographic group whose high school dropout rate has risen since 2000. Maine, a predominantly white state, is at 60-40 in college enrollment and is quickly reaching beyond it. There are now more female master's degree-earners than male, and in 10 years there will be more new female Ph.D.s, according to government projections. American colleges from Brown to Berkeley face a man shortage, and there's no end in sight.

5   Yet few alarm bells are ringing. In the early 1970s, when the college demographics were roughly reversed at 43 percent female and 57 percent male, federal education laws were reformed with the enactment in 1972 of Title IX, a provision that requires numerical parity for women in various areas of federally funded schooling. Feminist groups pushed the Equal Rights Amendment through the House and Senate. Universities opened women's studies departments. And the United Nations declared 1975 the International Year of the Woman. The problem was structural, feminists never tired of repeating: A system built by men, for men, was blocking women's way.

*Melana Zyla Vickers, *The Weekly Standard*, January 2, 2006.

6    Today's shortage of men, by contrast, is largely ignored, denied, or covered up. Talk to university administrators, and few will admit that the imbalance is a problem, let alone that they're addressing it. Consider the view of Stephen Farmer, director of undergraduate admissions at the University of North Carolina-Chapel Hill, where this year's enrollment is only 41.6 percent male. "We really have made no attempt to balance the class. We are gender blind in applications, very scrupulously so."

7    Why the blind devotion to gender-blindness? Because affirmative action for men is politically incorrect. And at universities receiving federal funding like UNC, it's also illegal. "My understanding of Title IX is that an admissions process that advantages men would be very difficult to defend," Farmer says.

8    The recent history at the University of Georgia, with its male enrollment of 42 percent, explains the situation further. In 2001, a federal appeals court struck down the university's use of gender and race criteria to try to boost its black, male numbers in undergraduate admissions. Three white women sued the school after being rejected, arguing they'd have gotten into the University of Georgia if they had been black men. The appeals court agreed with a lower court's finding that the admissions process in place at the time violated Title VI (race equity) and Title IX (gender equity) by "intentionally discriminating against them based on race and gender."

9    It didn't even take a court ruling to cause Brandeis University, which is 46 percent male, to abandon its lame effort to attract more men. A few years ago it offered free baseball caps to the first 500 male undergraduate applicants. Brandeis's new dean of admissions, Gil Villanueva, says "things were looking pretty low on the male end and so people said let's give it a shot and see what happens." Evidently not much—the promotion was never repeated. Says Villanueva, "We have no special recruitment plan for males. We are very much gender blind." He says the administrators won't worry about the gender balance unless "all of a sudden our applicant pool is 75 percent female."

10    Boston University, 40.8 percent male at the undergraduate level, shows even less official concern. The imbalance is a national trend that begins with fewer men graduating from high school and applying to college, says spokesman Colin Riley. "We can't do something about the pool if they're not applying."

11    BU's position wasn't always so passive. In the mid-'90s, then-president John Silber sought to take a few small steps to address the shortfall of males. He told staff that BU's publicity materials ought to be gender-neutral, and that an ROTC publicity photo showing a woman ought to show a man, because ROTC at the university was predominantly male. Asked this month about Silber's minor intervention, university spokesman Riley tried to downplay it, saying "most places would be impressed" to have a woman in the ROTC photo. He added that the gender ratio is not "discerned as a problem. We certainly don't view it as such." Interesting, then, that BU doesn't publicize the sex breakdown of its student body on its website.

12    Richard Nesbitt, admissions director at Williams College, which is just 52 percent female, sees things differently. "If we got to 60-40, that would set off some alarm bells because we would like to have a 50-50 split," he says, adding balance is desirable "in terms of the social atmosphere and so forth."

13    Nesbitt says Williams's past as an all-men's college, plus strong math and science departments and athletics programs, helps keep the male numbers higher than the average. A few other formerly all-male schools, such as Princeton, actually have male majorities. But

while the situation isn't yet alarming for such schools as Williams, Nesbitt calls it "alarming in terms of what's happening in our society."

14    The Department of Education doesn't appear to agree. The home of Title IX enforcement continues to be so preoccupied with advancing women that a recent 50-page study called Gender Differences in Participation and Completion of Undergraduate Education focuses not on the shortfall of men that's evident in practically every data point, but on tiny subpopulations of women who still have "risk characteristics," such as those entering university after age 29. And the department still spends money on studies such as Trends in Educational Equity of Girls and Women: 2004, while ignoring the eye-popping trends for boys and men.

15    The neglect has extended to the press as well, though there are a few signs that the blackout may be ending. The *Chronicle of Higher Education*, the bible of college and university news, has hardly touched the issue. *EdWeek*, while it has done better, still devotes less ink to the current gender gap than it does to women. And a recent piece in the *Washington Post* is an encouraging sign. As for state governments, inquiries around the country have turned up only a single public body studying the problem, a commission in Maine that is due to publish a study of boys' underperformance in education in January. It's true that President Bush mentioned boys' troubles in the 2005 State of the Union, but his aim was to "keep young people out of gangs, and show young men an ideal of manhood that respects women and rejects violence." Only a few business groups have looked at young men's academic performance, as have a handful of private researchers and authors.

16    Yet the trends are grave. Women outstrip men in education despite that there are 15 million men and 14.2 million women aged 18–24 in the country. Kentucky colleges enroll at least 67 first-year women for every 50 men. Delaware has 74 first-year women for every 50 men.

17    The gender gap is even more palpable within the colleges themselves, because women and men gravitate to different majors. While a split in preferences has always been the case, the gender imbalance in the overall college makes departments so segregated that campus life just ain't what it used to be. In North Carolina's public and private universities, a typical psychology class has four women for every man. In education, the ratio is five to one. The English and foreign language departments are heavily female as well.

The consequences go far beyond a lousy social life and the longer-term reality that many women won't find educated male peers to marry. There are also academic consequences, and economic ones.

18    Only a few fields, such as business and the social sciences, show men and women signing up at comparable rates. Math, computers, engineering, and the physical sciences continue to be male-dominated (in North Carolina, for example, engineering is 79 percent male), and the total number of graduates in these economically essential fields is often stagnant or declining. Thus, between 1992 and 2002, when the number of bachelor's degree-earners in California's public university system grew by 11 percent, the number of engineering bachelor's degrees shrank by 8 percent. California's private universities fared better, but the gap is still striking: bachelor's degrees grew by 41 percent overall, while bachelor's degrees in engineering grew only 27 percent.

19    It seems the education system is favoring quantity over quantitative skills. The result? American companies and research organizations that need to employ graduates in quantitative fields have to turn to foreigners. Already, an astounding 40 percent of all the master's

degrees awarded by American institutions in science, engineering, and information technology go to foreign students, as do 45 percent of all Ph.D.s in those fields, according to a study of the gender gap in education by the Business Roundtable in Washington, D.C.

20    The answer that education experts keep recycling is that American girls need to be encouraged to go into quantitative fields. After all, if there's one thing Harvard president Larry Summers taught the nation, it's that questioning women's aptitude for science is an absolute no-no. But surely some reflection is needed on whether science, mathematics, and engineering wouldn't be more attractive to American boys if more of them were encouraged to discover, at an early age, whether they have strengths in those fields and were warmly encouraged to pursue them in their schooling.

21    We're certainly not seeing any such encouragement these days. While much of the gender imbalance in higher education results from girls' advancing through high school and into university in greater proportions than boys, there are a few categories of boys who are stuck or losing ground. The high school dropout rate for white boys hovers around 7 percent, at a time when girls—black, white, and Hispanic—are making annual progress in cutting their dropout numbers, as are black and Hispanic boys. (To be sure, the Hispanic boys' high school dropout rate remains astonishingly high, and contributes to the overall college imbalance: 26.7 percent in 2003, a rate not seen since the early 1970s among black boys and girls.)

22    Young men also drop out of college more readily than young women do. And even in affluent, educated, white suburbs, fewer twelfth-grade boys make plans to attend college than girls do, according to a study by the Boston Private Industry Council. Unfortunately, a student who defers college enrollment increases his odds of never attending. All of this makes the pool of applicants to college predominantly female, and the pool of enrollees more female as well.

23    What is going on? Schools are not paying enough attention to the education of males. There's too little focus on the cognitive areas in which boys do well. Boys have more disciplinary problems, up to 10 percent are medicated for Attention Deficit Disorder, and they thrive less in a school environment that prizes what Brian A. Jacob of Harvard's Kennedy School of Government calls "noncognitive skills." These include the ability to pay attention in class, to work with others, to organize and keep track of homework, and to seek help from others. Where boys and girls score comparably on cognitive skills, boys get worse grades in the touchy-feely stuff. Perhaps not coincidentally, boys reportedly enjoy school less than girls do, and are less likely to perceive that their teachers support them, according to studies of Hispanic dropouts.

24    Harvard's Jacob is one of the few scholars to have studied the gender gap in higher education. His statistical analysis suggests it is boys' lack of skill in these noncognitive areas that is the principal cause of the gap. Other factors, which include young men choosing to go into the military or winding up in prison, account for only about one-sixth of the spread, according to his calculations.

25    Plain old economics is at work as well. Consider that among Hispanic boys, the wage gap between high school dropouts and high school graduates is much smaller than for whites and blacks. Hispanic boys may figure that high college tuition and four more years of touchy-feely classroom work is less appealing than a job and an immediate income. The economic draw of the workplace holds great sway over male college dropouts as well.

A "need to work" accounted for fully 28 percent of male dropouts' reasons for leaving college, but only 18 percent of women dropouts' reasons, according to a Department of Education study. The men were also more likely than women to report academic problems and dissatisfaction with classes as their reasons for leaving.

26    Whatever the precise combination of causes, the imbalance on today's campuses can only be harmful in its social and economic effects. In a rational world, the Bush administration would take a serious look at whether continued enforcement of Title IX is keeping men away from college. At a minimum, the federal Department of Education would follow the example of the state of Maine and mine its statistics for detailed information about boys. Only then would researchers be equipped to address the problem.

27    Even now, almost two decades after the failure of the effort to ratify the Equal Rights Amendment, the culture is still in thrall to feminist orthodoxy. The Bush administration declined to do battle against Title IX three years ago, essentially preserving the status quo when college sports teams sued for reforms. Meanwhile, the myopic bureaucrats at the Department of Education are unlikely to take their heads out of the sand unless forced to: As if prompted by the imminent release of Maine's report on how to help boys catch up, the National Center for Education Statistics led its website on December 1 with a colorful chart displaying the sex breakdown at a single high school—one in Bangor, where it just happens that boys outnumber girls.

## QUESTIONS FOR ANALYSIS AND DISCUSSION

1. In this essay, what accounts for the imbalance of men to women ratios at many institutions of higher learning?
2. According to Vickers, what problems will eventually rise due to the male/female imbalance in colleges and universities?
3. What examples does Vickers use to show that the government and other institutions are not reacting to the male/female imbalance in higher education appropriately?
4. Do you think the government should intervene to balance gender distribution on campus? If so, what steps could the government take to correct the problem?
5. In your opinion, are the institutions of higher education discriminating against males when they are "gender blind in applications"?

## Reading The Visual

## Asking for Directions
*Don Reilly*

This cartoon by Don Reilly first appeared in *The New Yorker* magazine.

"*Because my genetic programming prevents me from stopping to ask directions—that's why!*"

Copyright © The New Yorker Collection, 1991. Donald Reilly from cartoonbank.com. All Rights Reserved.

### QUESTIONS FOR ANALYSIS AND DISCUSSION

1. It has been a long-held adage that men don't stop to ask for directions. Is it self-reliance? independence? Or are men simply unwilling to admit that they need help? What social impressions may influence their reluctance? Explain.
2. Are women more likely to stop and ask for directions or other assistance? Or more importantly, why does this stereotype exist?
3. In the cartoon, the man tells the woman that it is his "genetic programming" that prevents him from stopping. How do you think the authors in this section would respond to this cartoon?
4. Explain why, in your opinion, the cartoon is—or isn't—true. Is this an American comedic situation, or does is it hold true for other cultures? Show this cartoon to some international students and ask for their reactions. Report your results in class for discussion.

# And May Your First Child Be a Feminine Child

*Aaron Traister*

Many of us have heard that China's "one-child rule" has led to a disparate ratio of males to females. But culturally, do Americans show similar gender bias? While we may not be terminating pregnancies or abandoning our girl babies, writer Aaron Traister argues that we still favor boys over girls when it comes to the birth announcement. Traister observes, "people did victory laps when my wife gave birth to a boy. Why was the reaction to our next baby, a girl, so cold?" *

**BEFORE YOU READ**

As a culture, do we still tend to favor one gender over another? Do we celebrate the birth of boys more than girls? Explain.

**AS YOU READ**

How does Traister feel about the birth of his daughter? The birth of his son? What bothers him about people's reactions to both births?

1   There is a scene in *The Godfather* in which the dim but faithful Luca Brasi congratulates Don Corleone on his daughter's wedding day. Nervous and eager to please, he finally delivers his much-practiced hope for the young couple: "And may their first child be a masculine child."

2   I'm not sure Luca Brasi would have ever found an occasion to offer his best wishes for a feminine child. He was a product of his times. Back then, you needed a male heir to inherit your sprawling crime syndicate. The idea of a woman whacking a drug-peddling upstart over a plate of clams never even crossed poor Luca's frontal lobes.

3   But those days, like Luca Brasi, swim with the fishes. Boys are falling behind in the workforce, in higher education, and at primary academics. According to the Associated Press, even the sprawling crime syndicates of Italy are now enjoying an era of unmatched chromosomal diversity at their highest levels. With the ascension of the double X and the supposed decline of the Y, you might expect the birth of a girl to be heralded with, at least, an equal sort of excitement to the announcement of the birth of a boy. And yet, as 18 million cracks appear on the highest of ceilings, perhaps we should train our gaze a little lower to the first ceiling our daughters encounter: the middling enthusiasm toward the impending arrival of a baby girl.

*Aaron Traister, *Salon Magazine*, November 15, 2009.

4  Or maybe it's just me.

5  I remember the sonogram tech revealing that our first child was a masculine child, in the same way I remember Oprah revealing she had given her audience members cars. "Look under your seats and you'll find your . . . BAY-BEE'S PEEE-NIS!!"

6  I screamed until I lost my voice and nearly knocked out the sonogram tech jumping up and down wildly, crying while clutching my keys close to my chest.

7  To be fair, "baby" was a foreign enough concept for my 27-year-old brain to deal with. Telling me that I had to figure out how to raise a "girl"—one of the other great mysteries of my life—would have seemed about as intimidating as informing me that it was my job to figure out how to fix the Large Hadron Collider. It would have ended with me living under an assumed name outside of New Braunfels, Texas.

8  Regardless, I found myself doing the baby boy victory lap.

9  I was excited about having a boy, but I was also excited because I had endured a good deal of ball-breaking from my guy friends before the gender had been determined. My buddies ribbed me about having a yucky girl baby. One friend went so far as to assure me my wife and I would only have girl babies for future pregnancies as well. It would be a plague on my house—a plague of girls.

10  When it turned out the curse had been lifted—or, more precisely, that it never existed—I admit: I crowed.

11  After that opening salvo of macho banter, I began to wonder if we speak about the sex of our impending children in vastly different ways and if the reservations about baby girls were not just limited to juvenile 20-something dudes. But it wasn't until we were expecting our second child, two years later, that the question transitioned from a passing curiosity to a legitimate concern.

12  From the time my wife announced her pregnancy, I knew she'd be having a girl. At 29, I had begun to experience a personal sea change, as the motivational speakers say. And maybe, on some level, I had known for a while a baby girl was coming, and I didn't want her to grow up with a lefty hypocrite father: "Baby girl, you can be anything you want to be . . . as long as it doesn't interfere with your brother's success." After all, I want my children to grow up and resent me for the right reasons, like my emotional unavailability and my middle-class white male rage.

13  The first eight months of my wife's pregnancy were full of bizarre and polarizing gender issues outside our home, unfolding as it did during the candidacies of Hillary Clinton and Sarah Palin. The less-than-stellar response to an estrogen-fused battle for the White House seemed to parallel, on a macro level, my one-time fear of welcoming a baby girl into my own house. And I found myself shifting from being a Howard Dean-style frat-house Democrat to a Jezebel-reading, Hillary-supporting Democrat who no longer used the word "bitch." Well, not every 15 minutes, anyway.

14  Armed with this new sense of feminine awareness (and, perhaps, a lingering embarrassment about my previous attitude), I became hypersensitive of how other people reacted to our little girl's imminent arrival.

15  A kind of pitying, you-lose sentiment was common among dads without daughters. They always delivered some polite variation of, "Dude, that sucks." Or, "What are you

gonna do with a girl?" I remember talking to a friend whose second son was born with a heart defect that required two open-heart surgeries before the kid's first birthday. When I mentioned how impressed I was with the way he and his wife shouldered such difficulty he said, with a sigh, "It's been rough." He then slapped me on the back before continuing, "I'm just glad we didn't have a girl. Good luck with all that!"

16    As for women, well, they never went that far, but even their enthusiasm seemed dialed down. During our son's birth, the blue-haired waitresses at our favorite diner had been kind enough to act as my wife's unofficial pregnancy support group. They doled out advice on anything from sleep deprivation to breast-feeding. And when it came to gender, the decision was unanimous from every waitress in the joint: Boys are easier than girls, and girls are difficult and demanding, and then they turn into teenage girls and then they're at their worst.

17    This line of thinking was not confined to the old-school atmosphere of Bob's Diner either. I remember one of our hipper neighbors responding to our news by griping about how easy her three boys were versus her 11-year-old daughter, a constant source of aggravation. The girl rolled her eyes but bore this proclamation with a surprising dignity, considering that her mother was standing next to her at the time.

18    Even my perpetually sensible Indian pediatrician ended my daughter's first checkup by saying, "Little girls are very special. But then they turn into teenage girls, and you want them to just go away."

19    This wasn't exactly the stuff of Maurice Chevalier.

20    It's true that an occasional mom without a daughter experienced an obvious moment of longing. Dads who already had girls were congratulatory enough. But dads who only had girls seemed, at times, to be overcompensating, trying too hard to prove just how cool they were with it. One gentleman earnestly regaled me with the hidden charms of "High School Musical" and the Jonas Brothers. It was petrifying. It just didn't seem like anyone was that pumped about the whole thing. I refuse to include grandparents here; they would have been happy if my wife had delivered a Labrador.

21    Maybe the reactions were muted for practical reasons. This was, after all, our second child. As a second child myself, I am acutely aware of the dip in excitement between the first kid and the second. (Although my sister might argue that she is acutely aware of the way boys are received as opposed to the way girls are.)

22    When my wife and I told people we were having a boy, their faces would light up, their eye-smiles would have made Tyra Banks proud. People radiated a sincere and palpable joy at the idea that another Y chromosome would be added to the global gene pool. But when it came to my daughter the only unbridled enthusiasm I remember came in relation to the fact that we already had a boy—thus creating the "Rich Man's Family" (a very important concept in my Philadelphia neighborhood). I'd never heard of it before. I have heard about it almost weekly since my daughter was born.

23    For my part, I can honestly say I was just as excited about my daughter as I was about my son. And she's even better out of the belly. Turns out, while we have years before we have to negotiate her first bare-midriff prom dress, none of the dire prophecies about her demands or attitude have come to pass. In fact, she is a calming counterbalance to my son, who takes after his hyperactive mother. My daughter is laid-back. At 10 months old, she's grunty and built like a linebacker and beautiful and perfect, and she makes me want to be

a better father, one who takes risks and stakes out my own success. Her first real word was "Orca," as in the whale, and that is awesome. I love her with every rapidly aging fiber of my being.

24    But I sometimes wonder if I would feel the same way if I did not already have my masculine child. If she had come first. Would I have been as excited about her arrival? Would I love her just as much? Or would I feel like something was missing?

### QUESTIONS FOR ANALYSIS AND DISCUSSION

1. What does Traister learn about himself when he realizes he and his wife will welcome a baby girl into his family? His friends and family? Society as a whole? Explain.
2. How do you think Kay Hymowitz would respond to this essay and his points. His description of his friends? His personal admission that he too feared a "plague of girls"?
3. Consider how you behave around members of the opposite sex. Are you relaxed? on guard? Do you act differently? Do you treat members of the opposite sex differently than your own? If so, in what ways, and why?
4. Traister notes that even women seem to be less enthusiastic about the birth of a girl. What reasons does he give for their reactions? How does he feel about them and what does he do? In your opinion, does he react appropriately to people's comments? Why or why not?
5. Evaluate Traister's introduction. Why does he reference *The Godfather*? What connection is he trying to make?

# The Men We Carry in Our Minds
## *Scott Russell Sanders*

Statistically, men tend to hold more positions of power and wealth than women do. Many women feel that simply being born male automatically confers status and power, or at the very least, makes life easier. This cultural assumption, however, may only apply to a very small segment of the male population. Is it fair to stereotype men this way? Writer Scott Russell Sanders grew up in rural Tennessee and Ohio, where men aged early from lives of punishing physical labor or died young in military service. When he got to college, Sanders was baffled when the daughters of lawyers, bankers and physicians accused him and his sex of "having cornered the world's pleasures." In this essay, Sanders explores the differences between the men and women in his life, and how male power is often dependent on class and social influence.*

---

*Scott Russell Sanders, *The Paradise of Bombs*, 1993.

A common complaint made by some women is that men tend to wield more power and privilege. Think about three men you know well, such as a father, brother, or friend. Do their everyday life experiences bear out this viewpoint? Why or why not?

**AS YOU READ**

Do you think Sanders feels women, not men, are the privileged class? Explain.

1  "This must be a hard time for women," I say to my friend Anneke.
2  "They have so many paths to choose from, and so many voices calling them."
3  "I think it's a lot harder for men," she replies.
4  "How do you figure that?"
5  "The women I know feel excited, innocent, like crusaders in a just cause. The men I know are eaten up with guilt."
6  "Women feel such pressure to be everything, do everything," I say. "Career, kids, art, politics. Have their babies and get back to the office a week later. It's as if they're trying to overcome a million years' worth of evolution in one lifetime."
7  "But we help one another. And we have this deep-down sense that we're in the right— we've been held back, passed over, used—while men feel they're in the wrong. Men are the ones who've been discredited, who have to search their souls."
8  I search my soul. I discover guilty feelings aplenty—toward the poor, Native Americans, the whales, an endless list of debts. But toward women I feel something more confused, a snarl of shame, envy, wary, tenderness, and amazement. This muddle troubles me. To hide my unease I say, "You're right, it's tough being a man these days."
9  "Don't laugh," Anneke frowns at me. "I wouldn't be a man for anything. It's much easier being the victim. All the victim has to do is break free. The persecutor has to live with his past."
10  How deep is that past? I find myself wondering. How much of an inheritance do I have to throw off?
11  When I was a boy growing up on the back roads of Tennessee and Ohio, the men I knew labored with their bodies. They were marginal farmers, just scraping by, or welders, steelworkers, carpenters; they swept floors, dug ditches, mined coal, or drove trucks, their forearms ropy with muscle; they trained horses, stoked furnaces, made tires, stood on assembly lines wrestling parts onto cars and refrigerators. They got up before light, worked all day long whatever the weather, and when they came home at night they looked as though somebody had been whipping them. In the evenings and on weekends they worked on their own places, tilling gardens that were lumpy with clay, fixing broken-down cars, hammering on houses that were always too drafty, too leaky, too small.

The bodies of the men I knew were twisted and maimed in ways visible and invisible. The nails of their hands were black and split, the hands tattooed with scars. Some had lost fingers. Heavy lifting had given many of them finicky backs and guts weak from hernias. Racing against conveyor belts had given them ulcers. Their ankles and knees ached from years of standing on concrete. Anyone who had worked for long around machines was hard of hearing. They squinted, and the skin of their faces was creased like the leather of old work gloves. There were times, studying them, when I dreaded growing up. Most of them coughed, from dust or cigarettes, and most of them drank cheap wine or whiskey, so their eyes looked bloodshot and bruised. The fathers of my friends always seemed older than the mothers. Men wore out sooner. Only women lived into old age.

12    As a boy I also knew another sort of men, who did not sweat and break down like mules. They were soldiers, and so far as I could tell they scarcely worked at all. But when the shooting started, many of them would die. This was what soldiers were for, just like a hammer was for driving nails. Warriors and toilers: those seemed, in my boyhood vision, to be the chief destinies for men. They weren't the only destinies, as I learned from having a few male teachers, from reading books, and from watching television. But the men on television—the politicians, the astronauts, the generals, the savvy lawyers, the philosophical doctors, the bosses who gave orders to both soldiers and laborers—seemed as remote and unreal to me as the figures in Renaissance tapestries. I could no more imagine growing up to become one of these cool, potent creatures than I could imagine becoming a prince.

13    A nearer and more hopeful example was that of my father, who had escaped from a red dirt farm to a tire factory, and from the assembly line to the front office. Eventually, he dressed in a white shirt and tie. He carried himself as if he had been born to work with his mind. But his body, remembering the earlier years of slogging work, began to give out on him in his fifties, and it quit on him entirely before he turned 65.

14    A scholarship enabled me not only to attend college, a rare enough feat in my circle, but even to study in a university meant for the children of the rich. Here I met for the first time young men who had assumed from birth that they would lead lives of comfort and power. And for the first time I met women who told me that men were guilty of having kept all the joys and privileges of the earth for themselves. I was baffled. What privileges? What joys? I thought about the maimed, dismal lives of most of the men back home. What had they stolen from their wives and daughters? The right to go five days a week, 12 months a year, for 30 or 40 years to a steel mill or a coal mine? The right to drop bombs and die in war? The right to feel every leak in the roof, every gap in the fence, every cough in the engine as a wound they must mend? The right to feel, when the layoff comes or the plant shuts down, not only afraid but ashamed?

15    I was slow to understand the deep grievances of women. This was because, as a boy, I had envied them. Before college, the only people I had ever known who were interested in art or music or literature, the only ones who read books, the only ones who ever seemed to enjoy a sense of ease and grace were the mothers and daughters. Like the menfolk, they fretted about money, they scrimped and made do. But, when the pay stopped coming in, they were not the ones who had failed. Nor did they have to go to war, and that seemed to me a blessed fact. By comparison with the narrow, ironclad days of fathers, there was an expansiveness, I thought, in the days of mothers. They went to see neighbors, to shop in town, to run errands at school, at the library, at church. No doubt, had I looked harder at their lives, I would have envied them less. It was not my fate to become a woman, so it was easier for me to see the graces. I didn't see, then, what a prison a house could be, since houses seemed to be brighter, handsomer places than any factory. I did not realize—because

such things were never spoken of—how often women suffered from men's bullying. Even then I could see how exhausting it was for a mother to cater all day to the needs of young children. But if I had been asked, as a boy, to choose between tending a baby and tending a machine, I think I would have chosen the baby. (Having now tended both, I know I would choose the baby.)

16      So I was baffled when the women at college accused me and my sex of having cornered the world's pleasures. I think something like my bafflement has been felt by other boys (and by girls as well) who grew up in dirt-poor farm country, in mining country, in black ghettoes, in Hispanic barrios, in the shadows of factories, in Third World nations—any place where the fate of men is just as grim and bleak as the fate of women.

17      When the women I met at college thought about the joys and privileges of men, they did not carry in their minds the sort of men I had known in my childhood. They thought of their fathers, who were bankers, physicians, architects, stockholders, the big wheels of the big cities. They were never laid off, never short of cash at month's end, never lined up for welfare. These fathers made decisions that mattered. They ran the world.

18      The daughters of such men wanted to share in this power, this glory. So did I. They yearned for a say over their future, for jobs worthy of their abilities, for the right to live at peace, unmolested, whole. Yes, I thought, yes, yes. The difference between me and these daughters was that they saw me, because of my sex, as destined from birth to become like their fathers, and therefore as an enemy to their desires. But I knew better. I wasn't an enemy, in fact or in feeling. I was an ally. If I had known, then, how to tell them so, would they have believed me? Would they now?

### QUESTIONS FOR ANALYSIS AND DISCUSSION

1. In paragraph 7, Sanders states he has feelings of guilt toward a number of minority groups or social causes, but his feelings toward women are more complicated. What do you think might be the reasons for his feelings? Can you identify with this perspective?

2. How do you think women from the different socioeconomic groups Sanders mentions in his essay would respond to his ideas? For example, how would the educated daughters of the lawyers and bankers respond? How about the women from Sanders's hometown?

3. What are the occupations and obligations of the men mentioned in the article? What socioeconomic segment of society is Sanders describing? What does this suggest about the relationship between gender and class?

4. Sanders relates his argument entirely in the first person, using personal anecdotes to illustrate his point. How does this approach influence the reader? Would this essay be different if he told it from a third-person point of view? Explain.

5. In paragraph 8, Sanders's friend Anneke says she "wouldn't be a man for anything. It is much easier being the victim." What does Anneke mean by this statement? Do you agree with her view? Why or why not?

6. What effect do Anneke's comments have on Sanders's audience? Why do you think he quotes her? How do her comments support his argument?

## WRITING ASSIGNMENTS

1. Write an essay exploring the effects of the perception of women as homemakers and mothers in the media. Some of the areas of your exploration might draw from television, film, art, advertising, newspapers, music, and other popular media. How do media representations of women enforce (or refute) the perception of women as mothers and homemakers rather than professionals?

2. Consider the ways Hollywood influences our cultural perspectives of gender and identity. Write an essay exploring the influence, however slight, film and television have had on your own perceptions of gender. If you wish, interview other students for their opinion on this issue, and address some of their points in your essay.

3. Thirty years ago, men were expected to earn more than women. Do we still hold such beliefs? Poll your classmates to find out their opinions regarding income status. Do men feel that they should earn more? Would they feel less masculine if their girlfriends or wives earned more then they did? Do women look for higher incomes when they consider a partner? Analyze your results and write an argument that draws conclusions from your survey and its connection to feminism in the twenty-first century.

4. In your own words, define the terms "masculine" and "feminine." You might include library research on the origins of the words or research their changing implications over the years. Develop your own definition for each word, and then discuss with the rest of the class how you arrived at your definitions.

5. Several of the authors in this section attribute youth's desire to act, dress, and look a certain way to media pressure. Write an essay discussing whether this is true or not true. Support your perspective using examples from the authors, and your own experiences and observations.

6. Is it harder to grow up male or female in America today? Using information from the articles in this section, as well as outside resources, write an essay explaining which gender faces the greatest and most daunting challenges, and why. Will this situation grow worse? Offer suggestions to help ease the gender-related challenges children face growing up in today's culture.

7. Write an essay in which you consider your own sense of cultural conditioning. Do you feel your behavior has been conditioned by sex-role expectations? In what ways? Is there a difference between the "real" you and the person you present to the world? If there is a difference, is it the result of cultural pressure? Explain.

8. Write an essay examining the role television and entertainment media has had on our perceptions of male and female social roles and how we fit in as men and as women in society today.

# 12

# In God We Trust?

The concept of the freedom of religion is in principle as old as the Constitution itself. However, different religious and secular groups have interpreted the phrase in vastly different ways, and it has only been over the last 50 years or so that the issue has received great national attention. At the center of the debate is the wording of the First Amendment:

> Congress shall make no law respecting an establishment of religion, or prohibiting the free exercise thereof; or abridging the freedom of speech, or of the press; or the right of the people peaceably to assemble, and to petition the Government for a redress of grievances.

Federal support of any religious cause may appear to be an endorsement of that religion and its belief system, and is viewed as a violation of the spirit of the Constitution. What did the founders mean when they wrote the Constitution? And are their intentions relevant to how we interpret the First Amendment?

Since 1947, stemming from a ruling related to *Everson v. Board of Education*, the U.S. judicial system has used the phrase "separation of church and state" to justify decisions on the constitutionality of the interaction between the state and matters of religion. Opponents of a strict separation between church and state (the phrase actually comes from a letter written by Thomas Jefferson to the Danbury Baptist Association in 1802 rather than the Constitution) argue that the founders wished to ensure that the new U.S. government did not establish a national religion, similar to that of the Church of England. Their intention was not to establish a strict separation of church and state, just to prevent one religion from trumping another. Supporters of literal separation claim that the clause ensures that no one is forced to accept the religious beliefs of another.

Beyond the immediate legality of the separation of church and state is the connected issue that expressions of religious belief are unacceptable in any civic arena—such as at political events, public greens, and in schools. Some towns, in an effort to include many faiths, have holiday displays that include Jewish symbols as well as Christian ones. But what happens when atheists, who do not believe in God at all, claim they are offended by such symbols? Does "under God" have any place in the Pledge of Allegiance? Should all mentions of religion be barred from the nation's courtrooms? What about the president's inaugural address? This chapter explores some of the many questions regarding the separation of church and state, how we balance religion and civic life, and the intersection of faith and the public sphere in American life.

# The Wall That Never Was

*Hugh Heclo*

Is religion a necessary part of American life? Should it have any role in civic life? While the principles of the separation of church and state are deeply valued and protected, it seems that many Americans—over half the population, in fact—would like to see religion's influence in American society grow. In the next essay, George Mason University professor and political scientist Hugh Heclo explains that the "wall" between church and state is not a constitutional principle. Moreover, it has only been over the last 50 years or so that the separation of church and state has become a matter of heated public debate for the courts to decide. Heclo argues that religion has traditionally played a role in public affairs, and will continue to do so, because cultural ideology will support it, even if society is unaware it is doing so.◆

## BEFORE YOU READ

Heclo notes that despite the opinion that church and state should be separate, both in America and in a global context, most modern political conflicts have their root in a religious cause or disagreement. Consider this statement. Try to identify as many international issues and conflicts as you can. Does Heclo's observation ring true? Why or why not?

## AS YOU READ

How does Heclo's essay provide a framework to explain the current trend in which religion seems to be playing a more prominent role in politics and modern culture? Do you think this is an isolated movement, or one of larger, more lasting implications?

1   A hundred years ago, advanced thinkers were all but unanimous in dismissing religion as a relic of mankind's mental infancy. What's being dismissed today is the idea that humanity will outgrow religion. Contrary to the expectations of Sigmund Freud, Max Weber, John Dewey, and a host of others, religion has not become a mere vestige of premodern culture. If anything, Americans at the dawn of the 21st century are more willing to contemplate a public place for religion than they have been for the past two generations. But what does it mean for religion to "reenter the public square"? What good might it do there—and what harm?

2   Mention religion and public policy in the same breath these days, and what will most likely spring to mind are specific controversies over abortion, school prayer, the death penalty, and stem cell research. All are issues of public choice that arouse the religious conscience of many Americans. They are also particular instances of a larger reality: the

◆Hugh Heclo, *Wilson Quarterly*, Winter 2003.

profound, troubled, and inescapable interaction between religious faith and government action in America.

3  For most of American history, the subject of religion and public policy did not need much discussion. There was a widespread presumption that a direct correspondence existed, or should exist, between Americans' religious commitments and their government public-policy choices. When the oldest of today's Americans were born (which is to say in the days of Bryan, McKinley, and Theodore Roosevelt), the "public-ness" of religion was taken for granted, in a national political culture dominated by Protestants. It was assumed that America was a Christian nation and should behave accordingly. Of course, what that meant in practice could arouse vigorous disagreement—for example, over alcohol control, labor legislation, child welfare, and foreign colonization. Still, dissenters had to find their place in what was essentially a self-confident Protestant party system and moralistic political culture.

4  Those days are long past. During the 20th century, religion came to be regarded increasingly as a strictly private matter. By mid-century, Supreme Court decisions were erecting a so-called wall of separation between church and state that was nationwide and stronger than anything known in the previous practice of the individual states' governments. National bans on state-mandated prayer (1962) and Bible reading in public schools (1963) soon followed. In 1960, presidential candidate John F. Kennedy was widely applauded for assuring convocation of Baptist ministers that his Catholic religion and his church's teachings on public issues were private matters unrelated to actions he might take in public office. Intellectual elites in particular were convinced that the privatization of religion was a natural accompaniment of modernization in any society.

5  But even as Kennedy spoke and Supreme Court justices wrote, strong crosscurrents were at work. Martin Luther King, Jr., and masses of civil rights activists asserted the very opposite of a disconnection between religious convictions and public-policy claims. King's crusade against segregation and his larger agenda for social justice were explicitly based on Christian social obligations, flowing from belief in the person of Jesus Christ. So, too, in antinuclear peace movements of the time atheists such as Bertrand Russell were probably far outnumbered by liberal religious activists. After the 1960s, the United States and many other countries witnessed a political revival of largely conservative fundamentalist religious movements. These, according to prevailing academic theories, were supposed to have disappeared with the steam engine. The horror of September 11, 2001, showed in the most public way imaginable that modernization had not relegated religion to an isolated sphere of private belief. On the contrary, religious convictions could still terrorize, as they could also comfort a nation and inspire beautiful acts of compassion.

6  It is nonetheless true that during much of the 20th century the dominant influences in American national culture—universities, media and literary elites, the entertainment industry—did move in the predicted secularist direction. What at mid-century had been mere embarrassment with old-fashioned religious belief had, by century's end, often become hostility to an orthodox Christianity that believed in fundamental, revealed truth. Noting that the inhabitants of the Indian subcontinent are the most religious society in the world and the inhabitants of Sweden the most secularized, sociologist Peter Berger has said, provocatively, that America might usefully be thought of as an Indian society ruled by a Swedish elite.

7    In contemporary discussions of religion and public affairs, the master concept has been secularization. The term itself derives from the Latin word *saeculum*, meaning "period of time" or "age" or "generation." The idea of the secular directs our attention to the place and time of this world rather than to things religious and beyond time. It supposes a demarcation between the sacred and the profane. The social sciences of the 19th century developed theories of secularization that dominated much of 20th-century thinking. In the disciplines' new scientific view of society, all human activities were to be analyzed as historical phenomena, rooted in particular places and times. Religion was simply another human activity to be understood historically, an evolutionary social function moving from primitive to higher forms.

8    The idea of secularization became tightly bound up with intellectuals' understanding of modernization. As the 20th century dawned, the secularization that religious traditionalists condemned, leading modernists of the day saw as a benign and progressive evolution of belief systems. Secular political organizations had already gone far in taking over the social functions (welfare and education, for example) of medieval religious institutions. As society modernized, science and enlightened humanitarianism would provide a creed to displace religion's superstitions, and religion would retreat to private zones of personal belief. Policymaking would deal with worldly affairs in a scientific manner, indifferent to religious faith. Public religion was something humanity would outgrow. Religion in the modern state would go about its private, one-on-one soul work; public life would proceed without passionate clashes over religious truth.

9    The foregoing, in very crude terms, is what came to be known as the secularization thesis. To be modern meant to disabuse the mind of religious superstitions (about miracles, for example) and recognize the psychological needs that prompt humankind to create religious commitments in the first place. Modern society might still call things sacred, but it was a private call. In public life, the spell of enchantment was broken-or soon would be.

10   But something happened on the way to privatizing religion in the 20th century. For about the first two-thirds of the century, secularization seemed to prevail as a plausible description of public life. Then, in the final third, the picture changed considerably. Religion re-engaged with political history and refused to stay in the private ghetto to which modernity had consigned it. Witness the Islamic Revolution in Iran, the role of the Catholic Church in communist Eastern Europe, and the growth of the Religious Right in the United States. Of this resurgence of public religion, the sociologist José Casanova has observed: "During the entire decade of the 1980s it was hard to find any serious political conflict anywhere in the world that did not show behind it the not-so-hidden hand of religion. . . . We are witnessing the 'deprivatization' of religion in the modern world."

11   This "going public" of religion, moreover, was not an expression of new religious movements or of the quasi-religions of modern humanism. Rather, it was a reentry into the political arena of precisely those traditional religions—the supposedly vestigial survivals of an unenlightened time—that secular modernity was supposed to have made obsolete.

12   Three powerful forces make this a particularly important time to take stock of the new status of religion in public life. The first is the ever-expanding role of national policy in Americans' mental outlook. During the 20th century, struggles over federal policy increasingly defined America's political and cultural order. In other words, conceptions of who we are as a people were translated into arguments about what Washington should do

or not do. The abortion debate is an obvious example, but one might also consider our thinking about race, the role of women, crime, free speech, economic security in old age, education, and our relationship with the natural environment. After the 1950s, academics, and then the public, began to make unprecedented use of the term *policy* as a conceptual tool for understanding American political life. But the entire century nourished and spread the modern syndrome of "policy-mindedness"—an addiction to the idea that everything preying on the public mind requires government to do or to stop doing something. It's a notion that allows almost any human activity to be charged with public relevance—from the design of toilets to sexual innuendo in the workplace (filigrees of environmental policy and civil rights policy, respectively). Like it or not, our cultural discussions and decisions are now policy-embedded. And this in turn inevitably implicates whatever religious convictions people may have.

13    The juggernaut of today's scientific applications is a second development that now compels us to think hard about religion in the public square. Technological advances have brought our nation to a point where momentous public choices are inescapable. To be sure, scientific knowledge has been accumulating over many generations. But in the latter years of the 20th century, much of modern society's earlier investment in basic research led to technological applications that will affect human existence on a massive scale. For example, though the human egg was discovered in 1827, the DNA structure of life did not become known until the middle of the 20th century. Since then, sweeping applications of that accumulated knowledge have cascaded with a rush. By 1978, the first human baby conceived in vitro had been born. By the 1990s, the first mammals had been cloned, the manipulation of genes had begun, and the first financial markets for human egg donors had developed. These and other scientific advances are forcing far-reaching decisions about the meaning of life forms, about artificial intelligence and reconstitution of the human brain, and even about the reconstruction of matter itself.

14    These choices at the micro-level have been accompanied by technology's challenge to human destiny at the macro-level. It was also in the mid-20th century that mankind became increasingly conscious that it held Earth's very life in its own contaminating hands. At the onset of the 1960s, Rachel Carson did much to overturn generations of unbridled faith in scientific progress when she publicized the first dramatic charges about humankind's disastrous impact on the environment in *Silent Spring*. By the end of the 1960s, people saw the first pictures from space of the fragile Earth home they share. The first Earth Day and the blossoming of the modern environmental movement soon followed. The point is not simply that issues such as ozone depletion, species extinction, global warming, and the like have not been thought about until now. It's that people have never before had to deal with them as subjects of collective decision-making—which is to say, as public-policy choices.

15    Our modern technological condition thus represents a double historical climacteric. Today's citizens must manage the first civilization with both the outward reach to bring all human societies within a common global destiny and the inward reach to put the very structures of life and matter into human hands. For more than 2,000 years, philosophers could talk abstractly about the problem of being and the nature of human existence. For 21st-century citizens, the problem of being is an ever-unfolding agenda of public-policy choices. The extent to which ethics leads or lags the scientific juggernaut will now be measured in the specific policy decisions our democratic political systems produce. And

the decisions are saturated with religious and cultural implications about what human beings are and how they should live.

16    Even as the policy choices are forcing citizens into a deeper search for common understandings, doubts about a shared cultural core of American values are pushing in precisely the opposite direction. Those doubts are the third challenge to religion in the public square. Thanks to the homogenization produced by mass markets throughout the 50 states, 20th-century America experienced a marked decline in traditional geographic and class differences. But with the uniformity in material culture has come a greater insistence on and acceptance of variation in the realm of nonmaterial meanings and values. The widespread use of phrases such as "identity politics," "culture wars," "inclusiveness," and "political correctness" reflects the extent to which affirmations of diversity have supplanted earlier assumptions about a cultural core. "Multiculturalism" is a label for a host of changes in mental outlook, group self-consciousness, and educational philosophy. And with Muslims almost as numerous as Presbyterians in today's America, multiculturalism is more than faddish academic terminology. It's true that self-identified Christians still outnumber all other faith categories of Americans by 8 to 1 (in 2001, 82 percent of the population reported themselves to be Christian, 10 percent non-Christian, and 8 percent nonbelievers). But the Christianity in the figures is often purely nominal, with little orthodox content. The cultural indicators show that, by and large, America is well on its way to becoming a post-Christian, multi-religion society of personally constructed moral standards.

17    These, then, are three developments that compel attention to the interrelations between religion and public policy: A vast and powerful political society is defining itself to an ever greater extent through self-conscious policy decisions about what to do and what not to do; a technological imperative is driving that society's policy agenda to raise ever more profound questions about the nature of life and the sustainability of our earthly existence; and an increasingly fragmented sense of cultural identity is taking hold among the self-governing people who are called upon to make and oversee these collective decisions.

18    In light of these developments, how are we to think about "public religion" in our self-proclaimed democratic world superpower (so much for Christian humility)? Ordinary Americans continue to profess a devotion to religion far greater than is found in other developed nations. At the beginning of the 21st century, some 90 percent of Americans say they believe in God and pray at least once a week. Sixty percent attend religious services at least once a month, and 43 percent do so weekly. Non-belief is a distinctly minority position; it's also a hugely unpopular position. Large majorities of Americans claim that they would vote for a presidential candidate who was female (92 percent), black (95 percent), Jewish (92 percent), or homosexual (59 percent)—but only 49 percent say they would do so for a candidate who was an atheist.

19    In the summer of 2002, a political firestorm greeted a federal appellate court's decision that the words "under God" (which Congress added to the Pledge of Allegiance in 1954) violated the constitutional separation of church and state. As the hapless Ninth Circuit Court backed off, delaying the decision's effect, polls showed that 87 percent of Americans supported keeping God in the pledge, and that 54 percent favored having government promote religion. These figures reflect a significant shift: After declining sharply between the mid-1960s and late 1970s, the proportion of Americans who say religion is very important to them grew to roughly two out of three by 2001. Seventy percent of

Americans want to see religion's influence on American society grow, and an even larger proportion, including two-thirds of Americans aged 17 to 35, are concerned about the moral condition of the nation. (And yet, by general agreement, the common culture has become more coarse and salacious. One may well wonder who's left to be making the popular culture so popular.)

20  However, the meaning of religious belief has also been changing in recent decades. A great many Americans find that the search for spirituality is more important to them than traditional religious doctrines, confessional creeds, or church denominations. Although most Americans say they want religion to play a greater public role so as to improve the moral condition of the nation, only 25 percent say that religious doctrines are the basis for their moral judgments about right and wrong. Even among born-again Christians, fewer than half say that they base their moral views on specific teachings of the Bible. To claim that there are absolute moral truths (a view rejected by three out of four American adults at the end of the 20th century), or that one religious faith is more valid than another, is widely regarded as a kind of spiritual racism. The new cornerstone of belief is that moral truths depend on what individuals choose to believe relative to their particular circumstances. Human choice has become the trump value and judgmentalism the chief sin. Thus, three-fourths of that large majority of Americans who want religion to become more influential in American society say that it does not matter to them which religion becomes more influential. Similarly, between 80 and 90 percent of Americans identify themselves as Christians, though most of them dismiss some of the central beliefs of Christianity as it has traditionally been understood. Father Richard John Neuhaus, editor of the journal *First Things*, recently summed up the situation: "To say that America is a Christian nation is like saying it's an English-speaking nation. There are not many people who speak the language well, but when they are speaking a language poorly, it is the English language they are speaking."

20  What all this means for the intertwining of religious faith and the politics of government policymaking is something of a mystery. It's mysterious because Americans both want and distrust religious convictions in the public arena. Thus, more than 60 percent want elected officials to compromise rather than to vote their religious beliefs, even on life-and-death issues such as abortion and capital punishment. And though Americans have become more open in recent decades to having religion talked about in the public arena, 70 percent of them also think that when political leaders talk about their faith, they're just saying what people want to hear. Most people surveyed are willing to have religious leaders speak out more on public issues, but they also don't care much whether they do so or not. In the spring of 2001, when President Bush's faith-based initiatives were being publicized, three-quarters of Americans expressed strong support for the idea that faith-based groups should receive government funds to provide social services. But that same proportion opposed having government-funded religious groups hire only people who shared their beliefs. This amounts to support for religion as long as religion does not really insist on believing anything. Then again, most Americans opposed funding American Muslim or Buddhist groups, and they regarded even Mormon groups as marginal.

21  So never mind thinking outside the box. When it comes to religion—their own or others'—in the public square, today's Americans have trouble thinking seriously even inside the box. The wonderfully rich history of religion and democracy in modern America

has been ignored and even suppressed in public-school textbooks and university curricula, both of which were largely purged of "God talk" after the mid-20th century. The sowing of traditional religious information in the school system has been so sparse that one national researcher on the topic has called younger cohorts of Americans a "seedless" generation. A less polite term for their religiously lobotomized view of culture would be heathen. Here is crooked timber indeed for building a framework to support the culture-shaping interactions between religion and public policy.

22      When Americans do think, however imprecisely, about religion and public decision-making, what do they commonly have in mind? Their predominant notion is probably of "a wall of separation between church and state." Most citizens would be surprised to learn that the phrase is not in the Constitution; it comes from a church building here, a government building there, distinctly separate institutions. And that, Americans have long believed, is as it should be. But even casual observation reveals that there's more going on in that square. Perched atop the ostensible wall of separation between the structures of church and state, we watch a public forum where religion and politics are anything but separate. There are not two kinds of people in the forum, some of them religious and some political. There are only citizens. And as they interact, they express themselves both religiously and politically. Religious, nonreligious, and antireligious ideas are all at work in their heads when they define problems and choose measures to deal with them collectively, as a people. Religious and irreligious ideas commingle in programs enacted in behalf of this or that vision of a good social order. Church and state, religion and politics, and ideas and social action are crosscutting elements whose presence, even if poorly articulated, we often sense in the public square.

23      To put it another way, the major interactions between religion and public policy occur across three domains. The first is institutional and focuses on the way organized structures of religion and government impinge on one another—and together impinge on society. This institutional perspective comes most naturally to Americans because it's encoded in their nation's constitutional understanding of itself. The bland phrase "separation of church and state" conceals what was the most audacious and historically unique element of America's experiment in self-government: the commitment to a free exercise of religion. In this institutional domain, one encounters, for example, groups claiming infringement on the unfettered exercise of their religious liberties and disputes over government sponsorship of religious organizations. Less obviously, it is where one also finds religious and public agencies jostling against one another as they pursue, for example, education and welfare policies.

24      The second domain where religion and public policy connect can be called behavioral. Here the term simply means that religious attachments move people to act in public ways (e.g., to vote, to organize within the community, to engage in other political activities). There's a direct, though paradoxical, link between the first and second domains. The distancing between religious and government institutions has allowed religion in America to be an immense resource for the nation's politics. Alexis de Tocqueville concluded that his American informants were correct in believing that the main reason religion held great sway over their country was the separation of church and state. He wrote, "by diminishing the apparent power of religion one increased its real strength." Since his visit in 1831, Americans in religious associations have created and sustained public movements to promote slavery's abolition, women's rights, prison and asylum reform, child welfare and worker protection, mothers' pensions, liquor regulation, racial desegregation, and civil rights

legislation. (Such associations have also been an important source of less savory causes, such as anti-Catholic and anti-Jewish laws.) And citizens moved to more routine political action through religious affiliations have done much to shape America's party system and election outcomes.

25    The third domain connecting religion and public policy is more difficult to describe, but one senses that something important is missing if we take account only of organized institutions and politically relevant behaviors. For lack of a better term, we might call the third domain philosophical. It reflects broad policy outlooks on the social order. At this intersection, ideas and modes of thought are expressed in programmatic courses of action. It's the realm in which people operate when they speak about culture wars in the schools, the work ethic in welfare, or the need for moral clarity in foreign policy. It's the basis on which some people cringe and others rejoice.

### QUESTIONS FOR ANALYSIS AND DISCUSSION

1. Heclo notes that at the turn of the twentieth century most U.S. citizens "assumed that America was a Christian nation and should behave accordingly." How did this assumption change during the twentieth century? What do you think caused a shift in thinking? Explain.
2. What did sociologist Peter Berger (paragraph 6) mean when he said America might be considered "an Indian society ruled by a Swedish elite"? How does "the intellectual elite" view religion?
3. What role has the concept of secularization played in the discussion of religion and public affairs? How did the principles of secularization shift during the last half of the twentieth century?
4. Based on his writing alone, can you tell how Heclo feels about the separation of church and state and the role of religion in civic life?
5. Why does Heclo feel now is an especially important time to "take stock of the new status of religion in public life"? To what trends should we be paying attention? How could these trends impact the future of the concept of separation between church and state? Explain.
6. Why, according to Heclo, is multiculturalism more than "faddish academic terminology"? What is multiculturalism? In your opinion, what influence, if any, has multiculturalism had on the issue of church and state?

---

## Why We're Not One Nation "Under God"
*David Greenberg*

In June of 2002, Alfred Goodwin issued an unpopular ruling declaring the recitation of the Pledge of Allegiance in public schools unconstitutional. Goodwin was deciding a lawsuit brought by Michael Newdow, who filed the lawsuit on behalf of his daughter "because I am an atheist and this offends me." The Senate was so outraged by Goodwin's decision that it passed a resolution 99–0 expressing full support for the

Pledge of Allegiance and voted 99–0 to recodify the "under God" language in the pledge. Goodwin stayed his decision even before an appeal was filed. In June of 2004, the Supreme Court overturned the decision but did so on a technicality that Newdow did not have the right to represent his daughter, leaving the issue wide open for future lawsuits. Should the Pledge of Allegiance be changed? Should "under God" be dropped? And would it surprise you to learn that these two words were not part of the original pledge? In this essay, historian David Greenberg explores the history of the Pledge of Allegiance, and how this history might just solve the problem.[*]

## BEFORE YOU READ

What do the words "under God" in the Pledge of Allegiance mean? Do they refer to a specific deity or endorse a particular faith? Do the words violate the separation of church and state as outlined in the First Amendment?

## AS YOU READ

Greenberg observes that the original Pledge of Allegiance was "meant as an expression of patriotism, not religious faith." Do you think the Pledge of Allegiance is an expression of faith? Why or why not?

1   Poor Alfred Goodwin! So torrential was the flood of condemnation that followed his opinion—which held that it's unconstitutional for public schools to require students to recite "under God" as part of the Pledge of Allegiance—that the beleaguered appellate-court judge suspended his own ruling until the whole 9th Circuit Court has a chance to review the case. Not one major political figure summoned the courage to rebut the spurious claims that America's founders wished to make God a part of public life. It's an old shibboleth of those who want to inject religion into public life that they're honoring the spirit of the nation's founders. In fact, the founders opposed the institutionalization of religion. They kept the Constitution free of references to God. The document mentions religion only to guarantee that godly belief would never be used as a qualification for holding office—a departure from many existing state constitutions. That the founders made erecting a church-state wall their first priority when they added the Bill of Rights to the Constitution reveals the importance they placed on maintaining what Isaac Kramnick and R. Laurence Moore have called a "godless Constitution." When Benjamin Franklin proposed during the Constitutional Convention that the founders begin each day of their labors with a prayer to God for guidance, his suggestion was defeated.

2   Given this tradition, it's not surprising that the original Pledge of Allegiance—meant as an expression of patriotism, not religious faith—also made no mention of God. The pledge was written in 1892 by the socialist Francis Bellamy, a cousin of the famous radical writer Edward Bellamy. He devised it for the popular magazine *Youth's Companion* on the occasion of the nation's first celebration of Columbus Day. Its wording omitted reference not only to God but also, interestingly, to the United States:

---

[*]David Greenberg, *Slate*, June 28, 2002.

3    "I pledge allegiance to my flag and the republic for which it stands, one nation indivisible, with liberty and justice for all."

4    The key words for Bellamy were "indivisible," which recalled the Civil War and the triumph of federal union over states' rights, and "liberty and justice for all," which was supposed to strike a balance between equality and individual freedom. By the 1920s, reciting the pledge had become a ritual in many public schools.

5    Since the founding, critics of America's secularism have repeatedly sought to break down the church-state wall. After the Civil War, for example, some clergymen argued that the war's carnage was divine retribution for the founders' refusal to declare the United States a Christian nation, and tried to amend the Constitution to do so.

6    The efforts to bring God into the state reached their peak during the so-called "religious revival" of the 1950s. It was a time when Norman Vincent Peale grafted religion onto the era's feel-good consumerism in his best-selling *The Power of Positive Thinking*; when Billy Graham rose to fame as a Red-baiter who warned that Americans would perish in a nuclear holocaust unless they embraced Jesus Christ; when Secretary of State John Foster Dulles believed that the United States should oppose communism not because the Soviet Union was a totalitarian regime but because its leaders were atheists.

7    Hand in hand with the Red Scare, to which it was inextricably linked, the new religiosity overran Washington. Politicians outbid one another to prove their piety. President Eisenhower inaugurated that Washington staple: the prayer breakfast. Congress created a prayer room in the Capitol. In 1955, with Ike's support, Congress added the words "In God We Trust" on all paper money. In 1956 it made the same four words the nation's official motto, replacing "E Pluribus Unum." Legislators introduced Constitutional amendments to state that Americans obeyed "the authority and law of Jesus Christ."

8    The campaign to add "under God" to the Pledge of Allegiance was part of this movement. It's unclear precisely where the idea originated, but one driving force was the Catholic fraternal society the Knights of Columbus. In the early '50s the Knights themselves adopted the God-infused pledge for use in their own meetings, and members bombarded Congress with calls for the United States to do the same. Other fraternal, religious, and veterans clubs backed the idea. In April 1953, Rep. Louis Rabaut, D-Mich., formally proposed the alteration of the pledge in a bill he introduced to Congress.

9    The "under God" movement didn't take off, however, until the next year, when it was endorsed by the Rev. George M. Docherty, the pastor of the Presbyterian church in Washington that Eisenhower attended. In February 1954, Docherty gave a sermon—with the president in the pew before him—arguing that apart from "the United States of America," the pledge "could be the pledge of any country." He added, "I could hear little Moscovites [sic] repeat a similar pledge to their hammer-and-sickle flag with equal solemnity." Perhaps forgetting that "liberty and justice for all" was not the norm in Moscow, Docherty urged the inclusion of "under God" in the pledge to denote what he felt was special about the United States.

10    The ensuing congressional speechifying—debate would be a misnomer, given the near-unanimity of opinion—offered more proof that the point of the bill was to promote religion. The legislative history of the 1954 act stated that the hope was to "acknowledge the dependence of our people and our Government upon . . . the Creator . . . [and] deny the atheistic and materialistic concept of communism." In signing the bill on June 14, 1954, Flag Day, Eisenhower delighted in the fact that from then on, "millions of our schoolchildren will daily proclaim in every city and town . . . the dedication of our nation and our

people to the Almighty." That the nation, constitutionally speaking, was in fact dedicated to the opposite proposition seemed to escape the president.

11    In recent times, controversies over the pledge have centered on the wisdom of enforcing patriotism more than on its corruption from a secular oath into a religious one. In the 1988 presidential race, as many readers will recall, George Bush bludgeoned Democratic nominee Michael Dukakis for vetoing a mandatory-pledge bill when he was governor of Massachusetts, even though the state Supreme Court had ruled the bill unconstitutional. Surely one reason for the current cravenness of Democratic leaders is a fear of undergoing Dukakis' fate in 2002 or 2004 at the hands of another Bush.

12    The history of the pledge supports Goodwin's decision. The record of the 1954 act shows that, far from a "de minimis" reference or a mere "backdrop" devoid of meaning, the words "under God" were inserted in the pledge for the express purpose of endorsing religion—which the U.S. Supreme Court itself ruled in 1971 was unconstitutional. Also according to the Supreme Court's own rulings, it doesn't matter that students are allowed to refrain from saying the pledge; a 2000 high court opinion held that voluntary, student-led prayers at school football games are unconstitutionally "coercive," because they force students into an unacceptable position of either proclaiming religious beliefs they don't share or publicly protesting.

13    The appeals court decision came almost 40 years to the day after the Supreme Court decision in *Engel v. Vitale*. In that case, the court ruled it unconstitutional for public schools to allow prayer, even though the prayer was non-denominational and students were allowed to abstain from the exercise. When asked about the unpopular decision, President John F. Kennedy replied coolly that he knew many people were angry, but that the decisions of the court had to be respected. He added that there was "a very easy remedy"—not a constitutional amendment but a renewed commitment by Americans to pray at home, in their churches, and with their families.

## QUESTIONS FOR ANALYSIS AND DISCUSSION

1. Were you surprised to learn that the original pledge made no mention of God? Do you think that restoring the original pledge could be the solution to the argument that the pledge violates the separation of church and state? Why or why not?

2. What does Greenberg mean "It's an old shibboleth of those who want to inject religion into public life that they're honoring the spirit of the nation's founders"? What is a shibboleth? Explain.

3. What official references to God were added during the 1950s? What motivated this movement? Do you think that social attitudes have changed sufficiently to drop these references? Why or why not?

4. Write an argument in which you either advocate to keep the pledge as it is, drop the words "under God," or drop the pledge entirely.

5. What is the author's position on the issue of "under God" in the Pledge of Allegiance? Identify statements in his essay in which he reveals his position. How does he use history to support his viewpoint? Explain.

6. How do you think Greenberg would respond to Heclo's essay, and vice versa? As fellow historians, on what points do you think they would agree and disagree?

## Reading the Visual

## Separation of Church and State

Rob Rogers

### QUESTIONS FOR ANALYSIS AND DISCUSSION

1. What is happening in this cartoon? What are the sculptures depicting? What issue does it raise?
2. What point is the cartoonist trying to make? Can you tell his position on the matter of church and state based upon this cartoon?
3. In your opinion, should the Ten Commandments be displayed outside of government buildings? Why or why not?

# God of Our Fathers

*Walter Isaacson*

Many arguments in favor of retaining references to "God" in government-directed areas of civic life cite the "intentions of the founding fathers" when the United States was an infant nation. However, drafts of the Declaration of Independence and of the Constitution indicate that religious references (such as "God," "Creator," and "Providence") were added later. The conspicuous lack of references to God in a culture that was highly religious could be significant. In the next essay, former chairman and CEO of CNN and current president of the Aspen Institute Walter Isaacson explores the colonial understanding of God and how the Colonialists might feel about the fury over the issue of church and state.*

**BEFORE YOU READ**

Should the intentions of the Founding Fathers—such as Jefferson, Washington, Adams, Franklin, Hancock—be considered when courts decide issues connected to the separation of church and state? Why or why not?

**AS YOU READ**

What does the crafting of the Declaration of Independence reveal about the possible religious intentions of the Founding Fathers?

1   Whenever an argument arises about the role that religion should play in our civic life, such as the dispute over the phrase "under God" in the Pledge of Allegiance or the display of the Ten Commandments in an Alabama courthouse, assertions about the faith of the founders are invariably bandied about. It's a wonderfully healthy debate because it causes folks to wrestle with the founders and, in the process, shows how the founders wrestled with religion.

2       The only direct reference to God in the Declaration of Independence comes in the first paragraph, in which Thomas Jefferson and his fellow drafters of that document—including Benjamin Franklin and John Adams—invoke the "laws of nature and of nature's god." (The absence of capitalization was the way Jefferson wrote it, though the final parchment capitalizes all four nouns.) The phrase "nature's god" reflected Jefferson's deism—his rather vague Enlightenment-era belief, which he shared with Franklin, in a Creator whose divine handiwork is evident in the wonders of nature. Deists like Jefferson did not believe in a personal God who interceded directly in the daily affairs of mankind.

3       In his first rough draft of the Declaration, Jefferson began his famous second paragraph: "We hold these truths to be sacred and undeniable." The draft shows Franklin's heavy printer's pen crossing out the phrase with backslashes and changing it to "We hold these truths to be self-evident." Our rights derive from nature and are secured "by the consent of the

---

*Walter Isaacson, *TIME*, July 5, 2004.

governed," Franklin felt, not by the dictates or dogmas of any particular religion. Later in that same sentence, however, we see what was likely the influence of Adams, a more doctrinaire product of Puritan Massachusetts. In his rough draft, Jefferson had written, after noting that all men are created equal, "that from that equal creation they derive rights inherent & inalienable." By the time the committee and then Congress finished, the phrase had been changed to "that they are endowed by their Creator with certain unalienable Rights." For those of us who have toiled as editors, it is wonderful to watch how ideas can be balanced and sharpened through the editing process (and also how even giants have trouble knowing whether the word is inalienable or unalienable). The final version of the sentence weaves together a respect for the role of the Almighty Creator with a belief in reason and rationality.

4    The only other religious reference in the Declaration comes in the last sentence, which notes the signers' "firm reliance on the protection of divine Providence." Most of the founders subscribed to the concept of Providence, but they interpreted it in different ways. Jefferson believed in a rather nebulous sense of "general Providence," the principle that the Creator has a benevolent interest in mankind. Others, most notably those who followed in the Puritan footsteps of Cotton Mather, had faith in a more specific doctrine, sometimes called "special Providence" which held that God has a direct involvement in human lives and intervenes based on personal prayer.

5    In any event, that phrase was not in Jefferson's original draft or the version as edited by Franklin and Adams. Instead, it was added by Congress at the last minute. Like the phrase "under God" in the Pledge, it got tucked into a resounding peroration and somewhat broke up the rhythm: ". . . for the support of this Declaration, with a firm reliance on the protection of divine Providence, we mutually pledge to each other our Lives, our Fortunes and our sacred Honor."

6    In the Constitution, the Almighty barely makes an appearance, except in the context of noting that it was written in "the Year of our Lord," 1787. (Jefferson was ambassador to France at the time, so he missed the convention.) The one clear proclamation on the issue of religion in the founding documents is, of course, the First Amendment. It prohibits the establishment of a state religion or any government interference in how people freely exercise their beliefs. It was Jefferson, the original spirit behind the Virginia Statute for Religious Freedom, who emphasized that this amounted to a wall between two realms. "I contemplate with sovereign reverence," he wrote after becoming President, "that act of the whole American people which declared that their legislature should 'make no law respecting an establishment of religion, or prohibiting the free exercise thereof,' thus building a wall of separation between church & State."

7    Colonial America had seen its share of religious battles, in which arcane theological disputes like the one over antinomianism caused Puritans to be banished from Massachusetts and have to go establish colonies like Rhode Island. The founders, however, were careful in their debates and seminal documents to avoid using God as a political wedge issue or a cause of civic disputes. Indeed, that would have appalled them. Instead they embraced a vague civic religion that invoked a depersonalized deity that most people could accept. "Religion is a subject on which I have ever been most scrupulously reserved," Jefferson once wrote. "I have considered it as a matter between every man and his Maker, in which no other, and far less the public, had a right to intermeddle." So it is difficult to know exactly what the founders would have felt about the phrase "under God" in the Pledge of Allegiance or about displaying the Ten Commandments. It is probable, however, that they

would have disapproved of people on either side who used the Lord's name or the Ten Commandments as a way to divide Americans rather than as a way to unite them.

### QUESTIONS FOR ANALYSIS AND DISCUSSION

1. Why does Isaacson feel that arguments about the intentions of the Founding Fathers' feelings regarding the separation of church and state stimulate "wonderfully healthy debate"? Why is such debate, in his opinion, important? Explain.

2. Did Isaacson's essay on the crafting of the Declaration of Independence and the Constitution influence your own opinions on the issue of the separation of church and state? Why or why not?

3. Isaacson observes, "The founders, however, were careful in their debates and seminal documents to avoid using God as a political wedge issue or a cause of civic disputes." Imagine that the Founding Fathers were able to witness the current controversies regarding church and state—religion in schools, the Ten Commandments in courthouses, "under God" in the Pledge, "In God we trust" on currency, or nativity scenes on town greens. Based on the information in this essay, write a short response to these issues from their point of view.

4. Do you think the intentions of the Founding Fathers have any relevance today? Does it matter what they were thinking when they wrote the Constitution? Why or why not?

## Public Prayers on State Occasions Need Not Be Divisive or Generic
### *Charles Haynes*

In January 2005, Michael Newdow, dubbed "America's least favorite atheist" by *Time* magazine, filed a lawsuit to try to prevent George W. Bush from placing his hand on the Bible or engaging in public prayer at his second inauguration. Newdow had gained fame with his 2004 lawsuit charging that the "under God" wording included in the Pledge of Allegiance violated the establishment clause of the U.S. Constitution. Attorneys representing Bush argued that prayers have been widely accepted at inaugurals for more than 200 years and that Bush's decision to have a minister recite the invocation was a personal choice the court had no power to prevent. A U.S. district judge determined that Newdow had no legal basis to pursue his claim because he could not show he would suffer any injury from hearing a prayer. Four years later, Newdow filed another lawsuit to prevent references to God and religion from being part of President Barak Obama's inauguration. While Newdow lost his bid to bar "all Christian religious acts" from both inaugurations, his lawsuit raises questions about how we legislate the separation of church and state. Is it possible for a politician to be religious upon state occasions, but not alienate people who do not share his or her beliefs? Author and First Amendment scholar Charles Haynes proposes some solutions.[*]

---

[*]Charles Haynes, *Freedom Forum*, 2001.

Do you think public prayer at state or public events is appropriate? If so, what kind of prayer do you think is acceptable? Should prayer be inclusive, without any religious preference, or may it be a prayer representing the religion of the person of honor, such as the president at an inauguration?

Have you ever attended a public event, such as an inauguration, a sporting event, a benefit, or a building dedication, in which a prayer was included as part of the program? If so, what was the nature of the prayer? How did you feel about it? Did you participate? Did anyone look uncomfortable?

1   The debate over the prayers offered at President Bush's inauguration is yet another reminder of just how diverse and contentious America has become in the 21st century. Prayers at inaugural ceremonies are nothing new, of course. The practice dates back to the day George Washington took the oath of office. And the Supreme Court has indicated that a prayer on such occasions is constitutional.

2   But we've just been through a long and bitter campaign full of charges and counter-charges about the influence of the "religious right" on George W. Bush. Now that the election is finally over, every symbolic gesture by the president is scrutinized for possible hidden messages and motives.

3   Why did these particular prayers spark debate? Because both ministers chosen to pray were evangelical Protestants, and both prayed in the name of Jesus Christ.

4   One writer criticized the prayers as "divisive, sectarian and inappropriate." Other commentators complained that millions of Americans were made to feel like "outsiders" at an official event.

5   On the other side of the argument are those who say that it is completely appropriate for the president to select clergy who share his faith. Besides, they point out, his inaugural address stressed unity and struck a note of inclusiveness by mentioning, "synagogues and mosques" as examples of faith communities working for the common good.

6   As this debate reveals, finding the "right" prayer for these occasions is a difficult, if not hopeless, task.

7   Some people propose general, non-sectarian prayers (common at many public events these days). While this approach has the advantage of being most inclusive, it still leaves out the growing number of Americans with no religious preference.

8   Moreover, many people of faith disparage generic prayers as meaningless addresses "to whom it may concern." In many religious traditions, how you pray and in whose name you pray determine whether or not the prayer is authentic and meaningful.

9   Since it's difficult to imagine any newly-elected president eliminating the tradition of opening and closing the inauguration with prayer, is there a way to pray that is genuine and yet somehow speaks to our nation's expanding diversity?

10   At the risk of making all sides mad, let me weigh in with two modest suggestions for public prayer at important state events.

11    First, why not consider the alternative offered by a number of religious leaders such as Bishop Krister Stendahl, former head of Harvard Divinity School, and Elder Dallin Oaks of the Mormon Church? They accept invitations to pray at public events on the condition that they be allowed to pray in ways that are authentic within their respective traditions. But they are careful to say "I," not "we" (e.g., "I pray in the name of Jesus").

12    I prefer this approach because it protects the integrity of religious traditions without assuming that we all share the same faith.

13    Second, it would be a civil and inclusive gesture for those leading the prayers—as well as for an incoming president—to acknowledge that we are a nation of many peoples and faiths.

14    It might be enough to simply say that although we have different beliefs (and prayers), under the First Amendment we share a commitment to uphold the right of every citizen to choose in matters of faith.

15    If there's going to be a religious message at inaugurations, let it be authentic. And let it be accompanied by a religious-liberty message reminding America that there are no "official prayers" in the land of the free.

## QUESTIONS FOR ANALYSIS AND DISCUSSION

1.  Haynes observes that following Bush's election, "every symbolic gesture is scrutinized for possible hidden messages and motives." Are George W. Bush's actions and words subjected to greater inspection than other modern presidents? If so, why do people watch him more closely? Do you think he could have "hidden motives"?

2.  Haynes admits that his two suggestions for prayer at public events risk "making all sides mad." What objections could both sides have to his solutions? What do you think of his suggestions? Explain.

3.  Why are the pronouns "I" and "we" so important to consider when engaging in publicly led prayer? Explain.

4.  Can you think of additional solutions to the issue of public prayer other than what Haynes suggests? If you think that public prayer is unacceptable under any circumstances, explain your point of view and how you would justify its removal to people who prefer to include prayer at state or public events.

5.  In 2008, Michael Newdow sued Supreme Court Chief Justice John G. Roberts to prevent the Chief Justice from saying "so help me God" when reading the oath the President traditionally repeats back. His argument was that these words are not included in the actual oath, but have been traditionally included. Judge Reggie Walton refused to grant Newdow's motion for a preliminary injunction. In your opinion, do you think the President should include a reference to God in taking the oath of office? Why or why not?

## Reading the Visual

## Church and State

### *USA TODAY/CNN/Gallup Poll*

In September 2003, *USA Today*/CNN/Gallup conducted a survey on public opinion regarding the separation of church and state. The results presented on below are based on telephone interviews conducted September 19–21 with 1,003 adults over the age of 18. Among other findings, the survey reported that 77 percent of the subjects polled disapproved of the decision by the U.S. District Court to have the Ten Commandments monument removed from the rotunda of the Alabama Justice Building, and 90 percent approved of nondenominational school prayer at public events such as graduations.*

---

***Please say whether you approve or disapprove of each of the following:***

The use of federal funds to support social programs like day care and drug rehabilitation run by Christian religious organizations

| Approve | Disapprove | No opinion |
|---------|------------|------------|
| 64% | 34% | 2% |

The inscription "In God We Trust" on U.S. coins

| Approve | Disapprove | No opinion |
|---------|------------|------------|
| 90% | 8% | 2% |

A non-denominational prayer as part of the official program at a public school ceremony such as a graduation or a sporting event

| Approve | Disapprove | No opinion |
|---------|------------|------------|
| 78% | 21% | 1% |

Display of a monument to the Ten Commandments in a public school or government building

| Approve | Disapprove | No opinion |
|---------|------------|------------|
| 70% | 29% | 1% |

Display of a monument with a verse from the Koran, the holy book of the Islamic religion, in a public school or government building

| Approve | Disapprove | No opinion |
|---------|------------|------------|
| 33% | 64% | 3% |

If you walked into a public school classroom and the teacher's desk had a Bible on it, would you consider that to be a good thing, or a bad thing?

| Good Thing | Bad thing | Doesn't matter | No opinion |
|------------|-----------|----------------|------------|
| 71% | 18% | 9% | 2% |

Do you think a monument to the Ten Commandments in a courthouse sends a message that the justice system gives special considerations to Jews and Christians over those who belong to other religions, or does it not send that message?

| Yes, it does | No, it does not | No opinion |
|--------------|-----------------|------------|
| 25% | 73% | 2% |

In your opinion, which comes closer to your view of why some people file lawsuits opposing such things as prayer in schools or displays of religious symbols in government buildings—they are trying to turn the United States into a godless society, or they are trying to protect themselves and others from having religion forced onto them?

| Turn the United States into a godless society | Protect themselves | No opinion |
|---|---|---|
| 31% | 62% | 7% |

Which comes closest to your opinion about displays of religion in public places or government buildings— it is acceptable to display only Christian symbols, as long as symbols of other religions are also displayed, or it is unacceptable to diaplay any religious symbols at all?

| Acceptable to display only Christian symbols | Acceptable to display symbols of all religions | Unacceptable | No opinion |
|---|---|---|---|
| 10% | 58% | 29% | 3% |

Which comes closest to your view—government can promote the teachings of a religion without harming the rights of people who do not belong to that religion, or any time government promotes the teachings of a religion, it can harm the rights of people who do not belong to that religion?

| Can promote without harming | Can harm any time it promotes | No opinion |
|---|---|---|
| 40% | 54% | 6% |

*For results based on the total sample of National Adults, one can say with 95% confidence that the margin of sampling error is ± 3 percentage points. In addition to sampling error, question wording and practical difficulties in conducting surveys can introduce error or bias into the findings of public opinion polls.*

## QUESTIONS FOR ANALYSIS AND DISCUSSION

1. On what issues connected to church and state do Americans seem to overwhelmingly agree? On which do they seem sharply divided? What do you think accounts for the areas of agreement and division? Explain.
2. Based on this poll, do Americans treat all religions equally, or favor one over others? Explain.
3. Answer each question in this poll expressing your own viewpoint. Include one or two sentences for each response explaining why you answered the way you did.
4. Conduct your own poll using the questions drafted by *USA Today*. Interview at least 30 people for their viewpoints. Do the opinions expressed in the poll mirror what you have heard yourself on campus? Analyze the data.

## What Happy Holidays?
*Cathy Young*

With the holiday decorations come the controversies. It is the season to argue about Christmas trees and menorahs on public greens, Santa Clauses on school property, and nativity scenes inside municipal rotaries. Do such public displays of religious celebrations oppress citizens who do not believe in the religions represented? Are cities and towns abusing the separation of church and state? Or do restrictions on such displays curtail citizens' rights to religious expression? In the next essay, columnist Cathy Young discusses the issue of the separation of church, state . . . and holiday decorations.*

### BEFORE YOU READ

Based on your personal experience consider how the issue of public expressions of religion during the holiday season has changed over the last 20 years. Do you think it is a good thing this issue has received so much attention recently, or is it much ado about nothing?

### AS YOU READ

In your opinion, does a public square that features a holiday display convey the message to people who do not celebrate the holiday that "they do not belong"? Why or why not?

1   Peace on Earth? Forget it. Nowadays, Christmas is a battlefield in the culture wars. "It's beginning to look a lot like Christmas" has come to mean that there are endless arguments about nativity scenes, Santa Claus and reindeer on public property, Christmas carols in public schools, and the greeting "Merry Christmas" vs. "Happy Holidays."

2   "Arguments" is, perhaps, too polite a term. These days, we can't argue about anything without name-calling, hyperbole, paranoia, and crude stereotyping. Christmas is no exception. One side sees a satanic peril in a store clerk's "Happy Holidays" greeting; the other sees a theocratic menace in a Christmas carol sung at a school concert.

3   On one side, we get lurid tales of political correctness run amok, of nothing less than a secularist crusade to expunge all traces of Christmas and Christianity itself from the public square. On the other side, we get counterclaims of a politically motivated hysteria about a mythical war on Christmas, with the ulterior motive of shoving the religious right's social values down everybody's throats.

4   The excesses of multicultural sensitivity do exist. In my home state of New Jersey, the South Orange-Maplewood school district banned even instrumental versions of Christmas carols from school holiday concerts. (One Jewish student who plays in a high

*Cathy Young, *Reason Online*, December 28, 2004.

school band in Maplewood told the Associated Press the ban was "silly.") New York City's public schools bizarrely permit menorah displays, which supposedly have a secular element, but not nativity scenes. In some towns, there have been attempts to banish even recognized secular festive symbols such as the Christmas tree and Santa from public grounds.

5    The hysteria about "Christmas under attack" is equally real, and equally silly. At the conservative website Townhall.com, one Dr. Donald May thunders that the new grinches want Americans to "accept the abolition of Christmas, close down our churches, and remove the crosses from our cemeteries." Fox News talk show host Bill O'Reilly refers, with a straight face, to "the media forces of darkness" attacking "the defenders of Christmas" (such as O'Reilly himself). He also warns that "the traditions of Christmas are under fire by committed secularists, people who do not want any public demonstration of spirituality."

6    Let's put things in perspective. Even the most far-reaching efforts to stamp out religious expression in "the public square" affect only government property. No one is seeking to stop churches from displaying nativity scenes on their front lawns or homeowners from putting up religiously themed decorations. If some private businesses such as stores decide to stick to secular holiday displays and salutations, that's their choice.

7    "Season's Greetings" and "Happy Holidays" may come across as bland and politically correct. But as James Lileks documents on his blog, the shift toward such nonsectarian greetings actually began in America in the 1950s, not as an attack on religion but in acknowledgment of an increasingly diverse society. At a recent press conference, President Bush wished everyone "Happy holidays" twice and never mentioned Christmas. He must be in on the left-wing plot.

Those Americans who don't celebrate Christmas obviously have to be tolerant of the vast majority who do; but they also have a right to a public square which does not loudly tell them they don't belong. It's worth noting, too, that quite a few non-Christian Americans celebrate Christmas as a cultural tradition, and being inclusive toward them is a good thing. Meanwhile, many Christians are genuinely concerned about the secularization and commercialization of the holiday. But for those who truly want to put Christ back into Christmas," the answer is in giving more time and attention to religious and charitable activities, not in demanding more Christian symbolism at the place where you shop. Macy's is not a temple.

Of course, the battle over Christmas isn't just over Christmas; it's part of the larger divide between liberal secularists and religious conservatives. Passions over such issues as same-sex marriage, abortion, and the teaching of evolution in schools are played out in clashes over crèches. On all those issues, there is precious little effort by either side to understand the other, and precious little respect for the other side's beliefs.

And so the Christmas wars are likely to continue, even though politicizing a religious holiday is surely just as bad as commercializing it. Dr. May's column at Townhall.com ends with the exhortation, "Merry Christmas to all, and to all a good fight." To this, one can only say: God help us, everyone.

QUESTIONS FOR ANALYSIS AND DISCUSSION

1. Young states "these days, we can't argue about anything without name-calling, hyperbole, paranoia, and crude stereotyping. Christmas is no exception." What sort of "name calling" and "crude stereotyping" is associated with the Christmas season? Explain.
2. What is Young's position on the "culture wars" over the holiday season? Does she present a balanced perspective on the issue?
3. What is the underlying issue over the "battle over Christmas"? To what broader issues does it connect? Explain.
4. Young observes that the "hysteria about 'Christmas under attack' is equally real and equally silly." How can it be both? Is Christmas indeed under attack? By whom? Do you agree that the "hysteria" is "silly"? Why or why not?
5. Is this issue likely to have a resolution that pleases everyone? If so, propose a solution you think would work. If not, explain why you believe the issue to be at an impasse.

## Deck the Halls?
*Bridget Samburg*

Arguments over holiday decorations in public spaces, including schools and in front of town halls, continue unabated into the second decade of the new millennium. In this next article, *Boston Globe* correspondent Bridget Samburg interviews two people with different opinions on the matter—a Massachusetts lawyer, and a professor of American Jewish history.*

### BEFORE YOU READ

What public holiday displays, if any, does your own home town erect? Are they on the town green or in front of the town hall? on public or school property? Do you think towns should or should not erect holiday displays on public or municipal property?

### AS YOU READ

In this interview, a Jewish professor explains why he feels that religion in the schools promotes tolerance and prepares students for the diversity of the real world. What do you think? Is it better to expose children to different religions and beliefs, or would such exposure subject them to "conflicting messages"?

*Bridget Samburg, *Boston Globe,* December 12, 2004.

1 It's holiday time again, and we've unpacked the dancing Santas, red-nosed reindeers, and big, shiny menorahs. But is it appropriate for them, kitschy and otherwise, religious and secular to be displayed in town squares, city halls, and public schools? Should such celebrations stay in private homes, or are they good for the community, if not an integral part of American tradition? Where some see an entanglement of government and religion, others see an opportunity to revel in our country's diversity. In any case, the post-election climate raises the temperature around these issues.

2 Melissa McWhinney is a lawyer who lives in Somerville, Massachusetts, and Jonathan Sarna is a professor of American Jewish history at Brandeis University.

3 **McWhinney:** There is a difference between decorating on generalized government property versus decorating in schools because children are more vulnerable to conflicting messages.

4 **Sarna:** While I think it is inappropriate to decorate for Christmas to the exclusion of Hanukkah, Kwanzaa, and other holidays, the notion that we have children from different cultural and religious backgrounds and that we recognize those backgrounds is legitimate. We are paying a huge price for the total removal of religion from schools. Helping youngsters understand diversity would be better for the schools and better for the youngsters.

5 **McWhinney:** It's essential that children learn about diversity. However, it tends to be pitted as a contest: "If I want to have my Christmas tree, how big a menorah do I need so I can get what I want?"

6 **Sarna:** Schools should be the arena where we work out peacefully those kinds of issues, so that we are well trained when we deal with them in society at large.

7 **McWhinney:** People who object to the denial to have Christmas parties in the schools are doing it because they remember how nice life was in the second grade. It's legally a problem, and it's culturally a problem. Winter decorations are fine. Crèches are out. Christmas trees play strongly on people's emotional sensitivities. I would prefer not to see them at all.

8 **Sarna:** The tension that we face is a larger tension about what the relationship of religion and state should be in America. We agree that the notion of a triumphant Christianity in society or in the classroom is inappropriate. Separationism in an extreme has turned out to neither work nor to reflect the kind of society most Americans want.

9 **McWhinney:** How do you compromise with the Christmas carols? What do you do with kids for whom this is a problem religiously?

10 **Sarna:** Any student should be allowed to bow out.

11 **McWhinney:** It's a small minority who actually bows out, but I think it's a larger minority who wishes they could.

12 **Sarna:** We respect the rights of children and their parents to make a variety of decisions.

13 **McWhinney:** I admire the families who stand up to it, but it puts them in a tremendous conflict situation, which is unnecessary. It's a question of the endorsement, the support, and the celebration with public funding that is of concern. There are some school districts that are not interested in this discussion and defend their right to do things as they always have.

14 **Sarna:** I'm arguing for a middle ground that would celebrate the religious diversity of the country.

15 **McWhinney:** What would be in your town square?

16 **Sarna:** A wide array of religious symbols: a Christmas tree, a menorah, symbols of other communities.

17 **McWhinney:** Everyone's symbol cannot stand in the public square. There is simply not enough room. I don't think it's possible to draw the line in a reasonable manner, which is why I would prefer that all these things retreat to the home and church. What I do in my home may be very different than what I expect to see at a town hall. To have my tax money spent on the promotion of what I consider a religious expression or endorsement of a particular religion does concern me.

18 **Sarna:** In some ways, that's what makes America great: that we do recognize various religious traditions, and we are not trying to create the sense that you are Christian at home or a Jew at home—and just a human being when you leave your home.

19 **McWhinney:** I don't think people are being asked to leave their religion at home. That's exactly why it's a problem to have Christmas parties at school. The Jewish kids, the Muslim kids, the Buddhist kids are who they are at school. How can they be asked to participate in a Christmas party?

20 **Sarna:** The goal should be to work very hard to preserve a religiously pluralistic America. I have faith in the American people that they are religiously tolerant, and given the opportunity to recognize and even venerate a full spectrum of world religions, they will do so.

21 **McWhinney:** I think they are religiously tolerant as long as you don't come along and mess with Christmas.

22 **Sarna:** The Supreme Court has approved the notion of religious diversity in the public square. It's about time we moved past these discussions and figure out how we can best carry out that ruling.

### QUESTIONS FOR ANALYSIS AND DISCUSSION

1. Samburg notes that the "post-election climate raises the temperature around" the issues of holiday displays in the public arena. What is the "post-election climate"? Why does it bring these issues to the forefront? Explain.
2. McWhinney argues that religious symbols and holidays must be kept out of schools "because children are more vulnerable to conflicting messages." What conflicting messages are children likely to experience with Christmas trees, menorahs, or carols in school? Respond to her claim with your own viewpoint and personal experience.
3. Sarna observes, "separationism in an extreme has turned out to neither work nor to reflect the kind of society most Americans want." In what ways has "separationism" failed? Should the majority ("most Americans") decide this issue? Why or why not?

4. Evaluate the following statements made by McWhinney:
   a. "Everyone's symbol cannot stand in the public square. There is simply not enough room."
   b. "People who object to the denial to have Christmas parties in the schools are doing it because they remember how nice life was in the second grade."
   c. "It's a small minority who actually bow out, but I think there's a larger minority who wishes they could."
   
   How do these statements support McWhinney's argument that religion should have no place in schools or public spaces?
5. Do you think McWhinney and Sarna would ever reach a consensus on this issue with further discussion? Why or why not?

## End the "War on Christmas"
### Edward Grinnan

*The war on Christmas.* Just about all of us have heard the phrase. Most of us know it has something to do with the removal of manger scenes on town greens and the re-phrasing of the traditional greeting "Merry Christmas" to "Happy Holidays." But in an ef-fort to include everyone, and offend no one, some people indeed feel excluded and offended. In this next essay, the editor of the religious magazine *Guideposts* appeals for an end to the annual controversies over Christmas displays, holiday greetings, and December celebrations.*

**BEFORE YOU READ**

Do you feel that there is indeed a "War on Christmas"? What implications does the word "war" have? How does it set the tone for the controversy? Explain.

**AS YOU READ**

Evaluate Grinnan's tone in this essay. Identify specific phrases and words that convey his tone. Where might you expect to hear this argument—in a magazine, in a lecture, over drinks? Explain.

1   This Christmas I would like to declare a ceasefire, a truce, nay an armistice on that ter-rible ongoing conflict known as "The War on Christmas."

2   Who declared this war anyway? Yet every year now it seems I hear the term bandied about as if it were Afghanistan or Iraq or Somalia we were talking about. Frankly the cou-pling of "Christmas" and "War" is offensive to me. I wish people would stop it.

3   In a pluralistic society the separation between state and religion can sometimes blur, people being the ambivalent creatures that we are. But to proclaim the existence of a war on Christmas and then start fighting it, on both sides, is odious, whether it's an atheist

*Edward Grinnan, *Washington Post,* December 2009.

taking umbrage over an innocuous nativity display or a Christian intolerant of any homogenization of the season. Let's not forget that many of the beloved trappings of Christmas are frankly pagan in origin and were folded into the Christian holy day by shrewd and pragmatic Roman politicians trying to market the new religion to the peoples of their far-flung and tottering empire.

4    We cut down trees and drag them inside our houses and adorn them. Can you say pantheism? There is no historical basis for December 25 being the birth date of Christ, other than the date coincided with Druidistic celebrations of the winter solstice that were already centuries if not millennia old. Yet isn't the solstice the point in annual time when light begins creeping back into our lives, just as Christians see the Christ child as the light of redemption divinely brought into a sin-darkened world? In this respect the evolution of Christmas makes perfect sense.

5    Do we say "Happy Holidays" or do we say "Merry Christmas?" Does it make a difference? I mean really. Sometimes this country sounds like a bickering old married couple arguing about things that don't matter to cover up the things that do.

6    I am reminded of a story published in *Guideposts* some time ago about an incident in WWI. On Christmas Eve, 1914, as British and German soldiers huddled miserably in their freezing, vermin-invested trenches in the French countryside, a sentry from the Fifth Scottish Rifles heard a familiar tune drifting across the cratered no-man's-land that separated the warring parties. "Heilige Nacht . . ." Holy night.

7    The British Tommy hummed along. Soon others on both sides of the murderous divide joined in, a chorus of voices rising above the shattered farmland. Then the British volleyed back with "God Rest Ye Merry Gentleman." And back and forth they went until the dawn of Christmas day broke. And a day later they resumed killing each other.

8    This is the great contradiction believers face, the human duality, our capacity for both great love and great hate, a metaphysical paradox we try to resolve through faith. Would the argument over the correctness of a seasonal salutation have made any sense to those soldiers? They only knew that a force stronger than fear, stronger than hatred, had briefly united them and offered a flicker of hope for the prospect of peace.

9    Christ was born not into a world of peace and prosperity but into a world roiling with conflict and uncertainty, a world riven by poverty and prejudice, war and oppression. It could have been no other way. It was a world and a race that needed him and still does, for the issues we face today are not so different from the ones the world grappled with then. What we celebrate as embodied by the Christ child is our yearning for hope and peace in our lives and in our world.

10    So please, no more talk of the so-called war on Christmas. Despite the vaguely pagan origins of its traditions, and our much worse coarsening of the holiday with rampant commercialization, at its golden heart Christmas is an embracing of joy and light and peace, something I think everyone can agree to celebrate together.

### QUESTIONS FOR ANALYSIS AND DISCUSSION

1.  Why does Grinnan object to the phrasing "war on Christmas." Explain.
2.  Grinnan's essay is the third viewpoint on the topic in this section (preceded by Young, McWhinney, and Sarna). In your opinion, who presents the most reasonable viewpoint, and why?

3. Why do you think Grinnan recounts the actions of the British and German soldiers during World War I? What relevance does this historical anecdote have on his overall argument?
4. What is Grinnan's call to action? How do you think McWhinney and Sarna from the previous interview would respond to Grinnan's appeal? Explain.

## Prayer and Creationism—Met with Supreme Hostility
*Stuart Taylor, Jr.*

It was only about a generation ago that most football games began with a prayer in the locker room. Most graduation ceremonies included an appeal by a religious figure to bless the commencement and its participants as they entered their new roles in life. Gradually, such public expressions of prayer have dwindled. The wording "under God" in the Pledge receives annual debate. Students need not recite the Pledge at all. In this next essay by *National Journal* columnist Stuart Taylor, Jr., describes how the Supreme Court is grappling with the controversy. Taylor wonders, with each decision it makes, can the Supreme Court somehow stop its slide down a slippery slope in which all expressions of prayer may be banned entirely?*

### BEFORE YOU READ

Should expressions of faith in school or in public spaces be banned? Who determines what is acceptable and what is not?

### AS YOU READ

In your opinion, did the Supreme Court decision create a "slippery slope"? Why or why not? Review page 56 in Chapter 2 in the first section for a discussion on slippery slope arguments.

1   It may now be unconstitutional for a public school teacher or student leader to recite the Pledge of Allegiance in class. Or at a football game. Or at a graduation. Or to recite the Declaration of Independence. Or to sing the national anthem.

2   At least, this is a plausible reading of the Supreme Court's 6-3 decision on June 19, 2000, that struck down a Texas high school's policy of allowing an elected student leader to pray over the public address system at football games. It seems most unlikely, of course, that the Justices would actually take the radical step of banishing the pledge from school ceremonies anytime soon—if only because it would be all too obvious that if the law says that, then the law is an ass. But the more-liberal Justices might have to strain to avoid carrying their logic that far. And the three dissenters had reason to complain that "the tone of the Court's opinion . . . bristles with hostility to all things religious in public life."

---
*Stuart Taylor, Jr., *National Journal*, July 18, 2000.

3      To be sure, the Texas school may have crossed the line into unconstitutional sponsorship of religion. Justice John Paul Stevens properly stressed in his opinion for the majority that various detailed provisions of the school's recently adopted policy—which authorized election of a single student leader for the entire season to deliver "a brief invocation and/or message" before each home game—rendered it "simply … a continuation" of the school's long-standing practice of sponsoring official prayers. That inference was enhanced by allegations that school officials had "chastis[ed] children who held minority religious beliefs" and had "distribut[ed] Gideon Bibles on school premises."

4      But Stevens did not stop there. He also implied strongly that the Court would strike down as an act of the state any prayer initiated by a majority vote of students, even at a school whose administrators have always eschewed endorsing any form of religion and have made it clear that nonreligious and religious messages are equally welcome. "The majoritarian process implemented by the district guarantees, by definition, that minority candidates will never prevail and that their views will be effectively silenced," Stevens asserted, leaving them "at the mercy of the majority" and feeling a "sense of isolation and affront."

5      Really? One Ben Marcus recalled in *Time* that far from "'isolation and affront' . . . I sometimes found an unexpected degree of the opposite: inclusion and camaraderie with my teammates after taking part in the pre-game prayers, a solemn connection that I wanted to scoff at but, because it moved me, could not."

6      The kind of prayer that Marcus found so benign is apparently too redolent of the Spanish Inquisition for the Supreme Court's taste: "Students . . . feel immense social pressure . . . to be involved in . . . high school football," Stevens explained, and thus "to risk facing a personally offensive religious ritual. . . . [So] the delivery of a pre-game prayer has the improper effect of coercing those present to participate in an act of religious worship." Wow.

7      Here we have two untenable propositions: that even though those present are free to sit or stand silently, turn their backs, or leave, any vote by a student majority to have prayers amounts to (1) "coercion" of nonbelievers and religious minorities to (2) "participate in an act of religious worship."

8      And that brings us to the Pledge of Allegiance. The most obvious problem is the phrase "under God," which was inserted in 1954 between "one nation" and "indivisible." Under the Court's reasoning, those two words alone would seem to make the thousands of teachers who regularly lead their students in the pledge into serial violators of the establishment clause. (The same could also be said of teachers who lead students in singing the national anthem. The last verse includes: "And this be our motto: 'In God is our trust.'") Well, we can fix that little problem by stripping "under God" out of the pledge, can't we? Nope. Not if we superimpose the logic of the June 19 Stevens opinion upon that of the famous 1943 decision striking down a West Virginia law that had compelled all students—on pain of expulsion and prosecution of their parents—to join in saluting and pledging allegiance to the flag.

9      Ruling that Jehovah's Witnesses had a right to refuse to salute or to recite the pledge (which did not then refer to God), Justice Robert H. Jackson penned some of the most stirring words in all of constitutional law: "If there is any fixed star in our constitutional constellation, it is that no official, high or petty, can prescribe what shall be orthodox in

politics, nationalism, religion, or other matters of opinion or force citizens to confess by word or act their faith therein." It violates the freedom of speech, Jackson held, to compel anybody to join in a public statement on any "matter of opinion" over his or her objection—whether or not religion is a factor.

10    "The refusal of these persons to participate in the ceremony," Jackson added, "does not interfere with or deny rights of others to do so." But now comes the June 19 Stevens opinion, which deems it "coercing those present to participate" when a student majority votes for a ceremony (at least a religious one) to which any student objects.

11    It's hard to see why a patriotic ceremony would be any less coercive than a religious one. So it might be logical (if dumb) to extend to patriotic ceremonies Stevens' assertion that "school sponsorship of a religious message is impermissible because it sends the ancillary message to members of the audience who are non-adherents that they are outsiders, not full members of the political community."

12    Suppose that the child of a Symbionese Liberation Army veteran, or of a Chinese diplomat, objects on political grounds to hearing the pledge recited at school. Under the 1943 decision, the child clearly could not be compelled to join in, and rightly so. But would Stevens also bar the school from allowing anyone to recite the pledge, with or without "under God," lest it send a message that those who object are "outsiders, not full members of the political community"?

13    A similar argument could be made for barring a recital of the Declaration of Independence if any student objects to the idea that "all men are created equal"—not to mention the neo-theocratic stuff that Thomas Jefferson threw in about being "endowed by their Creator with certain inalienable rights."

14    Far-fetched? Sure. But it's unclear how and where the Court can stop sliding down this slope. And "if the speech of the majority may be restricted to avoid giving offense to the minority," as Jeffrey Rosen suggests in *The New Republic*, some evangelical Christians might raise equally plausible objections to evolution being taught in their presence, "on the grounds that it offends their belief in creationism."

15    Speaking of which, consider another vote by the same 6-3 majority, also on June 19, involving a Louisiana school board's policy on teaching evolution. The policy did not bar such teaching, or require the teaching of creationism. It simply said that whenever "the scientific theory of evolution is to be presented," teachers should tell students three things: that it is "not intended to influence or dissuade the Biblical version of Creation or any other concept"; that each student has "the basic right and privilege . . . to form his/her own opinion or maintain beliefs taught by parents on this very important matter of the origin of life and matter"; and that "students are urged to exercise critical thinking and gather all information possible and closely examine each alternative toward forming an opinion."

16    That's it. Seems pretty innocuous—indeed, enlightened—to me. Yet six Justices voted without comment to let stand a federal appellate decision striking down the policy as yet another establishment of religion. The dissent, by Justice Antonin Scalia, seems persuasive: "Far from advancing religion . . . the [effect of the] disclaimer . . . is merely to advance freedom of thought . . . [by an] acknowledgment of beliefs widely held among the people of this country."

17    Yes, there really are a lot of people in the hinterland who still believe such stuff. Not many of them went to Ivy League schools, or hang out with Supreme Court Justices. Nor do their traditions and beliefs get much consideration in such sophisticated quarters. So now we have come, in Scalia's words, to "bar[ring] a school district from even suggesting to students that other theories besides evolution—including, but not limited to, the Biblical theory of creation—are worthy of their consideration."

18    Small wonder that some conservative Christians are starting to ask, as did an Illinois woman quoted by *the New York Times*, "How long it will be before they tell us we can't pray in public places"?

### QUESTIONS FOR ANALYSIS AND DISCUSSION

1. What objections might someone raise regarding the Pledge of Allegiance? The National Anthem? Explain.
2. Judge Stevens notes that despite what they say, students may feel inwardly pressured to participate in prayers at sporting events and other school activities. Have you ever felt pressured to participate in school prayer? Does public prayer add value for the players of a sporting activity? For a graduation? Explain.
3. What is Taylor's argument? What point is he trying to make? Explain.
4. What is Taylor's opinion of the Supreme Court's recent decisions regarding prayer and expressions of religion in school? Explain.
5. Respond to the question posed by the woman from Illinois "How long it will be before they tell us we can't pray in public places"? Is this likely to happen? Why or why not?

## A New Theology of Celebration
### *Francis S. Collins*

In this editorial, a renowned biologist reflects on the current battle between atheists and fundamentalist Christians. On the one hand, many atheists claim that intelligent people must reject religion as unreasonable and illogical. On the other hand, fundamentalist religious groups are forcing believers to agree that the world is 10,000 years old and any other interpretation is a rejection of their religious faith. Collins, himself a religious convert, describes his vision for a new theology in which faith and science cooperate and happily co-exist. Is his vision nothing more than wishful thinking?*

### BEFORE YOU READ

Are religious faith and acceptance of science compatible? Why or why not?

*Franscis S. Collins, *Science & Spirit*, September/October 2007.

**AS YOU READ**

Consider how Collins frames his argument. How does he define and identify the issue and controversy? How does he persuade readers to understand his point of view?

1   I have often been accused of being optimistic. In the early days of the Human Genome Project, some very wise people predicted that this audacious project would end in failure. But as the leader of the effort from 1993 until its conclusion in 2003 (ahead of schedule and under budget, no less), I never doubted that the best and brightest minds that were recruited to work on this historic project would prevail. And they did.

2   So my faith in the ability of science to answer questions about nature paid off. But that is not the most important area where faith is part of my life. After spending my young years as an atheist, I became convinced through reading the logical arguments of C.S. Lewis and the words of the Bible that belief in God was more plausible than atheism. After two years of struggle, I became a Christian at age twenty-seven. Since then, my faith in God has been the rock on which I stand, a means to answer critical questions on which science remains silent: What is the meaning of life? Is there a God? Do our concepts of right and wrong have any real foundation? What happens after we die?

3   As one of a large number of scientists who believe in God, I find it deeply troubling to watch the escalating culture wars between science and faith, especially in America. A spate of angry books by atheists, many of them using the compelling evidence of Darwin's theory of evolution as a rhetorical club over the heads of believers, argues that atheism is the only rational choice for a thinking person. Some go so far as to label religious faith as the root of all evil and insinuate that parents who teach their children about religion are committing child abuse.

4   Partially in response to these attacks, believers, especially evangelical Christians, have targeted evolution as godless and incompatible with the truths of the Bible. Many Americans see Earth as less than 10,000 years old, a "young Earth" belief that clashes with mountains of data from cosmology, physics, chemistry, geology, paleontology, anthropology, biology, and genetics. Intelligent Design, which proposes that evolution is insufficient to account for complexity, enjoys wide support in the church despite rejection in the scientific community.

5   What a sad situation. Are we not all seeking the truth? That is what God calls us to. It seems unlikely that God, the author of all creation, is threatened by what science is teaching us about the awesome complexity and grandeur of His creation. Can God be well served by lies about nature, no matter how noble the intentions of those who spread them?

6   The current circumstance is not tenable over the long run. Despite their claims to hardnosed objectivity, atheists have gone wildly outside the evidence by declaring God imaginary. They are proposing an impoverished perspective that will not satisfy most of their intended converts. For their part, fundamentalists who demand acceptance of a unilateral interpretation of Genesis are making that a litmus test for true faith, which wise theologians over the centuries have not found necessary.

7   Could we not step back from the unloving rhetoric of these entrenched positions and seek a path towards truth? If science is a way of uncovering the details of God's creation, then it may actually be a form of worship. Did not God, in giving us the intelligence to ask and answer questions about nature, expect us to use it? We should be able to learn about God in the laboratory as well as in the cathedral.

8    The shrill voices at the extremes of this debate have had the microphone for too long. Although they will no doubt continue to rail against each other, the rest of us should find ways to bring together scientists who are open to spiritual truths, theologians who are ready to embrace scientific findings about the universe, and pastors who know the real concerns and needs of their flocks. Together, in a loving and worshipful attitude, we could formulate a new and wondrous natural theology. This kind of theology celebrates God as the creator, embraces His majestic universe from the far-flung galaxies to the "fearfully and wonderfully made" nature of humanity, and accepts and incorporates the marvelous things that God has given us the chance to discover through science.

9    If we make a serious and prayerful attempt to do this together, perhaps in a few years this new "celebration theology" could eliminate the conflict between science and faith. God didn't start the conflict. We did. I may sound unrealistic, even a bit of a Pollyanna, by proposing that we could draw this unnecessary battle to a close. But, I remind you, I have often been accused of being optimistic.

### QUESTIONS FOR ANALYSIS AND DISCUSSION

1. Why does Collins open his editorial with a reference to his leadership of the Human Genome Project? Does this detailing his background help his argument? Why or why not?

2. Collins explains that the current debate over evolution has become so polarized that meaningful debate has become impossible. What problems does he identify, and what solutions does he offer?

3. Collins writes this editorial from the perspective of a believing Christian. Identify areas of his essay that reveal his religious stance.

4. Collins identifies himself as a convert to Christianity, but could his argument and his points appeal to people of other religious faiths? to atheists? to fundamentalists? Why or why not?

## WRITING ASSIGNMENTS

1. In the opening paragraph of his essay, Hugh Heclo wonders what it might mean for religion to "reenter the public square." He asks, "What good might it do there—and what harm?" Write an essay in which you answer his question. Refer to some of the issues in this section, as well as the concept of religion and civic life in general.

2. Do you think there is any room for religion in the public sphere? Who should decide what the rules are and determine the level of separation between church and state? Include public expressions of religion such as prayer in schools and at state occasions, swearing on the Bible in court or featuring the Ten Commandments on state property, Congressional prayer, and religious holiday displays on public lands. Write an essay presenting your position on this issue and support it with information from this chapter as well as outside research.

3. You are a judge asked to determine whether "In God We Trust" on U.S. currency is a violation of the First Amendment. Look up the history of this phrase at the U.S.

Treasury's website http://www.treas.gov (type in the phrase in the website's search bar). Make a ruling on the issue supporting your position on other church and state decisions.

4. Review the language of the First Amendment of the Constitution and present your own interpretation of its wording. You may include the history of the Constitution, the background of the Founding Fathers, and the spirit of the document in your response.

5. Write a research paper on the role religion plays in other nations' governments. For example, how does religion intersect with state in a European nation such as England, Sweden, or France? Or in a Middle Eastern nation such as Iraq or Jordan? Alternatively, you may prepare a research paper exploring the validity of Hugh Heclo's observation that most major political conflicts have a religious foundation. Research the conflict and its background. Can there ever be a true separation between church and state? Why or why not?

6. Before reading this chapter, did you already have an opinion on the separation of church and state? Did any of the essays in this section influence your current point of view or help you to form one? Why or why not?

# University Life

F or many students, college offers both an opportunity to learn about the world and a chance to exercise the personal freedoms and responsibilities of adulthood, when words and actions matter. The university opens the door to the millennia-old bodies of knowledge our intellectual history is based upon, as well as the cutting-edge thinking that will shape the future.

Despite the many new freedoms college students enjoy, a college campus is not truly the "real world." Campus policies often aim to control student behavior. Administrators may impose restrictions on students' right to assemble, implement speech codes, and enforce rules of behavior. At the same time, universities pledge to deliver a meaningful education and to prepare students for the challenges of adulthood. This chapter examines issues connected to the role of the university, students' personal rights and responsibilities, and the future of the American campus experience.

What exactly is role of the university? What does higher education owe to students? From the minute you take your PSAT as a junior in high school, the questions abound: Does everyone have the right to a college education? Should everyone go to college? Is today's college curriculum preparing students for the real world? Does college prepare students to compete in a new world economy and to think for themselves? Do the liberal arts matter? Do professors matter? And what should students expect after graduation? Great jobs? A lifetime of hard work?

Many students arrive on campus eager to learn and equally eager to party. Some readings in this chapter explore the issue of personal responsibility on campus. If college students are truly adults, do they need college administrators acting *in loco parentis*—controlling what they decide to do outside the classroom? With personal freedom comes responsibility. Are students expecting college to be an educational experience that will prepare them for the real world, or are they expecting merely a fun time? These readings consider the nuances of college life—what students might expect and what the university expects in return.

## Diversity: The Value of Discomfort
*Ronald D. Liebowitz*

In the next essay, Middlebury College president Ronald D. Liebowitz explains that college is not, and should not be, a sterile environment in which one is never challenged. Diversity of students and diversity of points of view encourage real-world experiences in which people must work together. There is value in discomfort because it encourages us to be critical thinkers and to challenge ourselves and the people around us to reach consensus—even if we don't always agree with each other. What follows is Liebowitz's baccalaureate address to the class of 2007 at Middlebury College on May 26, 2007. *

**BEFORE YOU READ**

How diverse is your campus population—both among students and faculty? How much is the diversity on campus connected to your regional location and college mission?

**AS YOU READ**

What were the "culture wars"? Do they still exist, in whole or in part, on college campuses today?

1    Good afternoon. On behalf of the faculty and staff of the College, I extend a warm welcome to the parents and families of our graduating seniors, and of course to members of the class of 2007, as well.

2    Both this baccalaureate service and commencement are joyous occasions celebrating an important transition in the lives of our graduates. Today's service is an occasion to reflect on what our graduating seniors have already done, on the experience and the accomplishments of the past four years, and what those years have meant to them and to this College community.

3    Let me begin, therefore, by telling you a few things about the Middlebury Class of 2007. There are 643 graduates in this class, 287 men and 356 women. Some 365 of you are graduating with honors, and 65 were elected to Phi Beta Kappa. The most popular majors for your class were economics, chosen by 92 students, and English, chosen by 74, and 135 of you majored in two subjects. About 77 percent of you—497 students—studied at least one foreign language, and 62 percent—405 students—studied abroad for at least one semester in 48 countries. Members of your class have earned three Watson Fellowships for research abroad, two Fulbright Scholarships, and a Keasbey Scholarship to study at Oxford University.

4    Your class has been characterized by an exceptional spirit of volunteerism. Collectively, approximately 70 percent of you contributed to the community through volunteer and service-learning projects, as well as through pro bono consulting work. Some of you have served on local fire departments and rescue squads; traveled to New Orleans in the wake of hurricane Katrina to assist in the rebuilding effort; served as Big Brothers or Big Sisters to local children; worked with the John Graham Community Shelter, providing meals and companionship to the homeless; and shared your expertise with local businesses and regional economic development groups based on what you learned in economics and geography courses.

5    Largely because of your energy, leadership, and dedication, Middlebury has been recognized by the Carnegie Foundation for its "community engagement" and by the Princeton Review, which named Middlebury as one of its "colleges with a conscience" for fostering

*Ronald D. Liebowitz, Baccalaureate Address to Middlebury College, 2007.

social responsibility and public service. I am enormously proud of all that you have done to bring positive changes to our community, our country, and our world.

6     I am also truly impressed by the imagination and scholarship of this class. These qualities were vividly demonstrated last month at our first College-wide symposium recognizing student research and creativity. About 60 members of your class participated in that symposium, where students presented the results of research on subjects ranging from solar power to social entrepreneurship to religious life at Middlebury. This symposium, which is going to be an annual event, exemplifies the spirit of intellectual risk-taking, independent thought, and a passion for learning that should characterize the best of a liberal arts education.

7     You've had impressive success in the arts, as well. For example, a number of members of this class belonged to the cast and crew that staged last year's remarkable production of *The Bewitched*, which was presented at the Kennedy Center in Washington as one of four finalists in the American College Theatre Festival. In addition, a member of your class relied on her work in the arts to become one of the winners of the Kathryn Wasserman Davis 100 Projects for Peace national fellowship program. She will use the study of architecture to analyze the border crossings between Israel and the West Bank and Gaza Strip, exploring how such crossings may be reconceived as points of connection rather than of division.

8     In athletics, too, you have excelled. Your class includes 30 athletes who have earned All American honors in intercollegiate sports and 50 who earned all-NESCAC academic honors. You helped to win 25 NESCAC championships and eight national titles for Middlebury over the past four years in intercollegiate sports, and this spring our rugby club won its first national championship.

9     There is yet one more notable thing about this class that I would like to mention. You have helped to make Middlebury a more diverse and inclusive place than it was four years ago—which brings me to the theme I particularly want to discuss this afternoon. Your class is statistically the most diverse, and the most international, ever to graduate from Middlebury. That has certainly affected—and I would say it has greatly improved—the education you have received here.

10     Why? In a nutshell: since so much of what you learn in college you learn from your fellow students, the broader the range of backgrounds and perspectives those students represent, the broader and richer the education one is likely to receive. Because of the residential and human-intensive nature of your Middlebury education, little of what you do that is related to your studies is done in solitude. You are always bouncing ideas off of classmates, roommates, hall-mates, housemates, teammates, or fellow members of student organizations.

11     The human-intensive nature of learning at liberal arts colleges was energized by the Civil Rights and other social movements of the 1960s. Formerly underrepresented groups began attending American colleges and universities in significantly greater numbers, and the breadth of learning experiences changed radically. The changes, at first, were by dint of the kinds of discussions that were taking place on a meaningful scale in the classroom. Those discussions, whether about a classical work of literature or an interpretation of some historical event, included new perspectives that had previously been absent from the classroom, and no doubt forced some people to rethink their opinions.

12    Over time, the fruits of a broadened scope of discussion extended to the curriculum and the faculty with similar results: a bigger tent of ideas within which to teach and learn. But that bigger tent brought intellectual conflict and discomfort. The so-called "culture wars" were an expression of the tension created by the challenge and inclusion of new interpretations of the curriculum. Some degree of conflict was inevitable given the new and vastly different perspectives that had been previously excluded from, or were, at best, on the margins of the academy. Through these changes, the academy became a richer, but also a more polarized, environment for learning.

13    Since the 1960s, small, rural liberal arts colleges have not experienced as rapid and extensive a change in the composition of their student bodies as public institutions or schools located in urban areas. Yet, many have changed quite significantly, especially with the arrival, more recently, of international students, many of whom come from the developing world.

14    I cite, for example, the changes that have taken place here at Middlebury since 1980. In 1980, less than 5 percent of the student population was either an American student of color or an international student . . . that is less than 1 in 20 students. Our incoming class, the Class of 2011, will be approximately 32 percent American students of color and international. Twenty-seven years ago it was 1 in 20; today, it is 1 in 3. In addition, the change in the percentage of students on need-based financial aid is noteworthy because a student body with greater socioeconomic diversity is essential to our students' exposure to a variety of perspectives. In 1980, the percentage was 24 percent, while for the incoming class this September, the percentage is 47 percent: the highest ever.

15    This change in the composition of the student body reflects, in part, the changing demographics of the United States. But more than that, it reflects the College's deliberate effort to provide the richest learning environment for students. The College's recently approved strategic plan has as its highest priority increasing access to Middlebury for the very strongest students by continuing to meet the full need of all admitted students, increasing the grant portion of our financial aid packages, and reducing the amount of debt a student will incur during four years at the College.

16    The strategic planning committee believed that, by removing some of the financial barriers to studying at Middlebury, the College would more easily matriculate students from rural areas, from developing countries, and from inner cities. The student body, as a result, would be more ethnically, racially, and socio-economically diverse. There would no doubt be a greater diversity of ideas coming from students with such varied backgrounds, which would once again energize the classroom with frequent exchanges rooted in our students' vastly different life experiences.

17    It is no longer a cliché to say that "the local is the global and the global the local." In fact, it should go without saying that all of you who are graduating tomorrow will no longer be competing with young men and women predominantly from your hometowns, from a particular region of this country, or even from the United States. In all likelihood, the majority of you will be trying to get a job, pursue a project, or secure a spot in a leading graduate or professional school that will bring you in direct competition with young people from . . . you name it: Shanghai, Tokyo, Madrid, Buenos Aires, Johannesburg, Dehli, or Berlin. Even those of you determined to do something independently, outside of official structures or institutions, will soon learn that you are now part of a global network,

and the sooner you adapt to what this means, the easier you will discover how to succeed within that network.

18    In other words, it is no longer adequate to understand only one's own culture, no matter how dominant that culture may seem; or one's political and economic system, no matter how much others claim to want to copy it; or a single approach to solving problems, no matter how sure you are that your approach is the best. To succeed in the 21st century— which means to be engaged in the world in a way that allows you to make a difference, to fulfill a sense of achievement, and to allow you to be true to yourself because you know who you are—you need to be multi-cultural, multi-national, and multi-operational in how you think. And you can only be multi-cultural, multi-national, and multi-operational if you feel comfortable with the notion of difference. And that is why we seek diversity.

19    But greater diversity means change, and change on college campuses is almost always difficult. Few 18 to 22 year olds are skilled in inviting or tolerating perspectives that are vastly different from than their own. Frankly, the same goes for 30-, 40-, and 50-something-year-old academics. Even though a campus may become more diverse in terms of the numbers of underrepresented groups present, the level of engagement can still be inconsequential if those representing different viewpoints are not encouraged and supported to express them. If an institution is not prepared to make space, figuratively speaking, for previously excluded groups, and support their presence on campus, its diversity efforts cannot succeed. And if the wariness about discomfort is stronger than the desire to hear different viewpoints because engaging difference is uncomfortable, then the quest for diversity is hollow no matter what the demographic statistics on a campus reflect.

20    In order for the pursuit of diversity to be intellectually defensible and valuable to those seeking a first-rate education, it needs to result in deliberation. It cannot simply facilitate the exchange of one orthodoxy or point of view for another. The best liberal arts education requires all voices, those of the old order as much as those of the new, and even those in between, to be subjected to the critical analysis that is supposed to make the academy a distinctive institution in society.

21    I know first hand of several incidents during your four years at the College that speak directly to the challenges of ensuring that a diverse spectrum of opinions can be voiced and considered within our academic community. To name just a few: the protest against the College's policy allowing military recruitment on campus; the complaints about the College's judicial procedures that were triggered by the suspension of an African-American student; the reaction to the College's decision to accept an endowed professorship in honor of a conservative former chief justice of the United States Supreme Court; and most recently, the rash of hateful homophobic graffiti and the resulting discussions about offensive stereotyping and free speech on a college campus.

22    Several of these issues were discussed at faculty meetings or in several large forums on campus. Though the depth of engagement at these gatherings may not have reached the level that many who were passionate about the issues would have liked, students and faculty did express themselves in ways that didn't happen on this campus 20, 15, or even 10 years ago. Issues were brought up by students and faculty that raised the collective consciousness of those in attendance, and, in some cases, had an impact on College policies and procedures.

23    The reaction to one gathering, in particular, was as instructive as the issues about which we learned at the open forum. Following a meeting in McCullough social space that was called to address several racial incidents on campus, I received a number of e-mails from students in which they apologized on behalf of their fellow students, whom the e-mail writers believed were disrespectful in how they engaged me. I found the e-mails— and there were a good number of them—surprising, because I found the meeting, which was attended by 300 students, more civil than I expected it to be, and in no case do I recall any student expressing their concerns in ways that I would consider disrespectful. Was it uncomfortable? Yes, for sure. Were the students disrespectful? I don't think so. But being uncomfortable, as many of us were made to feel that day, is a good thing; it needs to be part of one's education.

24    Similarly, this year's open discussions about homophobic graffiti and other anti-gay acts on campus did not delve as deeply into the root causes of such unacceptable stereotyping and the vicious treatment of individuals as one might expect given the incidents in question. Yet, the reactions to what was said at the open meetings created discomfort among those who were accused of contributing to homophobia on campus. The accusation—stereotyping recruited athletes as homophobic—highlights, once again, the challenges that greater diversity and openness bring to an academic community. Was the stereotyping of a single group a productive way to engage this important topic?

25    What emerged from our discussions of the homophobic incidents, at least thus far, is hardly what one might call neat and tidy. There was, however, much learned beginning with a far greater awareness of the bigotry that exists here as it does in society at-large, and that we have considerable work to do if we truly aspire to be a community that welcomes diversity and wishes to learn from it. We also witnessed how easy it can be for some members of an aggrieved group to fall into the same kind of stereotyping from which they themselves have suffered. Diversity sure can be messy.

26    The controversy surrounding the acceptance by the College of an endowed professorship in American history and culture in honor of William Rehnquist is one more example of the complexities that come with an increasingly diverse community. Because the former chief justice was conservative, and was on the side of several court decisions that ran counter to the positions held by several underrepresented groups on campus, there was a genuine feeling on the part of some that honoring Mr. Rehnquist was a repudiation of their presence on campus and a sign that the College did not value diversity. They felt, in their words, "invisible and disrespected" as a result of the College accepting the professorship. Though one can understand this perspective, especially given the history of underrepresented groups here and on other campuses, it is unfortunate that the Chief Justice's accomplishments and reputation as a brilliant jurist by liberal and conservative constitutional scholars alike were lost in the opposition to his politics.

27    Ironically, the stance taken by those who believed it was wrong to honor the Chief Justice because of his position on particular court cases undermines the very thing the protestors support most passionately—diversity. Some couched their protests in the name of the goals of liberal education, arguing that the ultimate goal should be about "advancing" social change. I do not share in that narrow definition of liberal education, especially liberal education in and for the 21st century. Rather, liberal education must be first and foremost about ensuring a broad range of views and opinions in the

classroom and across campus so that our students can question routinely both their preconceived and newly developed positions on important matters. Such deliberation will serve as the best foundation for enabling our graduates to contribute to the betterment of society.

28    In writing on the College's alumni online listserv about the Rehnquist controversy and the reported opposition of some to President Clinton speaking at tomorrow's Commencement ceremony, an alumnus from the Class of 2001 offered this perspective:

> "I always thought that the benefit of a place like Middlebury was that it opened your mind and helped you become more informed by allowing (or, forcing) you to interact with, listen to, and learn from people [with] different opinions—even if that meant welcoming those you disagree with onto your own turf."

29    I hope those of you in the audience who are graduating tomorrow have given, and will continue to give, this topic some thought. For sure, diversity is intellectually and socially challenging; it forces you to engage issues more broadly than you might otherwise. It often creates unintended consequences; and it surely can make one uncomfortable. But some discomfort, amidst all that is comfortable about college life, is the best preparation for a successful entry into our increasingly complex global world.

30    We have today few if any institutions that can claim a monopoly on how best to make the world a better, more tolerant, and just place. Talented, thoughtful, and well-educated individuals like yourselves, who have been made to feel uncomfortable and understand difference, are more likely than others to figure out how to discern right from wrong, acceptable from unacceptable behavior, and know the difference between ethical and unethical conduct.

31    As you leave college, the most important kind of confidence you must feel is the confidence that your education has prepared you to make sound judgments and to act on them. I believe because you have been exposed to diverse ideas, opinions, and people over the course of the past four years, and have been made to feel uncomfortable at times, you will discover that confidence and draw upon it so that it will serve you well in exercising your judgment and claiming your place in the wider world.

### QUESTIONS FOR ANALYSIS AND DISCUSSION

1.  According to Middlebury College president Ronald Liebowitz, what value does diversity add to a college education? What challenges does it present as well?

2.  Liebowitz cites several examples of issues raised during the graduates' four years at Middlebury. How do these examples support his theme of the importance of diversity on campus? Why is it important to permit and even support the expression of unpopular points of view? Do you agree?

3.  Liebowitz notes, "It is no longer a cliché to say that 'the local is the global and the global the local.' " What does he mean? Explain this statement and connect it to your own college experience.

4. Liebowitz leads his speech with a description of the graduates and their accomplishments. How does this introduction connect to the theme of his speech?
5. In October 2006, Middlebury College established the Justice William H. Rehnquist Professorship of American History and Culture—a controversial chair that met with some protest. Who was Rehnquist? Why did some students and faculty object to the creation of the professorship? What does Liebowitz say about the controversy, and the decision to create the professorship, despite the dispute?

# Who Should Get Into College?
*John H. McWhorter*

In 2003, the Supreme Court sided with the University of Michigan's admissions officers on the right to use race-based admission policies, which often involve different sets of admission criteria for minority students. Most of the arguments for and against race-based admissions hinge on fairness, with supporters claiming that inequalities in education put black students at a disadvantage and detractors claiming that such policies are unfair to white students as well as blacks. Following the Supreme Court's decision, then-Justice Sandra Day O'Connor noted her hope that "25 years from now the use of racial preferences will no longer be necessary." In the next essay, Manhattan Institute senior fellow and *New York Sun* columnist John H. McWhorter challenges the practice of race-based admission policies. He says that not only are they unnecessary today but also they're actually hurting the people they're supposed to help.*

### BEFORE YOU READ

What is your opinion of race-based admission policies? Do they help promote diversity on campus? Do they protect minority admissions? Are they necessary in a country where the quality of high schools is so varied? Or do they do more harm than good?

### AS YOU READ

What does "diversity" mean to McWhorter? What does it mean to you? Why is it important for colleges to embrace diversity on campus?

1   For many years now, elite colleges—taking their cue from the Supreme Court's 1978 Bakke decision—have justified racial preferences in admissions by saying that they are necessary to ensure campus "diversity." Get rid of preferences, "diversity" fans say, and top colleges will become minority-free enclaves; the spirit of segregation will be on the march again. The losers won't just be the folks with the brown pigmentation, now

---

* John H. McWhorter, *City Journal*, Spring 2003.

exiled from the good schools, but all those white students who now will never get to know the unique perspective of people of color.

2       Nonsense on all counts. Correctly understood, diversity encompasses the marvelous varieties of human excellence and vision in a modern civilization—from musical genius to civic commitment to big-brained science wizardry. People who recognize the folly of racial preferences are no more opposed to diversity in this sense than critics of "gangsta" rap are opposed to music. What they do reject is the condescending notion that a diverse campus demands lower admissions standards for brown students, and that, in 2003 America, brown students need crutches to make it.

3       With the Supreme Court about to decide a case that could overturn Bakke and require colorblind admissions, once and for all, it's a good time to describe what a post-affirmative-action admissions policy at a top school should look like—and explain why it would be fully compatible with minority success and real diversity.

4       The raison d'être of the nation's selective universities, at least from the standpoint of the public interest, is to forge a well-educated, national elite. Thus, our post-preferences approach to admissions must be meritocratic. But few people would want schools simply to choose students with the very best SAT scores and grades, and call it a day. The image of elite campuses populated solely by 1,600-SAT-scoring Ken Lays or Sam Waksalls, of whatever color, is unappealing.

5       Back in the early 1980s, at Simon's Rock Early College in Massachusetts, a smattering of my classmates fell into the 1,600 category. But thankfully, the school's administrators grasped that that kind of achievement represents only one of the forms of excellence that smart young people can bring to campus life. The school worked hard to attract a lively mix of students, who vastly enriched my years on campus. My cello playing, for example, took on new depth, because I had the opportunity to play with a brilliant musician whose talents on piano and violin scaled near-professional heights. A roommate was a splendid stage performer, and marinating (unwillingly at first) in his favorite music and historical anecdotes opened up a universe of vintage American popular music and theater that has been part of my life ever since.

6       At school, I also met my first Mennonite and my first white Southerner—there is no better way to get past a native sense of an accent as "funny," I discovered, than living with someone who speaks with one. There were other blacks among the school's 300 or so students, too. Most, like me, were middle-class kids, but there was one guy who had grown up in crumbling Camden, New Jersey. This student gave a lesson in one form of cultural "blackness" to his white classmates—he had real "street" cred. But far more important, after a rocky start and some coaching, he also proved he could do the schoolwork on the high level the school demanded.

7       This was real diversity—the full panoply of human variation, not just the tiny, superficial sliver of it represented by skin pigmentation. And Simon's Rock fostered it without surrendering academic standards.

8       Since my undergraduate days, however, elite universities have come to mean something much different when they speak of "diversity": having as many brown faces on campus as possible, regardless of standards. The origin of the current notion of "diversity," Peter Wood shows in his masterful *Diversity: The Invention of a Concept*, was Justice Lewis Powell's opinion for the court in Bakke. Though strict racial quotas were unconstitutional,

Powell argued, schools could still use race as an "important element" in admissions in order to create a "diverse" campus that would enhance the quality of all students' educational experiences by exposing them to minority "opinions."

9      Powell's argument was, in Wood's terms, a "self-contradictory mess." How, after all, does one make race an "important" factor in admissions while avoiding quotas? It was also dishonest, in that it wasn't at bottom about broadening white students' horizons but providing a rationale for admitting blacks and Hispanics much less qualified than other applicants. The decision has encouraged the Orwellian mindset by which the University of Michigan Law School can defend its admissions process, 234 times more likely to admit black applicants than similarly credentialed whites, as an expression of "diversity," not the obvious quota system it really is.

10      Even on its own terms, Powell's "diversity" argument is demeaning and offensive to minorities. What would be a black "opinion" on French irregular verbs? Or systolic pressure? The "black" views that most interest diversity advocates, of course, are those that illumine social injustice. But in my experience, white and Asian students are at least as likely to voice such PC opinions—often picked up in multiculturalism workshops when they first hit campus.

11      Diversity supporters sometimes reverse themselves 180 degrees and say that race preferences are necessary to show white students that there's no such thing as a "black" viewpoint. "By seeing firsthand that all black or Hispanic students in their classes do not act or think alike," argues Jonathan Alger, counsel for the American Association of University Professors, "white students can overcome learned prejudices." One can only hope that a warm corner of hell awaits anyone who would subject a race to lowered standards for a reason so callow.

12      Black students understandably can find this whole diversity regime repugnant and even racist. "Professor McWhorter," students have asked me, "what about when I am called on for my opinion as a black person in class? Is it fair that I have to deal with that burden?" A continent away, the undergraduate-written Black Guide to Life at Harvard insists: "We are not here to provide diversity training for Kate or Timmy before they go out to take over the world." Indeed, students in general are skeptical of the value of "diversity": a recent survey by Stanley Rothman and Seymour Martin Lipset of 4,000 students at 140 campuses shows that the more that racial "diversity" is emphasized on a campus, the less enthusiastic students are about the quality of education a school offers. What's more, Rothman and Lipset found that such "diversity"-focused schools had more reports of discrimination, not less.

13      The dismal failure of the "diversity" experiment of the last two decades offers an important lesson for a post-affirmative-action admissions policy. Even as we seek diversity in the worthy, Simon's Rock sense, we must recognize that students need to be able to excel at college-level studies. Nobody wins, after all, when a young man or woman of whatever color, unprepared for the academic rigors of a top university, flunks out, or a school dumbs down its curriculum to improve graduation rates. The problem, then, is to find some way to measure a student's potential that still leaves administrators enough leeway to ensure that campus life benefits from a rich variety of excellences and life experiences.

14      As it turns out, we have—and use—the measure: the Scholastic Aptitude Test. James Conant invented the SAT as a meritocratic tool to smoke out talented individuals from the

wide range of life circumstances in American society, not just the WASP elite who made up the vast majority of Ivy League student bodies in the pre-SAT era. Nowadays, a creeping fashion dismisses the SAT as culturally biased, claiming that it assesses only a narrow range of ability and is irrelevant to predicting students' future performance. But while it is true that the SAT is far from perfect—if it were, students wouldn't be able to boost their scores by taking SAT preparatory classes—the exam really does tend to forecast students' future success, as even William Bowen and Derek Bok admit in their valentine to racial preferences, *The Shape of the River*. In their sample of three classes from 1951 to 1989 at 28 selective universities, Bowen and Bok show that SAT scores correlated neatly with students' eventual class ranks.

15    For gauging student potential in the humanities, the verbal SAT, or SATV, seems particularly useful. Rutgers University English professor William Dowling compared the grades of kids in one of his classes over the years with how they did on the verbal test. "What I found," Dowling notes, "was that the SATV scores had an extraordinarily high correlation with final grades, and that neither, in the many cases where I had come to know my students' personal backgrounds, seemed to correlate very well with socio-economic status." The reason, Dowling thinks, is painfully obvious: having a strong command of English vocabulary, usually gained through a lifelong habit of reading, is hardly irrelevant to how one engages advanced reading material. As Dowling argues, a student of any socioeconomic background who can't answer correctly a relatively hard SAT question like this one—"The traditional process of producing an oil painting requires so many steps that it seems _____ to artists who prefer to work quickly: (A) provocative (B) consummate (C) interminable (D) facile (E) prolific"—will be fated to frustration at a selective university, at least in the humanities.

16    My own experience reinforces Dowling's. I've taught students who, though intelligent, possessed limited reading vocabularies and struggled with the verbal portion of the SAT. I have never known a single one of these students to reach the top ranks in one of my classes. "I think I understand what Locke is saying," one student told me in frustration while preparing for a big exam. But Locke isn't Heidegger—his prose, while sophisticated, is clear as crystal. This student confessed that he was "no reader" and possessed only a "tiny vocabulary." Without the vocabulary, he was at sea. Conversely, my textaholic students are usually the stars, gifted at internalizing material and interpreting it in fresh ways—and this is especially true of students immersed in high literature.

17    A post-preferences admissions policy, then, must accept that below a certain cut-off point in SAT scores, a student runs a serious risk of failing to graduate. As Thomas Sowell, among others, has shown, placing minorities in schools that expect a performance level beyond what they have been prepared to meet leads to disproportionate dropout rates—41 percent of the black students in Berkeley's class of 1988, to take one typical example, did not complete their education, compared with 16 percent of whites. Many of these students may have flourished at slightly less competitive schools. Moreover, when minority students attend schools beyond their level, note Stephen Cole and Elinor Barber in Increasing Faculty Diversity, poor grades often deter them from pursuing graduate degrees, contributing to the dearth of black Ph.D.s. Black and minority students overwhelmed on a too-demanding campus can succumb, too, to the bluster of seeing themselves as "survivors" in a racist country—becoming part of an embittered minority rather than proud

members of a national elite. To prevent this kind of damage, the SAT can supply us with the rough parameters within which our admissions search for different kinds of merit—diversity, rightly understood—will proceed. All this makes the recent efforts by the affirmative-action claque to get rid of the SAT misguided in the extreme.

18      Within our SAT range, and once in a while even a bit outside it, there will be plenty of room for judgment calls. Grades, extracurricular activities, and character will all be key. An applicant with a high GPA and a 1,480 SAT who plays the trumpet like Clifford Brown or who gives every indication of being a unique and charismatic individual may deserve admission over an applicant with a 1,600 SAT but no real interests and the individuality of a spoon. Our top universities seek to create a national elite, so geographical diversity will be important too: our admissions policy will seek a mix of students from all parts of the nation. As long as there is no coterie of students whose grades and test scores would have excluded them from consideration if they were white (or Asian), basic standards of excellence prevail.

19      And certainly, our admissions procedure won't immediately disqualify a student who is clearly bright and engaged, but whose test scores happen to fall slightly below the official cut-off, or whose GPA took a hit from one bad year, or who matured into a super student only late in his high school career. Fervent recommendation letters, attesting to leadership or virtue or strength of character, a flabbergastingly good writing sample, a demonstrated commitment to a calling—all will be significant in deciding whether to admit students whose grades and test scores put them on the borderline or slightly below.

20      Our admissions policy will be colorblind, but it won't ignore the working class and the poor (many of whom, as a practical matter, will be blacks or Hispanics). Of course, it's more likely that affluent children, growing up in print-rich homes, will score within our SAT parameters and have the tippy-top grades. But there have always been kids from hardscrabble backgrounds who show academic promise—by nature, by chance, or thanks to the special efforts of parents or other adults. Abraham Lincoln teaching himself to write on the back of a shovel, civil rights activist Fannie Lou Hamer growing up dust poor in the Mississippi Delta loving books—American history records many examples. Disadvantaged students of this stamp will sometimes get the nod in our admissions procedure over well-off applicants whose scores might be more impressive—provided that the disadvantaged kids' SAT scores are within our range (or close to it). That disadvantaged students have shown academic promise may be just a result of good genes, but it's often a sign of good character—a virtue that selective universities should recognize and cultivate.

21      The University of California at Berkeley, where I teach, is already on the right track here. Not so long ago, the admissions committee I sat on matter-of-factly chose middle-class brown students, essentially "white" culturally, over equally deserving white students. I felt tremendous discomfort over the practice. Since California voted in a 1997 referendum, led by anti-preferences activist Ward Connerly, to ban the use of race in admissions, things have changed. Berkeley still assesses students on grades and scores, of course, but instead of race, it now considers the "hardships" that young men and women may have overcome while excelling at school. We recently gave fellowships, for example, to two needy white students who had shown sterling promise. I felt fundamentally right about these fellowships. "This is a racially blind process," emphasizes Calvin Moore, chair of Berkeley's faculty committee on admissions.

22    The idea of a "racially blind process" makes today's "diversity" fans shudder, since they believe that it will lead to a tragic re-segregation of the best American universities and thus of American society. I'm sorry, but this is manipulative melodrama. In an America several decades past the Civil Rights Act, where far more black families are middle class than are poor, many black students will be ready for the top schools without dragging down the bar of evaluation.

23    For proof, consider the University of Washington. In 1998, the year before Washington State outlawed racial preferences in a citizen referendum (also led by Connerly), the school counted 124 African-American students in its freshman class. Two years after the ban, there were 119. Before Texas banned preferences in its schools in 1996, the University of Texas enrolled 266 black freshmen. After the ban and the debut of a new system that admits the top 10 percent of every high school in the state regardless of race, the number actually bounced, to 286. (The "top 10 percent" approach has serious problems, including treating huge discrepancies in school quality as if they did not exist, but it's better than what it replaced.) If this is re-segregation, bring it on.

24    The kind of colorblind admissions process I have outlined would likely just reshuffle the minority presence at selective schools, not reduce it. In Virginia, where racial preferences remain entrenched, black students currently make up 7.9 percent of the student body at the highly competitive University of Virginia Law School, 9.3 percent at the slightly less selective William and Mary Law School, and just 1.7 percent at the less elite, but still fine, George Mason Law School. George Mason's "diversity" deficit results from black students getting in to the more selective schools at a higher percentage than their dossiers would suggest in the absence of affirmative action. Bar preferences, and the number of black students at George Mason would rise; the overall number of blacks getting legal training in the three schools would probably remain the same.

25    What would be so bad about that? It's doubtful that the black students at George Mason's yearly commencement ceremony, feting their accomplishments as their parents beam beside them, worry that they will soon be on the street, selling pencils. In fact, nothing better underscores the progress made by black Americans than the prevalence in the affirmative-action camp of the bizarre notion that admission to a solid second-tier university somehow represents a tragic injustice.

26    Exactly this type of resorting took place after the end of preferences in California's schools. The state's flagship universities, Berkeley and UCLA, did see an initial plunge in the number of black freshmen. But minority presence rose at the same time at most state campuses. And minority admissions at the two top schools have gone up every year following the initial drop-off. Having watched this whole process play out at Berkeley, I can confidently say that the black student community is far from a lonely remnant of what it was in the "good old days" of affirmative action. Berkeley still boasts a thriving black community—the same African-American student groups, the same black dorm floors, the same African-American studies and ethnic studies departments.

27    Moreover, the minority presence at the flagships may have taken a bigger initial hit than the ban required. Immediately after the ban, black activists at the two schools lustily proclaimed their campuses "anti-black," doubtless discouraging some black students from applying—minority applications dropped off sharply for a spell. At UC Berkeley in 1998, the minority admissions office staff actually told some black students, already accepted to

the "racist" school, to enroll elsewhere. One of the motivations for writing my book *Losing the Race* was hearing a black student working in admissions casually say that she distrusted black applicants who did well enough in high school not to need preferences, since such students would not be committed to Berkeley's black community—as if it were somehow not "authentically black" to be a top student. No show lasts forever, however, and after the crowd crying "racism" had its fun and went home, minority applications have steadily climbed.

28    Most important of all, California's black students have started to do better now that they are going to schools that their academic background has prepared them to attend. As University of California at San Diego law professor Gail Heriot notes, before the preferences ban, 15 percent of the college's black freshmen undergraduates, compared with just 4 percent of whites, had GPAs below 2.0, which put them in academic jeopardy; only one black student had a GPA of 3.5 or better, compared with 20 percent of whites. The next year, after the outlawing of campus affirmative action, 20 percent of black freshmen reached the 3.5 or higher GPA level (compared with 22 percent of their white classmates), while black frosh with GPAs below 2.0 fell to 6 percent (about the same as all other racial groups). High freshmen dropout rates fell precipitously.

29    It's true that, with or without racial preferences, blacks will not make up as high a proportion of the student population at our better schools as they do of the overall population. But to worry unduly about this is ahistorical bean counting. Given the relatively short time since the nation rejected segregation, and the internal cultural factors that can hobble a group and keep it from seizing opportunities, it should surprise no one that our selective college campuses do not yet "look like America." But give it time. That's not a rhetorical statement, either: since the banning of racial preferences in California, there has been a 350 percent rise in the number of black teens taking calculus in preparation for college. Challenge people, and they respond.

30    Informed observers believe that the Supreme Court, in agreeing to decide two suits brought against the University of Michigan for reverse discrimination in its admissions, may be set to abolish all use of race in admissions, and move the nation toward the colorblind ideal that motivated the original civil rights movement. Especially in light of the stereotypes that blacks have labored under in this country, saddling black people with eternally lowered standards is immoral. We spent too much time suffering under the hideously unjust social experiments of slavery and segregation to be subjected to further social engineering that benefits the sentiments of liberal elites instead of bettering the conditions and spirits of minorities. Unfortunately, even some conservatives remain uncomfortable with this colorblind possibility: the Bush administration's amicus brief in the case, though it views the Michigan admissions policy as an unconstitutional quota system, still contemplates school officials "taking race into account."

31    It's time to step up to the plate. My years on college campuses have taught me that even those willing to acknowledge the injustices of preferences in private uphold the "diversity" party line in public—something Bakke allows them to do. "John, I get where you're coming from," a genial professor once told me, "but I reserve my right to be guilty." Indeed, 25 years of Bakke show that, in practice, even a hint that race can be "a" factor in admissions will give college administrators, ever eager to Do the Right Thing, the

go-ahead to continue fostering a second-tier class-within-a-class of "spunky" minorities on their campuses.

32    Justice Powell's Bakke opinion cited an amicus brief for "diversity" submitted by Harvard, Stanford, Columbia, and the University of Pennsylvania. The brief described how these schools had traditionally aimed to compose their classes with a mixture of "students from California, New York and Massachusetts; city dwellers and farm boys; violinists, painters and football players; biologists, historians and classicists; potential stockbrokers, academics and politicians." It's a wonderful, noble goal, this diversity—and we don't need to treat any group of citizens as lesser beings to accomplish it.

### QUESTIONS FOR ANALYSIS AND DISCUSSION

1. Summarize McWhorter's argument against race-based admission policies. Include in your summary his position and his supporting evidence.
2. McWhorter admits that diversity on campus adds value to a college education. What does McWhorter feel "diversity" means? How does his definition compare with Ronald Liebowitz's concept of diversity described in the previous essay? Explain.
3. McWhorter, who is himself black, writes on many issues connected to race and ethnicity. Does the fact that McWhorter is black and expressing this opinion against race-based admissions lend more credibility to his argument? Why or why not?
4. McWhorter points out that the original purpose of the SAT was to level the field for students from all socioeconomic backgrounds. How convincing is McWhorter's argument that the SAT still serves its purpose well?
5. Why are so many administrators adamant about maintaining race-based admissions? Explain.
6. In this essay, McWhorter makes his case for "colorblind" admissions. Present your own viewpoint on this issue, responding specifically to McWhorter's supporting evidence and your own from outside research and your personal perspective as a college student.

# What's Wrong with Vocational School?

*Charles Murray*

Are too many Americans going to college? Unlike students in Europe and Asia, over 70 percent of high school graduates intend to pursue some form of higher education, partially because many businesses have made a college degree a requirement for even entry-level office jobs. But are too many students trying to go to college? Are we making unreasonable demands of students and undervaluing the "vocational" trades? In the next essay, Charles Murray, a scholar at the conservative think-tank the American Enterprise Institute, discusses how the pressure to go to college hurts less gifted students as well as the extremely bright ones. Murray is perhaps best known for his controversial book *The Bell Curve* (1994), co-authored with Richard Herrnstein, which discusses the role of IQ in American society.[*]

**BEFORE YOU READ** —————————————————————————————

Much of the argument in the next essay hinges on the value of IQ. What is IQ? Do you think one's IQ should influence the decision of whether to pursue higher education?

**AS YOU READ** ———————————————————————————————

Is vocational school, as Murray suggests, indeed considered "second class"? What accounts for this judgment? How can this attitude hurt the United States in the long run?

1    My topic yesterday was education and children in the lower half of the intelligence distribution. Today I turn to the upper half, people with IQs of 100 or higher. Today's simple truth is that far too many of them are going to four-year colleges. Begin with those barely into the top half, those with average intelligence. To have an IQ of 100 means that a tough high-school course pushes you about as far as your academic talents will take you. If you are average in math ability, you may struggle with algebra and probably fail a calculus course. If you are average in verbal skills, you often misinterpret complex text and make errors in logic.

2    These are not devastating shortcomings. You are smart enough to engage in any of hundreds of occupations. You can acquire more knowledge if it is presented in a format commensurate with your intellectual skills. But a genuine college education in the arts and sciences begins where your skills leave off.

3    In engineering and most of the natural sciences, the demarcation between high-school material and college-level material is brutally obvious. If you cannot handle the math, you cannot pass the courses. In the humanities and social sciences, the demarcation is fuzzier. It is possible for someone with an IQ of 100 to sit in the lectures of Economics 1, read the textbook, and write answers in an examination book. But students who cannot follow complex arguments accurately are not really learning economics. They are taking away a mishmash of half-understood information and outright misunderstandings that probably leave them under the illusion that they know something they do not. (A depressing research literature documents one's inability to recognize one's own incompetence.) Traditionally and properly understood, a four-year college education teaches advanced analytic skills and information at a level that exceeds the intellectual capacity of most people.

4    There is no magic point at which a genuine college-level education becomes an option, but anything below an IQ of 110 is problematic. If you want to do well, you should have an IQ of 115 or higher. Put another way, it makes sense for only about 15% of the population, 25% if one stretches it, to get a college education. And yet more than 45% of recent high school graduates enroll in four-year colleges. Adjust that percentage to account

———————————————

* Charles Murray, *The Wall Street Journey*, January 17, 2007.

for high-school dropouts, and more than 40% of all persons in their late teens are trying to go to a four-year college—enough people to absorb everyone down through an IQ of 104.

5      No data that I have been able to find tell us what proportion of those students really want four years of college-level courses, but it is safe to say that few people who are intellectually unqualified yearn for the experience, any more than someone who is athletically unqualified for a college varsity wants to have his shortcomings exposed at practice every day. They are in college to improve their chances of making a good living. What they really need is vocational training. But nobody will say so, because "vocational training" is second class. "College" is first class.

6      Large numbers of those who are intellectually qualified for college also do not yearn for four years of college-level courses. They go to college because their parents are paying for it and college is what children of their social class are supposed to do after they finish high school. They may have the ability to understand the material in Economics 1 but they do not want to. They, too, need to learn to make a living—and would do better in vocational training.

7      Combine those who are unqualified with those who are qualified but not interested, and some large proportion of students on today's college campuses—probably a majority of them—are looking for something that the four-year college was not designed to provide. Once there, they create a demand for practical courses, taught at an intellectual level that can be handled by someone with a mildly above-average IQ and/or mild motivation. The nation's colleges try to accommodate these new demands. But most of the practical specialties do not really require four years of training, and the best way to teach those specialties is not through a residential institution with the staff and infrastructure of a college. It amounts to a system that tries to turn out televisions on an assembly line that also makes pottery. It can be done, but it's ridiculously inefficient.

8      Government policy contributes to the problem by making college scholarships and loans too easy to get, but its role is ancillary. The demand for college is market-driven, because a college degree does, in fact, open up access to jobs that are closed to people without one. The fault lies in the false premium that our culture has put on a college degree. For a few occupations, a college degree still certifies a qualification. For example, employers appropriately treat a bachelor's degree in engineering as a requirement for hiring engineers. But a bachelor's degree in a field such as sociology, psychology, economics, history or literature certifies nothing. It is a screening device for employers. The college you got into says a lot about your ability, and that you stuck it out for four years says something about your perseverance. But the degree itself does not qualify the graduate for anything. There are better, faster and more efficient ways for young people to acquire credentials to provide to employers.

9      The good news is that market-driven systems eventually adapt to reality, and signs of change are visible. One glimpse of the future is offered by the nation's two-year colleges. They are more honest than the four-year institutions about what their students want and provide courses that meet their needs more explicitly. Their time frame gives them a big advantage—two years is about right for learning many technical specialties, while four years is unnecessarily long.

10     Advances in technology are making the brick-and-mortar facility increasingly irrelevant. Research resources on the Internet will soon make the college library unnecessary.

Lecture courses taught by first-rate professors are already available on CDs and DVDs for many subjects, and online methods to make courses interactive between professors and students are evolving. Advances in computer simulation are expanding the technical skills that can be taught without having to gather students together in a laboratory or shop. These and other developments are all still near the bottom of steep growth curves. The cost of effective training will fall for everyone who is willing to give up the trappings of a campus. As the cost of college continues to rise, the choice to give up those trappings will become easier.

11      A reality about the job market must eventually begin to affect the valuation of a college education: The spread of wealth at the top of American society has created an explosive increase in the demand for craftsmen. Finding a good lawyer or physician is easy. Finding a good carpenter, painter, electrician, plumber, glazier, mason—the list goes on and on—is difficult, and it is a seller's market. Journeymen craftsmen routinely make incomes in the top half of the income distribution while master craftsmen can make six figures. They have work even in a soft economy. Their jobs cannot be outsourced to India. And the craftsman's job provides wonderful intrinsic rewards that come from mastery of a challenging skill that produces tangible results. How many white-collar jobs provide nearly as much satisfaction?

12      Even if forgoing college becomes economically attractive, the social cachet of a college degree remains. That will erode only when large numbers of high-status, high-income people do not have a college degree and don't care. The information technology industry is in the process of creating that class, with Bill Gates and Steve Jobs as exemplars. It will expand for the most natural of reasons: A college education need be no more important for many high-tech occupations than it is for NBA basketball players or cabinetmakers. Walk into Microsoft or Google with evidence that you are a brilliant hacker, and the job interviewer is not going to fret if you lack a college transcript. The ability to present an employer with evidence that you are good at something, without benefit of a college degree, will continue to increase, and so will the number of skills to which that evidence can be attached. Every time that happens, the false premium attached to the college degree will diminish.

13      Most students find college life to be lots of fun (apart from the boring classroom stuff), and that alone will keep the four-year institution overstocked for a long time. But, rightly understood, college is appropriate for a small minority of young adults—perhaps even a minority of the people who have IQs high enough that they could do college-level work if they wished. People who go to college are not better or worse people than anyone else; they are merely different in certain interests and abilities. That is the way college should be seen. There is reason to hope that eventually it will be.

## QUESTIONS FOR ANALYSIS AND DISCUSSION

1. Why does Murray feel that too many students are going to college? Why does he think this harms many students?
2. Murray's essay generated much controversy. He was accused of being "elitist" and of ignoring the benefits of a wider college-educated society. What do you think? Is he being elitist, or is he expressing a truth that is uncomfortable to hear and why?

3. This essay was written as part of a series for the *Wall Street Journal*. Does the content match the presumed audience? What assumptions based on readership does Murray make? Identify specific words/phrases/ideas in his essay that demonstrate how he writes to his audience.

4. Do you think that colleges are indeed "dumbing down" curricula to accommodate a broader range of students with lower abilities? Why or why not?

5. How, according to Murray, does government contribute to the problem of college over-enrollment? Explain.

6. Evaluate Murray's tone in paragraph 11 addressing the benefits of craftsmen. Do you agree that more value should be attributed to vocational trades so that students will be enticed to pursue careers in masonry and carpentry? Explain.

# Welcome to the Fun-Free University
*David Weigel*

Until the 1960s, the concept of colleges applying the principles of *in loco parentis*—acting in the place of a parent—was a generally accepted practice. But many students of the 1960s objected to controls that they felt were unfair violations of their rights as adults. For almost 30 years, colleges allowed students to assume personal responsibility for their actions, but in the wake of alcohol-related student deaths, unhealthy habits, and even medical conditions leading to suicide, many colleges are rethinking their "hands off" approach. Is the return of *in loco parentis* killing student freedom? In this next essay, David Weigel, associate editor of *Reason Magazine*, explores the differences between the college experience of the 1960s and university life in the 2000s.*

### BEFORE YOU READ

What rights and privileges do you expect to enjoy as a college student? Do you expect to be treated completely as an adult? Or do you expect the school to ensure certain protections and safeguards as part of your college experience? If so, what is the balance between safety and personal responsibility?

### AS YOU READ

How does the history of *in loco parentis* inform the current trend adopted by many colleges and universities to curtail student drinking on campus and enact other policies to ensure student safety?

1   In April 1968, student activists at Columbia University schemed to take over the dean's office as a protest against the Vietnam War and plans to build a new gym. More than 700 students were arrested, and the uprising won national attention. But the school's

---

* David Weigel, *Reason Online*, 2004.

buttoned-up administrators hadn't wanted to involve the police, and the rioters eventually were allowed to graduate. The mayor of New York, John Lindsay, even arrived in December to address the students and applaud "the urgent, authentically revolutionary work of this generation."

2    How much of that revolution has carried over to the Columbia of 2004? Registered students who occupy a building would get a dialogue with administrators, but the school wouldn't shy from expulsion. According to Ricardo Morales, the school's crime prevention specialist since 1983, nonstudent radicals wouldn't make it into the campus buildings. "If you want to bring a friend over," Morales explains, "you bring him to the lobby and swipe your ID cards. The guest leaves a piece of ID. If he wants to stay for a few days, you can apply for a guest pass."

3    Even when they're not keeping their borders sealed so tight, college administrators have been adopting harsh measures in response to unapproved student behavior. Last fall, students at Southern Methodist University saw their "affirmative action bake sale," a bit of political theater in which prices were determined by the races of buyers, shut down by the student center. They had failed to register with the university as a "protest" or to go to the officially designated "protest zone," on the south stairs outside of the Hughes-Trigg Student Center.

4    Many college administrators throughout the country are taking great pains to keep their students under tight control. Yet in the late 1960s and '70s, whether colleges could rein in students was an open question. Previously, America's universities had operated under the doctrine of *in loco parentis* ("in the place of a parent"). By the start of the '70s, thanks to a series of legal rulings and cultural shifts, courts and colleges were tossing out that policy, and universities that had been dealing with students as wards struggled to find a new approach.

5    That didn't last. *In loco parentis* has been rejuvenated and returned. Administrators have tapped into the devaluation of personal responsibility illustrated by smoking bans and fast food lawsuits, coupling it with bullish political correctness. The resulting dearth of individual liberties on campuses would have seemed impossible to college students of 25 years ago.

## Save the Children

6   In 1969 Sheldon Steinbach arrived at the American Council on Education, the catchall coordinating body for universities, just in time to weather the worst of the campus revolts. Elite schools such as Berkeley, Columbia, and Cornell were acquiescing to radical students and opening up their internal judicial processes. Students won seats on some boards of trustees. Administrators appeared to have lost their grip.

7    "The basic liberal arts education began to crumble," Steinbach says. "That's what it looked like. When the war ended, we could consolidate, sit back, and look at how to save the system."

8    An unexpected boon arrived in 1974, the year of the Kent State decision *Scheuer v. Rhodes*. Sens. John Warner (R-Va.) and James Buckley (Conservative-N.Y.) sponsored the Family Educational Rights and Privacy Act (FERPA) in the hope of empowering parents to keep tabs on their kids' academics. Committees amended the bill into a codification of student privacy rights, and Steinbach got a crack at it before FERPA moved on to the Senate.

When the bill passed, parents could peek into the records of their children until their 18th birthday, at which point those rights transferred to the student. But FERPA created exceptions: Schools could release records to providers of financial aid and to "appropriate officials in cases of health and safety emergencies." If a student was hit with a subpoena or legal charge, the school could peek into his criminal records. Yet college administrators and their advisers, Steinbach included, kept the champagne corked. It wasn't immediately clear what effect the law would have, outside of giving parents annual notice of their new rights.

9    Meanwhile, concern about the state of campuses was spreading. In March 1977, I ran a hand-wringing exposé titled "The End of Expulsion?," which gave the supposed academic apocalypse some context: "In just ten years, most of the rules that once governed student life *in loco parentis* have simply disappeared. Even serious scholastic offenses, such as cheating and plagiarism, seldom incur the harsh penalties that were once automatic. Most college administrators admit that they lean over backward to avoid expelling students." The irksome rites of passage that had been mandatory—core curricula, single-gender dorms, class attendance—fell away.

10    In the 1979 case *Bradshaw v. Rawlings*, the U.S. Court of Appeals for the 3rd Circuit spelled out the universities' weakness. When a Delaware Valley College sophomore three years under the Pennsylvania drinking age hitched a ride from a drunk driver and was injured in a car crash, he sued the school. The court shrugged him off. "The modern American college is not an insurer of the safety of its students," it said. "Rights formerly possessed by college administrations have been transferred to students." Expectations were pointless, because drinking by college students is a common experience. That this is true is not to suggest that reality always comports with state law and college rules. It does not."

11    The court's decision reflected the way students lived: They had a new relationship with their deans, who should treat them like the young adults they were.

## Just Say No

12 University administrators immediately started wringing their hands over the "kids will be kids" philosophy of *Bradshaw v. Rawlings*. When one of their wards was arrested, injured, or killed, whether a lawsuit resulted or not, the school felt a blow to its prestige and sense of community. Unchecked hedonism and recklessness among students increasingly free to skip classes or make their own schedules were perceived as a threat to the institution's reputation.

13    Brett Bokolow, manager of the National Center for Higher Education Risk Management (NCHERM), estimates that colleges have been seeking formulas to keep students out of actionable situations for 20 years. In the 1980s, they were increasingly finding themselves liable for providing services or sponsoring events that involved alcohol. After only a few legal wounds, schools sought methods to put the responsibility for drinking or drug use on the backs of students and fraternities and sororities. Two weapons fell into their laps.

14    As the Department of Education opened for business in 1980, an increasing number of students were turning to government aid and loans to pay for their college bills. From 1970 to 1980, federal aid to college students soared from $600 million to $4.5 billion. In 1978 Congress had passed legislation that entitled all college students to federally insured loans.

Suddenly, colleges had leverage to punish students for misusing their leisure time. If they were getting money from taxpayers, they were treated like any other employee found partying on the job. Since students were making use of their loans every minute of the academic year, all of their fun was suspect, and much of the adult behavior that vexed administrators was happening on the public dime.

15 Colleges became willing and able to shift some burden to Greek organizations, which had grown again after a marked falloff in the Vietnam era. Many schools created incentives for fraternities and sororities to go dry, or at least disincentives for them to stay wet. In one typical action in 1988, Rutgers University, which had just banned bringing kegs into dorms, responded to a student's death by embargoing all Greek events. In 1997, after first-year student Scott Kreuger drank himself to death at a pledge event, MIT banned freshmen from fraternities. More responsibility was shifted to fraternity and sorority members. By the mid-'90s, universities had become so strict that they were rarely found liable for student sins. Instead of threatening to punish their kids if they came home late, schools simply took away the car keys. If kids somehow got themselves into trouble, it was a police matter.

16 Colleges found the rest of their arsenal in 1987, when Congress threatened to withhold federal transportation money from states that allowed anyone below the age of 21 to buy alcohol, with the result that 21 became the de facto national drinking age. Across the country, the harshness many schools had formerly applied only to drug offenses began to apply to drinking as well, and the war on fraternities was ramped up. Finally, in 1998 FERPA was amended to make one provision clearer: Colleges could sidestep their students' wishes and inform parents whenever a drug or alcohol law was broken. Before that, less than 20 percent of schools had informed parents of such violations. Afterward, most of them did so.

17 In 2001 *The Chronicle of Higher Education* reviewed this phone-home policy and found great success. Reporters spotlighted the story of a University of Delaware freshman who pledged to quit drinking after police stopped him on the street for a Breathalyzer test. After he was caught, his parents began bringing him home each weekend and lecturing him on his mistakes. The student stopped drinking, but not because he worried about the effects of booze. If he was caught again, he would be suspended for a year.

## Back in Control

18 Four decades after *in loco parentis* started to stagger, college students would be hard pressed to name their new personal liberties. When administrators crack down, they will almost always at least provide a reason. But today's students may be punished just as hard as their predecessors—often harder. They've discovered that social engineers have a hard time turning down the opportunity to control things.

19 The expanding control over college students has had repercussions in the rest of America. Campuses are proving grounds for make-nice public programs. They've provided laboratories to test speech codes and small, designated "free speech zones" for protests. (Such zones marginalize and effectively silence dissent, which is one reason they've been adopted by the major political parties for their national conventions.) The stiffening of campus law also illustrates the trend toward greater control of adults' personal behavior.

20    *In loco parentis* could be overturned only once. After 1974, students should have had an arsenal of new rights. But parents never stopped believing that universities were responsible for shaping their kids, and schools have nervously assumed that too much freedom will bring about the system's collapse.

21    It won't. College students will drink, despair, play loose with hygiene, make dirty jokes. Before *in loco parentis* made its comeback, they were thriving. Meanwhile, the changes that really worried academics in the 1970s—demands for new disciplines, shrinking core curricula—are settling into permanence. It's the most enjoyable effect of the '60s student revolts that are being whittled away.

### QUESTIONS FOR ANALYSIS AND DISCUSSION

1. Do you think *in loco parentis* has a place on modern college campuses? Why or why not? Support your perspective on this issue with examples to back up personal viewpoints.

2. What did the decision of *Bradshaw v. Rawlings* reveal about administrators' views of student personal responsibility in the 1970s? Do you think a court today would make a similar pronouncement? Why or why not?

3. Weigel observes, "Four decades after *in loco parentis* started to stagger, college students would be hard pressed to name their new personal liberties. . . . They've discovered that social engineers have a hard time turning down the opportunity to control things." What are your personal liberties? Are any indeed new? Have any liberties enjoyed by your predecessors 10 or 20 years ago been revoked?

4. What does Weigel think of the resurrection of *in loco parentis* on college campuses? Identify specific areas where he makes his viewpoint clear.

# Parental Notification: Fact or Fiction

*Joel Epstein*

In 1998, Congress amended Section 444 of the General Education Provisions Act by adding *Sec. 952: Alcohol or Drug Possession Disclosure:* "Nothing in this Act or the Higher Education Act of 1965 shall be construed to prohibit an institution of higher education from disclosing, to a parent or legal guardian of a student, information regarding any violation of any Federal, State, or local law, or of any rule or policy of the institution, governing the use or possession of alcohol or a controlled substance, regardless of whether that information is contained in the student's education records, if (a) the student is under the age of 21; and (b) the institution determines that the student has committed a disciplinary violation with respect to such use or possession." Since the passage of this provision, some college administrators are warning students that their parents will be contacted if they are caught drinking alcohol or if they are deemed intoxicated by campus security. Should administrators notify parents of students' alcohol violations? Would notification reduce alcohol abuse? Joel Epstein, an attorney with the

U.S. Department of Education's Higher Education Center for Alcohol and Other Drug Prevention, explores both sides of this question in the next essay.*

## BEFORE YOU READ

Have you ever been in a situation, such as at a party, concert, or sporting event, in which either you or the people around you became unruly because of excessive alcohol consumption? How did college administrators respond? Were parents notified?

## AS YOU READ

In this essay, first-year student Jessica Kirshner is quoted as saying that alcohol is "just a way of life." What role does alcohol play in your student life? In your roommates' and friends' lives? How would your college experience be different if there were no alcohol at all? Explain.

1  It happens every weekend. A son or daughter, away at college for the first time, drinks him- or herself into a drunken stupor at an off-campus bar. Around 3:00 A.M. two less-intoxicated friends help their roommate, hardly able to stand, onto the Happy Bus, the local college shuttle, where they join nine other similarly inebriated undergraduates for the bumpy ride back to campus. This trip is an uneventful one. No major fights ensue and none of the dozen heavily besotted souls on this outing lose it on the way back to their dorm room.

2  Upon staggering off the bus at the college student union, several of the more intoxicated students are approached by campus police. What's happening here? Quickly the drunk and underage students are advised that they are being charged with violating the school's policy against underage drinking. The students are written up and told that under a newly enacted disciplinary policy their parents will be notified that the students have been charged with violating the school policy and state law.

3  Can a school really confront high-risk student drinking in this manner? Laws aimed at curtailing college student drinking and drug use was one of several major legislative initiatives passed during the 105th Congress. At first glance, these laws appear to represent important developments in the evolving attitude of the public toward student drinking and drug use and disorder. But some people question the conviction with which the new approaches will be embraced and the debate rages on about whether student privacy rights prohibit approaches like parental notification. Indeed, Section 952, Alcohol or Drug Possession Disclosure, of the Higher Education Act, is still being widely debated both on- and off-campus.

4  Signed into law in October 1998, the law clearly permits schools to disclose to parents violations of not only local, state, and federal laws but also school policies and rules governing the use or possession of alcohol or controlled substances. The parental notification amendment came about largely as a result of the efforts of Jeffrey Levy, the father

---

* Joel Epstein, *Prevention File*, Vol. 14, No.2.

of a college student killed in 1997 in an alcohol-related traffic crash. Levy lobbied hard for the proposal after his 20-year-old son, a student at Radford University in Virginia, was killed while riding as a passenger in a car driven by a drunk driver.

5     Appointed to a Virginia attorney general's task force on college drinking, Levy encouraged the task force to act forcefully with respect to parental notification. The other members of the task force listened. One of the group's leading recommendations was the parental notification idea and eventually the task force persuaded Virginia Senator John W. Warner to introduce legislation in the U.S. Senate. As enacted, the law permits but does not require schools to notify parents of a student's alcohol or other drug violation. [. . .]

## A Student's View

6 Opinions vary widely however as to whether schools should notify parents of their child's alcohol or drug violation. Jessica Kirshner, a first-year student at Harvard University, thinks maybe at a certain point parents should be notified, but not if the violation is just an isolated incident. "Perhaps after repeated incidents or if the incident is serious enough that the student has to be hospitalized, but otherwise I do not believe parents need to be notified," says Kirshner.

7     In Cambridge and Boston, undergraduates witness a great deal of drinking by underage students. "It permeates campus life," explains Kirshner. "Underage students definitely need fake IDs. Bars are conscious that these students are underage, but if the student has an ID to show at the door, they're in."

8     As for local enforcement efforts, Kirshner adds, "I know that liquor stores in Cambridge have 'Cops in Shops,' so it's a deterrent, but there are other ways to get around that."

9     One of the most common ways underage students obtain beer and liquor is simply by having of-age students purchase the alcohol. And a lot of the time students don't even have to buy it, "it's just around."

10     A close observer of campus alcohol policy, Kirshner is not aware of any disciplinary incidents this year at Harvard involving alcohol that resulted in parents being notified.

11     "I have seen underage students who got drunk at campus parties sent before the disciplinary board, but I have not seen any expulsions. Typically they get put on probation. It doesn't look good for the time being but assuming there is no subsequent violation, the charge gets taken off the student's record by the end of the term," Kirshner said. In her view, students are little concerned about underage drinking, and parental notification is not even on their radar. She adds, "I don't know if underage drinking would be considered a right of passage, it's just something to do."

12     As for the types of drinking taking place among underage students, "it tends to depend on the venue. Around the dorms it's not binge drinking or heavy drinking. Heavy drinking sitting around your room is not 'socially acceptable.' But once you get out in the bars, there it is heavier," explains Kirshner.

## Who's Responsible?

13 Before passage of the federal parental notification law, officials at most schools across the country had refused to tell parents about student drug and alcohol violations, citing the Family Educational Rights and Privacy Act (FERPA), also known as the Buckley Amendment, a 1974 law on the privacy of student records. Nonetheless, some parents had

for years argued that they have a right to be alerted to their children's life-threatening habits. Now the new law is causing many school administrators to rethink their position on parental notification, although a few schools, including Virginia's Radford University had changed their policy even before Congress acted.

14 Today, many university administrators believe that both students and their parents need to take more accountability and responsibility for their actions. But before the recent media focus on the problem of high-risk student drinking, most parents had little sense of the scope of the problem. Those who did know, more often than not saw it as the aberrant behavior of someone else's son or daughter.

15 While Jeffrey Levy views the parental notification amendment as an important first step, he remains skeptical about the willingness of most schools to take meaningful steps to address the heavy drinking that has become a way of life for too many college students. Levy fears that many universities will now simply make the empty promise that they have a notification policy in place. The bereaved father suspects that even at many of those schools that adopt a parental notification policy, no or few notifications will be made.

16 "What we had hoped for was a clear statement that schools will notify parents when their son or daughter has been involved in aggressive or binge drinking. Instead, at most colleges a report will only be made if there is evidence of a legal or disciplinary violation . . ." [Many campus police and school administrators would not even consider apprehending heavily intoxicated students as described in the fictional scenario above], explains Levy.

17 Advocates of parental notification warn that students know exactly what is going on. They fear that by not having a strong parental notification policy in place and by failing to say, "I will not tolerate abusive or binge drinking on my campus," schools may be sending the message that nothing has changed.

18 Levy says: "If the notifications were going out, the students would know about it and on most campuses the students can tell you that they do not."

19 Levy has had a hard time finding out how many notifications are actually being made. He says, "I've also spoken to many parents and I've never met a parent who had been notified."

20 A notable exception to what Levy has observed is the experience of the University of Delaware, which last year sent letters to the parents of 1,414 students who had violated the school's disciplinary rules. According to Timothy F. Brooks, Delaware's dean of students, most of these letters reported a student's alcohol or drug violation. Brooks notes that student recidivism has declined precipitously since Delaware enacted its three-strikes policy and initiated the practice of parental notification.

21 Parental notification advocates however are not persuaded by the exception to the general rule. Explains Levy, "A lot of schools have a three-strikes policy, but how many kids wander around campus drunk out of their minds and still there is no action. There's a big difference between, 'Oh, I had one too many to drink,' and 'I'm going to get wasted.' I can accept the first, I can't and I don't think any parent can accept the second. The whole attitude 'I'm going to open up the door, pick up a glass and drink as much as I can, as fast as I can, with the prime purpose of getting wasted,' that is different from the intention of going out to have fun. . . . The failure to stand up to that is unacceptable. Parents don't know about this and in failing to notify them, universities are not helping either the students or their parents."

In Levy's experience university presidents want this problem to go away, but they do
not want to be seen by students as the heavy. He predicts that on most campuses, for
parental notification to be triggered the student will have to have violated a state law, or
campus policy which mirrors state law. The catch is, most college officials believe they
must catch the student in the act of drinking and much campus drinking has been pushed
off-campus or underground. For all intents and purposes, there are no laws against public
intoxication on campus.

"The sight of two sober students carrying a passed-out student into the dorm should
trigger a college to say, 'you are in violation of my policy.' But it doesn't. I want to see
more colleges stand up and say, 'Binge or problem drinking is against our policy,'" says
Levy.

Advocates of parental notification will have to look carefully at campuses where problems continue and critically scrutinize how many parental notifications there have been.

Robert Metcalf, counsel to the Attorney General of Virginia and a prime mover behind
the parental notification amendment, is the first to admit the new law is not a silver bullet.

"It doesn't force colleges to do anything," notes Metcalf. "It should be called the
drunkenness in the sunshine amendment. The way the system was colleges were reluctant
to go after students who were clearly violating the law. This new law is just one of a number of methods schools can now use to address the problem. The law removes an artificial
barrier that some schools used in the past to not notify parents. Now they can. In Virginia,
the development of policy is still at the school level. We just hope that they adopt the
amendment approach."

With passage of the parental notification law many more schools are now considering
adopting a policy of parental notification. Not surprisingly, Virginia and District of
Columbia schools have been among the first to take advantage of parental notification.
Recently, Virginia Tech, where two students died last year in alcohol-related incidents, became the first major Virginia college to make use of the new federal law. Effective in
spring 1999, the new policy will permit the notification of parents of underage students
sanctioned for alcohol or drug violations on and off campus.

Virginia Tech's new policy is also noteworthy because it forges a partnership with the
local police who will notify the school if students are caught off campus with alcohol or
drugs. The new collaborative approach will mean students may face both campus disciplinary penalties and public prosecution. In Washington, D.C., both American University and
George Washington University are also reviewing their parental notification policies.

In considering adopting a parental notification policy, schools need to remember what
the amendment is not. Schools should know that the amendment does not impose any affirmative obligation on the institution to inform parents of the disciplinary violation. Rather,
it specifically states that such action does not violate FERPA or the Higher Education Act.
Basically, it's all up to the schools.

## QUESTIONS FOR ANALYSIS AND DISCUSSION

1. Epstein comments that the laws passed as a result of Section 952 "appear to
   represent important developments in the evolving attitude of the public toward student drinking and drug use and disorder." What does he mean by

"evolving attitude"? How has the attitude toward student drinking changed in recent years, and why?

2. What position does the author take on the issue of student drinking? Identify two statements in his essay that may be interpreted as revealing a position on this issue.

3. Do you think college administrators have the right to contact parents when the parents' underage children are caught drinking? Do you think that notification would reduce drinking? Would knowing that this could happen to you curtail your own drinking habits? Why or why not?

4. Epstein presents the student perspective of Jessica Kirshner and administrator Jeffrey Levy. Do these two perspectives present the issue in a balanced way? Whose perspective do you agree with more, and why?

# A's for Everyone!

*Alicia C. Shepard*

In an era of rampant grade inflation, some college students find it shocking to discover there are five letters in the grading system. It used to be that earning a B in a course was cause for celebration. But across college campuses nationwide, many students argue that an A is now the only acceptable grade. Increasingly, students are arguing with their professors to raise lower grades to higher ones, and urging them to consider their "hard work" rather than skill, talent, and performance, as the reason for an A grade. Today's parents are also putting pressure on their children to achieve high grades, adding to student anxieties. In this next essay, professor Alicia Shepard describes the trend from the perspective of a teacher and as a parent.*

## BEFORE YOU READ

What grades do you expect to earn in your college classes? In your opinion, what is a "good grade" and why?

## AS YOU READ

Professor Watson notes that many students believe that "working hard" should carry weight when factoring grades. What do you think? Is this a fair system? What is the line between talent and product and effort and earnestness?

1  It was the end of my first semester teaching journalism at American University. The students had left for winter break. As a rookie professor, I sat with trepidation in my office on a December day to electronically post my final grades.

---

* Alicia C. Shepard, *Washington Post*, June 5, 2005.

2    My concern was more about completing the process correctly than anything else. It took an hour to compute and type in the grades for three classes, and then I hit "enter." That's when the trouble started.

3    In less than an hour, two students challenged me. Mind you, there had been no preset posting time. They had just been religiously checking the electronic bulletin board that many colleges now use.

4    "Why was I given a B as my final grade?" demanded a reporting student via e-mail. "Please respond ASAP, as I have never received a B during my career here at AU and it will surely lower my GPA."

5    I must say I was floored. Where did this kid get the audacity to so boldly challenge a professor? And why did he care so much? Did he really think a prospective employer was going to ask for his GPA?

6    I checked the grades I'd meticulously kept on the electronic blackboard. He'd missed three quizzes and gotten an 85 on two of the three main writing assignments. There was no way he was A material. I let the grade mar his GPA because he hadn't done the required work.

7    I wasn't so firm with my other challenger. She tracked me down by phone while I was still in my office. She wanted to know why she'd received a B-plus. Basically, it was because she'd barely said a word in class, so the B-plus was subjective. She harangued me until, I'm ashamed to admit, I agreed to change her grade to an A-minus. At the time, I thought, "Geez, if it means that much to you, I'll change it." She thanked me profusely, encouraging me to have a happy holiday.

8    Little did I know the pressure was just beginning.

9    The students were relentless. During the spring semester, they showed up at my office to insist I reread their papers and boost their grades. They asked to retake tests they hadn't done well on. They bombarded me with e-mails questioning grades. More harassed me to change their final grade. I began to wonder if I was doing something wrong, sending out some sort of newbie signal that I could be pushed around. Then I talked to other professors in the School of Communication. They all had stories.

10    My colleague Wendy Swallow told me about one student who had managed to sour her Christmas break one year. Despite gaining entry into AU's honors program, the student missed assignments in Swallow's newswriting class and slept through her midterm. Slept through her midterm! Then she begged for lenience.

11    "I let her take it again for a reduced grade," Swallow says, "but with the warning that if she skipped more classes or missed more deadlines, the midterm grade would revert to the F she earned by missing it. She then skipped the last three classes of the semester and turned in all her remaining assignments late. She even showed up late for her final."

12    Swallow gave the student a C-minus, which meant she was booted out of the honors program. The student was shocked. She called Swallow at home hysterical about being dropped from the program. To Swallow, the C-minus was a gift. To the student, an undeserved lump of Christmas coal.

13    "She pestered me for several days by phone," says Swallow, who did not relent and suggested the student file a formal grievance. She didn't. "The whole exchange, though, made for a very unpleasant break. Now I wait to post my grades until the last minute before leaving for the semester, as by then most of the students are gone, and I'm less likely to get those instantaneous complaints."

14    Another colleague told me about a student she had failed. "He came back after the summer trying to convince me to pass him because other professors just gave him a C," says Leena Jayaswal, who teaches photography. Never mind that he didn't do her required work.

15    John Watson, who teaches journalism ethics and communications law at American, has noticed another phenomenon: Many students, he says, believe that simply working hard—though not necessarily doing excellent work—entitles them to an A. "I can't tell you how many times I've heard a student dispute a grade, not on the basis of in-class performance," says Watson, "but on the basis of how hard they tried. I appreciate the effort, and it always produces positive results, but not always the exact results the student wants. We all have different levels of talent."

16    It's a concept that many students (and their parents) have a hard time grasping. Working hard, especially the night before a test or a paper due date, does not necessarily produce good grades.

17    "At the age of 50, if I work extremely hard, I can run a mile in eight minutes," says Watson. "I have students who can jog through a mile in seven minutes and barely sweat. They will always finish before me and that's not fair. Or is it?"

18    Last September, AU's Center for Teaching Excellence hosted a lunchtime forum to provide faculty members tips on how to reduce stressful grade confrontations. I eagerly attended.

19    The advice we were given was solid: Be clear upfront about how you grade and what is expected, and, when possible, use a numerical grading system rather than letter grades. If the grade is an 89, write that on the paper rather than a B-plus.

20    "The key," said AU academic counselor Jack Ramsay, "is to have a system of grading that is as transparent as possible."

21    Yet even the most transparent grading system won't eliminate our students' desperate pursuit of A's. Of the 20 teachers who came to the session, most could offer some tale of grade harassment.

22    "Most of the complaints that colleagues tell me about come from B students," said James Mooney, special assistant to the dean for academic affairs in the College of Arts and Sciences. "They all want to know why they didn't get an A. Is there something wrong with a B?"

23    Apparently there is. "Certainly there are students who are victims of grade inflation in secondary school," said Mooney. "They come to college, and the grading system is much more rigorous. That's one of the most difficult things to convey to the students. If you're getting a B, you're doing well in a course."

24    But his interpretation is rarely accepted by students or their parents. And the pressure on professors to keep the A's coming isn't unique to AU. It's endemic to college life, according to Stuart Rojstaczer, a Duke University professor who runs a website called Gradeinflation.com. At Duke and many other colleges, A's outnumber B's, and C's have all but disappeared from student transcripts, his research shows.

25    Last spring, professors at Princeton University declared war on grade inflation, voting to slash the number of A's they award to 25 percent of all grades. At Harvard, where half of the grades awarded are A's, the university announced that it would cut the number of seniors graduating with honors from 91 percent to about 50 percent.

26    Despite those moves, Rojstaczer doesn't think it will be easy to reverse the rising tide of A's. He points out that in 1969, a quarter of the grades handed out at Duke were C's. By 2002, the number of C's had dropped to less than 10 percent.

27    Rojstaczer, who teaches environmental science, acknowledged in an op-ed piece he wrote for the *Post* two years ago that he rarely hands out C's, "and neither do most of my colleagues. And I can easily imagine a time when I'll say the same thing about B's."

28    Arthur Levine, president of Columbia University Teacher's College and an authority on grading, traces what's going on to the Vietnam War. "Men who got low grades could be drafted," Levine says. "The next piece was the spread of graduate schools where only A's and B's were passing grades. That soon got passed on to undergraduates and set the standard."

29    And then there's consumerism, he says. Pure and simple, tuition at a private college runs, on average, nearly $28,000 a year. If parents pay that much, they expect nothing less than A's in return. "Therefore, if the teacher gives you a B, that's not acceptable," says Levine, "because the teacher works for you. I expect A's, and if I'm getting B's, I'm not getting my money's worth."

30    Rojstaczer agrees: "We've made a transition where attending college is no longer a privilege and an honor; instead college is a consumer product. One of the negative aspects of this transition is that the role of a college-level teacher has been transformed into that of a service employee."

31    Levine argues that we "service employees" are doing students a disservice if we cave in to the demand for top grades. "One of the things an education should do is let you know what you do well in and what you don't," he says. "If everybody gets high grades, you don't learn that."

32    But, as I'd already seen, many students aren't interested in learning that lesson—and neither are their parents. When AU administrator James Mooney polled professors about grade complaints, he was appalled to learn that some overwrought parents call professors directly to complain. "One colleague told me he got a call from the mother of his student and she introduced herself by saying that she and her husband were both attorneys," said Mooney. "He thought it was meant to intimidate him."

33    Though I haven't received any menacing phone calls from parents, Mom and Dad are clearly fueling my students' relentless demand for A's. It's a learned behavior. I know, because I'm guilty of inflicting on my son the same grade pressure that now plays out before me as a university professor.

34    Last fall when my Arlington high school senior finally got the nerve to tell me that he'd gotten a C in the first quarter of his AP English class, I did what any self-respecting, grade-obsessed parent whose son is applying to college would do. I cried. Then I e-mailed his teacher and made an appointment for the three of us to meet. My son's teacher was accommodating. She agreed that if my son did A work for the second quarter, colleges would see a B average for the two quarters, not that ruinous C.

35    There's a term for the legions of parents like me. The parents who make sure to get the teacher's e-mail and home phone number on Back to School Night. The kind who e-mail teachers when their child fails a quiz. The kind who apply the same determination to making sure their child excels academically that they apply to the professional world.

36    We are called "helicopter parents" because we hover over everything our kids do like Secret Service agents guarding the president. (My son refers to me as an Apache attack helicopter, and he's Fallujah under siege.) Only we aren't worried about our kids getting taken out by wild-eyed assassins. We just want them to get into a "good" (whatever that means) college.

37    "Parents today have this intense investment in seeing their kids do well in school," says Peter Stearns, provost at George Mason University and author of Anxious Parenting: A History of Modern Childrearing in America. "This translates into teachers feeling direct and indirect pressure to keep parents off their backs by handing out reasonably favorable grades and making other modifications, like having up to 18 valedictorians."

38    High school administrators who haven't made those modifications sometimes find themselves defending their grading policies in court. Two years ago, a senior at New Jersey's Moorestown High School filed a $2.7 million lawsuit after she was told she'd have to share being valedictorian with another high-achieving student. A similar episode occurred in Michigan, where a Memphis High School senior who'd just missed being valedictorian claimed in a lawsuit that one of his A's should have been an A-plus.

39    That hyperconcern about grades and class rankings doesn't disappear when kids finally pack for college. Along with their laptops and cell phones, these students bring along the parental anxiety and pressure they've lived with for 18 years.

40    One of my students, Rachael Scorca, says that her parents have always used good grades as an incentive. And they've continued to do so during college. "In high school, my social life and curfew revolved around A's," explains Scorca, a broadcast journalism major. "I needed over a 90 average in order to go out during the week and keep my curfew as late as it was. Once college came and my parents couldn't control my hours or effort, they started controlling my bank account. If I wasn't getting good grades, they wouldn't put money in my account, and, therefore, I wouldn't have a social life."

41    But most of my students tell me the pressure to get top grades doesn't come from their parents any longer. They've internalized it. "I'd say most of the pressure just comes from my personal standards," says Molly Doyle. "It's also something I take pride in. When people ask me how my grades are, I like being able to tell them that I've got all A's and B's."

42    During my second semester of teaching, I received this e-mail from a student who'd taken my fall class on "How the News Media Shape History" and wasn't satisfied with his grade. He (unsuccessfully) tried bribery.

43    "Professor. I checked my grade once I got here and it is a B," he wrote. "I have to score a grade better than a B+ to keep my scholarship and I have no idea how I ended up with a B. In addition, to that I have brought you something from The GREAT INDIAN CONTINENT."

44    I invited him to come to my office so I could explain why he'd gotten a B, but after several broken appointments, he faded away.

45    Other students were more persistent, particularly a bright young man who'd been in the same class as the briber. He'd gotten an A-minus and made it clear in an e-mail he wasn't happy with it: "I have seen a number of the students from the class, and we inevitably got to talking about it. I had assumed that you are a tough grader and that earning an A-minus from you was a difficult task, but upon talking to other students, it appears that that grade was handed out more readily than I had thought. Not that other students did not deserve

a mark of that caliber, but I do feel as though I added a great deal to the class. I feel that my work, class participation, and consistency should have qualified me for a solid A."

46   When I ignored the e-mail, he pestered me a second time: "I know it's a great pain in the ass to have an A-minus student complain, but I'm starting to wonder about the way grades are given. I would be very curious to know who the A students were. While other students may have outdone me with quiz grades, I made up for it with participation and enthusiasm. I really feel that I deserved an A in your class. If I was an A-minus student, I assume that you must have handed out a lot of C's and D's. I don't mean to be a pain—I have never contested anything before. I feel strongly about this, though."

47   I shouldn't have done it, but I offered to change the grade. My student was thrilled. He wrote, "With grade inflation being what it is and the levels of competition being so high, students just can't afford to be hurt by small things. I thought that you did a great job with the course."

48   But when I completed the required paperwork, the grade change was rejected by a university official. Though no one questioned me the first time I did it, grades can be changed only if they are computed incorrectly. "How fair is it to change his grade?" an assistant dean asked me. "What about other kids who might be unhappy but didn't complain?"

49   I e-mailed my student to let him know that he would have to live with an A-minus. "The gods who make these decisions tell me that they rejected it because it's not considered fair to all the other students in the class," I wrote. "The grade you got was based on a numerical formula, and you can only change a grade if you made a mathematical error. I'm sorry."

50   "That seems illogical to me," he e-mailed back. "If a student feels that a grade was inappropriate and wishes to contest that grade, that student obviously must contact the person who gave it to them. Who was I supposed to contact? What was the process that I was to follow? The lack of logic in all this never fails to amaze me!"

51   I told him whom to contact. I'm not sure if he ever followed through, but I saw him recently and he smiled and stopped to talk. Nothing was mentioned about the grade.

52   The day before this spring semester's grades were due I bumped into another professor racing out of the building. What's the hurry? I asked.

53   She told me she had just posted her grades and wanted to get off campus fast. But she wasn't quick enough. Within eight minutes, a B-minus student had called to complain.

54   A few hours after I entered my final grades, I got an e-mail from a student, at 1:44 a.m. She was unhappy with her B. She worked so hard, she told me. This time, though, I was prepared. I had the numbers to back me up, and I wouldn't budge on her grade. No more Professor Softie.

## QUESTIONS FOR ANALYSIS AND DISCUSSION ————

1. Professor Shepard is shocked that a student would challenge the grade she assigned. Have you every felt that a grade you received was unfair? If so, did you ask your professor for clarification? Did you challenge the professor to change it? Explain.

2. The author changes one grade after the student challenges the subjective nature of "class participation." In your opinion, should class participation be a factor in grade determination? Why or why not?

3. How has electronic grade posting influenced the issue of grade challenging and grade inflation?

4. What are "helicopter parents"? Does it make Shepard's argument more credible when she admits that she is one?

5. Visit the Grade Inflation website at http://www.gradeinflation.com and review the data on its site. Discuss the issue of grade inflation with your group, and what it might mean to the value of grades in general. If your school appears on the website, discuss its ranking specifically.

6. Write about an experience you had as a student connected to a grade you receive in class. It could be about a poor grade you felt you didn't deserve, or the pressure to earn a grade because of parental influence or looming college admissions.

## Reading the Visual

### Passive Activism Ideal

The Gazette

### QUESTIONS FOR ANALYSIS AND DISCUSSION

1. What issue is this cartoon raising? Explain.
2. What visual cliché's does this cartoon use to convey its message? Who do the people in the cartoon represent? Could the characters be reversed? Why or why not?
3. This cartoon appeared in a campus newspaper. Would it be as effective in another publication? Why is context important to this cartoon?
4. What is your own opinion about campus activism? Do you participate in any groups? Do you volunteer for any causes? Why or why not?
5. In the 1960s, students were known for leading protests and pioneering social change. Do we still equate campus life with social change? Has the time for campus groups and activism passed? Why or why not?

# What's the Matter with College?

*Rick Perlstein*

In the turbulent late 1960s and early 1970s, college campuses played a major role in the culture and politics of the era. They shaped ideas, and provided a haven for students to challenge the status quo. They were the sites of student activism, marches, and protest as students learned to think for themselves and confront authority. Today, according to author and historian Rick Perlstein, colleges have lost their central place in the broader society and in the lives of undergraduates. Is the college experience less critical to the nation than it was a generation ago? In this next essay, Rick Perlstein compares his own college experience to that of students in the 1960s and today.*

**BEFORE YOU READ**

What are your expectations of the college experience? Do you anticipate being challenged? To discuss new ideas and be introduced to social and cultural issues you may not have considered before? Or do you have other expectations, such as job training and preparation for the workforce? Maybe a mixture of all these things? Explain.

**AS YOU READ**

Consider the students Perlstein interviews to support his essay's argument. Do they represent your college peers? Are they an accurate representation of college students today?

1   When Ronald Reagan ran against Pat Brown in 1966 for the governorship of California, the defining issue was college. Governor Brown was completing the biggest university expansion in modern history—nine new campuses. California's colleges and universities had been instrumental in turning the nation's biggest state into the world's seventh-biggest economy and an international cultural mecca and they formed the heart, Brown presumed, of his re-election appeal. Ronald Reagan's advisers agreed and sought to neutralize the higher-ed issue by having the actor announce his candidacy flanked by two Nobel Prize winners.

2   Reagan had other ideas. For months he told campaign-trail audiences horror stories about the building takeovers, antiwar demonstrations and sexual deviance "so vile that I cannot describe it to you" at Berkeley, the University of California's flagship campus. Reagan's advisers warned him that disparaging the jewel of California civilization was political suicide. The candidate snapped back: "Look, I don't care if I'm in the mountains, the desert, the biggest cities of this state, the first question: 'What are you going to do about Berkeley?' And each time the question itself would get applause."

* Rick Perlstein, *The New York Times*, July 30, 2007.

3    It's unimaginable now that a gubernatorial race in the nation's largest state would come down to a debate about what was happening on campus. But it seemed perfectly natural then. The nation was obsessed with college and college students. It wasn't just the building takeovers and the generation gap; the obsession was well in gear by the presidency of John F. Kennedy. (In October 1961, *Harper's* devoted an issue to the subject.) The fascination was rooted in reasons as fresh as yesterday's op-ed pages: in an increasingly knowledge-based economy, good colleges were a social-mobility prerequisite, and between 1957 and 1967, the number of college students doubled. Reagan actually cast himself as this new class's savior, asking whether Californians would allow "a great university to be brought to its knees by a noisy, dissident minority." To that, liberals responded that these communities' unique ability to tolerate noisy, dissident minorities was why universities were great.

4    Now, as then, everyone says higher education is more important than ever to America's future. But interesting enough to become a topic of national obsession? Controversial enough to fight a gubernatorial campaign over? Hardly. The kids do have their own war now, but not much of an antiwar movement, much less building takeovers. College campuses seem to have lost their centrality. Why do college and college students no longer lead the culture? Why does student life no longer seem all that important?

5    Here's one answer: College as America used to understand it is coming to an end.

6    For nine years I've lived in the shadow of the University of Chicago—as an undergraduate between 1988 and 1992 and again since 2002. After growing up in a suburb that felt like a jail to me, I found my undergraduate years delightfully noisy and dissident. I got involved with The Baffler, the journal of social criticism edited by Thomas Frank, who went on to write *What's the Matter With Kansas?*; every Sunday, I trekked down to the neighborhood jazz jam session, where '60s continuities were direct. The bass player was a former Maoist, the drummer a former beatnik.

7    Early in May of this year I had lunch with the beatnik, Doug Mitchell, who received his undergraduate degree in 1965 and then went to graduate school here and is now an editor at the University of Chicago Press. I suspect I got in this university primarily because I had a high school friend who got a pirated copy of Henry Miller's *Tropic of Capricorn,* he said. "I put that on my reading list. And the admissions counselor was utterly astonished: 'How did you get this?' It was truly banned in 1960." He settled into an alienated suburban kid's paradise. "We had a social life that kind of revolved around the dorm lounge, because that's where everybody hung out after midnight. And some people got way into it and didn't survive. They would never go to class. They would argue night and day in the lounge!"

8    Mitchell and his friends enhanced their social life with special celebrity guest speakers, lured to their dorm lounge with little more than chutzpah and a phone call—people like Anaïs Nin, Eudora Welty and Ralph Ellison. One kid, a loudmouthed New Yorker (overrepresented at Chicago, which didn't have Jewish quotas), confronted Ellison over the latter's distaste for Charlie Parker. Mitchell shakes his head in wonder. "It was extraordinary to see this kind of head-to-head thing go on practically the first week you showed up on campus. The scrappy kids who were there wanted to mix it up with whoever came in." Mitchell's stories tumbled forth: baiting rednecks by reciting Lenny Bruce routines; listening to Elaine May and Mike Nichols records (they helped invent modern sketch comedy

at the Compass Theater two blocks from campus in the 1950s); the midnight concert students organized in which John Cage shared the bill with Chicago jazz players. "We seemed to have boundless verve. I had a friend who said, 'Why don't we call Dexter Gordon and get him to come to our dorm lounge and play?' Then we called John Coltrane and said, 'Would you like to do a concert with Ravi Shankar?' The point I'm trying to make is that the adventure of going to college consisted of a kind of freedom that you couldn't imagine until you turned 18, you were no longer under adult control and you made your own schedule. This is the most liberating moment Americans have in life."

9    Mitchell was beaming, but his face fell when I told him about my conversation the previous evening with Hamilton Morris, a New Yorker finishing up his first year of college. His parents are documentary filmmakers; his father is Errol Morris. He attended a high school of the arts where "they sort of let me do whatever I wanted." He is a filmmaker, a painter, a photographer, an experienced professional stand-up comedian. His life precollege was exceptionally fulfilling, and he expected it to remain so here at one of the nation's great universities. Then what happened?

10    "I hated it from the first day," he told me. "People here are so insanely uncreative, and they're proud of it." His fellow students "had to spend their entire high-school experience studying for the SATs or something and didn't really get a chance to live life or experience things."

11    What was most harrowing was Hamilton's matter-of-fact description of a culture of enervation—"that so many people hate it with a passion and don't leave." I heard similar things from several bright, creative searchers on campus—the kind of people in whom I recognized my own (and Doug Mitchell's) 19-year-old self. I sat down with a group of them at the Medici cafe, a campus fixture for decades, and they described college as a small town they were eager to escape. "Everyone I talk to has that kind of feeling in their bones," Mike Yong, a Japanese-literature major, insisted. "Even if they're going into investment banking." Someone offered the word "infantilizing." Murmurs of assent, then the word "emasculating," to louder agreement. One even insisted his process of political, social and creative awakening had happened, yes, during college—not because of college but in spite of it.

12    Is their diagnosis a function of college itself today, or just this particular college? Hamilton Morris told me stories that suggest the former. He visited his adviser and described his frustrations with the university. Her response: "You're not meant for college. You should really drop out." He struck up a conversation with a student on his floor "who as far as I can tell doesn't have any friends at all, and nobody talks to him. He has no desire to transfer—even though he's unhappy. I feel like a lot of people are like that as well. You know: 'College sucks anyway, so I might as well stay here.' "

13    Most of my interviewees were happy. Caroline Ouwerkerk was ecstatically so. As I futzed with my digital recorder, she gushed, "I'll talk all day about the university, whether or not I'm being recorded!" She gushed about the housing system, which sorts students randomly into teamlike "houses," where "someone is caring for you right from the start." She gushed about her job with the university-sponsored Community Service Leadership Training Corps and about her volunteer work advising prospective students. We met in the spacious lobby of the campus art museum, where she had already been three times but had yet to see the paintings; she was always there for a reception or a meeting. I asked if many

of her fellow students felt alienated from society, as many young people did in the 1960s. "I don't think anyone really feels that," she responded. "I am so impressed with so many of my peers at the university, with what they've accomplished before they go there in their high-school years, what they've accomplished now."

14    Caroline is smart. She is passionate. She has a social conscience and a mature grasp of the extraordinary privileges life has handed her. A reporter slotting her in for an interview also discovers she's astonishingly overscheduled—"Right now it's probably the worst time to ask me what I do for fun!"—but even her fun is impressive: an anthropology major specializing in food culture, she has been all over the city discovering exotic new ethnic restaurants. Caroline is a pristine example of what the *Times* columnist David Brooks called, in a 2001 *Atlantic Monthly* article on college, an Organization Kid. She is, indeed, a cog in the organization—specifically, the bureaucracy that schedules students' self-exploration, the very facet of campus culture that Mike Yong and his friends find most "infantilizing." Organization Kids don't mind it.

15    Most people make their accommodation between the two extremes. Their numbers include, interestingly enough, most of the campus activists. Jonathan Hirsch is a right-of-center example. As the president of Chicago Friends of Israel, one of the actions he led was taking over the Q. and A. session at a panel on the Israeli-Palestinian conflict that the Friends considered unbalanced.

16    Hirsch is a case study of a phenomenon that wouldn't have made sense even to Ronald Reagan in 1966: the saturation of higher education with market thinking. It cuts against the presumption that the campus should be a place radically apart from the rest of society—its own "city-state," as the British poet Stephen Spender wrote in a 1968 essay entirely typical of the era's what's-happening-on-campus genre. A biology major, Hirsch is most passionate about biotechnology. His ambition is to work for a venture-capital firm. He became excited telling me about the summer job he had at the University of Chicago's Office of Technology and Intellectual Property and about sitting on a committee to help set up a university "biotech incubator, where a new biotechnology company can be started up." He also expresses disappointment in Chicago's relative lack of market mojo: "Stanford commercializes a lot of stuff very well. This university has a lot of stuff that would be great, but we don't act on it." I asked whether incentivizing science according to its marketability might distort the university's mission to nurture ideas on the basis of intellectual merit, regardless of commercial potential. He's a bright kid, but I'm not sure he understood the question.

17    Just before these interviews, there had been a wave of campus activism: Chicago was considering replacing its idiosyncratic Uncommon Application in favor of the so-called Common Application used by many top-tier schools. "I love the Uncommon Application," Hirsch said. Then he added, "But at the same time I want the value of my degree to go up." One thing that the *U.S. News & World Report* rankings measure, he explained, is "selectivity," and the Uncommon Application (goes the theory) kills Chicago's selectivity rate by keeping more people from applying. Interestingly enough, when I later spoke to a pro-Uncommon Application advocate, his argument for it was likewise couched in economic terms.

18    I brought up another goal of campus activists to Jonathan Hirsch: reversing Chicago's decision, unusual among top-tier universities, not to divest from the military government

of Sudan in protest against the genocide in Darfur. He responded: "I understand their whole position. But, well, I'm not going to intrude myself on the investment decisions of the university." He then began a sophisticated critique of the marginal utility limited, he says of the divestment strategy as politics. When I later presented his arguments to a group of Darfur activists, they laid out their own position in market language: "In terms of the prevailing trend in corporate social responsibility, as a large corporation, albeit a university, we want our university to remain competitive in that respect."

19    There is something that these very different students share. Just as the distance between the campus and the market has shrunk (perhaps not that surprising at Chicago, home of the market-based approach to almost everything), so has the gap between childhood and college and between college and the real world that follows. To me, to Doug Mitchell, to just about anyone over 30, going to college represented a break, sometimes a radical one and our immediate postcollege lives represented a radical break with college. Some of us ended up coming back to the neighborhood partly for that very fact: nostalgia for four years unlike any we had experienced or would experience again. Not for these kids.

20    Hamilton Morris, with his hip, creative parents, is an extreme case of a common phenomenon: college without the generation gap. (As I write this at a coffee shop near campus, a kid picks up her cellphone—"Hi, Dad!"—and chats amiably for 15 minutes. "When we went to college," a dean of students who was a freshman in 1971 tells me, "you called on Sunday—the obligatory 30-second phone call on the dorm phone—and you hoped not to hear from them for the rest of the week.")

21    Morris is an exaggeration too of another banal new reality. You used to have to go to college to discover your first independent film, read your first forbidden book, find freaks like yourself who shared, say, a passion for Lenny Bruce. Now for even the most provincial students, the Internet, a radically more democratic and diverse culture—and those hip baby-boomer parents—take care of the problem.

22    Caroline hopped on a community-service track in high school, continued in college and plans on a career working in the same kind of service bureaucracy after graduation as she does now. Jonathan will experience the same sort of continuity—he has embraced a worldview in which erasing the distinction between the university and the world outside it is the entire point. Some of these kids, indeed, might end up having more of a "college" experience when they enter the workplace than beforehand. The workplace may be more surprising and maybe even more creative.

23    Why aren't people paying attention to the campuses? Because, as a discrete experience, "college" has begun to disappear. My radical, alienated friends brought up the University of Chicago's marketing materials: bucolic images of a mystic world apart, where 18-year-olds discover themselves for the first time in a heady atmosphere of cultural and intellectual tumult. But college no longer looks like that. They wondered how long the admissions office thought it could get away with it before students started complaining they'd been swindled. I posed the question to a brilliant graduating senior, someone I've been friends with for years. "They're assuming that the marketing is for students," he explained. "It's not. It's for parents."

24    Who had, you know, gone to college back when it was college.

**QUESTIONS FOR ANALYSIS AND DISCUSSION**

1. Why does Perlstein begin his essay with the recounting of the 1966 gubernatorial race in California? What relevance does it have to his essay's argument
   that college as we know it has changed?
2. Perlstein graduated with his undergraduate degree in 1992. Does he identify
   himself more with college students from the 1960s, or college students today? Which college experience does he think is better, and why?
3. How does Perlstein describe students Hamilton Morris, Caroline Ouwerkerk,
   and Jonathan Hirsch? What opinion does he have of each student? Do you
   think they represent most college students today?
4. Summarize Perlstein's analysis of "what's the matter with college [today]".
5. The *New York Times* held an essay contest encouraging college students to
   respond to Perlstein's essay. Respond to Perlstein's essay with your own
   view in which you either agree or disagree, in whole or in part, with his assertion that college today is no longer relevant and the college students today
   are largely apathetic and uninvolved.

# The Post-Everything Generation

*Nicholas Handler*

In July 2007, the *New York Times Magazine* published "What's the Matter With College,"
an essay by historian Rick Perlstein (see page 465), and invited college students across
the United States to respond. Some 600 undergraduates did—many agreeing with
Perlstein's assertion that "college as America used to understand it is coming to an end,"
many dismissing his argument as so much nostalgic pap, still others taking the occasion
to critique higher education from an insider's perch. The next essay, by Yale University
student Nicholas Handler, won the competition. Handler, who hails from Glen Ridge,
New Jersey, graduated in 2009 and plans on pursuing a career in human rights law."*

**BEFORE YOU READ**

A generation is a group of people who were born around the same time and therefore share a similar cultural experience. Their political and cultural ideas and
social perspectives are often different from generations preceding them. What are
the defining elements of your generation? What things make your age group fundamentally different in thought and action than say, your parent's generation?

**AS YOU READ**

What makes Perlstein pay attention in his literary theory class? What encourages him to think about his generation and how he fits into a larger world-view?

---

* Nicholas Handler, *The New York Times Magazine*, September 27, 2009.

1 I never expected to gain any new insight into the nature of my generation, or the changing landscape of American colleges, in Lit Theory. Lit Theory is supposed to be the class where you sit at the back of the room with every other jaded sophomore wearing skinny jeans, thick-framed glasses, an ironic tee-shirt and over-sized retro headphones, just waiting for lecture to be over so you can light up a Turkish Gold and walk to lunch while listening to Wilco. That's pretty much the way I spent the course, too: through structuralism, formalism, gender theory, and post-colonialism, I was far too busy shuffling through my iPod to see what the patriarchal world order of capitalist oppression had to do with Ethan Frome. But when we began to study postmodernism, something struck a chord with me and made me sit up and look anew at the seemingly blasé college-aged literati of which I was so self-consciously one.

2 According to my textbook, the problem with defining postmodernism is that it's impossible. The difficulty is that it is so . . . . post. It defines itself so negatively against what came before it—naturalism, romanticism and the wild revolution of modernism—that it's sometimes hard to see what it actually is. It denies that anything can be explained neatly or even at all. It is parodic, detached, strange, and sometimes menacing to traditionalists who do not understand it. Although it arose in the post-war west (the term was coined in 1949), the generation that has witnessed its ascendance has yet to come up with an explanation of what postmodern attitudes mean for the future of culture or society. The subject intrigued me because, in a class otherwise consumed by dead-letter theories, postmodernism remained an open book, tempting to the young and curious. But it also intrigued me because the question of what postmodernism—what a movement so post-everything, so reticent to define itself—is spoke to a larger question about the political and popular culture of today, of the other jaded sophomores sitting around me who had grown up in a postmodern world.

3 In many ways, as a college-aged generation, we are also extremely post: post-Cold War, post-industrial, post-baby boom, post-9/11 . . . at one point in his famous essay, "Postmodernism, or the Cultural Logic of Late Capitalism," literary critic Frederic Jameson even calls us "post-literate." We are a generation that is riding on the tail-end of a century of war and revolution that toppled civilizations, overturned repressive social orders, and left us with more privilege and opportunity than any other society in history. Ours could be an era to accomplish anything.

4 And yet do we take to the streets and the airwaves and say 'here we are, and this is what we demand'? Do we plant our flag of youthful rebellion on the mall in Washington and say 'we are not leaving until we see change! Our eyes have been opened by our education and our conception of what is possible has been expanded by our privilege and we demand a better world because it is our right'? It would seem we do the opposite. We go to war without so much as questioning the rationale, we sign away our civil liberties, we say nothing when the Supreme Court uses *Brown v. Board of Education* to outlaw desegregation, and we sit back to watch the carnage on the evening news.

5 On campus, we sign petitions, join organizations, put our names on mailing lists, make small-money contributions, volunteer a spare hour to tutor, and sport an entire wardrobe's worth of Live Strong bracelets advertising our moderately priced opposition to everything from breast cancer to global warming. But what do we really stand for? Like a true postmodern generation we refuse to weave together an overarching narrative to our own political consciousness, to present a cast of inspirational or revolutionary characters on our public

stage, or to define a specific philosophy. We are a story seemingly without direction or theme, structure or meaning—a generation defined negatively against what came before us. When Al Gore once said "It's the combination of narcissism and nihilism that really defines postmodernism," he might as well have been echoing his entire generation's critique of our own. We are a generation for whom even revolution seems trite, and therefore as fair a target for bland imitation as anything else. We are the generation of the Che Geuvera tee-shirt.

6      Jameson calls it "Pastiche"—"the wearing of a linguistic mask, speech in a dead language." In literature, this means an author speaking in a style that is not his own—borrowing a voice and continuing to use it until the words lose all meaning and the chaos that is real life sets in. It is an imitation of an imitation, something that has been re-envisioned so many times the original model is no longer relevant or recognizable. It is mass-produced individualism, anticipated revolution. It is why postmodernism lacks cohesion, why it seems to lack purpose or direction. For us, the post-everything generation, pastiche is the use and reuse of the old cliches of social change and moral outrage—a perfunctory rebelliousness that has culminated in the age of rapidly multiplying non-profits and relief funds. We live our lives in masks and speak our minds in a dead language—the language of a society that expects us to agitate because that's what young people do.

7      But how do we rebel against a generation that is expecting, anticipating, nostalgic for revolution? How do we rebel against parents that sometimes seem to want revolution more than we do? We don't. We rebel by not rebelling. We wear the defunct masks of protest and moral outrage, but the real energy in campus activism is on the internet, with websites like moveon.org. It is in the rapidly developing ability to communicate ideas and frustration in chatrooms instead of on the streets, and channel them into nationwide projects striving earnestly for moderate and peaceful change: we are the generation of Students Taking Action Now Darfur; we are the Rock the Vote generation; the generation of letter-writing campaigns and public interest lobbies; the alternative energy generation.

8      College as America once knew it—as an incubator of radical social change—is coming to an end. To our generation the word 'radicalism' evokes images of al Qaeda, not the Weathermen. 'Campus takeover' sounds more like Virginia Tech in 2007 than Columbia University in 1968. Such phrases are a dead language to us. They are vocabulary from another era that does not reflect the realities of today. However, the technological revolution, the moveon.org revolution, the revolution of the organization kid, is just as real and just as profound as the revolution of the 1960's—it is just not as visible. It is a work in progress, but it is there. Perhaps when our parents finally stop pointing out the things that we are not, the stories that we do not write, they will see the threads of our narrative begin to come together; they will see that behind our pastiche, the post generation speaks in a language that does make sense. We are writing a revolution. We are just putting it in our own words.

### QUESTIONS FOR ANALYSIS AND DISCUSSION ────────

1. What is post-modern theory? Why does Handler connect to this theory and believe it represents his generation better than any other? Explain.
2. Handler points out that college students today have the opportunity to make a change in the world but often fail to do so because their post-modern world lacks inspiration. Respond to his idea with your own view.

3. As if you were a judge for the *New York Times* essay contest, identify this essay's strengths and weaknesses.
4. What is Handler's opinion of his generation? Identify words and phrases in his essay that demonstrate his view.
5. How do you think Neil Perlstein would respond to Handler's argument? Do you think Perlstein's essay would be any different if he had interviewed a student like Handler? Why or why not?
6. Handler's essay won the essay competition, but received a lot of criticism as being un-stimulating and even boring. Read the four runner-up essays posted on the *New York Times* website at http://essay.blogs.nytimes.com/2007/09/26/two-years-are-better-than-four/. Was Handler's essay the best? What distinguished it from the others? In your opinion, was one of the runner up essays better? Explain.

## WRITING ASSIGNMENTS

1. John H. McWhorter notes that although many admissions officers dislike the idea of race-based admissions in principle, they still believe they are necessary for a diverse campus. Assume the role of a college admissions officer and create a list of the academic standards, abilities, grades, and qualities you believe should be used to admit students to the college you currently attend. Explain why you think your standards and measures are important factors in the admissions process. Finally, explain the role race plays, or does not play, in your admission policies.

2. Write an essay on what a college education means to you. Include what skills, knowledge, and abilities you feel a college education should confer after four years of study.

3. One of the most pressing issues regarding student behavior is binge drinking. Binge drinking is defined as four drinks in a row for females, and five or six drinks in a row for males. Discuss this definition with your peers and determine whether you feel that it is realistic. Then discuss the seriousness of the issue of drinking at your own campus. What reputation does your school have? Is it considered a "party school" or a "drinking school"? Is it a dry campus? Research the issue of drinking on your campus and write a short essay exploring the issue as it relates specifically to your campus.

4. Review your student handbook and summarize your student rights and responsibilities. Do you agree with your college's rules and regulations? Write an essay in which you agree or disagree, in whole or in part, with the rules and regulations guiding student conduct.

5. Design a college core curriculum that every student must take before graduation, regardless of their major. Select 12 courses to be taken over the four-year time span of the average bachelor's degree. You may be general in your selection ("Western Civilization I & II") or very specific ("Gender and Power in Modern America"). After compiling your curriculum, share your list with other students in class to see which courses were chosen in common, and which ones were different. If your college or university has a core curriculum, compare your final list with that outlined in your student handbook.

6.  Neil Perlstein argues that "college students no longer rule the culture." Answer his assertion with your own view. As a college student, do you expect to "rule the culture"? How are your expectations of college different from previous generations, and why are they different?

7.  Write your own essay of no more than 1200 words explaining "Why College Matters."

# Race and Ethnicity

The United States is a union predicated on shared moral values, political and economic self-interest, and a common language. However, it is also a nation of immigrants— people of different races, ethnic identities, religions, and languages. It is a nation whose motto *e pluribus unum* ("one out of many") bespeaks a pride in its multicultural heritage. In this chapter, we explore some of the issues that arise from the diversity of our cultural and ethnic backgrounds.

This chapter examines the complex ways in which our assumptions about race and construction of stereotypes limit our relationships with others and distort how we define ourselves. By definition, stereotypes are generalizations about people based on characteristics such as race, ethnic origin, social class, religion, gender, or physical appearance. Often, stereotypes can lead one to make assumptions about others that are negative and demeaning. Sometimes even stereotypes that attribute positive qualities to certain groups, such as the assumption that Asian Americans are naturally smart, can deny individuals credit for their achievements.

Several readings in this chapter address the ways race can both unify and divide us. Although the United States has been a multiethnic and multiracial society since its founding, in the last few decades different groups of Americans have reasserted their ethnic and racial identities. And while we may glorify the memory of our own immigrant ancestors, we do not always welcome with open arms new waves of immigrants. But old ways of doing things linger on. For example, if race and ethnicity continue to be a question on employment forms and census data, can we ever really think of defining ourselves differently?

The election of Barack Obama to the nation's highest office raised new questions about racism in America. What does it mean for the United States to have a black president? Some people view Obama's election as proof that Americans have finally overcome institutionalized racism. Others view it as the end of a long struggle for equality and access to power. Still others say we have a long way to go. As you read this chapter, think about how the issue of race touches your daily life, including what Barack Obama's election to the presidency might mean to the dynamics of race in America.

## The Myth of the Latina Woman
*Judith Ortiz Cofer*

Racial stereotypes are often based on misperceptions and a lack of understanding of another group's cultural heritage. In this essay, novelist and writing professor Judith Ortiz Cofer explores how racial stereotypes are created by cultural misunderstandings, with often insulting results. She also describes how once stereotypes are established, they can perpetuate degrading popular opinions that, in turn, may damage the self-regard of an entire group of people.*

**BEFORE YOU READ**

Consider the ways the media perpetuate cultural stereotypes. Think about how various media, such as television and cinema, promote cultural clichés.

**AS YOU READ**

Ortiz Cofer comments that certain adjectives are often used to describe individuals from her ethnic background. What is the basis for these adjectives? What other words can you cite that are used to describe the personalities of women and men from other ethnic backgrounds?

1   On a bus trip to London from Oxford University where I was earning some graduate credits one summer, a young man, obviously fresh from a pub, spotted me and as if struck by inspiration went down on his knees in the aisle. With both hands over his heart he broke into an Irish tenor's rendition of "María" from *West Side Story*. My politely amused fellow passengers gave his lovely voice the round of gentle applause it deserved.

2   Though I was not quite as amused, I managed my version of an English smile: no show of teeth, no extreme contortions of the facial muscles—I was at this time of my life practicing reserve and cool. Oh, that British control, how I coveted it. But María had followed me to London, reminding me of a prime fact of my life: you can leave the Island, master the English language, and travel as far as you can, but if you are a Latina, especially one like me who so obviously belongs to Rita Moreno's gene pool, the Island travels with you.

3   This is sometimes a very good thing—it may win you that extra minute of someone's attention. But with some people, the same things can make you an island—not so much a tropical paradise as an Alcatraz, a place nobody wants to visit. As a Puerto Rican girl growing up in the United States and wanting like most children to "belong," I resented the stereotype that my Hispanic appearance called forth from many people I met.

*Judith Ortiz Cofer, *The Latin Deli* (excerpt), 1993.

4     Our family lived in a large urban center in New Jersey during the sixties, where life was designed as a microcosm of my parents' casas on the island. We spoke in Spanish, we ate Puerto Rican food bought at the bodega, and we practiced strict Catholicism complete with Saturday confession and Sunday mass at a church where our parents were accommodated into a one-hour Spanish mass slot, performed by a Chinese priest trained as a missionary for Latin America.

5     As a girl I was kept under strict surveillance, since virtue and modesty were, by cultural equation, the same as family honor. As a teenager I was instructed on how to behave as a proper señorita. But it was a conflicting message girls got, since the Puerto Rican mothers also encouraged their daughters to look and act like women and to dress in clothes our Anglo friends and their mothers found too "mature" for our age. It was, and is, cultural, yet I often felt humiliated when I appeared at an American friend's party wearing a dress more suitable to a semiformal than to a playroom birthday celebration. At Puerto Rican festivities, neither the music nor the colors we wore could be too loud. I still experience a vague sense of letdown when I'm invited to a "party" and it turns out to be a marathon conversation in hushed tones rather than a fiesta with salsa, laughter, and dancing—the kind of celebration I remember from my childhood.

6     I remember Career Day in our high school, when teachers told us to come dressed as if for a job interview. It quickly became obvious that to the barrio girls, "dressing up" sometimes meant wearing ornate jewelry and clothing that would be more appropriate (by mainstream standards) for the company Christmas party than as daily office attire. That morning I had agonized in front of my closet, trying to figure out what a "career girl" would wear because, essentially, except for Marlo Thomas on TV, I had no models on which to base my decision. I knew how to dress for school: At the Catholic school I attended we all wore uniforms; I knew how to dress for Sunday mass, and I knew what dresses to wear for parties at my relatives' homes. Though I do not recall the precise details of my Career Day outfit, it must have been a composite of the above choices. But I remember a comment my friend (an Italian-American) made in later years that coalesced my impressions of that day. She said that at the business school she was attending the Puerto Rican girls always stood out for wearing "everything at once." She meant, of course, too much jewelry, too many accessories. On that day at school, we were simply made the negative models by the nuns who were themselves not credible fashion experts to any of us. But it was painfully obvious to me that to the others, in their tailored skirts and silk blouses, we must have seemed "hopeless" and "vulgar." Though I now know that most adolescents feel out of step much of the time, I also know that for the Puerto Rican girls of my generation that sense was intensified. The way our teachers and classmates looked at us that day in school was just a taste of the cultural clash that awaited us in the real world, where prospective employers and men on the street would often misinterpret our tight skirts and jingling bracelets as a come-on.

7     Mixed cultural signals have perpetuated certain stereotypes—for example, that of the Hispanic woman as the "Hot Tamale" or sexual firebrand. It is a one-dimensional view that the media have found easy to promote. In their special vocabulary, advertisers have designated "sizzling" and "smoldering" as the adjectives of choice for describing not only the foods but also the women of Latin America. From conversations in my house I recall hearing about the harassment that Puerto Rican women endured in factories where the "boss

men" talked to them as if sexual innuendo was all they understood and, worse, often gave them the choice of submitting to advances or being fired.

8    It is custom, however, not chromosomes, that leads us to choose scarlet over pale pink. As young girls, we were influenced in our decisions about clothes and colors by the women—older sisters and mothers who had grown up on a tropical island where the natural environment was a riot of primary colors, where showing your skin was one way to keep cool as well as to look sexy. Most important of all, on the Island, women perhaps felt freer to dress and move more provocatively, since, in most cases, they were protected by the traditions, mores, and laws of a Spanish/Catholic system of morality and machismo whose main rule was: You may look at my sister, but if you touch her I will kill you. The extended family and church structure could provide a young woman with a circle of safety in her small pueblo on the island; if a man "wronged" a girl, everyone would close in to save her family honor.

9    This is what I have gleaned from my discussions as an adult with older Puerto Rican women. They have told me about dressing in their best party clothes on Saturday nights and going to the town's plaza to promenade with their girlfriends in front of the boys they liked. The males were thus given an opportunity to admire the women and to express their admiration in the form of piropos: erotically charged street poems they composed on the spot. I have been subjected to a few piropos while visiting the Island, and they can be outrageous, although custom dictates that they must never cross into obscenity. This ritual, as I understand it, also entails a show of studied indifference on the woman's part; if she is "decent," she must not acknowledge the man's impassioned words. So I do understand how things can be lost in translation. When a Puerto Rican girl dressed in her idea of what is attractive meets a man from the mainstream culture who has been trained to react to certain types of clothing as a sexual signal, a clash is likely to take place. The line I first heard based on this aspect of the myth happened when the boy who took me to my first formal dance leaned over to plant a sloppy overeager kiss painfully on my mouth, and when I didn't respond with sufficient passion said in a resentful tone: "I thought you Latin girls were supposed to mature early"—my first instance of being thought of as a fruit or vegetable—I was supposed to ripen, not just grow into womanhood like other girls.

10    It is surprising to some of my professional friends that some people, including those who should know better, still put others "in their place." Though rarer, these incidents are still commonplace in my life. It happened to me most recently during a stay at a very classy metropolitan hotel favored by young professional couples for their weddings. Late one evening after the theater, as I walked toward my room with my new colleague (a woman with whom I was coordinating an arts program), a middle-aged man in a tuxedo, a young girl in satin and lace on his arm, stepped directly into our path. With his champagne glass extended toward me, he exclaimed, "Evita!"

11    Our way blocked, my companion and I listened as the man half-recited, half-bellowed "Don't Cry for Me, Argentina." When he finished, the young girl said: "How about a round of applause for my daddy?" We complied, hoping this would bring the silly spectacle to a close. I was becoming aware that our little group was attracting the attention of the other guests. "Daddy" must have perceived this too, and he once more barred the way as we tried to walk past him. He began to shout-sing a ditty to the tune of

"La Bamba"—except the lyrics were about a girl named Maria whose exploits all rhymed with her name and gonorrhea. The girl kept saying "Oh, Daddy" and looking at me with pleading eyes. She wanted me to laugh along with the others. My companion and I stood silently waiting for the man to end his offensive song. When he finished, I looked not at him but at his daughter. I advised her calmly never to ask her father what he had done in the army. Then I walked between them and to my room. My friend complimented me on my cool handling of the situation. I confessed to her that I really had wanted to push the jerk into the swimming pool. I knew that this same man—probably a corporate executive, well educated, even wordly by most standards—would not have been likely to regale a white woman with a dirty song in public. He would perhaps have checked his impulse by assuming that she could be somebody's wife or mother, or at least somebody who might take offense. But to him, I was just an Evita or a María: merely a character in his cartoon-populated universe.

12    Because of my education and my proficiency with the English language, I have acquired many mechanisms for dealing with the anger I experience. This was not true for my parents, nor is it true for the many Latin women working at menial jobs who must put up with stereotypes about our ethnic group such as: "They make good domestics." This is another facet of the myth of the Latin woman in the United States. Its origin is simple to deduce. Work as domestics, waitressing, and factory jobs are all that's available to women with little English and few skills. The myth of the Hispanic menial has been sustained by the same media phenomenon that made "Mammy" from *Gone with the Wind* America's idea of the black woman for generations; María, the housemaid or counter girl, is now indelibly etched into the national psyche. The big and the little screens have presented us with the picture of the funny Hispanic maid, mispronouncing words and cooking up a spicy storm in a shiny California kitchen.

13    This media-engendered image of the Latina in the United States has been documented by feminist Hispanic scholars, who claim that such portrayals are partially responsible for the denial of opportunities for upward mobility among Latinas in the professions. I have a Chicana friend working on a Ph.D. in philosophy at a major university. She says her doctor still shakes his head in puzzled amazement at all the "big words" she uses. Since I do not wear my diplomas around my neck for all to see, I too have on occasion been sent to that "kitchen," where some think I obviously belong.

14    One such incident that has stayed with me, though I recognize it as a minor offense, happened on the day of my first public poetry reading. It took place in Miami in a boat-restaurant where we were having lunch before the event. I was nervous and excited as I walked in with my notebook in my hand. An older woman motioned me to her table. Thinking (foolish me) that she wanted me to autograph a copy of my brand new slender volume of verse, I went over. She ordered a cup of coffee from me, assuming that I was the waitress. Easy enough to mistake my poems for menus, I suppose. I know that it wasn't an intentional act of cruelty, yet of all the good things that happened that day, I remember that scene most clearly, because it reminded me of what I had to overcome before anyone would take me seriously. In retrospect I understand that my anger gave my reading fire, that I have almost always taken doubts in my abilities as a challenge—and that the result is, most times, a feeling of satisfaction at having won a convert when I see the cold, appraising eyes warm to my words, the body

language change, the smile that indicates that I have opened some avenue for communication. That day I read to that woman and her lowered eyes told me that she was embarrassed at her little faux pas, and when I willed her to look up at me, it was my victory, and she graciously allowed me to punish her with my full attention. We shook hands at the end of the reading, and I never saw her again. She has probably forgotten the whole thing but maybe not.

15    Yet I am one of the lucky ones. My parents made it possible for me to acquire a stronger footing in the mainstream culture by giving me the chance at an education. And books and art have saved me from the harsher forms of ethnic and racial prejudice that many of my Hispanic compañeras have had to endure. I travel a lot around the United States, reading from my books of poetry and my novel, and the reception I most often receive is one of positive interest by people who want to know more about my culture. There are, however, thousands of Latinas without the privilege of an education or the entrée into society that I have. For them life is a struggle against the misconceptions perpetuated by the myth of the Latina as whore, domestic or criminal. We cannot change this by legislating the way people look at us. The transformation, as I see it, has to occur at a much more individual level. My personal goal in my public life is to try to replace the old pervasive stereotypes and myths about Latinas with a much more interesting set of realities. Every time I give a reading, I hope the stories I tell, the dreams and fears I examine in my work, can achieve some universal truth which will get my audience past the particulars of my skin color, my accent, or my clothes.

16    I once wrote a poem in which I called us Latinas "God's brown daughters." This poem is really a prayer of sorts, offered upward, but also, through the human-to-human channel of art, outward. It is a prayer for communication, and for respect. In it, Latin women pray "in Spanish to an Anglo God / with a Jewish heritage," and they are "fervently hoping / that if not omnipotent, / at least He be bilingual."

## QUESTIONS FOR ANALYSIS AND DISCUSSION ——————————

1. How did Ortiz Cofer's cultural background prevent her from "fitting in"? What differences does she describe between Puerto Rican and "white" cultures?

2. How can cultural ideology and history hinder acceptance into "mainstream" corporate and social America? Explain.

3. How have the media promoted the image of the "Latina woman"? Evaluate Ortiz Cofer's analysis of why this stereotyping occurs. Do you agree?

4. What was the "Island system" of morality for Puerto Ricans? How did it both liberate and restrain them? Analyze Ortiz Cofer's connection between the island system of life and the cultural misunderstandings she encountered in urban America.

5. Explain the connection between Ortiz Cofer's poem at the end of her essay and the points she makes earlier. Is this an effective way to end the essay?

6. Why does Ortiz Cofer consider herself to be "one of the lucky ones" (paragraph 15)? Explain.

# Leaving Race Behind

## Amitai Etzioni

Caucasian, Black, Asian, Hispanic, Native American. . . .official forms ask us to indicate our race. In this next essay, author and sociology professor Amitai Etzioni explains why he hesitates to mark any specific race—why is this information important at all? He then explains why the growing Hispanic population raises troubling questions about why race matters to the government, and why the time has come to stop asking this question on forms. The U.S. Census Bureau estimates that there will be almost 50 million citizens claiming Hispanic origins living in the U.S., comprising 15 percent of the total population. It projects that within the next 40 years, Hispanics will represent one quarter of the total population in the U.S. Etzioni explains why this trend creates a golden opportunity to address the ills of racism in America.*

### BEFORE YOU READ

Have you ever felt discriminated against because of your race? Have you ever found yourself making stereotypical assumptions about others based on their ethnicity, even inadvertently? Explain.

### AS YOU READ

In his next essay, Amitai Etzioni recounts a personal experience in which race made him acutely aware of how disclosing this information can be abused. What role has race played in you life? Have you, like Etzioni, experienced a defining moment that changed or influenced your view of yourself or someone in your family connected to your ethnicity?

1   Some years ago the United States government asked me what my race was. I was reluctant to respond because my 50 years of practicing sociology—and some powerful personal experiences—have underscored for me what we all know to one degree or another, that racial divisions bedevil America, just as they do many other societies across the world. Not wanting to encourage these divisions, I refused to check off one of the specific racial options on the U.S. Census form and instead marked a box labeled "Other." I later found out that the federal government did not accept such an attempt to de-emphasize race, by me or by some 6.75 million other Americans who tried it. Instead the government assigned me to a racial category, one it chose for me. Learning this made me conjure up what I admit is a far-fetched association. I was in this place once before.

2   When I was a Jewish child in Nazi Germany in the early 1930s, many Jews who saw themselves as good Germans wanted to "pass" as Aryans. But the Nazi regime would have none of it. Never mind, they told these Jews, we determine who is Jewish and who is not.

---

*Amitai Etzioni, *The American Scholar*, September 1, 2006.

A similar practice prevailed in the Old South, where if you had one drop of African blood you were a Negro, disregarding all other facts and considerations, including how you saw yourself.

3    You might suppose that in the years since my little Census-form protest the growing enlightenment about race in our society would have been accompanied by a loosening of racial categories by our government. But in recent years the United States government has acted in a deliberate way to make it even more difficult for individuals to move beyond racial boxes and for American society as a whole to move beyond race.

4    Why the government perpetuates racialization and what might be done to diminish the role of race in our lives are topics that have become especially timely as Hispanics begin to take a more important role demographically, having displaced African-Americans as the largest American minority. How Hispanics view themselves and how they are viewed by others are among the most important factors affecting whether or not we can end race as a major social divide in America.

5    Treating people differently according to their race is as un-American as a hereditary aristocracy, and as American as slavery. The American ethos was formed by people who left the social stratification of the Old World to live in a freer, more fluid society. They sought to be defined by what they accomplished, not by what they were born with. As Arthur M. Schlesinger Jr. puts it in his book *The Disuniting of America*, one of the great virtues of America is that it defines individuals by where they are going rather than by where they have been. Achievement matters, not origin. The national ideal says that all Americans should be able to compete as equals, whatever their background. American society has been divided along racial lines since its earliest days.

6    Racial characterizations have trumped the achievement ideal; people born into a non-white race, whatever their accomplishments have been unable to change their racial status. Worse, race has often been their most defining characteristic, affecting most, if not all, aspects of their being.

7    As a result, we have been caught, at least since the onset of the civil rights movement, in ambivalence. On the one hand, we continue to dream of the day when all Americans will be treated equally, whatever their race; we rail against—and sometimes punish—those who discriminate according to race in hiring, housing, and social life. At the same time, we have ensconced in law many claims based on race: requirements that a given proportion of public subsidies, loans, job training, educational assistance, and admission slots at choice colleges be set aside for people of color. Many Americans, including African-Americans, are uneasy about what some people consider reverse discrimination. Courts have limited its scope; politicians have made hay by opposing it; and some of its beneficiaries feel that their successes are hollow because they are unsure whether their gains reflect hard-won achievements or special favors. There must be a better way to deal with past and current injustice. And the rapid changes in American demographics call for a reexamination of the place of race in America.

## Enter the Hispanic

8    We have grown accustomed to thinking about America in black and white, and might well have continued to do so for decades to come except that Hispanics complicate this simplistic scheme: they do not fit into the old racial categories. Some Hispanics appear to many

Americans to be black (for example, quite a few Cuban-Americans), others as white (especially immigrants from Argentina and Chile), and the appearance of still others is hard for many people to pigeonhole. Anyone seeing the lineup of baseball players honored as Major League Baseball's "Latino Legends Team" would find that the players vary from those who are as fair-skinned as Roger Clemens to those who are as dark-skinned as Jackie Robinson. More important by far, survey after survey shows that most Hispanics object to being classified as either black or white. A national survey conducted in 2002 indicated that 76 percent of Hispanics say the standard racial categories used by the U.S. Census do not address their preferences. The last thing most of those surveyed desire is to be treated as yet another race—as "brown" Americans.

9      Hispanics would have forced the question of how we define one another even if they were just another group of immigrants among the many that have made America what it is. But Hispanics are not just one more group of immigrants. Not only have Hispanic numbers surpassed those of black Americans, who until 2003 made up America's largest minority group, Hispanics have been reliably projected to grow much faster than African-Americans or any other American group. Thus, according to the Census, in 1990 blacks constituted 12 percent of the population and Hispanics 9 percent. By 2000, Hispanics caught up with blacks, amounting to 12.5 percent of the population compared to 12.3 percent for blacks. By 2050, Hispanics are projected to be 24.3 percent of the American population, compared to 14.7 percent for blacks. In many cities, from Miami to Los Angeles, in which African-Americans have been the largest minority group, Hispanics' numbers are increasingly felt. While once Hispanics were concentrated in the areas bordering Mexico, their numbers are now growing in places like Denver, St. Paul, and even New England.

10     Immigration fuels the growth of Hispanics relative to the growth of African-Americans because Latin American immigration, legal and illegal, continues at an explosive pace, while immigration from Africa is minuscule. Hispanics also have more children than African-Americans. During the most recent year for which data is available, 2003–2004, one of every two people added to America's population was Hispanic. And while black Americans have long been politically mobilized and active, Hispanics are just beginning to make their weight felt in American politics.

11     The rapid growth in the number, visibility, and power of Hispanics will largely determine the future of race in America, a point highlighted by Clara E. Rodriguez in her book *Changing Race: Latinos, the Census, and the History of Ethnicity in the U.S.* If Hispanics are to be viewed as brown or black (and some on the left aspire to color them), and above all if Hispanics develop the sense of disenfranchisement and alienation that many African-Americans have acquired (often for very good reasons), then America's immutable racial categories will only deepen.

12     If, on the other hand, most Hispanics continue to see themselves as members of one or more ethnic groups, then race in America might be pushed to the margins. Racial categories have historically set us apart; ethnic categories are part of the mosaic that makes up America. It has been much easier for an individual to assimilate from an ethnic perspective than from a racial one. Race is considered a biological attribute, a part of your being that cannot be dropped or modified. Ethnic origin, in contrast, is where you came from. All Americans have one hyphen or another attached to their ethnic status: we're Polish-, or

German-, or Anglo-, or Italian-Americans. Adding Cuban-Americans or Mexican-Americans to this collage would create more comfortable categories of a comparable sort.

## The Race Trap

13 Many people take it for granted that genes determine race, just as genes determine gender. And we also tend to believe that racial categories are easy to discern (though we all know of exceptions).

14    One way to show how contrived racial divisions actually are is to recall that practically all of the DNA in all human beings is the same. Our differences are truly skin deep. Moreover, the notion that most of us are of one race or another has little basis in science. The Human Genome Project informs us not only that 99.9 percent of genetic material is shared by all humans, but also that variation in the remaining 0.1 percent is greater within racial groups than across them. That is, not only are 99.9 percent of the genes of a black person the same as those of a white person, but the genes of a particular black person may be more similar to the genes of a white person than they are to another black person.

15    This point was driven home to college students in a sociology class at Penn State in April 2005. Following their professor's suggestion, the students took DNA tests that had surprising results. A student who identified himself as "a proud black man" found that only 52 percent of his ancestry traced back to Africa, while the other 48 percent was European. Another student who said she takes flak from black friends for having a white boyfriend found that her ancestry was 58 percent European and only 42 percent African. These two students are not alone: an estimated one-third of the African-American population has European ancestry.

16    Which people make up a distinct race and which are considered dark-skinned constantly changes as social prejudices change. Jewish-, Slavic-, Irish-, and Polish-Americans were considered distinct races in the mid-19th and early 20th centuries—and dark races at that, as chronicled in great detail in Matthew Frye Jacobson's book, *Whiteness of a Different Color: European Immigrants and the Alchemy of Race;* and in a well-documented book by Noel Ignatiev, *How the Irish Became White.* Ignatiev found that in the 1850s, Irish people were considered non-white in America and were frequently referred to as "niggers turned inside out." (Blacks were sometimes called "smoked Irish.")

17    The capriciousness of racial classifications is further highlighted by the way the U.S. Census, the most authoritative and widely used source of social classifications, divides Americans into races. When I ask my students how many races they think there are in America, they typically count four: white, black, Asian, and Native American. The Census says there are 15 racial categories: white, African-American, American Indian/Alaska Native, Asian Indian, Chinese, Filipino, Japanese, Korean, Vietnamese, "other Asian," Native Hawaiian, Guamanian/Chamorro, Samoan, and "other Pacific Islander," and as of 2000 one more for those who feel they are of some other race. (Hispanic is not on this list because the Census treats Hispanic as an ethnicity and asks about it on a separate question, but immediately following that question, the Census asks, "So what is your race, anyhow?")

18    The arbitrary nature of these classifications is demonstrated by the Census Bureau itself, which can change the race of millions of Americans by the stroke of a pen. The

Census changed the race of Indian- and Pakistani-Americans from white in 1970 to Asian in 1980. In 1930 the Census made Mexicans into a different race but then withdrew this category. Similarly, Hindu made a brief appearance as a race in the 1930 and 1940 Censuses but was subsequently withdrawn.

19    Anthropologists have found that some tribes do not see colors the way many of us do; for instance, they do not "see" a difference between brown and yellow. Members of these tribes are not colorblind, but some differences found in nature (in the color spectrum) simply don't register with them, just as young American children are unaware of racial differences until someone introduces them to these distinctions. We draw a line between white and black, but people's skin colors have many shades. It is our social prejudices that lead us to make sharp racial categories.

20    I am not one of those postmodernists who, influenced by Nietzsche and Foucault, claim that there are no epistemological truths, that all facts are a matter of social construction. I disagree with Nietzsche's description of truth as "a mobile army of metaphors, metonyms, and anthropomorphisms—in short a sum of human relations, which have been enhanced, transposed, and embellished poetically and rhetorically and which after long use seem firm, canonical, and obligatory to a people." However, there is no doubt that social construction plays a significant role in the way we "see" racial differences, although our views may in turn be affected by other factors that are less subject to construction, for example, historical differences.

21    Most important is the significance we attribute to race and the interpretations we impose on it. When we are told only that a person is, say, Asian-American, we often jump to a whole list of conclusions regarding that person's looks, intelligence, work ethic, character; we make the same sort of jumps for Native Americans, blacks, and other races. Many things follow from these kneejerk characterizations: whether we will fear or like this person, whether we will wish to have him or her as a neighbor or as a spouse for one of our children—all on the basis of race. In short, we load on to race a great deal of social importance that is not a reflection of the "objective" biological differences that exist. To paraphrase the UNESCO Constitution, racial divisions are made in the minds of men and women, and that is where they will have to be ended.

## Defining the Hispanic

22   If racial categories have long been settled, the social characterization of the Hispanic is up for grabs. We still don't know whether Hispanics will be defined as a brown race and align themselves with those in the United States who are or who see themselves as marginalized or victimized—or if they will be viewed as a conglomerate of ethnic groups, of Mexican-Americans, Cuban-Americans, Dominican-Americans, and so forth, who will fit snugly into the social mosaic.

23    The term Hispanic was first used in the Census in 1980. Before that, Mexican-Americans and Cuban-Americans were classified as white (except when a Census interviewer identified an individual as the member of a different racial group). Until 1980, Hispanics were part of the great American panorama of ethnic groups. Then the Census combined these groups into a distinct category unlike any other. It was as if the federal government were to one day lump together Spanish-, Italian-, and Greek-Americans into a

group called "Southern European" and begin issuing statistics on how their income, educational achievements, number of offspring, and so on compare to those of Northern Europeans.

24      And as we've seen, those who define themselves as Hispanic are asked to declare a race. In the 1980 Census, the options included, aside from the usual menu of races, that ambiguous category "Other." There were 6.75 million Americans, including me, who chose this option in 1980. Most revealing: 40 percent of Hispanics chose this option. (Note that they—and I—chose this category despite the nature of the word Other, which suggests the idea of "not being one of us." Had the category been accorded a less loaded label, say "wish not to be identified with any one group," it seems likely that many millions more would have chosen this box.)

25      To have millions of Americans choose to identify themselves as "Other" created a political backlash because Census statistics are used both to allocate public funds to benefit minority groups and to assess their political strength. Some African-American groups, especially, feared that if African-Americans chose "Other" instead of marking the "African-American" box, they would lose public allotments and political heft.

26      But never underestimate our government. The Census Bureau has used a statistical procedure to assign racial categories to those millions of us who sought to butt out of this divisive classification scheme. Federal regulations outlined by the Office of Management and Budget, a White House agency, ruled that the Census must "impute" a specific race to those who do not choose one. For several key public policy purposes, a good deal of social and economic data must be aggregated into five racial groups: white, black, Asian, American Indian or Alaska Native, and native Hawaiian or other Pacific Islander. How does the government pick a race for a person who checked the "Other" box? They turn to the answers for other Census questions: for example, income, neighborhood, education level, or last name. The resulting profiles of the U.S. population (referred to as the "age-race modified profile") are then used by government agencies in allotting public funds and for other official and public purposes.

27      But the Census isn't alone in oversimplifying the data. Increasingly, other entities, including the media, have treated Hispanics as a race rather than an ethnic group. This occurs implicitly when those who generate social data—such as government agencies or social scientists—break down the data into four categories: white, black, Asian, and Hispanic, which is comparable to listing apples, oranges, bananas, and yams. In their profile of jail inmates, the Bureau of Justice Statistics lists inmates' origins as "white, black, Hispanic, American Indian/Alaska Native, Asian/Pacific Islander, and more than one race." The *New York Times* ran a front-page story in September 2005 in which it compared the first names used by whites, blacks, Asians, and Hispanics. Replace the word Hispanics with the name of another ethnic group, say Jews, and the unwitting racial implication of this classification will stand out.

28      Still other studies include Hispanics when they explicitly refer to racial groups. For example, a 2001 paper by Sean Reardon and John T. Yun examines what they call "racial balkanization among suburban schools," where there is increased segregation among black, Hispanic, and Asian students. A 2005 *Seattle Times* story uses racial terminology when it reports "Latinos have the fewest numbers among racial groups in master's-of-business programs nationwide, with about 5,000 enrolling annually." Similarly, the *San Diego*

*Union Tribune* states: "A brawl between Latino and black students resulted in a lockdown of the school and revealed tensions between the two largest racial groups on campus."

29    A handful of others go a step further and refer to Hispanics as a brown race. For example, following the recent Los Angeles mayoral election, the *Houston Chronicle* informed us that "Villaraigosa's broad-based support has analysts wondering whether it is evidence of an emerging black-brown coalition." And, National Public Radio reported: "There is no black and brown alliance at a South Central Los Angeles high school."

30    One way or another, all of these references push us in the wrong direction—toward racializing Hispanics and deepening social divisions. America would be best served if we moved in the opposite direction.

## A New Taxonomy

31  Thus far, workers at the U.S. Census Bureau, following the White House's instructions, seem determined to prevent any de-emphasis of race. They are testing iterations of the wording for the relevant questions in the 2010 Census—but all of these possibilities continue to require people to identify themselves by race. Moreover, Census bureaucrats will continue to impute race to those who refuse to do so themselves, ignoring the ever-growing number of people, especially Hispanics, who do not fit into this scheme.

32    Imagine if instead the federal government classified people by their country (or countries) of origin. For some governmental purposes, it might suffice to use large categories, such as Africa (which would exclude other so-called black groups, such as Haitians and West Indians that are now included in references to "black" Americans), Asia, Europe, Central America, and South America (the last two categories would not, of course, include Spain). For other purposes, a more detailed breakdown might work better—using regions such as the Middle East and Southeast Asia, for example—and if still more detail was desired, specific countries could be used, as we do for identifying ethnic groups (Irish, Polish, Cuban, Mexican, Japanese, Ethiopian, and so on). Kenneth Prewitt, a former director of the U.S. Census Bureau, has suggested the use of ethnic categories. As we have seen, ethnic origins carry some implications for who we are, but these implications decline in importance over time. Above all, they do not define us in some immutable way, as racial categories do. A category called something like "wish not to be identified with any particular group" should be included for those who do not want to be characterized even by ethnicity or for others who view themselves as having a varied and combined heritage.

33    The classification of Americans who are second-generation, and beyond, highlights the importance of the no-particular-group category. Although a fourth-generation Italian-American might still wish to be identified as Italian, he might not, particularly if he has grandparents or parents who are, say, Greek, Korean, and Native American. Forcing such a person to classify himself as a member of one ethnic group conceals the significance of the most important American development in social matters: out-marriage. Out-marriage rates for all groups other than African-Americans are so high that most of us will soon be tied to Americans of a large variety of backgrounds by the closest possible social tie, the familial one. Approximately 30 percent of third-generation Hispanics and 40 percent of third-generation Asians marry people of a different racial or ethnic origin. Altogether, the proportion of marriages among people of different racial or ethnic origins has increased by 72 percent

since 1970. The trend suggests more of this in the future. Even if your spouse is of the same background, chances are high that the spouse of a sibling or cousin will represent a different part of the American collage. At holidays and other family events, from birthdays to funerals, we will increasingly be in close connection with "Others." Before too long most Americans will be "Tiger Woods" Americans, whose parental heritage is black, Native American, Chinese, Caucasian, and Thai. Now is the time for our social categories to reflect this trend—and its capacity for building a sense of one community—rather than conceal it.

## Where Do We Go from Here?

34 Changing the way we divide up society will not magically resolve our differences or abolish racial prejudices. Nor does a movement toward a colorblind nation mean that we should stop working for a more just America. A combination of three major approaches that deal with economic and legal change could allow us to greatly downgrade the importance of race as a social criterion and still advance social justice. These approaches include reparations, class-based social programs, and fighting discrimination on an individual basis.

35 To make amends for the grave injustice that has been done to African-Americans by slavery and racial prejudice, as well as to bring to a close claims based on past injustices—and the sense of victimhood and entitlement that often accompanies these claims—major reparations are called for. One possible plan might allot a trillion dollars in education, training, and housing vouchers to African-Americans over a period of 20 years. (The same sort of plan might be devised for Native Americans.)

36 Such reparations cannot make full compensation for the sins of slavery, of course. But nothing can. Even so, if Jews could accept restitution from Germany and move on (Germany and Israel now have normal international relations, and the Jewish community in Germany is rapidly growing), could not a similar reconciliation between black and white Americans follow reparations? A precedent in our own history is the payment of reparations to Japanese-Americans because of their internment in World War II. In 1988, the U.S. government issued a formal apology in the Civil Liberties Act and awarded $20,000 to each living person who had been interned. About 80,000 claims were awarded, totaling $1.6 billion.

37 Part of the deal should be that once reparations are made for the sins against African-Americans in the past, black people could no longer claim special entitlements or privileges on the basis of their race. Reparations thus would end affirmative action and minority set-asides as we have known them.

38 At the same time, Americans who are disadvantaged for any reason not of their own doing—the handicapped; those who grew up in parts of the country, such as Appalachia, in which the economy has long been lagging; those whose jobs were sent overseas who are too old to be retrained—would be given extra aid in applying for college admissions and scholarships, housing allowances, small-business loans, and other social benefits. The basis for such aid would be socio-economic status, not race. The child of a black billionaire would no longer be entitled to special consideration in college admissions, for instance, but the child of a poor white worker who lost his job to outsourcing and could not find new employment would be.

39    Social scientists differ in their estimates of the extent to which differences in opportunity and upward mobility between blacks and whites are due to racial prejudice and the extent to which they are due to economic class differences. But most scholars who have studied the matter agree that economic factors are stronger than racial ones, possibly accounting for as much as 80 percent of the differences we observe. A vivid example: In recent years, Wake County in North Carolina made sure that its public school classes were composed of students of different economic backgrounds, disregarding racial and ethnic differences. The results of this economic integration overshadowed previous attempts to improve achievement via racial integration. While a decade ago, only 40 percent of blacks in grades three through eight scored at grade level, in the spring of 2005, 80 percent did so.

40    Class differences affect not only educational achievement, health, and job selection, but also how people are regarded or stereotyped. Fifty years ago, a study conducted at Howard University showed that although adjectives used to describe whites and blacks were quite different, that variance was greatly reduced when class was held constant. People described upper-class whites and upper-class blacks in a remarkably similar fashion, as intelligent and ambitious. People also described lower-class whites and lower-class blacks in a similar way, as dirty and ignorant. The author concluded that "stereotypes vary more as a function of class than of race."

41    If race-based discrimination were a thing of the past, and black Americans were no longer subjected to it, then my argument that reparations can lead to closure would be easier to sustain. Strong evidence shows, however, that discrimination remains very much with us. A 1990 Urban Institute study found that when two people of different races applied for the same job, one in eight times the white was offered the job and an equally qualified African-American was not. Another Urban Institute study, released in 1999, found that racial minorities received less time and information from loan officers and were quoted higher interest rates than whites in most of the cities where tests were conducted.

42    The victims of current racial discrimination should be fully entitled to remedies in court and through such federal agencies as the Equal Employment Opportunity Commission. These cases should be dealt with on an individual basis or in a class-action suit where evidence exists to support one. Those who sense discrimination should be required to prove it. It shouldn't be assumed that because a given workplace has more people of race x than race y, discrimination must exist.

## A Vision of the Future

43  In the end, it comes down to what Americans envision for our future together: either an open society, in which everyone is equally respected (an elusive goal but perhaps closer at hand than we realize), or an even more racialized nation, in which "people of color" are arrayed in perpetual conflict with white people. The first possibility is a vision of America as a community in which people work out their differences and make up for past injustices in a peaceful and fair manner; the other is one in which charges of prejudice and discrimination are mixed with real injustices, and in which a frustrated sense of victimhood and entitlement on the one hand is met with guilt and rejection on the other.

44     A good part of what is at stake is all too real: the distribution of assets, income, and power, which reparations, class-based reforms, and the courts should be able to sort out. But don't overlook the importance of symbols, attitudes, and feelings, which can't be changed legislatively. One place to start is with a debate over the official ways in which we classify ourselves and the ways we gather social data, because these classifications and data are used as a mirror in which we see ourselves reflected.

45     Let us begin with a fairly modest request of the powers that be: Give us a chance. Don't make me define my children and myself in racial terms; don't "impute" a race to me or to any of the millions of Americans who feel as I do. Allow us to describe ourselves simply as Americans. I bet my 50 years as a sociologist that we will all be better for it.

### QUESTIONS FOR ANALYSIS AND DISCUSSION

1. Why does Etzioni decline to indicate his race? What point does he make by recounting his personal experiences?
2. Do you think the government and other institutions should change the "race" category to "ethnicity"? Should there be no section on race or ethnicity at all? Would this make the process of gathering information easier or more confusing?
3. Is Hispanic a "race"? Why does the government want to know this information? What issues connected to race are unique to this population?
4. What is the "race trap"? Why is it harmful? Explain.
5. What are reparations? What opinion does Etzioni have on reparations? Can they help address issues of race in America? In the world? Why or why not?
6. According to Etzioni, what unique opportunity do we now have to think "beyond race"? How are Hispanics connected to this opportunity? Explain.
7. Etzioni notes that "race" information has a history of causing more harm than good. Discuss as a group the ways that racial information on government forms could be abused. Then, discuss whether the time has come to eliminate this question from forms, no matter what good intentions (such as affirmative action) are behind it.

## Who Is a Whiz-Kid?
*Ted Gup*

> It is easy to spot negative and damaging racial stereotypes that are often the result of intolerance, misunderstanding, and even hate. But what about so-called "good" stereotypes, in which a particular group is dubbed smart, athletic, passionate, or musical? Are stereotypes permissible if they seem positive? How can these "good" stereotypes, in fact, cause harm? In this next essay, writer Ted Gup describes his personal brush with ethnic stereotypes, and how even good ones can hurt.*

---

*Ted Gup, *Newsweek*, April 27, 1997.

**BEFORE YOU READ**

In your experience, do you think society assumes that some races are inherently superior to others? What do you think accounts for such assumptions?

**AS YOU READ**

Is perpetuating a cultural stereotype acceptable if it promotes positive images? Or are all stereotypes unacceptable?

1  Shortly after joining a national magazine some years ago as a writer, I found myself watching in horror as the week's cover story was prepared. The story was about "Asian-American whiz kids," and it featured a series of six student portraits, each face radiating with an intellectual brilliance. Being new to the enterprise, I was at first tentative in my criticism, cautioning that such a story was inherently biased and fueled racial and ethnic stereotypes. My criticism was dismissed. "This is something good we are saying about them," one top editor remarked. I reduced my criticism to writing. "What," I asked, "would be the response if the cover were about 'Jewish whiz kids'? Would anyone really dare to produce such an obviously offensive story?" My memo was ignored. Not long after, the cover appeared on the nation's newsstands, and the criticism began to fly. The editors were taken aback.

2  As a former Fulbright Scholar to China I have long taken a strong interest in the portrayal of Asian-Americans. But my interest went well beyond the academic. Even as the cover was being prepared, I was waiting to adopt my first son from Korea. His name was to be David. He was 5 months old when he arrived. That did not stop even some otherwise sophisticated friends from volunteering that he would no doubt be a good student.

3  Probably a mathematician, they opined, with a tone that uncomfortably straddled jest and prediction. I tried to take it all with good humor, this idea that a 5-month-old who could not yet sit up, speak a word or control his bowels was already destined for academic greatness. Even his major seemed foreordained.

4  Many Asian-Americans seem to walk an uneasy line between taking pride in their remarkable achievements and needing to shake off stereotypes. The jokes abound. There is the apocryphal parent who asks "Where is the other point?" when his or her child scores a 99 on a test. Another familiar refrain has the young Asian-American student enumerating his or her hobbies: "studying, studying and more studying."

5  Several months after David arrived he and I entered a small mom-and-pop convenience store in our neighborhood. The owners were Korean. I noticed that the husband, standing behind the cash register, was eyeing my son. "Is he Korean?" he asked. "Yes," I nodded. He reached out for him and took him into his arms. "He'll be good in math," declared the man. "My God," I muttered. Not him, too!

6  It was preposterous. It was funny. And it was unnerving. Embedded in such elevated expectations were real threats to my son. Suppose, I wondered, he should turn out to be only a mediocre student, or, worse yet, not a student at all. I resented the stereotypes and saw them for what they were, the other side of the coin of racism. It is easy to delude one's self into thinking it harmless to offer racial compliments, but that is an inherent contradiction in

terms. Such sweeping descriptives, be they negative or positive, deny the one thing most precious to all peoples—individuality. These stereotypes are pernicious for two reasons. First, such attributes are relative and tend to pit one race against another. Witness the seething enmity in many inner cities between Korean store owners and their African-American patrons. Stereotypes that hint at superiority in one race implicitly suggest inferiority in another. They are ultimately divisive, and in their most virulent form, even deadly. Who can forget the costs of the Aryan myth?

7    Many stereotypes also place a crushing burden on Asian-Americans. Few would deny that disproportionate numbers of Asian surnames appear each year among the winners of the Westinghouse science prizes or in the ranks of National Merit Scholars. But it might be a reflection of parental influences, personal commitment and cultural predilections, not genetic predisposition. A decade ago, as a Fulbright Lecturer in Beijing, I saw firsthand the staggering hours my Chinese students devoted to their studies. Were my students in the United States to invest similar time in their books I would have every reason to expect similar results.

8    I have often been told that Koreans are the "Jews of Asia," a reference to both their reported skills in business and their inherent intelligence. As a Jew, I cannot help but wince at such descriptions. I remember being one of the very few of my faith in a Midwest boarding school. There were many presumptions weighing on me, most of them grounded in my religion. My own classroom performance almost singlehandedly disabused my teachers of the myth that Jews were academically gifted. I barely made it through. Whether it was a lack of intelligence or simple rebellion against expectation, I do not know. I do know that more than once the fact that I was Jewish was raised as evidence that I could and should be doing better. Expectations based on race, be they raised or lowered, are no less galling.

9    David is now in the first grade. He is already taking math with the second graders and asking me about square roots and percentiles. I think back to the Korean merchant who took him in his arms and pronounced him a math whiz. Was he right? Do Asian-Americans have it easier, endowed with some special strand of DNA? The answer is a resounding no. Especially in our house. My son David has learning disabilities to overcome and what progress he has made is individual in the purest and most heroic sense. No one can or should take that away from him, suggesting he is just another wunderkind belonging to a favored race.

10    A year after my first son arrived, we adopted his brother from Korea. His name is Matthew. Let it be known that Matthew couldn't care less about math. He's a bug man. Slugs and earthworms. I suspect he will never be featured on any cover stories about Asian-American whiz kids, but I will continue to resist anything and anyone who attempts to dictate either his interests or his abilities based on race or place of birth. Bugs are fine by me and should be more than fine by him.

### QUESTIONS FOR ANALYSIS AND DISCUSSION

1. When Gup questioned the decision to run a cover story on "Asian-American whiz kids," his editor dismissed his concerns with the comment, "This is something good we are saying about them." What does this statement say about Gup's editor? Why do you think Gup mentions this comment?

2. What pressures do stereotypes place on children? How can stereotypes affect race relations?

3. How are stereotypes "the other side of the coin of racism"?

4. Analyze Gup's comment that stereotypes contribute to strained relationships between Koreans and blacks in inner cities. Do you agree?

5. What is the "Aryan myth"? What were its costs? Is the myth active today? If so, what is its continued impact?

6. Link some of the opinions and observations on racial stereotypes Gup makes in this article to a personal experience you had with racial stereotypes. How did stereotypes apply to the situation, and how did you handle the incident?

## Why Racial Profiling Makes for Dumb Security
### Ahmed Rehab

Sometimes stereotypes can be more than simply insulting; they can interfere with the daily lives of the people victimized by such labels. Negative stereotypes continue to influence how many Americans view Muslims. The situation is made worse, each time we are faced with a new terror-threat made by a Muslim extremist. In this next editorial, Ahmed Rehab, a Chicago-based activist and writer specializing in American-Muslim affairs, explains why racial profiling is an ineffective tool in the fight against terrorism. Trying to solve a problem by introducing another problem will not fix anything. In fact, he argues, it is just plain "dumb."*

#### BEFORE YOU READ

Did the terrorist attacks of September 11 and the ensuing conflicts in Afghanistan and Iraq influence your view of Muslims? If you are Muslim, have you noticed a shift in opinion toward you? Explain.

#### AS YOU READ

Rehab notes that the December 25, 2009, terrorism attempt renewed the federal government's promise to improve airport security. How has terrorism affected our lives since Sept. 11? What freedoms are we willing to give up in the name of security?

1   By now, I am sure most people are privy to the raging public debate on racial profiling, reignited courtesy of a young Nigerian Muslim male's attempt to detonate an incendiary device aboard a Detroit-bound Northwest flight last Christmas.

2   After Umar Farouk Abdulmutallab slipped by airport security only to be stopped thanks to the vigilance of fellow passengers, a debate on the *effectiveness* of airport security and counter-terrorism intelligence is no doubt in order.

---

*Ahmed Rehab, *Huffington Post*, January 7, 2010.

3    But trying to fix a problem without actually fixing the problem is misguided. Trying to fix it by introducing a new problem is dumb.

4    This guy seemed to have left every clue short of to raise his hand and proclaim, "Arrest me, I am a terrorist!"

5    Can someone explain to me how he managed to purchase a one way ticket, pay for it in cash, board the plane with no luggage, have his own father report him as a radicalized threat to a CIA base in Nigeria, be denied a visa to the UK where he previously lived and worked, and on top of that be on an active U.S. terror watch list for two years, yet still not be flagged by the system as a security threat?

6    And can someone explain to me how after those six glaring red flags were missed— not to mention the explosive material in his underwear—the debate today is not about why and how they were missed, but about whether he could have been flagged for being of a certain skin color, hair texture, place of birth, faith, or namesake?

7    The racial profiling argument is lazy and unimaginative; most of all it is irresponsible because it evades the real problem starring us in the face: a fatal breakdown in communication between our intelligence units. Ironically, this is a problem so troubling that an entire new department, the National Homeland Security Department, was created with the sole mission to address it.

8    Make no mistake about it; it is hardly ever a case of not having the necessary intelligence. Even in the case of the 9/11 hijackers, we had security files on each of the 19 hijackers. The problem is in our repeated failure to act upon intelligence between our fingertips in a timely manner. Introducing new and untested wild card measures will not correct what's failing, though the debate makes for a convenient distraction from bearing responsibility.

9    The idea that there are some racial profiles we need to check out thoroughly in order to conclusively determine that they do not have bombs on them is not what troubles me most. What truly troubles me is the corollary of that idea: that we know of a way to conclusively determine whether someone has a bomb on them or not but we are going to exempt most people from it because we do not deem them suspicious enough, or we do not have the resources for it. How is that supposed to make us feel safer?

10    There is nothing comforting about a de facto admission by security officials that our primary airport security lines are a prop up and that secondary ones are where it's really at. So, what's the point of primary security? Placebo? Clearly, what will make us safer is beefing up our primary security measures so that they actually do what they are supposed to do for the entire population (conclusively determine that no bombs or explosive material makes it through). It certainly isn't adding a secondary layer that, by design, most passengers will end up skipping. As good as that layer may be it won't be good enough, given that it is only partially applied to the passenger population.

11    To begin with the notion that any security analyst will tell you that if we have a national security defense system that waits until an airport security gate to identify terrorists, then it's only a matter of time before it's good night and good luck. But even at security gates, our last-guard measures need to be scientific and objective, like improving bomb detecting machines; you know, the ones that didn't beep when dynamite underpants stepped through. Objective and scientific measures however do not include part-timers eyeballing passengers for people who look like characters out of Disney's Aladdin or whatever image their mind conjures of what a terror suspect looks like that day of the week.

12    So what *do* they look like? Presumably we are talking about Muslim men, but short of Muslims wearing green arm bands, what does that really mean?

13    Any Middle-Eastern looking person with an exotic sounding name?

14    Fine, this may work, provided we can count on Middle-Eastern terrorists with exotic sounding names being unaware of our little precautionary measure. Nobody tell them. As for non-terrorists who fit that profile (which would unfortunately include Jesus himself should he come back and try to enter the United States with his real name Yeshua Bin Yosef), get ready to take one for the team.

15    An African looking person with an exotic sounding name?

16    Well, fortunately for Barack Obama, he does not work for say Microsoft or Motorola, instead of the White House, otherwise he'd be spending his days at airports.

17    But never mind the absurdity in a system that is unfriendly to people who look like our president and Jesus, here's the real problem with racial profiling: it is ineffective. There are two main reasons for that, the first is scientific as concluded by what few studies on racial profiling have taken place.

18    The second is logical:

19    Think about it, the purpose of security checkpoints is to prevent future terror attacks not past ones. If it is future ones, then should we *limit* ourselves to what *did* happen or would it make more sense to address the possibilities of what *could* happen?

20    Racial profiling is an elusive game, and Al Qaeda can always racially profile too. This is not a probability game, one improbable situation is enough to do the damage we hope to prevent.

21    Do we really want a system where we are always one step behind?

22    Say we do go for the bearded brown guy, Al Qaeda will send a clean-shaven black one next. Oh wait, they already did; in fact, one that looks like your average all-state American high school athlete. Will that now be the next profile to look out for?

23    And when we've flagged all Middle-Eastern and black men with exotic names, they are going to send a white British guy with an Anglo name like Richard Reid. Oh wait, they already did that. And after they send a Russian recruit and a Chinese one and we start profiling all men of all races, they'll recruit a woman. Oh wait, there were two cases of women blowing up Russian airliners in 2004.

24    At this rate, the only profile that won't be racially profiled is that Scandinavian grandmother everyone keeps talking about.

25    Of course, after billions are spent and humanity inconvenienced to no avail, we could always go back to actually acting upon hard intelligence and actually detecting bomb material at airports.

26    Or, we could do that now.

## QUESTIONS FOR ANALYSIS AND CONSIDERATION

1. Rehab states that trying to fix a problem by introducing a new problem is "dumb." What solution to the problem does he find dumb, and why? Do you agree? Explain.
2. What are the stereotypes that most plague Muslim Americans? What are the roots of these stereotypes? Did they exist before September 11? Explain.

3. What dangers do Muslim Americans face because of ethnic stereotypes? Explain.

4. Rehab observes the "racial profiling argument is lazy and unimaginative." On what grounds does he object to racial profiling? Why is it lazy? Why will it fail to address the issue of terrorism and why does he feel it will not improve security?

5. How does Rehab frame his argument? What examples does he give of who would be profiled under current guidelines? How do his examples support his position that using racial profiling to deter terrorism is not only morally wrong, but distracts us from the real problem?

## Reading the Visual

## Is Your Mascot a Racial Stereotype?

Chief Wahoo is the official mascot of the Cleveland Indians. The team's history states that their name honors a Native American named Louis Sockalexis, who briefly played for the team when they were known as the Cleveland Spiders. Many Native Americans have disputed this claim, calling it "revisionist history." The image of Chief Wahoo has been bitterly disputed by many Native Americans who consider him a highly racist and unflattering stereotype. This blog entry discusses the use of Native American images as mascots. Are we taking things too seriously, or are we ignoring the dignity of a group of people with excuses that "it's all just for fun."*

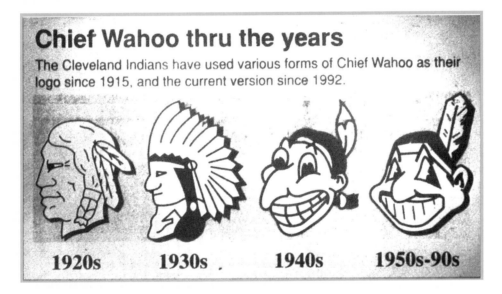

"Chief Illiniwek" of the University of Illinois will perform for the last time tonight. In fact, as I write this, the student who dances as Chief Illiniwek may have already made history as the last person to do so.

From *YahooSports:*

> The University of Illinois' controversial American Indian mascot was set to perform his last dance, and men who have previously portrayed Chief Illiniwek said they want the tradition to live on in some form.

> The mascot, whose fate was decided by school officials last week, will take center stage at Assembly Hall for one last performance during the men's basketball game between Illinois and Michigan on Wednesday night.

---

*PA Lady, www.palady.wordpress.com, February 22, 2007.

Removing the chief frees the university of NCAA sanctions after the organization deemed Illiniwek—portrayed by buckskin-clad students who dance at home football and basketball games and other athletic events—an offensive use of American Indian imagery and barred the school from hosting postseason athletic events.

1 I applaud the decision of the University of Illinois to comply with NCAA regulations and join the 21st century in ending the use of a stereotype. Now, it's past time for state and regional high school sports leagues to follow the NCAA's lead and mandate an end to "an offensive use of American Indian imagery."

2 My daughter's school calls itself, no kidding, *the Redskins.*

3 I have a lot of problems with this, and have since we first moved here. Let me give you a few examples of what I find offensive: 1) in the sports section of their website (which I won't link to, for privacy reasons) there are "cute" little caricatures of Indians in feathered headdress and buckskin leggings holding basketballs, pretending to be swimming, performing a split and holding pompoms, 2) their mascot is a chief in feathered headdress, 3) there's a tepee on the track/football field!

4 For one thing, they've mixed up their tribes. The Plains Indians wore the feathered headdress seen on the mascot, not the Susquehannas and/or the Lenni Lenape (Eastern Delaware Nation) which actually lived in my area. Also, the Native tribes of this area lived in *longhouses*, not tepees.

5 This is important to note because the school is about to celebrate its quasquicentennial (125 years) and thus, was founded about the time of the Indian wars. Back in the early years of the school, people weren't thinking about ethnic stereotypes, they were busy reading about the Bighorn, Sand Creek and Pine Ridge massacres. (Although, back then, they didn't call them massacres. They were "battles" won or lost by the Army.)

6 Second, the administrators, boosters, players, etc., don't seem to understand that the word "Redskin" *is* an ethnic slur. One of the most offensive phrases used by this school—and its faculty, students, and alumni—is: "Redskin Pride." Literally, this phrase makes me gag.

7 Let's be honest. This is a small school district, 95% or so white. There's little native ancestry here, if only because their ancestors wiped out the native populations with their diseases and their wars. These people have a misguided sense of pride if they can use the word "Redskin" as if it were some type of positive attribute—one to which they have no claim.

8 Over the summer, my mom got into a bit of a verbal tiff with a booster who had the utter audacity to say they weren't demeaning anyone. It was, she said, a way of "honoring" the Native peoples.

9 *Huh?*

10 How utterly stupid. As a person of Native ancestry, I don't feel "honored." I feel insulted. My Native ancestors were *not* "Redskins." Those ancestors were of the Bear Clan of the People of the Standing Stone (Oneida Nation) of the Six Nations of the Iroquois.

11 The Six Nations' Articles of Confederacy—creating the oldest known *participatory* democracy—later inspired the framing of the Constitution of the United

States. In fact, the Six Nations' confederation was considered so important to the writing, a delegation of Iroquois were asked to meet with the Continental Congress, and John Hancock was given an Iroquois name: *Karanduawn*, or the Great Tree.

12    Do you think those whose ancestors were slaves, would feel "honored" if the team was called the "Niggers"? Do you think anyone of Jewish ancestry would feel "honored" if the team was called the "Kikes"? Do you think any of the multitudes in this district who came from Irish and Italian immigrants would feel "honored" if the team was the "Micks" or the "Wops"?

13    Of course not!

14    Those are *all* derogatory words used to debase another race or belief or ethnic background, and are recognized as such by nearly every sentient being in this country. There is no such recognition for the constant slurs against Native peoples used by sports teams across the nation, professional or otherwise.

15    Let's put it this way, for those still so blind that they continue defending the use of "Redskins" for their high school teams: Would you feel comfortable calling anyone a "Redskin" while you were busy dumping money in a slot machine at a Native-run casino?

16    Ooh! I saw that! Made you a bit uncomfortable, eh? It's one thing to yell "Go Redskins" at a football game, and quite another to actually use it in a place where the owners are "Redskins."

17    It's past time for all sports teams to replace names and mascots which represent *"an offensive use of American-Indian imagery."*

### QUESTIONS FOR ANALYSIS AND DISCUSSION

1. What is the blogger's position on the use of Native Americans as school or sports mascots?
2. The blogger notes that in addition to the stereotypes we perpetuate visually with Native American mascots, the words we use are equally offensive. How does she support this viewpoint? Do you agree?
3. In what ways could Chief Wahoo (see inset) be considered offensive to Native Americans? What does his name mean? What image does the mascot project?
4. Could other ethnic groups be presented as mascots without incident? Why or why not?
5. In your opinion, can the disagreement over the Cleveland Indians' official mascot be resolved? How would you mediate this controversy?

# You Can't Judge a Crook by His Color
*Randall Kennedy*

Racial profiling is law enforcement's practice of considering race as an indicator of the likelihood of criminal behavior. Based on statistical assumptions, racial profiling presumes that certain groups of people are more likely to commit—or not to commit—certain crimes. The U.S. Supreme Court officially upheld the constitutionality of this practice, as long as race was only one of several factors leading to the detainment or arrest of an individual. In the next article, Harvard law professor Randall Kennedy argues that while racial profiling may seem justifiable, it is still morally wrong.*

**BEFORE YOU READ**

Do you consider racial profiling justifiable? If so, under what circumstances? If not, why?

**AS YOU READ**

Evaluate Kennedy's practice of posing questions to his readers and then providing them with the answers. In what ways could this article serve as a class lecture?

1   In Kansas City, a Drug Enforcement Administration officer stops and questions a young man who has just stepped off a flight from Los Angeles. The officer has focused on this man because intelligence reports indicate that black gangs in L.A. are flooding the Kansas City area with illegal drugs. Young, toughly dressed, and appearing nervous, he paid for his ticket in cash, checked no luggage, brought two carry-on bags, and made a beeline for a taxi when he arrived. Oh, and one other thing: The young man is black. When asked why he decided to question this man, the officer declares that he considered race, along with other factors, because doing so helps him allocate limited time and resources efficiently.

2   Should we applaud the officer's conduct? Permit it? Prohibit it? This is not a hypothetical example. Encounters like this take place every day, all over the country, as police battle street crime, drug trafficking, and illegal immigration. And this particular case study happens to be the real-life scenario presented in a federal lawsuit of the early '90s, *United States v. Weaver,* in which the 8th U.S. Circuit Court of Appeals upheld the constitutionality of the officer's action.

3   "Large groups of our citizens," the court declared, "should not be regarded by law enforcement officers as presumptively criminal based upon their race." The court went on to say, however, that "facts are not to be ignored simply because they may be unpleasant." According to the court, the circumstances were such that the young man's race, considered in conjunction with other signals, was a legitimate factor in the decision to approach and ultimately detain him. "We wish it were otherwise," the court maintained, "but we take the facts as they are presented to us, not as we would like them to be." Other courts have

*Randall Kennedy, *The New Republic*, 1999.

agreed that the Constitution does not prohibit police from considering race, as long as they do so for bona fide purposes of law enforcement (not racial harassment) and as long as it is only one of several factors.

4       These decisions have been welcome news to the many law enforcement officials who consider what has come to be known as racial profiling an essential weapon in the war on crime. They maintain that, in areas where young African-American males commit a disproportionate number of the street crimes, the cops are justified in scrutinizing that sector of the population more closely than others—just as they are generally justified in scrutinizing men more closely than they do women.

5       As Bernard Parks, chief of the Los Angeles Police Department, explained to Jeffrey Goldberg of the *New York Times Magazine:* "We have an issue of violent crime against jewelry salespeople. . . . The predominant suspects are Colombians. We don't find Mexican-Americans, or blacks, or other immigrants. It's a collection of several hundred Colombians who commit this crime. If you see six in a car in front of the Jewelry Mart, and they're waiting and watching people with briefcases, should we play the percentages and follow them? It's common sense."

6       Cops like Parks say that racial profiling is a sensible, statistically based tool. Profiling lowers the cost of obtaining and processing crime information, which in turn lowers the overall cost of doing the business of policing. And the fact that a number of cops who support racial profiling are black, including Parks, buttresses claims that the practice isn't motivated by bigotry. Indeed, these police officers note that racial profiling is race-neutral in that it can be applied to persons of all races, depending on the circumstances. In predominantly black neighborhoods in which white people stick out (as potential drug customers or racist hooligans, for example), whiteness can become part of a profile. In the southwestern United States, where Latinos often traffic in illegal immigrants, apparent Latin American ancestry can become part of a profile.

7       But the defenders of racial profiling are wrong. Ever since the Black and Latino Caucus of the New Jersey Legislature held a series of hearings, complete with testimony from victims of what they claimed was the New Jersey state police force's overly aggressive racial profiling, the air has been thick with public denunciations of the practice.

8       Unfortunately, though, many who condemn racial profiling do so without really thinking the issue through. One common complaint is that using race (say, blackness) as one factor in selecting surveillance targets is fundamentally racist. But selectivity of this sort can be defended on nonracist grounds. "There is nothing more painful to me at this age in my life," Jesse Jackson said in 1993, "than to walk down the street and hear footsteps and start to think about robbery and then look around and see somebody white and feel relieved." Jackson was relieved not because he dislikes black people, but because he estimated that he stood a somewhat greater risk of being robbed by a black person than by a white person. Statistics confirm that African-Americans—particularly young black men— commit a dramatically disproportionate share of street crime in the United States. This is a sociological fact, not a figment of a racist media (or police) imagination. In recent years, victims report blacks as perpetrators of around 25 percent of violent crimes, although blacks constitute only about 12 percent of the nation's population.

9       So, if racial profiling isn't bigoted, and if the empirical claim upon which the practice rests is sound, why is it wrong?

10    Racial distinctions are and should be different from other lines of social stratification. That is why, since the civil rights revolution of the 1960s, courts have typically ruled—based on the 14th Amendment's equal protection clause—that mere reasonableness is an insufficient justification for officials to discriminate on racial grounds. In such cases, courts have generally insisted on applying "strict scrutiny"—the most intense level of judicial review—to government actions. Under this tough standard, the use of race in governmental decision making may be upheld only if it serves a compelling government objective and only if it is "narrowly tailored" to advance that objective.

11    A disturbing feature of this debate is that many people, including judges, are suggesting that decisions based on racial distinctions do not constitute unlawful racial discrimination—as long as race is not the only reason a person was treated objectionably. The court that upheld the DEA agent's action at the Kansas City airport, for instance, declined to describe it as racially discriminatory and thus evaded strict scrutiny.

12    But racially discriminatory decisions typically stem from mixed motives. For example, an employer who prefers white candidates to black candidates—except for those black candidates with superior experience and test scores—is engaging in racial discrimination, even though race is not the only factor he considers (since he selects black superstars). In some cases, race is a marginal factor; in others it is the only factor. The distinction may have a bearing on the moral or logical justification, but taking race into account at all means engaging in discrimination.

13    Because both law and morality discourage racial discrimination, proponents should persuade the public that racial profiling is justifiable. Instead, they frequently neglect its costs and minimize the extent to which it adds to the resentment blacks feel toward the law enforcement establishment. When O. J. Simpson was acquitted, many recognized the danger of a large sector of Americans feeling cynical and angry toward the system. Such alienation creates witnesses who fail to cooperate with police, citizens who view prosecutors as the enemy, lawyers who disdain the rules they have sworn to uphold, and jurors who yearn to get even with a system that has, in their eyes, consistently mistreated them. Racial profiling helps keep this pool of accumulated rage filled to the brim.

14    The courts have not been sufficiently mindful of this risk. In rejecting a 1976 constitutional challenge that accused U.S. Border Patrol officers in California of selecting cars for inspection partly on the basis of drivers' apparent Mexican ancestry, the Supreme Court noted in part that, of the motorists passing the checkpoint, fewer than 1 percent were stopped. It also noted that, of the 820 vehicles inspected during the period in question, roughly 20 percent contained illegal aliens.

15    Justice William J. Brennan dissented, however, saying the Court did not indicate the ancestral makeup of all the persons the Border Patrol stopped. It is likely that many of the innocent people who were questioned were of apparent Mexican ancestry who then had to prove their obedience to the law just because others of the same ethnic background have broken laws in the past.

16    The practice of racial profiling undercuts a good idea that needs more support from both society and the law: Individuals should be judged by public authorities on the basis of their own conduct and not on the basis of racial generalization. Race-dependent policing retards the development of bias-free thinking; indeed, it encourages the opposite.

17      What about the fact that in some communities people associated with a given racial group commit a disproportionately large number of crimes? Our commitment to a just social order should prompt us to end racial profiling even if the generalizations on which the technique is based are supported by empirical evidence. This is not as risky as it may sound. There are actually many contexts in which the law properly enjoins us to forswear playing racial odds even when doing so would advance legitimate goals.

18      For example, public opinion surveys have established that blacks distrust law enforcement more than whites. Thus, it would be rational—and not necessarily racist—for a prosecutor to use ethnic origin as a factor in excluding black potential jurors. Fortunately, the Supreme Court has outlawed racial discrimination of this sort. And because demographics show that in the United States, whites tend to live longer than blacks, it would be perfectly rational for insurers to charge blacks higher life-insurance premiums. Fortunately, the law forbids that, too.

19      The point here is that racial equality, like all good things in life, costs something. Politicians suggest that all Americans need to do in order to attain racial justice is forswear bigotry. But they must also demand equal treatment before the law even when unequal treatment is defensible in the name of nonracist goals—and even when their effort will be costly.

20      Since abandoning racial profiling would make policing more expensive and perhaps less effective, those of us who oppose it must advocate a responsible alternative. Mine is simply to spend more money on other means of enforcement—and then spread the cost on some nonracial basis. One way to do that would be to hire more police officers. Another way would be to subject everyone to closer surveillance. A benefit of the second option would be to acquaint more whites with the burden of police intrusion, which might prompt more of them to insist on limiting police power. As it stands now, the burden is unfairly placed on minorities—imposing on Mexican-Americans, blacks, and others a special kind of tax for the war against illegal immigration, drugs, and other crimes. The racial element of that tax should be repealed.

21      I'm not saying that police should never be able to use race as a guideline. If a young white man with blue hair robs me, the police should certainly be able to use a description of the perpetrator's race. In this situation, though, whiteness is a trait linked to a particular person with respect to a particular incident. It is not a free-floating accusation that hovers over young white men practically all the time—which is the predicament young black men currently face. Nor am I saying that race could never be legitimately relied upon as a signal of increased danger. In an extraordinary circumstance in which plausible alternatives appear to be absent, officials might need to resort to racial profiling. This is a far cry from routine profiling that is subjected to little scrutiny.

22      Now that racial profiling is a hot issue, the prospects for policy change have improved. President Clinton directed federal law enforcement agencies to determine the extent to which their officers focus on individuals on the basis of race. The Customs Service is rethinking its practice of using ethnicity or nationality as a basis for selecting subjects for investigation. The Federal Aviation Administration has been re-evaluating its recommended security procedures; it wants the airlines to combat terrorism with computer profiling, which is purportedly less race-based than random checks by airport personnel.

Unfortunately, though, a minefield of complexity lies beneath these options. Unless we understand the complexities, this opportunity will be wasted.

23    To protect ourselves against race-based policing requires no real confrontation with the status quo, because hardly anyone defends police surveillance triggered solely by race. Much of the talk about police "targeting" suspects on the basis of race is, in this sense, misguided and harmful. It diverts attention to a side issue. Another danger is the threat of demagoguery through oversimplification. When politicians talk about "racial profiling," we must insist that they define precisely what they mean. Evasion—putting off hard decisions under the guise of needing more information—is also a danger.

24    Even if routine racial profiling is prohibited, the practice will not cease quickly. An officer who makes a given decision partly on a racial basis is unlikely to acknowledge having done so, and supervisors and judges are loath to reject officers' statements. Nevertheless, it would be helpful for President Clinton to initiate a strict anti-discrimination directive to send a signal to conscientious, law-abiding officers that there are certain criteria they ought not use.

25    To be sure, creating a norm that can't be fully enforced isn't ideal, but it might encourage us all to work toward closing the gap between our laws and the conduct of public authorities. A new rule prohibiting racial profiling might be made to be broken, but it could set a new standard for legitimate government.

## QUESTIONS FOR ANALYSIS AND DISCUSSION

1. Kennedy argues that racial profiling is racist. In what ways is it racist? Alternatively, how can it be defended on nonracist grounds? Is it always racist? Explain.
2. A critical reader may argue that Kennedy contradicts himself in some places, such as in paragraph 21 when he follows his argument that racial profiling is wrong with the statement that in "extraordinary circumstances" it may be permissible. Is this indeed a contradiction? Explain.
3. In paragraph 17, Kennedy presents two examples of how the law "properly enjoins us to forswear playing racial odds even when doing so would advance legitimate goals." Do these examples support his argument that all racial profiling should be illegal? Explain.
4. How plausible are the solutions Kennedy offers? For example, he proposes that to end racial profiling, cities should hire more police officers so that the "time-saving" element of racial profiling would no longer be a factor. What issues does he not address that an opponent could use to argue against this solution? What information would you recommend he include to deflect objections? Explain.
5. This essay refers to Jesse Jackson's remark that the negative stereotyping of their own race can influence even blacks. Why do you think Kennedy includes this admission?
6. Evaluate Kennedy's observation that the practice of racial profiling keeps "this pool of accumulated [minority] rage filled to the brim." How does this reaction affect other areas of law enforcement? How can racial profiling backfire in the courtroom and in the streets? Explain.

## Reading the Visual

## Pulling Teeth
*American Civil Liberties Union*

ADVERTISEMENT    ADVERTISEMENT    ADVERTISEMENT

# Getting the New Jersey State Police to Stop Racial Profiling is like Pulling Teeth.

photo by Sanford Luger

*Dr. Elmo Randolph, Dentist*

**"My name is Elmo Randolph** and I am a dentist. Within a five year period, **I was pulled over by New Jersey State Troopers approximately 100 times** without ever receiving a ticket. The police searched my car and I had to prove to the troopers that being an African-American man in a nice car doesn't mean that I am a drug dealer or car thief.

This kind of stereotyping is called **racial profiling, and it's wrong.** The State of New Jersey has admitted to racial profiling and has admitted that it's ongoing, but has yet to make amends to victims like me who are left with nothing but **fear of police and fear of driving on the Turnpike.**

**The ACLU represents me.** It may be able to help you, too. Please **CALL 1-877-6-PROFILE** or go to **aclu.org** to report your citation, stop or search to the ACLU and to seek assistance with any claim you have."

PAID FOR BY THE ACLU

As part of a larger campaign to bring attention to the issue of racial profiling in New Jersey, the American Civil Liberties Union ran this advertisement to raise awareness and inform victims of their rights. The ad features Dr. Elmo Randolph, a New Jersey dentist and a plaintiff in a racial profiling case in that state. Randolph, an African-American man, says he had been pulled over approximately 100 times over a five-year period without ever receiving a ticket. In the ad, Dr. Randolph describes his experience with the police, stating that, "The police searched my car and I had to prove to the troopers that being an African-American man in a nice car doesn't mean that I am a drug dealer or car thief." Deborah Jacobs, Executive Director of the ACLU of New Jersey, said of the ad, "We want to send a message to the victims about their rights, and to the state about its obligations." This ad ran in the October 29, 2001, edition of the *Newark Star-Ledger*.

## QUESTIONS FOR ANALYSIS AND DISCUSSION

1. What words are treated differently within the body text, and why? What is the effect of having certain words in bold or larger typeface than others?

2. How does the headline of the ad connect to the ad's content and message? Explain.

3. In this ad, Elmo Randolph states that he has been pulled over "approximately 100 times without ever receiving a ticket." What is the audience likely to infer from this statement?

4. Consider the photograph used in this ad. How is Dr. Randolph dressed? Where is he sitting? In what environment is he placed? Would this ad be as effective if Randolph were younger? Less professionally dressed? Explain.

5. A follow-up story in the *Newark Star-Ledger* reported that Randolph received a $75,000 settlement for his lawsuit against the state. The story notes, "Randolph said his story began soon after he bought his first BMW. Over the course of a decade, he estimated he was pulled over on North Jersey roads 50 to 100 times." In your opinion, did the ACLU skew the information in its ad? Does it matter if it gets an important point across? Explain.

# Welcome to the Dollhouse
*Francie Latour*

For generations of little girls, Barbie has been a toy both loved and loathed. Most often criticized are Barbie's ridiculous proportions. Still others lament Barbie's lack of varied ethnicity. The release of three new "So-In-Style" African-American Barbie dolls was heralded as progress by the toy industry. But many African-American women wondered why Barbie must still have the long flowing tresses sported by all three new dolls. In this essay, journalist Francie Latour challenges that this is not an issue for the toy industry to address, but one for the African-American community as a whole. As the mother of a young daughter, she notes, "It's easy to fill the blogosphere with Barbie commentary, and much more difficult to confront the messages we hand down ourselves. When we complain about how tough our daughters' hair is to comb. . . when we drag them to the swivel chair before they are ready, we tell them how important it is to try to be something besides who they are. Those messages predate Barbie."*

## BEFORE YOU READ

Consider our ideal standard of beauty. What is ideal? Is it a westernized image? A multicultural one? Which images of beauty are promoted by the media? How can these images reflect back issues of race?

## AS YOU READ

Latour observes that Mattel's new dolls have the hair many African-American women aspire to achieve through long hours at the beauty salon. What position does Latour take on this issue? Does she feel that Mattel is selling out to the status quo? Why or why not?

1   In every black family, there are two kinds of daughters: daughters who have good hair and daughters who don't. For much of my childhood, knowing this was as painful as raking a comb through my own locks, whose strands fell into the "don't" category: stubbornly short, easily broken, at war with the detanglers designed to tame them. And, like most black hair in its natural state, densely coiled and woolly. In the words of my aunties: coarse, bushy, difficult. In the words of history: nappy, picaninny, slave-girl.

2   It's no coincidence that the first black American self-made millionaire, Madame C. J. Walker, made her money turning that kind of hair into straight, shiny, behaving hair. That was 100 years ago, and black women everywhere have been on the same, self-denying quest ever since. Years ago, a cousin of mine perfectly articulated the power of hair over the psyches of black girls. When I told her about a new college boyfriend, who was white, she said, "You're so lucky. If you stay together and get married one day, your daughters will have the best hair." I acted shocked, but I was intimately familiar with the longing and loathing that prompted those words.

---

*Francie Latour, *Boston Globe Magazine*, October 25, 2009.

3    Now I'm a mother of three with a 2-year-old daughter of my own. (Yes, she's biracial and has smooth curls, but I swear that's a coincidence.) When it comes to cultural clashes over girls, beauty, blackness, and hair, I worry and pay attention. The latest controversy? The arrival of the new "So In Style" Barbie dolls, brought to you by Mattel. Created by an African-American mom and launched in stores last month, Grace, Kara, and Trichelle are black, and they're the new BFFs in Barbie-land. Like their fair-skinned friends, they have long, silky hair that is either bone-straight or loosely wavy.

4    Don't answer yet, there's more. To keep Barbie's new friends in style, Mattel offers a hair-straightening kit, with which girls can fantasize about a ritual of black womanhood most of us would gladly avoid if we could: regular, two-hour sessions at the hair salon to have our woolly manes straightened with harsh chemical straighteners. When that news hit the blogosphere, black mothers, scholars, and childhood experts everywhere got loud, many of them condemning Mattel for reinforcing white standards of beauty. Can't Barbie rock braids or an Afro just once? they cried. The controversy erupted up just as "Good Hair," comedian Chris Rock's new documentary about America's $9 billion black beauty industry, hit theaters.

5    For those of you unfamiliar with the complexities of black hair care, straightening is a process in which a stylist sections your hair and applies a cream that starts out cool but becomes unbearably hot. The cream contains sodium hydroxide, commonly found in drain and oven cleaners, and so corrosive that stylists have to use rubber gloves. When you absolutely can't stand the heat anymore, the stylist rinses it out. Straight hair, and sometimes scabs, result. The longer the cream stays in, the more you burn, but the straighter your hair gets; walk into a black salon and the most common thing you'll see is a woman gripping the armrests of a chair to manage her pain. In other words, hair-straightening is no ride in Ken's convertible or trip to your dreamhouse closet. (I'm not sure if Mattel was giving an ironic wink to the sisters out there, but like the real version of hair-straightening, "So In Style" hair kits are also wildly overpriced, costing more than a pair of the actual dolls.)

6    On the one hand, it seems that Mattel has finally awoken to the Sasha-and-Malia demographic of middle- and upper-class black America: The girls of "So In Style" have wider noses, fuller lips, and a spectrum of realistic skin tones. But one look at these dolls suggests that even in our so-called post-racial world, there are some places America's culture-makers still aren't willing to go. Among them, apparently, is the hair black girls are born with.

7    But is it really fair to expect a toy conglomerate to be at the vanguard of ideas about race and beauty? For that, we would presumably look to real black women leaders. And when we look up to them, what we find is more straight hair. Actually, straight hair with blinding sheen and cascading, otherworldly flow. Beyonce, Tyra, and Oprah all have it. Ditto for black women leaders in politics and business.

8    These are not dolls; these are the living, breathing role models of black America. But they all understand that straight hair is the key to unlocking mainstream success. It's the unspoken, elephant-in-the-room euphemism that remains as true today as it was during slavery: Straight hair is "good hair" because straight hair is white hair. And when blacks were slaves, straight hair could literally mean survival: Slaves who looked less African were treated better, often lifted from the fields to housework, which meant food, warmth, and maybe even education. Over time, straight hair became synonymous with nonthreatening hair. And that is the black Barbie formula Mattel has counted on going way back.

9     Mattel birthed the Barbie doll in 1959, a period when the notion of a black friend, real or pretend, was unthinkable for many white Americans. It was the same year a white journalist named John Howard Griffin took extreme measures to darken his skin and write about his travels through the deep South passing as a black man. The stories of the intense hatred he experienced were eventually published in the landmark book "Black Like Me." It's safe to say that when an entire race is struggling for recognition as human beings, nobody quibbles over whether a toy reflects their daughters' self-image.

10    I recently learned, to my amazement, that the first-ever brown-skinned Barbie Mattel dared to put on shelves bears my name. "Colored Francie" made a short-lived appearance in 1967, her dark-ish complexion painted onto a doll with the same features as her white counterpart, including a glistening mane of straight hair. Other versions came later, including the defining "Christie" in 1968 and the nameless "Black Barbie" in 1980. In 1997, Mattel took a turn that left some blacks outraged and others speechless when it teamed up with Nabisco to launch "Oreo Fun Barbie." The African-American version (also short-lived, it turns out) was strangely blue-black, which I'll chalk up to an effort to coordinate with the cookie's electric-blue packaging.

11    When "Black Barbie" arrived on the scene in 1980, I was 9, well within Mattel's target audience. But I never owned her or any other Barbie. I think it had something to do with the dolls I saw at my friends' houses. Whether the dolls were white or any other color, I got a creepy, not so-stylish feeling: Barbie wasn't black like me, or any other black girl or woman I knew. The makers of Grace, Kara, and Trichelle say the new dolls give black girls a truer mirror of themselves. But when I look at them, all these years later, that same feeling comes over me.

12    Here's what I remember about the black girls I knew: They had Mickey Mouse afro puffs tied in giant gumball barrettes or tight cornrow braids, or hair that was bound by nothing at all. For a little while, they had no idea what the word "nappy" meant, until one day they knew exactly what it meant. The black girls I knew marked their entry into womanhood reluctantly, with a first trip to the hair salon that often lived up to their worst fears. Caught in an in-between time when they were too old to sit for their mothers and too young to know what to do themselves, they climbed into swivel chairs and waited for the smell and then the feeling of chemicals that seared their scalps, leaving clumps of hair and Afro-puff innocence to be swept from the salon floor. As time goes on and products improve, many make peace with their unnatural states. Others find their way back to the beginning with locked, coiffed, or otherwise regal crowns. What I call Toni Morrison hair.

13    I haven't heard of anything in the works for a Toni Morrison doll. But I'm not waiting for one, either. Because here's the thing about black girls and hair: Dolls and straightening kits can scar, but so can people. And we do. It's easy to fill the blogosphere with Barbie commentary, and much more difficult to confront the messages we hand down ourselves. When we complain about how tough our daughters' hair is to comb, when we run our fingers through their cousins' smooth tresses and smile, when we drag them to the swivel chair before they are ready, we tell them how important it is to try to be something besides who they are. Those messages predate Barbie. They were shaped by blacks' need to survive in a white world, but how the messages began matters less than taking responsibility for them now.

14    I still straighten my hair, although I often wet it and let it dry naturally, making it weirdly wavy. For a long time, I believed that while straightening didn't make my hair

"good," it made it better. Then one day, a boyfriend (and now husband) perfectly articulated something that was totally new. He described a stray coil of my hair as "helicoptering" across his computer keyboard. I thought: My hair helicopters. My hair *helicopters*. And it occurred to me that a word of poetry could rewrite painful history. Straight hair may make black women more acceptable in the workplace or the White House. But straight hair can't helicopter.

15    Was I magically healed? Did I go off to my happily-ever-after dreamhouse, never to question my hair (or beauty) again? Well, no. That's for fairy tales. But for several moments, then and afterward, I felt detangled. It was the kind of hair balm you can't get from a bottle.

### QUESTIONS FOR ANALYSIS AND DISCUSSION

1. What words does Latour use to describe her own hair? How do these words connect to issues of race and ethnicity in the past, and today?
2. Latour notes that the new Barbie dolls have a deeper meaning in the ways we identify ourselves by race and the ways we think of race within our own communities. How important is race to your own sense of identity? In your opinion, on what criteria do the people you meet judge you? What do you want them to judge you by? By what criteria do you judge yourself?
3. What observations does Latour make about role models for young black America? For young girls? Explain.
4. Latour states "straight hair is 'good hair' because straight hair is white hair." Respond to her assertion with your own viewpoint. Is this a cultural truth, or is it an opinion? Explain.
5. How does Latour's description of her childhood and her feelings about her own hair connect to her argument? What does she hope to change by sharing her memories?

## Our Biracial President

*James Hannaham*

On January 20, 2009, America swore in its 44th President of the United States. Elected by the people, Barack Obama represented a striking departure—he was a democrat, one of his parents was not American, and he was black. His election has been hailed as a victory against institutionalized racism, and symbolic of new beginnings in which any native-born child—black, white, or brown—can aspire to the highest office in the land regardless of race. But while his election has been hailed as a victory by many, some critics warn that we must not mistakenly believe that racism is "over" in the U.S. In this next editorial, James Hannaham, a retired professor of international relations, explains why, when the starry glow around his election fades, Obama will allow us to see ourselves in black and white.*

*James Hannaham, *Salon*, November 6, 2008.

**BEFORE YOU READ** ——————————————————————

What does the expression "to see in black and white" mean? Why is this expression ironic when used in reference to race relations?

**AS YOU READ** ——————————————————————

Hannaham observes that electing a "black" man to the U.S. presidency is "a quantum leap unimaginable until this moment." What makes this election particularly significant? Could it have happened sooner? For example, do you think Colin Powell could have won the 2000 election eight years prior? Why or why not?

1    Voters across the United States and citizens around the world are calling the election of Barack Obama a historic moment, and it is indeed groundbreaking in many important ways. We have elected a man unashamed of his African blood into the nation's highest office. In historical terms, this is a milestone of race relations in the United States, a quantum leap unimaginable until this moment. For some cynics and paranoid supporters, it was impossible until the moment John McCain, in the most gracious and touching moment of his campaign, conceded.

2    Obama's presidency carries a huge burden of symbolic proof. As the president-elect's acceptance speech emphasized, his victory caresses America's image of itself as a place where equal opportunity exists for anyone who works hard enough. It helps erase a stigma against people of African descent that has lasted more than 500 years and included some of the lowest moments in our supposedly modern and enlightened age—Jim Crow, apartheid, slavery. It allows people of all colors around the globe to point to Obama and feel as if their struggle may not be a dead end after all, and that someone who shares at least some of their experiences and perspectives can offer genuine respect and perhaps even empathy to millions who have so frequently been overlooked and despised. It is a sign to humanity that the United States can walk democracy like we talk it. This is no small thing.

3    But this big-picture vision of the Global Village as the Kingdom of Obamaland is too starry-eyed to hold sway for long—maybe not even until he's sworn in. An Obama presidency by no means represents the end of racism, just a hopeful sign of the beginning of the end. To see it as proof that anyone can be president, no matter their origins, is ludicrous. It isn't as if Obama became president because the Electoral College has an affirmative action policy operating on a quota system. He is a man whose impeccable résumé, spotless personal history, elite education, leadership abilities, attractiveness, seriousness, sexual orientation, marriage to a woman of his own perceived race, whose gender, maybe even complexion and definitely choice of running mate have made him what some employers have a tendency to call "overqualified."

4    During his race for the presidency, many people had misgivings about Obama's supposed lack of experience, but few had anything to say about whether he had the appropriate qualifications to hold office, other than to wonder if America was ready for a president so suave he could play the first black James Bond. Perhaps if Obama were as inept as the man whose broken pretzels and hanging chads he will need to sweep up from the Oval Office carpet, yet still a contender for commander in chief, we could finally lay racial prejudice into its chilly crypt and be done with it. Because among other things, white

supremacy has meant that unqualified but well-connected and rich white people's dreams have fallen into their laps, while overqualified people of color have striven their whole lives to get nowhere. Obama has cleared a path for fairness.

5    Still, privilege is no Death Star, and one Luke Skywalker can't obliterate it with a couple of lasers, no matter how well-placed. It did not vaporize last night, so in the Obama presidency we can look forward to some amusing and possibly infuriating contretemps that will arise from an African-American family leading the country. (Why was this never the premise for a sitcom?) The same battles will rage over affirmative action—will we cheat ourselves out of the next Obama by cutting it back?—and issues of discrimination in representation, education, housing, etc. For me, racism won't be over until a bunch of black people can move into a neighborhood and watch the property values rise.

6    Nevertheless, there are plenty of immediate, serious sighs of relief that we can now legitimately heave. The pendulum has swung the other way. Obama's long coattails have given Democrats a majority in the Senate and the House. Sarah Palin will have to return her expensive wardrobe and go study the Republican foreign policy playbook for at least four years. We will have the most intriguing first lady since, well, Hillary Clinton. Perhaps most important, Republicans will not choose the next couple of Supreme Court justices. The likelihood of a conservative majority overturning *Roe v. Wade* or other pieces of legislation important to the left has been severely reduced.

7    We have an intelligent man in the White House, a literate guy who not only reads books but has written two himself. "That one" doesn't try to hide his background and attempt to broaden his appeal with a veneer of folksiness; instead he approaches others without pretense. He has a beautiful voice: calm, reassuring, persuasive, sexy. With just these superficial qualities, he has already done a great deal for America's image around the world. A McCain presidency, a Canadian warned me last night, would have made America "superfluous," the debt slaves of China. Already we've seen Obama's image on countless bootlegged T-shirts, chiseled into an FDR-like, constructivist symbol of progressive politics, creativity and open-mindedness. His election alone has rescued the world's opinion of America's ability to adapt and move forward.

8    But both radical leftists and radical right-wingers need to understand the same thing: Obama is not Malcolm X. He's not even Kanye West. His motorcade will not consist of souped-up cars with wheels that spin and bump up and down outside the White House; he will not sport a diamond grill that reads "PREZ." He's a moderate. The right has changed the definition of the liberalism over the last 40 years by hectoring Democratic candidates, saying that they will over-tax and -spend, even as the current administration chucks billions of dollars into the furnaces of Iraq and Afghanistan. It's hard to now imagine a president getting elected without claiming to be a fiscal conservative, certainly not as we climb out of the current financial disaster. As someone elected largely because of our failing economy, Obama will have to toe the line of fiscal policy pretty carefully and make a lot of practical and shrewd decisions fast.

9    On social issues, however, there's no comparison. John McCain's "health of the woman" air quotes could easily have lost him the support of even pro-life women. While there's no guarantee that Obama's brilliantly run, tech-savvy campaign will lead to a well-run White House, the decisions that we've watched Obama make have suggested reconciliation, sharpness, flexibility, ability to delegate responsibility to capable experts—in short,

a solid footing in the reality-based community. But one of Obama's great strengths can also melt into his most frustrating quality—he tries to hear all voices without prejudice. His desire to listen to the Rev. Jeremiah Wright's claptrap surely cost him the trust of many Americans. There is a point at which a leader should be able to make a judgment about whether he's listening to a real viewpoint or just plain crazy-talk, and Obama's high tolerance for nut-job rhetoric may return to haunt him in the coming years. He may not want to waste too much time listening to lunatics, even if they happen to run foreign countries.

10    Obama's acceptance of his Caucasian genes is another quality that sets him closer to the center than to Malcolm X. I've said it before and I'll keep saying it: Obama's biracial. He's an African-American, certainly—in strictly genetic terms, he's more literally African-American than other American black folks, whose veins are awash in various percentages of African, Native American and European blood. This is not to say that he hasn't received some of the same treatment as black Americans, or that he is not welcome among them, or that people should denigrate his need to make his background understandable to people who think that "biracial" means a type of airplane. It suggests something far less divisive. It means that black and white people (not to mention other ethnicities chained to the binary idiocy of American race relations) can share his victory equally.

11    As Obama gave his acceptance speech in Chicago, the media seemed to enjoy focusing on the elation of black communities in Harlem, in Kenya, and at Morehouse College, or on the tear-stained faces of Oprah and Jesse Jackson, as if black people had always been primarily invested in Obama's triumph. But we can't forget that the black political establishment and a big chunk of their constituency was initially very slow to warm to the candidate. (Well, except the Kenyans.) Here, he was the white man's black candidate, carefully vetted before winning the trust everyone seemed to think black people would lavish upon him based solely on his race.

12    Obama's Caucasian heritage has not evaporated just because he's the first American president to be unashamed to have a shot of espresso in his vanilla latte. By voting for him, whites have shown their acceptance on a major level, but if everyone continues to interpret his presidency primarily in terms of race, we're simply perpetuating the same old values. The Obama presidency gives us the opportunity to see more clearly into a future when the pain and injustice of the past, though it will not be forgotten, can be transformed into a shared purpose, and we can help the grand family squabble of American race relations to settle down. Like most American families, we'll have our differences, but we will be able to sit down at the same table and show each other some respect.

### QUESTIONS FOR ANALYSIS AND DISCUSSION

1. What does Hannaham mean when he says our new president has "a shot of espresso in his vanilla latte"? Do you think this is an apt metaphor?
2. Hannaham uses a reference to the film "Star Wars" in his article. Why do you think he uses this reference, and what analogy is he trying to make?
3. Find the passage when the author makes reference to former president George W. Bush. Which moments in Bush's presidency is the author directly referring to? Why does he highlight this aspect of the former president's tenure in office? Explain.

4. How does Hannaham define "white supremacy"? What does "white supremacy" mean to you and how does it compare to the author's version?

5. The author of this article states, "racism won't be over until a bunch of black people can move into a neighborhood and watch the property values rise." In your opinion how will we know when racism is "finally over."

6. Hannaham states, "Obama is not Malcolm X. He's not even Kanye West." What does Hannaham mean? Who are they? What do they represent culturally, socially and politically? Compare and contrast Barak Obama to Malcolm X and Kanye West and share your observations with the class as part of a broader discussion on race and society.

## WRITING ASSIGNMENTS

1. Teenagers often complain that they are watched more closely in stores because it is believed they are more likely to be shoplifters. Write an essay in which you consider the validity of other kinds of profiling, such as that based on age, income, or gender. What assumptions of criminal behavior correspond to these groups? If racial profiling is wrong, is it also wrong to profile on the basis of gender or age? Why or why not?

2. What is the government's official position on racial profiling? Visit the U.S. Department of Justice website and read the "Racial Profiling Fact Sheet". What exceptions does the government make concerning racial profiling, and why? Identify any areas of the document that you find questionable or particularly compelling and explain why.

3. Visit the ACLU's website on racial equality at http://www.aclu.org and review its information on racial profiling. What are the most pressing issues concerning racial profiling today? Select an issue or case described on the ACLU website and research it in greater depth. Write a short essay summarizing the situation or issue and your position on it.

4. Write a letter to the U.S. Government suggesting how race should be considered (or not) on documents, censuses, and other forms. Give concrete examples and detailed support for your point of view.

5. Consider the ways in which Hollywood influences our cultural perspectives of race and ethnicity. Write an essay exploring the influence, however slight, that film and television have had on your own perceptions of race and ethnicity. If you wish, interview other students for their opinions on this issue and address some of their points in your essay.

6. Think about the ways in which the social, intellectual, topographical, and religious histories of an ethnic group can influence the creation of stereotypes. Identify some current stereotypes that are active in American culture. What are the origins of these stereotypes? Write an essay in which you dissect these stereotypes and present ways to dispel them.

7. Write an essay discussing your own family's sense of ethnic or racial identity. What are the origins of some of your family's values, practices, and customs? Have these customs met with prejudice by people who did not understand them? Explain.

# CHAPTER 15

# Passing the Buck—Our Economy in Crisis?

Today's college graduates leave school facing some daunting financial challenges—namely, the toughest labor market the nation has witnessed in over 25 years with an unemployment rate close to 10 percent. While some experts no longer fear another Great Depression, an extended period of unemployment and national debt still looms. College tuition rates are at their highest, the housing market is in shambles, and a credit crisis still threatens to bankrupt a nation. Many people own homes "under water"—that is, what they owe on their mortgages exceeds the actual resale value of their houses. And while college graduates do have an edge—an unemployment rate of 6.1 percent vs. 19.6 percent for same-age people with only high-school diplomas—many carry a debt greater than their less educated peers.

To Laura Conway, executive editor of the *Village Voice*, the heirs to this financial crisis have been aptly labeled "Generation Debt." Twentysomethings are facing a complicated future as they transition into adulthood. On the one hand, today's graduates point out that student loans, credit card debt, employment instability, lack of affordable healthcare, and financial irresponsibility have melded into a foreboding landscape that they have unwillingly inherited. On the other hand, their elders may argue that today's youth has come to expect too many handouts, does not know real struggle, and is unwilling to sacrifice. It's a classic generational argument, but statistics point to a disturbing fact—that today's twentysomethings may be the first generation to be less successful than their parents.

What may the financial landscape look like in the next few years? How did it get this bad? This chapter examines the multi-faceted dimensions of the economic crisis young adults now face—from the mortgage meltdown to the credit card crunch. Should we just let the financial sector implode upon itself? Does it really help to bail out floundering businesses? Will things get even worse before they get better? One thing is clear: there are no easy answers as we examine the financial crisis many young Americans—indeed, Americans of every age—are facing today.

## How the Crash Will Reshape America

*Richard Florida*

The crash of 2008 continues to reverberate loudly nationwide—destroying jobs, bankrupting businesses, and displacing homeowners. But already, it has damaged some places much more severely than others. When the crisis is over, America's economic landscape will look very different than it does today. What fate will the coming years hold for New York City, Charlotte, Detroit, Las Vegas, Los Angeles? Will the suburbs be completely changed? Which cities and regions can come back strong? And which will never come back at all? In this essay, economist Richard Florida describes the impact the economy is having on our national identity, and how things might change in the not so distant future. Is recession simply the mother of reinvention?*

## BEFORE YOU READ

What impact, if any, did the recent "crash" have on your community? Were you personally affected by the recent economic downturn? Do you think your life or your priorities have changed at all? Explain.

## AS YOU READ

What multiple factors contribute to the rise and fall of communities? Can we influence the growth of cities, or prevent their decline? Why or why not?

1   My father was a child of the Great Depression. Born in Newark, New Jersey, in 1921 to Italian immigrant parents, he experienced the economic crisis head-on. He took a job working in an eyeglass factory in the city's Ironbound section in 1934, at age 13, combining his wages with those of his father, mother, and six siblings to make a single-family income. When I was growing up, he spoke often of his memories of breadlines, tent cities, and government-issued clothing. At Christmas, he would tell my brother and me how his parents, unable to afford new toys, had wrapped the same toy steam shovel, year after year, and placed it for him under the tree. In my extended family, my uncles occupied a pecking order based on who had grown up in the roughest economic circumstances. My Uncle Walter, who went on to earn a master's degree in chemical engineering and eventually became a senior executive at Colgate-Palmolive, came out on top—not because of his academic or career achievements, but because he grew up with the hardest lot.

2   My father's experiences were broadly shared throughout the country. Although times were perhaps worst in the declining rural areas of the Dust Bowl, every region suffered, and the residents of small towns and big cities alike breathed in the same uncertainty and distress. The Great Depression was a national crisis—and in many ways a nationalizing event. The entire country, it seemed, tuned in to President Roosevelt's fireside chats.

3   The current economic crisis is unlikely to result in the same kind of shared experience. To be sure, the economic contraction is causing pain just about everywhere. In October, less than a month after the financial markets began to melt down, Moody's Economy.com published an assessment of recent economic activity within 381 U.S. metropolitan areas. Three hundred and two were already in deep recession, and 64 more were at risk. Only 15 areas were still expanding. Notable among them were the oil- and natural-resource-rich regions of Texas and Oklahoma, buoyed by energy prices that have since fallen; and the greater Washington, D.C., region, where government bailouts, the nationalization of

*Richard Florida, *The Atlantic*, March 2009 (slightly abridged for space).

financial companies, and fiscal expansion are creating work for lawyers, lobbyists, political scientists, and government contractors.

4    No place in the United States is likely to escape a long and deep recession. Nonetheless, as the crisis continues to spread outward from New York, through industrial centers like Detroit, and into the Sun Belt, it will undoubtedly settle much more heavily on some places than on others. Some cities and regions will eventually spring back stronger than before. Others may never come back at all. As the crisis deepens, it will permanently and profoundly alter the country's economic landscape. I believe it marks the end of a chapter in American economic history, and indeed, the end of a whole way of life.

## Global Crises and Economic Transformation

5    "One thing seems probable to me," said Peer Steinbrück, the German finance minister, in September 2008. As a result of the crisis, "the United States will lose its status as the superpower of the global financial system." You don't have to strain too hard to see the financial crisis as the death knell for a debt-ridden, overconsuming, and underproducing American empire—the fall long prophesied by Paul Kennedy and others.

6    Big international economic crises—the crash of 1873, the Great Depression—have a way of upending the geopolitical order, and hastening the fall of old powers and the rise of new ones. In *The Post-American World* (published some months before the Wall Street meltdown), Fareed Zakaria argued that modern history's third great power shift was already upon us—the rise of the West in the 15th century and the rise of America in the 19th century being the two previous sea changes.

7    But Zakaria added that this transition is defined less by American decline than by "the rise of the rest." We're to look forward to a world economy, he wrote, "defined and directed from many places and by many peoples." That's surely true. Yet the course of events since Steinbrück's remarks should give pause to those who believe the mantle of global leadership will soon be passed. The crisis has exposed deep structural problems, not just in the U.S. but worldwide. Europe's model of banking has proved no more resilient than America's, and China has shown that it remains every bit the codependent partner of the United States. The Dow, down more than a third last year, was actually among the world's better-performing stock-market indices. Foreign capital has flooded into the U.S., which apparently remains a safe haven, at least for now, in uncertain times.

8    It is possible that the United States will enter a period of accelerating relative decline in the coming years, though that's hardly a foregone conclusion. What's more certain is that the recession, particularly if it turns out to be as long and deep as many now fear, will accelerate the rise and fall of specific places *within* the U.S.—and reverse the fortunes of other cities and regions.

9    By what they destroy, what they leave standing, what responses they catalyze, and what space they clear for new growth, most big economic shocks ultimately leave the economic landscape transformed. Some of these transformations occur faster and more violently than others. The period after the Great Depression saw the slow but inexorable rise of the suburbs. The economic malaise of the 1970s, on the other hand, found its embodiment in the vertiginous fall of older industrial cities of the Rust Belt, followed by an explosion of growth in the Sun Belt.

10    The historian Scott Reynolds Nelson has noted that in some respects, today's crisis most closely resembles the "Long Depression," which stretched, by one definition, from 1873 to 1896. It began as a banking crisis brought on by insolvent mortgages and complex financial instruments, and quickly spread to the real economy, leading to mass unemployment that reached 25 percent in New York.

11    During that crisis, rising industries like railroads, petroleum, and steel were consolidated, old ones failed, and the way was paved for a period of remarkable innovation and industrial growth. In 1870, New England mill towns like Lowell, Lawrence, Manchester, and Springfield were among the country's most productive industrial cities, and America's population overwhelmingly lived in the countryside. By 1900, the economic geography had been transformed from a patchwork of farm plots and small mercantile towns to a landscape increasingly dominated by giant factory cities like Chicago, Cleveland, Pittsburgh, Detroit, and Buffalo.

12    How might various cities and regions fare as the crash of 2008 reverberates into 2009, 2010, and beyond? Which places will be spared the worst pain, and which left permanently scarred? Let's consider how the crash and its aftermath might affect the economic landscape in the long run, from coast to coast—beginning with the epicenter of the crisis and the nation's largest city, New York.

## Whither New York?

13    At first glance, few American cities would seem to be more obviously threatened by the crash than New York. The city shed almost 17,000 jobs in the financial industry alone from October 2007 to October 2008, and Wall Street as we've known it has ceased to exist. "Farewell Wall Street, hello Pudong?" begins a recent article by Marcus Gee in the Toronto *Globe and Mail*, outlining the possibility that New York's central role in global finance may soon be usurped by Shanghai, Hong Kong, and other Asian and Middle Eastern financial capitals.

14    This concern seems overheated. In his sweeping history, *Capitals of Capital*, the economic historian Youssef Cassis chronicles the rise and decline of global financial centers through recent centuries. Though the history is long, it contains little drama: major shifts in capitalist power centers occur at an almost geological pace.

15    Amsterdam stood at the center of the world's financial system in the 17th century; its place was taken by London in the early 19th century, then New York in the 20th. Across more than three centuries, no other city has topped the list of global financial centers. Financial capitals have "remarkable longevity," Cassis writes, "in spite of the phases of boom and bust in the course of their existence."

16    The transition from one financial center to another typically lags behind broader shifts in the economic balance of power, Cassis suggests. Although the U.S. displaced England as the world's largest economy well before 1900, it was not until after World War II that New York eclipsed London as the world's preeminent financial center (and even then, the eclipse was not complete; in recent years, London has, by some measures, edged out New York). As Asia has risen, Tokyo, Hong Kong, and Singapore have become major financial centers—yet in size and scope, they still trail New York and London by large margins.

17    In finance, "there is a huge network and agglomeration effect," former assistant U.S. Treasury secretary Edwin Truman told *The Christian Science Monitor* in October—an advantage that comes from having a large critical mass of financial professionals, covering many different specialties, along with lawyers, accountants, and others to support them, all in close physical proximity. It is extremely difficult to build these dense networks anew, and very hard for up-and-coming cities to take a position at the height of global finance without them. "Hong Kong, Shanghai, Singapore, and Tokyo are more important than they were 20 years ago," Truman said. "But will they reach London and New York's dominance in another 20 years? I suspect not." Hong Kong, for instance, has a highly developed IPO market, but lacks many of the other capabilities—such as bond, foreign-exchange, and commodities trading—that make New York and London global financial powerhouses.

18    "A crucial contributory factor in the financial centers' development over the last two centuries, and even longer," writes Cassis, "is the arrival of new talent to replenish their energy and their capacity to innovate." All in all, most places in Asia and the Middle East are still not as inviting to foreign professionals as New York or London. Tokyo is a wonderful city, but Japan remains among the least open of the advanced economies, and admits fewer immigrants than any other member of the Organization for Economic Cooperation and Development, a group of 30 market-oriented democracies. Singapore remains for the time being a top-down, socially engineered society. Dubai placed 44th in a recent ranking of global financial centers, near Edinburgh, Bangkok, Lisbon, and Prague. New York's openness to talent and its critical mass of it—in and outside of finance and banking—will ensure that it remains a global financial center.

19    In the short run, the most troubling question for New York is not how much of its finance industry will move to other places, but how much will simply vanish altogether. At the height of the recent bubble, Greater New York depended on the financial sector for roughly 22 percent of local wages. But most economists agree that by then the financial economy had become bloated and overdeveloped. Thomas Philippon, a finance professor at New York University, reckons that nationally, the share of GDP coming from finance will probably be reduced from its recent peak of 8.3 percent to perhaps 7 percent—I suspect it may fall farther, to perhaps as little as 5 percent, roughly its contribution a generation ago. In either case, it will be a big reduction, and a sizable portion of it will come out of Manhattan.

20    Lean times undoubtedly lie ahead for New York. But perhaps not as lean as you'd think—and certainly not as lean as those that many lesser financial outposts are likely to experience. Financial positions account for only about 8 percent of the New York area's jobs, not too far off the national average of 5.5 percent. By contrast, they make up 28 percent of all jobs in Bloomington-Normal, Illinois; 18 percent in Des Moines; 13 percent in Hartford; 10 percent in both Sioux Falls, South Dakota, and Charlotte, North Carolina. Omaha, Nebraska; Macon, Georgia; and Columbus, Ohio, all have a greater percentage of population working in the financial sector than New York does.

21    New York is much, much more than a financial center. It has been the nation's largest city for roughly two centuries, and today sits in America's largest metropolitan area, as the hub of the country's largest mega-region. It is home to a diverse and innovative economy built around a broad range of creative industries, from media to design to arts and entertainment. It is home to high-tech companies like Bloomberg, and boasts a thriving Google

outpost in its Chelsea neighborhood. Elizabeth Currid's book, *The Warhol Economy,* provides detailed evidence of New York's diversity. Currid measured the concentration of different types of jobs in New York relative to their incidence in the U.S. economy as a whole. By this measure, New York is more of a mecca for fashion designers, musicians, film directors, artists, and—yes—psychiatrists than for financial professionals.

22    The great urbanist Jane Jacobs was among the first to identify cities' diverse economic and social structures as the true engines of growth. Although the specialization identified by Adam Smith creates powerful efficiency gains, Jacobs argued that the jostling of many different professions and different types of people, all in a dense environment, is an essential spur to innovation—to the creation of things that are truly new. And innovation, in the long run, is what keeps cities vital and relevant.

23    In this sense, the financial crisis may ultimately help New York by reenergizing its creative economy. The extraordinary income gains of investment bankers, traders, and hedge-fund managers over the past two decades skewed the city's economy in some unhealthy ways. In 2005, I asked a top-ranking official at a major investment bank whether the city's rising real-estate prices were affecting his company's ability to attract global talent. He responded simply: "We are the cause, not the effect, of the real-estate bubble." (As it turns out, he was only half right.) Stratospheric real-estate prices have made New York less diverse over time, and arguably less stimulating. When I asked Jacobs some years ago about the effects of escalating real-estate prices on creativity, she told me, "When a place gets boring, even the rich people leave." With the hegemony of the investment bankers over, New York now stands a better chance of avoiding that sterile fate.

## America's "FAST" Cities: Crisis and Reinvention

24  In his 2005 book, *The World Is Flat,* Thomas Friedman argues, essentially, that the global economic playing field has been leveled, and that anyone, anywhere, can now innovate, produce, and compete on a par with, say, workers in Seattle or entrepreneurs in Silicon Valley. But this argument isn't quite right, and doesn't accurately describe the evolution of the global economy in recent years.

25    In fact, place still matters in the modern economy—and the competitive advantage of the world's most successful city-regions seems to be growing, not shrinking. To understand how the current crisis is likely to affect different places in the United States, it's important to understand the forces that have been slowly remaking our economic landscape for a generation or more.

26    Worldwide, people are crowding into a discrete number of mega-regions, systems of multiple cities and their surrounding suburban rings like the Boston-New York-Washington Corridor. In North America, these mega-regions include Sun Belt centers like the Char-Lanta Corridor, Northern and Southern California, the Texas Triangle of Houston-San Antonio-Dallas, and Southern Florida's Tampa-Orlando-Miami area; the Pacific Northwest's Cascadia, stretching from Portland through Seattle to Vancouver; and both Greater Chicago and Tor-Buff-Chester in the old Rust Belt. Internationally, these mega-regions include Greater London, Greater Tokyo, Europe's Am-Brus-Twerp, China's Shanghai-Beijing Corridor, and India's Bangalore-Mumbai area. Economic output is ever-more concentrated in these places as well. The world's 40 largest mega-regions,

which are home to some 18 percent of the world's population, produce two-thirds of global economic output and nearly 9 in 10 new patented innovations.

27    Some (though not all) of these mega-regions have a clear hub, and these hubs are likely to be better buffered from the crash than most cities, because of their size, diversity, and regional role. Chicago has emerged as a center for industrial management and has rolled up many of the functions, such as finance and law, once performed in smaller midwestern centers. Los Angeles has a broad, diverse economy with global strength in media and entertainment. Miami, which is being hit hard by the collapse of the real-estate bubble, nonetheless remains the commercial center for the large South Florida mega-region, and a major financial center for Latin America. Each of these places is the financial and commercial core of a large mega-region with tens of millions of people and hundreds of billions of dollars in output. That's not going to change as a result of the crisis.

28    Along with the rise of mega-regions, a second phenomenon is also reshaping the economic geography of the United States and the world. The ability of different cities and regions to attract highly educated people—or human capital—has diverged, according to research by Edward Glaser of Harvard and Christopher Berry of the University of Chicago, among others. Thirty years ago, educational attainment was spread relatively uniformly throughout the country, but that's no longer the case. Cities like Seattle, San Francisco, Austin, Raleigh, and Boston now have two or three times the concentration of college graduates of Akron or Buffalo. Among people with postgraduate degrees, the disparities are wider still. The geographic sorting of people by ability and educational attainment, on this scale, is unprecedented.

29    Big, talent-attracting places benefit from accelerated rates of "urban metabolism," according to a pioneering theory of urban evolution developed by a multidisciplinary team of researchers affiliated with the Santa Fe Institute. The rate at which living things convert food into energy—their metabolic rate—tends to slow as organisms increase in size. But when the Santa Fe team examined trends in innovation, patent activity, wages, and GDP, they found that successful cities, unlike biological organisms, actually get faster as they grow. In order to grow bigger and overcome diseconomies of scale like congestion and rising housing and business costs, cities must become more efficient, innovative, and productive. The researchers dubbed the extraordinarily rapid metabolic rate that successful cities are able to achieve "super-linear" scaling. "By almost any measure," they wrote, "the larger a city's population, the greater the innovation and wealth creation per person." Places like New York with finance and media, Los Angeles with film and music, and Silicon Valley with high-tech are all examples of high-metabolism places.

30    Metabolism and talent-clustering are important to the fortunes of U.S. city-regions in good times, but they're even more so when times get tough. It's not that "fast" cities are immune to the failure of businesses, large or small. (One of the great lessons of the 1873 crisis—and of this one so far—is that when credit freezes up and a long slump follows, companies can fail unpredictably, no matter where they are.) It's that unlike many other places, they can overcome business failures with relative ease, reabsorbing their talented workers, growing nascent businesses, founding new ones.

31    Economic crises tend to reinforce and accelerate the underlying, long-term trends within an economy. Our economy is in the midst of a fundamental long-term transformation—similar to that of the late 19th century, when people streamed off farms and into new

and rising industrial cities. In this case, the economy is shifting away from manufacturing and toward idea-driven creative industries—and that, too, favors America's talent-rich, fast-metabolizing places.

## The Last Crisis of the Factory Towns

32 Sadly and unjustly, the places likely to suffer most from the crash—especially in the long run—are the ones least associated with high finance. While the crisis may have begun in New York, it will likely find its fullest bloom in the interior of the country—in older, manufacturing regions whose heydays are long past and in newer, shallow-rooted Sun Belt communities whose recent booms have been fueled in part by real-estate speculation, overdevelopment, and fictitious housing wealth. These typically less affluent places are likely to become less wealthy still in the coming years, and will continue to struggle long after the mega-regional hubs and creative cities have put the crisis behind them.

33 The Rust Belt in particular looks likely to shed vast numbers of jobs, and some of its cities and towns, from Cleveland to St. Louis to Buffalo to Detroit, will have a hard time recovering. Since 1950, the manufacturing sector has shrunk from 32 percent of nonfarm employment to just 10 percent. This decline is the result of long-term trends—increasing foreign competition and, especially, the relentless replacement of people with machines—that look unlikely to abate. But the job losses themselves have proceeded not steadily, but rather in sharp bursts, as recessions have killed off older plants and resulted in mass layoffs that are never fully reversed during subsequent upswings.

34 In November 2008, nationwide unemployment in manufacturing and production occupations was already 9.4 percent. Compare that with the professional occupations, where it was just a little over 3 percent. According to an analysis done by Michael Mandel, the chief economist at *BusinessWeek*, jobs in the "tangible" sector—that is, production, construction, extraction, and transport—declined by nearly 1.8 million between December 2007 and November 2008, while those in the intangible sector—what I call the "creative class" of scientists, engineers, managers, and professionals—increased by more than 500,000. Both sorts of jobs are regionally concentrated. Paul Krugman has noted that the worst of the crisis, so far at least, can be seen in a "Slump Belt," heavy with manufacturing centers, running from the industrial Midwest down into the Carolinas. Large swaths of the Northeast, with its professional and creative centers, have been better insulated.

35 Perhaps no major city in the U.S. today looks more beleaguered than Detroit, where in October the average home price was $18,513, and some 45,000 properties were in some form of foreclosure. A recent listing of tax foreclosures in Wayne County, which encompasses Detroit, ran to 137 pages in the *Detroit Free Press*. The city's public school system, facing a budget deficit of $408 million, was taken over by the state in December; dozens of schools have been closed since 2005 because of declining enrollment. Just 10 percent of Detroit's adult residents are college graduates, and in December the city's jobless rate was 21 percent.

36 To say the least, Detroit is not well positioned to absorb fresh blows. The city has of course been declining for a long time. But if the area's auto headquarters, parts manufacturers, and remaining auto-manufacturing jobs should vanish, it's hard to imagine anything replacing them.

37    When work disappears, city populations don't always decline as fast as you might expect. Detroit, astonishingly, is still the 11th-largest city in the U.S. "If you no longer can sell your property, how can you move elsewhere?" said Robin Boyle, an urban-planning professor at Wayne State University, in a December Associated Press article. But then he answered his own question: "Some people just switch out the lights and leave—property values have gone so low, walking away is no longer such a difficult option."

38    Perhaps Detroit has reached a tipping point, and will become a ghost town. I'd certainly expect it to shrink faster in the next few years than it has in the past few. But more than likely, many people will stay—those with no means and few obvious prospects elsewhere, those with close family ties nearby, some number of young professionals and creative types looking to take advantage of the city's low housing prices. Still, as its population density dips further, the city's struggle to provide services and prevent blight across an ever-emptier landscape will only intensify.

39    That's the challenge that many Rust Belt cities share: managing population decline without becoming blighted. The task is doubly difficult because as the manufacturing industry has shrunk, the local high-end services—finance, law, consulting—that it once supported have diminished as well, absorbed by bigger regional hubs and globally connected cities. In Chicago, for instance, the country's 50 biggest law firms grew by 2,130 lawyers from 1984 to 2006, according to William Henderson and Arthur Alderson of Indiana University. Throughout the rest of the Midwest, these firms added a total of just 169 attorneys. Jones Day, founded in 1893 and today one of the country's largest law firms, no longer considers its Cleveland office "headquarters"—that's in Washington, D.C.—but rather its "founding office."

40    Many second-tier midwestern cities have tried to reinvent themselves in different ways, with varying degrees of success. Pittsburgh, for instance, has sought to reimagine itself as a high-tech center, and has met with more success than just about anywhere else. Still, its population has declined from a high of almost 700,000 in the mid-20th century to roughly 300,000 today. There will be fewer manufacturing jobs on the other side of the crisis, and the U.S. economic landscape will be more uneven—"spikier"—as a result. Many of the old industrial centers will be further diminished, perhaps permanently so.

41    That's not to say that every factory town is locked into decline. You need only look at the geographic pattern of December's Senate vote on the auto bailout to realize that some places, mostly in the South, would benefit directly from the bankruptcy of GM or Chrysler and the closure of auto plants in the Rust Belt. Georgetown, Kentucky; Smyrna, Tennessee; Canton, Mississippi: these are a few of the many small cities, stretching from South Carolina and Georgia all the way to Texas, that have benefited from the establishment, over the years, of plants that manufacture foreign cars. Those benefits could grow if the Big Three were to become, say, the Big Two.

### Cities in the Sand: The End of Easy Expansion

42 For a generation or more, no swath of the United States has grown more madly than the Sun Belt. Of course, the area we call the "Sun Belt" is vast, and the term is something of a catch-all: the cities and metropolitan areas within it have grown for disparate reasons. Los Angeles is a mecca for media and entertainment; San Jose and Austin developed significant, innovative high-tech industries; Houston became a hub for energy production;

Nashville developed a unique niche in low-cost music recording and production; Charlotte emerged as a center for cost-effective banking and low-end finance.

43   But in the heady days of the housing bubble, some Sun Belt cities—Phoenix and Las Vegas are the best examples—developed economies centered largely on real estate and construction. With sunny weather and plenty of flat, empty land, they got caught in a classic boom cycle. Although these places drew tourists, retirees, and some industry—firms seeking bigger footprints at lower costs—much of the cities' development came from, well, development itself. At a minimum, these places will take a long, long time to regain the ground they've recently lost in local wealth and housing values. It's not unthinkable that some of them could be in for an extended period of further decline.

44   To an uncommon degree, the economic boom in these cities was propelled by housing appreciation: as prices rose, more people moved in, seeking inexpensive lifestyles and the opportunity to get in on the real-estate market where it was rising, but still affordable. Local homeowners pumped more and more capital out of their houses as well, taking out home-equity loans and injecting money into the local economy in the form of home improvements and demand for retail goods and low-level services. Cities grew, tax coffers filled, spending continued, more people arrived. Yet the boom itself neither followed nor resulted in the development of sustainable, scalable, highly productive industries or services. It was fueled and funded by housing, and housing was its primary product. Whole cities and metro regions became giant Ponzi schemes.

45   Phoenix, for instance, grew from 983,403 people in 1990 to 1,552,259 in 2007. One of its suburbs, Mesa, now has nearly half a million residents, more than Pittsburgh, Cleveland, or Miami. As housing starts and housing prices rose, so did tax revenues, and a major capital-spending boom occurred throughout the Greater Phoenix area. Arizona State University built a new downtown Phoenix campus, and the city expanded its convention center and constructed a 20-mile light-rail system connecting Phoenix, Mesa, and Tempe.

46   And then the bubble burst. From October 2007 through October 2008, the Phoenix area registered the largest decline in housing values in the country: 32.7 percent. (Las Vegas was just a whisker behind, at 31.7 percent. Housing in the New York region, by contrast, fell by just 7.5 percent over the same period.) Overstretched and overbuilt, the region is now experiencing a fiscal double whammy, as its many retirees—some 21 percent of its residents are older than 55—have seen their retirement savings decimated. Mortgages Limited, the state's largest private commercial lender, filed for bankruptcy last summer. The city is running a $200 million budget deficit, which is only expected to grow. Last fall, the city government petitioned for federal funds to help it deal with the financial crisis. "We had a big bubble here, and it burst," Anthony Sanders, a professor of economics and finance at ASU, told *USA Today* in December. "We've taken Kevin Costner's Field of Dreams and now it's Field of Screams. If you build it, nobody comes."

47   Will people wash out of these places as fast as they washed in, leaving empty sprawl and all the ills that accompany it? Will these cities gradually attract more businesses and industries, allowing them to build more-diverse and more-resilient economies? Or will they subsist on tourism—which may be meager for quite some time—and on the social security checks of their retirees? No matter what, their character and atmosphere are likely to change radically.

## The Limits of Suburban Growth

48 Every phase or epoch of capitalism has its own distinct geography, or what economic geographers call the "spatial fix" for the era. The physical character of the economy—the way land is used, the location of homes and businesses, the physical infrastructure that ties everything together—shapes consumption, production, and innovation. As the economy grows and evolves, so too must the landscape.

49 To a surprising degree, the causes of this crash are geographic in nature, and they point out a whole system of economic organization and growth that has reached its limit. Positioning the economy to grow strongly in the coming decades will require not just fiscal stimulus or industrial reform; it will require a new kind of geography as well, a new spatial fix for the next chapter of American economic history.

50 Suburbanization was the spatial fix for the industrial age—the geographic expression of mass production and the early credit economy. Henry Ford's automobiles had been rolling off assembly lines since 1913, but "Fordism," the combination of mass production and mass consumption to create national prosperity, didn't emerge as a full-blown economic and social model until the 1930s and the advent of Roosevelt's New Deal programs.

51 Before the Great Depression, only a minority of Americans owned a home. But in the 1930s and '40s, government policies brought about longer-term mortgages, which lowered payments and enabled more people to buy a house. Fannie Mae was created to purchase those mortgages and lubricate the system. And of course the tax deduction on mortgage-interest payments (which had existed since 1913, when the federal income-tax system was created) privileged house purchases over other types of spending. Between 1940 and 1960, the homeownership rate rose from 44 percent to 62 percent.

52 Demand for houses was symbiotic with demand for cars, and both were helped along by federal highway construction, among other infrastructure projects that subsidized a new suburban lifestyle and in turn fueled demand for all manner of household goods. More recently, innovations in finance like adjustable-rate mortgages and securitized subprime loans expanded homeownership further and kept demand high. By 2004, a record 69.2 percent of American families owned their home.

53 For the generation that grew up during the Depression and was inclined to pinch pennies, policies that encouraged freer spending were sensible enough—they allowed the economy to grow faster. But as younger generations, weaned on credit, followed, and credit availability increased, the system got out of hand. Housing, meanwhile, became an ever-more-central part of the American Dream: for many people, as the recent housing bubble grew, owning a home came to represent not just an end in itself, but a means to financial independence.

54 On one level, the crisis has demonstrated what everyone has known for a long time: Americans have been living beyond their means, using illusory housing wealth and huge slugs of foreign capital to consume far more than we've produced. The crash surely signals the end to that; the adjustment, while painful, is necessary.

55 But another crucial aspect of the crisis has been largely overlooked, and it might ultimately prove more important. Because America's tendency to overconsume and under-save has been intimately intertwined with our postwar spatial fix—that is, with housing

and suburbanization—the shape of the economy has been badly distorted, from where people live, to where investment flows, to what's produced. Unless we make fundamental policy changes to eliminate these distortions, the economy is likely to face worsening handicaps in the years ahead.

## The Next Economic Landscape

56    The housing bubble was the ultimate expression, and perhaps the last gasp, of an economic system some 80 years in the making, and now well past its "sell-by" date. The bubble encouraged massive, unsustainable growth in places where land was cheap and the real-estate economy dominant. It encouraged low-density sprawl, which is ill-fitted to a creative, postindustrial economy. And not least, it created a workforce too often stuck in place, anchored by houses that cannot be profitably sold, at a time when flexibility and mobility are of great importance.

57    So how do we move past the bubble, the crash, and an aging, obsolescent model of economic life? What's the right spatial fix for the economy today, and how do we achieve it?

58    The solution begins with the removal of homeownership from its long-privileged place at the center of the U.S. economy. Substantial incentives for homeownership (from tax breaks to artificially low mortgage-interest rates) distort demand, encouraging people to buy bigger houses than they otherwise would. That means less spending on medical technology, or software, or alternative energy—the sectors and products that could drive U.S. growth and exports in the coming years. Artificial demand for bigger houses also skews residential patterns, leading to excessive low-density suburban growth. The measures that prop up this demand should be eliminated.

59    If anything, our government policies should encourage renting, not buying. Homeownership occupies a central place in the American Dream primarily because decades of policy have put it there. A recent study by Grace Wong, an economist at the Wharton School of Business, shows that, controlling for income and demographics, homeowners are no happier than renters, nor do they report lower levels of stress or higher levels of self-esteem.

60    As homeownership rates have risen, our society has become less nimble: in the 1950s and 1960s, Americans were nearly twice as likely to move in a given year as they are today. Last year fewer Americans moved, as a percentage of the population, than in any year since the Census Bureau started tracking address changes, in the late 1940s. This sort of creeping rigidity in the labor market is a bad sign for the economy, particularly in a time when businesses, industries, and regions are rising and falling quickly.

61    The foreclosure crisis creates a real opportunity here. Instead of resisting foreclosures, the government should seek to facilitate them in ways that can minimize pain and disruption. Banks that take back homes, for instance, could be required to offer to rent each home to the previous homeowner, at market rates—which are typically lower than mortgage payments—for some number of years. (At the end of that period, the former homeowner could be given the option to repurchase the home at the prevailing market price.) A bigger,

healthier rental market, with more choices, would make renting a more attractive option for many people; it would also make the economy as a whole more flexible and responsive.

62     Next, we need to encourage growth in the regions and cities that are best positioned to compete in the coming decades: the great mega-regions that already power the economy, and the smaller, talent-attracting innovation centers inside them—places like Silicon Valley, Boulder, Austin, and the North Carolina Research Triangle.

63     Whatever our government policies, the coming decades will likely see a further clustering of output, jobs, and innovation in a smaller number of bigger cities and city-regions. But properly shaping that growth will be one of the government's biggest challenges. In part, we need to ensure that key cities and regions continue to circulate people, goods, and ideas quickly and efficiently. This in itself will be no small task; increasing congestion threatens to slowly sap some of these city-regions of their vitality.

64     Just as important, though, we need to make elite cities and key mega-regions more attractive and affordable for all of America's classes, not just the upper crust. High housing costs in these cities and in the more convenient suburbs around them, along with congested sprawl farther afield, have conspired to drive lower-income Americans away from these places over the past 30 years. This is profoundly unhealthy for our society.

65     If there is one constant in the history of capitalist development, it is the ever-more-intensive use of space. Today, we need to begin making smarter use of both our urban spaces and the suburban rings that surround them—packing in more people, more affordably, while at the same time improving their quality of life. That means liberal zoning and building codes within cities to allow more residential development, more mixed-use development in suburbs and cities alike, the in-filling of suburban cores near rail links, new investment in rail, and congestion pricing for travel on our roads. Not everyone wants to live in city centers, and the suburbs are not about to disappear. But we can do a much better job of connecting suburbs to cities and to each other, and allowing regions to grow bigger and denser without losing their velocity.

66     Finally, we need to be clear that ultimately, we can't stop the decline of some places, and that we would be foolish to try. Places like Pittsburgh have shown that a city can stay vibrant as it shrinks, by redeveloping its core to attract young professionals and creative types, and by cultivating high-growth services and industries. And in limited ways, we can help faltering cities to manage their decline better, and to sustain better lives for the people who stay in them.

67     The Stanford economist Paul Romer famously said, "A crisis is a terrible thing to waste." The United States, whatever its flaws, has seldom wasted its crises in the past. On the contrary, it has used them, time and again, to reinvent itself, clearing away the old and making way for the new. Throughout U.S. history, adaptability has been perhaps the best and most quintessential of American attributes. Over the course of the 19th century's Long Depression, the country remade itself from an agricultural power into an industrial one. After the Great Depression, it discovered a new way of living, working, and producing, which contributed to an unprecedented period of mass prosperity. At critical moments, Americans have always looked forward, not back, and surprised the world with our resilience. Can we do it again?

## QUESTIONS FOR ANALYSIS AND DISCUSSION

1. Why does Florida recount his father's experiences during the Great Depression? How does the story of his father set up the points he raises in his essay?
2. Florida quotes German finance minister Peer Steinbrück's observation (paragraph 5) that the U.S. will "lose its status as the superpower of the global financial system." Based on your current knowledge and information in this essay, explain why you agree or disagree with Steinbrück's projection.
3. What is the "rise of the rest"? Will it be at the expense of countries currently in power?
4. How will our landscape be transformed as a result of the current economic crisis? Explain.
5. Why does Florida locate the "epicenter" of the current economic crisis in New York City? How will NYC change as a result of the downturn?
6. How has urban sprawl contributed to the current economic crisis? How will the suburban landscape change in the next decade and beyond?
7. Review the "solutions" that Florida offers in his conclusion. How feasible are his solutions? Do some seem more plausible than others? How might residents of Detroit or Silicon Valley respond to his solutions? Explain.

## Saving Yourself
*Daniel Akst*

America's enduring love affair with big spending is coming up against some unromantic realities. The spending of the Baby Booms, coupled with the instant gratification demanded by Gen-Xers and Millennials have created unheard of levels of personal debt. But a life-long saver assures us that there are worse fates than socking it away for a rainy day. Writer Daniel Akst defines what it means to be thrifty and explains how thrift can be much sexier than the alternative—poverty.*

### BEFORE YOU READ

In this next article, the author describes "spenders" and "savers." Which are you and why?

### AS YOU READ

What cultural influences drive our spending habits? How does where we live and with whom contribute to our ideas of thrift? Explain.

*Daniel Akst, *Wilson Quarterly*, Summer 2009.

1   Remember Jack Benny? Cheapness was his shtick; on his radio and television shows he occasionally made hilarious subterranean visits to his money, which was protected by locks, alligators, and an ancient security guard who, from the look of him, had last seen action at the Second Battle of Bull Run. "Your money or your life," to the rest of us, is Hobson's choice; to Benny, it was an existential crisis.

2   Ah, those were the days—a halcyon time when, the Depression still a fresh memory, Americans enjoyed both affluence and restraint. Willy Loman's refrigerator payments notwithstanding, consumer indebtedness at midcentury now looks like a mere flyspeck, at least from the towering mountain of debt atop which we sit.

3   We have managed since Benny's heyday to get a little carried away. Alan Greenspan and the Chinese gave us too much credit, unfettered bankers chose greed over sobriety, and consumers snapped up McMansions financed by loans they could never repay. In 1980, American household debt stood at what must have seemed the enormous sum of $1.4 trillion. Last year the figure was 10 times as large, only 24 percent of us were debt free, and more than half of college students carried at least four credit cards. Is it any wonder there were more than a million consumer bankruptcy filings last year? Or that the nation's banking system came close to collapse? The result of all this excess is a people hung-over from its recent intoxication with spending and flabbergasted by the bill from the wine merchant.

4   So thrift, supposedly, is back, implying, as the dictionary tells us, "using money and other resources carefully and not wastefully." (The word's etymological connection to "thrive" may come as a shock to some big spenders, but not to the truly thrifty.) Personally, I'm not certain that the resurrection of thrift—heralded on the covers of *Time* and *Business Week,* among other places—is anything more than temporary. But as a lifelong cheapskate, I'm grateful that at least thrift no longer carries quite the musty and ungenerous connotations it once did. If we skinflints are the last ones to step out of the closet, it only means we can appreciate all the more heartily how nice it is to escape the smell of mothballs.

5   I'm talking here about real thrift, which for the most part involves *not spending money.* It's not to be confused with the smug species of faux thrift that's been in vogue for a while. You see it in shelter magazines and newspaper home sections, where rich people boast of furnishing their multimillion-dollar homes with zany castoffs and repurposed industrial *objects.* Or how about the children of one Joan Asher? The *Wall Street Journal* reports that after three had inpatient nose jobs—attended by a private nurse each time—the fourth had to suffer through an outpatient procedure after which she was nursed at home by mom.

6   Real thrift, the skeptical, calculating kind that can make a difference between being solvent and not, is not a matter of cut-rate rhinoplasty. The quotidian penny-pinching I'm talking about used to have a bad name indeed, in much the same way as "spinster" and "cardigan," as we know very well from Jack Benny. Like his preening insistence that he was always 39—or that he was an accomplished violinist—Benny's pretend niggardliness was funny but also geriatric, unsexy, and possibly even emasculating. Men do in fact make passes at women who wear glasses, but do women melt for men who hoard gelt?

7   Evolutionary biologists, who seem to know everything about everything, suggest otherwise. The males of many species, including our own, evolved to attract females by means of costly displays—for example, the tail of the peacock, which he drags around to demonstrate his vitality to peahens. Lacking such plumage, human males resort to exotic European automobiles, pricey dinners, vulgar wristwatches, and other forms of showiness.

(Human females are supposed to be seeking signs in such ostentation that a mate will spend on them and their offspring. In the modern world, of course, women themselves earn and spend plenty, often supposedly in answer to their own evolutionary imperative to look young and beautiful.)

8      Spending and sex thus are inextricably connected. "Easy come, easy go" might well have been our motto on both fronts until relatively recently. During the boom, people spent freely and were implored to do so on every side by purveyors of every conceivable thing, in terms designed to penetrate directly to the unrestrained limbic brain. Sex, after all, sells, and thrift is the opposite of sexy. Kooky Scotsmen are thrifty. Flinty New England farmers are thrifty. Elderly pensioners are thrifty. Brad Pitt isn't thrifty.

9      This lack of sex appeal is one reason modern life has produced no great constituency for saving. Like dentists and Jews, saving has often found itself the subject of negative stereotyping in popular culture. In *McTeague* (1899), the novelist Frank Norris tars all three with the same broad brush in a melodramatic portrait of greed and its tragic consequences. *McTeague* is a good example of how, in literature, the prudently thrifty (who are perhaps inherently too boring for drama) tend to be overshadowed by the fanatically miserly. From Shylock through Silas Marner and Ebenezer Scrooge right up to Mr. Potter (*It's a Wonderful Life*), Fred C. Dobbs (*Treasure of the Sierra Madre*) and C. Montgomery Burns *(The Simpsons),* it's clear that writers have always taken seriously St. Paul's assertion that the love of money is the root of all evil. Financial profligacy, it would seem, is nothing compared with being a greedy skinflint.

10      To the extent that thrift produces wealth, it breeds envy. The thrift, future-mindedness, and sobriety of the Jews have fueled prodigious achievements and equally prodigious anti-Semitism, and the association of thrift with a despised minority probably didn't do any good for the trait's public image. Shylock was far from the last moneygrubbing Jew to besmirch popular culture; a coarse and monied Jewish stock manipulator is at the center of Anthony Trollope's *The Way We Live Now* (1875)*,* and lesser such figures flitted in and out of books and movies well into the 20th century. Before Harold Lloyd finds himself hanging from the hands of a clock high above the sidewalk in the silent classic *Safety Last* (1923), he encounters such a character practically salivating with greed behind the counter of a jewelry store. One wonders uneasily whether it was by sheer chance that Jack Benny—né Benjamin Kubelsky—chose a penny-pinching stage persona for himself. The man was by all accounts as generous in his private life as he was tightfisted on screen.

11      There was a time, of course, when thrift was in favor. It was practically a matter of life and death for the Puritans and a cornerstone of their work ethic, along with temperance, diligence, and piety. They excelled at deferring gratification, and it is one of the great ironies of American history that their preternatural self-discipline and industry launched us on the path to such unimaginable riches that thrift would be forgotten in the stampede to the mall. (On the other hand, if you have to be a victim of something, it might as well be your own success.)

12      Benjamin Franklin, who was hardly puritanical in any modern sense of the term, nonetheless embraced thrift and famously reminded us that "a penny saved is a penny earned" even before the advent of income taxes (which have made a penny saved worth *even more* than a penny earned). A relentless self-improver, Franklin as a young man "conceived the bold and arduous project of arriving at moral perfection," and as an aid in this venture developed a kind of moral spreadsheet, writing the days of the week across the top

and listing 13 virtues along the side, so he could plot his failings by date and category in a grid. Frugality ("waste nothing") was number five on the list.

13    Thrift was so important to Samuel Smiles, the great 19th-century Scottish self-help guru, that in 1875 he published an entire book devoted to it. Smiles's *Thrift* was a sequel to his earlier bestseller, *Self-Help,* which appeared in the landmark literary year of 1859 (when readers first encountered John Stuart Mill's *On Liberty* and Charles Darwin's *Origin of Species).* Smiles's oeuvre, which also included *Duty* and *Character,* made the case for the overriding Victorian virtue of self-control, a characteristic then associated not with the timid but the strong. For in those days, people understood the connection between money and virtue. "No man can be free who is in debt," Smiles tells us in *Thrift.* "The inevitable effect of debt is not only to injure personal independence, but, in the long-run, to inflict moral degradation."

14    We have self-help gurus today, of course, and some of them (the ubiquitous Suze Orman, for example) even stress the connection between money and morals, but that's not why they are known or attended. We simply want the advantages of financial security and a higher standard of living. The reward for good financial management is a big house, a nice car—all the things that come from bad financial management, without the debt.

15    How did we get here? The transformation of thrift from a virtue into something verging on a social disorder occurred sometime between the 1880s and 1920s, when America transformed itself from a nation of want into one of, well, *wants.* Unbridled economic growth (fueled by decades of self-restraint and invested savings) undermined the Protestant ethos of self-denial and reticence, while the rising merchant class did its best to change the country's long-ingrained aversion to luxury. Consumer credit became more widely available, and religious denominations laid off the hellfire and brimstone in favor of a therapeutic approach to happiness in the present. Vast new big-city "department stores" leveled the full force of their merchandising grandeur at women, who understandably preferred to purchase items they had once laboriously made. Catalyzed by mass communications (which made possible the stimulation of mass desire through advertising) and the rise of an urbanized middle class, consumerism exploded.

16    The loud noise caught the attention of two important social theorists, one of them famous and the other largely forgotten. It's yet another irony in the saga of America's love/hate relationship with thrift that we live by the precepts of the thinker whose name hardly anyone remembers.

17    First, the one you know about. Thorstein Veblen, the peripatetic Norwegian-American economist (he died in 1929, shortly before the great crash that might have brought him grim satisfaction), is best known today for his theory of conspicuous consumption, which argued that a lot of spending is just a wasteful attempt to impress. In effect, Veblen explained consumerism in terms of status and display, bringing evolutionary ideas to bear on economics and consumer behavior to powerful effect. Reading Veblen is a little like reading Freud or Darwin, albeit on a smaller scale: Do so and you'll never look at the world in quite the same way again.

18    As you might imagine, the iconoclastic Veblen took a dim view of all the conspicuous consumption around him, regarding it as a species of giant potlatch in which competitive waste had run amok. You might call Veblen's the voice of thrift, and it is still heard today from leftist intellectuals who, from their tenured pulpits and Arts and Crafts homes, reliably denounce the spending of others. The truth is that nobody listens to these people, except to submit to their periodic floggings as a kind of penance for sins we have no intention of ceasing.

19     But there was another voice heard back when thrift was in its death throes—that of Simon Patten (1852–1922), like Veblen a maladjusted economist who had strong ideas about spending. Patten can seem naive and even crass to us today, for he used his pulpit at the University of Pennsylvania's Wharton School to advocate the very thing that Marx feared: that business and consumer spending should sweep away all the old arrangements and remake the world according to the doctrine of plenty. And he imagined a large role for economists in the running of it.

20     Unlike Veblen, Patten came on the scene not to praise thrift but to bury it. The old values that "inculcated a spirit of resignation" and "emphasized the repression of wants" must be abandoned, Patten argued, adding, "The principle of sacrifice continues to be exalted by moralists at the very time when the social structure is being changed by the slow submergence of the primeval world, and the appearance of a land of unmeasured resources with a hoard of mobilized wealth."

21     Patten was hugely influential in his time, especially in helping liberals to see that something like Adam Smith's "universal opulence" should be a goal and not a cause for shame. His genius was in recognizing capitalism's potential for realizing something like a modern Cockaigne, the mythical land of plenty that beguiled the suffering masses in the Middle Ages. Patten's thinking opened the door to such later fulfillment-oriented intellectuals as Abraham Maslow and Herbert Marcuse, who implicitly (or explicitly) disparaged the idea of deferring gratification—a notion that would come to seem as pointlessly self-sacrificial as postponing happiness until the afterlife.

22     In important ways Patten and Veblen were both right about consumerism, but of the two Patten was the true radical. Beside his starry-eyed utopianism Veblen's sour conservatism is plain to see. As things turned out, it's Patten's world we live in, even if we use the language of Veblen to understand it.

23     Patten and Veblen both died in the 1920s, a decade when affluence, technology, and changing social mores joined forces to drive a stake through the heart of pecuniary restraint. Since then, modern America has effectively banished thrift by foisting on the world those four horsemen of the financial apocalypse: the automobile, the television, the credit card, and the shopping cart. Besides costing money to buy and operate, cars opened up the landscape so that more Americans could have bigger houses on bigger lots. To fill them up, people enjoyed the dubious guidance of television, which helped them figure out what they should want. Credit cards enabled us to conjure money on the spot to pay for stuff. And the shopping cart, unthinkable in traditional department stores but indispensable in their demotic successors—Wal-Mart and Target—gave Americans a way to get all that booty out to the automobile, which they could use to drive it home.

24     After the hardships of the Great Depression and the rationing and other deprivations of World War II (during which Americans saved roughly a quarter of their income), nobody was too focused on thrift, and I can't say I blame them. Besides, spending stimulated the economy, which was something like a patriotic duty. In his 1954 study *People of Plenty: Economic Abundance and the American Character,* David M. Potter said of the contemporary American that "society expects him to consume his quota of goods—of automobiles, of whiskey, of television sets—by maintaining a certain standard of living, and it regards him as a 'good guy' for absorbing his share, while it snickers at the prudent, self-denying, abstemious thrift that an earlier generation would have respected." Or as William H. Whyte put it in *The Organization Man* (1956), "Thrift is becoming a little un-American."

25    Unfortunately, for a people who love money, we've become very good at making it disappear, a task to which we've brought characteristic ingenuity and verve. Reckless overspending was until recently a course open to practically every American, just like reckless investing. And suddenly we were all Emma Bovary, bent on financial suicide. "It is because she feels that society is fettering her imagination, her body, her dreams, her appetites," Mario Vargas Llosa once wrote, "that Emma suffers, commits adultery, lies, steals, and in the end kills herself."

26    He might well have been describing America, circa 2007. Four-dollar coffee drinks? Fourteen-dollar cocktails? Bottled water from Fiji, priced higher than gasoline? You've got to be kidding. Now that it's safe to come clean, I will confess to having been a bit of a refusenik about all this for most of my, er, 39 years on this earth. Every stick of furniture in my house is second-hand, as are many of my family's clothes, computers, bicycles, books, pieces of art, and other items. We've mostly had used cars, and we still have the new ones we bought in a single mad burst in 2001. The funny thing is, it's amazing what a nice life you can have with a middle-class income and Jack Benny's attitude about money.

27    More people are waking up to this particular old-time religion. Since early 2008 personal saving has crept back up a few percentage points above zero (much to the consternation of stimulus-minded economists), and some long-term trends are likely to reinforce today's renewed interest in controlling spending.

28    It helps that conspicuous consumption, like tobacco, has fallen into social disrepute, a change that removes some of the pressure felt by many families to keep up with the Joneses (who may well have been foreclosed by now). Veblen was right that much spending is meant to be conspicuous, and if the display incentives surrounding consumption have changed, so will consumption.

27    Rising environmental consciousness ought to be a further spur to thrift, for what could possibly be greener—or more demonstrative of piety—than eschewing wasteful consumption? Although cutting global greenhouse emissions by building new power plants and the like can be expensive, many of the ways individuals can make a difference will actually put money in your pocket: eating less red meat, driving a fuelefficient car, and taking fewer planet-warming plane trips, to name a few. The same goes for buying less stuff; making do with what you have or going secondhand uses fewer resources and of course reduces spending as well. A rising scavenger subculture threatens to erase the stigma that was associated with "garbage picking" when I was a kid, transforming shame into virtue. Like so many other things, this "freecycling" is abetted by Craigslist.

28    You'll need to consider garbage picking now and then because in the years ahead we'll have to pay not only for our individual and collective overspending in the boom years, but also for our gigantic national outlays during the ensuing crash to bail out banks, insurers, and automakers and stimulate the economy to stave off a depression. We've been paying for all this by borrowing, so expect to pay higher taxes to retire these debts. Speaking of retirement, have I mentioned Social Security and Medicare? Maybe I shouldn't.

29    So do our straitened circumstances give Jack Benny any more sex appeal? It's hard to believe he could make it on *American Idol,* but we might learn something from him nonetheless, for as any behavioral economist can tell you, there was method in his money-storing madness. From whom, after all, was he protecting his savings if not himself? Self-protective "commitment devices" like Benny's moats and alligators are already being used

here and there—deposits to your retirement account are defended by hungry tax collectors, after all—and if we're smart, we'll use them even more in the future.

30    Fortunately, thrift is far from the worst thing we can have thrust upon us. To be thrifty, after all, is to save, and to save is not only to keep but to rescue. Thrift is thus a way to redeem yourself not just from the unsexy bondage of indebtedness but also from subjugation to people and efforts that are meaningless to you, or worse. Debt means staying in a pointless job, failing to support needy people or worthwhile causes, accepting the strings that come with dependence, and gritting your teeth when your boss asks you to do something unethical (instead of saying "drop dead"). Ultimately, thrift delivers not just freedom but salvation—which makes it a bargain even Jack Benny could love.

### QUESTIONS FOR ANALYSIS AND DISCUSSION

1. What assumptions does Daniel Akst make about his readers? Would you consider yourself Akst's target audience? For example, what do you need to know in order to understand Akst's first paragraph? His historical references? Explain.
2. What is thrift? What associations does the word have for you? Is it negative, positive, or neutral? Is being thrifty "un-American"? Why has it gained a bad reputation, despite sage advice that saving is a good thing to do?
3. Akst uses many synonyms in his essay to define thrift and thrifty. Which other words does he use in its place? What words have more negative meanings, and which ones have a more positive meaning?
4. The author states that going green is equal to becoming thrifty. What are some examples he gives that prove his point? Besides the examples that Akst lists in his essay, which other ways can leaving a smaller carbon footprint actually put money in your pocket?
5. According to Akst, you can have a "nice life" with a middle-class income and Jack Benny's attitude about money. What is your definition of a "nice life"? Do you agree with the author that a nice life can be had this way?
6. Do you agree with Akst's thesis: being thrifty is more honorable and intelligent than being a spend-thrift? Is there a middle ground? Explain.

## Let It Die
*Douglas Rushkoff*

Over the last 100 years, the United States has weathered the Great Depression, the burst of the tech bubble, as well as several other "crashes" in our economy. Each time, we managed to work ourselves and move on toward dreams of greater prosperity. We are told by financial gurus to "buy low, and sell high," to invest in our 401K plans, and to trust the government with our Social Security and healthcare. We are told that if we play by the rules all will be well. And we believe that the government is there to hold everything together. But maybe the time has come to re-examine our financial system.

Should our government continue to intervene to save banks and businesses from bankruptcy? While we may initially think so, in the next essay, author Douglas Rushkoff explains why he feels that our entire economic system is based on a fragile foundation and why he feels it is time to just "let it die."*

### BEFORE YOU READ

Do big corporations have too much influence over our economy and our daily lives? What role, if any, should our government play in regulating the influence of industry on our economy?

### AS YOU READ

Rushkoff outlines the system upon which our economy is based. Did his information surprise you? Do you think our current system is in need of an update?

1   With any luck, the economy will never recover.

2   In a perfect world, the stock market would decline another 70 or 80 percent along with the shuttering of about that fraction of our nation's banks. Yes, unemployment would rise as hundreds of thousands of formerly well-paid brokers and bankers lost their jobs; but at least they would no longer be extracting wealth at our expense. They would need to be fed, but that would be a lot cheaper than keeping them in the luxurious conditions they're enjoying now. Even Bernie Madoff costs us less in jail than he does on Park Avenue.

3   Alas, I'm not being sarcastic. If you had spent the last decade, as I have, reviewing the way a centralized economic plan ravaged the real world over the past 500 years, you would appreciate the current financial meltdown for what it is: a comeuppance. This is the sound of the other shoe dropping; it's what happens when the chickens come home to roost; it's justice, equilibrium reasserting itself, and ultimately a good thing.

4   I started writing a book three years ago through which I hoped to help people see the artificial and ultimately dehumanizing landscape of corporatism on which we conduct so much of our lives. It's not just that I saw the downturn coming—it's that I feared it wouldn't come quickly or clearly enough to help us wake up from the self-destructive fantasy of an eternally expanding economic frontier. The planet, and its people, were being taxed beyond their capacity to produce. Try arguing that to a banker whose livelihood is based on perpetuating that illusion, or to people whose retirement incomes depend on just one more generation falling for the scam. It's like arguing to Brooklyn's latest crop of brownstone buyers that they've invested in real estate at the very moment the whole market is about to tank. (I did; it wasn't pretty.)

5   Now that the scheme we have mistaken for the real economy is collapsing under its own weight, however, it's a whole lot easier to make these arguments. And, if anything, it's even more important for us to come to grips with the fact that the system in peril is not a natural one, or even one that we should be attempting to revive and restore. The thing that

---

*Douglas Rushkoff, *Arthur Magazine*, March 15, 2009.

is dying—the corporatized model of commerce—has not, nor has it ever been, supportive of the real economy. It wasn't meant to be. And before we start lamenting its demise or, worse, spending good money after bad to resuscitate it, we had better understand what it was for, how it nearly sucked us all dry, and why we should put it out of our misery.

## Chartered Corporations

6 Back in the good ol' days—I mean as far back as the late middle ages—people just did business with each other. As traveling got easier and people got access to new resources and markets, a middle class of merchants and small businesspeople started to get wealthy. So wealthy that they threatened the power of the aristocracy. Monarchs needed to come up with a way to stabilize their own wealth before the free market unseated them.

7     They invented the corporate charter. By granting an exclusive charter, a king could give one of his friends in the merchant class monopoly control over a region or sector. In exchange, he'd get shares in the company. So the businessperson no longer had to worry about competition—his position at the top of the business hierarchy was locked in place, by law. And the monarch never had to worry about losing his authority; businesses with crown-guaranteed charters tend to support the crown.

8     But this changed the shape of business fundamentally. Instead of thriving on innovation and progress, corporate monopolies simply sought to extract wealth from the regions they controlled. They didn't need to compete, anymore, so they just sucked resources from places and people. Meanwhile, people living and working in the real world lost the ability to generate value by or for themselves.

9     For example: In the 1700s, American colonists were allowed to grow corn but they weren't allowed to do anything with it–except sell it at fixed prices to the British East India Trading Company, the corporation sanctioned by England to do business in the colonies. Colonists weren't allowed to sell their cotton to each other or, worse, make clothes out of it. They were mandated, by law, to ship it back to England where clothes were fabricated by another chartered monopoly, then shipped back to America where they could be purchased. The American war for independence was less a revolt against England than a revolt against her chartered corporations.

10     The other big innovation of the early corporate era was monopoly currency. There used to be lots of different kinds of money. Local currencies, which helped regions reinvest in their own activities, and centralized currencies, for long distance transactions. Local currencies were earned into existence. A farmer would grow a bunch of grain, bring it to the grain store, and get receipts for how much grain he had deposited. The receipts could be used as money—even by people who didn't need grain at that particular moment. Everyone knew what it was worth.

11     The interesting thing about local, grain-based currencies was that they lost value over time. The people at the grain store had to be paid, and a certain amount of grain was lost to rain or rodents. So every year, the money would be worth less. This encouraged people to spend it rather than save it. And they did. Late Middle Ages workers were paid more for less work time than at any point in history. Women were taller in England in that era than they are today—an indication of their relative health. People did preventative maintenance

on their equipment, and invested in innovation. There was so much extra money looking for productive investment, that people built cathedrals. The great cathedrals of Europe were not paid for with money from the Vatican; they were local investments, made by small towns looking for ways to share their prosperity with future generations by creating tourist attractions.

12    Local currencies favored local transactions, and worked against the interests of large corporations working from far away. In order to secure their own position as well as that of their chartered monopolies, monarchs began to make local currencies illegal, and force locals to instead use "coin of the realm." These centralized currencies worked the opposite way. They were not earned into existence, they were lent into existence by a central bank. This meant any money issued to a person or business had to be paid back to the central bank, with interest.

13    What does that do to an economy? It bankrupts it. Think of it this way: A business borrows 1000 dollars from the bank to get started. In ten years, say, it is supposed to pay back 2000 to the bank. Where does the other 1000 come from? Some other business that has borrowed 1000 from the bank. For one business to pay back what it owes, another must go bankrupt. That, or borrow yet another 1000, and so on.

14    An economy based on an interest-bearing centralized currency must grow to survive, and this means extracting more, producing more and consuming more. Interest-bearing currency favors the redistribution of wealth from the periphery (the people) to the center (the corporations and their owners). Just sitting on money—capital—is the most assured way of increasing wealth. By the very mechanics of the system, the rich get richer on an absolute and relative basis.

15    The biggest wealth generator of all was banking itself. By lending money at interest to people and businesses who had no other way to conduct transactions or make investments, banks put themselves at the center of the extraction equation. The longer the economy survived, the more money would have to be borrowed, and the more interest earned by the bank.

## Financial Meltdown

16 Which is pretty much how things have worked over the past 500 years to today. So what went wrong? Nothing. The system worked exactly as it was supposed to. The problem was that after America's post WWII expansion, there was really no longer any real growth area in the economy from which to extract wealth. We were producing and consuming about as much as we could. Almost no commercial activity was occurring outside the corporate system. There was no room left to grow. Sure, outsourcing, lay-offs, and technology created some efficiencies, but wars, rising costs of health care, and exchange rates essentially offset any gains.

17    Making matters worse, all that capital that the wealthy had accumulated needed markets—even fake markets—in which to be invested. There was a ton of money out there—just nowhere to put it. Nothing on which to speculate.

18    The dot.com boom seemed to offer the promise of a new market, but it fizzled almost as quickly as it rose. So speculators turned instead to real assets, like corn, oil, even real estate. They started investing speculatively on the things that real people need to stay alive.

What real people didn't understand was that there is no way to compete against speculators. Speculators aren't buying homes in which to live—they are buying houses to flip. Speculators aren't buying corn to eat or oil to burn, but bushels to hoard and tankers to park off shore until prices rise. The fact that the speculative economy for cash and commodities accounts for over 95% of economic transactions, while people actually using money and consuming commodities constitute less than 5%, tells us something important. Real supply and demand have almost nothing to do with prices. We do not live in an economy, we live in a Ponzi scheme.

19    Luckily for us, the banks, and the speculators depending on them, made a bad wager: they bet on our continuing capacity to provide a reality on which to base their highly leveraged schemes. We just couldn't do it. They put us between a rock and a hard place. With George W.'s help, they sold us on the notion of home ownership as a prerequisite to the American dream. And they created a number of loan products which made it look as if we could actually afford over-priced homes. The banking industry spent hundreds of millions of dollars lobbying for laws making bankruptcy difficult or impossible for average people to accomplish—while simultaneously selling average people loans that they would never be able to pay back.

20    The banks didn't really care, anyway, since they never meant to keep these loans. They simply provided the cash to mortgage companies, who then packaged the loans. In return for putting up the original cash, the banks also won the right to underwrite the sale of those mortgage packages to investors—investors like pension funds, retirement funds, or you and me. Get it? The banks get all the interest, but we put up all the money. Our retirement accounts and pension funds invest in the very mortgages that we can't pay back. The bank collects any interest, playing both sides of the equation but responsible for neither.

21    And when the whole scheme begins to break down, what do we do? We try to bail out the very banks that created the mess, under the premise that we need these banks in order for business to come back, since only banks can lend the capital required for businesses to flourish.

## Yes, It is Wrong

22 President Obama may be smarter than most of us, but he's still attempting to rescue the very institutions that robbed us in the first place. He's not a socialist, as conservatives may be arguing, but he is a corporatist. Using future tax dollars to fund government job programs is one thing. Using future tax dollars to give banks more money to lend out at interest is robbing from the poor to pay the rich to rob from the poor.

23    As painful as it might be to watch, and as irritating as it might be to those with shrinking retirement savings, the collapse of the centralized corporate economy is ultimately a good thing. It makes room for a real economy to rise up in its place. And while it may be temporarily uncomfortable for the rich, and even temporarily devastating for the poor, it may be the fastest and least violent way to dismantle a system set in place for the benefit of 14th century monarchs who have long since left this earth.

24    If the corporate supermarket chain's debt structure renders it incapable of stocking its shelves this spring, this may be the wake-up call that consumers need to finally subscribe to a Community Supported Agriculture farmer. If the former associate fund analyst at Lehman realizes that he is unable to get a job not just because his industry is contracting but because his work day creates no real value for anyone at all, he will be forced to learn how to do something that does. If an urban elite parent realizes he can no longer pay private school tuition for his kids, maybe he'll consider donating to public school the time he would have spent earning that tuition.

25    In short, the less we are able to depend on business-as-usual to provide for our basic needs, the more we will be forced to provide them for ourselves and one another. Sometimes we'll do this for free, because we like each other, or live in the same community. Sometimes we'll exchange services or favors. Sometimes we'll use one of the alternative, local currencies coming into use across the country as central bank-issued currencies become too hard to get without a corporate job.

26    Deprived of centralized banks and corporations, we'll be forced to do things again. And in the process, we'll find out that these institutions were not our benefactors at all. They were never meant to be. They were invented to mediate transactions between people, and extract the value that would have passed between us. Far from making commerce or industry more efficient, they served to turn the real world into a set of speculative assets, and real people into debtors.

27    The current financial crisis is the best opportunity we have had in a very long time for a bloodless revolution against the faceless fascism under which we have been living, unaware, for much too long. Let us seize the day.

## QUESTIONS FOR ANALYSIS AND CONSIDERATION

1. According to Rushkoff, "we live in a Ponzi scheme." Look up the actual definition of a Ponzi scheme on the Internet. What is a Ponzi scheme? Do you agree that "a Ponzi scheme" applies to our current economic system?
2. Locate and list the many clichés Rushkoff uses in this essay. Do you find this writing style effective?
3. Rushkoff suggests that our society should return to the old way of economics once practiced in the Middle Ages. Do you see this suggestion as viable? Is it logical? Is the old way really better? Why or why not?
4. What did you think when you read the first sentence of Rushkoff's essay? Did it grab your attention? If you were reading a magazine, would it draw you into the article? How does Rushkoff explain what he means by this controversial statement?
5. The "Tea Party Movement" has recently emerged as a counter response to the government's bailout of the banks. Research the "Tea Party Movement." What is it and what are its goals? In your opinion, is this movement capable of changing the course of our economy and government? Why or why not?

## Reading the Visual

### Scenes from the Depression

Photos from the *Boston Globe*

A sign informing readers that Fremont Pontiac GMC is permanently closed is seen on a door at the Newark, Calif. dealership, Tuesday, March 3, 2009. The dealership closed due to economic conditions earlier this year. (AP Photo/Paul Sakuma)

A RE/MAX Central bus advertises tours of foreclosed homes March 7, 2009 in Las Vegas, Nevada. The real estate group began giving tours for prospective buyers three times a week in February 2008, in an effort to clear inventory of foreclosed properties. They have seen a steady decrease in foreclosure listings since the summer of 2008 in the Las Vegas area. (Ethan Miller/Getty Images)

As new home sales and housing starts hit record lows, empty lots, partially constructed homes, and abandoned ones are seen in a subdivision on January 30, 2009 near Homestead, Florida. Prices in November of 2008 declined 8.7 percent from a year earlier, the biggest drop in records going back to 1991, the Federal Housing Finance Agency reported. (Joe Raedle/ Getty Images)

## QUESTIONS FOR ANALYSIS AND DISCUSSION

1. Why do you think the *Boston Globe* chose these photos, among others, to represent the recession? What exactly do these photos represent?
2. "A picture is worth a thousand words." In a single paragraph for each, summarize what story these photographs are trying to visually convey.
3. Richard Florida observes that during times of economic hardship, certain areas of the country are hit harder than others. Has this recession been more equalizing than others? Why or why not?

# Generation Debt
*Anya Kamenetz*

Many young Americans report that they are trapped by low-end jobs with low wages, few opportunities, high taxes, and huge student loans. Many fear that they are facing a lifetime of recycled debt. Sometime over the last 20 years, something happened: The cost of a college education skyrocketed. It became acceptable to carry large debt. People stopped expecting to work in one company for their entire career and started hopping around in search of a better deal. Unable to get on solid financial footing, college graduates started putting off marriage plans and moved back in with their parents. In this excerpt from the book with the same title, Anya Kamenetz explores some of the challenges her generation faces in an economic landscape vastly different from that of her parents' only a generation before.*

## BEFORE YOU READ

In this essay, Anya Kamenetz observes that young adulthood is emerging as a "new" distinct phase of life, similar to the recognition of childhood and adolescence in centuries before. What are your expectations from this phase of your life? What challenges do you face, and what benefits might you expect? If you are past young adulthood, compare your experience with the trend now emerging. What might average young adulthood look like 20 years from now?

## AS YOU READ

Kamenetz describes the typical college student. Summarize the characteristics she cites, and then describe how you and your fellow classmates compare.

1   The simplest definition of a "generation" is those people who pass through a specific stage of life at the same time. We tend to think of human life stages as natural demarcations of growth, like the rings on a tree. Yet social and economic structures also determine the divisions between infancy and old age. Since 1960, when historian Philippe Aries published the book *Centuries of Childhood*, scholars have been writing about how childhood was "discovered" for sentimental and moralistic reasons in eighteenth and nineteenth-century Europe. Before this historical turning point, infants were often farmed out to indifferent wet nurses, and seven-year-olds herded sheep.

2   Likewise, for most of human history, sexual maturity occurred just a year or two before marriage, and adolescence, as we know it, didn't exist. As Thomas Hine chronicles in *The Rise and Fall of the American Teenager,* when the United States was industrializing in the nineteenth century, people thirteen and up were the backbone of the semiskilled workforce. Teenagers came to America alone as immigrants. They ran weaving machines, dug

---

*Anya Kamenetz, *Generation Debt* (excerpt), 2007.

mines, herded cattle, picked cotton, and fought wars. If they weren't slaves or indentured servants, they contributed their earnings to their families of origin until they got married and started families of their own.

3    American psychologist G. Stanley Hine popularized the term "adolescent" in 1904, as the rise of compulsory schooling and the move away from an agricultural economy began to lengthen the expected period of youthful preparation. It wasn't until the Great Depression, though, that teenagers' economic life assumed the limits it has today. Hine points out that Roosevelt's New Deal was explicitly designed to take jobs away from young people and give them to heads of households. Teenagers were thus compelled to enroll in high school in much larger numbers than ever before. Young people's secondary economic role has persisted ever since. The affluence and restiveness of postwar America gave new cultural prominence in the 1950s to the modern version of teenhood, a distinct stage of life, a subculture, and a commercial market, funded ultimately by parents. The accepted age of independence for the middle class and above was pushed forward to twenty-one.

4    Now the postmillennial years are bringing in an entirely new life stage: "emerging adulthood," a term coined by developmental psychologist Jeffrey Jensen Arnett in a 2000 article. The Research Network on Transitions to Adulthood at the University of Pennsylvania is a group of a dozen or so experts in various fields: sociologists, policy experts, developmental psychologists, and economists. Their 2005 book, *On the Frontier of Adulthood*, explores emerging adulthood in depth. "More youth are extending education, living at home longer, and moving haltingly, or stopping altogether, along the stepping stones of adulthood," writes Frank F. Furstenberg, chair of the network. "A new period of life is emerging in which young people are no longer adolescents but not yet adults. . . . It is simply not possible for most young people to achieve economic and psychological autonomy as early as it was half a century ago." The underlying reason, once again, is an economic shift, this time to a labor market that rewards only the highly educated with livable and growing wages.

5    In 2002, there were 68 million people in the United States aged eighteen to thirty-four. The social and economic upheaval of the past three decades, not to mention that of the past five years, affects us in complex ways. We have all come of age as part of Generation Debt.

6    The Penn researchers use five milestones of maturity: leaving home, finishing school, becoming financially independent, getting married, and having a child. By this definition, only 46 percent of women and 31 percent of men were grown up by age thirty in 2000, compared to 77 percent of women and 65 percent of men of the same age in 1960.

7    "I went from being a child to being a mother," says Doris, now in her fifties. "I was married at twenty. By thirty I had four children and was divorced." Doris completed college and a master's degree while keeping house and raising her children, then supported her family as a medical physicist. Doris' youngest daughter, Miriam, graduated from Southern Connecticut State University in 2000, after six years of work and school, with $20,000 in student loans and $5,000 in credit card debt. Now, at twenty-nine, she is living in Madison, Wisconsin, and training to be a commodities broker, a job she could have pursued with only a high school diploma. Her mother, who bought her first house with her

husband in her early twenties, helped Miriam pay off her credit cards and gave her the down payment on the condo she lives in. Miriam earns $28,000 a year and just manages the minimum payments on her loans. She is single. She hasn't passed the five milestones of adulthood; she is barely out to the driveway.

8     Young people are falling behind first of all because of money. College tuition has grown faster than inflation for three decades, and faster than family income for the past fifteen years. Federal aid has lagged behind. An unprecedented explosion of borrowing has made up the difference between what colleges charge and what families can afford. Between 1995 and 2005, the total volume of federal student loans rose 249 percent after inflation, to over $61 billion. Two-thirds of four-year students are graduating with loan debt, an average of up to $19,200 in 2004 and growing every year. Three out of four college students have credit cards, too, carrying an average unpaid balance of $2,169 in 2005. Nearly a quarter of all students, according to a 2004 survey, are actually putting their tuition directly on plastic.

9     Even as the price has risen, more young people than ever aspire to college. Over 90 percent of high school graduates of all backgrounds say in national surveys that they hope to go on to college. Yet the inadequacy of aid shoots down their hopes. As a direct consequence of the decline in public investment in education at every level, young people today are actually less educated than their parents. The nationwide high school graduation level peaked in 1970 at 77 percent. It was around 67 percent in 2004. According to a recent study cited in the 2004 book *Double the Numbers*, by Richard Kazis, Joel Vargas, and Nancy Hoffman, of every 100 younger people who begin their freshman year of high school, just 38 eventually enroll in college, and only 18 graduate within 150 percent of the allotted time—six years for a bachelor's degree or three years for an associates' degree. Only 24.4 percent of the adult population has a B.A., according to the 2000 Census, and those 25 to 34 years old are a little less likely to have one than 45- to 54-year-olds. Sociologists call noncollege youth "the forgotten majority."

10     Statistically, the typical college student is a striving young adult; nearly half are 24 or older. She (56 percent are women) is spending several years in chronic exhaustion splitting her days between a nearly full-time, low-wage job, and part-time classes at a community college or four-year public university. She uses her credit cards to make ends meet—for books, meals, and clothes—and barely manages the minimum payments. Overloaded and falling behind, she is likely to drop out for a semester or for good. Almost one in three Americans in his or her twenties is a college dropout, compared with one in five in the late 1960s.

11     What happens to the three out of four young people who don't get a four-year degree? They are much more likely to remain in the working class than previous generations. Youths eighteen to twenty-four are the most likely to hold minimum wage jobs, giving them a poverty rate of 30 percent in 2000, according to the U.S. Census; that's the highest of any age group. For those aged twenty-five to thirty-four, the poverty rate is 15 percent, compared with 10 percent for older working adults.

12     Policy analyst Heather McGhee, formerly of the think tank Demos, points out, when the Boomers were entering the workforce in 1970, the nations' largest private employer was General Motors. They paid an average wage of $17.50 an hour in today's dollars. The largest employer in the post-industrial economy is Wal-Mart.

13    Their average wage? Eight dollars an hour. The service-driven economy is also a youth-driven economy, burning young people's energy and potential over a deep-fat fryer. McDonalds is the nation's largest youth employer; workers under 24 make up nearly half of the food services, department store, and grocery store workforce nationwide. The working world has always been tough for those starting out, but today's economy relies on a new element—a "youth class." The entire labor market is downgrading toward what was once entry level.

14    For better-off, college-educated sons and daughters, it's the same song, different verse. An astonishing 44 percent of dependent students from families making over $100,000 a year borrowed money for school in 2002. Credit card debt is higher for the middle class than for the poor. Unable to find good jobs with a bachelor's degree, young people are swelling graduate school classes, only to join the ranks of the unemployed or underemployed, after all.

15    The middle class has been shrinking for two decades. On a family-by-family basis, this means that many people my age who grew up in comfort and security are experiencing a startling decline in their standard of living. Median annual earnings for male workers 25 to 34 sank nearly 20 percent in constant dollars between 1971 and 2002. We start out in the working world with large monthly debt payments but without health insurance, pension benefits, or dependable jobs. It is impossible to predict whether we will be able to make up these deficits with higher earnings later on, but the evidence suggests that most of us will not.

16    In the 1960s the phrase "midlife crisis" captured the malaise of educated middleclass man confronting his mortality and an unfulfilling job or family life. Today "quarter-life crisis" has entered the lexicon for a generation whose unbelievably expensive educations didn't guarantee them success, a sense of purpose, or even a livable income.

      When we talk about economics, we are also talking about ambition, responsibility, trust, and family. The new economic realities are distorting the life paths and relationships of the young. We are spending more time moving in and out of school, finding and losing jobs. Some of us move back home, and we put off marriage, children, and home buying. The older generation's response to these changes has been a chorus of disapproval and dismay.

17    The scholars of the Research Network on Transitions to Adulthood, relying on hard data, make the point that economic factors far outweigh psychological ones in explaining what has happened to young adults. "The current changing timetable of adulthood has given rise to a host of questions about whether current generations of young people are more dependent on their parents, less interested in growing up, and more wary of making commitments," they write. Our generation's delay in entering adulthood is often interpreted as a reflection of the narrowed generation gap.

18    In the 1980s, President Ronald Reagan began to dismantle the welfare state and put to rest the liberal dream of ending poverty on a large scale in America. His rhetorical ace was the Cadillac driving, government-cheating "welfare queen." Creating this infamous bogeywoman blamed the poor for their own problems and made taking away their means of support into the morally right thing to do.

19    The lazy, irresponsible, possibly sociopathic "twixter" is this decade's welfare queen, an insidious image obscuring public perception of a real inequity. If you look at where public resources are directed—toward the already wealthy, toward building prisons and expanding the military, away from education and jobs programs—it is easy to see a prejudice against young people as a class.

20    This is not to say that the phenomenon of emerging adulthood in and of itself is exclusively bad. It's a fact of history, like the so-called discoveries of childhood and adolescence before it. This change in the way we experience the life cycle brings upsides and downsides that we may not realize for decades to come. My friends and I overwhelmingly relish the time that we have, as postmillennial young adults, to try out prospective jobs, travel, volunteer, study, and form strong friendships before settling down into career and family responsibilities. Young women, especially, tend to appreciate the way their options have widened, and the chance that medical science gives us to possibly delay motherhood into our thirties and forties. The more money and education you start out with, the better this time of uncertainty starts to look.

21    The problems arise because our society does not recognize this new state of life, and is instead withdrawing resources from young people. Therefore, the majority of us faces obstacles that make it harder to see the bright side of emerging adulthood. In the past few decades, the trend in the United States has been toward smaller families and looser kinship ties. The bonds of kinship in our national family are weakening too. It's not too dramatic to say that the nation is abandoning its children. In everything from national budget deficits to the rise of household debt to cuts in student aid and public funds for education, Americans are living in the present at the expense of the future.

### QUESTIONS FOR ANALYSIS AND DISCUSSION

1. What is the purpose of Kamenetz's recounting of the history of childhood and how childhood has been viewed over the centuries? What point is she trying to support by providing us with this background?

2. Kamenetz observes that the New Deal was largely responsible for our expectations of teenhood today. What factor does she identify as responsible for another shift that marks young adulthood?

3. What are the "five milestones of maturity"? Where are you on the timeline? Have you followed a linear timeline, or have you hopped around, reaching some milestones out of order? At what age would you expect to reach all five milestones? Explain.

4. What reasons does Kamenetz give for why young people are "falling behind"? Explain.

5. What is the "the forgotten majority"? Why are they forgotten? What does this segment of people represent now and in the future? Explain.

6. What is the author's opinion of low-wage and/or service-driven employment? What does she imply happens to young workers who do not earn college degrees?

## Millennials' Heads Under a Rock

*Ed Schipul*

Today's college graduates face one of the toughest labor markets since the Great Depression. Raised as part of the "praise" generation in which they were told they were special and could achieve almost anything, many young adults are left wondering what went wrong. In this next article, blogger and marketing consultant Ed Schipul explains why things are different for this generation, why they need to change their expectations, and why they have reason to be more than a little upset with the Baby Boomers.*

### BEFORE YOU READ

What are your expectations of employment after college?

### AS YOU READ

How did the spending habits of the Baby Boomers set the stage for the current economic crisis? Why do members of the millennial generation have reason to be upset with the consumer habits of the Baby Boomers?

1 The GI generation, by all accounts, appears to have raised one of the biggest groups of spoiled kids our country has ever seen. The Baby Boomers. And the Boomers are burying the Millennial generation and their grandkids in debt and chaos. Pretending deficit spending isn't just a deferred tax increase (it is). And that seems wrong to this Gen X'er.

2 In the book *Generations, The History of America's Future*, the authors describe the Boomers as:

The Boomers, who came to college after Eisenhower and before the Carter malaise of 1979. These were the babies of optimism and hubris, Beaver Cleaver and Musketeers, the

*Ed Schipul, *The List*, August 8, 2009.

## Recession a Dose of Reality for Young Workers
*Megan K. Scott*

Molly Stach thought she was doing everything right until she got laid off from her public relations job in December. Since then, the 26-year-old has been struggling with self-doubt.

"Why don't they want to hire me?" she asked of the companies not responding to the résumés she sends out. "I went through four years of college, graduated. You get praised while you are working and then all the sudden you are not employable."

For 20-somethings who are losing their first or second jobs because of the recession, the economic downturn has been an especially bitter pill. Many of them have been raised to believe they can do anything and be anything, and are finding their high expectations dashed.

"Many were raised to believe that the world was their oyster," said Alexandra Robbins, author of *Conquering Your Quarterlife Crisis*. "And in this kind of economy, that's just not the case."

The national unemployment rate for people ages 20 to 24 was 12.9 percent in February, up from 9 percent a year ago and higher than the overall unemployment rate of 8.1 percent, according to Bureau of Labor Statistics. For those ages 25 to 29, the rate—not seasonally adjusted—was 10.6 percent.

Getting laid-off is a humbling experience for Gen Yers, many of whom have never experienced real financial hardship or big disappointment, said Nancy Molitor, a clinical psychologist in Wilmette, Ill. "A lot of these kids grew up thinking they were going to be able to have it all."

While 20-somethings don't generally have the responsibilities of older workers, getting laid off is in other ways a harder blow because they are still trying to figure out what to do with their lives and are "ardent about doing something meaningful for a living," Robbins said.

Craig Hengel, 27, of St. Cloud,

post-Sputnik high school kids whose SAT scores declined for seventeen straight years, student strikers, flower-child hippies and draft resisters (30).

3    Much of this can be summed up from the famous line from the musical *Hair* that goes:

"... I ain't dying for no one!"

4    Of course that's not exactly true. While some boomers were at Woodstock, many were in Vietnam (including my father who proudly served). And being a complex group of people some Boomers were in both Vietnam and Woodstock! *But overall they are divided. They don't like each other.*

5    Let's be blunt. *The Baby Boomers as a group have been divided and the conservatives and the liberals in this generation will NEVER agree. **Ever***. Except on one thing they agree—that their generation is somehow special and warrants deficit spending. They will slide into home plate at the end of life having spent every penny and lived life to the fullest. Whoohoo!

6    Yet can you imagine Andrew Carnegie spending every penny on the way out the door? Or any parent from the 50s? The values changed from "build a legacy," "provide for the family" to "have a helluva ride!" A generation that proudly says: "Spending My Children's Inheritance" on the bumper sticker of their RV. Towing their jeep.

7    Or rather, they did have that bumper sticker. Until the economy went to hell in a hand basket built on no-money-down mortgages (because everyone has a right to a house!?) that were then securitized (translation: no accountability). And it all blew up. Oooops. This has been documented in thousands of ways in the media. OK, let's have a moment: "Transcendental meditation ... on the ocean of reality ... is LOVE!"

9    Again from *Hair* of course.

10   Gah. Checking the deficit clock as I type this, we are at 11,174,021,379,855. I had to type that because the online clock was going too fast for me to copy-paste. Really. And according to the *Urban Dictionary*, the Federal Deficit/Debt is defined as:

The perpetual and perpetually increasing debt that the United States of America has due to the federal government's unlimited debting power with the Federal Reserve.

11   So what does this have to do with the Millennials? Well, they don't see what is happening yet. They haven't quite figured out they are being HOSED! With their internal focus they haven't looked up from their uber cool sushi twitter meetup at the storms on the horizon yet. (Photos posted on Facebook later!) *Yes, there are clouds there my friends.* And they are owned by the Chinese. And I love the Chinese, especially the food, but we don't get to elect their leaders (does anyone?) and this is influence without representation, right?

12   Megan K. Scott wrote a recent AP article titled "A bitter pill for 20-somethings" in which the subject asks:

Minn., was surprised to be let go from his job at a printing company.

"Losing my job is something I never thought about because I am educated, very hard working and have never had to deal with something like this," he said.

In previous recessions, companies tended to let go of more senior workers because of their high salaries, said Andrew Sum, director of the Center for Labor Market Studies at Northeastern University. But he said younger workers are faring worse this time around as employers hold on to the workers who have knowledge, experience and better work habits.

Brianna D'Amico, 23, was the first to go at the high-end retail group where she landed a job in Washington, D.C. She had been there six months when the company restructured; everyone else had five or more years of experience.

D'Amico spends hours looking for jobs each week. "I know something will come for me, something good is around the corner," she said.

"Why don't they want to hire me?" she asked of the companies not responding to the resumes she sends out. "I went through four years of college, graduated. You get praised while you are working and then all the sudden you are not employable."

13    Because ToTo, this isn't Fun-Fair-Positive-Work where there is no-score-keeping and an everyone-gets-a-trophy award dinner at the end. Companies have REAL competitors. It's called capitalism and it is tough! Why hire a 39.5-hour-per-week-I'm-doing-you-a-favor-if-I-show-up employee when you can hire an experienced 40 year old? The article continues:

> "In previous recessions, companies tended to let go of more senior workers because of their high salaries, said Andrew Sum, director of the Center for Labor Market Studies at Northeastern University. But he said younger workers are faring worse this time around as *employers hold on to the workers who have knowledge, experience and better work habits.*"

14    Ouch. So when the Millennials figure out that the world is in fact not their oyster. And that they have been sold into debt by the Baby Boomers. Will they get mad? Probably not. Because as Ellen Goodman points out in "Meltdown stoking fears of generational conflict" (originally called "The Virtue of Working Longer"), people don't think in generations. She says:

> The folks revving up generational conflict overlook the fact that most of us do not live or think in age cohort groups. We belong to families. If public money is transferred upward from younger workers to older retirees, private money flows downward from older parents to adult children and grandchildren. In this economy, some older workers are clinging to their jobs to keep the younger employed members of their own families afloat.

15    In summary, the Baby Boomers in self-congratulations deficit spent to have a good life. They bought the house in Florida on money stolen from the future in the form of deficits. And their politicians call it "deficit spending" instead of "a future tax increase" so they can be re-elected. And while the deficit isn't going away, the Millennials have stolen the money back from the boomers because the Boomer's Florida house is worth 40 cents on the dollar. But as a family and a tribe everyone has less money and less time.

16    It's like two fishermen fighting over money on the way back to shore, only to have it fall over board lost forever. They spend the rest of the ride back to shore mad at each other, but it doesn't change the fact that the money is GONE. Truly neither won. The Boomers are going to have to keep working. ("Wah! I was promised I wouldn't have to!!") And the Millennials are going to have to work much harder. ("Not fair! I should get a trophy even if I work less than everyone else!") And everyone is mad at everyone. Just friggin' great.

Another line from *Hair*.

> What do we want? PEACE!
> When do we want it? NOW!

17    I suspect the Boomers will continue to act in their own self interest. Which won't get us to the desired "peace." When exactly will the Millennials figure out what is going on? And what will they do about it?

## QUESTIONS FOR ANALYSIS AND DISCUSSION

1. How are the Baby Boomers "burying their grandkids"? How does Schipul twist this phrase to apply to his overarching point that the Baby Boomers have created a mess for the younger generation to clean up?

2. Why does Schipul reference the 1970s musical *Hair*? How does this musical apply to the points he raises? If necessary, look up the theme and context of the musical online before you answer this question.

3. What is Schipul's opinion of the Baby Boomers? Of Gen-Y and the Millennial generation? What generation do you think he is from and how does his age help shape his view of the generations he cites?

4. What response does Schipul give the student cited by Megan Scott in her AP article? What tone does he use? Why?

5. What does Schipul hope to achieve with this article? What change does he hope to influence? Explain.

## Maxed Out

*James D. Scurlock*

1 *much easier to get in college.*
2 *learn how to manage their money.*
3 *Out of money to pay emergency situation*

Many of us know that feeling overwhelmed by debt is awful. This next piece describes how some college students felt so helpless and hopeless because of their debt that they took their own lives. Director James Scurlock interviewed bereft parents for his documentary, *Maxed Out*, and uncovered a predatory world in which credit card companies target students they know have no income, because they believe "Mommy and Daddy" will bail their kids out. But when parents have their own financial burdens, or when kids are too embarrassed to reveal their panic, the results can be deadly. *

### BEFORE YOU READ

Consider the psychology of credit cards. What does it mean to own them? How does it make you feel? If you have a card, how does it influence your purchasing decisions? How do you feel when you use it?

### AS YOU READ

What does the term "low-hanging fruit" mean? How are college students "low-hanging fruit" to credit card companies?

1  Janne O'Donnell remembers when she took her son Sean to college. A National Merit Scholar from a small town in Oklahoma, Sean, she remembers, "was so excited to be in the big city. *Dallas*." As they carried Sean's belongings across the relatively small

---

*James D. Scurlock, *Maxed Out: Hard Times in the Age of Easy Credit*, 2007.

campus of the University of Texas at Dallas (UTD), she noticed a number of tables advertising credit cards. "But I didn't worry," she recalls. "Sean was 18, he didn't have a job. Who would give him a credit card?"

2    What she has learned since that day makes the question seem impossibly naïve. Not only would they give him a credit card, they would practically shove it down his throat. And as soon as he maxed that one out, they'd reward him with another one, and another. In the industry's parlance, he was "building his credit history." "Sean was a smart kid," Janne says, "but he didn't know how he got in, or how to get out." Sean would drop out of UTD, move back home, and find himself working two minimum-wage jobs, paying down $12,000 in debt on ten credit cards and saving money—to declare bankruptcy. "I just didn't understand," Janne says. "It was something that was never in my world." Back in Janne's day, you and your husband could both work full-time jobs and still not qualify for a single credit card.

3    The Visa and MasterCard offers Sean received as he was digging himself deeper and deeper into desperation describe an extraordinarily responsible young man, one who had "graduated into adulthood," whose "responsible use of credit" was to be rewarded by a coveted spot on a number of VIP lists—in short, a platinum young man who deserved a limitless supply of credit. What exactly he did to deserve that credit remains a mystery to his mother.

4    "If you're working, or if you're in a trade school," Janne tells me, "they don't want you. Maybe they realize that you know the value of a dollar. It's the *college* students who get the credit card offers. So we're setting up a two-tiered system and I believe that they're manipulating the students. An easy market."

5    Several years ago Janne met another mother, Trisha, from the Oklahoma City area whose daughter had hanged herself in her dorm room after racking up a modest $2,500 in credit card debt (the young woman, Mitzi, didn't leave a note but did spread her credit card bills on her bed by way of explanation). Trisha and Janne had separately written their children's schools demanding that credit card companies be kicked off campus, and they had both been ignored. Then they took their stories to the newspapers, to *60 Minutes,* and finally, with the help of a local congressman, to the Oklahoma state legislature. A bill was introduced prohibiting credit card companies from marketing on college campuses, an idea which has since been made law in several other states. When it came time to testify, Trisha and Janne found themselves opposing the financial industry and its lobbyists. "We were sitting across a table from them," Janne recalls, "and they were discussing how much money they contributed to each congressman's campaign. That bill didn't have a chance. They didn't want to listen to these two mothers. They wanted to listen to the money." As it turns out, Janne was right: Congressmen have their own preferred customer lists.

6    In one of her last appearances before Congress, Julie Williams, the comptroller of the currency and thus the nation's top banking regulator, assured the Senate Banking Committee that credit card companies have not only developed complex models that determine exactly how much credit to extend to a particular student at a particular school, but that these models have appropriate risk metrics built in. I would be curious to see her explain this to Janne and Trisha. I would be even more curious to know the magic number these banks and credit card companies had assigned to Sean and Mitzi—in other words, their price. What that company expected to make over a lifetime from Janne's and Trisha's kids by selling them more credit—not just credit cards but home mortgages (and then equity lines of credit), auto loans, student loans, credit insurance, late fees, and so

on. No one has ever asked the credit card companies for that particular number, but one thing is certain: It is much larger than most people realize, and the competition for young customers is getting more and more intense.

7    Ten years ago, First USA paid the University of Tennessee $19 million for access to its students and alumni—their telephone numbers, Social Security numbers, and addresses— setting off a bidding war for access to college students. In 2000, the company raised the stakes again by purchasing two high school students from New Jersey who'd offered to sell themselves as human billboards to any company willing to pay their college tuitions. If positioning the two friends—"Chris" and "Luke"—as a couple of hip surfer dudes who just happened to love First USA seemed a tad corny, the two students, who were working at a public relations firm, had already developed the perfect angle. Chris (who was photographed driving a brand-new BMW convertible) and Luke (the edgier one, with the mutton chops and board shorts to prove it) would position themselves as spokesmen for financial responsibility (wink, nod)! Even for a credit card company, this was an act of extraordinary chutzpah, meaning that the media ate it up. Chris and Luke appeared on FOX News, the *Today* show, and *Good Morning America,* to name a few. Their website, www.chrisandluke.com, was featured on *Yahoo!* and received millions of hits. The financially responsible "celebrity surfers" from New Jersey who were ferried to photo ops in limos were a hit, at least for a few months.

8    In the end, the marriage of credit card behemoth and surfer-dude students turned sour. Chris dropped out of Pepperdine to start a career in the independent film business, and Luke tired of being manipulated by bossy PR people from First USA, though he does admit that being flown in a private jet for lunch at the company's headquarters in Chicago was pretty cool. Plus, First USA was more about boring business mags like *Forbes* and *BusinessWeek* than about MTV and *Rolling Stone.* "We wanted to delve deeper into the aspect of financial responsibility but we got the feeling that First USA was just a little more interested in getting credit card sign-ups," Chris relates in one of the less shocking revelations I'll hear in my lifetime. He estimates that, in exchange for the $50,000 First USA spent on the duo's freshman-year college tuition, the company has received roughly $20 million in free publicity and hundreds of thousands of new, college-age cardholders. Despite this appearing to be a fairly awesome deal for First USA, Luke says the company paid their tuition weeks late, nearly causing an early end to both his and Chris's college careers. "It was just weird," Luke says with a straight face.

9    Ultimately, there is one customer far more valuable to the corporations than the 18-to-24 demographic, and that customer is Wall Street, which supplies the funds that lenders like First USA resell in small chunks to people like Chris and Luke and Sean and Mitzi. At the time Chris and Luke were being hyped on the pages of *The Wall Street Journal* and *Fortune,* First USA had just been acquired by a larger bank, Bank One, for close to $8 billion. One of First USA's major selling points had been its access to the student market. Perhaps Bank One recognized the perfect opportunity to justify its big purchase, to show analysts that its new brand was hip with the kids, that it would continue to aggressively pick the low-hanging fruit—the easy market, as Janne put it.

10   Like Chris, Janne's son eventually dropped out of college. Sean moved back home and tried to figure out a way to declare bankruptcy, finish school, and somehow get a law degree, his dream. Living at home and working more low-wage jobs must have been humiliating for a National Merit Scholar who'd left for the big city with so much potential, but it

was harder on Janne and her husband, who were forced to choose between bailing out Sean or helping their younger son through college.)In the end Janne couldn't see denying her other son the same opportunity they'd given Sean. Sean accepted the decision, told his mother he felt like a failure, and two days later hung himself. Thereafter Sean's memory was commemorated by a constant stream of phone calls from bill collectors, threatening letters, and more offers for credit, one of which read, "We want you back!" One day a collector called up and suggested that Janne should pay up to honor Sean's memory.

11     "I gave you my son," she replied. "What more do you want?"

### QUESTIONS FOR ANALYSIS AND DISCUSSION

1. Sean's mother dismisses the credit card tables on campus, because she knows that her son doesn't have job, so she presumes he would not be given a credit card. Yet Sean does get a card. Why are credit card companies giving cards to students without jobs? How do they assume balances will be paid? Do you think it makes sense to give a credit card to an unemployed student? Is it a matter of self-management of one's finances? Explain.

2. Review the story of Chris and Luke, who sold themselves to First USA in exchange for college tuition. What accounted for their success? Why did they discontinue their relationship with the credit card company? Would you be more likely to sign up for a credit card promoted by another college student?

3. Janne mentions that the language used in letters offering Sean more credit made him seem like an outstanding credit card user worthy of obtaining even more credit. How do credit cards market themselves to students? If possible try to gather some offers on your own campus, such as near the campus bookstore, on tables, or even online. How does the language appeal to students and entice them to obtain a card?

4. Most people never read the fine print on their credit card agreements. Go online and locate the user agreement for a credit card from a major credit card issuer such as MasterCard, Visa, or Discover. Review the agreement and discuss whether the terms are clear. Identify any policies that seem particularly noteworthy.

*what Is average debt*

## Why Won't Anyone Give Me a Credit Card?
*Kevin O'Donnell*

Many of today's graduates carry credit card debt. For many years, credit card companies were falling over themselves trying to entice college students to sign on the dotted line, much to the chagrin of credit counselors and parents alike. While carrying credit card debt is never a good idea it turns out that college may be the best time to start building your credit profile. As recent graduate Kevin O'Donnell explains, he doesn't have bad credit, but the companies keep turning him down. Why the change of heart?

**BEFORE YOU READ**

Do you have a credit card? If so, did you get it through a campus offer? Through a department store? How old were you when you got your first card, and how well have you managed your credit profile?

**AS YOU READ**

O'Donnell complains that no one will offer him a credit card. Why are credit card companies so eager to offer college students cards while they are still in school, but reluctant once these students graduate?

1 While picking up a new shirt at J.Crew a few months ago, I asked about opening one of those store credit cards—you know, the ones that give you a discount on the first purchase. I filled out the paperwork, and the cashier phoned the lending bank and gave them my information. "You'll hear if you've been approved by mail in a few days," he said. A few weeks later, I got a letter from World Financial Network National Bank (how dubious does that sound?) saying they would not be able to extend me a line of credit.

2 The J.Crew card was the fourth one I'd applied for over the past year, and it was my third rejection. I am a 27-year-old professional with a full-time job, no mortgage, no children, and no student loans. With the exception of one outstanding dental bill, I have absolutely no debt. I pay my bills on time; I never miss rent. I should be an ideal candidate for a credit card, right? Not so.

3 With the economy in the dumps, it's harder than ever to get a card. The amount of credit card offers mailed to U.S. households has dropped precipitously in 2009, from an estimated 1.13 billion in the first fiscal quarter of 2008 to 372.4 million in the same period this year. Why the decline in junk mail? Last month, credit card default rates reached their highest point since the recession began. Bank of America claimed its rate hit 14.54 percent, while Citigroup (which issues MasterCard) saw its default rate go from 10.03 percent to 12.14 percent. American Express, however, reported a slight decrease—from 8.9 percent to 8.4 percent—in default rates. Perhaps that decline is related to AmEx offering certain customers a $300 bribe to *close* their accounts.

4 Well, that explains why my American Express application got rejected. But why, despite my decent financial record, am I a particularly bad candidate for a credit card? I've got no credit history. Typically, the best time to get your first credit card is in college, when banks litter campuses with offers. One study estimated that students receive 25 to 50 applications per semester. I was always wary of getting a credit card as an undergrad. I was living hand-to-mouth, and it was always easy enough to pick up a bar tab with a debit card. What I didn't realize was that I'd very soon need a credit card to live. If I'm doomed to a life without plastic, what am I going to do if I want to buy a house or lease a car? There are certain things you can't put on a debit card.

5 My quest for credit is a paradoxical one: How can I establish a credit history when banks won't let me create one in the first place? When my American Express, MasterCard, and Continental Chase Rewards applications were denied, I did what friends and relatives advised—try to take out a card with a department store, hence the J.Crew Card. It turns out they gave me bad advice—J.Crew, just like everybody else I had tried before, requires

applicants to have a prior credit history. Gail Cunningham, the spokeswoman for the National Foundation for Credit Counseling, told me that, historically, gas cards and department store cards have been relatively easy to get because the companies' "risk is pretty small—how much can you charge at the filling station?" But in this time of economic decline, even those once-freewheeling retailers are cutting back on the number of applications they approve. Standard & Poor's recently reported that U.S. retail outlets that extend credit claimed losses of 12.2 percent in May, the highest since S&P started tracking such data in January 2000.

6    So what *should* I do to get a credit card? I could just keep filling out applications—and I'd probably have a better chance with smaller community banks, as they didn't suffer the financial blows that the larger institutions did. But sending in loads of applications will probably hurt me in the end. When lenders review applicants, they look at five factors: identification, account history, public records (bankruptcy filings, court records of tax liens), consumer statements (challenges to the status of an account with a lender), and inquiries. That last item is the most crucial for those of us with no credit: It shows how many times lenders have requested to review an applicant's credit history. The more times that information has been reviewed (and rejected), the more suspicious you look as an applicant. Since I have no credit history, I basically don't exist to these lenders—and since I've only started applying for credit in earnest since the start of the credit crunch, I pose more of a gamble to these banks, who aren't willing to take risks on applicants who can't prove their fiscal prudence.

7    As a last resort, I went to a branch of Chase Bank, the place that happily accepts my twice-monthly direct deposits. "You don't have credit?" the costumer service rep asked. "Well, it's going to be very hard to get [a card]." I had heard about secured credit cards, which require you to put up cash as collateral—think of it as a credit card with training wheels. When I asked the financial adviser about that option, she laughed—laughed!—and said Chase didn't offer those. It was like that scene in *Pee-wee's Big Adventure*, when Pee-wee asks to see the basement of the Alamo and gets heckled off the grounds by the tour guide.

8    My quest for credit does have a happy ending, however. Bank of America actually does offer one of those secured credit cards, the BankAmericard Visa Secured Card. Mine just arrived three weeks ago. First purchase? A hotel stay for a friend's wedding out of town. (My balance is almost maxed out for the month, alas.) It will take about a year before I've proven my worth and can get those ridiculous credit-card training wheels removed— my account will be evaluated periodically and, provided I'm in good standing, my credit score will increase. And you know what? If my mailbox suddenly becomes flooded with offers, I promise I won't complain.

## QUESTIONS FOR ANALYSIS AND DISCUSSION

1. Some students are given credit cards by their parents "for emergencies." Do you think this is a good idea? If you have such an arrangement, have you ever used your card for something other than an emergency? What constituted an "emergency"?

2. O'Donnell is very eager to get a credit card. Why does he want one? Is it a marker of adult life? Simply a way of life? Can you survive in this world without credit cards and the debt that comes with them? Explain.

3. O'Donnell experiences difficulties in getting a credit card after he graduates. In light of the points raised by James Scurlock in the previous essay, what advice would you give him?

4. Why is credit important? How can it be useful and valuable? Explain.

## WRITING ASSIGNMENTS

1. Research recent articles on the current financial crisis. Have things improved since the articles in this chapter were written? Based on your research and the information in this chapter, write a short essay in which you forecast what your personal economic future might look like over the next five to ten years.

2. Several writers in this chapter accuse the Baby Boomers for much of the current economic crisis. Why is this particular group scapegoated? How might Baby Boomers respond to these accusations? Identify several points raised in the articles in this section and interview at least three people between 55 and 65 about their views on the economy and the reasons why things got so bad. Do they admit any culpability?

3. Anya Kamentz calls postmillennial youth "generation debt." Is this an appropriate title for this generation? Explain why or why not.

4. Write about a time when you had to make a personal choice that involved incurring debt. Describe the circumstances and your feelings about the incident.

5. What, if anything, can the younger generation learn from the older generation about debt? Speak to a few people older than you about their views of debt, including student loans, credit card debt, and car loans. What is their view of debt? Does it differ from your view? Explain.

6. Several authors refer to parents or grandparents who came of age during the Great Depression with reverence and hold them as examples of a time when people lived better, more financially responsible lives. Research the social impact of the Great Depression. What are the merits of thrift? What role does it play in our social consciousness? Is it as important today as it was 50 years ago? As America once again faces the most challenging economic climate since the Great Depression, how might your generation measure up?

7. Several writers in this chapter cite government and corporate policies that have contributed to the current generation's debt crisis. How can students turn the tide of the "Era of Debt"? Include grassroots efforts, political policy, and campus initiatives in your discussion.

8. Learn more about the history of credit cards at www.PBS.org—The Secret History of the Credit Card. Based on what you learn in the documentary, write an essay in which you explore the ethics of credit card marketing on college campuses.

# Our Lives Online

B efore 1990, very few people had ever heard of the Internet. Only a handful had a cell-phone, and those that were available were clunky and cumbersome, requiring a suitcase-sized transmitter. Social networking meant meeting your friends after work at the local bar where you might exchange a home telephone number or a business card, which was filed in a card index called a Rolodex. No one could have guessed how different things would be in 2010, or how much the Internet age would change American culture, education, personal and business relationships, journalism, commerce and medicine. Today, three-quarters of the U.S. and Canadian population is online.

Today we use the Internet to network for business, friendships, and dating. It is inextricably connected to the daily life and social experience of most Americans. Web communities have changed the way many of us think about meeting people and sharing information. Social networking sites such as MySpace and Facebook have revolutionized the way we communicate with friends and share information. Online databases and encyclopedias have transformed the way we research information and share ideas. Almost 80% of charitable contributions come through the Web. And the brevity required for text messaging and "tweeting" is changing the way the younger generation spells and speaks.

This chapter explores how technology, the Internet, and especially social networking sites influence our relationships with each other and how we relate to the world around us. Is the Internet redefining friendships and what it means to be a "friend"? Is it changing the way we think and speak? Is it rewiring our brains? And if so, should we be worried? The arguments may surprise you.

## "Is Google Making Us Stoopid?"
*Nicholas Carr*

Only a generation ago, researching information could take weeks or months, and consisted of countless hours of reading through mounds of printed magazines, newspapers, and academic journals. To find original sources for research papers students waded through microfiche, card catalogues, and volumes of reference books, reading every detail, looking for just the right phrase or statistic that could prove their point or help make their case. Now researching takes only a few hours working with databases and search engines to find that perfect phrase or statistic to cut and paste into a research paper. The Internet has changed the way we work and study, and it may even be changing the way we think. Are we getting more efficient, or are our brains getting lazy? In this next essay, author Nicholas Carr discusses what the Internet is doing to our brains and how new ways of thinking will change us forever—for better or for worse.*

## BEFORE YOU READ

Do you tend to skim through long pieces of writing or do you become deeply involved in longer works? Which do you prefer—long novels or short abstracts of information and why?

## AS YOU READ

How is society affected by the media? How do new technologies change our way of thinking?

1  "Dave, stop. Stop, will you? Stop, Dave. Will you stop, Dave?" So the supercomputer HAL pleads with the implacable astronaut Dave Bowman in a famous and weirdly poignant scene toward the end of Stanley Kubrick's *2001: A Space Odyssey*. Bowman, having nearly been sent to a deep-space death by the malfunctioning machine, is calmly, coldly disconnecting the memory circuits that control its artificial brain. "Dave, my mind is going," HAL says, forlornly. "I can feel it. I can feel it."

2  I can feel it, too. Over the past few years I've had an uncomfortable sense that someone, or something, has been tinkering with my brain, remapping the neural circuitry, reprogramming the memory. My mind isn't going—so far as I can tell—but it's changing. I'm not thinking the way I used to think. I can feel it most strongly when I'm reading. Immersing myself in a book or a lengthy article used to be easy. My mind would get caught up in the narrative or the turns of the argument, and I'd spend hours strolling through long stretches of prose. That's rarely the case anymore. Now my concentration often starts to drift after two or three pages. I get fidgety, lose the thread, begin looking for something else to do. I feel as if I'm always dragging my wayward brain back to the text. The deep reading that used to come naturally has become a struggle.

3  I think I know what's going on. For more than a decade now, I've been spending a lot of time online, searching and surfing and sometimes adding to the great databases of the Internet. The Web has been a godsend to me as a writer. Research that once required days in the stacks or periodical rooms of libraries can now be done in minutes. A few Google searches, some quick clicks on hyperlinks, and I've got the telltale fact or pithy quote I was after. Even when I'm not working, I'm as likely as not to be foraging in the Web's info-thickets reading and writing e-mails, scanning headlines and blog posts, watching videos and listening to podcasts, or just tripping from link to link to link. (Unlike footnotes, to which they're sometimes likened, hyperlinks don't merely point to related works; they propel you toward them.)

---

*Nicholas Carr, *Atlantic*, Jul./Aug. 2008.

4    For me, as for others, the Net is becoming a universal medium, the conduit for most of the information that flows through my eyes and ears and into my mind. The advantages of having immediate access to such an incredibly rich store of information are many, and they've been widely described and duly applauded. "The perfect recall of silicon memory," *Wired*'s Clive Thompson has written, "can be an enormous boon to thinking." But that boon comes at a price. As the media theorist Marshall McLuhan pointed out in the 1960s, media are not just passive channels of information. They supply the stuff of thought, but they also shape the process of thought. And what the Net seems to be doing is chipping away my capacity for concentration and contemplation. My mind now expects to take in information the way the Net distributes it: in a swiftly moving stream of particles. Once I was a scuba diver in the sea of words. Now I zip along the surface like a guy on a Jet Ski.

5    I'm not the only one. When I mention my troubles with reading to friends and acquaintances—literary types, most of them—many say they're having similar experiences. The more they use the Web, the more they have to fight to stay focused on long pieces of writing. Some of the bloggers I follow have also begun mentioning the phenomenon. Scott Karp, who writes a blog about online media, recently confessed that he has stopped reading books altogether. "I was a lit major in college, and used to be [a] voracious book reader," he wrote. "What happened?" He speculates on the answer: "What if I do all my reading on the web not so much because the way I read has changed, i.e. I'm just seeking convenience, but because the way I THINK has changed?"

6    Bruce Friedman, who blogs regularly about the use of computers in medicine, also has described how the Internet has altered his mental habits. "I now have almost totally lost the ability to read and absorb a longish article on the Web or in print," he wrote earlier this year. A pathologist who has long been on the faculty of the University of Michigan Medical School, Friedman elaborated on his comment in a telephone conversation with me. His thinking, he said, has taken on a "staccato" quality, reflecting the way he quickly scans short passages of text from many sources online. "I can't read *War and Peace* anymore," he admitted. "I've lost the ability to do that. Even a blog post of more than three or four paragraphs is too much to absorb. I skim it."

7    Anecdotes alone don't prove much. And we still await the long-term neurological and psychological experiments that will provide a definitive picture of how Internet use affects cognition. But a recently published study of online research habits, conducted by scholars from University College London, suggests that we may well be in the midst of a sea change in the way we read and think. As part of the five-year research program, the scholars examined computer logs documenting the behavior of visitors to two popular research sites, one operated by the British Library and one by a U.K. educational consortium, that provide access to journal articles, e-books, and other sources of written information. They found that people using the sites exhibited "a form of skimming activity," hopping from one source to another and rarely returning to any source they'd already visited. They typically read no more than one or two pages of an article or book before they would "bounce" out to another site. Sometimes they'd save a long article, but there's no evidence that they ever went back and actually read it. The authors of the study report:

>    It is clear that users are not reading online in the traditional sense; indeed there are signs that new forms of "reading" are emerging as users "power browse" horizontally

through titles, contents pages and abstracts going for quick wins. It almost seems that they go online to avoid reading in the traditional sense.

8    Thanks to the ubiquity of text on the Internet, not to mention the popularity of text-messaging on cell phones, we may well be reading more today than we did in the 1970s or 1980s, when television was our medium of choice. But it's a different kind of reading, and behind it lies a different kind of thinking—perhaps even a new sense of the self. "We are not only *what* we read," says Maryanne Wolf, a developmental psychologist at Tufts University and the author of *Proust and the Squid: The Story and Science of the Reading Brain*. "We are *how* we read." Wolf worries that the style of reading promoted by the Net, a style that puts "efficiency" and "immediacy" above all else, may be weakening our capacity for the kind of deep reading that emerged when an earlier technology, the printing press, made long and complex works of prose commonplace. When we read online, she says, we tend to become "mere decoders of information." Our ability to interpret text, to make the rich mental connections that form when we read deeply and without distraction, remains largely disengaged.

9    Reading, explains Wolf, is not an instinctive skill for human beings. It's not etched into our genes the way speech is. We have to teach our minds how to translate the symbolic characters we see into the language we understand. And the media or other technologies we use in learning and practicing the craft of reading play an important part in shaping the neural circuits inside our brains. Experiments demonstrate that readers of ideograms, such as the Chinese, develop a mental circuitry for reading that is very different from the circuitry found in those of us whose written language employs an alphabet. The variations extend across many regions of the brain, including those that govern such essential cognitive functions as memory and the interpretation of visual and auditory stimuli. We can expect as well that the circuits woven by our use of the Net will be different from those woven by our reading of books and other printed works.

10    Sometime in 1882, Friedrich Nietzsche bought a typewriter—a Malling-Hansen Writing Ball, to be precise. His vision was failing, and keeping his eyes focused on a page had become exhausting and painful, often bringing on crushing headaches. He had been forced to curtail his writing, and he feared that he would soon have to give it up. The typewriter rescued him, at least for a time. Once he had mastered touch-typing, he was able to write with his eyes closed, using only the tips of his fingers. Words could once again flow from his mind to the page.

11    But the machine had a subtler effect on his work. One of Nietzsche's friends, a composer, noticed a change in the style of his writing. His already terse prose had become even tighter, more telegraphic. "Perhaps you will through this instrument even take to a new idiom," the friend wrote in a letter, noting that, in his own work, his "'thoughts' in music and language often depend on the quality of pen and paper."

12    "You are right," Nietzsche replied, "our writing equipment takes part in the forming of our thoughts." Under the sway of the machine, writes the German media scholar Friedrich A. Kittler, Nietzsche's prose "changed from arguments to aphorisms, from thoughts to puns, from rhetoric to telegram style."

13    The human brain is almost infinitely malleable. People used to think that our mental meshwork, the dense connections formed among the 100 billion or so neurons inside our

skulls, was largely fixed by the time we reached adulthood. But brain researchers have discovered that that's not the case. James Olds, a professor of neuroscience who directs the Krasnow Institute for Advanced Study at George Mason University, says that even the adult mind "is very plastic." Nerve cells routinely break old connections and form new ones. "The brain," according to Olds, "has the ability to reprogram itself on the fly, altering the way it functions."

14    As we use what the sociologist Daniel Bell has called our "intellectual technologies"—the tools that extend our mental rather than our physical capacities—we inevitably begin to take on the qualities of those technologies. The mechanical clock, which came into common use in the 14th century, provides a compelling example. In *Technics and Civilization*, the historian and cultural critic Lewis Mumford described how the clock "disassociated time from human events and helped create the belief in an independent world of mathematically measurable sequences." The "abstract framework of divided time" became "the point of reference for both action and thought."

15    The clock's methodical ticking helped bring into being the scientific mind and the scientific man. But it also took something away. As the late MIT computer scientist Joseph Weizenbaum observed in his 1976 book, *Computer Power and Human Reason: From Judgment to Calculation*, the conception of the world that emerged from the widespread use of timekeeping instruments "remains an impoverished version of the older one, for it rests on a rejection of those direct experiences that formed the basis for, and indeed constituted, the old reality." In deciding when to eat, to work, to sleep, to rise, we stopped listening to our senses and started obeying the clock.

16    The process of adapting to new intellectual technologies is reflected in the changing metaphors we use to explain ourselves to ourselves. When the mechanical clock arrived, people began thinking of their brains as operating "like clockwork." Today, in the age of software, we have come to think of them as operating "like computers." But the changes, neuroscience tells us, go much deeper than metaphor. Thanks to our brain's plasticity, the adaptation occurs also at a biological level.

17    The Internet promises to have particularly far-reaching effects on cognition. In a paper published in 1936, the British mathematician Alan Turing proved that a digital computer, which at the time existed only as a theoretical machine, could be programmed to perform the function of any other information-processing device. And that's what we're seeing today. The Internet, an immeasurably powerful computing system, is subsuming most of our other intellectual technologies. It's becoming our map and our clock, our printing press and our typewriter, our calculator and our telephone, and our radio and TV.

18    When the Net absorbs a medium, that medium is re-created in the Net's image. It injects the medium's content with hyperlinks, blinking ads, and other digital gewgaws, and it surrounds the content with the content of all the other media it has absorbed. A new e-mail message, for instance, may announce its arrival as we're glancing over the latest headlines at a newspaper's site. The result is to scatter our attention and diffuse our concentration.

19    The Net's influence doesn't end at the edges of a computer screen, either. As people's minds become attuned to the crazy quilt of Internet media, traditional media have to adapt to the audience's new expectations. Television programs add text crawls and pop-up ads, and magazines and newspapers shorten their articles, introduce capsule summaries, and crowd their pages with easy-to-browse info-snippets. When, in March of this year, the *New*

*York Times* decided to devote the second and third pages of every edition to article abstracts, its design director, Tom Bodkin, explained that the "shortcuts" would give harried readers a quick "taste" of the day's news, sparing them the "less efficient" method of actually turning the pages and reading the articles. Old media have little choice but to play by the new-media rules.

20    Never has a communications system played so many roles in our lives—or exerted such broad influence over our thoughts—as the Internet does today. Yet, for all that's been written about the Net, there's been little consideration of how, exactly, it's reprogramming us. The Net's intellectual ethic remains obscure.

21    About the same time that Nietzsche started using his typewriter, an earnest young man named Frederick Winslow Taylor carried a stopwatch into the Midvale Steel plant in Philadelphia and began a historic series of experiments aimed at improving the efficiency of the plant's machinists. With the approval of Midvale's owners, he recruited a group of factory hands, set them to work on various metalworking machines, and recorded and timed their every movement as well as the operations of the machines. By breaking down every job into a sequence of small, discrete steps and then testing different ways of performing each one, Taylor created a set of precise instructions—an "algorithm," we might say today—for how each worker should work. Midvale's employees grumbled about the strict new regime, claiming that it turned them into little more than automatons, but the factory's productivity soared.

22    More than a hundred years after the invention of the steam engine, the Industrial Revolution had at last found its philosophy and its philosopher. Taylor's tight industrial choreography—his "system," as he liked to call it—was embraced by manufacturers throughout the country and, in time, around the world. Seeking maximum speed, maximum efficiency, and maximum output, factory owners used time-and-motion studies to organize their work and configure the jobs of their workers. The goal, as Taylor defined it in his celebrated 1911 treatise, *The Principles of Scientific Management*, was to identify and adopt, for every job, the "one best method" of work and thereby to effect "the gradual substitution of science for rule of thumb throughout the mechanic arts." Once his system was applied to all acts of manual labor, Taylor assured his followers, it would bring about a restructuring not only of industry but of society, creating a utopia of perfect efficiency. "In the past the man has been first," he declared; "in the future the system must be first."

23    Taylor's system is still very much with us; it remains the ethic of industrial manufacturing. And now, thanks to the growing power that computer engineers and software coders wield over our intellectual lives, Taylor's ethic is beginning to govern the realm of the mind as well. The Internet is a machine designed for the efficient and automated collection, transmission, and manipulation of information, and its legions of programmers are intent on finding the "one best method"—the perfect algorithm—to carry out every mental movement of what we've come to describe as "knowledge work."

24    Google's headquarters, in Mountain View, California—the Googleplex—is the Internet's high church, and the religion practiced inside its walls is Taylorism. Google, says its chief executive, Eric Schmidt, is "a company that's founded around the science of measurement," and it is striving to "systematize everything" it does. Drawing on the terabytes of behavioral data it collects through its search engine and other sites, it carries out thousands of experiments a day, according to the *Harvard Business Review*, and it uses the

results to refine the algorithms that increasingly control how people find information and extract meaning from it. What Taylor did for the work of the hand, Google is doing for the work of the mind.

25   The company has declared that its mission is "to organize the world's information and make it universally accessible and useful." It seeks to develop "the perfect search engine," which it defines as something that "understands exactly what you mean and gives you back exactly what you want." In Google's view, information is a kind of commodity, a utilitarian resource that can be mined and processed with industrial efficiency. The more pieces of information we can "access" and the faster we can extract their gist, the more productive we become as thinkers.

26   Where does it end? Sergey Brin and Larry Page, the gifted young men who founded Google while pursuing doctoral degrees in computer science at Stanford, speak frequently of their desire to turn their search engine into an artificial intelligence, a HAL-like machine that might be connected directly to our brains. "The ultimate search engine is something as smart as people—or smarter," Page said in a speech a few years back. "For us, working on search is a way to work on artificial intelligence." In a 2004 interview with *Newsweek*, Brin said, "Certainly if you had all the world's information directly attached to your brain, or an artificial brain that was smarter than your brain, you'd be better off." Last year, Page told a convention of scientists that Google is "really trying to build artificial intelligence and to do it on a large scale."

27   Such an ambition is a natural one, even an admirable one, for a pair of math whizzes with vast quantities of cash at their disposal and a small army of computer scientists in their employ. A fundamentally scientific enterprise, Google is motivated by a desire to use technology, in Eric Schmidt's words, "to solve problems that have never been solved before," and artificial intelligence is the hardest problem out there. Why wouldn't Brin and Page want to be the ones to crack it?

28   Still, their easy assumption that we'd all "be better off" if our brains were supplemented, or even replaced, by an artificial intelligence is unsettling. It suggests a belief that intelligence is the output of a mechanical process, a series of discrete steps that can be isolated, measured, and optimized. In Google's world, the world we enter when we go online, there's little place for the fuzziness of contemplation. Ambiguity is not an opening for insight but a bug to be fixed. The human brain is just an outdated computer that needs a faster processor and a bigger hard drive.

29   The idea that our minds should operate as high-speed data-processing machines is not only built into the workings of the Internet, it is the network's reigning business model as well. The faster we surf across the Web—the more links we click and pages we view—the more opportunities Google and other companies gain to collect information about us and to feed us advertisements. Most of the proprietors of the commercial Internet have a financial stake in collecting the crumbs of data we leave behind as we flit from link to link—the more crumbs, the better. The last thing these companies want is to encourage leisurely reading or slow, concentrated thought. It's in their economic interest to drive us to distraction.

30   Maybe I'm just a worrywart. Just as there's a tendency to glorify technological progress, there's a countertendency to expect the worst of every new tool or machine. In Plato's *Phaedrus*, Socrates bemoaned the development of writing. He feared that, as

people came to rely on the written word as a substitute for the knowledge they used to carry inside their heads, they would, in the words of one of the dialogue's characters, "cease to exercise their memory and become forgetful." And because they would be able to "receive a quantity of information without proper instruction," they would "be thought very knowledgeable when they are for the most part quite ignorant." They would be "filled with the conceit of wisdom instead of real wisdom." Socrates wasn't wrong—the new technology did often have the effects he feared—but he was shortsighted. He couldn't foresee the many ways that writing and reading would serve to spread information, spur fresh ideas, and expand human knowledge (if not wisdom).

31    The arrival of Gutenberg's printing press, in the 15th century, set off another round of teeth gnashing. The Italian humanist Hieronimo Squarciafico worried that the easy availability of books would lead to intellectual laziness, making men "less studious" and weakening their minds. Others argued that cheaply printed books and broadsheets would undermine religious authority, demean the work of scholars and scribes, and spread sedition and debauchery. As New York University professor Clay Shirky notes, "Most of the arguments made against the printing press were correct, even prescient." But, again, the doomsayers were unable to imagine the myriad blessings that the printed word would deliver.

32    So, yes, you should be skeptical of my skepticism. Perhaps those who dismiss critics of the Internet as Luddites or nostalgists will be proved correct, and from our hyperactive, data-stoked minds will spring a golden age of intellectual discovery and universal wisdom. Then again, the Net isn't the alphabet, and although it may replace the printing press, it produces something altogether different. The kind of deep reading that a sequence of printed pages promotes is valuable not just for the knowledge we acquire from the author's words but for the intellectual vibrations those words set off within our own minds. In the quiet spaces opened up by the sustained, undistracted reading of a book, or by any other act of contemplation, for that matter, we make our own associations, draw our own inferences and analogies, foster our own ideas. Deep reading, as Maryanne Wolf argues, is indistinguishable from deep thinking.

33    If we lose those quiet spaces, or fill them up with "content," we will sacrifice something important not only in our selves but in our culture. In a recent essay, the playwright Richard Foreman eloquently described what's at stake:

34    I come from a tradition of Western culture, in which the ideal (my ideal) was the complex, dense and "cathedral-like" structure of the highly educated and articulate personality—a man or woman who carried inside themselves a personally constructed and unique version of the entire heritage of the West. [But now] I see within us all (myself included) the replacement of complex inner density with a new kind of self—evolving under the pressure of information overload and the technology of the "instantly available."

35    As we are drained of our "inner repertory of dense cultural inheritance," Foreman concluded, we risk turning into "'pancake people'—spread wide and thin as we connect with that vast network of information accessed by the mere touch of a button."

36    I'm haunted by that scene in *2001*. What makes it so poignant, and so weird, is the computer's emotional response to the disassembly of its mind: its despair as one circuit after another goes dark, its childlike pleading with the astronaut—"I can feel it. I can feel it.

I'm afraid"—and its final reversion to what can only be called a state of innocence. HAL's outpouring of feeling contrasts with the emotionlessness that characterizes the human figures in the film, who go about their business with an almost robotic efficiency. Their thoughts and actions feel scripted, as if they're following the steps of an algorithm. In the world of *2001*, people have become so machinelike that the most human character turns out to be a machine. That's the essence of Kubrick's dark prophecy: as we come to rely on computers to mediate our understanding of the world, it is our own intelligence that flattens into artificial intelligence.

### QUESTIONS FOR ANALYSIS AND DISCUSSION

1. In this essay, Nicholas Carr uses a full-circle approach in which he links his introduction to his conclusion. What hook does Carr use in the introduction and how does he revisit it in his conclusion? Do you find the full-circle approach to be an effective writing strategy? Explain.

2. The psychologist Maryanne Wolf is quoted as saying, "We are not only *what* we read . . .We are *how* we read." What does she mean by this statement? How might this effect the reading of literature for future generations?

3. The article illustrates several examples of how technology has given us great advancements, but in the process has taken something away from our ability to think. Find three textual examples of this phenomenon. In the author's opinion is the price we are paying worth the gain? What do you think?

4. Sergey Brin, one of the founders of Google, says, "Certainly if you had all the world's information directly attached to your brain, or an artificial brain that was smarter than your brain, you'd be better off." What is Nicholas Carr's opinion of this statement? What is your opinion of this statement?

5. According to Carr, Google seeks to develop the perfect search engine that will "understand exactly what you mean and gives you back exactly what you want." Which search engine do you commonly use? Try experimenting with at least three different search engines to see which one is most effective. What makes one search engine better than another?

6. How does Nicholas Carr show that money may be the underlining cause of the recent change in the way we are reading and thinking? Summarize this section of the article, and then state if you find this business model to be ethical. What, if anything, can individuals do to influence the trend?

## In the Beginning Was the Word
### *Christine Rosen*

The book, that dusty old technology, seems rigid and passé as we daily consume a diet of information bytes and digital bits. The fault, says sociologist Christine Rosen, is not in our books but in ourselves.

**BEFORE YOU READ**

Do you enjoy reading? What things do you like to read and why? Do you like to read novels or books of non-fiction?

**AS YOU READ**

Do you own an e-reader such as a Kindle or a Nook? Does an e-reader offer the same experience as a paper volume? Why or why not? Why does Rosen object to e-readers on principle?

1    In August, the company that owns *Reader's Digest* filed for bankruptcy protection. The magazine, first cobbled together with scissors and paste in a Greenwich Village basement in 1922 by De Witt Wallace and his wife, Lila, was a novel experiment in abridgement—in 62 pages, it offered Americans condensed versions of current articles from other periodicals. The formula proved wildly successful, and by midcentury *Reader's Digest* was a publishing empire, with millions of subscribers and ventures including Reader's Digest Condensed Books, which sold abridged versions of best-selling works by authors such as Pearl Buck and James Michener. *Reader's Digest* both identified and shaped a peculiarly American approach to reading, one that emphasized convenience, entertainment, and the appearance of breadth. An early issue noted that it was "not a magazine in the usual sense, but rather a co-operative means of rendering a time-saving device."

2    The fate of *Reader's Digest* would have been of interest to the late historian and Librarian of Congress Daniel Boorstin. In his renowned 1962 book *The Image: A Guide to Pseudo-Events in America,* Boorstin used *Reader's Digest* as an example of what was wrong with a culture that had learned to prefer image to reality, the copy to the original, the part to the whole. Publications such as the *Digest,* produced on the principle that any essay can be boiled down to its essence, encourage readers to see articles as little more than "a whiff of literary ectoplasm exuding from print," he argued, and an author's style as littered with unnecessary "literary embellishments" that waste a reader's time.

3    Today, of course, abridgement and abbreviation are the norm, and our impatience for information has trained even those of us who never cracked an issue of *Reader's Digest* to prefer 60-second news cycles to 62 condensed pages per month. Free "aggregator" Web sites such as The Huffington Post link to hundreds of articles from other publications every day, and services such as DailyLit deliver snippets of novels directly to our e-mail in-boxes every morning.

4    Our willingness to follow a writer on a sustained journey that may at times be challenging and frustrating is less compelling than our expectation of being conveniently entertained. Over time, this attitude undermines our commitment to the kind of "deep reading" that researcher Maryanne Wolf, in *Proust and the Squid: The Story and Science of the Reading Brain* (2007), argues is important from an early age, when readers learn to identify with characters and to "expand the boundaries of their lives."

5    As Boorstin surveyed the terrain nearly half a century ago, his overarching concern was that an image-saturated culture would so distort people's sense of judgment that they

would cease to distinguish between the real and the unreal. He criticized the creation of what he called "pseudo-events" such as politicians' staged photo-ops, and he traced the ways in which our pursuit of illusion transforms our experience of travel, clouds our ability to discern the motivations of advertisers, and encourages us to elevate celebrities to the status of heroes. "This is the appealing contradiction at the heart of our passion for pseudo-events: for made news, synthetic heroes, prefabricated tourist attractions, homogenized interchangeable forms of art and literature (where there are no 'originals,' but only the shadows we make of other shadows)," Boorstin wrote. "We believe we can fill our experience with new-fangled content."

6      Boorstin wrote *The Image* before the digital age, but his book still has a great deal to teach us about the likely future of the printed word. Some of the effects of the Internet appear to undermine Boorstin's occasionally gloomy predictions. For example, an increasing number of us, instead of being passive viewers of images, are active participants in a new culture of online writing and opinion mongering. We comment on newspaper and magazine articles, post our reviews of books and other products online, write about our feelings on personal blogs, and bombard our friends and acquaintances with status updates on Facebook. As the word migrates from printed page to pixilated screen, so too do more of our daily activities. Online we find news, work, love, social interaction, and an array of entertainment. We have embraced new modes of storytelling, such as the interactive, synthetic world of video games, and found new ways to share our quotidian personal experiences, in hyperkinetic bursts, through microblogging services such as Twitter.

7      Many observers have loudly and frequently praised the new technologies as transformative and democratic, which they undoubtedly are. But their widespread use has sparked broader questions about the relevance and value of the printed word and the traditional book. The book, like the wheel, is merely a technology, these enthusiasts argue, and thus we should welcome improvements to it, even if those improvements eventually lead to the book's obsolescence. After all, the deeply felt human need for storytelling won't fade; it will merely take on new forms, forms we should welcome as signs of progress, not decay. As Boorstin observed in the foreword to the 25th-anniversary edition of *The Image,* "We Americans are sensitive to any suggestion that progress may have its price."

8      Our screen-intensive culture poses three challenges to traditional reading: distraction, consumerism, and attention-seeking behavior. Screen technologies such as the cell phone and laptop computer that are supposedly revolutionizing reading also potentially offer us greater control over our time. In practice, however, they have increased our anxiety about having too little of it by making us available anytime and anywhere. These technologies have also dramatically increased our opportunities for distraction. It is a rare Web site that presents its material without the clutter of advertisement, and a rare screen reader who isn't lured by the siren song of an incoming e-mail's "ping!" to set aside her work to see who has written. We live in a world of continuous partial attention, one that prizes speed and brandishes the false promise of multitasking as a solution to our time management challenges. The image-driven world of the screen dominates our attention at the same time that it contributes to a kind of experience pollution that is challenging our ability to engage with the printed word.

9      The digital revolution has also transformed the experience of reading by making it more consumer oriented. With the advent of electronic readers (and cell phones that can

double as e-readers), the book is no longer merely a thing you purchase, but a service to which you subscribe. With the purchase of a traditional book, your consumer relationship ends when you walk out of the bookstore. With a wirelessly connected Kindle or iPhone, or your Wi-Fi-enabled computer, you exist in a perpetual state of potential consumerism. To be sure, for most people reading has never been a pure, quasi-monastic activity; everyday life has always presented distractions to the person keen on losing herself in a book. But for the first time, thanks to new technologies, we are making those distractions an integral part of the experience of reading. Embedded in these new versions of the book are the means for constant and elaborate demands on our attention. And as our experience with other screen media, from television to video games to the Internet, suggests, such distractions are difficult to resist.

10    Finally, the transition from print reading to screen reading has increased our reliance on images and led to a form of "social narcissism" that Boorstin first identified in his book. "We have fallen in love with our own image, with images of our making, which turn out to be images of ourselves," he wrote. We become viewers rather than readers, observers rather than participants. The "common reader" Virginia Woolf prized, who is neither scholar nor critic but "reads for his own pleasure, rather than to impart knowledge or correct the opinions of others," is a vanishing species. Instead, an increasing number of us engage with the written word not to submit ourselves to another's vision or for mere edification, but to have an excuse to share our own opinions.

11    In August, Stanford University released preliminary results from its Stanford Study of Writing, which examined in-class and out-of-class writing samples from thousands of students over five years. One of the study's lead researchers, Andrea Lunsford, concluded, "We're in the midst of a literacy revolution the likes of which we haven't seen since Greek civilization." The source of this revolution, Lunsford proposed, is the "life writing" students do every day online: The study found that 38 percent of their writing occurred outside the classroom.

12    But as Emory University English professor Mark Bauerlein pointed out in a blog post on *The Chronicle of Higher Education's,* Web site, this so-called revolution has not translated into concrete improvements in writing skills as measured by standardized tests such as the ACT; nor has it led to a reduction in the number of remedial writing courses necessary to prepare students for the workplace. Of greater concern was the attitude students expressed about the usefulness of writing: Most of them judged the quality of writing by the size of the audience that read it rather than its ability to convey ideas. One of the most prolific contributors to the study, a Stanford undergraduate who submitted more than 700 writing samples ranging from Facebook messages to short stories, told the *Chronicle* that for him a class writing assignment was a "soulless exercise" because it had an audience of one, the professor. He and other students in the study, raised on the Internet, consistently expressed a preference for writing that garnered the most attention from as many people as possible.

13    Our need for stories to translate our experience hasn't changed. Our ability to be deeply engaged readers of those stories is changing; For at least half a century, the image culture has trained us to expect the easily digestible, the quickly paced, and the uncomplicated. As our tolerance for the inconvenient or complex fades, images achieve even more prominence, displacing the word by appealing powerfully to a different kind of emotional

sensibility, one whose vividness and urgency are undeniable but whose ability to explore nuance are not the same as that of the printed word.

14    What Boorstin feared—that a society beholden to the image would cease to distinguish the real from the unreal—has not come to pass. On the contrary, we acknowledge the unique characteristics of the virtual world and have eagerly embraced them, albeit uncritically. But Boorstin's other concern—that a culture that craves the image will eventually find itself mired in solipsism and satisfied by secondhand experiences—has been borne out. We follow the Twitter feeds of protesting Iranians and watch video of Michael Jackson's funeral and feel connected to the rest of the world, even though we lack context for that feeling and don't make much effort to achieve it beyond logging on. The screen offers us the illusion of participation, and this illusion is becoming our preference. As Boorstin observed, "Every day seeing there and hearing there takes the place of being there."

15    This secondhand experience is qualitatively different from the empathy we develop as readers. "We read to know we are not alone," C. S. Lewis once observed, and by this he meant that books are a gateway to a better understanding of what it means to be human. Because the pace is slower and the rewards delayed, the exercise of reading on the printed page requires a commitment unlike that demanded by the screen, as anyone who has embarked on the journey of an ambitiously long novel can attest. What the screen gives us is pleasurable, but it is not the same kind of experience as deeply engaged reading; the "screen literacy" praised by techno-enthusiasts should be seen as a complement to, not a replacement of, traditional literacy.

16    Since the migration of the word from page to screen is still in its early stages, predictions about the future of print are hazardous at best. When *Time* magazine named "YOU!" its person of the year in 2006, the choice was meant as a celebratory recognition of our new digital world and its many opportunities for self-expression. We are all writers now, crafters of our own images and creators of our own online worlds. But so far this power has made us less, not more, willing to submit ourselves to the singular visions of writers and artists and to learn from them difficult truths about the human condition. It has encouraged us to substitute images and simplistic snippets of text for the range, precision, and peculiar beauty of written language, with its unique power to express complex and abstract ideas. Recent surveys by the National Endowment for the Arts reveal that fewer Americans read literature for pleasure than in the past; writers of serious fiction face a daunting publishing market and a reading public that has come to prefer the celebrity memoir to the new literary novel.

17    There is a reason that the metaphor so often invoked to describe the experience of reading is one of escape: An avid reader can recall the book that first unlocked the door of his imagination or provided a sense of escape from the everyday world. The critic Harold Bloom has written that he was forever changed by his early encounters with books: "My older sisters, when I was very young, took me to the library, and thus transformed my life." As Maryanne Wolf notes, "Biologically and intellectually reading allows the species to go 'beyond the information given' to create endless thoughts most beautiful and wonderful."

18    The proliferation of image and text on the Internet has exacerbated the solipsism Boorstin feared, because it allows us to read in a broad but shallow manner. It endorses rather than challenges our sensibilities, and substitutes synthetic images for our own peculiar form of imagination. Over time, the ephemeral, immediate quality of this constant

stream of images undermines the self-control required to engage with the written word. And so we find ourselves in the position of living in a highly literate society that chooses not to exercise the privilege of literacy—indeed, it no longer views literacy as a privilege at all.

19    In *Essays on His Own Times* (1850), Samuel Taylor Coleridge observed, "The great majority of men live like bats, but in twilight, and know and feel the philosophy of their age only by its reflections and refractions." Today we know our age by its tweets and text messages, its never-ending litany of online posts and ripostes. Judging by the evidence so far, the content we find the most compelling is what we produce about ourselves: our tastes, opinions, and habits. This has made us better interpreters of our own experience, but it has not made us better readers or more empathetic human beings.

### QUESTIONS FOR ANALYSIS AND DISCUSSION

1.  What is "deep reading"? Why is it important? In what ways, according to Rosen, does modern communication inhibit the practice of "deep reading"? Explain.
2.  Rosen extensively references Daniel Boorstin. Specifically, Boorstin was critical of "pseudo events" that make it difficult to distinguish the real from the unreal. How does modern communication technology challenge our ability to critically assess the world around us? Provide some examples from both the essay and your personal experience.
3.  According to Rosen, what challenges to traditional reading does our screen-intensive culture pose? How is it changing the way we think?
4.  One goal of persuasive writing is to encourage readers to think about something differently and to get them to take a new position or action. After reading this article, did Rosen change the way you view digital technology? Did her article encourage you to take any action or consider an issue in a different light? Why or why not?
5.  According to Rosen, why is reading a text on a screen different from reading it on paper? Do you agree with her viewpoint?

## My Facebook, My Self
*Jessica Helfand*

Many people feel that there is no better way of keeping in contact with high school friends, old neighbors, and new acquaintances than on Facebook. Facebook allows us to keep in touch with as many people as we wish, and in different ways. We see posts about everything from our friends' most recent travels, their comments on world news, to what they had for dinner. Social networking has allowed us to not only view others, but also to present ourselves to the world. More than simply connecting us with each other, social networking sites allow us to present a persona to the world—publicly sharing who we know, what we think, what we do, and even what we own. However, in the next essay, writer Jessica Helfand warns us that we need to think carefully about what we put on Facebook, how we create our "Profile" and how privacy on Facebook may just be an oxymoron.*

*[handwritten notes]*

### BEFORE YOU READ

Have you ever thought about what your Facebook profile says about you? What image do you project? What do you hope people will learn about you from what you share?

### AS YOU READ

Have you ever put anything on a social networking page or blog that could potentially embarrass you in five, ten, even twenty years? Consider the information you have personally shared online (include emails) and the ramifications of having a record of your online activity possibly accessible in the future.

1  n a recent interview on the *Today Show*, Mark Zuckerberg—the young founder of Facebook—observed that the single most distinctive feature of his revolutionary social networking site was its capacity to let users control various degrees of privacy.

2  I would have listened to more of the interview were it not for my laptop notifying me that I was being invited to chat by someone I went to high school with. For anyone unfamiliar with this practice, Facebook also has a questionable feature displaying everyone who you've "friended" who happens to be online while you're online, which in turn allows them to spontaneously engage you in an online chat. (Even if you're sitting in your pajamas, watching the *Today Show*.) Mind you, the sheer fascination of this surprise encounter—this particular guy never uttered a single word to me when I was a teenager—struck me then, as it does now, as remarkably un-private.

3  Turns out, the very perception of what is public versus what is private is a fundamentally generational conceit. It is also, as it happens, a visual one.

4  I am often asked whether people made scrapbooks, a century ago, intending to share them with others. There's no explicit visual cue that tells us people wanted their stories projected to the world, nor is it clear that any single scrapbook maker believed this to be a clear-cut, black-and-white issue. (Couldn't it be both?)

5  What it does point to is perhaps the more profound question of the projected self: who, after all, doesn't want to look a certain way to others? Scrapbooks and photo albums represent a genre unto themselves because they are unique autobiographical efforts—unvalidated by external approvals, often asynchronous and even wrong in their depiction of real-world events, and stunningly prone to.the occasional willfully-constructed fiction. Among other things, this explains why so many scrapbooks celebrate a kind of curious "episodic" time —leapfrogging from happy event to happy event and ignoring the arguably more revealing, if banal, moments in between. Reconstructing biographical narratives within the context of so much idiosyncrasy is ridiculously hard. (And devilishly fun.) There's also something deeply engaging in the ebbs and flows of personal stories in which actual truth

---

*Jessica Helfand, *Observatory,* March 11, 2009.

is gloriously trumped by an individual's own flawed, if heartfelt rendition of life as he or she deems fit. The resulting palimpsest-like volumes offer extraordinary reflections of authors no longer here to speak for themselves, in which visual cues become biographical cues: pictures speak at least as loud as the words that accompany them. Often, they speak louder.

6    Where Facebook is concerned, the line between public and private exists in a sort of parallel (though oddly torqued) universe: like scrapbooks, Facebook is comprised of pages with amalgamations of diverse content, all held together by an individual's own process of selection. Generally speaking, there is a pronounced appreciation for nostalgia, alternately endearing (how adorable you were at 15!) and excruciating (how appalling you look at 50!). Just like scrapbooks, there is a fair amount of posturing and proselytizing, bad grammar and bizarre juxtapositions. There's a scarcity of snark. And an almost evangelical devotion to stuff: where scrapbook-makers once pasted in pictures of their favorite film stars, Facebook encourages the construction of fan pages, as well as groups to join, causes to support, and so forth.

7    But when it comes to posting actual images, the similarity ends somewhat abruptly: first, because the emphasis on networked sharing is Facebook's *lingua franca*, whereas scrapbooks inhabit a more diary-driven personal landscape; and second, because online, the degree to which pictures are deployed takes the projected self and splinters it into millions of tiny satellite identities leading who knows where.

8    And it begins with the no-holds-barred domain of the Facebook portrait, or portraits *plural*, since that is more the rule than the exception for most users. Why have one self-portrait when you can have twenty or thirty or more? I predict—within the next ten years or so—a magnificent exhibition in some great museum that examines the aesthetic permutations of the iterative self-portrait: retouched and re-engineered, Googled and canoodled and oh-so-public. But the social consequences of such wanton picture-posting are not without concern: paradoxically, while this endless and myopic self-branding may breed a generation of really thoughtful image-makers, what are they jeopardizing, even sacrificing, in the process?

9    For anyone under the age of, say thirty or so, the whole notion of open-source thinking is a native habitat that can be applied to everything from group-table seating in restaurants to sharing playlists to data clouds (I tag, you tag, we all tag)—in short, there's nothing proprietary because people in this particular demographic group don't perceive space as anything you can own. They see it as infinite real estate, to be grazed but not commandeered, shared but not colonized. The beauty of this thinking, besides the fact that it is inherently democratic and gracious, is that it lends itself to a kind of progressive evolution in which everyone wins. It's commendable, really, and speaks well for us all.

10    On the other hand (and I'm not the first, nor will I be the last to mention it) there are implicit pitfalls in this rapidly growing virtual arena, particularly for those for whom social skills have not caught up with, say, their computational skills. On Facebook, this leads to huge numbers of pictures by kids of kids at parties acting stupid—yes, stupid—with cigarettes and sunglasses and cans of beer and face paint. It's kind of sweet and sort of sad and probably meaningless (or so way too many parents of teenagers tell me) and lighten up, I'm told, because they're just posturing, showing the world just how radical they can be. It's safe, because after all, they're not drinking and driving. They're just on screen.

11     Or are they? Even if you are super-careful—ell, even if you don't have a Facebook account yourself—say you find yourself at some random party where there's someone brandishing a mobile phone. And that someone (or, for that matter, someone else) snaps your picture. Soon thereafter, somebody *with* a Facebook account "tags" you and there you are—*whammo*—your questionable behavior rendered spectacularly public. Sure, the same thing can happen on Flickr (and does) but there's something about those interconnected six-degrees-of-separation orbits on Facebook that make a seemingly innocent act like "posting" a random image seem both insidious and scary. (Scarier still, many of the more provocative pictures being posted are actually seen as badges of honor by the people posting them.)

12     Naturally, people in their thirties and forties (and fifties and sixties) are just as likely to parade themselves through their Facebook albums, and do. But the control mechanism is more conscious, and the editorial process itself is typically a bit more cogent. Sure, there are people my age posting images of themselves with big hair back in the 1980s, but this seems more silly (and sentimental) than self-destructive. (After all, those of us who re-member a world before Starbucks are old enough to know better.) No—self-destructive is a thirteen-year old girl posting images of herself in a bikini, and all the boys in her class, and her school, and her neighborhood, and even her friends' friends commenting on it, all of it screamingly public. Self-destructive is a seventeen-year old high school senior posting images of himself with a bong, or downing shots of whiskey, or lap-dancing with that thir-teen-year old in the bikini. Self-destructive is the as-yet unknown ramifications of so much self-publishing, when what we're publishing is our selves.

13     Who is to say what's right or wrong, what's appropriate or not, what's shared, what's seen, what's hidden? Plenty of what's taking place on Facebook is inherently innocuous, and most of us are willing to take responsibility for what we post and where we post it. A lot of Facebook is seamless and fast, streamlined and effective and fun. But as projections of ourselves, a Facebook identity, made manifest through a person's posted photo albums, inhabits a public trajectory that goes way beyond who and what we are. And it all starts with what—and more critically, who—we actually show.

## QUESTIONS FOR ANALYSIS AND DISCUSSION

1. The founder of Facebook, Mark Zuckerberg, contends that Facebook lets "users control various degrees of privacy." On the other hand, the author of this essay shows how Facebook allows for very little privacy. In your opin-ion, which is the stronger argument? Have the new privacy features recently added by Facebook addressed the issue, or made it more complicated?

2. The author states that one of her Facebook friends "never uttered a single word to me when I was a teenager." Why would someone want to "friend" someone with whom they have little connection? Is Facebook redefining the definition of a "friend"? Explain.

3. Helfand compares and contrasts traditional scrapbooks to Facebook. How are they are similar and different? Add your own observations.

4. Helfand predicts that one day a great museum will exhibit the iterative self-portrait, such as seen on Facebook. What predictions do you make about

how Facebook will evolve in the future? Will it perhaps lend itself to great art or will it eventually become obsolete? Explain.

5. Jessica Helfand belongs to the older generation, which she views as "cogent"; whereas she views the younger generation as in part "democratic and gracious" and in part "self-destructive." Is Hefand fair in her assessment?

6. Evaluate your own internet relationships and friendships. Are you a different person online than you are in "real" life?

# Scientific Truth in the Age of Wikipedia

*T. J. Kelleher*

For many people, Wikipedia is *the* go-to website for finding information on just about everything. For many students, it is the first place to look to get an overview of a concept, geographic region, or historical person. However, in countless classrooms across the United States, teachers are telling their students *not* to use Wikipedia in their research, and not to rely on what they describe as a very unreliable source of information. But what if they were told that wikis may exactly be what students should be using for scientific data? In this next essay, science writer T. J. Kelleher explains how public consensus in science is creating the voice of authority, and why the authorities are growing concerned.[*]

## BEFORE YOU READ

Who determines what is the truth? Do we depend on experts or authorities for "truth"? Is there more truth in consensus? Who are you more likely to believe— a single expert or many people who seem to agree?

## AS YOU READ

How should wikis be viewed in academic arenas and in our search for knowledge? Is there a way to make wikis better?

1 Consensus might be an effective means of choosing leaders, but as a method of discerning the truth, philosophers have long found it wanting. The standard critique is simple enough to state and grasp: The fact that everyone decides to act as though something is true does not make it true. Nevertheless, consensus is an important facet of modern science; the notion looms especially large in climate science. It's become a sort of best-guess assessment of how the world works when a controlled test of a master hypothesis—for example, that humans are the leading contributors to climate change—is not possible. It's not perfect, and to many philosophers not even desirable, but it has proved a useful concept, especially as human society can't afford to test the models by waiting for events to vindicate them.

---

[*]T. J. Kelleher, *Seed Magazine*, February 9, 2009.

2    Consensus is also the defining characteristic of epistemology on the internet, thanks to the awesome growth of the wiki. From the humble beginnings of the WikiWikiWeb, the open-source wiki movement has achieved near-total saturation of public consciousness on the strength of its most famous progeny, Wikipedia. Much of the world thinks of it as an indispensable first step for researching anything, but it still has its critics: Some have called Wikipedia "a public toilet" and its editorial style "digital Maoism," and more temperate concerns hold that the bottom-up model of content generation at the heart of the wiki, and its mass-consensus model of knowledge, seem to threaten our ability to verify facts and know the truth. As scientists move toward embracing the wiki—which they are doing, through sites such as OpenWetWare and Proteopedia—it would be reasonable to worry that a consensus of the uninformed could overwhelm the knowledge derived from hard-won expertise. The possibility of verification would seem undermined, the reality of truth and facts buried under an epistemological sludge. But, whatever the flaws of Wikipedia, those worries seem unfounded. It is not scientific rigor that is accommodating the wiki, but the wiki that is accommodating science.

3    One of Wikipedia's most persistent critics is the man who first proposed the creation of a wiki-based reference guide. Larry Sanger, cofounder of Wikipedia and self-described "wiki-apostate," thinks the encyclopedia exists in a state in which the "know-nothings can drive off the know-somethings" with a bankrupt founding principle of "radical egalitarianism." That a meaningful consensus can derive from "a project that has millions of participants is ridiculous," he says. One of the system's biggest supporters, Clay Shirky, author of *Here Comes Everybody: the Power of Organizing Without Organizations*, holds the opposite opinion of its value, but a similar opinion of the wiki's strength. Shirky argues that authority and expertise are only "social facts." "Works are only authoritative because everybody agrees they are," he says. "It's circular. That's what's going on with Wikipedia now. To the degree that people begin to take it seriously, it's going to acquire the patina of authority."

4    Many scholars dispute the notion that wikis will eliminate more traditional models of scientific authority, but the wiki model is nonetheless exerting a gravitational influence on some of the core principles of epistemology. "I think it's changing how we think about authority," says Tyler Cowen, a professor of economics at George Mason University. But that may not be the case for science wikis. The opinion of an authority, however well informed, is no more a hallmark of the truth than consensus is. Two primary methodological pillars of science—peer review and the pursuit of replication of results—and its philosophy of falsifiability, rather than being threatened by the wiki, might actually be well served by it.

5    For Seth Lloyd, MIT professor of mechanical engineering, the wiki model is "reasonably good" at discerning, if not what is true, then what is false. The notion of falsifiability, thanks to the massively influential work of Karl Popper, sits at the core of many conceptions of how science operates; scientists may not be able to prove what is true, but by repetition of prediction, trial, and analysis, scientists can at least discern what is false. Indeed, Shirky's description of the wiki as a rapidly evolving "process, not a product," speaks to the power of the wiki to act as a chronicler and creator of repositories for science, to create a home for what we haven't proved to be false and for what we think to be true. Constant checking, a ceaseless selection of good information and argumentation over bad, could accelerate falsification.

6　　The key is who gets to participate. Sheila Jasanoff, a professor of science and technology studies at Harvard's Kennedy School of Government, argues that those tools are undergoing more of an evolution than a revolution. "It's not that the peer-review system is breaking down so much as getting remade into some different kind of thing," she says. According to Jasanoff, one problem wikis face is the absence of clear methods for quality control. That uncertainty, Jasanoff argues, has meant that wikis have inadvertently enhanced the status of peer-reviewed journals. "People want to know who's good and who's bad and who's better and who's worse," she says, and thanks to the prestige of journals such as *Science* and *Nature*, they remain the place to find out who's what. And if scientific wikis were in fact like Wikipedia, then those journals would probably forever remain the best places to find those answers, and the wikis, insofar as anyone used them, would present real problems for notions of truth and reasonable consensus, for figuring out what work is better and what work is worse. Fortunately, the people building scientific wikis have taken those concerns into account. Proteopedia, for example, was introduced to the world this past August in the journal *Genome Biology*, and its founding principles were laid out for inspection. Would-be contributors have to petition the site's editors for the ability to create and edit pages, and even then they work only on specific topics in which the editors have accredited them as expert. Furthermore, as is also the case with OpenWetWare, a wiki established by Drew Endy and Tom Knight at MIT in 2005, now host to more than a hundred research laboratories, no one writes from behind a veil of anonymity. However little Wikipedia cares for authority, and however much that encyclopedia has dispensed with peer review in favor of a dictatorship of the persistent, authority and peer review are concepts built into the core of science wikis.

7　　Sanger himself is using those same principles in his latest venture, the Citizendium. Shirky calls the failure of Sanger's new project a "foregone conclusion," because it wants mass participation while eliminating the openness that has encouraged Wikipedia's mind-boggling growth. Indeed, for something to get as big as Wikipedia, there can be few barriers to entry. For wikified science, Sanger may just have the ticket.

## QUESTIONS FOR ANALYSIS AND DISCUSSION

1. Why do some critics refer to Wikipedia as a "public toilet" and "digital Maoism"? Do you agree with these assessments?
2. Explain the concept of consensus. How might it help with proving scientific authority?
3. According to the author, why are scientists moving toward embracing wikis?
4. How would you rate Wikipedia for accuracy? What checks and balances are in place to ensure that the information you find on Wikipedia is accurate? Try looking something up on Wikipedia that you already know a lot about: perhaps your hometown, a certain sport, a celebrity, etc. Is the information correct? Is there anything you would add or take away? Explain.
5. According to Kelleher, what is the biggest problem that wikis currently face, and how is this problem being addressed in order to make sure the sites better serve the public?

6. The author mentions Larry Sanger's new encyclopedia project "Citizendium," which claims to have no vandalism due to a more selective editing process. Are you already familiar with this site? Visit the site and compare it to Wikipedia. In your opinion is this site bound to replace Wikipedia in the future? Explain.

## Three Tweets for the Web
*Tyler Cowen*

It's an age-old grievance—the older generation grumbles that the younger one has so many problems—they have limited attention spans, they have no manners, they lack culture, they sit around all day, they don't read and now, with texting and Twitter, they can't even write a coherent sentence. In the next essay, economics professor Tyler Cowen explains that the younger generation may be different not because they are lazy, but because they are doing things in new and exciting ways. They navigate information and communication in ways their grandparents could not have imagined. The future is now, and they are steering a new course through the information age. Cowan encourages everyone to welcome the new world with open arms—and browsers.*

### BEFORE YOU READ

Evaluate your own online communication style. Are you brief and to the point, or do you compose in more detail? What do you think your style says about you? What does it communicate to others? Do you have different styles for different situations? Explain.

### AS YOU READ

In which ways does modern technology help enhance and deepen our life experiences? Can you imagine your life without a cell phone, hand-held communication devices, the Internet, or social networking tools like Facebook and Twitter? How would your life be different?

1  The printed word is not dead. We are not about to see the demise of the novel or the shuttering of all the bookstores, and we won't all end up on Twitter. But we are clearly in the midst of a cultural transformation. For today's younger people, Google is more likely to provide a formative cultural experience than *The Catcher in the Rye* or *Catch-22* or even the Harry Potter novels. There is no question that books are becoming less central to our cultural life.

2  The relative decline of the book is part of a broader shift toward short and to the point. Small cultural bits—written words, music, video—have never been easier to record, store, organize, and search, and thus they are a growing part of our enjoyment and education. The

---
*Tyler Cowen, *Wilson Quarterly*, Autumn 2009.

classic 1960s rock album has given way to the iTunes single. On YouTube, the most popular videos are usually just a few minutes long, and even then 2viewers may not watch them through to the end. At the extreme, there are Web sites offering five-word movie and song reviews, six-word memoirs ("Not Quite What I Was Planning"), seven-word wine reviews, and fifty-word minisagas.

3      The new brevity has many virtues. One appeal of following blogs is the expectation of receiving a new reward (and finishing off that reward) every day. Blogs feature everything from expert commentary on politics or graphic design to reviews of new Cuban music CDs to casual ruminations on feeding one's cat. Whatever the subject, the content is replenished on a periodic basis, much as 19th-century novels were often delivered in installments, but at a faster pace and with far more authors and topics to choose from. In the realm of culture, a lot of our enjoyment has always come from the opening and unwrapping of each gift. Thanks to today's hypercurrent online environment, this is a pleasure we can experience nearly constantly.

4      It may seem as if we have entered a nightmarish attention-deficit culture, but the situation is not nearly as gloomy as you have been told. Our culture of the short bit is making human minds more rather than less powerful.

5      The arrival of virtually every new cultural medium has been greeted with the charge that it truncates attention spans and represents the beginning of cultural collapse—the novel (in the 18th century), the comic book, rock 'n' roll, television, and now the Web. In fact, there has never been a golden age of all-wise, all-attentive readers. But that's not to say that nothing has changed. The mass migration of intellectual activity from print to the Web has brought one important development: We have begun paying more attention to information. Overall, that's a big plus for the new world order.

6      It is easy to dismiss this cornucopia as information overload. We've all seen people scrolling with one hand through a BlackBerry while pecking out instant messages (IMs) on a laptop with the other and eyeing a television (I won't say "watching"). But even though it is easy to see signs of overload in our busy lives, the reality is that most of us carefully regulate this massive inflow of information to create something uniquely suited to our particular interests and needs—a rich and highly personalized blend of cultural gleanings.

7      The word for this process is *multitasking*, but that makes it sound as if we're all over the place. There is a deep coherence to how each of us pulls out a steady stream of information from disparate sources to feed our long-term interests. No matter how varied your topics of interest may appear to an outside observer, you'll tailor an information stream related to the continuing "stories" you want in your life—say, Sichuan cooking, health care reform, Michael Jackson, and the stock market. With the help of the Web, you build broader intellectual narratives about the world. The apparent disorder of the information stream reflects not your incoherence but rather your depth and originality as an individual.

8      My own daily cultural harvest usually involves listening to music and reading—novels, nonfiction, and Web essays—with periodic glances at the *New York Times* Web site and an e-mail check every five minutes or so. Often I actively don't want to pull apart these distinct activities and focus on them one at a time for extended periods. I *like* the blend I assemble for myself, and I like what I learn from it. To me (and probably no one else, but that is the point), the blend offers the ultimate in interest and suspense. Call me an addict, but if I am torn away from these stories for even a day, I am very keen to get back for the next "episode."

9     Many critics charge that multitasking makes us less efficient. Researchers say that periodically checking your e-mail lowers your cognitive performance level to that of a drunk. If such claims were broadly correct, multitasking would pretty rapidly disappear simply because people would find that it didn't make sense to do it. Multitasking is flourishing, and so are we. There are plenty of lab experiments that show that distracting people reduces the capacity of their working memory and thus impairs their decision making. It's much harder to show that multitasking, when it results from the choices and control of an individual, does anyone cognitive harm. Multitasking is not a distraction from our main activity, it is our main activity.

10    Consider the fact that IQ scores have been rising for decades, a phenomenon known as the Flynn effect. I won't argue that multitasking is driving this improvement, but the Flynn effect does belie the common impression that people are getting dumber or less attentive. A harried multitasking society seems perfectly compatible with lots of innovation, lots of high achievers, and lots of high IQ scores.

11    With the help of technology, we are honing our ability to do many more things at once and do them faster. We access and absorb information more quickly than before, and, as a result, we often seem more impatient. If you use Google to look something up in ten seconds rather than spend five minutes searching through an encyclopedia, that doesn't mean you are less patient. It means you are creating more time to focus on other matters. In fact, we're devoting more effort than ever before to big-picture questions, from the nature of God to the best age for marrying and the future of the U.S. economy.

12    Our focus on cultural bits doesn't mean we are neglecting the larger picture. Rather, those bits are building-blocks for seeing and understanding larger trends and narratives. The typical Web user doesn't visit a gardening blog one day and a Manolo Blahnik shoes blog the next day, and never return to either. Most activity online, or at least the kind that persists, involves continuing investments in particular long-running narratives—about gardening, art, shoes, or whatever else engages us. There's an alluring suspense to it. *What's next?* That is why the Internet captures so much of our attention.

13    Indeed, far from shortening our attention spans, the Web *lengthens* them by allowing us to follow the same story over many years' time. If I want to know what's new with the NBA free-agent market, the debate surrounding global warming, or the publication plans of Thomas Pynchon, Google quickly gets me to the most current information. Formerly I needed personal contacts—people who were directly involved in the action—to follow a story for years, but now I can do it quite easily.

14    Sometimes it does appear I am impatient. I'll discard a half-read book that twenty years ago I might have finished. But once I put down the book, I will likely turn my attention to one of the long-running stories I follow online. I've been listening to the music of Paul McCartney for more than thirty years, for example, and if there is some new piece of music or development in his career, I see it first on the Internet. If our Web surfing is sometimes frantic or pulled in many directions, that is because we care so much about so many long-running stories. It could be said, a bit paradoxically, that we are impatient to return to our chosen programs of patience.

15    Another way the Web has affected the human attention span is by allowing greater specialization of knowledge. It has never been easier to wrap yourself up in a long-term intellectual project without at the same time losing touch with the world around you. Some

critics don't see this possibility, charging that the Web is destroying a shared cultural experience by enabling us to follow only the specialized stories that pique our individual interests. But there are also those who argue that the Web is doing just the opposite—that we dabble in an endless variety of topics but never commit to a deeper pursuit of a specific interest. These two criticisms contradict each other. The reality is that the Internet both aids in knowledge specialization and helps specialists keep in touch with general trends.

16    The key to developing your personal blend of all the "stuff" that's out there is to use the right tools. The quantity of information coming our way has exploded, but so has the quality of our filters, including Google, blogs, and Twitter. As Internet analyst Clay Shirky points out, there is no information overload, only filter failure. If you wish, you can keep all the information almost entirely at bay and use Google or text a friend only when you need to know something. That's not usually how it works. Many of us are cramming ourselves with Web experiences—videos, online chats, magazines—and also fielding a steady stream of incoming e-mails, text messages, and IMs. The resulting sense of time pressure is not a pathology; it is a reflection of the appeal and intensity of what we are doing. The Web allows you to enhance the meaning and importance of the cultural bits at your disposal; thus you want to grab more of them, and organize more of them, and you are willing to work hard at that task, even if it means you sometimes feel harried.

17    It's true that many people on the Web are not looking for a cerebral experience, and younger people especially may lack the intellectual framework needed to integrate all the incoming bits into a meaningful whole. A lot of people are on the Web just to have fun or to achieve some pretty straightforward personal goals—they may want to know what happened to their former high school classmates or the history of the dachshund. "It's still better than watching TV" is certainly a sufficient defense of these practices, but there is a deeper point: The Internet is supplementing and intensifying real life. The Web's heralded interactivity not only furthers that process but opens up new possibilities for more discussion and debate. Anyone can find space on the Internet to rate a product, criticize an idea, or review a new movie or book.

18    One way to understand the emotional and intellectual satisfactions of the new world is by way of contrast. Consider Mozart's opera *Don Giovanni*. The music and libretto express a gamut of human emotions, from terror to humor to love to the sublime. With its ability to combine so much in a single work of art, the opera represents a great achievement of the Western canon. But, for all *Don Giovanni*'s virtues, it takes well over three hours to hear it in its entirety, perhaps four with an intermission. Plus, the libretto is in Italian. And if you want to see the performance live, a good seat can cost hundreds of dollars.

19    Instead of experiencing the emotional range of *Don Giovanni* in one long, expensive sitting, on the Web we pick the moods we want from disparate sources and assemble them ourselves. We take a joke from YouTube, a terrifying scene from a Japanese slasher movie, a melody from iTunes, and some images—perhaps our own digital photos—capturing the sublime beauty of the Grand Canyon. Even if no single bit looks very impressive to an outsider, to the creator of this assemblage it is a rich and varied inner experience. The new wonders we create are simply harder for outsiders to see than, say, the fantastic cathedrals of Old Europe.

20    The measure of cultural literacy today is not whether you can "read" all the symbols in a Rubens painting but whether you can operate an iPhone and other Web-related technologies.

One thing you can do with such devices is visit any number of Web sites where you can see Rubens's pictures and learn plenty about them. It's not so much about having information as it is about knowing how to get it. Viewed in this light, today's young people are very cultur-ally literate indeed—in fact, they are very often cultural leaders and creators.

21    To better understand contemporary culture, consider an analogy to romance. Although many long-distance relationships survive, they are difficult to sustain. When you have to travel far to meet your beloved, you want to make every trip a grand and glorious occasion. Usually you don't fly from one coast to another just to hang out and share downtime and small talk. You go out to eat and to the theater, you make passionate love, and you have in-tense conversations. You have a lot of thrills, but it's hard to make it work because in the long run it's casually spending time together and the routines of daily life that bind two people to each other. And of course, in a long-distance relationship, a lot of the time you're not together at all. If you really love the other person you're not consistently happy, even though your peak experiences may be amazing.

22    A long-distance relationship is, in emotional terms, a bit like culture in the time of Cervantes or Mozart. The costs of travel and access were high, at least compared to mod-ern times. When you did arrive, the performance was often very exciting and indeed mon-umental. Sadly, the rest of the time you didn't have that much culture at all. Even books were expensive and hard to get. Compared to what is possible in modern life, you couldn't be as happy overall but your peak experiences could be extremely memorable, just as in the long-distance relationship.

23    Now let's consider how living together and marriage differ from a long-distance rela-tionship. When you share a home, the costs of seeing each other are very low. Your partner is usually right there. Most days include no grand events, but you have lots of regular and predictable interactions, along with a kind of grittiness or even ugliness rarely seen in a long-distance relationship. There are dirty dishes in the sink, hedges to be trimmed, maybe diapers to be changed.

24    If you are happily married, or even somewhat happily married, your internal life will be very rich. You will take all those small events and, in your mind and in the mind of your spouse, weave them together in the form of a deeply satisfying narrative, dirty diapers and all. It won't always look glorious on the outside, but the internal experience of such a mar-riage is better than what's normally possible in a long-distance relationship.

25    The same logic applies to culture. The Internet and other technologies mean that our favorite creators, or at least their creations, are literally part of our daily lives. It is no longer a long-distance relationship. It is no longer hard to get books and other written ma-terial. Pictures, music, and video appear on command. Culture is there all the time, and you can receive more of it, pretty much whenever you want.

26    In short, our relationship to culture has become more like marriage in the sense that it now enters our lives in an established flow, creating a better and more regular daily state of mind. True, culture has in some ways become uglier, or at least it would appear so to the outside observer. But when it comes to how we actually live and feel, contemporary culture is more satisfying and contributes to the happiness of far more people. That is why the pub-lic devours new technologies that offer extreme and immediate access to information.

27    Many critics of contemporary life want our culture to remain like a long-distance rela-tionship at a time when most of us are growing into something more mature. We assemble

culture for ourselves, creating and committing ourselves to a fascinating brocade. Very often the paper-and-ink book is less central to this new endeavor; it's just another cultural bit we consume along with many others. But we are better off for this change, a change that is filling our daily lives with beauty, suspense, and learning.

28      Or if you'd like the shorter version to post to your Twitter account (140 characters or less): "Smart people are doing wonderful things."

## QUESTIONS FOR ANALYSIS AND DISCUSSION

1. How many complete novels have you read in the past year? Do you agree or disagree with the author "that books are becoming less central to our cultural life"? Explain. Could books still be seen as a part of our social lives? Explain.

2. This essay is in direct opposition to Nicholas Carr's article, "Is Google Making Us Stoopid?" For instance, Cowen argues that the Internet helps us think creatively and encourages debate, whereas Nicholas Carr feels that the Internet is taking away our ability to be deeply involved in lengthy prose, curtailing our creative thinking. After reading both articles, determine who makes the stronger overall argument.

3. Cowen explains his daily multitasking as involving "listening to music and reading—novels, nonfiction, and Web essays—with periodic glances at the *New York Times* Web site and an e-mail check every five minutes or so. Describe your own "daily cultural harvest." Do you agree with the author that "Multitasking is not a distraction from our main activity, it is our main activity"? Explain.

4. According to the author, the Web actually lengthens our attention spans "by allowing us to follow the same story over many years' time." Which stories have you been following consistently for at least a year? Does the author's statement seem to be consistent with your own experience?

5. Define what it means to be cultured. Which analogy does Cowen use to support his point that today's young people are indeed cultured?

6. At the conclusion of his essay, Cowen jokingly sums up his main point for a posting to a Twitter account—in 140 characters or less. Do you agree with Cowen's own summation of his article? Write your own version of Cowen's essay in 140 characters or less.

## Reading the Visual

### My Kids, MySpace

*Marty Bucella*

"When my kids get out of line, I threaten to start a 'My Space' page and invite their friends."

### QUESTIONS FOR ANALYSIS AND DISCUSSION

1. What is the woman's "threat"? Why would her kids be concerned if she followed through with this threat?
2. What do you need to know in order to understand the point of this cartoon? Explain.
3. Would this cartoon have made any sense ten years ago? Why or why not?

# Treading Water in a Sea of Data
*Peter Suderman*

We live in a technology age that only a few generations ago would have seemed unimaginable. We can communicate with people around the world in seconds, we can find information—even photos—on events as they happen, we can purchase almost any item or service without getting off the couch, we can download songs and video in an instant, we can even direct and star in our own movies, and share them with the entire world in seconds. But for all these remarkable advances, we also must live tied to our desktops, laptops, BlackBerrys, and iPhones. Information flows in and out of our lives at a constant speed. But how are we adapting to this technology? In the next essay, author Peter Suderman wonders if we have too much of a good thing. Is there such a thing as information overload? And if so, what do we propose to do about it?*

## BEFORE YOU READ

Consider the differences in technology over the last 20 or 30 years. Speak to a few people over 40 about the technical devices they now use, and what they used when they were 18. How have things changed?

## AS YOU READ

How much time do you spend using electronic devices? Do you think that you could live without all of the information that comes to you through these devices? Without the ability to instantly communicate?

## Staying Afloat

1 In March 1997, *Wired* magazine, ever the zealous prophet of near-future consumer tech, breathlessly trumpeted the imminent death of the Internet browser and the rise of so-called "push media." In short, the idea was that the Web would expand beyond the confines of the browser, both to additional desktop applications and to a host of other devices: phones, televisions, appliances, and even wallpaper. Next, all of these devices would coordinate their information delivery, transforming the Web from a passive medium, in which users request information, to an active medium, in which information "pushes" itself toward users. This new medium, we learn, would not "wait for clicks": it's "always-on, mildly in-your-face" and will "bombard you with an intensity that invitational media never muster." Content, we are promised—or warned?—"will not hesitate to find you."

2 A decade later, some of these predictions have not come to pass: thankfully, our toasters don't yet deliver the latest political headlines. Yet in the most important ways, the *Wired* piece has proven accurate. Although the computer monitor is still the primary way by which we view the Web, other devices—BlackBerrys; iPhones; and big-screen,

---

*Peter Suderman, *New Atlantis*, Number 22, Fall 2008.

media-center televisions—also increasingly play a role. And the browser has not disappeared, but it has certainly evolved: rather than acting solely as a picture window through which to view static Web pages, it now also serves as a frame for an array of applications which sort, filter, and manipulate information for its users.

3   The purpose of these applications is to assist us in staying afloat as the vast tides of information continue to rise. The programs can be divided into two broad categories. First, there are programs for news and blog updates. Chief among these is a news reader, an application that uses an electronic syndication protocol known as RSS (Really Simple Syndication) to continuously collect and organize news stories and blog posts from the sources to which the user subscribes. The program pulls information from these sources and reformats it so that, instead of visiting a hundred Websites, the user need only open the browser and skim the headlines it presents him, organized by category—politics, technology, arts and entertainment, economics, and so on. Additionally, other tools may feed constant updates, turning the side of the screen into a sort of ongoing, customized news scroll.

4   There are also programs designed to facilitate personal communications: e-mail applications; social networking sites like Facebook and MySpace; and Twitter (a "micro-blogging" system that lets users send and read very short messages via cell phones or Websites). Add in chat applications, customized e-mail news alerts (essentially digital clipping services), newsletter subscriptions, and online calendars, and the result is a great welter of information demanding immediate attention. Intended to ease the work of wading through the information now available, these tools have instead yielded a different sort of informational deluge, pushing upon us so much information at such great speed that reading and communication have accelerated into hectic, frantic activities.

5   We have entered the age of push technologies. But the problem is that they turn out to be, well, pushy. The Web once seemed to be little more than a simple catalogue of linked, non-linear information, neatly organized and searchable. But in just over a decade it has, for many users, shed any trace of its former stillness. Like most commercial developments, the movement is toward louder, brighter, and more overwhelming, as each application must work harder to engage the user's attention.

6   And what is the key selling point for this sort of media delivery? According to the authors of that 1997 *Wired* essay:

> Foremost is relief from boredom. Push media will penetrate environments that have, in the past, been media-free—work, school, church, the solitude of a country walk. Through cheap wireless technologies, push media are already colonizing the world's last quiet nooks and crannies.

7   Leaving aside the suggestion that church, school, and country walks are boring, the larger problem here is the conflation of boredom with lack of stimulus. The idea hinges on the notion that humans at rest are intrinsically lacking in some way, that a mind cannot be at peace with itself. Moreover, it inverts the long-settled relationship between humans and the information they collect. Thanks to these tools, information no longer merely responds to your requests. Instead, it chases you.

8   The greatest toll is exacted on habits of mind. A regular user of these tools is likely to grow accustomed to consuming information in tiny, disparate chunks, and even these

tiny chunks are often further broken up. Reading in such an environment lends itself to perpetual distraction; there is always some new piece of information insistent on grabbing the user's attention. It becomes nearly impossible to finish, much less dwell on, a single thought.

9    The habits of mind this environment promotes do not recede when one leaves the screen behind. Just drawing on my own experience, I've found it increasingly difficult in recent years to read books; my eyes, trained by hours each day in front of screens, jump fitfully around the page, impatiently flicking downward as if in hopes of a notification popping up from the bottom of the page. It has become harder for me to follow lengthy arguments, and more difficult to memorize important details. As others have noted—Christine Rosen, for example, and Nicholas Carr in *The Atlantic*—our electronic tools have made distraction a way of life.

10    These changes should come as no great surprise. They are, in a sense, natural: the human mind is tremendously adaptable, able to reshape itself to match our situations. But in adapting, our minds take on the qualities of the tools they use. Scientific research has confirmed what everyday experience has shown to be obviously true: external inputs—soothing music, bright lights, and countless other environmental factors—can alter not just a person's moods but even his thought processes. Given this, it seems entirely reasonable to suppose that persistent exposure to an environment of agitation and distraction can have a transformative, and generally damaging, effect on the mind.

11    Indeed, there is a growing recognition that the modern Web's torrent of information can be deeply wearying. Technology workers—particularly the small number of full-time professional bloggers who spend much of each day swimming the riptide currents of the Web's heaviest information streams—seem particularly susceptible. The *New York Times* reported a few months ago that since cybermogul Michael Arrington began blogging, "he has gained 30 pounds . . . developed a severe sleeping disorder and turned his home into an office for him and four employees." Arrington reports that he receives more than one thousand e-mails a day, in addition to numerous messages through other services. His lifestyle is "not sustainable," he says: "At some point, I'll have a nervous breakdown and be admitted to the hospital, or something else will happen." A handful of bloggers, the *Times* article suggests, have been killed by the stress of their work—drowned in the information flood.

12    It's no wonder, then, that there is a small movement of tech-workers who have vowed to take a single day each week as a break from technology: no e-mail, no RSS, no phones, no computers. It's a Sabbath with the rest but without the reverence; the idea is to clear one's mind, to refresh, to unplug. This "Digital Day of Rest" represents an attempt at balance—an approach that avoids an outright rejection of information technology, but that recognizes the value of carving out time for psychic rejuvenation.

13    The informational rhythms of modernity sometimes lead people to forget that in addition to managing information, they must also manage themselves. The best of today's information-organizing technologies serve up an astonishing amount of news and other media; yet even as these devices insinuate themselves into everyday life and reshape how we understand the world, the fact remains that the most crucial tool for information management is one's own commonsense judgment. Increasingly, this means that the best way to manage the endless flow of information is, from time to time, to close the spigot.

1. Suderman uses an extended metaphor to describe how information has taken over our lives. Which extended metaphor does he use? Find textual evidence throughout his essay to show how he keeps revisiting this metaphor.
2. According to Suderman, some tech-workers have started to take a day off from all technology each week. Do you find this possible? Is this a solution to information overload? Do you think you personally could go without technology for one full day each week? Explain.
3. The author notices that when he is trying to read a book, his eyes "jump fitfully around the page, impatiently flicking downward as if in hopes of a notification popping up from the bottom of the page." Have you noticed any changes in your own reading habits after looking at a computer screen for long periods of time? Explain.
4. Even though it hasn't quite happened yet, do you think "push media" as defined by *Wired* magazine will become the wave of the future? Explain.
5. How many different forms of information technology do you typically use? The Web, BlackBerrys, iPhones, media-center televisions, blogs, RSS feeds, Facebook, MySpace, Twitter, others? Would you consider any of these "pushy"?
6. Suderman asserts, " . . . it seems entirely reasonable to suppose that persistent exposure to an environment of agitation and distraction can have a transformative, and generally damaging, effect on the mind." Which examples does Suderman give to support his point? Do you agree or disagree that information overload is becoming a serious problem? Explain.

# Facebook Sees Dead People
*Sandip Roy*

For most people, keeping the memories of their loved ones alive after death is very important. For some, it may be a simple headstone marking a place of burial and photos left on a piano. Other people may create memorials, fund scholarships, write biographies, and for the wealthy, name buildings. Online, Facebook has many sites to memorialize the deceased, and the Internet has provided a free and easy way to "visit" those we have lost. But our digital footprints may linger long after we are gone, haunting the living and reminding others that we are no longer alive. In this next essay, Sandip Roy an editor with New America Media and host of its radio show *New America Now*, discusses how the dead live online.*

Are you "friends" with anyone who has died but is still on Facebook, whether through a memorial page or otherwise?

---

*Sandip Roy, *New American Media*, October 27, 2009.

**AS YOU READ** ─────────────────────────────────

Is Facebook responsible for protecting the privacy of its users who have died? Should it control who has the rights over a dead person's pages?

1    When William showed up as a suggested friend on Facebook I almost clicked on the link. He was an acquaintance. We had friends in common. Then I remembered I had gotten a mail about his memorial service months ago. In the eternal sunshine of Facebook's mind we could still become friends. There was something simultaneously soothing and creepy about it all.

2    Others have complained about how a new feature on Facebook tells them to reconnect with friends they haven't talked to for awhile. Except some of those friends are actually dead.

3    Now Facebook says dead people won't show up as suggested friends anymore. But if their friends and family request it, their pages can be preserved for eternity—a sort of virtual memorial.

4    I wonder who qualifies as friends and family here, who gets the power to preserve someone's page. Do already-approved friends get precedence here? My mother and my sister are not on Facebook. If something happens to me, do they have the right to demand my page be taken down? Or do one of my Facebook friends (many of whom are really Facebook acquaintances) get precedence?

5    And how do you prove someone has died? Facebook requires an obituary or a news article. But what if there is neither?

6    Ashley Gilbertson, who wrote an amazing book about being a war photographer in Iraq once talked about his new project. It was photographing the bedrooms of young soldiers who had died in Iraq. The rooms were frozen in time, preserved by grieving mothers—a jumble of photographs of high school sweethearts, posters of rock stars, college jerseys, sports trophies.

7    Facebook is creating its own versions of those bedrooms, preserved in Internet ether—messages on the wall, links they had shared, quizzes they had taken (what kind of superhero are you). They are there forever (as long as the storage lasts).

8    And their approved friends, a sort of exclusive club, are the only ones allowed to post on their wall. It sounds a little spooky, a sort of online planchette, leaving messages for the beyond on the dead person's wall. This is not like leaving teddy bears and candles at a memorial shrine. That shrine eventually disappears. The teddy bear gets grubby. The candles melt. But the Facebook shrine never ages, never fades. Can the friends unfriend themselves if it gets too much, trapped in the mausoleum?

9    It makes me curious what else can happen with the pages of people who died. Facebook says they won't be searchable anymore. But a report on NPR just talked about how those endless quizzes we take on Facebook actually can allow an application to mine our profiles for all kinds of information—religion, sexual preference, school, groups we belong to etc. All that information can then be sold to marketers. These people won't know that William has died. He will live forever in their database, memorialized whether he wanted to be or not.

10   Facebook has really altered our notion of privacy. Work colleagues, lovers, cousins, parents, casual acquaintances you met at a party, members of your book club are suddenly all swimming in the same pool. Some of them might even know each other.

11    There have already been stories of people posting about playing hooky from work without realizing work colleagues were on it. I went to an event the other day that was rather ridiculous but I stopped myself from posting about it because I knew the organizer was a Facebook friend. I have realized that when I enter the social networking world I am visible in ways I didn't count on. I am searchable. I have no real privacy even though it gives me the illusion of intimacy. That's the price I pay for connection.

Now even in death we are not private. Facebook sees dead people.

### QUESTIONS FOR ANALYSIS AND DISCUSSION

1. What pop cultural reference is this essay's title making? Is this title a good choice for this essay?
2. Facebook allows for the deceased to have their pages preserved for eternity. Do you agree or disagree with Facebook's decision? Explain.
3. In his essay, Roy makes reference to the NPR *All Things Considered* report, "Is Your Facebook Profile as Private As you Think?" broadcast on October 27, 2009, by Martin Kaste. Listen to this 6-minute webcast at http://www.npr.org. Does it influence the way you think about Facebook and the issue of privacy?
4. Consider your digital footprint. What social networking pages do you maintain? Do you have pages you no longer access, but may still have information? What impression will be left on the Internet if something suddenly happened to you?
5. In order to make his point, Sandip Roy asks a series of questions but doesn't supply many direct answers. Is this a valuable method for argumentative essay writing? Explain.
6. The author states that a loss of privacy is the price he pays for connection. Are there other ways besides Facebook in which we have been losing more and more of our privacy?

## Facebook, the Mean Girls and Me
*Taffy Brodesser-Akner*

Films such as *Mean Girls*, *John Tucker Must Die*, and *Bring it On* highlight female aggression in high school. There are the popular "queen bees" who bully and control the popular crowd, and everyone else who takes the abuse or risks getting singled out for ridicule. For the underdogs in Hollywood films, the unpopular usually prevail and the "mean girls" get their due. What about in real life? Our experiences in middle school and high school can influence our self-image even into adulthood. In this next essay, Taffy Brodesser-Akner explains her own experience as a not-so-popular girl who now finds that at 34 years old, she finally feels "like a popular seventh-grader" thanks to networking on Facebook.*

---

*Taffy Brodesser-Akner, *Salon*, November 20, 2009.

BEFORE YOU READ

When you were in high school, was there a particularly popular group of kids? Did you belong to this popular crowd? Did you know any "mean girl" type of kids and did they affect you?

AS YOU READ

What can *Facebook* tell you about your friends? Is it a superficial way to stay in touch or do you get to know people on a deeper level? When someone asks to be your Facebook friend, how much thought do you put into the decision to say "yes"?

1   I sit at my computer and wait for Barbara, who once poured yogurt on my head in front of the entire field hockey team, to tell me the details of her breakup with her current boyfriend. While I wait, I chat with Alison, who, years ago, stole my pants during gym and cut a hole in the crotch area, and who needs advice on how to sleep-train her baby. Still, while all this is going on, I play online Scrabble with Rachel, who, when I was 12, told everyone I had faked getting my period for attention.

2   I am someone with a life. I have a career, a son, a husband, an active volunteer life, and many current and real-life friendships that need maintenance. I have a work deadline in three hours, plus dinner isn't ready. The laundry remains unlaundered. Why, then, am I sitting at my computer, concerned to distraction over the activities of the people who were cruelest to me during my formative years?

3   They weren't always horrible to me. I loved fifth and sixth grades. I had a clique of friends, complete with secret nicknames, passed notes, knowing looks, friendship bracelets, friendship pens, friendship songs. We moved through the school as a group and took turns slumber-partying at each other's houses.

4   We traded the title "best friend" regularly among different pairings in our group. Nancy and Barbara had spent two weeks together in Nantucket over the summer, and though Nancy

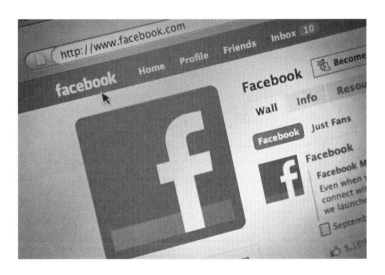

and I had been best friends prior to that, apparently they had decided that their time had come to be best friends. They made this announcement to me via conference call the week before school started. I took it OK; after all, I'd been meaning to get to know Amy better.

5    Late in sixth grade, something changed, and I wasn't a part of it. One day, all my friends came in with matching training bras. "I didn't know we were getting bras," I said. They looked at each other, a shared glance I used to be on the comfy side of, and my heart sank with the unspoken answer: *We* weren't. *They* were.

6    Seventh grade began, and I found out we had grown out of things like changing best friends. I met a girl named Emily who had transferred to our school. After a good day of getting to know her, I asked if she wanted to be best friends. "You're such a loser," she spat. I looked around one day, and my group of friends had wandered away. Adults like to generalize and say things like, "Aren't kids cruel?" But we kids, the ones who are left out in the cold, have a role in what happens to us. Not necessarily a fair one, but the facts of our unpopularity are not mysterious. We get fat, we say the wrong thing, we wear outdated clothing. Me, I was too needy. Long after my friends stopped needing superlative titles to know how much they meant to each other, I still did.

7    I did not go quietly into that lonely and unpopular night. Each morning, I tried to assume a casual air of friendship. Big mistake. My efforts backfired, and my former friends' apathy toward me turned to hatred. Soon, I was not just ignored at school. I was tripped as I came out of the shower. People made flatulent noises when I sat down in class. My locker was magic-markered with the word "loser." We are tempted to remember this behavior and make light of it. Oh, it couldn't have been that bad, we said. But I remember it well. It was that bad.

8    Now, all these years later, there's Facebook, allowing us to put the past to rest, to erase the mystery that used to be inherent in the subject of wondering whatever happened to those people you once knew.

9    After accumulating college friends and ex-boyfriends, as we all do when we join Facebook, I took a chance and looked up Barbara. With the nervousness that accompanied me on every bus trip to school following my fall from grace, I pressed the button that would send her a friend request. Immediately, I received confirmation: She had agreed, finally, to be my friend. Brave now, I found Alison, then Amy, then Nancy. I was euphoric. Here I am, back in the inner sanctum. I sort through their pictures, their posts, their lives. I cheer their triumphs, their babies' birthdays, photos from their ski trips. I cobble together the story of how life has been since we knew each other, deliberately, forcefully forgetting how it was we parted.

10    I check their updates and their statuses with eagerness each day. Like an addict, I am euphoric when I am practicing my addiction, remorseful and self-hating when I'm not. I am shocked at how easily I have forgiven these people. I am filled with the warm light of acceptance; I am wrapped in the cozy blanket of belonging.

11    In my imagination, my old clique's renewed friendship tells me that they know they were wrong, that they were just being cruel. They're sorry, they say with every LOL or emoticon. We were wrong, they say when they press the "like" button on my status update. If I'm honest, I bet they don't think about it. I bet they regard me as a name that is familiar— a new person in their lives, more than an old one.

12    There is no way to go back in time and undo things—not the insults, not the humiliations. We can pretend some events never happened, though we are always still a little plagued. But, sometimes, we can also find a way to make what happened in the past right.

I'm not saying you can do that with everything that haunts your past. But some things, you can. Maybe the way women in the '90s took back the word "bitch," calling themselves and each other by the ugly slur so that it wouldn't hold power when men said it, maybe that's what I'm doing with my former friends.

13    Why do you need to be loved by people who rejected you a hundred years ago, asks my husband, though I have explained it. He believes I have Stockholm syndrome, that I have fallen in love with my torturers. I tell him that these are just old friends, that I'm over it, that it's nice to be in touch with a piece of my past. But I'm not exactly over it, am I? What I am, though, is someone who has finally found a way to put my life's ugliest social chapter to rest. Maybe I didn't come by it the honest way—through a true reckoning with my past, a fearless inventory of what happened that year and why I can't get over it. But who is to say that we shouldn't try to find peace any way we can? Who says it always has to be so hard?

14    Whatever my intention was when I contacted my former friends, it's different now. I no longer want validation; I no longer am testing the waters to see if they now find me worth their time. These women are not who I thought they'd be. They're people having a hard time in the economy, people who are struggling through their days, their relationships. I don't have enough in common with them to think that, had we not fallen out, our friendships would have survived. But here, now, I am someone who also struggles with these things. I have stretched across a social divide that was narrower than I thought, and I found community where I least expected it. Am I pathetic? Maybe. But what I also am, finally, is a popular seventh-grader. I think of my younger self, eating her lunch alone, wondering when this agony will be over. I wish I could tell her I haven't forgotten about her. I wish I could tell her I've made it OK.

## QUESTIONS FOR ANALYSIS AND DISCUSSION

1. Brodesser-Akner comments in her essay that she no longer wants or needs validation. Describe what she means by this statement. Do you believe her? Draw from textual evidence to support your point.
2. The author states that she is finally "a popular seventh-grader" due to Facebook. What does it mean to be "popular"? Can you be truly popular on Facebook? Can Facebook or other social networking sites help people right the wrongs in their past?
3. Most narratives essays use chronological order to tell their stories. Show how Brodesser-Akner progresses through her own essay. Do you find the author's style to be effective?
4. What was the author's purpose for writing this essay? Explain. Use textual evidence in your explanation.
5. Look up the definition of "Stockholm Syndrome." Why does the author's husband use this term to describe her relationship with her "friends" on Facebook?
6. Brodesser-Akner asserts that in the 1990's women "took back the word, 'bitch,' calling themselves and each other by the ugly slur so that it wouldn't hold power when men said it." She then claims that this is what she's doing with her former friends. Explain what she means by this analogy.

## WRITING ASSIGNMENTS

1. Track all of your online correspondence—received and sent—for a period of one week. This should include email, IM, text messaging, and posting on social networking sites. Develop categories for the communication (social, family, work, school, junk, etc.) and chart how many of each you receive and send in each category. Keep track of how much time you spend online. In a short essay, discuss how the Internet both enhances and complicates life, and whether it is indeed changing your personal relationships for better or for worse.

2. Several of the writers in this chapter are critical of social networking sites, noting that they promote self-centeredness, reduce our ability to cope with emotions, and cheapen what it means to be "a friend." Interview at least ten people of different age groups about how they use online communication and their views of social networking sites. Create simple questions, but make them broad enough to allow for the expression of detailed viewpoints and options. Write a short essay evaluating the role of social networking on the lives of people today. Include any differences or similarities you noticed between age groups, professions, and/or social backgrounds. Based on your surveys, can you predict the role social networking will have in our lives in the next decade?

3. Is there a connection between how we communicate and relate to others online and how we develop our own sense of identity? How others perceive us? Print the profiles of at least ten people you know (you may need to ask for permission if you are not part of a social network) and compare the profiles they present to the people you know in "real life." Alternatively, you could ask an acquaintance to share five profiles of people you don't know for analysis.

4. A popular television commercial for an Internet employment agency features a man writing an insulting letter to his boss only to have a toy fall off his monitor and hit the "enter" key, sending his message. Have you ever had a mishap with online communication, or found yourself sending a message that you shouldn't have simply because you hit the "enter" key in the heat of the moment? Describe your experience. Did it influence your future use of online communication?

5. Evaluate your own online communication style. Are you brief and to the point, or do you compose in more detail? What do you think your style says about you? What does it communicate to others? Do you have different styles for different situations? Explain.

6. Write about a relationship, romantic or merely friendly, in which online networking was an essential component of the connection you had with the other person. Cite examples of how social networking contributed to your relationship, and how it enriched its quality.

7. Research how the Internet is influencing how we think and how it may be even changing our brains. Will the Internet be the next influence on our physical evolution? Explain.

# Human Rights and Wrongs

Our concept of freedom is deeply connected to our understanding of human rights—those basic rights to which all people are entitled. The idea that all people everywhere should enjoy the same rights is relatively new. For millennia, different groups of people have been denied many of the rights we now take for granted. Until very recently, for instance, African-Americans had been denied some basic civil liberties. Even today, women in many parts of the world do not enjoy the same rights and freedoms as men. Likewise, some groups of people are still oppressed because of their ethnicity or religious views.

Human rights advocates maintain that our rights are basic and universal, granted to us because we are human, and independent of any legal systems or government rules. Although debates continue as to which rights are universal, basic human rights include civil rights such as the right to life, liberty, freedom of expression, the right to be treated with respect, the right to work, the right to be afforded equal protection under the law, the right to education, and the right to food, shelter, and health. In 1948, the United Nations attempted to codify human rights in an attempt to encourage their adoption and recognition internationally. Since then, the Human Rights Declaration has been rendered in at least 375 languages and dialects, making it the most widely translated document in the world.

Disagreement continues over whether some rights, such as the right to have a family and to marry, are inalienable and basic, and whether some rights are legal but mutable based upon the cultural mores of a people. Some Islamic countries have criticized the Universal Declaration of Human Rights, claiming that it is based on Judeo-Christian tradition and fails to take into account the cultural and religious context of Islam. In June 2000, Muslim countries that are members of the Organization of the Islamic Conference adopted the Cairo Declaration on Human Rights in Islam, which states that people have "freedom and the right to a dignified life in accordance with the Islamic Shari'ah." Clearly the debate over the definition of human rights will continue and, perhaps, never be settled.

This chapter examines some current debates concerning human rights and freedoms. To prepare for the readings in this section, you may wish to review the history of human rights and civil rights. A good resource is www.humanrights.com, a site maintained by United for Human Rights (UHR), an organization that promotes the Universal Declaration of Human Rights at local, regional, national and international levels. As you read the essays in this chapter, consider your view of human rights, the freedoms you expect, and the ambiguity surrounding what you understand human rights to be.

## Universal Declaration of Human Rights
*United Nations*

On December 10, 1948, following the Second World War, the General Assembly of the United Nations adopted and proclaimed the Universal Declaration of Human Rights, the full text of which appears in the following pages. Following this historic act, the Assembly called upon all member countries to publicize the text of the Declaration and "to cause it to be disseminated, displayed, read and expounded principally in schools and other educational institutions, without distinction based on the political status of countries or territories." Since its creation, the Declaration has been translated into 375 languages and dialects. While not enforceable (not part of binding international law), international lawyers refer to it in applying diplomatic pressure to governments violating its articles.

### BEFORE YOU READ

Think about what you consider to be basic freedoms and rights. Make a list of the things you believe should be inalienable to all people. After reading the Universal Declaration of Human Rights, compare your list to the document. What did you leave out? Did the UN document leave out anything you had on *your* list?

### AS YOU READ

Why is a document like this necessary? What does it seek to define and whom does it aim to protect?

## Preamble

1 Whereas recognition of the inherent dignity and of the equal and inalienable rights of all members of the human family is the foundation of freedom, justice and peace in the world,

2 Whereas disregard and contempt for human rights have resulted in barbarous acts which have outraged the conscience of mankind, and the advent of a world in which human beings shall enjoy freedom of speech and belief and freedom from fear and want has been proclaimed as the highest aspiration of the common people,

3 Whereas it is essential, if man is not to be compelled to have recourse, as a last resort, to rebellion against tyranny and oppression, that human rights should be protected by the rule of law,

4 Whereas it is essential to promote the development of friendly relations between nations,

5 Whereas the peoples of the United Nations have in the Charter reaffirmed their faith in fundamental human rights, in the dignity and worth of the human person and in the equal rights of men and women and have determined to promote social progress and better standards of life in larger freedom,

6    Whereas Member States have pledged themselves to achieve, in co-operation with the United Nations, the promotion of universal respect for and observance of human rights and fundamental freedoms,

7    Whereas a common understanding of these rights and freedoms is of the greatest importance for the full realization of this pledge,

8    Now, Therefore THE GENERAL ASSEMBLY proclaims THIS UNIVERSAL DECLARATION OF HUMAN RIGHTS as a common standard of achievement for all peoples and all nations, to the end that every individual and every organ of society, keeping this Declaration constantly in mind, shall strive by teaching and education to promote respect for these rights and freedoms and by progressive measures, national and international, to secure their universal and effective recognition and observance, both among the peoples of Member States themselves and among the peoples of territories under their jurisdiction.

### Article 1.

9 All human beings are born free and equal in dignity and rights. They are endowed with reason and conscience and should act towards one another in a spirit of brotherhood.

### Article 2.

10 Everyone is entitled to all the rights and freedoms set forth in this Declaration, without distinction of any kind, such as race, color, sex, language, religion, political or other opinion, national or social origin, property, birth or other status. Furthermore, no distinction shall be made on the basis of the political, jurisdictional or international status of the country or territory to which a person belongs, whether it is independent, trust, non-self-governing or under any other limitation of sovereignty.

### Article 3.

11 Everyone has the right to life, liberty and security of person.

### Article 4.

12 No one shall be held in slavery or servitude; slavery and the slave trade shall be prohibited in all their forms.

### Article 5.

13 No one shall be subjected to torture or to cruel, inhuman or degrading treatment or punishment.

### Article 6.

14 Everyone has the right to recognition everywhere as a person before the law.

### Article 7.

15 All are equal before the law and are entitled without any discrimination to equal protection of the law. All are entitled to equal protection against any discrimination in violation of this Declaration and against any incitement to such discrimination.

### Article 8.

16 Everyone has the right to an effective remedy by the competent national tribunals for acts violating the fundamental rights granted him by the constitution or by law.

### Article 9.

17 No one shall be subjected to arbitrary arrest, detention or exile.

### Article 10.

18 Everyone is entitled in full equality to a fair and public hearing by an independent and impartial tribunal, in the determination of his rights and obligations and of any criminal charge against him.

### Article 11.

19 1. Everyone charged with a penal offence has the right to be presumed innocent until proved guilty according to law in a public trial at which he has had all the guarantees necessary for his defense.

20 2. No one shall be held guilty of any penal offence on account of any act or omission which did not constitute a penal offence, under national or international law, at the time when it was committed. Nor shall a heavier penalty be imposed than the one that was applicable at the time the penal offence was committed.

### Article 12.

21 No one shall be subjected to arbitrary interference with his privacy, family, home or correspondence, nor to attacks upon his honor and reputation. Everyone has the right to the protection of the law against such interference or attacks.

### Article 13.

22 1. Everyone has the right to freedom of movement and residence within the borders of each state.

23 2. Everyone has the right to leave any country, including his own, and to return to his country.

### Article 14.

1. Everyone has the right to seek and to enjoy in other countries asylum from persecution.

24 2. This right may not be invoked in the case of prosecutions genuinely arising from non-
25 political crimes or from acts contrary to the purposes and principles of the United Nations.

### Article 15.

26 1. Everyone has the right to a nationality.

27 2. No one shall be arbitrarily deprived of his nationality nor denied the right to change his nationality.

## Article 16.

29  1.  Men and women of full age, without any limitation due to race, nationality or religion, have the right to marry and to found a family. They are entitled to equal rights as to marriage, during marriage and at its dissolution.

30  2.  Marriage shall be entered into only with the free and full consent of the intending spouses.

31  3.  The family is the natural and fundamental group unit of society and is entitled to protection by society and the State.

## Article 17.

32  1.  Everyone has the right to own property alone as well as in association with others.

33  2.  No one shall be arbitrarily deprived of his property.

## Article 18.

34  Everyone has the right to freedom of thought, conscience and religion; this right includes freedom to change his religion or belief, and freedom, either alone or in community with others and in public or private, to manifest his religion or belief in teaching, practice, worship and observance.

## Article 19.

35  Everyone has the right to freedom of opinion and expression; this right includes freedom to hold opinions without interference and to seek, receive and impart information and ideas through any media and regardless of frontiers.

## Article 20.

36  1.  Everyone has the right to freedom of peaceful assembly and association.

37  2.  No one may be compelled to belong to an association.

## Article 21.

38  1.  Everyone has the right to take part in the government of his country, directly or through freely chosen representatives.

39  2.  Everyone has the right of equal access to public service in his country.

40  3.  The will of the people shall be the basis of the authority of government; this will shall be expressed in periodic and genuine elections which shall be by universal and equal suffrage and shall be held by secret vote or by equivalent free voting procedures.

## Article 22.

41  Everyone, as a member of society, has the right to social security and is entitled to realization, through national effort and international co-operation and in accordance with the organization and resources of each State, of the economic, social and cultural rights indispensable for his dignity and the free development of his personality.

## Article 23.

41  1. Everyone has the right to work, to free choice of employment, to just and favorable conditions of work and to protection against unemployment.

42  2. Everyone, without any discrimination, has the right to equal pay for equal work.

43  3. Everyone who works has the right to just and favorable remuneration ensuring for himself and his family an existence worthy of human dignity, and supplemented, if necessary, by other means of social protection.

44  4. Everyone has the right to form and to join trade unions for the protection of his interests.

## Article 24.

45  Everyone has the right to rest and leisure, including reasonable limitation of working hours and periodic holidays with pay.

## Article 25.

46  1. Everyone has the right to a standard of living adequate for the health and well-being of himself and of his family, including food, clothing, housing and medical care and necessary social services, and the right to security in the event of unemployment, sickness, disability, widowhood, old age or other lack of livelihood in circumstances beyond his control.

47  2. Motherhood and childhood are entitled to special care and assistance. All children, whether born in or out of wedlock, shall enjoy the same social protection.

## Article 26.

48  1. Everyone has the right to education. Education shall be free, at least in the elementary and fundamental stages. Elementary education shall be compulsory. Technical and professional education shall be made generally available and higher education shall be equally accessible to all on the basis of merit.

49  2. Education shall be directed to the full development of the human personality and to the strengthening of respect for human rights and fundamental freedoms. It shall promote understanding, tolerance and friendship among all nations, racial or religious groups, and shall further the activities of the United Nations for the maintenance of peace.

50  3. Parents have a prior right to choose the kind of education that shall be given to their children.

## Article 27.

51  1. Everyone has the right freely to participate in the cultural life of the community, to enjoy the arts and to share in scientific advancement and its benefits.

52  2. Everyone has the right to the protection of the moral and material interests resulting from any scientific, literary or artistic production of which he is the author.

## Article 28.

53  Everyone is entitled to a social and international order in which the rights and freedoms set forth in this Declaration can be fully realized.

## Article 29.

54  1.  Everyone has duties to the community in which alone the free and full development of his personality is possible.

55  2.  In the exercise of his rights and freedoms, everyone shall be subject only to such limitations as are determined by law solely for the purpose of securing due recognition and respect for the rights and freedoms of others and of meeting the just requirements of morality, public order and the general welfare in a democratic society.

56  3.  These rights and freedoms may in no case be exercised contrary to the purposes and principles of the United Nations.

## Article 30.

57  Nothing in this Declaration may be interpreted as implying for any State, group or person any right to engage in any activity or to perform any act aimed at the destruction of any of the rights and freedoms set forth herein.

### QUESTIONS FOR ANALYSIS AND DISCUSSION

1.  What are the basic, main principles upheld by the Declaration?
2.  What is the goal and function of this document? Who is the audience?
3.  Some countries have argued that the rights outlined in this document disregard some religious laws that define and govern those particular countries. Therefore, some of the rights do not apply if they counter the religious beliefs of such countries. Do you agree with all of the rights outlined in this document? Are there some that are questionable?
4.  Do you think anything is missing from this document? If you were a member of the International Council for Human Rights Policy, what changes would you suggest, and why?
5.  Countries may employ sanctions against other countries that violate the principles outlined in the Universal Declaration of Human Right. Research some countries against which the U.S. has instituted an economic embargo (Iran, North Korea, Cuba, Myanmar, etc.). Select one such country and, using the Declaration as the foundation for your argument, explain why an embargo is justifiable.

## Don't Close Gitmo
*Judith Miller*

Guantanamo Bay Naval Base, more commonly referred to as "Gitmo," is located in Guantanamo Bay in the southeastern end of Cuba. It has leased the area since 1903, despite opposition from the Cuban government, who challenges the presence of the naval base claiming that the lease is invalid under international law. Of national attention is the military detention camp, created in 2002, to incarcerate people captured in

Afghanistan and Iraq charged as unlawful combatants. The closing of the detention center has been requested by Amnesty International (May 2005), the United Nations (February 2006), and the European Union (May 2006), citing human rights violations, including inhumane confinement, sleep deprivation, religious defamation, and indefinite detention. President Barack Obama has indicated his intention to close the prison, but at publication, the center remains in operation. In this next essay, journalist Judith Miller explains why she believes that we still need detention centers like Gitmo as long as our war on terror lasts.*

### BEFORE YOU READ

If a person violates the rights of others, and poses a threat to the lives of others, what basic human rights should be retained, and what rights do you think should be forfeited? Explain.

### AS YOU READ

How does Miller describe the Guantanamo Bay detention center after taking the journalist's tour of the facility? How does her description compare to reports of inhumane conditions and activities we have seen from the media?

1   It's been a busy summer at the detention center at the Guantánamo Bay Naval Base. The joint task force in charge of the 226 remaining detainees—they are never called "prisoners"—is spending about $440,000 to expand the recreation yards at Camp 6, a medium-security facility. At nearby Camp 4, which offers communal living for the most "compliant" captives, the soccer yard is being enlarged. At Camp 5, a maximum-security facility, another new, $73,000 classroom is under construction, and satellite TV cables have just been installed. In March, Joint Task Force Guantánamo added art classes to the thrice-weekly instruction it offers in Arabic, Pashtu, and English. And the estimated 16 detainees who have been cleared for release as soon as Washington can find countries willing to accept them have just received training on new laptop computers, courtesy of the U.S. taxpayer.

2   Though President Obama vowed on his second day in office to close the detention center within a year—January 22, 2010—Gitmo's officers say they intend to continue spending previously budgeted funds to improve life at the center until the last detainee leaves. "It's business as usual around here," the task force's deputy commander, Brigadier General Rafael O'Ferrall, said during one of the weekly tours that Gitmo offers journalists, legislators, military and other officials, human-rights groups, and other "distinguished visitors," more than 1,800 of whom visited last year.

3   The point of the tour is to show that Gitmo, which President Obama called a "stain" on America's reputation, has become a model, if somewhat surreal, detention center. But another message is implicit in the barrage of statistics about the services and amenities being offered to such ostensibly dangerous people: closing Gitmo, now that it has been transformed

---

*Judith Miller, *City Journal*, September 24, 2009.

into a first-class detention facility, is a largely empty political gesture that makes little sense for either the detainees or tax-paying Americans.

4    My hosts would never dare publicly challenge their commander-in-chief's orders. But they clearly believe that Gitmo no longer deserves to be seen as a symbol of human-rights abuses. "This place is synonymous with military abuse and it's just not fair," says Rear Admiral Thomas H. Copeman III, the task force's commander, who took charge only two months ago. "In the last five and a half years, there has not been a single substantiated allegation of abuse."

5    Officers here are eager to distance themselves from the "enhanced interrogation techniques" that defense secretary Donald Rumsfeld and other senior Bush administration officials approved soon after 9/11, one of the most notorious of which was quickly rescinded. "No one was ever waterboarded at Gitmo," says Army colonel Bruce E. Vargo, commander of Gitmo's Joint Detention Group (a division of the joint task force).

6    The issue is fresh in the public mind. Attorney General Eric Holder has appointed a prosecutor to investigate alleged CIA abuse of detainees in the wake of last month's Justice Department decision, prompted by an ACLU lawsuit, to release more of a CIA inspector general's 2004 report documenting detainee abuses. Most of those abuses, however, apparently did not take place at Gitmo. A 2005 Pentagon report concluded, after examining 26 complaints from FBI agents involving a small portion of over 24,000 interrogations here, that while some "special interrogation plans" against a few "high-value detainees" were cumulatively "degrading and abusive," they "did not rise to the level of prohibited inhumane treatment" or torture. Further, those techniques—such as loud music, sleep deprivation, temperature manipulation, strip searches, prolonged shackling, and being doused with water—ended long ago, officers say. Since 2004, interrogation methods have adhered to the U.S. Army field manual, says Paul B. Rester, the Pentagon official in charge of interrogations: "Loud music has no place in my world."

7    Officers seem intent on restoring the center's image, sparing little effort or expense to improve Gitmo. In addition to providing captives with prayer rugs, beads, caps, and Korans in their native languages, soldiers are instructed not to interrupt prayer five times a day. Arrows point toward Mecca. Female journalists are asked not to wear perfume near the cells. The center spends roughly $4 million a year—or $17,467 a prisoner at its current occupancy rate—offering detainees a choice of six different halal meals a day, totaling between 4,500 and 5,500 calories. The kitchen prepares two Islamic "feast" meals a week and offers fresh food—such as yogurt, veggie-burger patties with fresh garlic and onion, and scrambled eggs and waffles.

8    In fact, obesity is increasingly a problem, says Gitmo's chief physician, a reservist who volunteered for this six-month assignment and found the "professional and compassionate" medical care offered here stunning. The detainees make roughly 7,800 visits per year to receive state-of-the-art medical care. That includes colonoscopies for "age-appropriate" detainees, 25 of which have been performed so far.

9    Hunger strikes are allowed here, but only along with "voluntary force-feeding"—a phrase admittedly worthy of Orwell. Each day, most of the protesters (about 18 percent of the detainees, according to Vargo) line up for Ensure nutritional supplements. They ingest the supplements not through the mouth but through the nostril, via a yellow, spaghetti-size tube lubricated with olive oil, which detainees prefer to the petroleum jelly commonly

used in American hospitals. (Butter pecan is the most popular of the five available flavors, the doctor says.) A full meal can be consumed in as little as 15 minutes. However grue-some this sounds, the procedure is neither inhumane nor painful, Copeman asserts. He has tried it himself: "It's a big nothing sandwich." Of course, those who don't "volunteer" are shackled and force-fed anyway. "They have a right to protest, and we have an obligation to keep them alive and healthy while they do so," Copeman explains.

10    The physician calls Gitmo's medical care far superior to what most Americans get, even his own relatively pampered patients back in Beverly Hills. A fact sheet states that the center has one medical staff member for every two detainees and a licensed provider for every 57, compared with the U.S. national average of one primary-care provider for every 390 people (or the one-to-5,300 ratio in Afghanistan). Eight detainees have been fitted with prosthetic devices. Detainees are also screened for, and when possible vaccinated against, a variety of illnesses—diphtheria, tuberculosis, H1N1 and other flu viruses, and HIV—most of which went undiagnosed in their own countries. Four detainees have hearing aids. "This place embodies the best of what we do as Americans," the doctor tells me, without a trace of irony. Are the detainees grateful for this care? "Some are, some aren't," he says. But like his clientele back in California, "most detainees don't want to die."

11    Still, some clearly do: there have been five documented suicides so far at Gitmo and many more unsuccessful attempts. The latest—Muhammad Ahmad Abdallah Salih, a 31-year-old Yemeni held here since 2002—killed himself in June, apparently by hoarding pills and downing them all at once, despite monitoring in the facility's psychiatric ward. (An internal investigation is ongoing.) Depression and other mental ailments among detainees are common, doctors acknowledge, and afflict some 13 percent of detainees.

12    So Gitmo continues to expand its "intellectual stimulation program" for detainees, whose education ranges from nonexistent to postgraduate. In addition to a library of over 15,000 books in a dozen languages, magazines, puzzles, electronic games, and newspapers—two mainstream Arabic dailies are offered twice weekly along with *USA Today*—there are over 315 movies on DVD and up to five hours a day of five-channel satellite TV. Detainees may order between two and eight books a week. Librarians black out pictures of scantily clad women and other photos that detainees find offensive.

13    What Gitmo is *not* doing, however, is trying to rehabilitate or de-radicalize its remaining detainees, as does the detention program in Iraq headed last year by General Douglas Stone. There, less than 1 percent of the 26,000 Iraqis detained went back to the fight after being released. Recidivism among Gitmo detainees released so far is higher—from a low estimate of 2.5 percent to the Pentagon's estimate of at least 5 percent and perhaps as high as 14 percent. "We must recognize that we are engaged in an ideological war and that these detainees have been warriors on that front," Stone tells me. "In a battlefield of the mind, no matter how humanely we treat these people—and we must do so as Americans—they will continue hating us unless they lose faith in their extremist interpretation of Islam."

14    But Gitmo has shunned de-radicalization programs, perhaps because of the political heat to which it has already been subjected. There are, for instance, no classes that offer detainees alternative mainstream interpretations of the Koran, as the program that Stone led provides in Iraq. And militant prisoners of all nationalities and ideological strains—from Wahhabi-oriented Yemenis to hard-core Pakistani Taliban—are housed together at Gitmo and hence have ample opportunity to reinforce militant religious doctrines. Without

rehabilitation, Stone worries, Gitmo's concentration on simply "humane custody and care" may not be enough to overcome radicalism.

15    Gitmo's detainees are permitted between two and 20 hours of recreational activity per day—soccer, volleyball, basketball, foosball, ping-pong, aerobic exercise on machines, and gardening. Rec time depends not on what detainees may have allegedly done to have been sent here, but on their degree of compliance with Gitmo's rules. As a result, Colonel Vargo says, most of the "compliant"—about 30 percent of the detainees—spend only four hours a day in their dorm-style communal housing. Those deemed less compliant reside in a maximum-security facility up to 20 hours a day. "Noncompliant" detainees are confined to individual cells, about ten feet long by eight feet wide, for 22 hours a day, but still have two hours of daily recreation. That's an hour more than most civilian prisoners get in American maximum-security prisons, officers point out—but then American civilian prisoners have been tried and convicted of crimes.

16    This is the real problem with Gitmo—the fact that most of the detainees have not yet been charged with terrorism or any other crime. "So what if they have satellite TV!" says Karen Greenberg, author of *The Least Worst Place*, about Gitmo's first 100 days. "Just charge them, try them and put them away, or release them," she adds, noting that despite all the time, money, and effort spent on Gitmo, only three detainees have been convicted— "hardly a record of judicial success."

17    H. Candace Gorman, who is representing two detainees, challenges the Pentagon's rosy portrait of Gitmo—one, she claims, was held for years in what any layman would call solitary confinement and had hepatitis B, tuberculosis, and untreated liver problems (Gitmo spokesmen say his ailments have been treated). But more disturbing, she tells me, is the violation of their human and civil rights by the absence of independent judicial review of their detention. Calling Guantánamo's two internal reviews "kangaroo courts," she argues that both—Combatant Status Review Tribunals and the annual Administrative Review Boards—rely on hearsay evidence and information acquired though coercion. And detainees are allowed to see no evidence against them deemed "secret." Gitmo officers counter that these "kangaroo courts" have nonetheless already freed over 500 detainees.

18    While detention conditions have improved, Gorman says, ending the detainees' legal limbo is far more important than changing where they are detained: "What we're looking for is some justice for these men, not a new prison." But President Obama seems to feel no urgency about that. The task force he created to consider the detention process has had its deadline extended as the complexity of the issues involved sinks in.

19    And there is little difference between Obama and his predecessor on some key civil-liberties issues. Jonathan Hafetz of the ACLU complains that Obama still defends the Bush idea that the "terrorism battlefield is unlimited, and hence that people can be picked up and held indefinitely anywhere, anyplace, and anytime." Not only has Obama embraced George W. Bush's notion of military commissions to try some detainees, with ostensibly bolstered rights for the defendants; he has also endorsed Bush's position on "renditions" to countries with suspect human-rights records.

20    And he agrees with Bush on preventive detention for a so-called "fifth category" of detainee: captives who supposedly cannot be prosecuted by a civilian court or even by a military commission because of torture-tainted evidence or the need to protect intelligence sources and methods, but who "pose a clear danger to the American people," as Obama puts

it, and may be too dangerous to release. It is unclear how many detainees fall into this category. In April, defense secretary Robert Gates estimated their numbers at Gitmo between 50 and 100; in July, Assistant Attorney General David Kris told Congress that though half of the Gitmo detainees' cases had been reviewed, none fell into the "fifth category." By mid-September, after all the cases had gotten an initial review, at least 100 detainees were being examined a second time for potential inclusion in the "can't transfer or prosecute" category.

21    While the administration ponders the detainees' legal fate, it seems pointless and even counterproductive to spend more money and energy moving them to "Gitmo North"—maximum-security prisons in the United States where they may be far more harshly treated. Though four to six attacks on Gitmo's guards take place each week—suggesting that detainees may not appreciate their art classes that much—Lieutenant Commander Brook DeWalt, the joint task force's director of public affairs, says that the military guards are taught never to respond to provocations, even the "cocktails" of excrement that detainees hurl at them. Soldiers are also trained to return quickly to their posts.

22    Would even veteran civilian guards react as stoically to such abuse? "If the detainees are transferred to a maximum-security prison in the U.S., they'll wish they were back at Gitmo," says Brigadier General Thomas L. Hemingway, the former legal advisor in the Pentagon's Office of Military Commissions.

23    Officials also stress the continuing intelligence value of the 60 to 70 interrogations a week conducted at Gitmo. Over the years, 46,000 such interrogations have produced an estimated 6,000 reports. At one time, intelligence officials say, some 37 different al-Qaeda-related groups were represented in the camp, and there is still an active al-Qaeda cell here. Some 60 current or former detainees had residences in the U.S., relatives here, or other direct ties.

24    Representative Pete Hoekstra, the ranking Republican on the House Intelligence Committee, supports the Senate's refusal to authorize $80 million that the Obama administration requested to close Gitmo or the use of any funds to release or transfer prisoners to the United States. Hoekstra says that the military estimates that it will cost over $100 million to rehab the soon-to-be closed maximum-security prison at Standish, Michigan, or the army base at Fort Leavenworth, Kansas. Given the $185 million already invested in Gitmo and its $120 million annual operating budget, he says, closing Gitmo now would be "an utter waste of taxpayer money."

25    It's time for the Obama administration to acknowledge that Gitmo, or another center like it, will be needed as long as the War on Terror—no matter what our commander-in-chief calls it—endures. As a result, we will need to detain foreign fighters who under national and international law can be held without charge until the "end of hostilities," which in this case means indefinitely. But to ensure that such places do not become legal black holes, detainees—whether we call them prisoners of war, enemy combatants, or "enemy criminals," as lawyer Noah Feldman once suggested—should be assured of some kind of periodic, independent review of the allegations against them. As civilian detainees or prisoners of an unconventional war in which the battlefield can be anywhere or everywhere, they should have not only decent physical treatment, but also some legal right to challenge their detention in a way that does not jeopardize intelligence sources and methods.

26    Several legal experts, among them Benjamin Wittes of the Brookings Institution, have proposed legal compromises that would authorize preventive detention for terrorism suspects like many of those at Gitmo. Such detention schemes, with bolstered rights

for detainees and a guaranteed, periodic impartial review of the intelligence information or actions that led to their detention, may not be perfect. But they may be the most effective way to protect American values while we continue fighting a war that we cannot afford to abandon.

## QUESTIONS FOR ANALYSIS AND DISCUSSION

1. According to Miller, what is the "real problem" with Gitmo?
2. Organizations that have called for the closing of Guantanamo Bay Detention Center claim that "indefinite detention" is a form of torture. Respond to this assertion with your own viewpoint.
3. Miller notes that the detainees at Gitmo are never called "prisoners." Consider the importance of language in describing a situation. What is the difference between a detainee and a prisoner? A detention center and a prison? Explain.
4. What is the "battlefield of the mind"? Why is this term important to our understanding of the role of Gitmo and the conflict in the Middle East?
5. What is Miller's opinion of Barack Obama? What does she say about his position on Gitmo? His understanding of the War on Terror? Explain.
6. Research the issues surrounding the Guantanamo Bay Detention Center and explain why you think it should or should not be closed. Refer to points raised by Miller as well as outside research. Support your view with as much evidence as you can.

# The Torture Memos
## Noam Chomsky

In 2009, President Barack Obama released the "torture memos"—documents that revealed that the Justice Department's Office of the Legal Council authorized the use of torture as part of interrogation tactics used on political prisoners held in Abu Ghraib, Guantanamo Bay, and other sites. The memos outlined that the CIA could use practices that were defined as torture, such as waterboarding, in their interrogation of suspected terrorists, practices that were clearly against U.S. law. The memo's authors have not been charged. Human rights activists have called for the disbarment of the attorneys who authorized the practices with the argument that they should not have overwritten legal policy. Who is more culpable, the authors of the memo or the CIA who asked if they could use torture tactics in the first place? In this next essay, linguist, professor, and political activist Noam Chomsky, a well-known critic of U.S. foreign policy, argues that the U.S., much to its shame, has a long history of justifying torture in the name of justice.*

*Noam Chomsky, chomsky.info, May 24, 2009.

BEFORE YOU READ

Is torture ever justifiable? If so, under what circumstances?

AS YOU READ

What is the "idea" of America? What does the United States represent? How do the torture memos undermine that idea?

1   The torture memos released by the White House elicited shock, indignation, and surprise. The shock and indignation are understandable—particularly the testimony in the Senate Armed Services Committee report on Cheney-Rumsfeld desperation to find links between Iraq and al-Qaeda, links that were later concocted as justification for the invasion, facts irrelevant. Former Army psychiatrist Maj. Charles Burney testified that "a large part of the time we were focused on trying to establish a link between al-Qaeda and Iraq. The more frustrated people got in not being able to establish this link . . . there was more and more pressure to resort to measures that might produce more immediate results"; that is, torture. The McClatchy press reported that a former senior intelligence official familiar with the interrogation issue added that "The Bush administration applied relentless pressure on interrogators to use harsh methods on detainees in part to find evidence of cooperation between al-Qaeda and the late Iraqi dictator Saddam Hussein's regime . . . [Cheney and Rumsfeld] demanded that the interrogators find evidence of al Qaida-Iraq collaboration . . . 'There was constant pressure on the intelligence agencies and the interrogators to do whatever it took to get that information out of the detainees, especially the few high-value ones we had, and when people kept coming up empty, they were told by Cheney's and Rumsfeld's people to push harder'."[1]

2   These were the most significant revelations, barely reported.

3   While such testimony about the viciousness and deceit of the administration should indeed be shocking, the surprise at the general picture revealed is nonetheless surprising. A narrow reason is that even without inquiry, it was reasonable to suppose that Guantanamo was a torture chamber. Why else send prisoners where they would be beyond the reach of the law—incidentally, a place that Washington is using in violation of a treaty that was forced on Cuba at the point of a gun? Security reasons are alleged, but they are hard to take seriously. The same expectations held for secret prisons and rendition, and were fulfilled.

4   A broader reason is that torture has been routine practice from the early days of the conquest of the national territory, and then beyond, as the imperial ventures of the "infant empire"—as George Washington called the new Republic—extended to the Philippines, Haiti, and elsewhere. Furthermore, torture was the least of the many crimes of aggression, terror, subversion and economic strangulation that have darkened U.S. history, much as in the case of other great powers. Accordingly, it is surprising to see the reactions even by some of the most eloquent and forthright critics of Bush malfeasance: for example, that we used to be "a nation of moral ideals" and never before Bush "have our leaders so utterly betrayed everything our nation stands for" (Paul Krugman). To say the least, that common view reflects a rather slanted version of history.

5   Occasionally the conflict between "what we stand for" and "what we do" has been forthrightly addressed. One distinguished scholar who undertook the task is Hans

Morgenthau, a founder of realist international relations theory. In a classic study written in the glow of Camelot, Morgenthau developed the standard view that the U.S. has a "transcendent purpose": establishing peace and freedom at home and indeed everywhere, since "the arena within which the United States must defend and promote its purpose has become world-wide." But as a scrupulous scholar, he recognized that the historical record is radically inconsistent with the "transcendent purpose" of America.

6   We should not, however, be misled by that discrepancy, Morgenthau advises: in his words, we should not "confound the abuse of reality with reality itself." Reality is the unachieved "national purpose" revealed by "the evidence of history as our minds reflect it." What actually happened is merely the "abuse of reality." To confound abuse of reality with reality is akin to "the error of atheism, which denies the validity of religion on similar grounds." An apt comparison.

7   The release of the torture memos led others to recognize the problem. In the *New York Times*, columnist Roger Cohen reviewed a book by British journalist Geoffrey Hodgson, who concludes that the U.S. is "just one great, but imperfect, country among others." Cohen agrees that the evidence supports Hodgson's judgment, but regards it as fundamentally mistaken. The reason is Hodgson's failure to understand that "America was born as an idea, and so it has to carry that idea forward." The American idea is revealed by America's birth as a "city on a hill," an "inspirational notion" that resides "deep in the American psyche"; and by "the distinctive spirit of American individualism and enterprise" demonstrated in the Western expansion. Hodgson's error is that he is keeping to "the distortions of the American idea in recent decades," the "abuse of reality" in recent years.

8   Let us then turn to "reality itself": the "idea" of America from its earliest days.

9   The inspirational phrase "city on a hill" was coined by John Winthrop in 1630, borrowing from the Gospels, and outlining the glorious future of a new nation "ordained by God." One year earlier his Massachusetts Bay Colony established its Great Seal. It depicts an Indian with a scroll coming out of his mouth. On it are the words "Come over and help us." The British colonists were thus benevolent humanists, responding to the pleas of the miserable natives to be rescued from their bitter pagan fate.

10   The Great Seal is a graphic representation of "the idea of America," from its birth. It should be exhumed from the depths of the psyche and displayed on the walls of every classroom. It should certainly appear in the background of all of the Kim il-Sung-style worship of the savage murderer and torturer Ronald Reagan, who blissfully described himself as the leader of a "shining city on the hill" while orchestrating some of the more ghastly crimes of his years in office, leaving a hideous legacy.

11   This early proclamation of "humanitarian intervention," to use the currently fashionable phrase, turned out to be very much like its successors, facts that were not obscure to the agents. The first Secretary of War, General Henry Knox, described "the utter extirpation of all the Indians in most populous parts of the Union" by means "more destructive to the Indian natives than the conduct of the conquerors of Mexico and Peru." Long after his own significant contributions to the process were past, John Quincy Adams deplored the fate of "that hapless race of native Americans, which we are exterminating with such merciless and perfidious cruelty . . . among the heinous sins of this nation, for which I believe God will one day bring [it] to judgment." The merciless and perfidious cruelty continued until "the West was won." Instead of God's judgment, the heinous sins bring only praise for the fulfillment of the American "idea."[2]

12    There was, to be sure, a more convenient and conventional version, expressed for example by Supreme Court Justice Joseph Story, who mused that "the wisdom of Providence" caused the natives to disappear like "the withered leaves of autumn" even though the colonists had "constantly respected" them.[3]

13    The conquest and settling of the West indeed showed individualism and enterprise. Settler-colonialist enterprises, the cruelest form of imperialism, commonly do. The outcome was hailed by the respected and influential Senator Henry Cabot Lodge in 1898. Calling for intervention in Cuba, Lodge lauded our record "of conquest, colonization, and territorial expansion unequalled by any people in the 19th century," and urged that it is "not to be curbed now," as the Cubans too are pleading with us to come over and help them.[4] Their plea was answered. The U.S. sent troops, thereby preventing Cuba's liberation from Spain and turning it into a virtual colony, as it remained until 1959.

14    The "American idea" is illustrated further by the remarkable campaign, initiated virtually at once, to restore Cuba to its proper place: economic warfare with the clearly articulated aim of punishing the population so that they would overthrow the disobedient government; invasion; the dedication of the Kennedy brothers to bring "the terrors of the earth" to Cuba (the phrase of historian Arthur Schlesinger, in his biography of Robert Kennedy, who took the task as one of his highest priorities); and other crimes continuing to the present, in defiance of virtually unanimous world opinion.

15    There are to be sure critics, who hold that our efforts to bring democracy to Cuba have failed, so we should turn to other ways to "come over and help them." How do these critics know that the goal was to bring democracy? There is evidence: so our leaders proclaim. There is also counter-evidence: the declassified internal record, but that can be dismissed as just "the abuse of history."

16    American imperialism is often traced to the takeover of Cuba, Puerto Rico, and Hawaii in 1898. But that is to succumb to what historian of imperialism Bernard Porter calls "the salt water fallacy," the idea that conquest only becomes imperialism when it crosses salt water. Thus if the Mississippi had resembled the Irish Sea, Western expansion would have been imperialism. From Washington to Lodge, those engaged in the enterprise had a clearer grasp.

17    After the success of humanitarian intervention in Cuba in 1898, the next step in the mission assigned by Providence was to confer "the blessings of liberty and civilization upon all the rescued peoples" of the Philippines (in the words of the platform of Lodge's Republican party)—at least those who survived the murderous onslaught and the large-scale torture and other atrocities that accompanied it. These fortunate souls were left to the mercies of the U.S.-established Philippine constabulary within a newly devised model of colonial domination, relying on security forces trained and equipped for sophisticated modes of surveillance, intimidation, and violence.[5] Similar models were adopted in many other areas where the U.S. imposed brutal National Guards and other client forces, with consequences that should be well-known.

18    In the past sixty years, victims worldwide have also endured the CIA's "torture paradigm," developed at a cost reaching $1 billion annually, according to historian Alfred McCoy, who shows that the methods surfaced with little change in Abu Ghraib. There is no hyperbole when Jennifer Harbury entitles her penetrating study of the U.S. torture record Truth, Torture, and the American Way. It is highly misleading, to say the least,

when investigators of the Bush gang's descent into the sewer lament that "in waging the war against terrorism, America had lost its way."[6]

19     Bush-Cheney-Rumsfeld et al. did introduce important innovations. Ordinarily, torture is farmed out to subsidiaries, not carried out by Americans directly in their government-established torture chambers. Alain Nairn, who has carried out some of the most revealing and courageous investigations of torture, points out that "What the Obama [ban on torture] ostensibly knocks off is that small percentage of torture now done by Americans while retaining the overwhelming bulk of the system's torture, which is done by foreigners under U.S. patronage. Obama could stop backing foreign forces that torture, but he has chosen not to do so." Obama did not shut down the practice of torture, Nairn observes, but "merely repositioned it," restoring it to the norm, a matter of indifference to the victims. Since Vietnam, "the U.S. has mainly seen its torture done for it by proxy—paying, arming, training and guiding foreigners doing it, but usually being careful to keep Americans at least one discreet step removed." Obama's ban "doesn't even prohibit direct torture by Americans outside environments of 'armed conflict,' which is where much torture happens anyway since many repressive regimes aren't in armed conflict . . . his is a return to the status quo ante, the torture regime of Ford through Clinton, which, year by year, often produced more U.S.- backed strapped-down agony than was produced during the Bush/Cheney years."[7]

20     Sometimes engagement in torture is more indirect. In a 1980 study, Latin Americanist Lars Schoultz found that U.S. aid "has tended to flow disproportionately to Latin American governments which torture their citizens, . . . to the hemisphere's relatively egregious violators of fundamental human rights." That includes military aid, is independent of need, and runs through the Carter years. Broader studies by Edward Herman found the same correlation, and also suggested an explanation. Not surprisingly, U.S. aid tends to correlate with a favorable climate for business operations, and this is commonly improved by murder of labor and peasant organizers and human rights activists, and other such actions, yielding a secondary correlation between aid and egregious violation of human rights.[8]

21     These studies precede the Reagan years, when the topic was not worth studying because the correlations were so clear. And the tendencies continue to the present.

22     Small wonder that the President advises us to look forward, not backward—a convenient doctrine for those who hold the clubs. Those who are beaten by them tend to see the world differently, much to our annoyance.

23     An argument can be made that implementation of the CIA's "torture paradigm" does not violate the 1984 Torture Convention, at least as Washington interprets it. Alfred McCoy points out that the highly sophisticated CIA paradigm, based on the "KGB's most devastating torture technique," keeps primarily to mental torture, not crude physical torture, which is considered less effective in turning people into pliant vegetables. McCoy writes that the Reagan administration carefully revised the international Torture Convention "with four detailed diplomatic 'reservations' focused on just one word in the convention's 26-printed pages," the word "mental." These intricately-constructed diplomatic reservations redefined torture, as interpreted by the United States, to exclude sensory deprivation and self-inflicted pain—the very techniques the CIA had refined at such great cost." When Clinton sent the UN Convention to Congress for ratification in 1994, he included the Reagan reservations.

The President and Congress therefore exempted the core of the CIA torture paradigm from the U.S. interpretation of the Torture Convention; and those reservations, McCoy observes, were "reproduced verbatim in domestic legislation enacted to give legal force to the UN Convention." That is the "political land mine" that "detonated with such phenomenal force" in the Abu Ghraib scandal and in the shameful Military Commissions act that was passed with bipartisan support in 2006. Accordingly, after the first exposure of Washington's resort to torture, constitutional law professor Sanford Levinson observed that it could perhaps be justified in terms of the "interrogator-friendly" definition of torture adopted by Reagan and Clinton in their revision of international human rights law.[9]

24    Bush, of course, went beyond his predecessors in authorizing prima facie violations of international law, and several of his extremist innovations were struck down by the Courts. While Obama, like Bush, eloquently affirms our unwavering commitment to international law, he seems intent on substantially reinstating the extremist Bush measures. In the important case of Boumediene v. Bush in June 2008, the Supreme Court rejected as unconstitutional the Bush administration claim that prisoners in Guantanamo are not entitled to the right of habeas corpus. Glenn Greenwald reviews the aftermath. Seeking to "preserve the power to abduct people from around the world" and imprison them without due process, the Bush administration decided to ship them to Bagram, treating "the Boumediene ruling, grounded in our most basic constitutional guarantees, as though it was some sort of a silly game—fly your abducted prisoners to Guantanamo and they have constitutional rights, but fly them instead to Bagram and you can disappear them forever with no judicial process." Obama adopted the Bush position, "filing a brief in federal court that, in two sentences, declared that it embraced the most extremist Bush theory on this issue," arguing that prisoners flown to Bagram from anywhere in the world—in the case in question, Yemenis and Tunisians captured in Thailand and the UAE—"can be imprisoned indefinitely with no rights of any kind—as long as they are kept in Bagram rather than Guantanamo."

25    In March, a Bush-appointed federal judge "rejected the Bush/Obama position and held that the rationale of Boumediene applies every bit as much to Bagram as it does to Guantanamo." The Obama administration announced that it would appeal the ruling, thus placing Obama's Department of Justice "squarely to the Right of an extremely conservative, pro-executive-power, Bush 43-appointed judge on issues of executive power and due-process-less detentions," in radical violation of Obama's campaign promises and earlier stands.[10]

26    The case of Rasul v. Rumsfeld appears to be following a similar trajectory. The plaintiffs charged that Rumsfeld and other high officials were responsible for their torture in Guantanamo, where they were sent after they were captured by Uzbeki warlord Rashid Dostum. Dostum is a notorious thug who was then a leader of the Northern Alliance, the Afghan faction supported by Russia, Iran, India, Turkey, and the Central Asian states, joined by the U.S. as it attacked Afghanistan in October 2001. Dostum then turned him over to U.S. custody, allegedly for bounty money. The plaintiffs claimed that they had traveled to Afghanistan to offer humanitarian relief. The Bush administration sought to have the case dismissed. Obama's Department of Justice filed a brief supporting the Bush position that government officials are not liable for torture and other violations of due process in this case, because the Courts had not yet clearly established the rights that prisoners enjoy.[11]

27    It is also reported that Obama intends to revive military commissions, one of the more severe violations of the rule of law during the Bush years. There is a reason. "Officials who work on the Guantanamo issue say administration lawyers have become concerned that they would face significant obstacles to trying some terrorism suspects in federal courts. Judges might make it difficult to prosecute detainees who were subjected to brutal treatment or for prosecutors to use hearsay evidence gathered by intelligence agencies."[12] A serious flaw in the criminal justice system, it appears.

28    There is much debate about whether torture has been effective in eliciting information— the assumption being, apparently, that if it is effective then it may be justified. By the same argument, when Nicaragua captured U.S. pilot Eugene Hasenfuss in 1986 after shooting down his plane delivering aid to Reagan's contra forces, they should not have tried him, found him guilty, and then sent him back to the U.S., as they did. Rather, they should have applied the CIA torture paradigm to try to extract information about other terrorist atrocities being planned and implemented in Washington, no small matter for a tiny and poor country under terrorist attack by the global superpower. And Nicaragua should certainly have done the same if they had been able to capture the chief terrorism coordinator, John Negroponte, then Ambassador in Honduras, later appointed counterterrorism Czar, without eliciting a murmur. Cuba should have done the same if they had been able to lay hands on the Kennedy brothers. There is no need to bring up what victims should have done to Kissinger, Reagan, and other leading terrorist commanders, whose exploits leave al-Qaeda far in the distance, and who doubtless had ample information that could have prevented further "ticking bombs."

29    Such considerations, which abound, never seem to arise in public discussion. Accordingly, we know at once how to evaluate the pleas about valuable information.

30    There is, to be sure, a response: our terrorism, even if surely terrorism, is benign, deriving as it does from the city on the hill. Perhaps the most eloquent exposition of this thesis was presented by New Republic editor Michael Kinsley, a respected spokesman of "the left." America's Watch (Human Rights Watch) had protested State Department confirmation of official orders to Washington's terrorist forces to attack "soft targets"—undefended civilian targets—and to avoid the Nicaraguan army, as they could do thanks to CIA control of Nicaraguan airspace and the sophisticated communications systems provided to the contras. In response, Kinsley explained that U.S. terrorist attacks on civilian targets are justified if they satisfy pragmatic criteria: a "sensible policy [should] meet the test of cost-benefit analysis," an analysis of "the amount of blood and misery that will be poured in, and the likelihood that democracy will emerge at the other end"[13]—"democracy" as U.S. elites determine. His thoughts elicited no comment, to my knowledge, apparently deemed acceptable. It would seem to follow, then, that U.S. leaders and their agents are not culpable for conducting such sensible policies in good faith, even if their judgment might sometimes be flawed.

31    Perhaps culpability would be greater, by prevailing moral standards, if it were discovered that Bush administration torture cost American lives. That is, in fact, the conclusion drawn by U.S. Major Matthew Alexander [pseudonym], one of the most seasoned interrogators in Iraq, who elicited "the information that led to the U.S. military being able to locate Abu Musab al-Zarqawi, the head of al-Qa'ida in Iraq," correspondent Patrick Cockburn reports. Alexander expresses only contempt for the harsh interrogation methods: "The use of torture by the U.S.," he believes, not only elicits no useful information but "has

proved so counter-productive that it may have led to the death of as many U.S. soldiers as
civilians killed in 9/11." From hundreds of interrogations, Alexander discovered that foreign fighters came to Iraq in reaction to the abuses at Guantanamo and Abu Ghraib, and
that they and their domestic allies turned to suicide bombing and other terrorist acts for the
same reason.[14]

32      There is also mounting evidence that Cheney-Rumsfeld torture created terrorists. One
carefully studied case is that of Abdallah al-Ajmi, who was locked up in Guantanamo on
the charge of "engaging in two or three fire fights with the Northern Alliance." He ended
up in Afghanistan after having failed to reach Chechnya to fight against the Russian invasion. After four years of brutal treatment in Guantanamo, he was returned to Kuwait. He
later found his way to Iraq, and in March 2008 drove a bomb-laden truck into an Iraqi military compound, killing himself and 13 soldiers—"the single most heinous act of violence
committed by a former Guantanamo detainee," the *Washington Post* reports, the direct result
of his abusive imprisonment, his Washington lawyer concludes.[15]

33      All much as a reasonable person would expect.

34      Another standard pretext for torture is the context: the "war on terror" that Bush declared after 9/11, a "crime against humanity" carried out with "wickedness and awesome
cruelty," as Robert Fisk reported. That crime rendered traditional international law
"quaint" and "obsolete," Bush was advised by his legal counsel Alberto Gonzales, later appointed Attorney-General. The doctrine has been widely reiterated in one or another form
in commentary and analysis.

35      The 9/11 attack was doubtless unique, in many respects. One is where the guns were
pointing: typically it is in the opposite direction. In fact that was the first attack of any consequence on the national territory since the British burned down Washington in 1814.
Another unique feature is the scale of terror by a non-state actor. But horrifying as it was,
it could have been worse. Suppose that the perpetrators had bombed the White House,
killed the president and established a vicious military dictatorship that killed 50–100,000
people and tortured 700,000, set up a huge international terror center that carried out assas-
sinations and helped impose comparable military dictatorships elsewhere, and implemented economic doctrines that destroyed the economy so radically that the state had to
virtually take it over a few years later. That would have been a lot worse than 9/11 2001.
And it happened, in what Latin Americans often call "the first 9/11," in 1973. The numbers
have been changed to per capita equivalents, a realistic way of measuring crimes.
Responsibility traces straight back to Washington. Accordingly, the—quite appropriate—
analogy is out of consciousness, while the facts are consigned to the "abuse of reality" that
the naive call history.

36      It should also be recalled that Bush did not declare the "war on terror"; he re-
declared it. Twenty years earlier, the Reagan administration came into office declaring
that a centerpiece of its foreign policy would be a war on terror, "the plague of the modern age" and "a return to barbarism in our time," to sample the fevered rhetoric of the
day. That war on terror has also been deleted from historical consciousness, because the
outcome cannot readily be incorporated into the canon: hundreds of thousands slaugh-
tered in the ruined countries of Central America and many more elsewhere. Among
them an estimated 1.5 million in the terrorist wars sponsored in neighboring countries

by Reagan's favored ally apartheid South Africa, which had to defend itself from Nelson Mandela's African National Congress, one of the more world's "more notorious terrorist groups," Washington determined in 1988. In fairness, it should be added that 20 years later Congress voted to remove the ANC from the list of terrorist organizations, so that Mandela is now at last able to enter the U.S. without obtaining a waiver from the government.[16]

37   The reigning doctrine is sometimes called "American exceptionalism." It is nothing of the sort. It is probably close to universal among imperial powers. France was hailing its "civilizing mission" while the French Minister of War called for "exterminating the indigenous population" of Algeria. Britain's nobility was a "novelty in the world," John Stuart Mill declared, while urging that this angelic power delay no longer in completing its liberation of India. This classic essay on humanitarian intervention was written shortly after the public revelation of Britain's horrifying atrocities in suppressing the 1857 Indian rebellion. The conquest of the rest of India was in large part an effort to gain a monopoly of opium for Britain's huge narcotrafficking enterprise, by far the largest in world history, designed primarily to compel China to accept Britain's manufactured goods.

38   Similarly, there is no reason to doubt the sincerity of Japanese militarists who were bringing an "earthly paradise" to China under benign Japanese tutelage, as they carried out the rape of Nanking. History is replete with similar glorious episodes.

39   As long as such "exceptionalist" theses remain firmly implanted, the occasional revelations of the "abuse of history" can backfire, serving to efface terrible crimes. The My Lai massacre was a mere footnote to the vastly greater atrocities of the post-Tet pacification programs, ignored while indignation focused on this single crime. Watergate was doubtless criminal, but the furor over it displaced incomparably worse crimes at home and abroad—the FBI-organized assassination of black organizer Fred Hampton as part of the infamous COINTELPRO repression, or the bombing of Cambodia, to mention two egregious examples. Torture is hideous enough; the invasion of Iraq is a far worse crime. Quite commonly, selective atrocities have this function.

40   Historical amnesia is a dangerous phenomenon, not only because it undermines moral and intellectual integrity, but also because it lays the groundwork for crimes that lie ahead.

## ENDNOTES

1. http://documents.nytimes.com/report-by-the-senate-armed-services-committee-on-detainee-treatment#p=72. Jonathan Landay, "Abusive tactics used to seek Iraq-al Qaida link," *McClatchy News 21 Apr.* Gordon Trowbridge, "Levin: Iraq link goal of torture," *Detroit News 22 Apr 2009.*

2. Reginald Horsman, *Expansion and American Indian Policy* (Michigan State, 1967); William Earl Weeks, *John Quincy Adams and American Global Empire* (Kentucky, 1992).

3. On the record of Providentialist justifications for the most shocking crimes, and its more general role in forging "the American idea," see Nicholas Guyatt, *Providence and the Invention of the United States, 1607-1876* (Cambridge, 2007).

4. Cited by Lars Schoultz, *That Infernal Little Cuban Republic* (North Carolina, 2009).

5. Ibid. Alfred McCoy, *Policing America's Empire* (Wisconsin, 2009).

6. McCoy, *A Question of Torture* (Metropolitan, 2006). Also McCoy, "The U.S. Has a History of Using Torture," http://hnn.us/articles/32497.html. Harbury (Beacon, 2005). Jane Mayer, "The Battle for a Country's Soul," *NY Review,* 14 Aug. 2008.

7. *News and Comment,* 24 Jan. 2009, www.allannairn.com.

8. Schoultz, Comparative Politics, Jan. 1981. Herman, in Chomsky and Herman, *Political Economy of Human Rights I,* ch. 2.1.1 (South End, 1979); Herman, *Real Terror Network,* 1 (South End, 1982), 26ff.

9. McCoy, "US has a history." Levinson, "Torture in Iraq & the Rule of Law in America," *Daedalus,* Summer 2004.

10. Greenwald, "Obama and habeas corpus—then and now," http://www.salon.com/opinion/greenwald/2009/04/11/bagram/index.html?source=newsletter

11. Daphne Eviatar, "Obama Justice Department Urges Dismissal of Another Torture Case," *Washington Independent,* 12 Mar. 2009, http://washingtonindependent.com/33679/obama-justice-department-urges-dismissal-of-another-torture-case.

12. William Glaberson, "U.S. May Revive Guantanamo Military Courts," NYT, May 1, 2009; http://www.nytimes.com/2009/05/02/us/politics/02gitmo.html?scp=1&sq=%22military%20commissions%22&st=cse.

13. Kinsley, *Wall Street Journal* 26 Mar. 1987.

14. Cockburn, "Torture? It probably killed more Americans than 9/11," *Independent* 6 Apr. 2009.

15. Anonymous (Rajiv Chandrasekaran), "From Captive to Suicide Bomber," WP 22 Feb. 2009.

16. Joseba Zulaika and William Douglass, *Terror and Taboo* (Routledge, 1996). Jesse Holland, *AP* 9 May. 2009. NYT.

## QUESTIONS FOR ANALYSIS AND DISCUSSION

1. Chomsky explains that the torture memos highlight the conflict between "what we stand for" and "what we do." In your opinion, what does the U.S. stand for? Explain.

2. What is Chomsky's view of the United States in general? Of its foreign policy? Identify areas of his essay in which his words and tone reveal his position. Do his feelings about the U.S. strengthen or undermine his argument? Explain.

3. What does Chomsky's final sentence mean? How does "historical amnesia" undermine our moral integrity? How could it create even more damage in the future?

4. According to Chomsky, what is "American exceptionalism"? What does he mean by this term? How does it apply to human rights violations and the torture memos?

5. Why does Chomsky feel that arguments in support of torture as the lesser evil in light of the "war on terror" are invalid? Explain.

6. What historical background for U.S. use of torture does Chomsky provide? Why does he detail this history? How does it support his essay?

7. Summarize Chomsky's essay in a single paragraph. Distill his primary points into six sentences or less.

# The Meaning of Freedom

*The Economist*

U.S. citizens understand that the First Amendment to the U.S. Constitution affords them the right of freedom of speech, including the right to express their views without fear of government censorship. The free and open exchange of ideas and viewpoints is held by many people, as fundamental to our ability to debate and explore issues. What happens, however, when one group perceives free speech as threatening to their dignity? How does one define offensive speech, and should offensive speech be subjected to censure? At the beginning of 2009, the UN Human Rights Council passed a resolution condemning "defamation of religion" as a human rights violation. Proposed by Pakistan on behalf of Muslim nations, the goal was to prevent the defamation of Islam, as in the case of the cartoons of the prophet Muhammad, which sparked angry Muslims in 2006. Opponents to the resolution argued that the resolution restricted freedom of speech. The next editorial, by the editors of *The Economist*, explains that freedom of speech extends to even the right to "defame" religions. When we censure speech, they argue, we end up violating one right in favor of another.*

## BEFORE YOU READ

Is free speech a basic human right? Should you have the right to express yourself without fear of reprisal, or do you think that censorship is sometimes justifiable?

## AS YOU READ

What reasons does the editor offer for protecting even religious defamation? Do you agree? Why or why not?

1   At first glance, the resolution on "religious defamation" adopted by the UN's Human Rights Council on March 26, 2009, mainly at the behest of Islamic countries, reads like another piece of harmless verbiage churned out by a toothless international bureaucracy. What is wrong with saying, as the resolution does, that some Muslims faced prejudice in the aftermath of September 2001? But a closer look at the resolution's language, and the context in which it was adopted (with an unholy trio of Pakistan, Belarus and Venezuela acting as sponsors), makes clear that bigger issues are at stake.

2   The resolution says "defamation of religions" is a "serious affront to human dignity" which can "restrict the freedom" of those who are defamed, and may also lead to the incitement of violence. But there is an insidious blurring of categories here, which becomes plain when you compare this resolution with the more rigorous language of the Universal Declaration of Human Rights, adopted in 1948 in a spirit of revulsion over the evils of

*The Economist*, April 2, 2009.

fascism. This asserts the right of human beings in ways that are now entrenched in the theory and (most of the time) the practice of liberal democracy. It upholds the right of people to live in freedom from persecution and arbitrary arrest; to hold any faith or none; to change religion; and to enjoy freedom of expression, which by any fair definition includes freedom to agree or disagree with the tenets of any religion.

3    In other words, it protects individuals—not religions, or any other set of beliefs. And this is a vital distinction. For it is not possible systematically to protect religions or their followers from offence without infringing the right of individuals.

4    What exactly is it the drafters of the council resolution are trying to outlaw? To judge from what happens in the countries that lobbied for the vote—like Saudi Arabia, Egypt and Pakistan—they use the word "defamation" to mean something close to the crime of blasphemy, which is in turn defined as voicing dissent from the official reading of Islam. In many of the 56 member states of the Organization of the Islamic Conference, which has led the drive to outlaw "defamation," both non-Muslims and Muslims who voice dissent (even in technical matters of Koranic interpretation) are often victims of just the sort of persecution the 1948 declaration sought to outlaw. That is a real human-rights problem. And in the spirit of fairness, laws against blasphemy that remain on the statute books of some Western countries should also be struck off; only real, not imaginary, incitement of violence should be outlawed.

## Good manners, please; not censorship

5  In much of the Muslim world, the West's reaction to the attacks of September 2001, including the invasions of Afghanistan and Iraq, has been misread as an attack on Islam itself. This is more than regrettable; it is dangerous. Western governments, and decent people everywhere, should try to ensure that the things they say do not entrench religious prejudice or incite acts of violence; being free to give offence does not mean you are wise to give offence. But no state, and certainly no body that calls itself a Human Rights Council, should trample on the right to free speech enshrined in the Universal Declaration. And in the end, given that all faiths have undergone persecution at some time, few people have more to gain from the protection of free speech than sincere religious believers.

6    The United States, with its tradition of combining strong religious beliefs and religious freedom, is well placed to make that case. Having taken a politically risky decision (see article) to re-engage with the Human Rights Council and seek election as one of its 47 members, America should now make the defense of real religious liberty one of its highest priorities.

### QUESTIONS FOR ANALYSIS AND DISCUSSION  ————————

1.  Why the authors of this editorial believe that the UN Council's resolution is guilty of an "insidious blurring of categories" becomes clear when you review the Universal Declaration of Human Rights. According to the authors, how does the resolution violate the spirit of very document it intends to support?

2. The author calls for "good manners," not amendments. Are good manners likely to prevail? Are they a weak, but still better solution than the resolution adopted by the UN Council?

3. According to the authors, what bigger issue is at stake? What examples do the authors use to prove the point that religious defamation should not be censured? Explain.

4. Summarize the authors' argument and the call to action. Do you agree with the position taken by the editors of the *Economist* on this issue? Why or why not?

5. Research the March 26, 2009 resolution described in this editorial. Then write your own editorial in which you either defend or challenge the decision by the UN's Human Rights Council.

## Reading the Visual

## Media Blitz

*Piero Tonin*

### QUESTIONS FOR ANALYSIS AND DISCUSSION

1. What is this cartoon trying to convey? What is its point? How long does it take for the viewer to realize what the cartoon's point is?
2. What do you need to know in order to understand this cartoon? Explain.
3. How much media attention is given to human rights issues? What sort of coverage is granted to human rights issues in general?
4. Research human rights violations in Darfur. What is happening and how much coverage has it received?
5. In your opinion, does American media focus on the wrong things? Should it include more human rights issues and international news? Why or why not?

# The Detention Debacle: Toward Reform with Civility
*Arlene Roberts*

Guantanamo Bay isn't the only detention center that President Barack Obama must deal with. Every year, thousands of illegal immigrants are locked up in detention centers across the country. Some have families in the United States. Others are arrested in huge sweeps that separated mothers from their young children. In August 2009, Obama announced his plans to overhaul the immigration detention system. In this next short editorial, attorney and freelance speechwriter Arlene Roberts explains why reform is long overdue. Deplorable conditions, coupled by inhumane separation from families and support networks would seem to violate human rights. Robert's editorial is accompanied by a letter by a Marlene Jaggernauth, a detainee who describes her experience firsthand.*

**BEFORE YOU READ**

What rights, if any, are illegal immigrants entitled to? How should they be treated? Should they be arrested? Incarcerated? Explain.

**AS YOU READ**

Is it a basic right to be able to live where you wish? In any country you wish? Why or why not?

1   Anyone currently subject to an immigration detainer or who still has a loved one ensconced in detention at some far away location, most likely waited with bated breath for President Obama's report on proposed reforms for immigration detention. No discussion of detention reform can be complete without addressing the establishment of a uniform standard of accountability.

2   Across the nation detention facilities are run by private companies that are not held accountable for what transpires within the confines of their facilities. As a result, former detainees recount tales of horror and abuse. Just ask Marlene Jaggernauth, an immigrant from Trinidad and Tobago who spent eleven months in detention before being deported to the country of her birth. In a statement provided to the Women's Refugee Commission, Marlene said,

3   *Had I not personally experienced detention, I would never have believed such inhumane conditions existed in the United States. I was trapped in a cruel unjust system, and I could only watch, powerless, as lives unraveled around me . . . While in detention, I got to know many other women who were also being held by ICE, often for many months. They included mothers like myself, many of whom were separated from their children, and their families were destroyed. This effect was driven by the fact that women could not always locate their children because they did not have*

*Arlene Roberts, *The Huffington Post*, October 6, 2009.

*access to resources, including phone calls, legal materials, consulates and legal counsel. Additionally, parents are not always allowed contact visits with their children . . . In addition to the trauma of separation and deportation women face inhumane conditions while they are detained, especially in the areas of medical and mental health care. Often, our requests for care were ignored by guards and medical staff . . . I also repeatedly witnessed the inhumane treatment of the elderly and mentally ill.*

4   President Obama's 35-page report addresses some of these concerns. According to the report, Immigration and Customs Enforcement (ICE) will provide "sound medical care." Additionally, ICE will detain immigrants "in settings commensurate with the risk of flight and danger they present." Let's hope that implementation and enforcement of proposed reform policies translate into tangible benefits for individuals in detention.


## Marlene Jaggernauth's Statement

5   *My name is Marlene Jaggernauth. I was born in Trinidad, but I came to the U.S. as a lawful permanent resident when I was very young. During a very difficult time in my life over a decade ago, I was convicted of two shoplifting crimes. I am very ashamed of what I did, but thankfully through counseling and belief in my family, I moved forward with my life. Many years later, in 2003, ICE arrested me. At that point, I had lived legally in the United States for 27 years. ICE detained me because they claimed my conviction was an aggravated felony.*

6   *On March 23, 2003, my 17-year-old daughter woke me up to say that her car had just been hit in our driveway by a police officer. I went out with my 6-year-old twin girls, and my 16-year-old son and my nephew were also outside. As soon as I stepped out the front door, I was grabbed by a male officer, and he pulled my hands behind my back and snapped handcuffs on me while my four children watched in disbelief. When I asked what was going on, they told me I would find out when I got to Miami. In the meantime, my son went to get my parents, who came to my home to see what was happening. I can still see the vision of my blind mother hobbling up my driveway, still in her nightclothes, with total fear on her face, and the pain in my children's eyes still haunts me.*

7   *My parents took my children and ICE took me away. During the next 11 months I was moved to four different county jails. I was ultimately deported to Trinidad, a country I left in 1977 and where I had no family ties. Had I not personally experienced detention, I would never have believed that such inhumane conditions existed in the United States. I was trapped in a cruel unjust system, and I could only watch, powerless, as lives unraveled around me.*

8   *Prior to my detention, my four U.S. citizen children were honor-roll students, who were very active in the community as volunteers. However, due to my detention, my children felt abandoned, and developed many issues including depression, anxiety, and self-destructive behavior. This was further complicated by the fact that my children were left with my mother, who is blind and had many medical problems, and was in no position to support four very active minor children. My children were affected so*

*profoundly that, had I not returned, I think they would have ended up as yet another juvenile statistic.*

9     *While in detention, I got to know many other women who were also being held by ICE, often for many months. They included mothers like myself, many of whom were victims of abuse and trauma, who were separated from their children, and their families were destroyed. This effect was driven by the fact that women could not locate their children because they did not have access to resources, including phone calls, legal materials, consulates and legal counsel. Additionally, parents are not always allowed contact visits with their children, and I often had great difficulty arranging visits with my children due to the location where I was detained and constraints on contact visits.*

10     *In detention, I met a young mother whose child was taken into foster care because she was unable to coordinate child-care with family members since she could not afford a phone card to contact them. I remember another mother confiding in me that she was forced to leave her daughter with her ex-husband, who was molesting the girl, because she lacked the resources to coordinate care.*

11     *Even when families are reunited in the parent's home country following deportation the effects of our immigration policies on U.S. citizen children continue. I met one mother who brought her four U.S. citizen children with her to Trinidad. The children were having problems coping, difficulty in school, and faced ridicule from an unfamiliar and unwelcoming culture.*

12     *In addition to the trauma of separation and deportation women face inhumane conditions while they are detained, especially in the areas of medical and mental health care. Often, our requests for care were ignored by guards and medical staff, even in emergency situations, and in some desperate cases, detainees actually had to ask someone from the outside to call 911.*

13     *I also repeatedly witnessed the inhumane treatment of the elderly and the mentally ill. As a mental health caseworker, I recognized that a German woman who was detained for several months was likely a paranoid schizophrenic. During her delusions, the guards humiliated her, joined in making fun of her, and used excessive force when transferring her. At another facility, I remember waking up in the middle of the night to loud, painful screams by another mentally ill women held in a confined space without being let out for fresh air. These women clearly lacked access to proper medical and psychiatric care.*

14     *Communication barriers, such as lack of translation services and illiteracy, as well as fear of retaliation and a negative impact on immigration proceedings also prevented women from getting care. On more than one occasion, I was placed in solitary confinement and transferred to different facilities because I was labeled a "troublemaker," for advocating for myself and others. During these times I could not see my children and sometimes for weeks my family did not know where I was.*

15     *I eventually won my immigration case and am back with my family thanks to the Florida Immigrant Advocacy Center, who took my case all the way up to the Eleventh Circuit Court of Appeals, which ruled that my conviction was not an aggravated felony. When I was finally brought back to the United States, I was placed in detention again until my cancellation of removal hearing. If the judge had had discretionary powers to grant cancellation of removal in the first place my entire ordeal might have been avoided, saving tax payers a great deal of money and preventing my children from*

*suffering. Congress needs to give immigration judges back their discretionary powers in immigration cases, especially for those who have strong familial ties in the United States.*

16    *In addition, after four years, I had hoped to find that conditions in detention facilities had improved, but in fact they had actually gotten worse. I observed a glaring lack of accountability on the part of ICE officials and facility staff. In part I believe this is due to a lack of proper training. Officers are not trained to deal with immigrants in civil proceedings and they don't differentiate between immigration detainees and criminal inmates. The general attitude seems to be that because immigration detainees are going to be deported and are not U.S. citizens they do not deserve humane treatment and should not be protected under the Constitution. I'm now working as a mental health caseworker and I am incredibly grateful to be reunited with my children. What makes my story unique is that I was able to return after being deported.*

17    *The incredible loss and desperation that my children faced is a story that plays out again and again every day with so many other families, especially with increased immigration enforcement. I still think about the thousands of other women being held in immigration detention. Many of them are suffering in silence. I truly hope this might make a difference in getting them the care and respect they deserve, with the ultimate hope of having them reunited with their loved ones. Immigration is not only about immigrants, it is about the American families they are forced to leave behind.*

### QUESTIONS FOR CONSIDERATION AND DISCUSSION

1. Read the report Roberts refers to in her final paragraph (see www.ice.gov). What concerns does the report address. Does it assist illegal immigrants? Does it attempt to address their human rights?

2. This article includes a letter written by a woman who, although a legal resident, is subjected to harsh treatment at the hands of immigration authorities. How does this letter support the case for immigration reform?

3. Should illegal immigrants who have children in the U.S. be afforded special considerations when they are detained? For example, should mothers not be separated from their children? Explain.

4. Jaggernauth states that had she not experienced such conditions, she never would have believed they existed in the U.S. To what standard do we hold our detention facilities? If taxpayer money is used to support them, what conditions should detainees expect? Medical care? Education? Recreation? Explain.

5. What was your initial reaction to Jaggernauth's letter? Explain.

6. Roberts' editorial appears on the blog site *The Huffington Post*. Write a response to her posting expressing your own view. Refer to her comments and the statement provided by Jaggernauth in your posting.

# Immigration Quotas vs. Individual Rights: The Moral and Practical Case for Open Immigration

*Harry Binswanger*

When people raise the issue of immigration, it usually focuses on illegal immigration—people who enter the country without going through proper legal channels. As of 2007, the United States accepts more legal immigrants as permanent residents than any other country in the world. The U.S. grants legal immigrant status to over 700,000 people each year, not including refugee admissions. While it is difficult to determine exact numbers, another estimated 500,000 people come to the U.S. illegally. Estimates of the number of illegal immigrants currently residing in the U.S. range from 10 to 13 million. In the next essay, philosophy professor Harry Binswanger explains why he feels all people, regardless of immigration quotas, should be allowed to immigrate to the U.S. No one, he explains should be considered illegal, and all people, with a few exceptions he outlines, should be granted residency rights. It is not an issue of law, but an issue of human rights.*

**BEFORE YOU READ**

Do you think that the United States should limit the number of immigrants allowed to enter the country? What about restrictions on the number of refugees who can enter the U.S.?

**AS YOU READ**

What distinction does Binswanger make between free and open residency and U.S. citizenship? Explain.

1 This is a defense of phasing-in open immigration into the United States. Entry into the U.S. should ultimately be free for any foreigner, with the exception of criminals, would-be terrorists, and those carrying infectious diseases. (And note: I am defending freedom of entry and residency, not the automatic granting of U.S. citizenship).

2 An end to immigration quotas is demanded by the principle of individual rights. Every individual has rights as an individual, not as a member of this or that nation. One has rights not by virtue of being an American, but by virtue of being human.

3 One doesn't have to be a resident of any particular country to have a moral entitlement to be secure from governmental coercion against one's life, liberty, and property. In the words of the Declaration of Independence, government is instituted "to secure these rights"—to protect them against their violation by force or fraud.

4 A foreigner has rights just as much as an American. To be a foreigner is not to be a criminal. Yet our government treats as criminals those foreigners not lucky enough to win the green-card lottery.

---

*Harry Binswanger, *Capitalism Magazine*, April 2, 2006.

5    Seeking employment in this country is not a criminal act. It coerces no one and violates no one's rights (there is no "right" to be exempt from competition in the labor market, or in any other market).

6    It is not a criminal act to buy or rent a home here in which to reside. Paying for housing is not a coercive act—whether the buyer is an American or a foreigner. No one's rights are violated when a Mexican, or Canadian, or Senegalese rents an apartment from an American owner and moves into the housing he is paying for. And what about the rights of those American citizens who want to sell or rent their property to the highest bidders? Or the American businesses that want to hire the lowest cost workers? It is morally indefensible for our government to violate their right to do so, just because the person is a foreigner.

7    Immigration quotas forcibly exclude foreigners who want not to seize but to purchase housing here, who want not to rob Americans but to engage in productive work, raising our standard of living. To forcibly exclude those who seek peacefully to trade value for value with us is a violation of the rights of both parties to such a trade: the rights of the American seller or employer and the rights of the foreign buyer or employee.

8    Thus, immigration quotas treat both Americans and foreigners as if they were criminals, as if the peaceful exchange of values to mutual benefit were an act of destruction.

9    To take an actual example, if I want to invite my Norwegian friend Klaus to live in my home, either as a guest or as a paying tenant, what right does our government have to stop Klaus and me? To be a Norwegian is not to be a criminal. And if some American business wants to hire Klaus, what right does our government have to interfere?

10    The implicit premise of barring foreigners is: "This is our country, we let in who we want." But who is "we"? The government does not own the country. Jurisdiction is not ownership. Only the owner of land or any item of property can decide the terms of its use or sale. Nor does the majority own the country. This is a country of private property, and housing is private property. So is a job.

11    American land is not the collective property of some entity called "the U.S. government." Nor is there such thing as collective, social ownership of the land. The claim, "We have the right to decide who is allowed in" means some individuals—those with the most votes—claim the right to prevent other citizens from exercising their rights. But there can be no right to violate the rights of others.

12    Our constitutional republic respects minority rights. 60 percent of the population cannot vote to enslave the other 40 percent. Nor can a majority dictate to the owners of private property. Nor can a majority dictate on whom private employers spend their money. Not morally, not in a free society. In a free society, the rights of the individual are held sacrosanct, above any claim of even an overwhelming majority.

13    The rights of one man end where the rights of his neighbor begin. Only within the limits of his rights is a man free to act on his own judgment. The criminal is the man who deliberately steps outside his rights-protected domain and invades the domain of another, depriving his victim of his exclusive control over his property, or liberty, or life. The criminal, by his own choice, has rejected rights in favor of brute violence. Thus, an immigration policy that excludes criminals is proper.

14    Likewise, a person with an infectious disease, such as smallpox, threatens with serious physical harm those with whom he comes into proximity. Unlike the criminal, he may not

intend to do damage, but the threat of physical harm is clear, present, and objectively demonstrable. To protect the lives of Americans, he may be kept out or quarantined until he is no longer a threat. But what about the millions of Mexicans, South Americans, Chinese, Canadians, etc. seeking entry who are not criminal and not bearing infectious diseases? By what moral principle can they be excluded? Not on the grounds of majority vote, not on the grounds of protecting any American's rights, not on the grounds of any legitimate authority of the state.

## The Moral and the Practical

15 That's the moral case for phasing out limits on immigration. But some ask: "Is it practical? Wouldn't unlimited immigration—even if phased in over a decade—be disastrous to our economic well being and create overcrowding? Are we being told to just grit our teeth and surrender our interests in the name of morality?"

16 This question is invalid on its face. It shows a failure to understand the nature of rights, and of moral principles generally. Rational moral principles reflect a recognition of the basic nature of man, his nature as a specific kind of living organism, having a specific means of survival. Questions of what is practical, what is to one's self-interest, can be answered only in that context. It is neither practical nor to one's interest to attempt to live and act in defiance of one's nature as a human being.

17 Yet that is the meaning of the moral-practical dichotomy. When one claims, "It is immoral but practical," one is maintaining, "It cripples my nature as a human being, but it is beneficial to me"—which is a contradiction.

18 Rights, in particular, are not something pulled from the sky or decreed by societal whim. Rights are moral principles, established by reference to the needs inherent in man's nature qua man. "Rights are conditions of existence required by man's nature for his proper survival." (Ayn Rand)

19 Every organism has a basic means of survival; for man, that means is: reason. Man is the rational animal, homo sapiens. Rights are moral principles that spell out the terms of social interaction required for a rational being to survive and flourish. Since the reasoning mind cannot function under physical coercion, the basic social requirement of man's survival is: freedom. Rights prescribe freedom by proscribing coercion.

20 "If man is to live on earth, it is right for him to use his mind, it is right to act on his own free judgment, it is right to work for his values and to keep the product of his work." (Ayn Rand)

21 Rights reflect the fundamental alternative of voluntary consent or brute force. The reign of force is in no one's interest; the system of voluntary cooperation by mutual consent is the precondition of anyone achieving his actual interests.

22 To ignore the principle of rights means jettisoning the principled, moral resolution of conflicts, and substituting mere numbers (majority vote). That is not to anyone's interest. Tyranny is not to anyone's self-interest.

23 Rights establish the necessary framework within which one defines his legitimate self-interest. One cannot hold that one's self-interest requires that he be "free" to deprive others of their freedom, treating their interests as morally irrelevant. One cannot hold that recognizing the rights of others is moral but "impractical."

24    Since rights are based on the requirements of man's life as a rational being, there can be no conflict between the moral and the practical here: if respecting individual rights requires it, your interest requires it.

25    Freedom or force, reason or compulsion—that is the basic social alternative. Immigrants recognize the value of freedom—that's why they seek to come here.

26    The American Founders defined and implemented a system of rights because they recognized that man, as a rational being, must be free to act on his own judgment and to keep the products of his own effort. They did not intend to establish a system in which those who happen to be born here could use force to "protect" themselves from the peaceful competition of others.

## Economics

27  One major fear of open immigration is economic: the fear of losing one's job to immigrants. It is asked: "Won't the immigrants take our jobs?" The answer is: "Yes, so we can go on to better, higher-paying jobs."

28    The fallacy in this protectionist objection lies in the idea that there is only a finite amount of work to be done. The unstated assumption is: "If Americans don't get to do that work, if foreigners do it instead, we Americans will have nothing to do."

29    But work is the creation of wealth. A job is a role in the production of goods and services—the production of food, of cars, computers, the providing of internet content— all the items that go to make up our standard of living. A country cannot have too much wealth. The need for wealth is limitless, and the work that is to be done is limitless.

30    From a grand, historical perspective, we are only at the beginning of the wealth-creating age. The wealth Americans produce today is as nothing compared to what we'll have two hundred years from now—just as the standard of living 200 years in the past, in 1806, was as nothing compared to ours today.

31    Unemployment is not caused by an absence of avenues for the creation of wealth. Unemployment is caused by government interference in the labor market. Even with that interference, the number of jobs goes relentlessly upward, decade after decade. This bears witness to the fact that there's no end to the creation of wealth and thus no end to the useful employment of human intelligence and the physical effort directed by that intelligence. There is always more productive work to be done. If you can give your job to an immigrant, you can get a more valuable job.

32    What is the effect of a bigger labor pool on wage rates? If the money supply is constant, nominal wage rates fall. But real wage rates rise, because total output has gone up. Economists have demonstrated that real wages have to rise as long as the immigrants are self-supporting. If immigrants earn their keep, if they don't consume more than they produce, then they add to total output, which means that prices fall (if the money supply is constant).

33    And, in fact, rising real wages was the history of our country in the nineteenth century. Before the 1920s, there were no limits on immigration, yet our standard of living rocketed upward. Self-supporting immigrants were an economic benefit not an injury. The protectionist objection that immigrants take away jobs and harm our standard of living is a solid economic fallacy.

## Welfare

34 A popular misconception is that immigrants come here to get welfare. To the extent that is true, immigrants do constitute a burden. But this issue is mooted by the passage, under the Clinton Administration, of the Personal Responsibility and Work Opportunity and Reconciliation Act (PRWORA), which makes legal permanent residents ineligible for most forms of welfare for five years. I support this kind of legislation.

35    Further, if the fear is of non-working immigrants, why is the pending legislation aimed at employers of immigrants?

## Overcrowding

36 America is a vastly under-populated country. Our population density is less than one-third of France's.

37    Take an extreme example. Suppose a tidal wave of immigrants came here. Suppose that half of the people on the planet moved here. That would mean an unthinkable eleven-fold increase in our population—from 300 million to 3.3 billion people. That would make America almost as "densely" populated as today's England (360 people/sq. km. vs. 384 people/sq. km.). In fact, it would make us less densely populated than the state of New Jersey (453 per sq. km.). And these calculations exclude Alaska and Hawaii, and count only land area.

38    Contrary to widespread beliefs, high population density is a value not a disvalue. High population density intensifies the division of labor, which makes possible a wider variety of jobs and specialized consumer products. For instance, in Manhattan, there is a "doll hospital"—a store specializing in the repair of children's dolls. Such a specialized, niche business requires a high population density in order to have a market. Try finding a doll hospital in Poughkeepsie. In Manhattan, one can find a job as a Pilates Method teacher or as a "Secret Shopper" (two jobs actually listed on Craig's List). Not in Paducah.

39    People want to live near other people, in cities. One-seventh of England's population lives in London. If population density is a bad thing, why are Manhattan real-estate prices so high?

## The Value of Immigrants

40 Immigrants are the kind of people who refresh the American spirit. They are ambitious, courageous, and value freedom. They come here, often with no money and not even speaking the language, to seek a better life for themselves and their children.

41    The vision of American freedom, with its opportunity to prosper by hard work, serves as a magnet drawing the best of the world's people. Immigrants are self-selected for their virtues: their ambitiousness, daring, independence, and pride. They are willing to cast aside the tradition-bound roles assigned to them in their native lands and to re-define themselves as Americans. These are the people America needs in order to keep alive the individualist, hard-working attitude that made America.

42    Here is a short list of some great immigrants: Alexander Hamilton, Alexander Graham Bell, Andrew Carnegie, most of the top scientists of the Manhattan Project, Igor Sikorsky (the inventor of the helicopter), Ayn Rand.

43    Open immigration: the benefits are great. The right is unquestionable. So let them come.

1. Why does Binswanger believe immigration should be open to everyone? Do you agree with his perspective that entrance to the U.S. is a human right? Why or why not?

2. Binswanger observes that foreigners do not deserve to be treated as criminals, yet U.S. citizens often think of them in this light. Comment on this observation with your own viewpoint. Do you think of illegal aliens as criminals? Why or why not?

3. Who, according to Binswanger, should be excluded from entry to the U.S.? Does his criteria for exclusion run counter to his explanation of why all people should be allowed to emigrate? Why or why not?

4. Binswanger, who taught philosophy at the Ayn Rand Institute, quotes her several times in this essay. How do these quotes support the position he takes in his essay?

5. Evaluate Binswanger's tone, style and language in this essay. How does he try to persuade his readers to his point of view? What appeals does he make? Does he explore both sides of the issue? Explain.

6. Binswanger's argument hinges on his audience's agreement that he is stating obvious moral truths. Create a list of reasons why foreigners should, or should not, be allowed unlimited access to the United States. Give at least one reason why you think each item on your list is an obvious moral truth.

# Why Feminism is AWOL on Islam
*Kay Hymowitz*

In the United States, most women will agree that they are afforded the same rights as men, at least in theory. But do women take their freedoms for granted? And more importantly, do they think that women in other countries deserve the same rights that women in the U.S. do? Cultural and social mores aside, in many parts of the world, women have severe restrictions placed on their freedoms and basic rights. Their bodies can be mutilated in observance of religious or cultural traditions. They are denied access to education, the right to go out in public unescorted, to drive a motor vehicle, to hold a job, or to run for office. They are told what to wear and to cover their bodies and even their faces from public view. They can even be murdered by their fathers, husbands, and brothers for failure to conform. Author Kay S. Hymowitz wonders why women in the United States, who have so little to complain about here, aren't advocating more for their sisters abroad.*

**BEFORE YOU READ**

How has feminism changed our view of rights for women? Do we take these rights for granted?

---

*Kay Hymowitz, *City Journal*, Winter 2003.

**AS YOU READ**

What are the three major feminist theories and how do they relate to what is happening in the Middle East at this time?

1   Argue all you want with many feminist policies, but few quarrel with feminism's core moral insight, which changed the lives (and minds) of women forever: that women are due the same rights and dignity as men. So, as news of the appalling miseries of women in the Islamic world has piled up, where are the feminists? Where's the outrage? For a brief moment after September 11, when pictures of those blue alien-creaturely shapes in Afghanistan filled the papers, it seemed as if feminists were going to have their moment. And in fact the Feminist Majority, to its credit, had been publicizing since the mid-90s how Afghan girls were barred from school, how women were stoned for adultery or beaten for showing an ankle or wearing high-heeled shoes, how they were prohibited from leaving the house unless accompanied by a male relative, how they were denied medical help because the only doctors around were male.

2   But the rest is feminist silence. You haven't heard a peep from feminists as it has grown clear that the Taliban were exceptional not in their extreme views about women but in their success at embodying those views in law and practice. In the United Arab Emirates, husbands have the right to beat their wives in order to discipline them—" provided that the beating is not so severe as to damage her bones or deform her body," in the words of the Gulf News. In Saudi Arabia, women cannot vote, drive, or show their faces or talk with male non-relatives in public. (Evidently they can't talk to men over the airwaves either; when Prince Abdullah went to George Bush's ranch in Crawford in 2003, he insisted that no female air-traffic controllers handle his flight.) Yes, Saudi girls can go to school, and many even attend the university; but at the university, women must sit in segregated rooms and watch their professors on closed-circuit televisions. If they have a question, they push a button on their desk, which turns on a light at the professor's lectern, from which he can answer the female without being in her dangerous presence. And in Saudi Arabia, education can be harmful to female health. In 2002 in Mecca, members of the mutaween, the Commission for the Promotion of Virtue, pushed fleeing students back into their burning school because they were not properly covered in abaya. Fifteen girls died.

3   You didn't hear much from feminists when in the northern Nigerian province of Katsina a Muslim court sentenced a woman to death by stoning for having a child outside of marriage. The case might not have earned much attention—stonings are common in parts of the Muslim world—except that the young woman, who had been married off at 14 to a husband who ultimately divorced her when she lost her virginal allure, was still nursing a baby at the time of sentencing. During her trial she had no lawyer, although the court did see fit to delay her execution until she weans her infant.

4   You didn't hear much from feminists as it emerged that honor killings by relatives, often either ignored or only lightly punished by authorities, are also commonplace in the Muslim world. In September, Reuters reported the story of an Iranian man, "defending my honor, family, and dignity," who cut off his seven-year-old daughter's head after suspecting she had been raped by her uncle. The postmortem showed the girl to be a virgin. In another family mix-up, a Yemeni man shot his daughter to death on her wedding night when her

husband claimed she was not a virgin. After a medical exam revealed that the husband was mistaken, officials concluded he was simply trying to protect himself from embarrassment about his own impotence. According to the Human Rights Commission of Pakistan, every day two women are slain by male relatives seeking to avenge the family honor.

5      The savagery of some of these murders is worth a moment's pause. In 2000, two Punjabi sisters, 20 and 21 years old, had their throats slit by their brother and cousin because the girls were seen talking to two boys to whom they were not related. In one especially notorious case, an Egyptian woman named Nora Marzouk Ahmed fell in love and eloped. When she went to make amends with her father, he cut off her head and paraded it down the street. Several years back, according to the *Washington Post,* the husband of Zahida Perveen, a 32-year-old pregnant Pakistani, gouged out her eyes and sliced off her earlobe and nose because he suspected her of having an affair.

6      In a related example widely covered last summer, a teenage girl in the Punjab was sentenced by a tribal council to rape by a gang that included one of the councilmen. After the hour-and-a-half ordeal, the girl was forced to walk home naked in front of scores of onlookers. She had been punished because her 11-year-old brother had compromised another girl by being been seen alone with her. But that charge turned out to be a ruse: it seems that three men of a neighboring tribe had sodomized the boy and accused him of illicit relations—an accusation leading to his sister's barbaric punishment—as a way of covering up their crime.

7      Nor is such brutality limited to backward, out-of-the-way villages. Muddassir Rizvi, a Pakistani journalist, says that, though always common in rural areas, in recent years honor killings have become more prevalent in cities "among educated and liberal families." In relatively modern Jordan, honor killings were all but exempt from punishment until the penal code was modified last year; unfortunately, a young Palestinian living in Jordan, who had recently stabbed his 19-year-old sister 40 times "to cleanse the family honor," and another man from near Amman, who ran over his 23-year-old sister with his truck because of her "immoral behavior," had not yet changed their ways. British psychiatrist Anthony Daniels reports that British Muslim men frequently spirit their young daughters back to their native Pakistan and force the girls to marry. Such fathers have been known to kill daughters who resist. In Sweden, in one highly publicized case, Fadima Sahindal, an assimilated 26-year-old of Kurdish origin, was murdered by her father after she began living with her Swedish boyfriend. "The whore is dead," the family announced.

8      As you look at this inventory of brutality, the question bears repeating: Where are the demonstrations, the articles, the petitions, the resolutions, the vindications of the rights of Islamic women by American feminists? The weird fact is that, even after the excesses of the Taliban did more to forge an American consensus about women's rights than 30 years of speeches by Gloria Steinem, feminists refused to touch this subject. They have averted their eyes from the harsh, blatant oppression of millions of women, even while they have continued to stare into the Western patriarchal abyss, indignant over female executives who cannot join an exclusive golf club and college women who do not have their own lacrosse teams.

9      But look more deeply into the matter, and you realize that the sound of feminist silence about the savage fundamentalist Muslim oppression of women has its own perverse logic. The silence is a direct outgrowth of the way feminist theory has developed in recent

years. Now mired in self-righteous sentimentalism, multicultural non-judgmentalism, and internationalist utopianism, feminism has lost the language to make the universalist moral claims of equal dignity and individual freedom that once rendered it so compelling. No wonder that most Americans, trying to deal with the realities of a post-9/11 world, are paying feminists no mind.

10    To understand the current sisterly silence about the sort of tyranny that the women's movement came into existence to attack, it is helpful to think of feminisms plural rather than singular. Though not entirely discrete philosophies, each of three different feminisms has its own distinct reasons for causing activists to "lose their voice" in the face of women's oppression.

11    The first variety—radical feminism (or gender feminism, in Christina Hoff Sommers's term)—starts with the insight that men are, not to put too fine a point upon it, brutes. Radical feminists do not simply subscribe to the reasonable-enough notion that men are naturally more prone to aggression than women. They believe that maleness is a kind of original sin. Masculinity explains child abuse, marital strife, high defense spending, every war from Troy to Afghanistan, as well as Hitler, Franco, and Pinochet. As Gloria Steinem informed the audience at a Florida fundraiser last March: "The cult of masculinity is the basis for every violent, fascist regime."

12    Gender feminists are little interested in fine distinctions between radical Muslim men who slam commercial airliners into office buildings and soldiers who want to stop radical Muslim men from slamming commercial airliners into office buildings. They are both examples of generic male violence—and specifically, male violence against women. "Terrorism is on a continuum that starts with violence within the family, battery against women, violence against women in the society, all the way up to organized militaries that are supported by taxpayer money," according to Roxanne Dunbar-Ortiz, who teaches "The Sexuality of Terrorism" at California State University in Hayward. Violence is so intertwined with male sexuality that, she tells us, military pilots watch porn movies before they go out on sorties. The war in Afghanistan could not possibly offer a chance to liberate women from their oppressors, since it would simply expose women to yet another set of oppressors, in the gender feminists' view. As Sharon Lerner asserted bizarrely in the Village Voice, feminists' "discomfort" with the Afghanistan bombing was "deepened by the knowledge that more women than men die as a result of most wars."

13    If guys are brutes, girls are their opposite: peace-loving, tolerant, conciliatory, and reasonable—"Antiwar and Pro-Feminist," as the popular peace-rally sign goes. Feminists long ago banished tough-as-nails women like Margaret Thatcher and Jeanne Kirkpatrick (and these days, one would guess, even the fetching Condoleezza Rice) to the ranks of the imperfectly female. Real women, they believe, would never justify war. "Most women, Western and Muslim, are opposed to war regardless of its reasons and objectives," wrote the Jordanian feminist Fadia Faqir on OpenDemocracy.net. "They are concerned with emancipation, freedom (personal and civic), human rights, power sharing, integrity, dignity, equality, autonomy, power-sharing [sic], liberation, and pluralism."

14    Sara Ruddick, author of Maternal Thinking, is perhaps one of the most influential spokeswomen for the position that women are instinctually peaceful. According to Ruddick (who clearly didn't have Joan Crawford in mind), that's because a good deal of mothering is naturally governed by the Gandhian principles of nonviolence such as

"renunciation," "resistance to injustice," and "reconciliation." The novelist Barbara Kingsolver was one of the first to demonstrate the subtleties of such universal maternal thinking after the United States invaded Afghanistan. "I feel like I'm standing on a playground where the little boys are all screaming 'He started it!' and throwing rocks," she wrote in the *Los Angeles Times*. "I keep looking for somebody's mother to come on the scene saying, 'Boys! Boys!'"

15     Gender feminism's tendency to reduce foreign affairs to a Lifetime Channel movie may make it seem too silly to bear mentioning, but its kitschy naiveté hasn't stopped it from being widespread among elites. You see it in widely read writers like Kingsolver, Maureen Dowd, and Alice Walker. It turns up in our most elite institutions. Swanee Hunt, head of the Women in Public Policy Program at Harvard's Kennedy School of Government wrote, with Cristina Posa in Foreign Policy: "The key reason behind women's marginalization may be that everyone recognizes just how good women are at forging peace." Even female elected officials are on board. "The women of all these countries should go on strike, they should all sit down and refuse to do anything until their men agree to talk peace," urged Ohio representative Marcy Kaptur to the Arab News last spring, echoing an idea that Aristophanes, a dead white male, proposed as a joke 2,400 years ago. And President Clinton is an advocate of maternal thinking, too. "If we'd had women at Camp David," he said in July 2000, "we'd have an agreement."

16     Major foundations too seem to take gender feminism seriously enough to promote it as an answer to world problems. Last December, the Ford Foundation and the Soros Open Society Foundation helped fund the Afghan Women's Summit in Brussels to develop ideas for a new government in Afghanistan. As Vagina Monologues author Eve Ensler described it on her website, the summit was made up of "meetings and meals, canvassing, workshops, tears, and dancing." "Defense was mentioned nowhere in the document," Ensler wrote proudly of the summit's concluding proclamation—despite the continuing threat in Afghanistan of warlords, bandits, and lingering al-Qaida operatives. "[B]uilding weapons or instruments of retaliation was not called for in any category," Ensler cooed. "Instead [the women] wanted education, health care, and the protection of refugees, culture, and human rights."

17     Too busy celebrating their own virtue and contemplating their own victimhood, gender feminists cannot address the suffering of their Muslim sisters realistically, as light years worse than their own petulant grievances. They are too intent on hating war to ask if unleashing its horrors might be worth it to overturn a brutal tyranny that, among its manifold inhumanities, treats women like animals. After all, hating war and machismo is evidence of the moral superiority that comes with being born female.

18     Yet the gender feminist idea of superior feminine virtue is becoming an increasingly tough sell for anyone actually keeping up with world events. Kipling once wrote of the fierceness of Afghan women: "When you're wounded and left on the Afghan plains/And the women come out to cut up your remains/Just roll to your rifle and blow out your brains." Now it's clearer than ever that the dream of worldwide sisterhood is no more realistic than worldwide brotherhood; culture trumps gender any day. Mothers all over the Muslim world are naming their babies Usama or praising Allah for their sons' efforts to kill crusading infidels. Last February, 28-year-old Wafa Idris became the first female Palestinian suicide bomber to strike in Israel, killing an elderly man and wounding

scores of women and children. And in April, Israeli soldiers discovered under the maternity clothes of 26-year-old Shifa Adnan Kodsi a bomb rather than a baby. Maternal thinking, indeed.

19    The second variety of feminism, seemingly more sophisticated and especially prevalent on college campuses, is multiculturalism and its twin, post colonialism. The postcolonial feminist has even more reason to shy away from the predicament of women under radical Islam than her maternally thinking sister. She believes that the Western world is so sullied by its legacy of imperialism that no Westerner, man or woman, can utter a word of judgment against former colonial peoples. Worse, she is not so sure that radical Islam isn't an authentic, indigenous—and therefore appropriate—expression of Arab and Middle Eastern identity.

20    The postmodern philosopher Michel Foucault, one of the intellectual godfathers of multiculturalism and post colonialism, first set the tone in 1978 when an Italian newspaper sent him to Teheran to cover the Iranian revolution. As his biographer James Miller tells it, Foucault looked in the face of Islamic fundamentalism and saw . . . an awe-inspiring revolt against "global hegemony." He was mesmerized by this new form of "political spirituality" that, in a phrase whose dark prescience he could not have grasped, portended the "transfiguration of the world." Even after the Ayatollah Khomeini came to power and reintroduced polygamy and divorce on the husband's demand with automatic custody to fathers, reduced the official female age of marriage from 18 to 13, fired all female judges, and ordered compulsory veiling, whose transgression was to be punished by public flogging, Foucault saw no reason to temper his enthusiasm. What was a small matter like women's basic rights, when a struggle against "the planetary system" was at hand?

21    Post colonialists, then, have their own binary system, somewhat at odds with gender feminism—not to mention with women's rights. It is not men who are the sinners; it is the West. It is not women who are victimized innocents; it is the people who suffered under Western colonialism, or the descendants of those people, to be more exact. Caught between the rock of patriarchy and the hard place of imperialism, the postcolonial feminist scholar gingerly tiptoes her way around the subject of Islamic fundamentalism and does the only thing she can do: she focuses her ire on Western men.

22    To this end, the post colonialist eagerly dips into the inkwell of gender feminism. She ties colonialist exploitation and domination to maleness; she might refer to Israel's "masculinist military culture"—Israel being white and Western—though she would never dream of pointing out the "masculinist military culture" of the jihadi. And she expends a good deal of energy condemning Western men for wanting to improve the lives of Eastern women. At the turn of the twentieth century Lord Cromer, the British vice consul of Egypt and a pet target of postcolonial feminists, argued that the "degradation" of women under Islam had a harmful effect on society. Rubbish, according to the post colonialist feminist. His words are simply part of "the Western narrative of the quintessential otherness and inferiority of Islam," as Harvard professor Leila Ahmed puts it in *Women and Gender in Islam*. The same goes for American concern about Afghan women; it is merely a "device for ranking the 'other' men as inferior or as 'uncivilized,'" according to Nira Yuval-Davis, professor of gender and ethnic studies at the University of Greenwich, England. These are all examples of what renowned Columbia professor Gayatri Spivak called "white men saving brown women from brown men."

23    Spivak's phrase, a great favorite on campus, points to the postcolonial notion that brown men, having been victimized by the West, can never be oppressors in their own right. If they give the appearance of treating women badly, the oppression they have suffered at the hands of Western colonial masters is to blame. In fact, the worse they treat women, the more they are expressing their own justifiable outrage. "When men are traumatized [by colonial rule], they tend to traumatize their own women," Miriam Cooke, a Duke professor and head of the Association for Middle East Women's Studies, told me. And today, Cooke asserts, brown men are subjected to a new form of imperialism. "Now there is a return of colonialism that we saw in the nineteenth century in the context of globalization," she says. "What is driving Islamist men is globalization."

24    It would be difficult to exaggerate the through-the-looking-glass quality of post colonialist theory when it comes to the subject of women. Female suicide bombers are a good thing, because they are strong women demonstrating "agency" against colonial powers. Polygamy too must be shown due consideration. "Polygamy can be liberating and empowering," Cooke answered sunnily when I asked her about it. "Our norm is the Western, heterosexual, single couple. If we can imagine different forms that would allow us to be something other than a heterosexual couple, we might imagine polygamy working," she explained murkily. Some women, she continued, are relieved when their husbands take a new wife: they won't have to service him so often. Or they might find they now have the freedom to take a lover. But, I ask, wouldn't that be dangerous in places where adulteresses can be stoned to death? At any rate, how common is that? "I don't know," Cooke answers, "I'm interested in discourse." The irony couldn't be darker: the very people protesting the imperialist exploitation of the "Other" endorse that Other's repressive customs as a means of promoting their own uniquely Western agenda—subverting the heterosexual patriarchy.

25    The final category in the feminist taxonomy, which might be called the world-government utopian strain, is in many respects closest to classical liberal feminism. Dedicated to full female dignity and equality, it generally eschews both the biological determinism of the gender feminist and the cultural relativism of the multicultural post colonialist. Stanford political science professor Susan Moller Okin, an influential, subtle, and intelligent spokeswoman for this approach, created a stir among feminists in 1997 when she forthrightly attacked multiculturalists for valuing "group rights for minority cultures" over the well-being of individual women. Okin admirably minced no words attacking arranged marriage, female circumcision, and polygamy, which she believed women experienced as a "barely tolerable institution." Some women, she went so far as to declare, "might be better off if the culture into which they were born were either to become extinct . . . or preferably, to be encouraged to alter itself so as to reinforce the equality of women."

26    But though Okin is less shy than other feminists about discussing the plight of women under Islamic fundamentalism, the typical U.N. utopian has her own reasons for keeping quiet as that plight fills Western headlines. For one thing, the utopian is also a bean-counting absolutist, seeking a pure, numerical equality between men and women in all departments of life. She greets Western, and particularly American, claims to have achieved freedom for women with skepticism. The motto of the 2002 International Women's Day—"Afghanistan Is Everywhere"—was in part a reproach to the West about its superior airs. Women in Afghanistan might have to wear burqas, but don't women in the West parade around in bikinis? "It's equally disrespectful and abusive to have women prancing

around a stage in bathing suits for cash or walking the streets shrouded in burqas in order to survive," columnist Jill Nelson wrote on the MSNBC website about the murderously fanatical riots that attended the Miss World pageant in Nigeria.

27    As Nelson's statement hints, the utopian is less interested in freeing women to make their own choices than in engineering and imposing her own elite vision of a perfect society. Indeed, she is under no illusions that, left to their own democratic devices, women would freely choose the utopia she has in mind. She would not be surprised by recent Pakistani elections, where a number of the women who won parliamentary seats were Islamist. But it doesn't really matter what women want. The universalist has a comprehensive vision of "women's human rights," meaning not simply women's civil and political rights but "economic rights" and "socioeconomic justice." Cynical about free markets and globalization, the U.N. utopian is also unimpressed by the liberal democratic nation-state "as an emancipatory institution," in the dismissive words of J. Ann Tickner, director for international studies at the University of Southern California. Such nation-states are "unresponsive to the needs of [their] most vulnerable members" and seeped in "nationalist ideologies" as well as in patriarchal assumptions about autonomy. In fact, like the (usually) unacknowledged socialist that she is, the U.N. utopian eagerly awaits the withering of the nation-state, a political arrangement that she sees as tied to imperialism, war, and masculinity. During war, in particular, nations "depend on ideas about masculinized dignity and feminized sacrifice to sustain the sense of autonomous nationhood," writes Cynthia Enloe, professor of government at Clark University.

28    Having rejected the patriarchal liberal nation-state, with all the democratic machinery of self-government that goes along with it, the utopian concludes that there is only one way to achieve her goals: to impose them through international government. Utopian feminists fill the halls of the United Nations, where they examine everything through the lens of the "gender perspective" in study after unreadable study. (My personal favorites: "Gender Perspectives on Landmines" and "Gender Perspectives on Weapons of Mass Destruction," whose conclusion is that landmines and WMDs are bad for women.)

29    The 1979 U.N. Convention on the Elimination of Discrimination Against Women (CEDAW), perhaps the first and most important document of feminist utopianism, gives the best sense of the sweeping nature of the movement's ambitions. CEDAW demands many measures that anyone committed to democratic liberal values would applaud, including women's right to vote and protection against honor killings and forced marriage. Would that the document stopped there. Instead it sets out to impose a utopian order that would erase all distinctions between men and women, a kind of revolution of the sexes from above, requiring nations to "take all appropriate measures to modify the social and cultural patterns of conduct of men and women" and to eliminate "stereotyped roles" to accomplish this legislative abolition of biology. The document calls for paid maternity leave, nonsexist school curricula, and government-supported child care. The treaty's 23-member enforcement committee hectors nations that do not adequately grasp that, as Enloe puts it, "the personal is international." The committee has cited Belarus for celebrating Mother's Day, China for failing to legalize prostitution, and Libya for not interpreting the Qur'an in accordance with "committee guidelines."

30    Confusing "women's participation" with self-determination, and numerical equivalence with equality, CEDAW utopians try to orchestrate their perfect society through quotas

and affirmative-action plans. Their bean-counting mentality cares about whether women participate equally, without asking what it is that they are participating in or whether their participation is anything more than ceremonial. Thus at the recent Women's Summit in Jordan, Rima Khalaf suggested that governments be required to use quotas in elections "to leapfrog women to power." Khalaf, like so many illiberal feminist utopians, has no hesitation in forcing society to be free. As is often the case when elites decide they have discovered the route to human perfection, the utopian urge is not simply antidemocratic but verges on the totalitarian.

31    That this combination of sentimental victimhood, postcolonial relativism, and utopian overreaching has caused feminism to suffer so profound a loss of moral and political imagination that it cannot speak against the brutalization of Islamic women is an incalculable loss to women and to men. The great contribution of Western feminism was to expand the definition of human dignity and freedom. It insisted that all human beings were worthy of liberty. Feminists now have the opportunity to make that claim on behalf of women who in their oppression have not so much as imagined that its promise could include them, too. At its best, feminism has stood for a rich idea of personal choice in shaping a meaningful life, one that respects not only the woman who wants to crash through glass ceilings but also the one who wants to stay home with her children and bake cookies or to wear a veil and fast on Ramadan. Why shouldn't feminists want to shout out their own profound discovery for the world to hear?

32    Perhaps, finally, because to do so would be to acknowledge the freedom they themselves enjoy, thanks to Western ideals and institutions. Not only would such an admission force them to give up their own simmering resentments; it would be bad for business.

33    The truth is that the free institutions—an independent judiciary, a free press, open elections—that protect the rights of women are the same ones that protect the rights of men. The separation of church and state that would allow women to escape the burqa would also free men from having their hands amputated for theft. The education system that would teach girls to read would also empower millions of illiterate boys. The capitalist economies that bring clean water, cheap clothes, and washing machines that change the lives of women are the same ones that lead to healthier, freer men. In other words, to address the problems of Muslim women honestly, feminists would have to recognize that free men and women need the same things—and that those are things that they themselves already have. And recognizing that would mean an end to feminism as we know it.

34    There are signs that, outside the academy, middlebrow literary circles, and the United Nations, feminism has indeed met its Waterloo. Most Americans seem to realize that September 11 turned self-indulgent sentimental illusions, including those about the sexes, into an unaffordable luxury. Consider, for instance, women's attitudes toward war, a topic on which politicians have learned to take for granted a gender gap. But according to the Pew Research Center, in January 2002, 57 percent of women versus 46 percent of men cited national security as the country's top priority. There has been a "seismic gender shift on matters of war," according to pollster Kellyanne Conway. In 1991, 45 percent of U.S. women supported the use of ground troops in the Gulf War, a substantially smaller number than the 67 percent of men. But as of November, a CNN survey found women were more likely than men to support the use of ground troops against Iraq, 58 percent to 56 percent. The numbers for younger women were especially dramatic. Sixty-five percent of women

between 18 and 49 support ground troops, as opposed to 48 percent of women 50 and over. Women are also changing their attitudes toward military spending: before September 11, only 24 percent of women supported increased funds; after the attacks, that number climbed to 47 percent. An evolutionary psychologist might speculate that, if females tend to be less aggressively territorial than males, there's little to compare to the ferocity of the lioness when she believes her young are threatened.

35  Even among some who consider themselves feminists, there is some grudging recognition that Western, and specifically American, men are sometimes a force for the good. The Feminist Majority is sending around urgent messages asking for President Bush to increase American security forces in Afghanistan. The influential left-wing British columnist Polly Toynbee, who just 18 months ago coined the phrase "America the Horrible," went to Afghanistan to figure out whether the war "was worth it." Her answer was not what she might have expected. Though she found nine out of ten women still wearing burqas, partly out of fear of lingering fundamentalist hostility, she was convinced their lives had greatly improved. Women say they can go out alone now.

36  As we sink more deeply into what is likely to be a protracted struggle with radical Islam, American feminists have a moral responsibility to give up their resentments and speak up for women who actually need their support. Feminists have the moral authority to say that their call for the rights of women is a universal demand—that the rights of women are the Rights of Man.

## QUESTIONS FOR ANALYSIS AND DISCUSSION

1. What message is the author intending to give her audience by the use of sexist language in her conclusion? Do you find this ironic? Explain.

2. In Islamic controlled countries, there are many actions which are illegal for women of these countries to do. List as many of these illegal actions as you can find from the reading. How would life be different for you if these actions were also illegal here in the U.S.?

3. Is feminism in the U.S. obsolete? Should feminists from the United States only worry about what is happening outside of this country and just concern themselves with their global sisterhood? Explain.

4. Summarize the three different feminist theories according to the author. Do you agree with the author that none of these theories is sufficient in helping women nowadays? Explain.

5. According to CSU Professor Roxanne Dunbar-Ortiz, violence is intertwined with male sexuality. Can you give examples from personal experience or your own education to refute this statement or to show it to be true? Explain.

6. According to educator Swanee Hunt, women are good at forging peace. Can you give examples from personal experience or your own education to refute this statement or to show it to be true? Explain.

7. Hymowitz states, "culture trumps gender any day." Which examples does she use to prove this point? Can you think of any examples of your own which would refute or prove this point? Explain.

## WRITING ASSIGNMENTS

1. What rights should be granted to everyone? Do human rights extend beyond national borders? Write an essay in which you outline your own definition of human rights and how these rights extend to immigration. Reference the Universal Declaration of Human Rights ratified by the United Nations in 1948 at the beginning of this chapter.

2. Watch a movie that addresses human rights issues, such as *The Kite Runner, Hotel Rwanda*, or *War Dance*. Summarize the issues it raises and then research media coverage on the issue. Write a short essay evaluating the role media coverage has in educating or failing to educate the American public on human rights issues.

3. Visit Amnesty International USA's website (http://www.amnestyusa.org). What issues does Amnesty International address? What are the most pressing issues today? How aware were you of current human rights issues? Pick an issue and write a short media plan to increase awareness of that issue on your college campus.

4. In January 2010, Haiti suffered a devastating earthquake that drew worldwide attention to this small impoverished nation that is located just south of Cuba. The devastation caused by the earthquake was compounded by the fact that Haiti is the poorest nation in the western hemisphere. Read more about Haiti and human rights violations suffered by its people in "2008 Human Rights Report: Haiti" on the U.S. Department of State site (http://www.state.gov/g/drl/rls/hrrpt/2008/wha/119163.htm). Using the Universal Declaration of Human Rights, identify what basic rights are being violated in Haiti. If you wish, you may make recommendations on how to leverage the international attention Haiti received in 2010 to address the violations you cite in your report.

5. In her essay, Kay Hymowitz mentions the ancient Greek play *Lysistrata* by Aristophanes. Read the play and write a short essay in which you compare the issues highlighted by the women in the play 2,400 years ago to issues today.

6. Review the first reading in this chapter, the Universal Declaration of Human Rights, and write a short essay explaining which rights are the most important to society and why.

7. In many parts of the world, children are forced to work long hours, denied an education, and even forced to serve in the military. Visit the Human Rights Watch's web pages on children's rights (http://www.hrw.org/en/topics) and select a children's rights issue that interests you. Write a letter to your congressional representative explaining the problem, and why it deserves our attention.

# Credits

## Image Credits

Page 205: Pablo Picasso/Museo Nacional Centro de Arte Reina Sofia, Madrid, Spain/Art Resource. © 2009 Estate of Pablo Picasso/Artists Rights Society (ARS), New York; Page 208: Printed by permission of the Norman Rockwell Family Agency. Copyright © 1943, the Norman Rockwell Family Entities; Page 210: Courtesy Toyota Motors North America, Dentsu America; Page 215: "FRESH STEP" is a registered trademark of The Clorox Pet Products Company. Used with Permission. (C) The Clorox Pet Products Company. Reprinted with permission; Page 217: Courtesy of ForestEthics/Half-Full; Page 220: By permission of Mike Luckovich and Creators Syndicate, Inc.; Page 222: Courtesy of Pat Bagley; Page 223: Daryl Cagle, MSNBC.com/Cagle Cartoons; Page 224: Larry Downing/Reuters/Landov; Page 226: Suzanne Kreiter/Boston Globe/Landov; Page 237: David Bunting; Page 279: Courtesy of Mkie Cramer; Page 319: Courtesy Adbusters; Page 339: Advertising Archives; Page 341: Courtesy People in Need & Dentsu; Page 342: Courtesy Friday Monkey Wine; Page 343: Advertising Archive; Page 344: Maximilian Pinegger and Justin Salice-Stephan; Page 345: Courtesy Tobacco Free Florida & Accent Marketing Miami; Page 361: Reprinted with permission, National Eating Disorders Association; Page 362: Advertising Archives; Page 387: Copyright © The New Yorker Collection, 1991. Donald Reilly from cartoonbank.com. All Rights Reserved; Page 408: Rob Rogers/United Media Syndicate; Page 464: Brice Hall; Page 497: AP Images; Page 505: Courtesy of the American Civil Liberties Union Foundation; Page 540: Paul Sakuma/AP Images; Page 541: Ethan Miller/Getty; Page 542: Joe Raedle/Getty; Page 584: Marty Bucella/Cartoonstock; Page 591: PSL Images/Alamy; Page 620: Piero Tonin/Cartoonstock

## Text Credits

**Arthur Allen.** "Prayer in Prison: Prison: Religion as Rehabilitation." Religion as Rehabilitation" by permission of the author.

**Daniel Askt.** "Saving Yourself." *The Wilson Quarterly*, Summer 2009. Reprinted by permission.

**Harry Binswanger.** "Immigration Quotas vs. Individual Rights: The Moral and Practical Case for Open Immigration," from *Capitalism Magazine*, April 2, 2006. Reprinted by permission of the author.

**Stephanie Bower.** "What's the Rush?: Speed and Mediocrity in Local TV News." Reprinted by permission of the author.

**Taffy Brodesser-Akner.** "Facebook, the mean girls, and me," from *Salon*, November 29, 2009. Reprinted with permission.

**Nicolas Carr.** "Is Google Making Us Stoopid?" *The Atlantic*, July/August 2008. Copyright 2008 by Nicholas Carr. Reprinted with permission of author.

**Danise Cavallaro.** "Smoking: Offended by the Numbers." Reprinted by permission of the author.

**Noam Chomsky.** "The Torture Memos," from *Chomsky.info*, May 24, 2009. Reprinted with permission.

**Judith Ortiz Cofer.** "The Myth of the Latina Woman," from *The Latin Deli: Prose and Poetry*. Copyright © by Judith Ortiz Cofer. Reprinted with permission of the University of Chicago Press.

**Amanda Collins.** "Bring East Bridgewater Elementary into the World." Reprinted by permission of Amanda Collins.

**Francis S. Collins.** "A New Theology of Celebration," from *Science & Spirit*, September/October 2007. Reprinted with permission of the Helen Dwight Reid Educational Foundation. Published by Heldref Publications, 1319 Eighteenth St., NW, Washington, DC 20036-1802. Copyright © 2007.

**Tyler Cowan.** "Three Tweets for the Web." *The Wilson Quarterly*, Autumn 2009. Reprinted with permission of the author.

**Joel Epstein.** "Parental Notification: Fact or Fiction?" from *Prevention File*, Vol. 14, No. 2. Reprinted with permission of the publisher.

**Amitai Etzioni.** "Spent: America after consumerism," from *The New Republic*, June 17, 2009. Reprinted with permission.

**Jerry Fensterman.** "I See Why Others Choose to Die." from *The Boston Globe*, January 31, 2006. Reprinted by permission of the author's widow, Lisa Bevilaqua.

**Richard Florida.** "How the Crash Will Reshape America," from *The Atlantic*, March 2009. Reprinted with permission.

**Sean Flynn.** "Is Anything Private Anymore?" from *Parade Magazine*, September 16, 2007. © 2007 Sean Flynn. All rights reserved.

**Ted Gup.** "Who is a Whiz Kid?" from *Newsweek*, April 21, 1997. Reprinted with permission.

**David Greenberg.** "A Very Ecumenical Christmas," from *Slate*, December 15, 2006. Reprinted with permission.

**David Greenberg.** "Why We're Not One Nation Under 'God,'" *Slate.com*, June 28, 2002. Reprinted by permission.

**Edward Grinnan, Editor-in-Chief, Guideposts Magazine.** Copyright © 2009 by Edward Grinnan. All rights reserved.

**Stephen S. Hall.** "The Bully in the Mirror," *New York Times*, August 22, 1999. Copyright © 1999. The New York Times Company. Reprinted by permission.

**Nicholas Handler.** "The Post-Everything Generation," from *The New York Times Magazine*, September 30, 2007. Reprinted with permission.

**James Hannaham.** "Our biracial president," from *Salon*, November 6, 2008. Reprinted with permission.

**Charles Haynes.** "Public Prayers on State Occasions Need Not Be Divisive or Generic," from *www.firstamendment.org*, February 11, 2001. Reprinted by permission of the author.

**Hugh Heclo.** "The Wall that Never Was," from *The Wilson Quarterly*, Winter 2003. Reprinted by permission of the author.

**Jessica Helfand.** "My Facebook, My Self," from *Observatory*, March 11, 2009. Reprinted with permission.

**Robert Horning.** "The Design Imperative," from *PopMatters*, January 29, 2008. Reprinted with permission.

**Dan Hoskins.** "Tapped Out: Bottled Water's Detrimental Side." Reprinted by permission of the author.

**Kay Hymowitz.** "Child-Man in the Promised Land," from *City Journal*, Winter 2008, vol. 18, no. 1. Reprinted by permission.

**Kay S. Hymowitz.** "Why Feminism is AWOL on Islam," from *City Journal*, Winter 2003. Reprinted with permission.

**Lee Innes.** "A Double Standard of Olympic Proportion." Reprinted by permission of the author.

**Walter Isaacson.** "God of Our Fathers," from *Time Magazine*, July 5, 2004. Reprinted by permission of the author.

**Derrick Jackson.** Let's Ban All Flavors of Cigarettes," from *The Boston Globe*, September 30, 2009.

**Liz Jones.** "What I Think of the Fashion World," *You Magazine*, April 15, 2001. Copyright © You Magazine. Reprinted with permission.

**Anya Kamenetz.** "Why Generation Debt?: from *Generation Debt* by Anya Kamenetz © 2006 by Anya Kamenetz. Used by permission of Riverhead Books, and imprint of Penguin Group (USA) Inc.

**T.J. Kelleher.** "Scientific Proof in an Age of Wikipedia." *Seed Magazine*, February 9, 2009. Reprinted with permission.

**Michael Kelly.** "Arguing for Infanticide," from *The Washington Post*, November 6, 1997. PermissionOrders@parsintl.com.

**Randall Kennedy.** "You Can't Judge a Crook By His Color," *The New Republic*, September 13, 1999. Copyright © 1999 The New Republic, LLC. Reprinted by permission.

**Francie Latour.** "Welcome to the dollhouse," from *Boston Magazine*, October 25, 2009. Reprinted with permission.

**Michael Levine.** "Brand Leaders Case Study: Nike," from *A Branded World: Adventures in Public Relations and the Creation of Superbrands*, 2003, John Wiley & Sons, Inc. Reprinted with permission.

**Ronald D. Liebowitz.** "Diversity: The Value of Discomfort." *Baccalaureate address*, Middlebury College, May 26, 2007. Reprinted with permission of the author.

**Michael Lewis.** "The Case Against Tipping," from the "The Case Against New York Times, Tipping" September 23, 1997. Reprinted with permission from the author.

**William Lutz.** "With These Words I Can Sell You Anything," from *Doublespeak* by William Lutz. Copyright © 1989 by Blond Bear, Inc. Reprinted by permission of the author.

**Bill McKibben.** "The $100 Christmas," from *Mother Jones*, November/December 1997, © 1997. Foundation for National Progress.

**John H. McWhorter.** "Who Should Get Into College," from *City Journal*, Spring 2003. Reprinted by permission of the publisher. Reprinted from The Wall Street Journal © 2007. Dow Jones & Company. All rights reserved."

**Judith Miller.** "Don't Close Gitmo," from *City Journal*, September 24, 2009. Reprinted by Permission.

**Kevin O'Donnell.** "Why Won't Anyone Give Me a Credit Card," from *Slate*, Section, 9/18/2009 issue.

**Shannon O'Neil.** "Literature Hacked and Torn Apart: Censorship in Public Schools." Reprinted by permission of the author.

**Charles O'Neill.** "The Language of Advertising." Reprinted by permission of the author.

**Rick Perlstein.** "What's the Matter with College?" from *The New York Times*, September 30, 2007. Reprinted with permission.

**Kari Peterson.** "The Statistic Speaks: A Real Person's Argument for Universal Healthcare." Reprinted by permission of the author.

**Stephen Pinker.** "Why They Kill Their Newborns," *New York Times Sunday Magazine*, November 2, 1997. By permission of the author.

**Mary Pipher.** "Saplings in the Storm," from *Reviving Ophelia* by Mary Pipher, Ph.D., copyright © 1994 by Mary Pipher, Ph.D. Used by permission of G.P. Putnam's Sons, a division of Penguin Group (USA) Inc.

**Ahmed Rehab.** "Why Racial Profiling Makes for Dumb Security," from *The Huffington Post*, January 7, 2010. Reprinted with permission.

**Arlene Roberts.** "The Detention Debacle," from *The Huffington Post*, October 6, 2009. Reprinted with permission.

**Christine Rosen.** "In the Beginning was the Word," *The Wilson Quarterly*, Autumn 2009. Reprinted by permission.

**Sandip Roy.** "Facebook Sees Dead People," *New America Media*, October 27, 2009. Reprinted by permission of the author.

**Douglas Rushkoff.** "Let it Die." *Arthur Magazine*, March 2009. Reprinted by permission.

**Douglas Rushkoff.** "Which One of These Sneakers is Me? How Marketers Outsmart Our Media-Savvy Children," *The London Times*, May 6, 2000. Reprinted with permission.

**Bridget Samburg.** "Deck the Halls?" *The Boston Globe*, December 12, 2004. Reprinted with permission of the author.

**Scott Russell Sanders.** "The Men We Carry in Our Minds," Copyright © 1984 by Scott Russell Sanders; Milkweed Chronicle; from The Paradise of Bombs; reprinted by permission of the author and the author's agents, the Virginia Kidd Agency, Inc.

**Ed Schipul.** "Millennials head under a rock," from "The List" blog, Chron.com, *Houston Chronicle*, April 8, 2009.

**Megan Scott.** "Recession is a Dose of Reality for Young Workers," from *The Associated Press*, March 21, 2009. Reprinted by permission.

**David Scurlock.** From "Maxed Out: Hard Times in the age of Easy." Copyright © 2007 James D. Scurlock. Reprinted with permission of Scribner, a Division of Simon & Schuster. All rights reserved.

**Alicia C. Shepard.** "A's for Everyone!" from *The Washington Post*, June 5, 2005. Copyright © 2005, by the author.

**Leslie Marmon Silko.** "In the Combat Zone." Copyright © 1996 by Leslie Marmon Silko. Included with permission of The Wylie Agency, Inc.

**S. Fred Singer.** "The Great Global Warming Swindle," from *The San Francisco Examiner*, May 22, 2007. Reprinted by permission of the author.

**Peter Suderman.** "Staying Afloat: Treading Water in a Sea of Data," from *The New Atlantis*, Fall 2008. Reprinted with permission.

**Stuart Taylor, Jr.** "Prayer and Creationism," *National Journal*, July 15, 2000. Reprinted with permission from National Journal. Copyright © 2010 by National Journal Group. All rights reserved.

**Aaron Traister.** "And May Your First Child be a Feminine Chile," from *Salon*, November 15, 2009. Reprinted by permission.

**Joseph Turow.** "Targeting a New World," from *Breaking Up America: Advertisers and the New Media World*. University of Chicago Press, 1997. Reprinted with permission.

**"Universal Declaration of Human Rights."** General Assembly of the United Nations, 1948. "The Meaning of Freedom," from *The Economist*, April 2, 2009. Reprinted with permission.

**Melana Zyla Vickers.** "Where the Boys Aren't," from *The Weekly Standard*, January 2, 2006. Reprinted by permission of the publisher.

**Henry Wechsler.** "Binge Drinking Must Be Stopped," from *The Boston Globe*, October 2, 1997. Reprinted by permission of the author.

**David Weigel.** "Welcome to the Fun Free University," from *Reason Magazine*, October 2004. Reprinted with permission.

**Cathy Young.** "What Happy Holidays?" from *Reason Online*, December 28, 2004. Reprinted by permission of the author.

# Index

Page numbers followed by an *f* refer to figures.